# Data Structures And Algorithms Made Easy

-To All My Readers and Parents

By
Narasimha Karumanchi

☼ Problems ☼ Interview Questions

Copyright© 2023 by *CareerMonk.com*

All rights reserved.

Designed by *Narasimha Karumanchi*

Copyright© 2023 CareerMonk Publications. All rights reserved.

All rights reserved. No part of this book may be reproduced in any form or by any electronic or mechanical means, including information storage and retrieval systems, without written permission from the publisher or author.

This book has been published with all the efforts taken to make the material error-free after the consent of the author. However, the author and the publisher do not assume and hereby disclaim any liability to any party for any loss, damage, or disruption caused by errors or omissions, whether such errors or omissions result from negligence, accident, or any other cause.

While every effort has been made to avoid any mistake or omission, this publication is being sold on the condition and understanding that neither the author nor the publishers or printers would be liable in any manner to any person by reason of any mistake or omission in this publication or for any action taken or omitted to be taken or advice rendered or accepted on the basis of this work. For any defect in printing or binding the publishers will be liable only to replace the defective copy by another copy of this work then available.

# Acknowledgements

Dear *Mother* and *Father*, I cannot find the words to express my gratitude for everything you have done for me. Your unwavering love and dedication in providing a stable and nurturing household has allowed me to flourish and embrace life with open arms. Your traditional values and persistent efforts have instilled in me the belief that with faith, hard work, and determination, anything is possible. You are not just my parents, but my role models, and I feel blessed to have you in my life.

I would like to acknowledge the many people who have contributed to the creation of this book. Without their support, advice, feedback, and assistance in editing, proofreading, and design, this book would not have been possible. Thank you for everything.

—*Narasimha Karumanchi*
M-Tech, *IIT Bombay*
Founder, *CareerMonk.com*

# Preface

**Dear Reader,**

I urge you to pause for a moment! Although many individuals tend to skip the Preface when reading a book, I implore you to make an exception and read this particular preface.

The primary aim of this book is not to provide you with a comprehensive list of theorems and proofs on data structures and algorithms. Instead, I have adopted a method of enhancing problem-solving skills by presenting multiple solutions for each problem, each with varying complexities. Essentially, this book is an enumeration of potential solutions that will assist you in your thought process when approaching new questions. Whether you are preparing for interviews, competitive exams, or campus interviews, you will find this book to be an invaluable resource.

If you are a job seeker and read this book in its entirety, I am confident that you will be well-equipped to impress your interviewers with your knowledge and skills. As an instructor, this book will enable you to deliver lectures in a clear and straightforward manner, resulting in your students developing a greater appreciation for their chosen field of study in Computer Science/Information Technology.

This book is a valuable resource not only for students pursuing a degree in Engineering or Masters, but also for those preparing for competitive exams in Computer Science/Information Technology. The book places a greater emphasis on problem-solving and analysis, rather than just theory. Each chapter begins with an introduction to the necessary theory, followed by a range of problem sets. There are approximately 700 algorithmic problems, each with its solution, presented in the book.

My primary focus in writing this book was to aid students in their preparation for competitive exams. For each problem, multiple solutions are provided, each with varying levels of complexity. The solutions start with a brute force approach and gradually progress to the most efficient solution. For each problem, we also explore the time and memory complexities of the algorithm.

To gain a complete understanding of all the topics covered, it is recommended that the reader does at least one complete reading of the book. Subsequently, readers can refer to specific chapters or topics as required. While we have made every effort to eliminate errors, there may still be minor typos in the book. Corrections can be found on www.CareerMonk.com, along with new problems and solutions. I also welcome your valuable suggestions at: Info@CareerMonk.com.

I wish you the best of luck and am confident that you will find this book to be an invaluable resource.

—*Narasimha Karumanchi*
M-Tech, *IIT Bombay*
Founder, *CareerMonk.com*

# Other Books by Narasimha Karumanchi

- IT Interview Questions
- Data Structures and Algorithms Made Easy in Java
- Coding Interview Questions
- Data Structures and Algorithmic Thinking with Python
- Data Structures and Algorithmic Thinking with Go
- Algorithm Design Techniques

# Data Structure Operations Cheat Sheet

| Data Structure Name | Average Case Time Complexity | | | | Worst Case Time Complexity | | | | Space Complexity |
|---|---|---|---|---|---|---|---|---|---|
| | Accessing $n^{th}$element | Search | Insertion | Deletion | Accessing $n^{th}$element | Search | Insertion | Deletion | Worst Case |
| Arrays | O(1) | O($n$) | O($n$) | O($n$) | O(1) | O($n$) | O($n$) | O($n$) | O($n$) |
| Stacks | O($n$) | O($n$) | O(1) | O(1) | O($n$) | O($n$) | O(1) | O(1) | O($n$) |
| Queues | O($n$) | O($n$) | O(1) | O(1) | O($n$) | O($n$) | O(1) | O(1) | O($n$) |
| Binary Trees | O($n$) | O($n$) | O($n$) | O($n$) | O($n$) | O($n$) | O($n$) | O($n$) | O($n$) |
| Binary Search Trees | O($logn$) | O($logn$) | O($logn$) | O($logn$) | O($n$) | O($n$) | O($n$) | O($n$) | O($n$) |
| Balanced Binary Search Trees | O($logn$) | O($logn$) | O($logn$) | O($logn$) | O($logn$) | O($logn$) | O($logn$) | O($logn$) | O($logn$) |
| Hash Tables | N/A | O(1) | O(1) | O(1) | N/A | O($n$) | O($n$) | O($n$) | O($n$) |

**Note**: For best case operations, the time complexities are O(1).

# Sorting Algorithms Cheat Sheet

| Sorting Algorithm Name | Time Complexity | | | Space Complexity | Is Stable? | Sorting Class Type | Remarks |
|---|---|---|---|---|---|---|---|
| | Best Case | Average Case | Worst Case | Worst Case | | | |
| Bubble Sort | O($n$) | O($n^2$) | O($n^2$) | O(1) | Yes | Comparison | Not a preferred sorting algorithm. |
| Insertion Sort | O($n$) | O($n^2$) | O($n^2$) | O(1) | Yes | Comparison | In the best case (already sorted), every insert requires constant time |
| Selection Sort | O($n^2$) | O($n^2$) | O($n^2$) | O(1) | Yes | Comparison | Even a perfectly sorted array requires scanning the entire array |
| Merge Sort | O($nlogn$) | O($nlogn$) | O($nlogn$) | O($n$) | Yes | Comparison | On arrays, it requires O($n$) space; and on linked lists, it requires constant space |
| Heap Sort | O($nlogn$) | O($nlogn$) | O($nlogn$) | O(1) | No | Comparison | By using input array as storage for the heap, it is possible to achieve constant space |
| Quick Sort | O($nlogn$) | O($nlogn$) | O($n^2$) | O($logn$) | No | Comparison | Randomly picking a pivot value can help avoid worst case scenarios such as a perfectly sorted array. |
| Tree Sort | O($nlogn$) | O($nlogn$) | O($n^2$) | O($n$) | Yes | Comparison | Performing inorder traversal on the balanced binary search tree. |
| Counting Sort | O($n + k$) | O($n + k$) | O($n + k$) | O($k$) | Yes | Linear | Where $k$ is the range of the non-negative key values. |
| Bucket Sort | O($n + k$) | O($n + k$) | O($n^2$) | O($n$) | Yes | Linear | Bucket sort is stable, if the underlying sorting algorithm is stable. |
| Radix Sort | O($dn$) | O($dn$) | O($dn$) | O($d + n$) | Yes | Linear | Radix sort is stable, if the underlying sorting algorithm is stable. |

# Table of Contents

# INTRODUCTION

The objective of this chapter is to explain the importance of the analysis of algorithms, their notations, relationships and solving as many problems as possible. Let us first focus on understanding the basic elements of algorithms, the importance of algorithm analysis, and then slowly move toward the other topics as mentioned above. After completing this chapter, you should be able to find the complexity of any given algorithm (especially recursive functions).

## 1.1 Variables

Before going to the definition of variables, let us relate them to old mathematical equations. All of us have solved many mathematical equations since childhood. As an example, consider the following equation:

$$x^2 + 2y - 2 = 1$$

We don't have to worry about the use of this equation. The important thing that we need to understand is that the equation has names ($x$ and $y$), which hold values (data). That means the *names* ($x$ and $y$) are placeholders for representing data. Similarly, in computer science programming we need something for holding data, and *variables* is the way to do that.

## 1.2 Data Types

In the above-mentioned equation, the variables $x$ and $y$ can take any values such as integral numbers (10, 20), real numbers (0.23, 5.5), or just 0 and 1. To solve the equation, we need to relate them to the kind of values they can take, and *data type* is the name used in computer science programming for this purpose. A *data type* in a programming language is a set of data with predefined values. Examples of data types are: integer, floating point, unit number, character, string, etc.

Computer memory is all filled with zeros and ones. If we have a problem and we want to code it, it's very difficult to provide the solution in terms of zeros and ones. To help users, programming languages and compilers provide us with data types. For example, *integer* takes 2 bytes (actual value depends on compiler), *float* takes 4 bytes, etc. This says that in memory we are combining 2 bytes (16 bits) and calling it an *integer*. Similarly, combining 4 bytes (32 bits) and calling it a *float*. A data type reduces the coding effort. At the top level, there are two types of data types:

- System-defined data types (also called *Primitive* data types)
- User-defined data types

### System-defined data types (Primitive data types)

Primitive data types are data types that are defined by the system. Many programming languages provide primitive data types such as int, float, char, double, and bool. The number of bits assigned to each primitive data type varies depending on the programming language, compiler, and operating system. Even for the same primitive data type, different languages may use different bit sizes. The available values (domain) for a primitive data type will also vary depending on its size.

For example, "*int*" may take 2 bytes or 4 bytes. If it takes 2 bytes (16 bits), then the total possible values are minus 32,768 to plus 32,767 ($-2^{15}$ *to* $2^{15}-1$). If it takes 4 bytes (32 bits), then the possible values are between −2,147,483,648 and +2,147,483,647 ($-2^{31}$ *to* $2^{31}-1$). The same is the case with other data types.

## User defined data types

If the system-defined data types are not enough, then most programming languages allow the users to define their own data types, called *user – defined data types*. Good examples of user defined data types are: structures in *C/C++* and classes in *Java*. For example, in the snippet below, we are combining many system-defined data types and calling the user defined data type by the name "*newType*". This gives more flexibility and comfort in dealing with computer memory.

```
struct newType {
    int data1;
    float data 2;
    ...
    char data;
};
```

## 1.3 Data Structures

Based on the discussion above, once we have data in variables, we need some mechanism for manipulating that data to solve problems. *Data structure* is a particular way of storing and organizing data in a computer so that it can be used efficiently. A *data structure* is a special format for organizing and storing data. General data structure types include arrays, files, linked lists, stacks, queues, trees, graphs and so on.

Depending on the organization of the elements, data structures are classified into two types:

1) *Linear data structures*: Elements are accessed in a sequential order, but it is not compulsory to store all elements sequentially. *Examples*: Linked Lists, Stacks and Queues.
2) *Non – linear data structures*: Elements of this data structure are stored/accessed in a non-linear order. *Examples*: Trees and graphs.

## 1.4 Abstract Data Types (ADTs)

Before defining abstract data types, let us consider the different view of system-defined data types. We all know that, by default, all primitive data types (int, float, etc.) support basic operations such as addition and subtraction. The system provides the implementations for the primitive data types. For user-defined data types we also need to define operations. The implementation for these operations can be done when we want to actually use them. That means, in general, user defined data types are defined along with their operations.

To simplify the process of solving problems, we combine the data structures with their operations, and we call this *Abstract Data Types* (ADTs). An ADT consists of *two parts*:

1. Declaration of data
2. Declaration of operations

Commonly used ADTs *include*: Linked Lists, Stacks, Queues, Priority Queues, Binary Trees, Dictionaries, Disjoint Sets (Union and Find), Hash Tables, Graphs, and many others. For example, stack uses LIFO (Last-In-First-Out) mechanism while storing the data in data structures. The last element inserted into the stack is the first element that gets deleted. Common operations of it are: creating the stack, pushing an element onto the stack, popping an element from stack, finding the current top of the stack, finding number of elements in the stack, etc.

While defining the ADTs do not worry about the implementation details. They come into the picture only when we want to use them. Different kinds of ADTs are suited to different kinds of applications, and some are highly specialized to specific tasks. By the end of this book, we will go through many of them, and you will be in a position to relate the data structures to the kind of problems they solve.

## 1.5 What is an Algorithm?

Let us consider the problem of preparing an *omelette*. To prepare an omelette, we follow the steps given below:

1) Get the frying pan.
2) Get the oil.
    a. Do we have oil?
        i. If yes, put it in the pan.
        ii. If no, do we want to buy oil?
            1. If yes, then go out and buy.
            2. If no, we can terminate.
3) Turn on the stove, etc...

What we are doing is, for a given problem (preparing an omelette), we are providing a step-by-step procedure for solving it. The formal definition of an algorithm can be stated as:

An algorithm is the step-by-step unambiguous instructions to solve a given problem.

In the traditional study of algorithms, there are two main criteria for judging the merits of algorithms: correctness (does the algorithm give solution to the problem in a finite number of steps?) and efficiency (how much resources (in terms of memory and time) does it take to execute the).

**Note**: We do not have to prove each step of the algorithm.

## 1.6 Why the Analysis of Algorithms?

To go from city *"A"* to city *"B"*, there can be many ways of accomplishing this: by flight, by bus, by train and also by bicycle. Depending on the availability and convenience, we choose the one that suits us. Similarly, in computer science, multiple algorithms are available for solving the same problem (for example, a sorting problem has many algorithms, like insertion sort, selection sort, quick sort and many more). Algorithm analysis helps us to determine which algorithm is most efficient in terms of time and space consumed.

## 1.7 Goal of the Analysis of Algorithms

The analysis of an algorithm can help us understand it better and can suggest informed improvements. The main and important role of analysis of algorithm is to predict the performance of different algorithms in order to guide design decisions. The goal of the *analysis of algorithms* is to compare algorithms (or solutions) mainly in terms of running time but also in terms of other factors (e.g., memory, developer effort, etc.).

In theoretical analysis of algorithms, it is common to estimate their complexity in the asymptotic sense, i.e., to estimate the complexity function for arbitrarily large input. The term "analysis of algorithms" was coined by Donald Knuth.

Algorithm analysis is an important part of computational complexity theory, which provides theoretical estimation for the required resources of an algorithm to solve a specific computational problem. Most algorithms are designed to work with inputs of arbitrary length. Analysis of algorithms is the determination of the amount of time and space resources required to execute it.

Usually, the efficiency or running time of an algorithm is stated as a function relating the input length to the number of steps, known as time complexity, or volume of memory, known as space complexity.

## 1.8 What is Running Time Analysis?

It is the process of determining how processing time increases as the size of the problem (input size) increases. Input size is the number of elements in the input, and depending on the problem type, the input may be of different types. The following are the common types of inputs.

- Size of an array
- Polynomial degree
- Number of elements in a matrix
- Number of bits in the binary representation of the input
- Vertices and edges in a graph.

## 1.9 How to Compare Algorithms

To compare algorithms, let us define a few *objective measures*:

**Execution times?** *Not a good measure* as execution times are specific to a particular computer.

**Number of statements executed?** *Not a good measure*, since the number of statements varies with the programming language as well as the style of the individual programmer.

**Ideal solution?** Let us assume that we express the running time of a given algorithm as a function of the input size $n$ (i.e., $f(n)$) and compare these different functions corresponding to running times. This kind of comparison is independent of machine time, programming style, etc.

## 1.10 What is Rate of Growth?

The rate at which the running time increases as a function of input is called *rate of growth*. Let us assume that you go to a shop to buy a car and a bicycle. If your friend sees you there and asks what you are buying, then in general you say *buying a car*. This is because the cost of the car is high compared to the cost of the bicycle (approximating the cost of the bicycle to the cost of the car).

$$Total\ Cost\ = cost\_of\_car + cost\_of\_bicycle$$
$$Total\ Cost\ \approx cost\_of\_car\ (approximation)$$

For the above-mentioned example, we can represent the cost of the car and the cost of the bicycle in terms of function, and for a given function ignore the low order terms that are relatively insignificant (for large value of input size, $n$). As an example, in the case below, $n^4$, $2n^2$, $100n$ and 500 are the individual costs of some function and approximate to $n^4$ since $n^4$ is the highest rate of growth.

$$n^4 + 2n^2 + 100n + 500 \approx n^4$$

## 1.11 Commonly Used Rates of Growth

Below is the list of growth rates you will come across in the following chapters.

| Time Complexity | Name | Description |
|---|---|---|
| 1 | Constant | Whatever is the input size $n$, these functions take a constant amount of time. |
| $logn$ | Logarithmic | These are slower growing than even linear functions. |
| $n$ | Linear | These functions grow linearly with the input size $n$. |
| $nlogn$ | Linear Logarithmic | Faster growing than linear but slower than quadratic. |
| $n^2$ | Quadratic | These functions grow faster than the linear logarithmic functions. |
| $n^3$ | Cubic | Faster growing than quadratic but slower than exponential. |
| $2^n$ | Exponential | Faster than all of the functions mentioned here except the factorial functions. |
| $n!$ | Factorial | Fastest growing than all these functions mentioned here. |

The diagram below shows the relationship between different rates of growth.

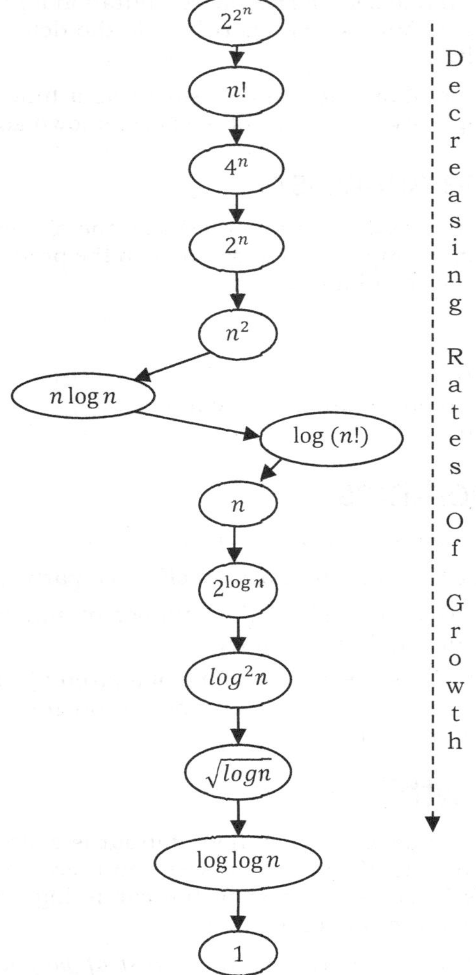

## 1.12 Types of Analysis

To effectively analyze an algorithm, it is crucial to identify the inputs that yield favorable performance as well as those that result in longer execution times. Algorithms can be expressed through different expressions that represent their performance in various scenarios, including a best-case expression for optimal performance and a worst-case expression for suboptimal performance. Asymptotic analysis/notation serves as the foundation for algorithm analysis, categorized into three types of analysis.

- **Worst case**
  - Defines the input for which the algorithm takes a long time (slowest time to complete).
  - Input is the one for which the algorithm runs the slowest.
- **Best case**
  - Defines the input for which the algorithm takes the least time (fastest time to complete).
  - Input is the one for which the algorithm runs the fastest.
- **Average case**
  - Provides a prediction about the running time of the algorithm.
  - Run the algorithm many times, using many different inputs that come from some distribution that generates these inputs, compute the total running time (by adding the individual times), and divide by the number of trials.
  - Assumes that the input is random.

$$Lower\ Bound <= Average\ Time <= Upper\ Bound$$

For a given algorithm, we can represent the best, worst and average cases in the form of expressions. As an example, let $f(n)$ be the function which represents the given algorithm.

$$f(n) = n^2 + 500, \text{ for worst case}$$
$$f(n) = n + 100n + 500, \text{ for best case}$$

Similarly for the average case. The expression defines the inputs with which the algorithm takes the average running time (or memory).

## 1.13 Asymptotic Notation

Once we have determined the expressions for the best, average, and worst cases of an algorithm, we must then identify the upper and lower bounds for each of these cases. This requires the use of a specific syntax, which will be discussed below. For the purposes of this discussion, we will assume that the algorithm has been represented as a function, denoted as $f(n)$.

## 1.14 Big-O Notation

This notation gives the *tight* upper bound of the given function. Generally, it is represented as $f(n) = O(g(n))$. That means, at larger values of $n$, the upper bound of $f(n)$ is $g(n)$. For example, if $f(n) = n^4 + 100n^2 + 10n + 50$ is the given algorithm, then $n^4$ is $g(n)$. That means $g(n)$ gives the maximum rate of growth for $f(n)$ at larger values of $n$.

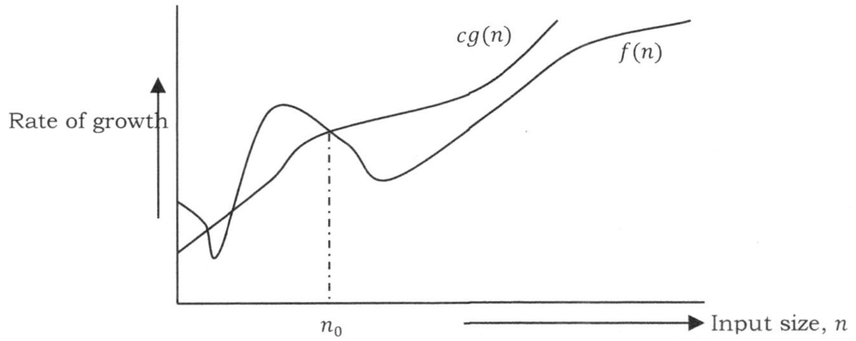


Let us see the O−notation with a little more detail. O−notation defined as $O(g(n)) = \{f(n)$: there exist positive constants $c$ and $n_0$ such that $0 \leq f(n) \leq cg(n)$ for all $n \geq n_0\}$. $g(n)$ is an asymptotic tight upper bound for $f(n)$. Our objective is to give the smallest rate of growth $g(n)$ which is greater than or equal to the given algorithms' rate of growth $f(n)$.

Generally, we discard lower values of $n$. That means the rate of growth at lower values of $n$ is not important. In the figure, $n_0$ is the point from which we need to consider the rate of growth for a given algorithm. Below $n_0$, the rate of growth could be different. $n_0$ is called threshold for the given function.

## Big-O Visualization

$O(g(n))$ is the set of functions with smaller or the same order of growth as $g(n)$. For example; $O(n^2)$ includes $O(1), O(n), O(nlogn)$, etc.

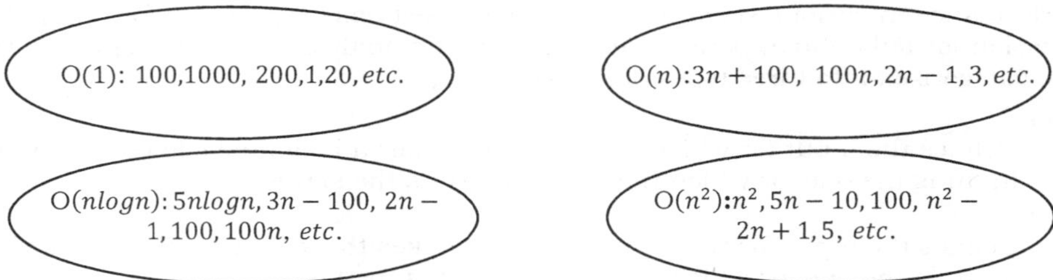


**Note:** Focus on analyzing the algorithms for larger values of n, as the rate of growth below $n_0$ is not of concern to us.

## Big-O Examples

**Example-1** Find upper bound for $f(n) = 3n + 8$

**Solution:** $3n + 8 \leq 4n$, for all $n \geq 8$
$\therefore 3n + 8 = O(n)$ with c = 4 and $n_0 = 8$

**Example-2** Find upper bound for $f(n) = n^2 + 1$

**Solution:** $n^2 + 1 \leq 2n^2$, for all $n \geq 1$
$\therefore n^2 + 1 = O(n^2)$ with $c = 2$ and $n_0 = 1$

**Example-3** Find upper bound for $f(n) = n^4 + 100n^2 + 50$

**Solution:** $n^4 + 100n^2 + 50 \leq 2n^4$, for all $n \geq 11$
$\therefore n^4 + 100n^2 + 50 = O(n^4)$ with $c = 2$ and $n_0 = 11$

**Example-4** Find upper bound for $f(n) = 2n^3 - 2n^2$

**Solution:** $2n^3 - 2n^2 \leq 2n^3$, for all $n \geq 1$
$\therefore 2n^3 - 2n^2 = O(n^3)$ with $c = 2$ and $n_0 = 1$

**Example-5** Find upper bound for $f(n) = n$

**Solution:** $n \leq n$, for all $n \geq 1$
$\therefore n = O(n)$ with $c = 1$ and $n_0 = 1$

**Example-6** Find upper bound for $f(n) = 410$

**Solution:** $410 \leq 410$, for all $n \geq 1$
$\therefore 410 = O(1)$ with $c = 1$ and $n_0 = 1$

## No Uniqueness?

There is no unique set of values for $n_0$ and $c$ in proving the asymptotic bounds. Let us consider, $100n + 5 = O(n)$. For this function there are multiple $n_0$ and $c$ values possible.

**Solution1:** $100n + 5 \leq 100n + n = 101n \leq 101n$, for all $n \geq 5$, $n_0 = 5$ and $c = 101$ is a solution.

**Solution2:** $100n + 5 \leq 100n + 5n = 105n \leq 105n$, for all $n \geq 1$, $n_0 = 1$ and $c = 105$ is also a solution.

# 1.15 Omega-Ω Notation [Lower Bounding Function]

Similar to the O discussion, this notation gives the tighter lower bound of the given algorithm and we represent it as $f(n) = \Omega(g(n))$. That means, at larger values of $n$, the tighter lower bound of $f(n)$ is $g(n)$. For example, if $f(n) = 100n^2 + 10n + 50$, $g(n)$ is $\Omega(n^2)$.

The Ω notation can be defined as $\Omega(g(n))$ = {f(n): there exist positive constants c and $n_0$ such that $0 \leq cg(n) \leq f(n)$ for all $n \geq n_0$}. $g(n)$ is an asymptotic tight lower bound for $f(n)$. Our objective is to give the largest rate of growth $g(n)$ which is less than or equal to the given algorithm's rate of growth $f(n)$.

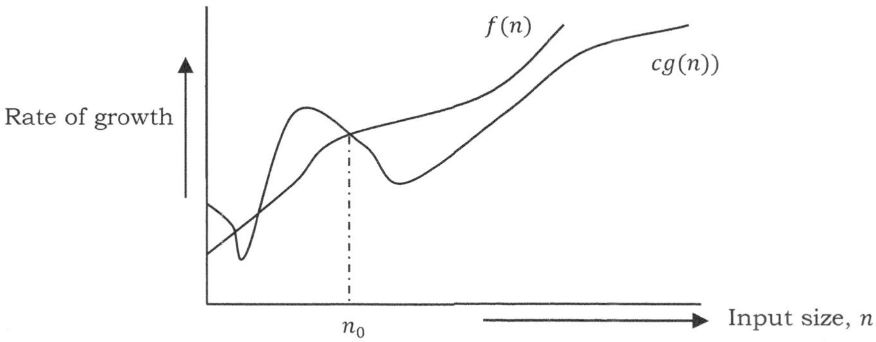


### Ω Examples

**Example-1** Find lower bound for $f(n) = 5n^2$.

**Solution:** $\exists\, c,\ n_0$ Such that: $0 \le cn^2 \le 5n^2 \Rightarrow cn^2 \le 5n^2 \Rightarrow c = 5$ and $n_0 = 1$
$\therefore\ 5n^2 = \Omega(n^2)$ with $c = 5$ and $n_0 = 1$

**Example-2** Prove $f(n) = 100n + 5 \ne \Omega(n^2)$.

**Solution:** $\exists$ c, $n_0$ Such that: $0 \le cn^2 \le 100n + 5$
$100n + 5 \le 100n + 5n\ (\forall n \ge 1) = 105n$
$cn^2 \le 105n \Rightarrow n(cn - 105) \le 0$
Since $n$ is positive $\Rightarrow cn - 105 \le 0 \Rightarrow n \le 105/c$
$\Rightarrow$ Contradiction: $n$ cannot be smaller than a constant

**Example-3** $2n = \Omega(n)$, $n^3 = \Omega(n^3)$, $logn = \Omega(logn)$.

## 1.16 Theta-Θ Notation

This notation decides whether the upper and lower bounds of a given function (algorithm) are the same. The average running time of an algorithm is always between the lower bound and the upper bound. If the upper bound (O) and lower bound (Ω) give the same result, then the Θ notation will also have the same rate of growth. As an example, let us assume that $f(n) = 10n + n$ is the expression. Then, its tight upper bound $g(n)$ is $O(n)$. The rate of growth in the best case is $g(n) = O(n)$.

In this case, the rates of growth in the best case and worst case are the same. As a result, the average case will also be the same. For a given function (algorithm), if the rates of growth (bounds) for O and Ω are not the same, then the rate of growth for the Θ case may not be the same. In this case, we need to consider all possible time complexities and take the average of those (for example, for a quick sort average case, refer to the *Sorting* chapter).

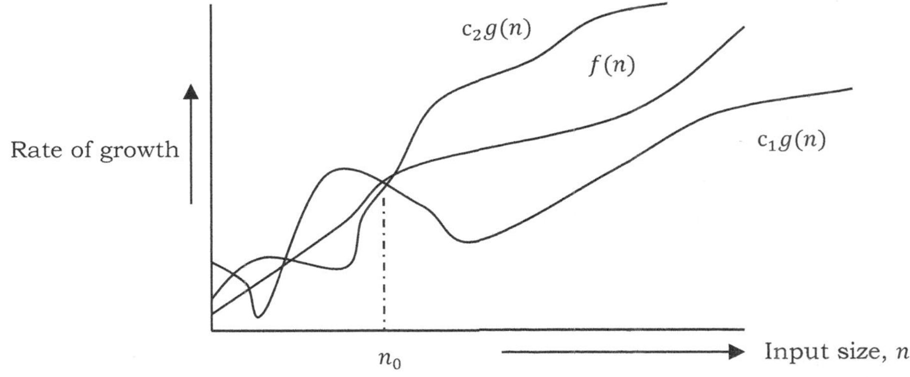


Now consider the definition of Θ notation. It is defined as $\Theta(g(n)) = \{f(n)$: there exist positive constants $c_1, c_2$ and $n_0$ such that $0 \le c_1g(n) \le f(n) \le c_2g(n)$ for all $n \ge n_0\}$. $g(n)$ is an asymptotic tight bound for $f(n)$. $\Theta(g(n))$ is the set of functions with the same order of growth as $g(n)$.

### Θ Examples

**Example 1** Find Θ bound for $f(n) = \frac{n^2}{2} - \frac{n}{2}$

**Solution:** $\frac{n^2}{5} \le \frac{n^2}{2} - \frac{n}{2} \le n^2$, for all, $n \ge 2$
$\therefore\ \frac{n^2}{2} - \frac{n}{2} = \Theta(n^2)$ with $c_1 = 1/5, c_2 = 1$ and $n_0 = 2$

**Example 2** Prove $n \neq \Theta(n^2)$

**Solution:** $c_1 n^2 \leq n \leq c_2 n^2 \Rightarrow$ only holds for: $n \leq 1/c_1$

$\therefore n \neq \Theta(n^2)$

**Example 3** Prove $6n^3 \neq \Theta(n^2)$

**Solution:** $c_1 n^2 \leq 6n^3 \leq c_2 n^2 \Rightarrow$ only holds for: $n \leq c_2/6$

$\therefore 6n^3 \neq \Theta(n^2)$

**Example 4** Prove $n \neq \Theta(logn)$

**Solution:** $c_1 logn \leq n \leq c_2 log n \Rightarrow c_2 \geq \frac{n}{\log n}, \forall n \geq n_0$ – Impossible

### Important Notes

For analysis (best case, worst case and average), we try to give the upper bound (O) and lower bound (Ω) and average running time (Θ). From the above examples, it should also be clear that, for a given function (algorithm), getting the upper bound (O) and lower bound (Ω) and average running time (Θ) may not always be possible. For example, if we are discussing the best case of an algorithm, we try to give the upper bound (O) and lower bound (Ω) and average running time (Θ).

In the remaining chapters, we generally focus on the upper bound (O) because knowing the lower bound (Ω) of an algorithm is of no practical importance, and we use the Θ notation if the upper bound (O) and lower bound (Ω) are the same.

## 1.17 Why is it called Asymptotic Analysis?

From the discussion above (for all three notations: worst case, best case, and average case), we can easily understand that, in every case for a given function $f(n)$ we are trying to find another function $g(n)$ which approximates $f(n)$ at higher values of $n$. That means $g(n)$ is also a curve which approximates $f(n)$ at higher values of $n$.

In mathematics we call such a curve an *asymptotic curve*. In other terms, $g(n)$ is the asymptotic curve for $f(n)$. For this reason, we call algorithm analysis *asymptotic analysis*.

## 1.18 Guidelines for Asymptotic Analysis

There are some general rules to help us determine the running time of an algorithm.

1) **Loops**: The running time of a loop is, at most, the running time of the statements inside the loop (including tests) multiplied by the number of iterations.

```
// executes n times
for (i=1; i<=n; i++)
    m = m + 2; // constant time, c
```

Total time = a constant $c \times n = c\,n = O(n)$.

2) **Nested loops:** Analyze from the inside out. Total running time is the product of the sizes of all the loops.

```
//outer loop executed n times
for (i=1; i<=n; i++) {
    // inner loop executes n times
    for (j=1; j<=n; j++)
        k = k+1; //constant time
}
```

Total time = $c \times n \times n = cn^2 = O(n^2)$.

3) **Consecutive statements:** Add the time complexities of each statement.

```
x = x +1; //constant time
// executes n times
for (i=1; i<=n; i++)
    m = m + 2; //constant time
//outer loop executes n times
for (i=1; i<=n; i++) {
    //inner loop executed n times
    for (j=1; j<=n; j++)
        k = k+1; //constant time
}
```

Total time = $c_0 + c_1 n + c_2 n^2 = O(n^2)$.

4) **If-then-else statements:** Worst-case running time: the test, plus *either* the *then* part *or* the *else* part (whichever is the larger).

```
//test: constant
```

```
if(length( ) == 0 ) {
    return false; //then part: constant
}
else {// else part: (constant + constant) * n
    for (int n = 0; n < length( ); n++) {
      // another if : constant + constant (no else part)
      if(!list[n].equals(otherList.list[n]))
          //constant
        return false;
    }
}
```

Total time $= c_0 + (c_1 + c_2) * n = O(n)$.

5) **Logarithmic complexity:** An algorithm is $O(logn)$ if it takes a constant time to cut the problem size by a fraction (usually by ½). As an example, let us consider the following program:

```
for (i=1; i<=n;)
    i = i*2;
```

If we observe carefully, the value of $i$ is doubling every time. Initially $i = 1$, in next step $i = 2$, and in subsequent steps $i = 4, 8$ and so on. Let us assume that the loop is executing some $k$ times. At $k^{th}$ step $2^k = n$, and at $(k+1)^{th}$ step we come out of the *loop*. Taking logarithms on both sides, gives

$log(2^k) = logn$
$klog2 = logn$
$k = logn$ //if we assume base-2

Total time $= O(logn)$.

**Note:** Similarly, for the case below, the worst-case rate of growth is $O(logn)$ [discussion holds good for the decreasing sequence as well].

```
for (i=n; i>=1;)
    i = i/2;
```

Another example: binary search (finding a word in a dictionary of $n$ pages)

- Look at the center point in the dictionary.
- Is the word towards the left or right of center?
- Repeat the process with the left or right part of the dictionary until the word is found.

## 1.19 Simplifying properties of asymptotic notations

- Transitivity: $f(n) = \Theta(g(n))$ and $g(n) = \Theta(h(n)) \Rightarrow f(n) = \Theta(h(n))$. Valid for O and $\Omega$ as well.
- Reflexivity: $f(n) = \Theta(f(n))$. Valid for O and $\Omega$.
- Symmetry: $f(n) = \Theta(g(n))$ if and only if $g(n) = \Theta(f(n))$.
- Transpose symmetry: $f(n) = O(g(n))$ if and only if $g(n) = \Omega(f(n))$.
- If $f(n)$ is in $O(kg(n))$ for any constant $k > 0$, then $f(n)$ is in $O(g(n))$.
- If $f_1(n)$ is in $O(g_1(n))$ and $f_2(n)$ is in $O(g_2(n))$, then $(f_1 + f_2)(n)$ is in $O(\max(g_1(n), g_1(n)))$.
- If $f_1(n)$ is in $O(g_1(n))$ and $f_2(n)$ is in $O(g_2(n))$ then $f_1(n)\, f_2(n)$ is in $O(g_1(n)\, g_1(n))$.

## 1.20 Commonly used Logarithms and Summations

Logarithms

$log\, x^y = y\, log\, x$ $\quad logn = log_{10}^n$

$log\, xy = logx + logy$ $\quad log^k n = (logn)^k$

$log\, logn = log(logn)$ $\quad log\frac{x}{y} = logx - logy$

$a^{log_b^x} = x^{log_b^a}$ $\quad log_b^x = \frac{log_a^x}{log_a^b}$

Arithmetic series

$$\sum_{K=1}^{n} k = 1 + 2 + \cdots + n = \frac{n(n+1)}{2}$$

Geometric series

$$\sum_{k=0}^{n} x^k = 1 + x + x^2 \ldots + x^n = \frac{x^{n+1} - 1}{x - 1} (x \neq 1)$$

### Harmonic series

$$\sum_{k=1}^{n} \frac{1}{k} = 1 + \frac{1}{2} + \ldots + \frac{1}{n} \approx \log n$$

### Other important formulae

$$\sum_{k=1}^{n} \log k \approx n\log n$$

$$\sum_{k=1}^{n} k^p = 1^p + 2^p + \cdots + n^p \approx \frac{1}{p+1} n^{p+1}$$

## 1.21 Master Theorem for Divide and Conquer Recurrences

All divide and conquer algorithms (also discussed in detail in the *Divide and Conquer* chapter) divide the problem into sub-problems, each of which is part of the original problem, and then perform some additional work to compute the final answer. As an example, a merge sort algorithm [for details, refer to *Sorting* chapter] operates on two sub-problems, each of which is half the size of the original, and then performs $O(n)$ additional work for merging. This gives the running time equation:

$$T(n) = 2T\left(\frac{n}{2}\right) + O(n)$$

The following theorem can be used to determine the running time of divide and conquer algorithms. For a given program (algorithm), first we try to find the recurrence relation for the problem. If the recurrence is of the below form then we can directly give the answer without fully solving it. If the recurrence is of the form $T(n) = aT(\frac{n}{b}) + \Theta(n^k \log^p n)$, where $a \geq 1$, $b > 1, k \geq 0$ and $p$ is a real number, then:

1) If $a > b^k$, then $T(n) = \Theta(n^{\log_b^a})$
2) If $a = b^k$
   a. If $p > -1$, then $T(n) = \Theta(n^{\log_b^a} \log^{p+1} n)$
   b. If $p = -1$, then $T(n) = \Theta(n^{\log_b^a} \log\log n)$
   c. If $p < -1$, then $T(n) = \Theta(n^{\log_b^a})$
3) If $a < b^k$
   a. If $p \geq 0$, then $T(n) = \Theta(n^k \log^p n)$
   b. If $p < 0$, then $T(n) = O(n^k)$

## 1.22 Divide and Conquer Master Theorem: Problems & Solutions

For each of the following recurrences, give an expression for the runtime $T(n)$ if the recurrence can be solved with the Master Theorem. Otherwise, indicate that the Master Theorem does not apply.

Problem-1 $T(n) = 3T(n/2) + n^2$

**Solution:** $T(n) = 3T(n/2) + n^2 \Rightarrow T(n) = \Theta(n^2)$ (Master Theorem Case 3.a)

Problem-2 $T(n) = 4T(n/2) + n^2$

**Solution:** $T(n) = 4T(n/2) + n^2 \Rightarrow T(n) = \Theta(n^2 \log n)$ (Master Theorem Case 2.a)

Problem-3 $T(n) = T(n/2) + n^2$

**Solution:** $T(n) = T(n/2) + n^2 \Rightarrow \Theta(n^2)$ (Master Theorem Case 3.a)

Problem-4 $T(n) = 2^n T(n/2) + n^n$

**Solution:** $T(n) = 2^n T(n/2) + n^n$ => Does not apply ($a$ is not constant)

Problem-5 $T(n) = 16T(n/4) + n$

**Solution:** $T(n) = 16T(n/4) + n \Rightarrow T(n) = \Theta(n^2)$ (Master Theorem Case 1)

Problem-6 $T(n) = 2T(n/2) + n\log n$

**Solution:** $T(n) = 2T(n/2) + n\log n \Rightarrow T(n) = \Theta(n\log^2 n)$ (Master Theorem Case 2.a)

Problem-7 $T(n) = 2T(n/2) + n/\log n$

**Solution:** $T(n) = 2T(n/2) + n/\log n \Rightarrow T(n) = \Theta(n\log\log n)$ (Master Theorem Case 2.b)

Problem-8 $T(n) = 2T(n/4) + n^{0.51}$

**Solution:** $T(n) = 2T(n/4) + n^{0.51} \Rightarrow T(n) = \Theta(n^{0.51})$ (Master Theorem Case 3.b)

Problem-9 $T(n) = 0.5T(n/2) + 1/n$

**Solution:** $T(n) = 0.5T(n/2) + 1/n$ => Does not apply ($a < 1$)

Problem-10 $T(n) = 6T(n/3) + n^2 logn$

**Solution:** $T(n) = 6T(n/3) + n^2 logn$ => $T(n) = \Theta(n^2 logn)$ (Master Theorem Case 3.a)

Problem-11 $T(n) = 64T(n/8) - n^2 logn$

**Solution:** $T(n) = 64T(n/8) - n^2 logn$ => Does not apply (function is not positive)

Problem-12 $T(n) = 7T(n/3) + n^2$

**Solution:** $T(n) = 7T(n/3) + n^2$ => $T(n) = \Theta(n^2)$ (Master Theorem Case 3.as)

Problem-13 $T(n) = 4T(n/2) + logn$

**Solution:** $T(n) = 4T(n/2) + logn$ => $T(n) = \Theta(n^2)$ (Master Theorem Case 1)

Problem-14 $T(n) = 16T(n/4) + n!$

**Solution:** $T(n) = 16T(n/4) + n!$ => $T(n) = \Theta(n!)$ (Master Theorem Case 3.a)

Problem-15 $T(n) = \sqrt{2}T(n/2) + logn$

**Solution:** $T(n) = \sqrt{2}T(n/2) + logn$ => $T(n) = \Theta(\sqrt{n})$ (Master Theorem Case 1)

Problem-16 $T(n) = 3T(n/2) + n$

**Solution:** $T(n) = 3T(n/2) + n$ => $T(n) = \Theta(n^{log3})$ (Master Theorem Case 1)

Problem-17 $T(n) = 3T(n/3) + \sqrt{n}$

**Solution:** $T(n) = 3T(n/3) + \sqrt{n}$ => $T(n) = \Theta(n)$ (Master Theorem Case 1)

Problem-18 $T(n) = 4T(n/2) + cn$

**Solution:** $T(n) = 4T(n/2) + cn$ => $T(n) = \Theta(n^2)$ (Master Theorem Case 1)

Problem-19 $T(n) = 3T(n/4) + nlogn$

**Solution:** $T(n) = 3T(n/4) + nlogn$ => $T(n) = \Theta(nlogn)$ (Master Theorem Case 3.a)

Problem-20 $T(n) = 3T(n/3) + n/2$

**Solution:** $T(n) = 3T(n/3) + n/2$ => $T(n) = \Theta(nlogn)$ (Master Theorem Case 2.a)

## 1.23 Master Theorem for Subtract and Conquer Recurrences

Let $T(n)$ be a function defined on positive $n$, and having the property

$$T(n) = \begin{cases} c, & \text{if } n \le 1 \\ aT(n-b) + f(n), & \text{if } n > 1 \end{cases}$$

for some constants $c, a > 0, b > 0, k \ge 0$, and function $f(n)$. If $f(n)$ is in $O(n^k)$, then

$$T(n) = \begin{cases} O(n^k), & \text{if a} < 1 \\ O(n^{k+1}), & \text{if a} = 1 \\ O\left(n^k a^{\frac{n}{b}}\right), & \text{if a} > 1 \end{cases}$$

## 1.24 Variant of Subtraction and Conquer Master Theorem

The solution to the equation $T(n) = T(\alpha\, n) + T((1-\alpha)n) + \beta n$, where $0 < \alpha < 1$ and $\beta > 0$ are constants, is $O(nlogn)$.

## 1.25 Method of Guessing and Confirming

Now, let us discuss a method which can be used to solve any recurrence. The basic idea behind this method is:

*guess* the answer; and then *prove* it correct by induction.

In other words, it addresses the question: What if the given recurrence doesn't seem to match with any of these (master theorem) methods? If we guess a solution and then try to verify our guess inductively, usually either the proof will succeed (in which case we are done), or the proof will fail (in which case the failure will help us refine our guess).

As an example, consider the recurrence $T(n) = \sqrt{n}\, T(\sqrt{n}) + n$. This doesn't fit into the form required by the Master Theorems. Carefully observing the recurrence gives us the impression that it is similar to the divide and conquer method (dividing the problem into $\sqrt{n}$ subproblems each with size $\sqrt{n}$). As we can see, the size of the subproblems at the first level of recursion is $n$. So, let us guess that $T(n) = O(nlogn)$, and then try to prove that our guess is correct.

Let's start by trying to prove an *upper* bound $T(n) \le cnlogn$:

$$\begin{aligned} T(n) &= \sqrt{n}\, T(\sqrt{n}) + n \\ &\leq \sqrt{n}.\, c\sqrt{n}\, log\sqrt{n} + n \\ &= n.\, c\, log\sqrt{n} + n \\ &= n.c.\tfrac{1}{2}.logn + n \\ &\leq cnlogn \end{aligned}$$

The last inequality assumes only that $1 \leq c.\frac{1}{2}.logn$. This is correct if $n$ is sufficiently large and for any constant $c$, no matter how small. From the above proof, we can see that our guess is correct for the upper bound. Now, let us prove the *lower* bound for this recurrence.

$$\begin{aligned} T(n) &= \sqrt{n}\, T(\sqrt{n}) + n \\ &\geq \sqrt{n}.\, k\sqrt{n}\, log\sqrt{n} + n \\ &= n.\, k\, log\sqrt{n} + n \\ &= n.k.\tfrac{1}{2}.logn + n \\ &\geq knlogn \end{aligned}$$

The last inequality assumes only that $1 \geq k.\frac{1}{2}.logn$. This is incorrect if $n$ is sufficiently large and for any constant $k$. From the above proof, we can see that our guess is incorrect for the lower bound.

From the above discussion, we understood that $\Theta(nlogn)$ is too big. How about $\Theta(n)$? The lower bound is easy to prove directly:

$$T(n) = \sqrt{n}\, T(\sqrt{n}) + n \quad \geq n$$

Now, let us prove the upper bound for this $\Theta(n)$.

$$\begin{aligned} T(n) &= \sqrt{n}\, T(\sqrt{n}) + n \\ &\leq \sqrt{n}.c.\sqrt{n} + n \\ &= n.\, c + n \\ &= n\,(c + 1) \\ &\nleq cn \end{aligned}$$

From the above induction, we understood that $\Theta(n)$ is too small and $\Theta(nlogn)$ is too big. So, we need something bigger than $n$ and smaller than $nlogn$. How about $n\sqrt{logn}$?

Proving the upper bound for $n\sqrt{logn}$:

$$\begin{aligned} T(n) &= \sqrt{n}\, T(\sqrt{n}) + n \\ &\leq \sqrt{n}.c.\sqrt{n}\sqrt{log\sqrt{n}} + n \\ &= n.\, c.\tfrac{1}{\sqrt{2}}\, log\sqrt{n} + n \\ &\leq cnlog\sqrt{n} \end{aligned}$$

Proving the lower bound for $n\sqrt{logn}$:

$$\begin{aligned} T(n) &= \sqrt{n}\, T(\sqrt{n}) + n \\ &\geq \sqrt{n}.k.\sqrt{n}\sqrt{log\sqrt{n}} + n \\ &= n.\, k.\tfrac{1}{\sqrt{2}}\, log\sqrt{n} + n \\ &\ngeq knlog\sqrt{n} \end{aligned}$$

The last step doesn't work. So, $\Theta(n\sqrt{logn})$ doesn't work. What else is between $n$ and $nlogn$? How about $nloglogn$?

Proving upper bound for $nloglogn$:

$$\begin{aligned} T(n) &= \sqrt{n}\, T(\sqrt{n}) + n \\ &\leq \sqrt{n}.c.\sqrt{n}loglog\sqrt{n} + n \\ &= n.\, c.loglogn\text{-}c.n + n \\ &\leq cnloglogn, \text{ if } c \geq 1 \end{aligned}$$

Proving lower bound for $nloglogn$:

$$\begin{aligned} T(n) &= \sqrt{n}\, T(\sqrt{n}) + n \\ &\geq \sqrt{n}.k.\sqrt{n}loglog\sqrt{n} + n \\ &= n.\, k.loglogn\text{-}k.n + n \\ &\geq knloglogn, \text{ if } k \leq 1 \end{aligned}$$

From the above proofs, we can see that $T(n) \leq cnloglogn$, if $c \geq 1$ and $T(n) \geq knloglogn$, if $k \leq 1$. Technically, we're still missing the base cases in both proofs, but we can be fairly confident at this point that $T(n) = \Theta(nloglogn)$.

## 1.26 Amortized Analysis

Amortized analysis refers to determining the time-averaged running time for a sequence of operations. It is different from average case analysis, because amortized analysis does not make any assumption about the distribution of the data values, whereas average case analysis assumes the data are not "bad" (e.g., some sorting algorithms do well *on average* over all input orderings but very badly on certain input orderings). That is, amortized analysis is a worst-case analysis, but for a sequence of operations rather than for individual operations.

The motivation for amortized analysis is to better understand the running time of certain techniques, where standard worst case analysis provides an overly pessimistic bound. Amortized analysis generally applies to a method that consists of a sequence of operations, where the vast majority of the operations are cheap, but some of the operations are expensive. If we can show that the expensive operations are particularly rare we can *change them* to the cheap operations, and only bound the cheap operations.

The general approach is to assign an artificial cost to each operation in the sequence, such that the total of the artificial costs for the sequence of operations bounds the total of the real costs for the sequence. This artificial cost is called the amortized cost of an operation. To analyze the running time, the amortized cost thus is a correct way of understanding the overall running time — but note that particular operations can still take longer so it is not a way of bounding the running time of any individual operation in the sequence.

When one event in a sequence affects the cost of later events:

- One particular task may be expensive.
- But it may leave data structure in a state that the next few operations become easier.

**Example**: Let us consider an array of elements from which we want to find the $k^{th}$ smallest element. We can solve this problem using sorting. After sorting the given array, we just need to return the $k^{th}$ element from it. The cost of performing the sort (assuming comparison based sorting algorithm) is $O(nlogn)$. If we perform $n$ such selections then the average cost of each selection is $O(nlogn/n) = O(logn)$. This clearly indicates that sorting once is reducing the complexity of subsequent operations.

## 1.27 Algorithms Analysis: Problems & Solutions

**Note:** From the following problems, try to understand the cases which have different complexities ($O(n)$, $O(logn)$, $O(loglogn)$ etc.).

Problem-21 Find the complexity of the recurrence below:

$$T(n) = \begin{cases} 3T(n-1), if\ n > 0, \\ 1, \qquad otherwise \end{cases}$$

**Solution:** Let us try solving this function with substitution.

$T(n) = 3T(n-1)$
$T(n) = 3\big(3T(n-2)\big) = 3^2T(n-2)$
$T(n) = 3^2(3T(n-3))$

$T(n) = 3^nT(n-n) = 3^nT(0) = 3^n$

This clearly shows that the complexity of this function is $O(3^n)$.

**Note:** We can use the *Subtraction and Conquer* master theorem for this problem.

Problem-22 Find the complexity of the recurrence below:

$$T(n) = \begin{cases} 2T(n-1) - 1, if\ n > 0, \\ 1, \qquad otherwise \end{cases}$$

**Solution:** Let us try solving this function with substitution.

$T(n) = 2T(n-1) - 1$
$T(n) = 2(2T(n-2) - 1) - 1 = 2^2T(n-2) - 2 - 1$
$T(n) = 2^2(2T(n-3) - 2 - 1) - 1 = 2^3T(n-4) - 2^2 - 2^1 - 2^0$
$T(n) = 2^nT(n-n) - 2^{n-1} - 2^{n-2} - 2^{n-3} \ldots .2^2 - 2^1 - 2^0$
$T(n) = 2^n - 2^{n-1} - 2^{n-2} - 2^{n-3} \ldots .2^2 - 2^1 - 2^0$
$T(n) = 2^n - (2^n - 1)\ [note: 2^{n-1} + 2^{n-2} + \cdots + 2^0 = 2^n]$
$T(n) = 1$

∴ Time Complexity is $O(1)$. Note that while the recurrence relation looks exponential, the solution to the recurrence relation here gives a different result.

Problem-23 What is the running time of the following function?

```
void function(int n) {
    int i=1, s=1;
    while( s <= n) {
        i++;
        s= s+i;
        printf("*");
```

```
        }
    }
```

**Solution:** Consider the comments in the below function:

```
void function (int n) {
    int i=1, s=1;
    // s is increasing not at rate 1 but i
    while( s <= n) {
        i++;
        s= s+i;
        printf("*");
    }
}
```

We can define the *'s'* terms according to the relation $s_i = s_{i-1} + i$. The value of *'i'* increases by 1 for each iteration. The value contained in *'s'* at the $i^{th}$ iteration is the sum of the first *'i'* positive integers. If $k$ is the total number of iterations taken by the program, then the *while* loop terminates if:

$$1 + 2 + \ldots + k = \frac{k(k+1)}{2} > n \Rightarrow k = O(\sqrt{n}).$$

Problem-24 Find the complexity of the function given below.

```
void function(int n) {
    int i, count =0;
        for(i=1; i*i<=n; i++)
            count++;
}
```

**Solution:**

```
void function(int n) {
    int i, count =0;
    for(i=1; i*i<=n; i++)
        count++;
}
```

In the above-mentioned function the loop will end, if $i^2 > n \Rightarrow T(n) = O(\sqrt{n})$. This is similar to Problem-23.

Problem-25 What is the complexity of the program given below:

```
void function(int n) {
    int i, j, k , count =0;
    for(i=n/2; i<=n; i++)
        for(j=1; j + n/2<=n; j= j+1)
            for(k=1; k<=n; k= k * 2)
                count++;
}
```

**Solution:** Consider the comments in the following function.

```
void function (int n) {
    int i, j, k, count = 0;
    //outer loop execute n/2 times
    for (i = n / 2; i <= n; i++)
        //middle loop executes n/2 times
        for (j = 1; j + n / 2 <= n; j = j + 1)
            //inner loop execute logn times
            for (k = 1; k <= n; k = k * 2)
                count++;
}
```

The complexity of the above function is $O(n^2 logn)$.

Problem-26 What is the complexity of the program given below:

```
void function(int n) {
    int i, j, k , count =0;
    for(i=n/2; i<=n; i++)
        for(j=1; j<=n; j= 2 * j)
            for(k=1; k<=n; k= k * 2)
                count++;
}
```

**Solution:** Consider the comments in the following function.

```
void function(int n) {
```

```
    int i, j, k , count =0;
    //outer loop execute n/2 times
    for(i=n/2; i<=n; i++)
      //middle loop executes logn times
      for(j=1; j<=n; j= 2 * j)
        //inner loop execute logn times
        for(k=1; k<=n; k= k*2)
          count++;
}
```

The complexity of the above function is $O(nlog^2n)$.

Problem-27 Find the complexity of the program below.

```
function( int n ) {
    if(n == 1) return;
    for(int i = 1 ; i <= n ; i + + ) {
        for(int j= 1 ; j <= n ; j + + ) {
            printf("*" );
            break;
        }
    }
}
```

**Solution:** Consider the comments in the function below.

```
function( int n ) {
  //constant time
  if( n == 1 ) return;
  //outer loop execute n times
  for(int i = 1 ; i <= n ; i + + ) {
    // inner loop executes only time due to break statement.
    for(int j= 1 ; j <= n ; j + + ) {
      printf("*" );
      break;
    }
  }
}
```

The complexity of the above function is $O(n)$. Even though the inner loop is bounded by $n$, due to the break statement it is executing only once.

Problem-28 Write a recursive function for the running time $T(n)$ of the function given below. Prove using the iterative method that $T(n) = \Theta(n^3)$.

```
void function( int n ) {
    if( n == 1 ) return;
    for(int i = 1 ; i <= n ; i + + )
        for(int j = 1 ; j <= n ; j + + )
            printf("*");
    function( n-3 );
}
```

**Solution:** Consider the comments in the function below:

```
void function (int n) {
  if( n == 1 ) return; //constant time
  //outer loop execute n times
  for(int i = 1 ; i <= n ; i + + )
    //inner loop executes n times
    for(int j = 1 ; j <= n ; j + + )
      //constant time
      printf("*" ) ;
  function( n-3 );
}
```

The recurrence for this code is clearly $T(n) = T(n - 3) + cn^2$ for some constant $c > 0$ since each call prints out $n^2$ asterisks and calls itself recursively on $n$ - 3. Using the iterative method we get: $T(n) = T(n - 3) + cn^2$. Using the *Subtraction and Conquer* master theorem, we get $T(n) = \Theta(n^3)$.

Problem-29 Determine $\Theta$ bounds for the recurrence relation: $T(n) = 2T\left(\frac{n}{2}\right) + nlogn$.

**Solution:** Using Divide and Conquer master theorem, we get $O(nlog^2n)$.

Problem-30 Determine Θ bounds for the recurrence: $T(n) = T\left(\frac{n}{2}\right) + T\left(\frac{n}{4}\right) + T\left(\frac{n}{8}\right) + n$.

**Solution:** Substituting in the recurrence equation, we get: $T(n) \leq c1 * \frac{n}{2} + c2 * \frac{n}{4} + c3 * \frac{n}{8} + cn \leq k * n$ , where $k$ is a constant. This clearly says $\Theta(n)$.

Problem-31 Determine Θ bounds for the recurrence relation: $T(n) = T(\lceil n/2 \rceil) + 7$.

**Solution:** Using Master Theorem we get: $\Theta(logn)$.

Problem-32 Prove that the running time of the code below is $\Omega(logn)$.

```
void Read(int n) {
        int k = 1;
        while( k < n )
                k = 3*k;
}
```

**Solution:** The *while* loop will terminate once the value of *'k'* is greater than or equal to the value of *'n'*. In each iteration the value of *'k'* is multiplied by 3. If $i$ is the number of iterations, then *'k'* has the value of $3^i$ after $i$ iterations. The loop is terminated upon reaching $i$ iterations when $3^i \geq n \leftrightarrow i \geq \log_3 n$, which shows that $i = \Omega\ (logn)$.

Problem-33 Solve the following recurrence.

$$T(n) = \begin{cases} 1, & if\ n = 1 \\ T(n-1) + n(n-1), & if\ n \geq 2 \end{cases}$$

**Solution:** By iteration:

$$T(n) = T(n-2) + (n-1)(n-2) + n(n-1)$$

...

$$T(n) = T(1) + \sum_{i=1}^{n} i(i-1)$$

$$T(n) = T(1) + \sum_{i=1}^{n} i^2 - \sum_{i=1}^{n} i$$

$$T(n) = 1 + \frac{n((n+1)(2n+1)}{6} - \frac{n(n+1)}{2}$$

$$T(n) = \Theta(n^3)$$

**Note:** We can use the *Subtraction and Conquer* master theorem for this problem.

Problem-34 Consider the following program:

```
Fib[n]
if(n==0) then return 0
else if(n==1) then return 1
else return Fib[n-1]+Fib[n-2]
```

**Solution:** The recurrence relation for the running time of this program is: $T(n) = T(n-1) + T(n-2) + c$. Note $T(n)$ has two recurrence calls indicating a binary tree. Each step recursively calls the program for $n$ reduced by 1 and 2, so the depth of the recurrence tree is $O(n)$. The number of leaves at depth $n$ is $2^n$ since this is a full binary tree, and each leaf takes at least $O(1)$ computations for the constant factor. Running time is clearly exponential in $n$ and it is $O(2^n)$.

Problem-35 Running time of following program?

```
void function(n) {
    for(int i = 1; i <= n ; i + + )
        for(int j = 1 ; j <= n ; j+ = i )
            printf(" * ");
}
```

**Solution:** Consider the comments in the function below:

```
void function (n) {
    //this loop executes n times
    for(int i = 1;  i <= n ; i + + )
        //this loop executes j times with j increase by the rate of i
        for(int j = 1 ; j <= n ; j+ = i )
            printf( " * " );
}
```

In the above code, inner loop executes $n/i$ times for each value of $i$. Its running time is $n \times (\sum_{i=1}^{n} n/i) = O(nlogn)$.

Problem-36 What is the complexity of $\sum_{i=1}^{n} log\ i$ ?

**Solution:** Using logarithmic property, $logxy = logx + logy$, we can see that this problem is equivalent to

$$\sum_{i=1}^{n} logi = log\ 1 + log\ 2 + \cdots + log\ n = log\,(1 \times 2 \times ... \times n) = log\,(n!) \ \le log\,(n^n\,) \le nlogn$$

This shows that the time complexity = $O(nlogn)$.

Problem-37 What is the running time of the following recursive function (specified as a function of the input value $n$)? First write the recurrence formula and then find its complexity.

```
void function(int n) {
        if(n <= 1) return;
        for (int i=1 ; i <= 3; i++ )
                f(⌈n/3⌉);
}
```

**Solution:** Consider the comments in the function below:

```
void function (int n) {
    if(n <= 1) return;   // constant time
    //this loop executes with recursive loop of n/3 value
    for (int i=1 ; i <= 3; i++ )
        f(⌈n/3⌉);
}
```

We can assume that for asymptotical analysis $k = \lceil k \rceil$ for every integer $k \ge 1$. The recurrence for this code is $T(n) = 3T(\frac{n}{3}) + \Theta(1)$. Using master theorem, we get $T(n) = \Theta(n)$.

Problem-38 What is the running time of the following recursive function (specified as a function of the input value $n$)? First write a recurrence formula and show its solution using induction.

```
void function(int n) {
        if(n <= 1) return;
        for (int i=1 ; i <= 3 ; i++ )
                function (n − 1).
}
```

**Solution:** Consider the comments in the function below:

```
void function (int n) {
    //constant time
    if(n <= 1) return;
    //this loop executes 3 times with recursive call of n-1 value
    for (int i=1 ; i <= 3 ; i++ )
        function (n − 1).
}
```

The *if* statement requires constant time [O(1)]. With the *for* loop, we neglect the loop overhead and only count three times that the function is called recursively. This implies a time complexity recurrence:

$$T(n) = c, if\ n \le 1;$$
$$= c + 3T(n-1), if\ n > 1.$$

Using the *Subtraction and Conquer* master theorem, we get $T(n) = \Theta(3^n)$.

Problem-39 Write a recursion formula for the running time $T(n)$ of the function whose code is below.

```
void function (int n) {
        if(n <= 1)  return;
        for(int i = 1; i < n; i + +)
                printf(" * ");
        function ( 0.8n ) ;
}
```

**Solution:** Consider the comments in the function below:

```
function (int n) {
    if(n <= 1)  return;   //constant time
    // this loop executes n times with constant time loop
    for(int i = 1; i < n; i + +)
        printf(" * ");
    //recursive call with 0.8n
    function ( 0.8n ) ;
}
```

The recurrence for this piece of code is $T(n) = T(.8n) + O(n) = T(4/5n) + O(n) = 4/5\,T(n) + O(n)$. Applying master theorem, we get $T(n) = O(n)$.

Problem-40 Find the complexity of the recurrence: $T(n) = 2T(\sqrt{n}) + logn$

**Solution:** The given recurrence is not in the master theorem format. Let us try to convert this to the master theorem format by assuming $n = 2^m$. Applying the logarithm on both sides gives, $logn = mlog2 \Rightarrow m = logn$. Now, the given function becomes:

$$T(n) = T(2^m) = 2T(\sqrt{2^m}) + m = 2T\left(2^{\frac{m}{2}}\right) + m.$$

To make it simple we assume $S(m) = T(2^m) \Rightarrow S(\frac{m}{2}) = T(2^{\frac{m}{2}}) \Rightarrow S(m) = 2S\left(\frac{m}{2}\right) + m$.
Applying the master theorem format would result in $S(m) = O(mlogm)$.
If we substitute $m = logn$ back, $T(n) = S(logn) = O((logn)\ loglogn)$.

Problem-41 Find the complexity of the recurrence: $T(n) = T(\sqrt{n}) + 1$

**Solution:** Applying the logic of Problem-40 gives $S(m) = S\left(\frac{m}{2}\right) + 1$. Applying the master theorem would result in $S(m) = O(logm)$. Substituting $m = logn$, gives $T(n) = S(logn) = O(loglogn)$.

Problem-42 Find the complexity of the recurrence: $T(n) = 2T(\sqrt{n}) + 1$

**Solution:** Applying the logic of Problem-40 gives: $S(m) = 2S\left(\frac{m}{2}\right) + 1$. Using the master theorem results $S(m) = O\left(m^{log_2^2}\right) = O(m)$. Substituting $m = logn$ gives $T(n) = O(logn)$.

Problem-43 Find the complexity of the below function.

```
int function (int n) {
        if(n <= 2) return 1;
        else return (Function (floor(sqrt(n))) + 1);
}
```

**Solution:** Consider the comments in the function below:

```
int function (int n) {
   if(n <= 2) return 1;              //constant time
   else                              // executes √n + 1 times
      return (Function (floor(sqrt(n))) + 1);
}
```

For the above code, the recurrence function can be given as: $T(n) = T(\sqrt{n}) + 1$. This is the same as that of Problem-41.

Problem-44 Analyze the running time of the following recursive pseudo-code as a function of $n$.

```
void function(int n) {
  if( n < 2 ) return;
  else counter = 0;
  for i = 1 to 8 do
     function (n/2);
     for i =1 to n^3 do
        counter = counter + 1;
}
```

**Solution:** Consider the comments in below pseudo-code and call running time of function(n) as $T(n)$.

```
void function(int n) {
   if( n < 2 ) return;    //constant time
   else counter = 0;
   // this loop executes 8 times with n value half in every call
   for i = 1 to 8 do
      function(n/2);
   // this loop executes n^3 times with constant time loop
   for i =1 to n^3 do
      counter = counter + 1;
}
```

$T(n)$ can be defined as follows:

$$T(n) = 1\ if\ n < 2,$$
$$= 8T(\frac{n}{2}) + n^3 + 1\ otherwise.$$

Using the master theorem gives: $T(n) = \Theta(n^{log_2^8}logn) = \Theta(n^3logn)$.

Problem-45 Find the complexity of the pseudocode below:

```
temp = 1
repeat
     for i z 1 to n
```

```
        temp =  temp + 1;
        n  = n/2;
    until n <= 1
```

**Solution:** Consider the comments in the pseudocode below:

```
temp  = 1  //const time
repeat          // this loops executes n times
   for i = 1 to n
      temp =  temp + 1;
      //recursive call with n/2 value
      n  = n/2;
until n <= 1
```

The recurrence for this function is $T(n) = T(n/2) + n$. Using master theorem, we get $T(n) = O(n)$.

Problem-46 Running time of the following program?

```
void function(int n) {
      for(int i = 1 ; i <= n ; i + + )
        for(int j = 1 ; j <= n ; j * = 2 )
          printf( " * " );
}
```

**Solution:** Consider the comments in the below function:

```
void function(int n) {
   for(int i = 1 ; i <= n ; i + + ) // this loops executes n times
     // this loops executes logn times from our logarithms guideline
     for(int j = 1 ; j <= n ; j * = 2 )
         printf( " * " );
}
```

Complexity of above program is: $O(nlogn)$.

Problem-47 Running time of the following program?

```
void function(int n) {
    for(int i = 1 ; i <= n/3 ; i + + )
        for(int j = 1 ; j <= n ; j += 4 )
          printf( " * " );
}
```

**Solution:** Consider the comments in the function below:

```
void function(int n) {           // this loops executes n/3 times
   for(int i = 1 ; i <= n/3 ; i + + )
     for(int j = 1 ; j <= n ; j += 4)          // this loops executes n/4 times
         printf( " * " );
}
```

The time complexity of this program is: $O(n^2)$.

Problem-48 Find the complexity of the below function:

```
void function(int n) {
    if(n <=  1) return;
    if(n > 1) {
        printf (" * ");
        function( n/2 );
        function( n/2 );
      }
}
```

**Solution:** Consider the comments in the function below:

```
void function(int n) {
    if(n <= 1) return; //constant time
    if(n > 1) {
        //constant time
        printf (" * ");
        function( n/2 );               //recursion with n/2 value
        function( n/2 );               //recursion with n/2 value
    }
}
```

The recurrence for this function is: $T(n) = 2T\left(\frac{n}{2}\right) + 1$. Using master theorem, we get $T(n) = O(n)$.

**Problem-49** Find the complexity of the function below:

```
void function(int n) {
    int i=1;
    while (i < n) {
        int j=n;
        while(j > 0)
            j = j/2;
        i=2*i;
    } // i
}
```

**Solution:**

```
void function(int n) {
    int i=1;
    while (i < n) {
        int j=n;
        while(j > 0)
            j = j/2;   //logn code
        i=2*i; //logn times
    } // i
}
```

Time Complexity: $O(logn * logn) = O(log^2n)$.

**Problem-50** $\sum_{1 \le k \le n} O(n)$, where $O(n)$ stands for order $n$ is:

(A) $O(n)$ (B) $O(n^2)$ (C) $O(n^3)$ (D) $O(3n^2)$ (E) $O(1.5n^2)$

**Solution: (B)**. $\sum_{1 \le k \le n} O(n) = O(n) \sum_{1 \le k \le n} 1 = O(n^2)$.

**Problem-51** Which of the following three claims are correct?

I $(n + k)^m = \Theta(n^m)$, where $k$ and $m$ are constants II $2^{n+1} = O(2^n)$ III $2^{2n+1} = O(2^n)$

(A) I and II (B) I and III (C) II and III (D) I, II and III

**Solution: (A)**. (I) $(n + k)^m = n^k + c1*n^{k-1} + \dots k^m = \Theta(n^k)$ and (II) $2^{n+1} = 2*2^n = O(2^n)$

**Problem-52** Consider the following functions:

$f(n) = 2^n$ $g(n) = n!$ $h(n) = n^{logn}$

Which of the following statements about the asymptotic behavior of f(n), g(n), and h(n) is true?

(A) $f(n) = O(g(n))$; $g(n) = O(h(n))$ (B) $f(n) = \Omega(g(n))$; $g(n) = O(h(n$ (C) $g(n) = O(f(n))$; $h(n) = O(f(n))$ (D) $h(n) = O(f(n))$; $g(n) = \Omega(f(n))$

**Solution**: **(D)**. According to the rate of growth: $h(n) < f(n) < g(n)$ ($g(n)$ is asymptotically greater than $f(n)$, and $f(n)$ is asymptotically greater than $h(n)$). We can easily see the above order by taking logarithms of the given 3 functions: $lognlogn < n < log(n!)$. Note that, $log(n!) = O(nlogn)$.

**Problem-53** Consider the following segment of C-code:

```
int j=1, n;
while (j <=n)
    j = j*2;
```

The number of comparisons made in the execution of the loop for any $n > 0$ is:

(A) ceil($log_2^n$)+ 1 (B) $n$ (C) ceil($log_2^n$) (D) floor($log_2^n$) + 1

**Solution: (a)**. Let us assume that the loop executes $k$ times. After $k^{th}$ step the value of $j$ is $2^k$. Taking logarithms on both sides gives $k = log_2^n$. Since we are doing one more comparison for exiting from the loop, the answer is ceil($log_2^n$)+ 1.

**Problem-54** Consider the following C code segment. Let $T(n)$ denote the number of times the for loop is executed by the program on input $n$. Which of the following is true?

```
int isPrime(int n){
    for(int i=2;i<=sqrt(n);i++)
    if(n%i == 0){
        printf("Not Prime\n");
        return 0;
    }
    return 1;
}
```

(A) $T(n) = O(\sqrt{n})$ and $T(n) = \Omega(\sqrt{n})$ (B) $T(n) = O(\sqrt{n})$ and $T(n) = \Omega(1)$ (C) $T(n) = O(n)$ and $T(n) = \Omega(\sqrt{n})$ (D) None of the above

**Solution: (B)**. Big O notation describes the tight upper bound and Big Omega notation describes the tight lower bound for an algorithm. The *for* loop in the question is run maximum $\sqrt{n}$ times and minimum 1 time. Therefore, $T(n) = O(\sqrt{n})$ and $T(n) = \Omega(1)$.

Problem-55 In the following C function, let $n \geq m$. How many recursive calls are made by this function?

```
int gcd(n,m){
    if (n%m ==0)
        return m;
    n = n%m;
    return gcd(m,n);
}
```

(A) $\Theta(log_2^n)$ (B) $\Omega(n)$ (C) $\Theta(log_2 log_2^n)$ (D) $\Theta(n)$

**Solution:** No option is correct. Big O notation describes the tight upper bound and Big Omega notation describes the tight lower bound for an algorithm. For $m = 2$ and for all $n = 2^i$, the running time is O(1) which contradicts every option.

Problem-56 Suppose $T(n) = 2T(n/2) + n$, T(0)=T(1)=1. Which one of the following is false?

(A) $T(n) = O(n^2)$ (B) $T(n) = \Theta(nlogn)$ (C) $T(n) = \Omega(n^2)$ (D) $T(n) = O(nlogn)$

**Solution:** (**C**). Big O notation describes the tight upper bound and Big Omega notation describes the tight lower bound for an algorithm. Based on master theorem, we get $T(n) = \Theta(nlogn)$. This indicates that tight lower bound and tight upper bound are the same. That means, $O(nlogn)$ and $\Omega(nlogn)$ are correct for given recurrence. So, option (C) is wrong.

Problem-57 Find the complexity of the function below:

```
void function(int n) {
    for (int i = 0; i<n; i++)
        for(int j=i; j<i*i; j++)
            if (j %i == 0){
                for (int k = 0; k < j; k++)
                    printf(" * ");
            }
}
```

**Solution:**

```
void function(int n) {
    for (int i = 0; i<n; i++)              // Executes n times
        for(int j=i; j<i*i; j++)           // Executes n*n times
            if (j %i == 0){
                for (int k = 0; k < j; k++)    // Executes j times = (n*n) times
                    printf(" * ");
            }
}
```

Time Complexity: $O(n^5)$.

Problem-58 To calculate $9^n$, give an algorithm and discuss its complexity.

**Solution:** Start with 1 and multiply by 9 until reaching $9^n$.

Time Complexity: There are $n - 1$ multiplications and each takes constant time giving a $\Theta(n)$ algorithm.

Problem-59 For Problem-58, can we improve the time complexity?

**Solution:** Refer to the *Divide and Conquer* chapter.

Problem-60 Find the time complexity of recurrence $T(n) = T(\frac{n}{2}) + T(\frac{n}{4}) + T(\frac{n}{8}) + n$.

**Solution**: Let us solve this problem by method of guessing. The total size on each level of the recurrence tree is less than $n$, so we guess that $f(n) = n$ will dominate. Assume for all $i < n$ that $c_1 n \leq T(i) \leq c_2 n$. Then,

$$c_1\frac{n}{2} + c_1\frac{n}{4} + c_1\frac{n}{8} + kn \leq T(n) \leq c_2\frac{n}{2} + c_2\frac{n}{4} + c_2\frac{n}{8} + kn$$

$$c_1 n(\frac{1}{2} + \frac{1}{4} + \frac{1}{8} + \frac{k}{c_1}) \leq T(n) \leq c_2 n(\frac{1}{2} + \frac{1}{4} + \frac{1}{8} + \frac{k}{c_2})$$

$$c_1 n(\frac{7}{8} + \frac{k}{c_1}) \leq T(n) \leq c_2 n(\frac{7}{8} + \frac{k}{c_2})$$

If $c_1 \geq 8k$ and $c_2 \leq 8k$, then $c_1 n = T(n) = c_2 n$. So, $T(n) = \Theta(n)$. In general, if you have multiple recursive calls, the sum of the arguments to those calls is less than n (in this case $\frac{n}{2} + \frac{n}{4} + \frac{n}{8} < n$), and $f(n)$ is reasonably large, a good guess is $T(n) = \Theta(f(n))$.

Problem-61 Find the complexity of the below function:

```
void function(int n) {
    int sum = 0;
    for (int i = 0; i<n; i++)
        if (i>j)
            sum = sum +1;
```

```
        else {
            for (int k = 0; k < n; k++)
                sum = sum -1;
        }
    }
}
```

**Solution:** Consider the worst-case.

```
void function(int n) {
    int sum = 0;
        for (int i = 0; i<n; i++)                  // Executes n times
        if (i>j)
            sum = sum +1;                          // Executes n times
        else {
            for (int k = 0; k < n; k++)            // Executes n times
                sum = sum -1;
        }
    }
}
```

Time Complexity: $O(n^2)$.

Problem-62 Solve the following recurrence relation using the recursion tree method: $T(n)=T(\frac{n}{2}) + T(\frac{2n}{3}) + n^2$.

**Solution:** How much work do we do in each level of the recursion tree?

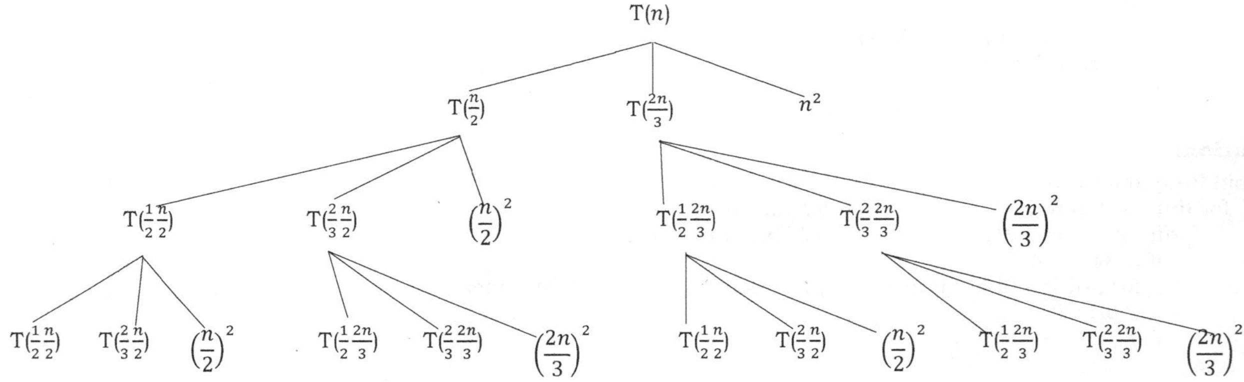

In level 0, we take $n^2$ time. At level 1, the two subproblems take time:

$$\left(\frac{1}{2}n\right)^2 + \left(\frac{2}{3}n\right)^2 = \left(\frac{1}{4}+\frac{4}{9}\right)n^2 = \left(\frac{25}{36}\right)n^2$$

At level 2 the four subproblems are of size $\frac{1}{2}\frac{n}{2}$, $\frac{2}{3}\frac{n}{2}$, $\frac{1}{2}\frac{2n}{3}$, and $\frac{2}{3}\frac{2n}{3}$ respectively. These two subproblems take time:

$$\left(\frac{1}{4}n\right)^2 + \left(\frac{1}{3}n\right)^2 + \left(\frac{1}{3}\right)n^2 + \left(\frac{4}{9}\right)n^2 = \frac{625}{1296}n^2 = \left(\frac{25}{36}\right)^2 n^2$$

Similarly, the amount of work at level $k$ is at most $\left(\frac{25}{36}\right)^k n^2$.

Let $\alpha = \frac{25}{36}$, the total runtime is then:

$$\begin{aligned} T(n) &\leq \sum_{k=0}^{\infty} \alpha^k n^2 \\ &= \frac{1}{1-\alpha} n^2 \\ &= \frac{1}{1-\frac{25}{36}} n^2 \\ &= \frac{1}{\frac{11}{36}} n^2 \\ &= \frac{36}{11} n^2 \\ &= O(n^2) \end{aligned}$$

That is, the first level provides a constant fraction of the total runtime.

Problem-63 Rank the following functions by order of growth: $(n+1)!$, n!, $4^n$, $n \times 3^n$, $3^n + n^2 + 20n$, $(\frac{3}{2})^n$, $4n^2$, $4^{lgn}$, $n^2 + 200$, $20n + 500$, $2^{lgn}$, $n^{2/3}$, 1.

**Solution**:

| Function | Rate of Growth | |
|---|---|---|
| $(n+1)!$ | $O(n!)$ | Decreasing rate of growths |
| $n!$ | $O(n!)$ | |
| $4^n$ | $O(4^n)$ | |
| $n \times 3^n$ | $O(n3^n)$ | |
| $3^n + n^2 + 20n$ | $O(3^n)$ | |
| $(\frac{3}{2})^n$ | $O((\frac{3}{2})^n)$ | |
| $4n^2$ | $O(n^2)$ | |
| $4^{lgn}$ | $O(n^2)$ | |
| $n^2 + 200$ | $O(n^2)$ | |
| $20n + 500$ | $O(n)$ | |
| $2^{lgn}$ | $O(n)$ | |
| $n^{2/3}$ | $O(n^{2/3})$ | |
| 1 | $O(1)$ | |

Problem-64 Can we say $3^{n^{0.75}} = O(3^n)$?

**Solution**: Yes: because $3^{n^{0.75}} < 3^{n^1}$.

Problem-65 Can we say $2^{3n} = O(2^n)$?

**Solution**: No: because $2^{3n} = (2^3)^n = 8^n$ not less than $2^n$.

# RECURSION AND BACKTRACKING

## 2.1 Introduction

In this chapter, we will look at one of the important topics, "*recursion*", which will be used in almost every chapter, and also its relative "*backtracking*".

## 2.2 What is Recursion?

Any function which calls itself is called *recursive*. A recursive method solves a problem by calling a copy of itself to work on a smaller problem. This is called the recursion step. The recursion step can result in many more such recursive calls.

It is important to ensure that the recursion terminates. Each time the function calls itself with a slightly simpler version of the original problem. The sequence of smaller problems must eventually converge on the base case.

## 2.3 Why Recursion?

Recursion is a useful technique borrowed from mathematics. Recursive code is generally shorter and easier to write than iterative code. Generally, loops are turned into recursive functions when they are compiled or interpreted.

Recursion is most useful for tasks that can be defined in terms of similar subtasks. For example, sort, search, and traversal problems often have simple recursive solutions.

## 2.4 Format of a Recursive Function

A recursive function performs a task in part by calling itself to perform the subtasks. At some point, the function encounters a subtask that it can perform without calling itself. This case, where the function does not recur, is called the *base case*. The former, where the function calls itself to perform a subtask, is referred to as the *recursive case*. We can write all recursive functions using the format:

```
if(test for the base case)
    return some base case value
else if(test for another base case)
    return some other base case value
// the recursive case
else
    return (some work and then a recursive call)
```

As an example consider the factorial function: $n!$ is the product of all integers between $n$ and 1. The definition of recursive factorial looks like:

$$n! = 1, \quad \text{if } n = 0$$
$$n! = n * (n-1)! \quad \text{if } n > 0$$

This definition can easily be converted to recursive implementation. Here the problem is determining the value of $n!$, and the subproblem is determining the value of $(n-l)!$. In the recursive case, when $n$ is greater than 1, the function calls itself to determine the value of $(n-l)!$ and multiplies that with $n$. In the base case, when $n$ is 0 or 1, the function simply returns 1. This looks like the following:

```
// calculates factorial of a positive integer
int Fact(int n) {
  if(n == 1)    // base cases: fact of 0 or 1 is 1
    return 1;
  else if(n == 0)
```

```
        return 1;
    else    // recursive case: multiply n by (n – 1) factorial
        return n*Fact(n-1);
}
```

## 2.5 Recursion and Memory (Visualization)

Each recursive call makes a new copy of that method (actually only the variables) in memory. Once a method ends (that is, returns some data), the copy of that returning method is removed from memory. The recursive solutions look simple but visualization and tracing takes time. For better understanding, let us consider the following example.

```
//print numbers 1 to n backward
int printFunc(int n) {
  if( n = = 0) return 0;           // this is the terminating base case
  else {
      printf ("%d",n);
      return printFunc(n-1);       // recursive call to itself again
  }
}
```

For this example, if we call the print function with n=4, visually our memory assignments may look like:

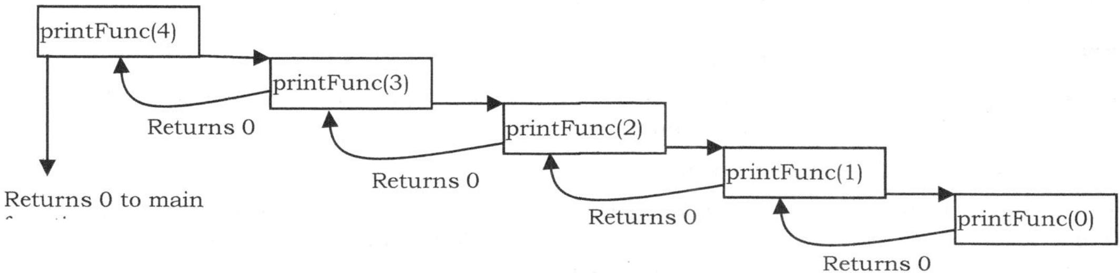


Now, let us consider our factorial function. The visualization of factorial function with n=4 will look like:

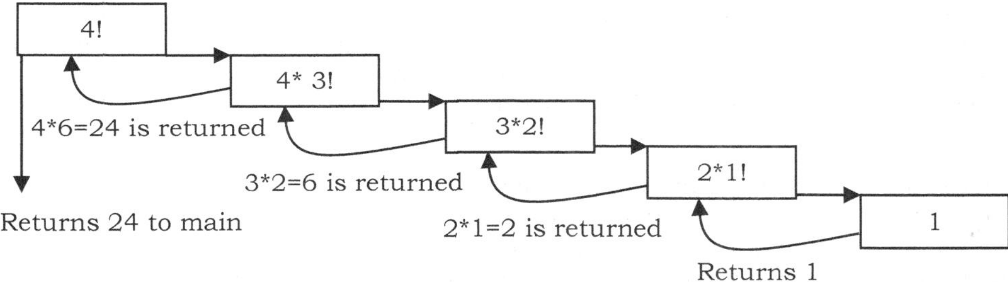


## 2.6 Recursion versus Iteration

While discussing recursion, the basic question that comes to mind is: which way is better? – iteration or recursion? The answer to this question depends on what we are trying to do. A recursive approach mirrors the problem that we are trying to solve. A recursive approach makes it simpler to solve a problem that may not have the most obvious of answers. But, recursion adds overhead for each recursive call (needs space on the stack frame).

### Recursion

- Terminates when a base case is reached.
- Each recursive call requires extra space on the stack frame (memory).
- If we get infinite recursion, the program may run out of memory and result in stack overflow.
- Solutions to some problems are easier to formulate recursively.

### Iteration

- Terminates when a condition is proven to be false.
- Each iteration does not require extra space.
- An infinite loop could loop forever since there is no extra memory being created.
- Iterative solutions to a problem may not always be as obvious as a recursive solution.

## 2.7 Notes on Recursion

- Recursive algorithms have two types of cases, recursive cases and base cases.

- Every recursive function case must terminate at a base case.
- Generally, iterative solutions are more efficient than recursive solutions [due to the overhead of function calls].
- A recursive algorithm can be implemented without recursive function calls using a stack, but it's usually more trouble than its worth. That means any problem that can be solved recursively can also be solved iteratively.
- For some problems, there are no obvious iterative algorithms.
- Some problems are best suited for recursive solutions while others are not.

## 2.8 Example Algorithms of Recursion

- Fibonacci Series, Factorial Finding
- Merge Sort, Quick Sort
- Binary Search
- Tree Traversals and many Tree Problems: InOrder, PreOrder PostOrder
- Graph Traversals: DFS [Depth First Search] and BFS [Breadth First Search]
- Dynamic Programming Examples
- Divide and Conquer Algorithms
- Towers of Hanoi
- Backtracking Algorithms [we will discuss in next section]

## 2.9 Recursion: Problems & Solutions

In this chapter we cover a few problems with recursion, and we will discuss the rest in other chapters. By the time you complete reading the entire book, you will encounter many recursion problems.

Problem-1 Discuss Towers of Hanoi Puzzle.

**Solution:** The Towers of Hanoi is a mathematical puzzle. It consists of three rods (or pegs or towers), and several disks of different sizes which can slide onto any rod. The puzzle starts with the disks on one rod in ascending order of size, the smallest at the top, thus making a conical shape. The objective of the puzzle is to move the entire stack to another rod, satisfying the following rules:

- Only one disk may be moved at a time.
- Each move consists of taking the upper disk from one of the rods and sliding it onto another rod, on top of the other disks that may already be present on that rod.
- No disk may be placed on top of a smaller disk.

**Algorithm:**

- Move the top $n-1$ disks from $Source$ to $Auxiliary$ tower,
- Move the $n^{th}$ disk from $Source$ to $Destination$ tower,
- Move the $n-1$disks from $Auxiliary$ tower to $Destination$ tower.
- Transferring the top $n-1$ disks from $Source$ to $Auxiliary$ tower can again be thought of as a fresh problem and can be solved in the same manner. Once we solve $Towers\ of\ Hanoi$ with three disks, we can solve it with any number of disks with the above algorithm.

```
void TowersOfHanoi(int n, char frompeg, char topeg, char auxpeg) {
    /* If only 1 disk, make the move and return */
    if(n==1) {
        printf("Move disk 1 from peg %c to peg %c",frompeg, topeg);
        return;
    }
    /* Move top n-1 disks from A to B, using C as auxiliary */
    TowersOfHanoi(n-1, frompeg, auxpeg, topeg);
    /* Move remaining disks from A to C */
    printf("\nMove disk %d from peg %c to peg %c", n, frompeg, topeg);
    /* Move n-1 disks from B to C using A as auxiliary */
    TowersOfHanoi(n-1, auxpeg, topeg, frompeg);
}
```

Problem-2 Given an array, check whether the array is in sorted order with recursion.

**Solution**:

```
int isArrayInSortedOrder(int A[],int n){
    if(n == 1)
      return 1;
```

```
        return (A[n-1] < A[n-2])?0:isArrayInSortedOrder(A,n-1);
}
```

Time Complexity: O($n$). Space Complexity: O($n$) for recursive stack space.

## 2.10 What is Backtracking?

Backtracking is an improvement of the brute force approach. It systematically searches for a solution to a problem among all available options. In backtracking, we start with one possible option out of many available options and try to solve the problem if we are able to solve the problem with the selected move then we will print the solution else we will backtrack and select some other option and try to solve it. If none if the options work out we will claim that there is no solution for the problem.

Backtracking is a form of recursion. The usual scenario is that you are faced with a number of options, and you must choose one of these. After you make your choice, you will get a new set of options; just what set of options you get depends on what choice you made. This procedure is repeated over and over until you reach a final state. If you made a good sequence of choices, your final state is a goal state; if you didn't, it isn't.

Backtracking can be thought of as a selective tree/graph traversal method. The tree is a way of representing some initial starting position (the root node) and a final goal state (one of the leaves). Backtracking allows us to deal with situations in which a raw brute-force approach would explode into an impossible number of options to consider. Backtracking is a sort of refined brute force. At each node, we eliminate choices that are obviously not possible and proceed to recursively check only those that have potential.

What's interesting about backtracking is that we back up only as far as needed to reach a previous decision point with an as-yet-unexplored alternative. In general, that will be at the most recent decision point. Eventually, more and more of these decision points will have been fully explored, and we will have to backtrack further and further. If we backtrack all the way to our initial state and have explored all alternatives from there, we can conclude the particular problem is unsolvable. In such a case, we will have done all the work of the exhaustive recursion and known that there is no viable solution possible.

- Sometimes the best algorithm for a problem is to try all possibilities.
- This is always slow, but there are standard tools that can be used to help.
- Tools: algorithms for generating basic objects, such as binary strings [$2^n$ possibilities for $n$-bit string], permutations [$n!$], combinations [$n!/r!\,(n-r)!$], general strings [$k$ –ary strings of length $n$ has $k^n$ possibilities], etc...
- Backtracking speeds the exhaustive search by pruning.

## 2.11 Example Algorithms of Backtracking

- Binary Strings: generating all binary strings
- Generating $k$ –ary Strings
- N-Queens Problem
- The Knapsack Problem
- Generalized Strings
- Hamiltonian Cycles [refer to *Graphs* chapter]
- Graph Coloring Problem

## 2.12 Backtracking: Problems & Solutions

Problem-3 Generate all the strings of $n$ bits. Assume $A[0..n-1]$ is an array of size $n$.

**Solution:**

```
void binary(int n) {
    if(n < 1)
            printf("%s", A);            // Assume array A is a global variable
    else {
            A[n-1] = 0;
            binary(n - 1);
            A[n-1] = 1;
            binary(n - 1);
    }
}
```

Let $T(n)$ be the running time of $binary(n)$. Assume function $printf$ takes time O(1).

$$T(n) = \begin{cases} c, & \text{if } n < 0 \\ 2T(n-1) + d, & \text{otherwise} \end{cases}$$

Using Subtraction and Conquer Master theorem we get: $T(n) = O(2^n)$. This means the algorithm for generating bit-strings is optimal.

Problem-4 Generate all the strings of length $n$ drawn from $0...k - 1$.

**Solution:** Let us assume we keep current k-ary string in an array $A[0..n-1]$. Call function $k\text{-}string$(n, k):

```
void k_strings(int n, int k) {
    //process all k-ary strings of length m
    if (n < 1)
        printf(" %s ", A); //Assume array A is a global variable
    else {
        for (int j = 0; j < k; j++) {
            A[n - 1] = j;
            k_strings(n - 1, k);
        }
    }
}
```

Let $T(n)$ be the running time of $k - string(n)$. Then,

$$T(n) = \begin{cases} c, & if\ n < 0 \\ kT(n-1) + d, otherwise \end{cases}$$

Using Subtraction and Conquer Master theorem we get: $T(n) = O(k^n)$.

**Note:** For more problems, refer to *String Algorithms* chapter.

Problem-5 **Finding the length of connected cells of 1s (regions) in an matrix of 0s and 1s**: Given a matrix, each of which may be 1 or 0. The filled cells that are connected form a region. Two cells are said to be connected if they are adjacent to each other horizontally, vertically or diagonally. There may be several regions in the matrix. How do you find the largest region (in terms of number of cells) in the matrix?

Sample Input: 11000 Sample Output: 5
01100
00101
10001
01011

**Solution:** The simplest idea is: for each location traverse in all 8 directions and in each of those directions keep track of the maximum region found.

```
int getval(int (*A)[5],int i,int j,int L, int H){
    if (i< 0 || i >= L || j< 0 || j >= H)
        return 0;
    else
        return A[i][j];
}
void findMaxBlock(int (*A)[5], int r, int c,int L,int H,int size, bool **cntarr,int &maxsize){
    if ( r >= L || c >= H)
        return;
    cntarr[r][c]=true;
    size++;
    if (size > maxsize)
        maxsize = size;
    //search in eight directions
    int direction[][2]={{-1,0},{-1,-1},{0,-1},{1,-1},{1,0},{1,1},{0,1},{-1,1}};
    for(int i=0; i<8; i++)     {
        int newi =r+direction[i][0];
        int newj=c+direction[i][1];
        int val=getval (A,newi,newj,L,H);
        if (val>0  && (cntarr[newi][newj]==false)){
            findMaxBlock(A,newi,newj,L,H,size,cntarr,maxsize);
        }
    }
    cntarr[r][c]=false;
}
int getMaxOnes(int (*A)[5], int rmax, int colmax){
    int maxsize=0;
    int size=0;
    bool **cntarr=create2darr(rmax,colmax);
```

```
        for(int i=0; i< rmax; i++){
            for(int j=0; j< colmax; j++){
                if (A[i][j] == 1){
                    findMaxBlock(A,i,j,rmax,colmax, 0,cntarr,maxsize);
                }
            }
        }
        return maxsize;
}
```

*Test Call:*

```
int zarr[][5]={{1,1,0,0,0},{0,1,1,0,1},{0,0,0,1,1},{1,0,0,1,1},{0,1,0,1,1}};
cout << "Number of maximum 1s are " << getMaxOnes(zarr,5,5) << endl;
```

Problem-6 Solve the recurrence $T(n) = 2T(n - 1) + 2^n$.

**Solution**: At each level of the recurrence tree, the number of problems is double from the previous level, while the amount of work being done in each problem is half from the previous level. Formally, the $i^{th}$ level has $2^i$ problems, each requiring $2^{n-i}$ work. Thus the $i^{th}$ level requires exactly $2^n$ work. The depth of this tree is $n$, because at the $i^{th}$ level, the originating call will be $T(n - i)$. Thus the total complexity for $T(n)$ is $T(n2^n)$.

CHAPTER

# LINKED LISTS

## 3.1 What is a Linked List?

One disadvantage of using arrays to store data is that arrays are static structures and therefore cannot be easily extended or reduced to fit the data set. Arrays are also expensive to maintain new insertions and deletions. In this chapter we consider another data structure called Linked Lists that addresses some of the limitations of arrays. A linked list is a data structure used for storing collections of data. A linked list has the following properties.

The linked list is a linear dynamic data structure. The number of nodes in a list is not fixed and can grow and shrink demand. Each node of a linked list is made up of two items - the data and a reference to the next node. The last node has a reference to null. The entry point into a linked list is called the head of the list. It should be noted that the *head* is not a separate node, but the reference to the first node. If the list is empty, then the head is a null reference.

- Pointers connect successive elements.
- The final element points to NULL.
- Size can change during program execution.
- It can be made as long as necessary (until system memory is depleted).
- It avoids wasting memory space but requires additional memory for pointers. Memory is allocated as the list expands.

4 → 15 → 7 → 40 → NULL

head

## 3.2 Linked Lists ADT

The following operations make linked lists an ADT:

### Main Linked Lists Operations

- Insert: inserts an element into the list
- Delete: removes and returns the specified position element from the list

### Auxiliary Linked Lists Operations

- Delete List: removes all elements of the list (disposes the list)
- Count: returns the number of elements in the list
- Find $n^{th}$ node from the end of the list

## 3.3 Why Linked Lists?

There exist numerous other data structures that can perform similar functions as linked lists. However, it is imperative to first grasp the dissimilarities between linked lists and arrays before delving into the topic of linked lists. Arrays and linked lists are both utilized for storing collections of data, but it is essential to differentiate their usage and determine which structure is suitable for a particular task. This includes understanding the specific scenarios in which arrays or linked lists are most appropriate.

## 3.4 Arrays Overview

To store the elements of an array, a single memory block is allocated. Accessing any particular element in the array is achieved in constant time by using the index of the element as the subscript.

| | 3 | 2 | 1 | 2 | 2 | 3 |
|---|---|---|---|---|---|---|
| Index → | 0 | 1 | 2 | 3 | 4 | 5 |

## Why Constant Time for Accessing Array Elements?

To access an array element, the address of an element is computed as an offset from the base address of the array and one multiplication is needed to compute what is supposed to be added to the base address to get the memory address of the element. First the size of an element of that data type is calculated and then it is multiplied with the index of the element to get the value to be added to the base address. This process takes one multiplication and one addition. Since these two operations take constant time, we can say the array access can be performed in constant time.

## Advantages of Arrays

- Simple and easy to use
- Faster access to the elements (constant access)

## Disadvantages of Arrays

- Preallocates all needed memory up front and wastes memory space for indices in the array that are empty.
- **Fixed size:** The size of the array is static (specify the array size before using it).
- **One block allocation**: To allocate the array itself at the beginning, sometimes it may not be possible to get the memory for the complete array (if the array size is big).
- **Complex position-based insertion**: To insert an element at a given position, we may need to shift the existing elements. This will create a position for us to insert the new element at the desired position. If the position at which we want to add an element is at the beginning, then the shifting operation is more expensive.

## Dynamic Arrays

Dynamic array (also called as *growable array*, *resizable array*, *dynamic table*, or *array list*) is a random access, variable-size list data structure that allows elements to be added or removed.

One simple way of implementing dynamic arrays is to initially start with some fixed size array. As soon as that array becomes full, create the new array double the size of the original array. Similarly, reduce the array size to half if the elements in the array are less than half.

**Note:** We will see the implementation for *dynamic arrays* in the *Stacks*, *Queues* and *Hashing* chapters.

## Advantages of Linked Lists

Linked lists have both advantages and disadvantages. The advantage of linked lists is that they can be *expanded* in constant time. To create an array, we must allocate memory for a certain number of elements. To add more elements to the array when full, we must create a new array and copy the old array into the new array. This can take a lot of time.

We can prevent this by allocating lots of space initially but then we might allocate more than we need and waste memory. With a linked list, we can start with space for just one allocated element and *add* on new elements easily without the need to do any copying and reallocating.

## Issues with Linked Lists (Disadvantages)

There are a number of issues with linked lists. The main disadvantage of linked lists is *access time* to individual elements. Array is random-access, which means it takes O(1) to access any element in the array. Linked lists take $O(n)$ for access to an element in the list in the worst case. Another advantage of arrays in access time is *spacial locality* in memory. Arrays are defined as contiguous blocks of memory, and so any array element will be physically near its neighbors. This greatly benefits from modern CPU caching methods.

Although the dynamic allocation of storage is a great advantage, the *overhead* with storing and retrieving data can make a big difference. Sometimes linked lists are *hard to manipulate*. If the last item is deleted, the last but one must then have its pointer changed to hold a NULL reference. This requires that the list is traversed to find the last but one link, and its pointer set to a NULL reference.

Finally, linked lists waste memory in terms of extra reference points.

# 3.5 Comparison of Linked Lists with Arrays and Dynamic Arrays

As with most choices in computer programming and design, no method is well suited to all circumstances. A linked list data structure might work well in one case, but cause problems in another. This is a list of some of the common tradeoffs involving linked list structures. In general, if you have a dynamic collection, where elements are frequently being added and deleted, and the location of new elements added to the list is significant, then benefits of a linked list increase.

| Parameter | Linked list | Array | Dynamic array |
|---|---|---|---|
| Indexing | O($n$) | O(1) | O(1) |
| Insertion/deletion at beginning | O(1) | O($n$), if array is not full (for shifting the elements) | O($n$) |
| Insertion at ending | O($n$) | O(1), if array is not full | O(1), if array is not full<br>O($n$), if array is full |
| Deletion at ending | O($n$) | O(1) | O($n$) |
| Insertion in middle | O($n$) | O($n$), if array is not full (for shifting the elements) | O($n$) |
| Deletion in middle | O($n$) | O($n$), if array is not full (for shifting the elements) | O($n$) |
| Wasted space | O($n$) (for pointers) | 0 | O($n$) |

# 3.6 Singly Linked Lists

The linked list consists of a series of structures called nodes. We can think of each node as a record. The first part of the record is a field that stores the data, and the second part of the record is a field that stores a pointer to a node. So, each node contains two fields: a *data* field and a *next* field which is a pointer used to link one node to the next node. Typically, the term "linked list" refers to a singly linked list comprising multiple nodes, with each node having a next pointer that points to the subsequent element in the list. The link of the last node in the list is NULL, which indicates the end of the list.

Each node is allocated in the heap with a call to *malloc*(), so the node memory continues to exist until it is explicitly deallocated with a call to *free*(). The node called a *head* is the first node in the list. The last node's next pointer points to NULL value.

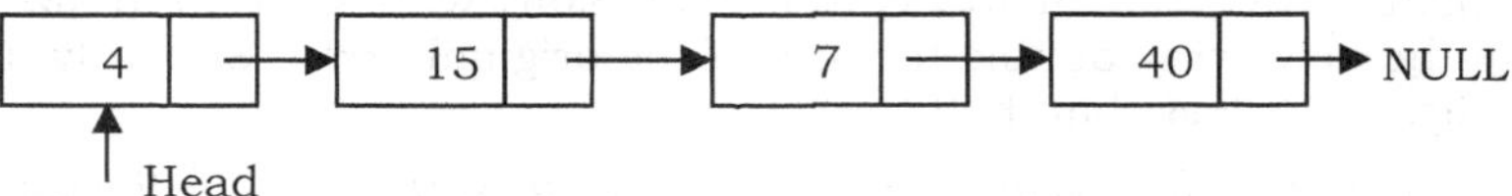


The following is a type declaration for a linked list of integers:

```
struct ListNode {                 // defines a ListNode in a linked list
    int data;                     // the datum
    struct ListNode *next;        // pointer to the next ListNode
};
```

## Basic Operations on a List

- Traversing the list
- Inserting an item in the list
- Deleting an item from the list

## Traversing the Linked List

Let us assume that the *head* points to the first node of the list. To traverse the list, we do the following.

- Follow the pointers.
- Display the contents of the nodes (or count) as they are traversed.
- Stop when the next pointer points to NULL.

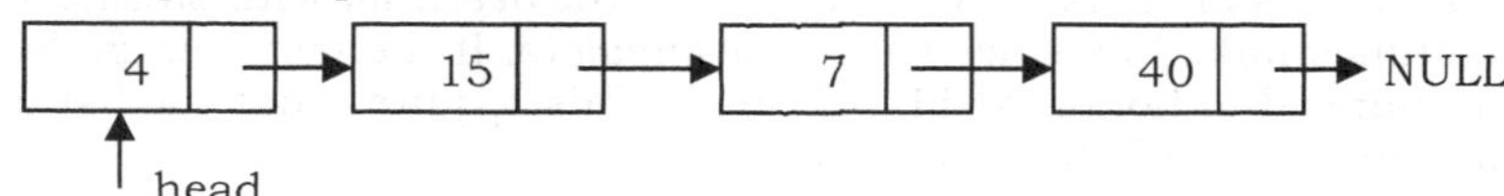


The length() function takes a linked list as input and counts the number of nodes in the list. The function given below can be used for printing the list data with extra print function.

```
void print(struct ListNode *head) {
    struct ListNode *cur = head;
    for (cur = head; cur != NULL; cur = cur->next) {
        printf("%d ", cur->data);
    }
```

```
    printf("\n");
}
// Calculating the size of the list
int length(struct ListNode *head) {
    struct ListNode *cur = head;
    int count = 0;
    for (cur = head; cur != NULL; cur = cur->next) {
        count++;
        cur = cur->next;
    }
    return count;
}
```

Time Complexity: $O(n)$, for scanning the list of size $n$. Space Complexity: $O(1)$, for creating a temporary variable.

## Singly Linked List Insertion

Insertion into a singly-linked list has three cases:

- Inserting a new node before the head (at the beginning)
- Inserting a new node after the tail (at the end of the list)
- Inserting a new node at the middle of the list (random location)

**Note:** To insert an element in the linked list at some position $p$, assume that after inserting the element the position of this new node is $p$.

### Inserting a Node in Singly Linked List at the Beginning

In this case, a new node is inserted before the current head node. *Only one next pointer* needs to be modified (new node's next pointer) and it can be done in two steps:

- Update the next pointer of new node, to point to the current head.

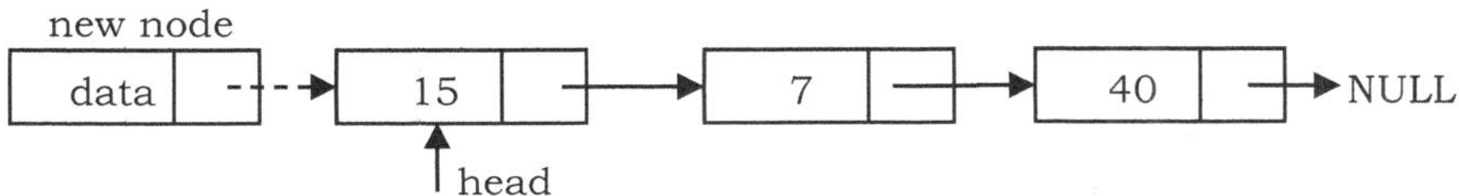


- Update head pointer to point to the new node.

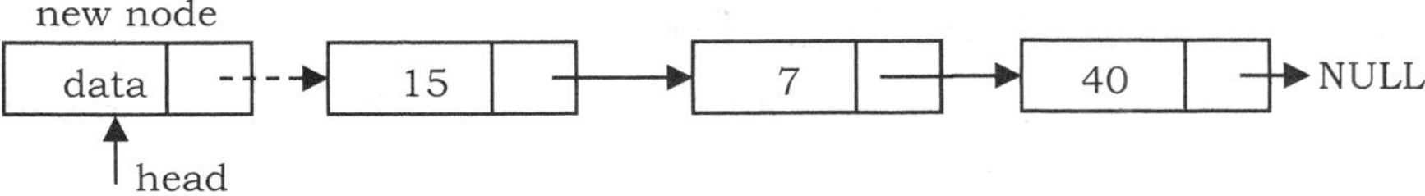


```
struct ListNode  *insertAtBeginning(struct ListNode *head, int data){ // add to beginning of list
    struct ListNode *temp;
    // create a new temp node
    temp=(struct ListNode *)malloc(sizeof(struct ListNode)); //create unnamed node and pointer
    temp->data=data;  //set temp data value
    temp->next=NULL;  // set as end of list
    if (head== NULL){  // then list empty, so set as head node
        head=temp;
        head->next=NULL;
    }
    else{  // else add to left of list
        temp->next=head;
        head=temp;
    }
    return head;
}
```

Time Complexity: $O(1)$. Space Complexity: $O(1)$.

### Inserting a Node in Singly Linked List at the Ending

In this case, we need to modify *two next pointers* (last nodes next pointer and new nodes next pointer).

- New nodes next pointer points to NULL.
- Last nodes next pointer points to the new node.

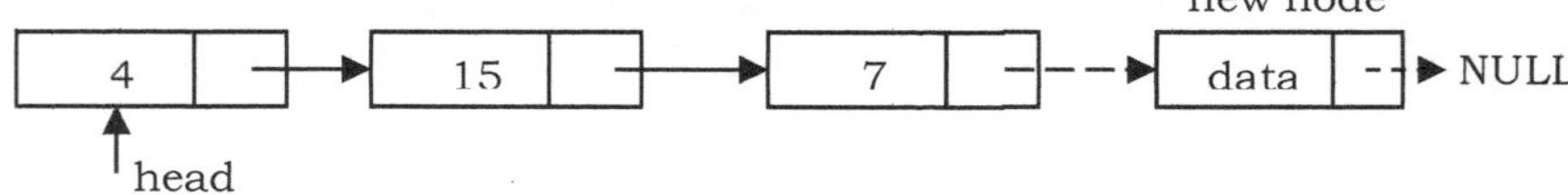


```
struct ListNode *insertAtEnd(struct ListNode *head, int data){ //add to end of list
   struct ListNode *temp,*cur;
   // create a new temp node
   temp= (struct ListNode *)malloc(sizeof(struct ListNode)); //create temp node
   temp->data=data; //set temp value
   temp->next=NULL; // set as end of list
   *cur = head;
   if (cur==NULL){
      // then no head node exists yet, so set temp as head
      head=temp;
   }
   else{
      // find end of current list
      while(cur->next != NULL)
         cur=cur->next;
      // cur is now the last node in list (next==NULL)
      // set temp as new next node
      cur->next =temp;
   }
   return head;
}
```

Time Complexity: O($n$), for scanning the list of size $n$. Space Complexity: O(1).

## Inserting a Node in Singly Linked List at the Given Position

Let us assume that we are given a position where we want to insert the new node. In this case also, we need to modify two next pointers.

- To add an element at position 3 then we stop at position 2. That means, traverse 2 nodes and insert the new node. For simplicity let us assume that *pred* will point to the predecessor of new node. The next pointer of new node points to the next node of the *pred* node.

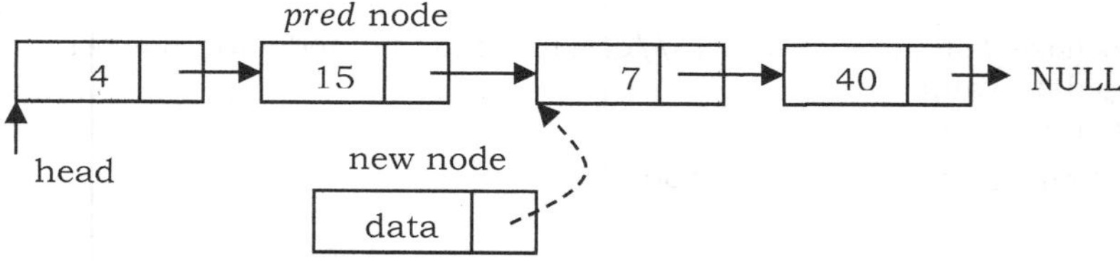


- *pred* node's next pointer now points to the new node.

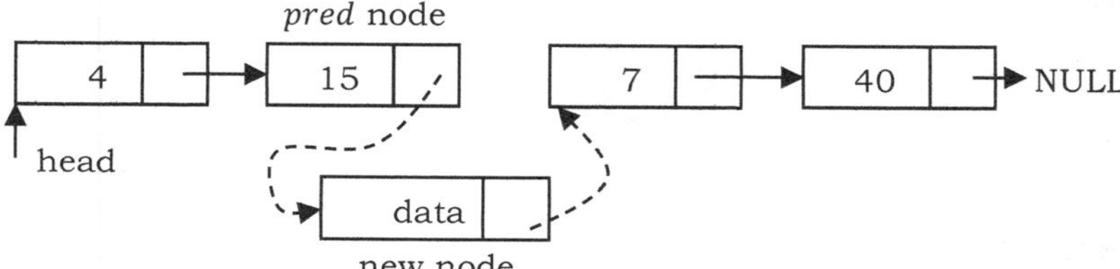


Let us write the code for all three cases. We must update the first element pointer in the calling function, not just in the called function. As a result, we require a double pointer to be passed. The subsequent code is used to insert a node into a singly linked list.

```
// Inserts a new node (new) at position n and returns head.
struct ListNode *insertAtGivenPosition( struct ListNode *head, struct ListNode *new, int n ) {
    // pred will point to the predecessor of new
    struct ListNode *pred = head;
    // Special case: adding at position 1 (inserting at head)
    if ( n <= 1 ) {
        new -> next = head;
        return new;
    }
    // find the n-1 node (predecessor): decrement n and move down the list
    // until either the list has ended or n becomes 0
    while ( --n && pred != NULL )
        pred = pred -> next; // repoint temp to the next element
    if ( pred == NULL )
        return NULL;
    // if it is not NULL, insert new after its predecessor
    new -> next = pred -> next;
    pred -> next = new;
    return head;
}
```

Time Complexity: O($n$). In the worst case, we may need to insert the item at the end of the list.
Space Complexity: O(1).

**Note:** We can implement the three variations of the *insert* operation separately.

Time Complexity: O($n$), since, in the worst case, we may need to insert the node at the end of the list.
Space Complexity: O(1).

As with insertion, there are also three cases to consider here..

- Deleting the first node
- Deleting the last node
- Deleting an intermediate node.

## Deleting the First Node in Singly Linked List

First node (current head node) is removed from the list. It can be done in two steps:

- Create a temporary node which will point to the same node as that of head.

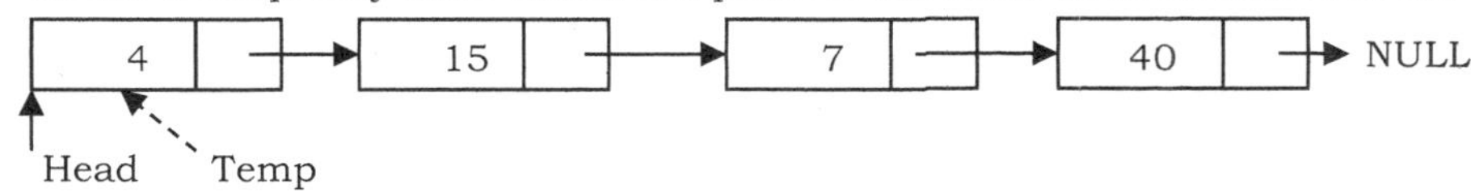


- Now, move the head nodes pointer to the next node and dispose of the temporary node.

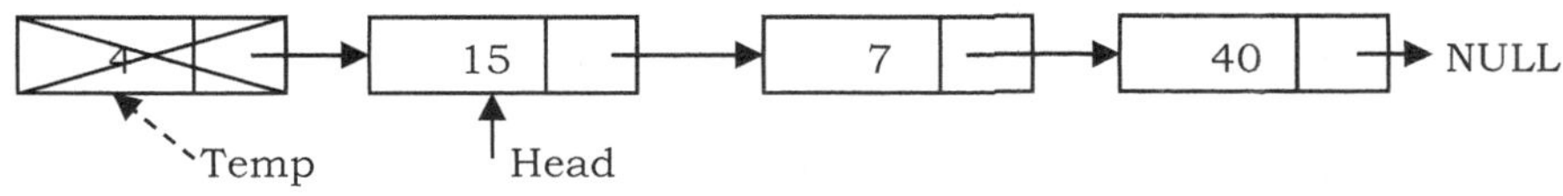


```
void *deleteFirst(struct ListNode **head){
    struct ListNode *temp;
    if (*head == NULL)
        return;
    temp = *head;
    *head = (*head)->next;
    free(temp);
    return;
}
```

Time Complexity: O(1). Space Complexity: O(1).

## Deleting the Last Node in Singly Linked List

In this instance, the final node in the list is being removed. This procedure is somewhat more complex than removing the first node, as the algorithm must locate the node that precedes the tail. This can be achieved in three steps:

- Traverse the list and while traversing maintain the previous node address also. By the time we reach the end of the list, we will have two pointers, one pointing to the *tail* node and the other pointing to the node *before* the tail node.

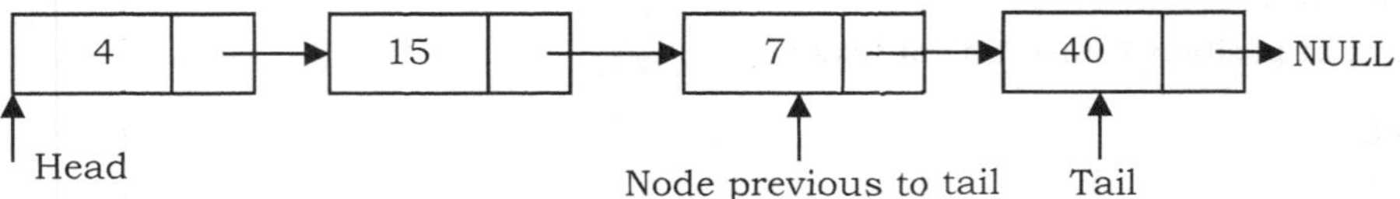


- Update previous node's next pointer with NULL.

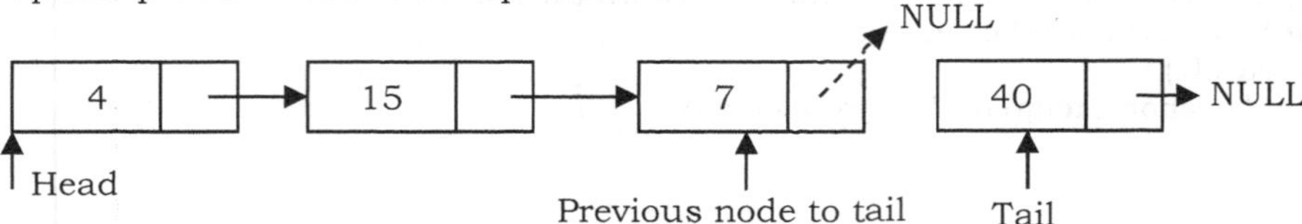


- Dispose of the tail node.

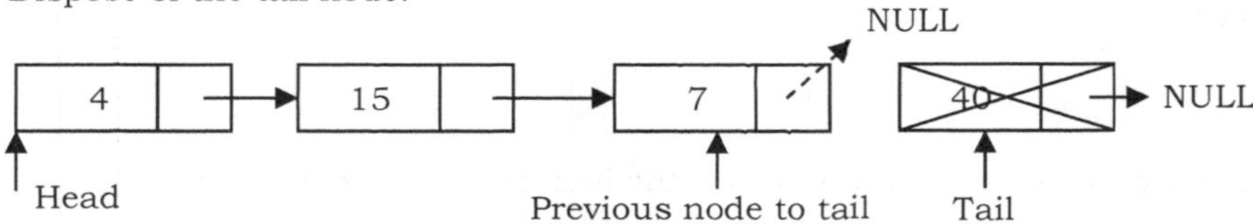


```
void *deleteLast(struct ListNode **head){
    struct ListNode *temp=NULL;
    struct ListNode *current=*head;
    if (*head == NULL)
        return;
    while(current->next){
        temp = current;
        current = current->next;
    }
    temp->next = NULL;
    free(current);
    return;
}
```

Time Complexity: O($n$), for scanning the list of size $n$. Space Complexity: O(1).

## Deleting an Intermediate Node in Singly Linked List

In this case, the node to be removed is *always located between* two nodes. Head and tail links are not updated in this case. Such a removal can be done in two steps:

- Similar to the previous case, maintain the previous node while traversing the list. Once we find the node to be deleted, change the previous node's next pointer to the next pointer of the node to be deleted.

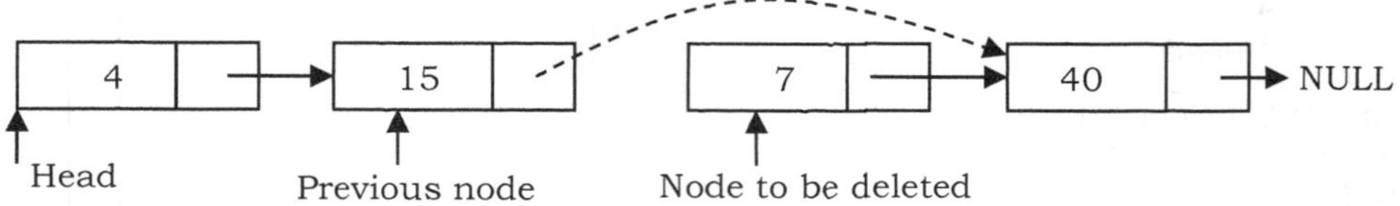


- Dispose of the current node to be deleted.

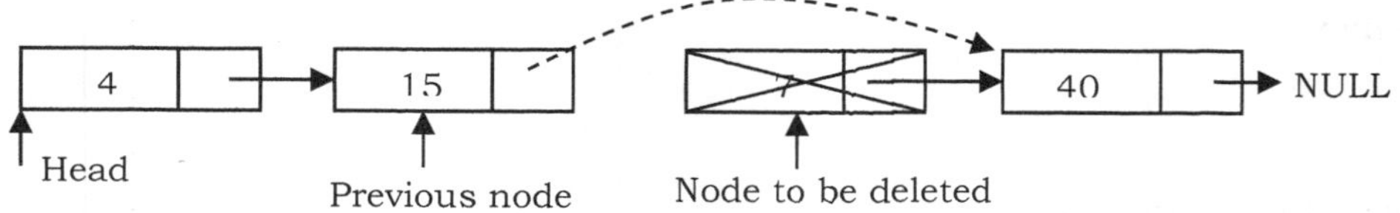


```
void *delete(struct listNode **head, int position) {
    int k = 1;
    struct listNode *p, *q;
    if(*head == NULL) {
        printf ("List Empty");
        return;
```

```
        }
        p = *head;

        if(position == 1) {                          /* from the beginning */
           *head = (*head)->next;
           free (p);
           return;
        }
        else {
           while ((p != NULL) && k < position ) { // traverse the list to the position from which we want to delete
              k++;
              q = p;
              p = p->next;
           }
           if(p == NULL){                           /* at the end */
              printf ("Position does not exist.\n");
              return;
           }
           else {                                   /* from the middle */
              q->next = p->next;
              free(p);
           }
           return;
        }
    }
```

Time Complexity: O($n$). In the worst case, we may need to delete the node at the end of the list.
Space Complexity: O(1).

## Deleting Singly Linked List

This works by storing the current node in some temporary variable and freeing the current node. After freeing the current node, go to the next node with a temporary variable and repeat this process for all nodes.

```
void deleteLinkedList(struct ListNode **head) {
    struct ListNode *auxilaryNode, *iterator;
    iterator = *head;
    while (iterator) {
       auxilaryNode = iterator→next;
       free(iterator);
       iterator = auxilaryNode;
    }
    *head = NULL;                // to affect the real head back in the caller.
}
```

Time Complexity: O($n$), for scanning the complete list of size $n$. Space Complexity: O(1).

# 3.7 Doubly Linked Lists

A doubly linked list, also known as a two-way linked list, is a type of linked list where each node contains both a pointer to the previous node and a pointer to the next node in the sequence. In a doubly linked list, a node is comprised of three parts: data, a next pointer, and a previous pointer. Each node has two links: one that points to the previous node (or to a null value or empty list if it is the first node), and another that points to the next node (or to a null value or empty list if it is the final node).

One of the main advantages of a doubly linked list is that it allows for navigation in both directions. Unlike a singly linked list, where a node cannot be removed unless we have the pointer to its predecessor, a node in a doubly linked list can be deleted even if we do not have the previous node's address. This is possible because each node has a left pointer that points to the previous node and enables backward movement.

The primary *disadvantages* of doubly linked lists are:

- Each node requires an extra pointer, requiring more space.
- The insertion or deletion of a node takes a bit longer (more pointer operations).

Just like a singly linked list, we can implement a doubly linked list with its own set of operations. If you are familiar with the operations of a singly linked list, then the operations for a doubly linked list will be straightforward. Below is the type declaration for a node in a doubly linked list:

```
struct DLLNode {
    int data;
    struct DLLNode *next;
    struct DLLNode *prev;
};
```

## Doubly Linked List Insertion

Insertion into a doubly-linked list has three cases (same as singly linked list):

- Inserting a new node before the head (at beginning).
- Inserting a new node after the tail (at the end of the list).
- Inserting a new node at the given position.

### Inserting a Node in Doubly Linked List at the Beginning

In this case, the new node is inserted before the head node. Previous and next pointers need to be updated and it can be done with the following steps:

- Create a new node and initialize both previous and next pointers to NULL.

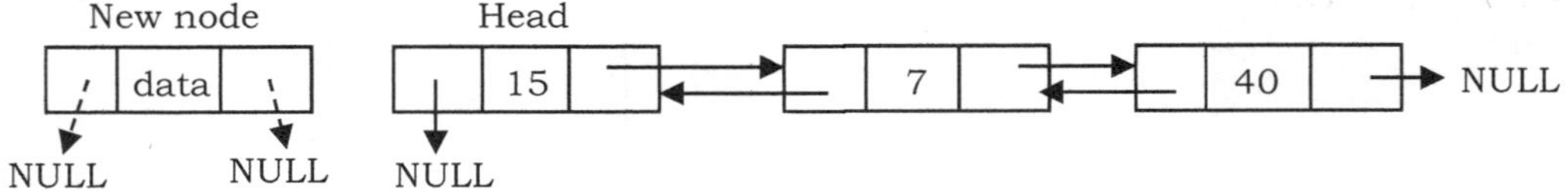


- Update the right pointer of the new node to point to the current head node (dotted link in below figure).

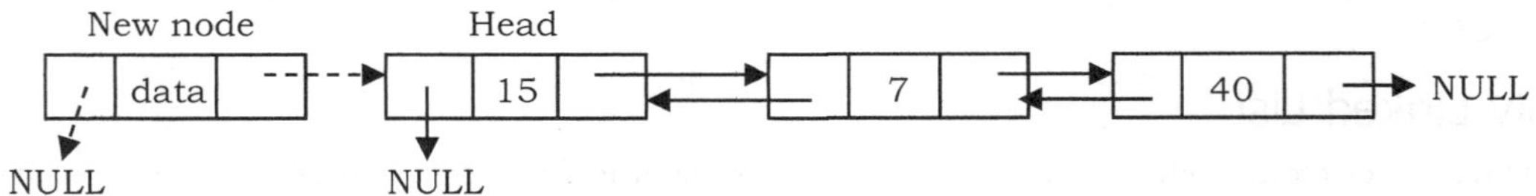


- Update head node's left pointer to point to the new node and make new node as head.

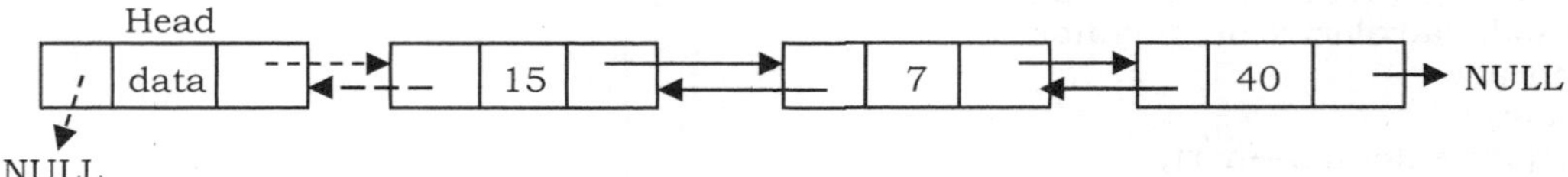


```
// Insert at the beginning of the list
void insertAtBeginning(struct DLLNode **head, int data){
    struct DLLNode *current = *head;
    struct DLLNode *newNode = (struct DLLNode *) (malloc(sizeof(struct DLLNode)));
    if(!newNode) {
        printf("Memory Error");
        return;
    }
    newNode->prev = NULL;
    newNode->data = data;
    newNode->next = NULL;
    if(current == NULL){
        *head = newNode;
        return;
    }
    newNode->next = *head;
    (*head)->prev = newNode;
    *head = newNode;
}
```

Time Complexity: O(1). Space Complexity: O(1).

### Inserting a Node in Doubly Linked List at the Ending

In this case, traverse the list till the end and insert the new node.

- Create a new node and initialize both previous and next pointers to NULL.

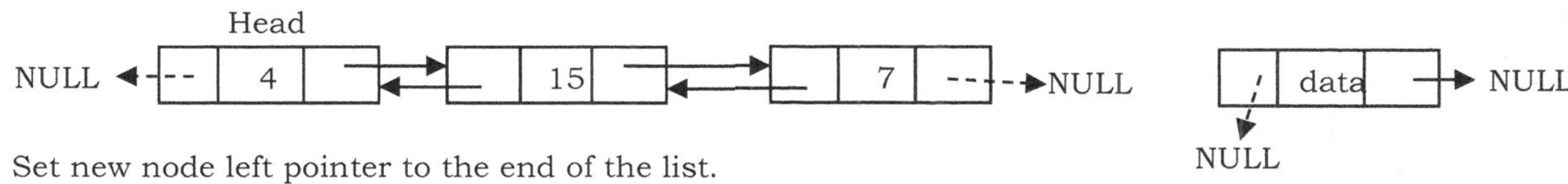


- Set new node left pointer to the end of the list.

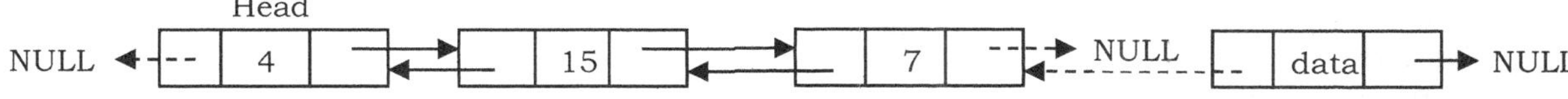


- Update right pointer of last node to point to new node.

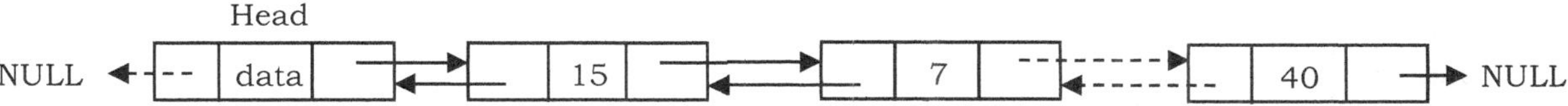


```
// Insert item at the end of the list
void insertAtEnd(struct DLLNode **head, int data){
    struct DLLNode *current = *head;
    struct DLLNode *newNode = (struct DLLNode *)(malloc(sizeof(struct DLLNode)));
    if(!newNode) {
        printf("Memory Error");
        return;
    }
    newNode->prev = NULL;
    newNode->data = data;
    newNode->next = NULL;
    if(*head == NULL){
        *head = newNode;
        return;
    }
    while (current->next != NULL)
        current = current->next;
    // current points to tail node
    newNode->prev = current;
    current->next = newNode;
}
```

Time Complexity: $O(n)$. Space Complexity: $O(1)$.

## Inserting a Node in Doubly Linked List at the Given Position

As discussed in singly linked lists, traverse the list to the position node and insert the new node.

- *New node* right pointer points to the next node of the *position node* where we want to insert the new node. Also, *new node* left pointer points to the *position node*.

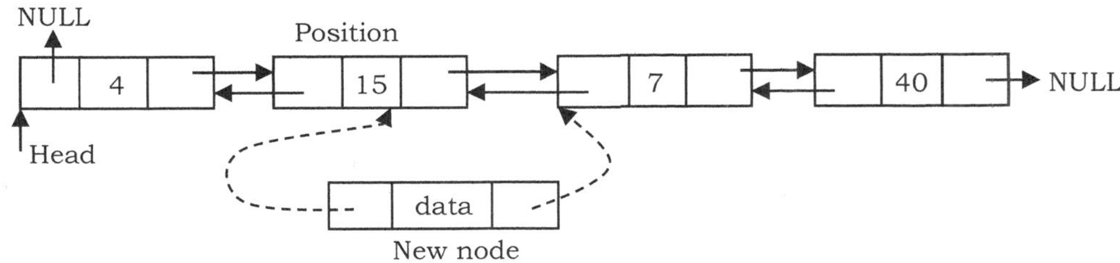


- Position node right pointer points to the new node and the left of position nodes' *next node* points to new node.

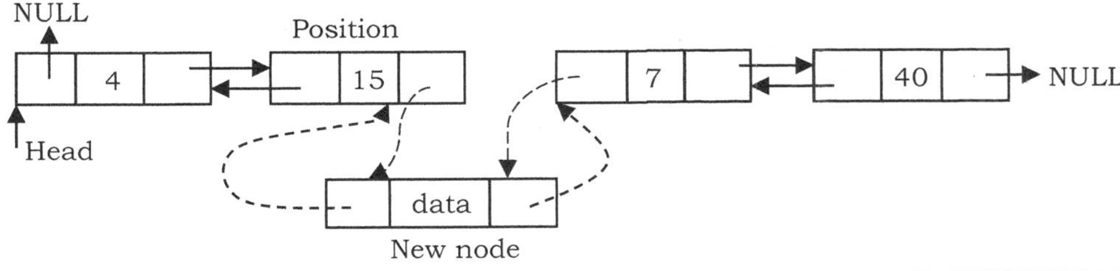

Next, we will provide code for all three cases. It is important to note that we must update the first element pointer in the calling function and not just within the called function. Therefore, we need to pass a double pointer to ensure proper updating. The code below demonstrates how to insert a node into a doubly linked list.

```
void insert(struct DLLNode **head, int data, int position) {
    int k = 1;
    struct DLLNode *temp, *newNode;
    newNode = (struct DLLNode *) malloc(sizeof ( struct DLLNode ));
    if(!newNode) {                          //Always check for memory errors
        printf ("Memory Error");
        return;
    }
    newNode->prev = NULL;
    newNode->data = data;
    newNode->next = NULL;
    if(position == 1) {                     //Inserting a node at the beginning
        newNode->next = *head;
        newNode->prev = NULL;
        if(*head)
            (*head)->prev = newNode;
        *head = newNode;
        return;
    }
    temp = *head;
    while (k < position-1 && temp->next != NULL) {
        temp = temp->next;
        k++;
    }
    if(k < position-1){
        printf("Desired position does not exist\n");
        return;
    }
    newNode->next = temp->next;
    newNode->prev = temp;
    if(temp->next)
        temp->next->prev = newNode;
    temp->next = newNode;
    return;
}
```

Time Complexity: $O(n)$. In the worst case, we may need to insert the item at the end of the list. Space Complexity: $O(1)$.

## Doubly Linked List Deletion

As with deleting a node from a singly linked list, there are three cases to consider here as well:

- Deleting the first node
- Deleting the last node
- Deleting an intermediate node

## Deleting the First Node in Doubly Linked List

In this case, the first node (current head node) is removed from the list. It can be done in two steps:

- Create a temporary node which will point to the same node as that of head.

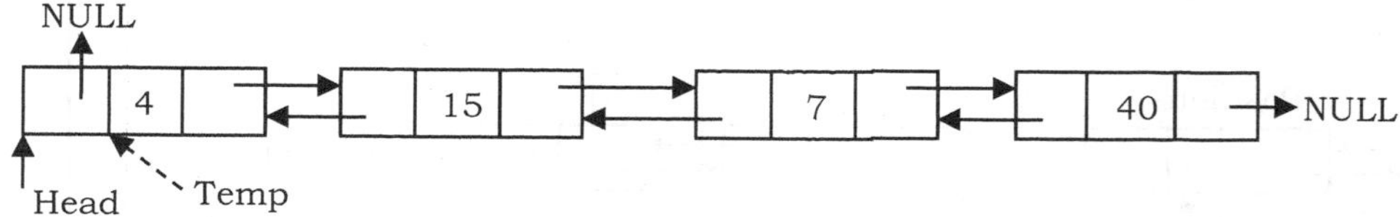


- Now, move the head nodes pointer to the next node and change the heads previous pointer to NULL. Then, dispose of the temporary node.

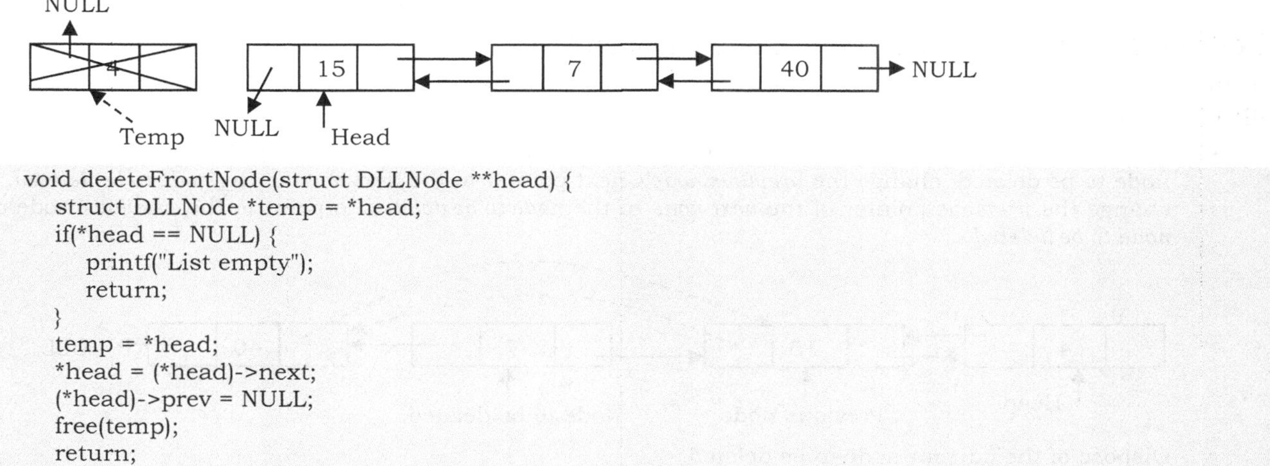


```
void deleteFrontNode(struct DLLNode **head) {
    struct DLLNode *temp = *head;
    if(*head == NULL) {
        printf("List empty");
        return;
    }
    temp = *head;
    *head = (*head)->next;
    (*head)->prev = NULL;
    free(temp);
    return;
}
```

Time Complexity: O(1). Space Complexity: O(1).

## Deleting the Last Node in Doubly Linked List

This operation is a bit trickier than removing the first node, because the algorithm should find a node, which is previous to the tail first. This can be done in three steps:

- Traverse the list, and while traversing maintain the previous node address. By the time we reach the end of the list, we will have two pointers, one pointing to the tail and the other pointing to the node before the tail.

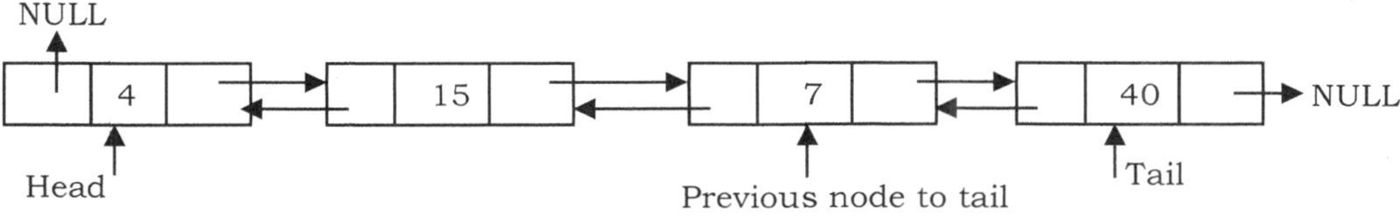


- Update the next pointer of previous node to the tail node with NULL.

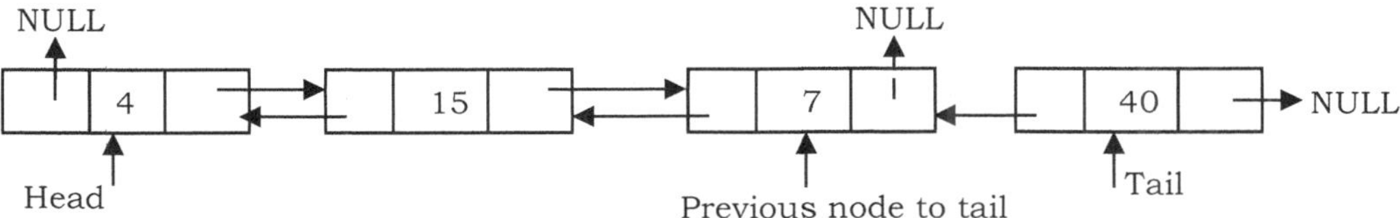


- Dispose the tail node.

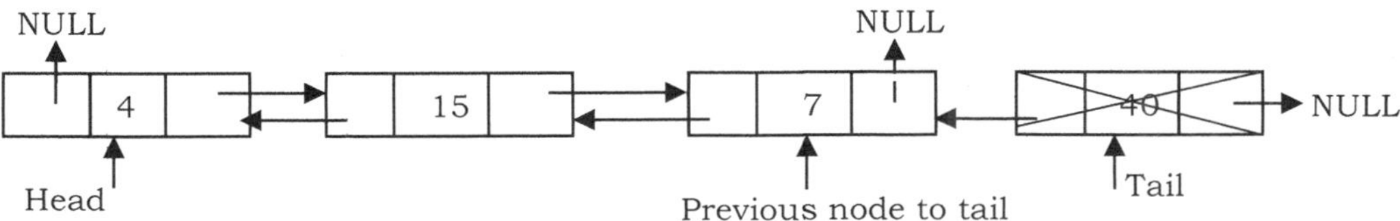


```
void deleteLastNode(struct DLLNode **head) {
    struct DLLNode *temp = *head, *current = *head;
    if(*head == NULL) {
        printf( "List empty!");
        return;
    }
    while (current->next != NULL)
        current = current->next;
    temp = current->prev;
    temp->next = current->next;
    free(current);
    return;
}
```

Time Complexity: O($n$). Space Complexity: O(1).

### Deleting an Intermediate Node in Doubly Linked List

In this case, the node to be removed is *always located between* two nodes, and the head and tail links are not updated. The removal can be done in two steps:

- Similar to the previous case, maintain the previous node while also traversing the list. Upon locating the node to be deleted, change the *previous node's* next pointer to the *next node* of the *node to be deleted*. Also, change the *previous* pointer of the *next node* to the *node to be deleted* to point to the *previous* node of the *node to be deleted*.

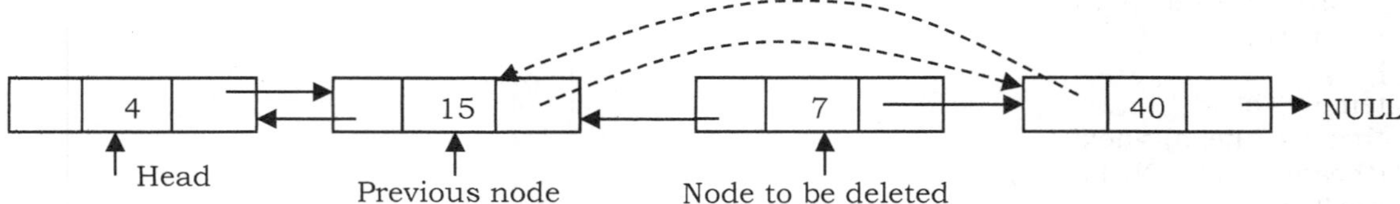


- Dispose of the current node to be deleted.

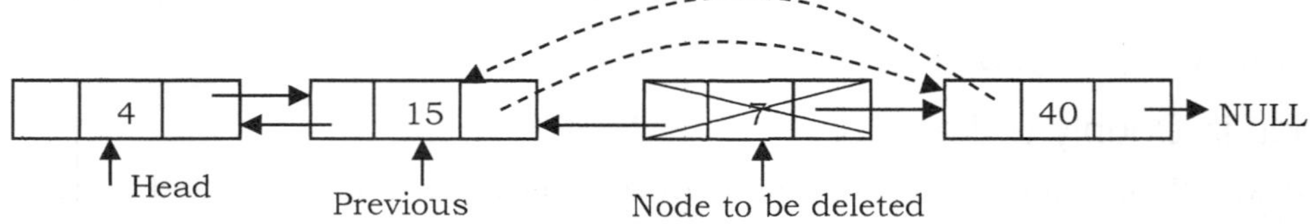


```
void delete(struct DLLNode **head, int position) {
    struct DLLNode *temp2, *temp = *head;
    int k = 1;
    if(*head == NULL) {
        printf("List is empty");
        return;
    }
    if(position == 1) {
        *head = (*head)->next;
    if(*head != NULL)
         (*head)->prev = NULL;
        free(temp);
        return;
    }
    while(k < position && temp->next!=NULL) {
        temp = temp->next;
        k++;
    }
    if(k < position-1){
        printf("Desired position does not exist\n");
        return;
    }
    temp2 = temp->prev;
    temp2->next = temp->next;
    if(temp->next) // Deletion from Intermediate Node
        temp->next->prev = temp2;
    free(temp);
    return;
}
```

Time Complexity: O($n$), for scanning the complete list of size $n$. Space Complexity: O(1).

## 3.8 Circular Linked Lists

In a singly-circularly-linked list, each node has one link, similar to an ordinary singly-linked list, except that the next link of the last node points back to the first node. In singly linked lists and doubly linked lists, the end of lists are indicated with NULL value. But, circular linked lists do not have ends. While traversing the circular linked lists we should be careful; otherwise we will be traversing the list indefinitely.

In circular linked lists, each node has a successor. In a circular linked list, every node points to its next node in the sequence but the last node points to the first node in the list.

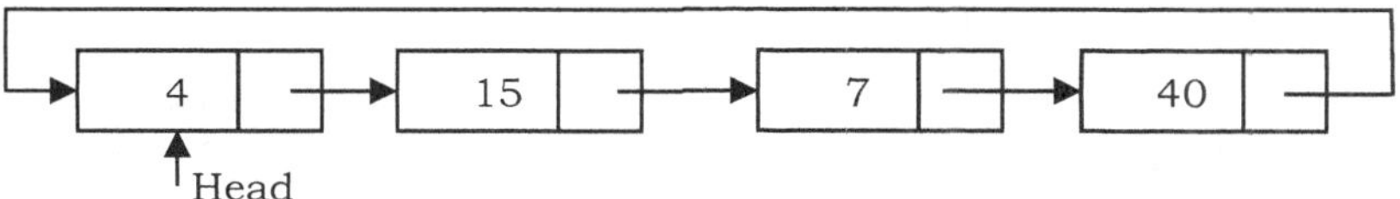


In some situations, circular linked lists are useful. For example, when several processes are using the same computer resource (say, CPU) for the same amount of time, we have to assure that no process accesses the resource before all other processes do (round robin algorithm). The following is a type declaration for a circular linked list of integers:

```
typedef struct CLLNode {
    int data;
    struct CLLNode *next;
};
```

In a circular linked list, we access the elements using the *head* node (similar to *head* node in singly linked list and doubly linked lists).

## Counting Nodes in a Circular Linked List

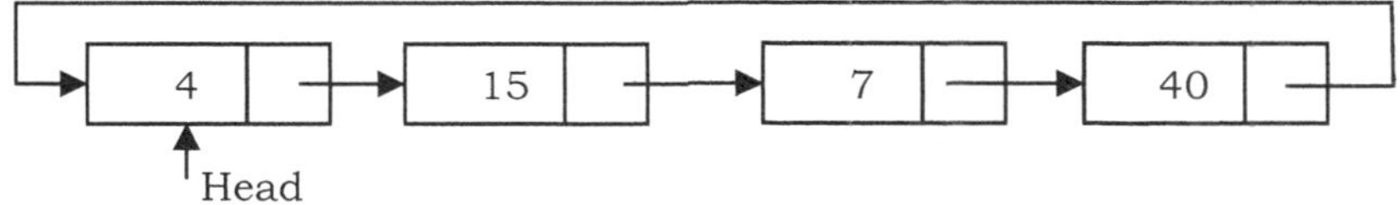


The circular list is accessible through the node marked *head*. To count the nodes, the list has to be traversed from the node marked *head*, with the help of a dummy node *current*, and stop the counting when *current* reaches the starting node *head*. If the list is empty, *head* will be NULL, and in that case set *count* = 0. Otherwise, set the current pointer to the first node, and keep on counting till the current pointer reaches the starting node.

```
int length(struct CLLNode *head) {
    struct CLLNode *current = head;
    int count = 0;
    if(head == NULL) return 0;
    do {
        current = current→next;
        count++;
    } while (current != head);
    return count;
}
```

Time Complexity: $O(n)$, for scanning the complete list of size $n$. Space Complexity: $O(1)$, for creating one temporary variable.

## Printing the Contents of a Circular Linked List

We assume here that the list is being accessed by its *head* node. Since all the nodes are arranged in a circular fashion, the *tail* node of the list will be the node previous to the *head* node. Let us assume we want to print the contents of the nodes starting with the *head* node. Print its contents, move to the next node and continue printing till we reach the *head* node again.

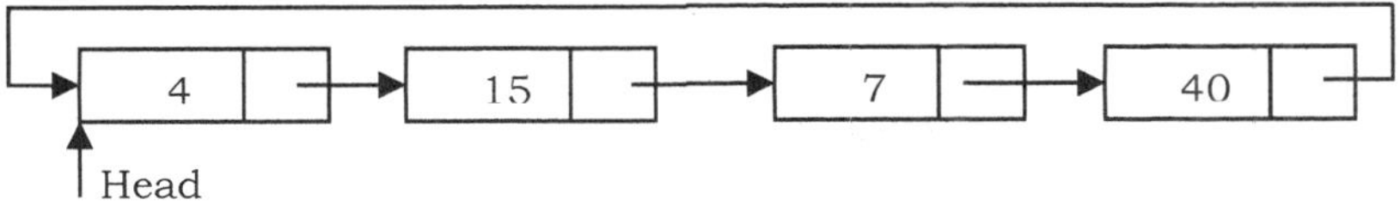


```
void printList(struct CLLNode *head) {
    struct CLLNode *current = head;
    if(head == NULL) return;
    do {
        printf ("%d-->", current->data);
        current = current->next;
    } while(current != head);
}
```

Time Complexity: $O(n)$, for scanning the complete list of size $n$. Space Complexity: $O(1)$, for the temporary variable.

## Inserting a Node at the End of a Circular Linked List

Let us add a node containing *data*, at the end of a list (circular list) headed by *head*. The new node will be placed just after the tail node (which is the last node of the list), which means it will have to be inserted in between the tail node and the first node.

- Create a new node and initially keep its next pointer pointing to itself.

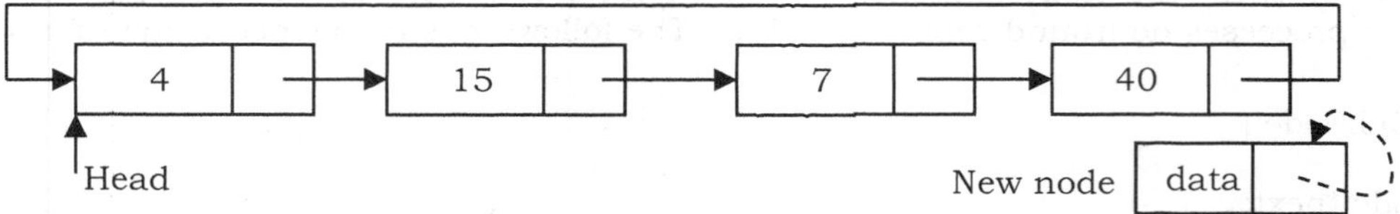


- Update the next pointer of the new node with the head node and also traverse the list to the tail. That means, in a circular list we should stop at the node whose next node is head.

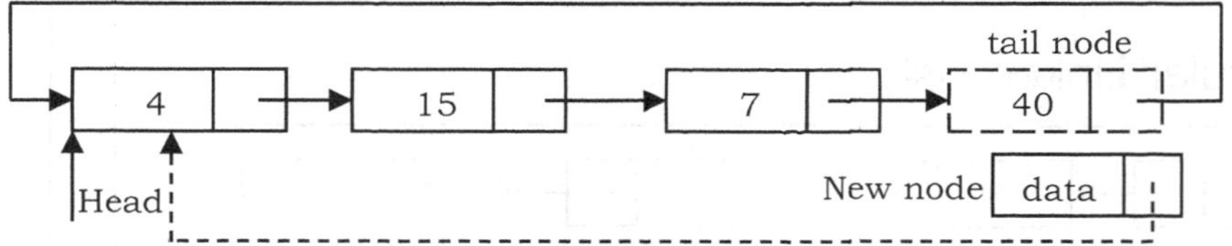


- Update the next pointer of the tail node to point to the new node and we get the list as shown below.

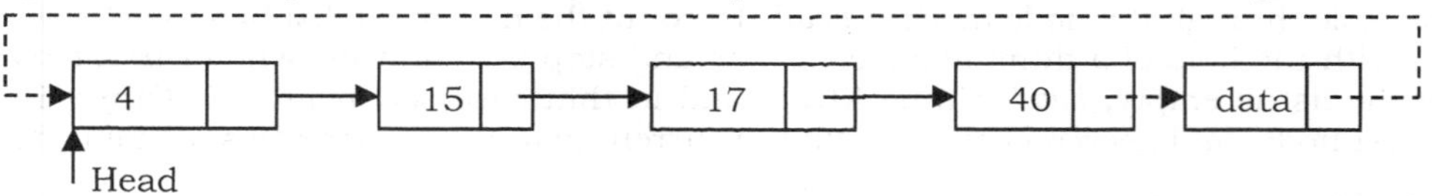


```
void insertAtEnd(struct CLLNode **head, int data){
    struct CLLNode *current = *head;
    struct CLLNode *newNode = (struct CLLNode *) (malloc(sizeof(struct CLLNode)));
    if(!newNode) {
        printf("Memory Error");
        return;
    }
    newNode->data = data;
    while (current->next != *head)
        current = current->next;
    newNode->next = newNode;
    if(*head ==NULL)
        *head = newNode;
    else {
        newNode->next = *head;
        current->next = newNode;
    }
}
```

Time Complexity: $O(n)$, for scanning the complete list of size $n$. Space Complexity: $O(1)$, for temporary variable.

## Inserting a Node at the Front of a Circular Linked List

The only difference between inserting a node at the beginning and at the end is that, after inserting the new node, we just need to update the pointer. The steps for doing this are given below:

- Create a new node and initially keep its next pointer pointing to itself.

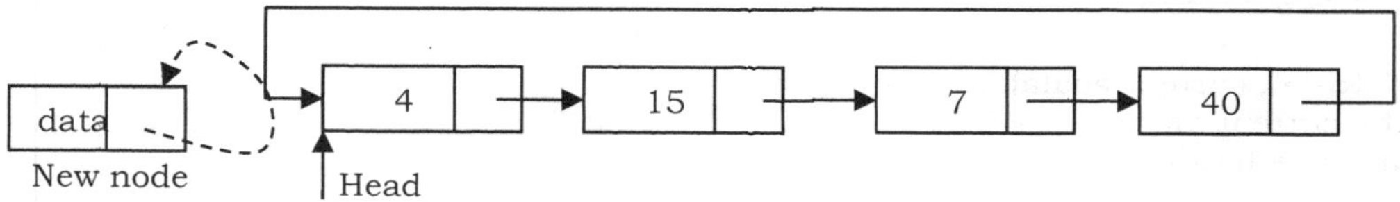


- Update the next pointer of the new node with the head node and also traverse the list until the tail node (node with data 40).

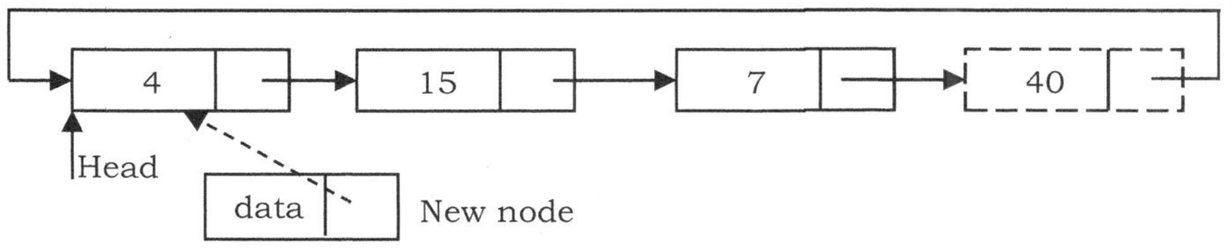


- Update the tail node in the list to point to the new node.

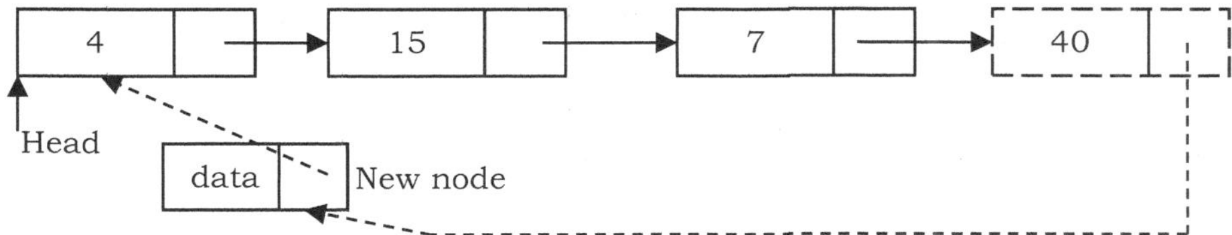


- Make the new node as the head.

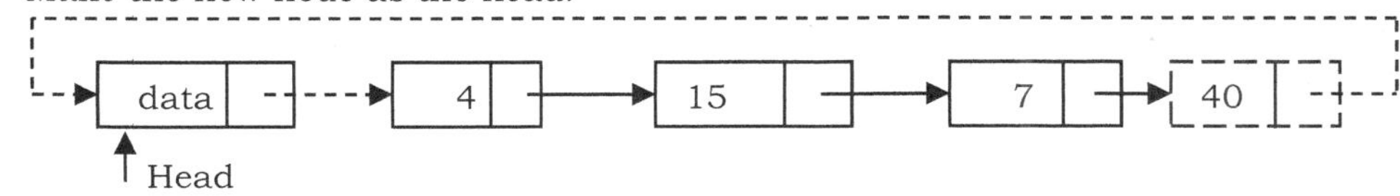


```
void insertAtBegin(struct CLLNode **head, int data){
    struct CLLNode *current = *head;
    struct CLLNode *newNode = (struct CLLNode *) (malloc(sizeof(struct CLLNode)));
    if(!newNode) {
        printf("Memory Error");
        return;
    }
    newNode->data = data;
    newNode->next = newNode;
    if(current == NULL){
        *head = newNode;
        return;
    }
    while (current->next != *head)
        current = current->next;
    newNode->next = *head;
    current->next = newNode;
    *head = newNode;
}
```

Time Complexity: O($n$), for scanning the complete list of size $n$. Space Complexity: O(1), for temporary variable.

## Deleting the Last Node in a Circular Linked List

The list has to be traversed to reach the last but one node. This has to be named as the tail node, and its next field has to point to the first node. Consider the following list. To delete the last node 40, the list has to be traversed till you reach 7. The next field of 7 has to be changed to point to 60, and this node must be renamed *pTail*.

- Traverse the list and find the tail node and its previous node.

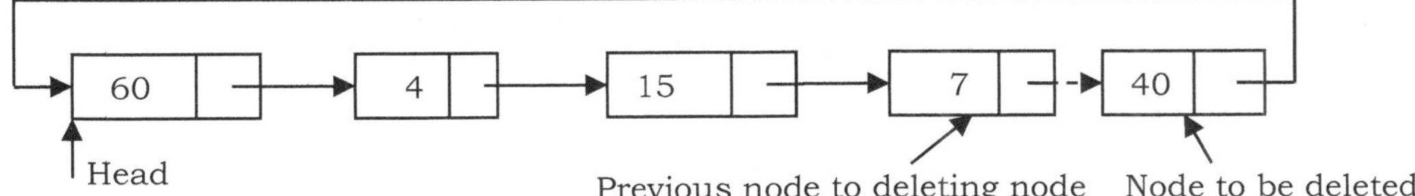


- Update the next pointer of tail node's previous node to point to head.

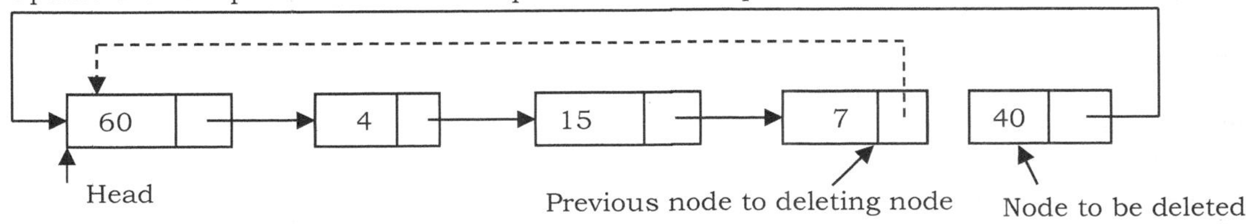

- Dispose of the tail node.

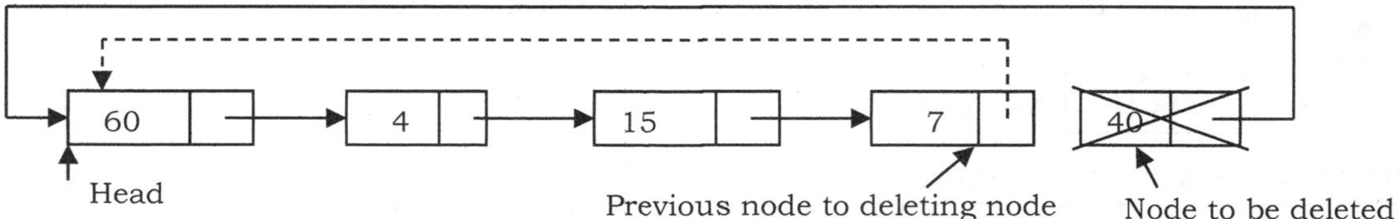


```
void deleteLastNode(struct CLLNode **head) {
    struct CLLNode *temp = *head, *current = *head;
    if(*head == NULL) {
        printf( "List empty!");  return;
    }
    while (current->next != *head) {
        temp = current;
        current = current->next;
    }
    temp->next = current->next;
    free(current);
    return;
}
```

Time Complexity: $O(n)$, for scanning the complete list of size $n$. Space Complexity: $O(1)$, for a temporary variable.

## Deleting the First Node in a Circular List

The first node can be deleted by simply replacing the next field of the tail node with the next field of the first node.

- Find the tail node of the linked list by traversing the list. Tail node is the previous node to the head node which we want to delete.

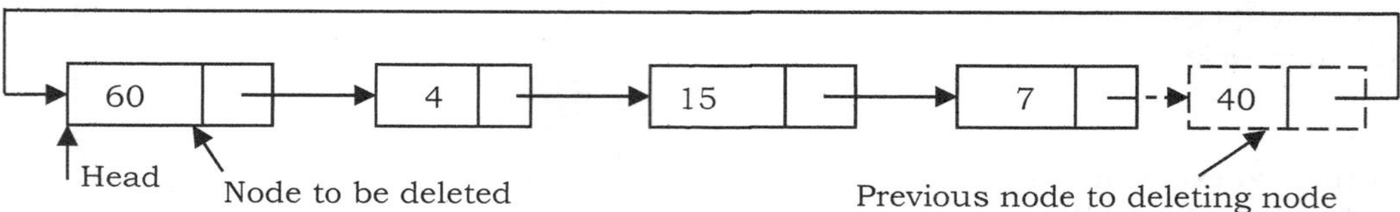


- Create a temporary node which will point to the head. Also, update the tail nodes next pointer to point to next node of head (as shown below).

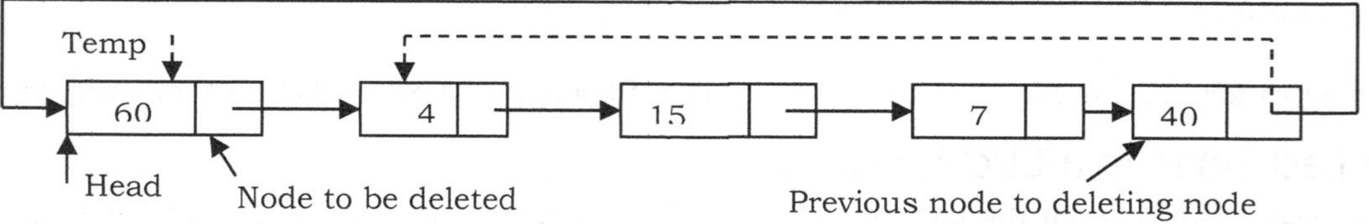


- Now, move the head pointer to next node and dispose the temporary node (as shown below).

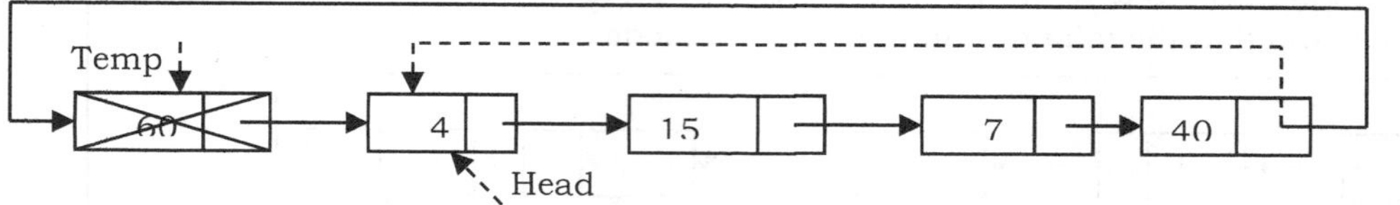


```
void deleteFrontNode(struct CLLNode **head) {
    struct CLLNode *temp = *head, current = *head;
    if(*head == NULL) {
        printf("List empty");
        return;
    }
    while (current->next != *head)
        current = current->next;
    current->next = (*head)->next;
    *head = (*head)->next;
```

```
        free(temp);
        return;
    }
```

Time Complexity: $O(n)$, for scanning the complete list of size $n$. Space Complexity: $O(1)$, for a temporary variable.

## Applications of Circular List

Circular linked lists are used in managing the computing resources of a computer. We can use circular lists for implementing stacks and queues.

## 3.9 A Memory-efficient Doubly Linked List

In conventional implementation, we need to keep a forward pointer to the next item on the list and a backward pointer to the previous item. That means elements in doubly linked list implementations consist of data, a pointer to the next node and a pointer to the previous node in the list as shown below.

**Conventional Doubly Linked List Node Definition**

```
typedef struct ListNode {
    int data;
    struct ListNode * prev;
    struct ListNode * next;
};
```

Recently a journal (Sinha) presented an alternative implementation of the doubly linked list ADT, with insertion, traversal and deletion operations. This implementation is based on pointer difference. Each node uses only one pointer field to traverse the list back and forth.

**New Node Definition**

```
typedef struct ListNode {
  int data;
  struct ListNode * ptrdiff;
};
```

The *ptrdiff* pointer field contains the difference between the pointer to the next node and the pointer to the previous node. The pointer difference is calculated by using exclusive-or (⊕) operation.

$$ptrdiff = pointer\ to\ previous\ node \oplus pointer\ to\ next\ node.$$

The *ptrdiff* of the start node (head node) is the ⊕ of NULL and *next* node (next node to head). Similarly, the *ptrdiff* of end node is the ⊕ of *previous* node (previous to end node) and NULL. As an example, consider the following linked list.

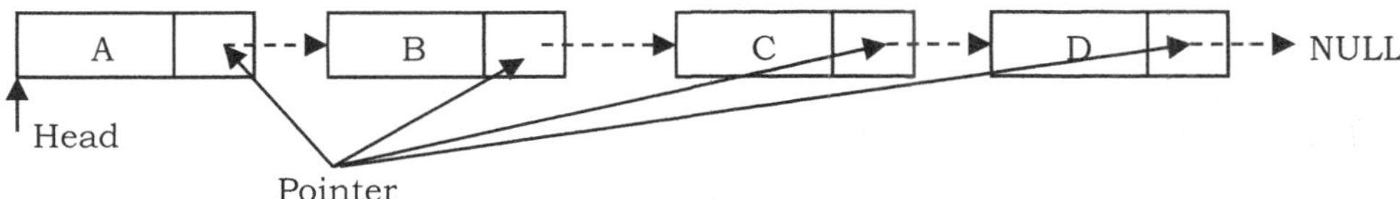


In the example above,

- The next pointer of A is: NULL ⊕ B
- The next pointer of B is: A ⊕ C
- The next pointer of C is: B ⊕ D
- The next pointer of D is: C ⊕ NULL

**Why does it work?**

To find the answer to this question let us consider the properties of ⊕:

$X \oplus X = 0$
$X \oplus 0 = X$
$X \oplus Y = Y \oplus X$ (symmetric)
$(X \oplus Y) \oplus Z = X \oplus (Y \oplus Z)$ (transitive)

For the example above, let us assume that we are at C node and want to move to B. We know that C's *ptrdiff* is defined as B ⊕ D. If we want to move to B, performing ⊕ on C's *ptrdiff* with D would give B. This is due to the fact that

$$(B \oplus D) \oplus D = B \text{ (since, } D \oplus D=0)$$

Similarly, if we want to move to D, then we have to apply ⊕ to C's *ptrdiff* with B to give D.

$$(B \oplus D) \oplus B = D \text{ (since, } B \oplus B = 0)$$

From the above discussion we can see that just by using a single pointer, we can move back and forth. A memory-efficient implementation of a doubly linked list is possible with minimal compromising of timing efficiency.

## 3.10 Unrolled Linked Lists

One of the biggest advantages of linked lists over arrays is that inserting an element at any location takes only O(1) time. However, it takes O($n$) to search for an element in a linked list. There is a simple variation of the singly linked list called *unrolled linked lists*.

An unrolled linked list stores multiple elements in each node (let us call it a block for our convenience). In each block, a circular linked list is used to connect all nodes.

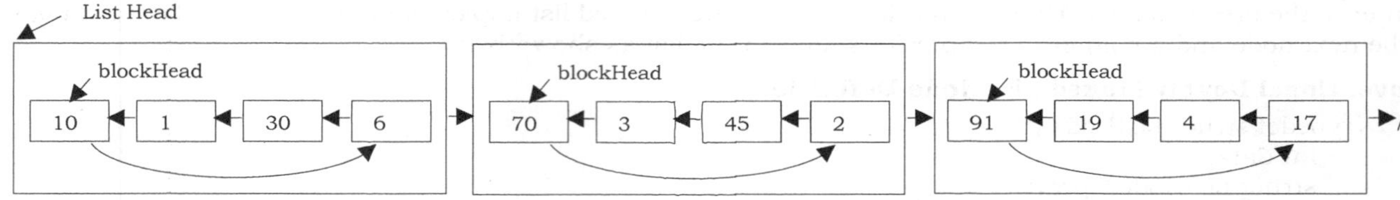


Assume that there will be no more than $n$ elements in the unrolled linked list at any time. To simplify this problem, all blocks, except the last one, should contain exactly $\lceil\sqrt{n}\rceil$ elements. Thus, there will be no more than $\lfloor\sqrt{n}\rfloor$ blocks at any time.

### Searching for an element in Unrolled Linked Lists

In unrolled linked lists, we can find the $k^{th}$ element in O($\sqrt{n}$):

1. Traverse the *list of blocks* to the one that contains the $k^{th}$ node, i.e., the $\left\lceil\frac{k}{\lceil\sqrt{n}\rceil}\right\rceil^{th}$ block. It takes O($\sqrt{n}$) since we may find it by going through no more than $\sqrt{n}$ blocks.
2. Find the ($k$ mod $\lceil\sqrt{n}\rceil$)$^{th}$ node in the circular linked list of this block. It also takes O($\sqrt{n}$) since there are no more than $\lceil\sqrt{n}\rceil$ nodes in a single block.

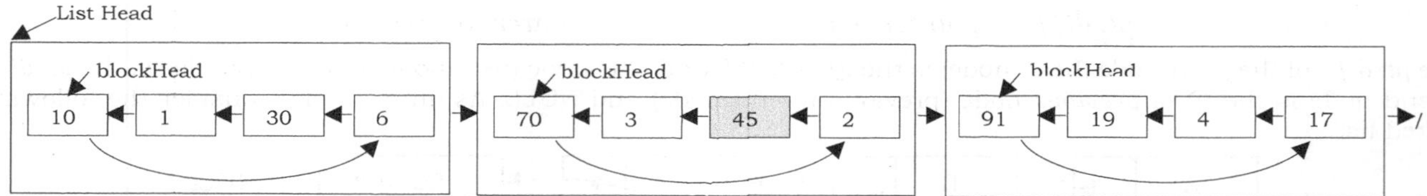


### Inserting an element in Unrolled Linked Lists

When inserting a node, we have to re-arrange the nodes in the unrolled linked list to maintain the properties previously mentioned, that each block contains $\lceil\sqrt{n}\rceil$ nodes. Suppose that we insert a node $x$ after the $i^{th}$ node, and $x$ should be placed in the $j^{th}$ block. Nodes in the $j^{th}$ block and in the blocks after the $j^{th}$ block have to be shifted toward the tail of the list so that each of them still have $\lceil\sqrt{n}\rceil$ nodes. In addition, a new block needs to be added to the tail if the last block of the list is out of space, i.e., it has more than $\lceil\sqrt{n}\rceil$ nodes.

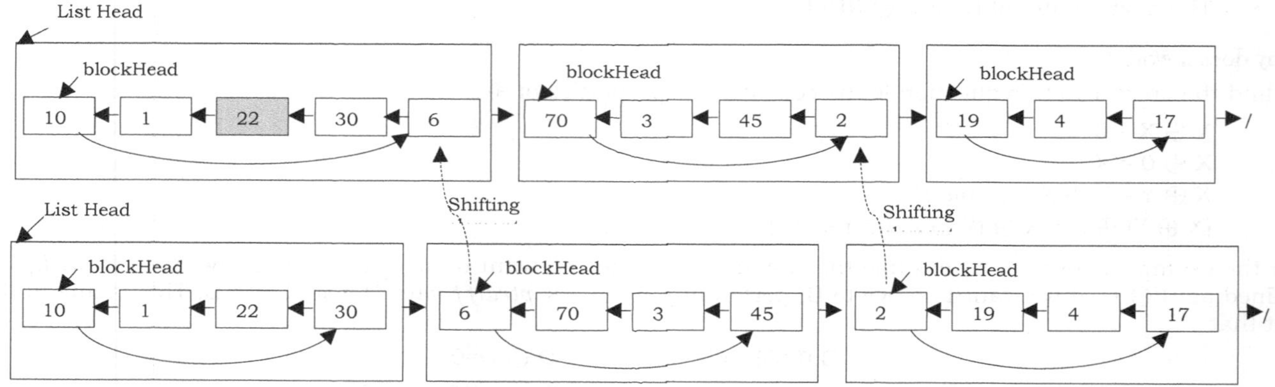

## Performing Shift Operation

Note that each *shift* operation, which includes removing a node from the tail of the circular linked list in a block and inserting a node to the head of the circular linked list in the block after, takes only O(1). The total time complexity of an insertion operation for unrolled linked lists is therefore $O(\sqrt{n})$; there are at most $O(\sqrt{n})$ blocks and therefore at most $O(\sqrt{n})$ shift operations.

1. A temporary pointer is needed to store the tail of *A*.

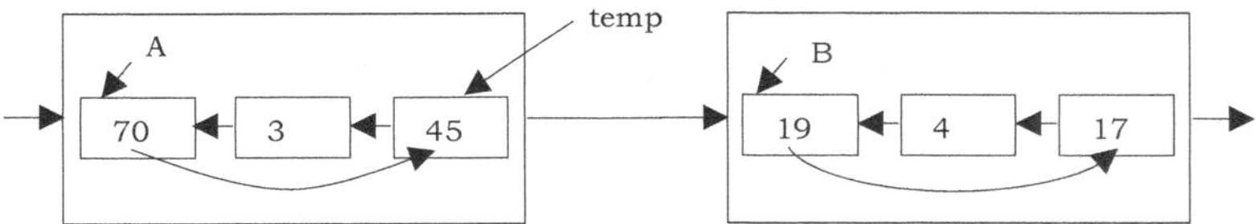


2. In block *A*, move the next pointer of the head node to point to the second-to-last node, so that the tail node of *A* can be removed.

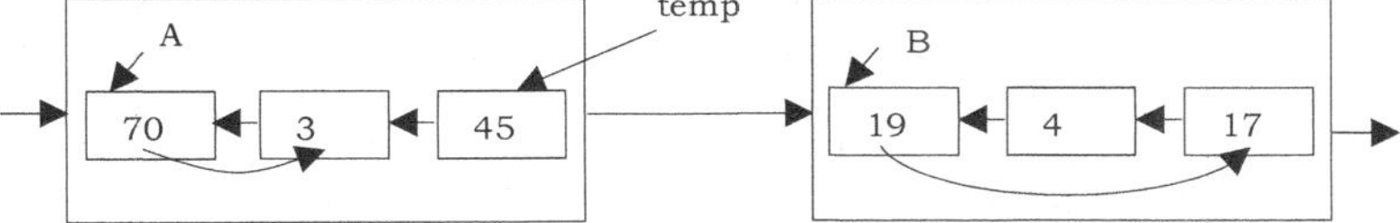


3. Let the next pointer of the node, which will be shifted (the tail node of *A*), point to the tail node of *B*.

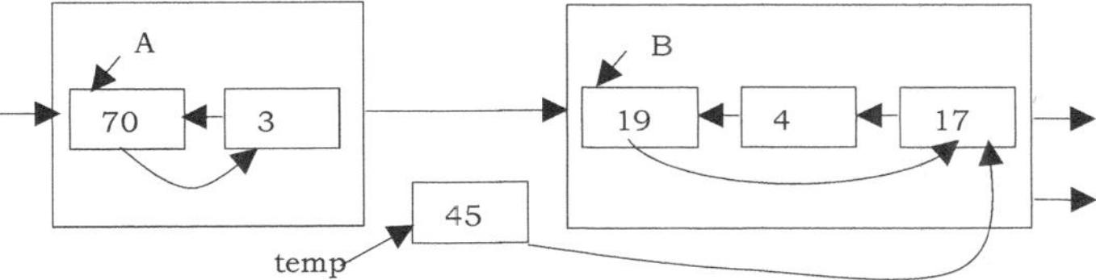


4. Let the next pointer of the head node of *B* point to the node *temp* points to.

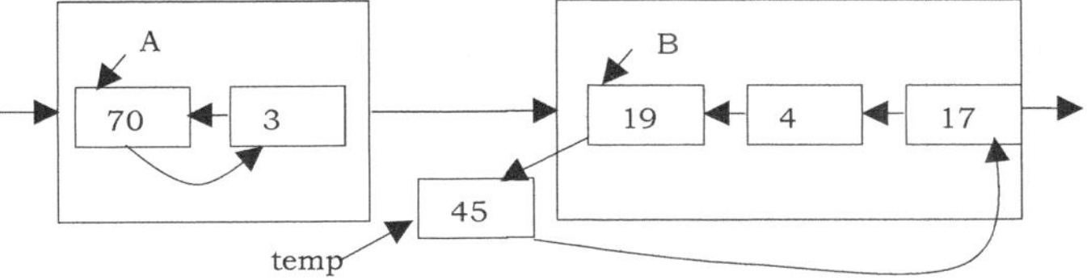


5. Finally, set the head pointer of *B* to point to the node *temp* points to. Now the node *temp* points to becomes the new head node of *B*.

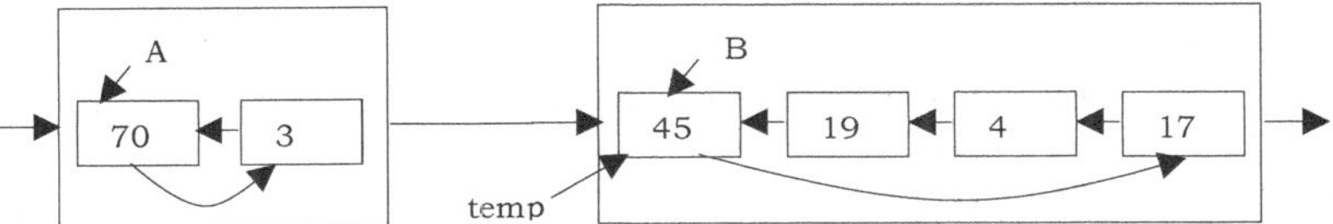


6. *temp* pointer can be thrown away. We have completed the shift operation to move the original tail node of *A* to become the new head node of *B*.

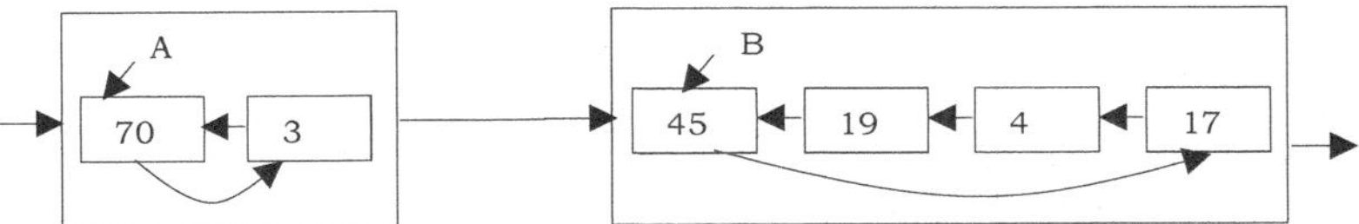


## Performance

With unrolled linked lists, there are a couple of advantages, one in speed and one in space. First, if the number of elements in each block is appropriately sized (e.g., at most the size of one cache line), we get noticeably better cache performance from the improved memory locality. Second, since we have $O(n/m)$ links, where $n$ is the number of elements in the unrolled linked list and $m$ is the number of elements we can store in any block, we can also save an appreciable amount of space, which is particularly noticeable if each element is small.

## Comparing Linked Lists and Unrolled Linked Lists

To compare the overhead for an unrolled list, elements in doubly linked list implementations consist of data, a pointer to the next node, and a pointer to the previous node in the list, as shown below.

```
struct ListNode {
    int data;
    struct ListNode *prev;
    struct ListNode *next;
};
```

Assuming we have 4 byte pointers, each node is going to take 8 bytes. But the allocation overhead for the node could be anywhere between 8 and 16 bytes. Let's go with the best case and assume it will be 8 bytes. So, if we want to store 1K items in this list, we are going to have 16KB of overhead.

Now, let's think about an unrolled linked list node (let us call it *LinkedBlock*). It will look something like this:

```
struct LinkedBlock{
    struct LinkedBlock *next;
    struct ListNode *head;
    int nodeCount;
};
```

Therefore, allocating a single node (12 bytes + 8 bytes of overhead) with an array of 100 elements (400 bytes + 8 bytes of overhead) will now cost 428 bytes, or 4.28 bytes per element. Thinking about our 1K items from above, it would take about 4.2KB of overhead, which is close to 4x better than our original list. Even if the list becomes severely fragmented and the item arrays are only 1/2 full on average, this is still an improvement. Also, note that we can tune the array size to whatever gets us the best overhead for our application.

## Implementation

```
#include <stdio.h>
#include <stdlib.h>
#define MAXSKIPLEVEL 5
struct ListNode {
    int data;
    struct ListNode *next[1];
};
struct SkipList {
    struct ListNode *header;
    int listLevel;              //current level of list */
};
struct SkipList list;
struct ListNode *insertElement(int data) {
    int i, newLevel;
    struct ListNode *update[MAXSKIPLEVEL+1];
    struct ListNode *temp;
    temp = list.header;
    for (i = list.listLevel; i >= 0; i--) {
        while (temp→next[i] !=list.header && temp→next[i]→data < data)
            temp = temp→next[i];
        update[i] = temp;
    }
    temp = temp→next[0];
    if (temp != list.header && temp→data == data)
        return(temp);
    //determine level
    for (newLevel = 0; rand() < RAND_MAX/2 && newLevel < MAXSKIPLEVEL; newLevel++);
    if (newLevel > list.listLevel) {
        for (i = list.listLevel + 1; i <= newLevel; i++)
            update[i] = list.header;
        list.listLevel = newLevel;
    }
    // make new node
    if ((temp = malloc(sizeof(Node) +
     newLevel*sizeof(Node *))) == 0) {
        printf ("insufficient memory (insertElement)\n");
        exit(1);
    }
    temp→data = data;
    for (i = 0; i <= newLevel; i++) {   // update next links
        temp→next[i] = update[i]→next[i];
```

```
            update[i]→next[i] = temp;
        }
        return(temp);
    }
    // delete node containing data
    void deleteElement(int data) {
        int i;
        struct ListNode *update[MAXSKIPLEVEL+1], *temp;
        temp = list.header;
        for (i = list.listLevel; i >= 0; i--) {
            while (temp→next[i] != list.header && temp→next[i]→data < data)
                temp = temp→next[i];
            update[i] = temp;
        }
        temp = temp→next[0];
        if (temp == list.header || !(temp→data == data) return;
        //adjust next pointers
        for (i = 0; i <= list.listLevel; i++) {
            if (update[i]→next[i] != temp) break;
            update[i]→next[i] = temp→next[i];
        }
        free (temp);
        //adjust header level
        while ((list.listLevel > 0) && (list.header→next[list.listLevel] == list.header))
            list.listLevel--;
    }
    // find node containing data
    struct ListNode *findElement(int data) {
        struct ListNode *temp = list.header;
        for (int i = list.listLevel; i >= 0; i--) {
            while (temp→next[i] != list.header
             && temp→next[i]→data < data)
                temp = temp→next[i];
        }
        temp = temp→next[0];
        if (temp != list.header && temp→data == data) return (temp);
        return(0);
    }
    // initialize skip list
    void initList() {
        int i;
        if ((list.header = malloc(sizeof(struct ListNode) + MAXSKIPLEVEL*sizeof(struct ListNode *))) == 0) {
            printf ("Memory Error\n");
            exit(1);
        }
        for (i = 0; i <= MAXSKIPLEVEL; i++)
            list.header→next[i] = list.header;
        list.listLevel = 0;
    }
    /* command-line: skipList maxnum skipList 2000: process 2000 sequential records */
    int main(int argc, char **argv) {
        int i, *a, maxnum = atoi(argv[1]);
        initList();
        if ((a = malloc(maxnum * sizeof(*a))) == 0) {
            fprintf (stderr, "insufficient memory (a)\n");
            exit(1);
        }
        for (i = 0; i < maxnum; i++) a[i] = rand();
            printf ("Random, %d items\n", maxnum);
        for (i = 0; i < maxnum; i++) {
            insertElement(a[i]);
        }
        for (i = maxnum-1; i >= 0; i--) {
```

```
            findElement(a[i]);
        }
        for (i = maxnum-1; i >= 0; i--) {
            deleteElement(a[i]);
        }
        return 0;
    }
```

## 3.11 Skip Lists

Binary trees can be used for representing abstract data types such as dictionaries and ordered lists. They work well when the elements are inserted in a random order. Some sequences of operations, such as inserting the elements in order, produce degenerate data structures that give very poor performance. If it were possible to randomly permute the list of items to be inserted, trees would work well with high probability for any input sequence. In most cases queries must be answered on-line, so randomly permuting the input is impractical. Balanced tree algorithms re-arrange the tree as operations are performed to maintain certain balance conditions and assure good performance.

Skip lists are a probabilistic alternative to balanced trees. Skip list is a data structure that can be used as an alternative to balanced binary trees (refer to *Trees* chapter). As compared to a binary tree, skip lists allow quick search, insertion and deletion of elements. This is achieved by using probabilistic balancing rather than strictly enforce balancing. It is basically a linked list with additional pointers such that intermediate nodes can be skipped. It uses a random number generator to make some decisions.

In an ordinary sorted linked list, search, insert, and delete are in O($n$) because the list must be scanned node-by-node from the head to find the relevant node. If somehow we could scan down the list in bigger steps (skip down, as it were), we would reduce the cost of scanning. This is the fundamental idea behind Skip Lists.

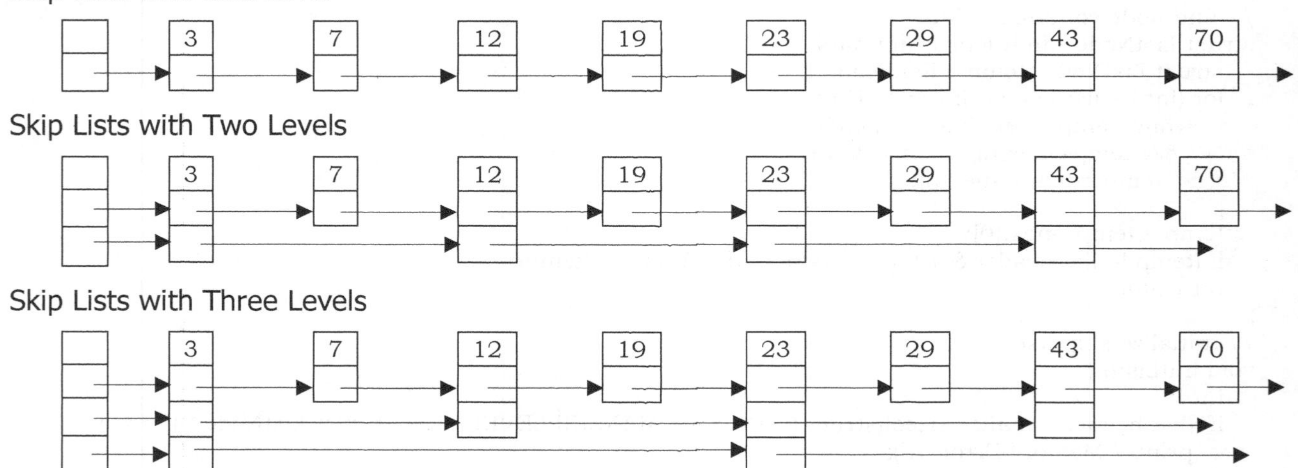


### Performance

In a simple linked list that consists of $n$ elements, to perform a search $n$ comparisons are required in the worst case. If a second pointer pointing two nodes ahead is added to every node, the number of comparisons goes down to $n/2 + 1$ in the worst case.

Adding one more pointer to every fourth node and making them point to the fourth node ahead reduces the number of comparisons to $\lceil n/4 \rceil + 2$. If this strategy is continued so that every node with $i$ pointers points to $2 * i - 1$ nodes ahead, O($logn$) performance is obtained and the number of pointers has only doubled ($n + n/2 + n/4 + n/8 + n/16 + .... = 2n$).

The find, insert, and remove operations on ordinary binary search trees are efficient, O($logn$), when the input data is random; but less efficient, O($n$), when the input data is ordered. Skip List performance for these same operations and for any data set is about as good as that of randomly-built binary search trees - namely O($logn$).

### Comparing Skip Lists and Unrolled Linked Lists

In simple terms, Skip Lists are sorted linked lists with two differences:

- The nodes in an ordinary list have one next reference. The nodes in a Skip List have many *next* references (also called *forward* references).

- The number of *forward* references for a given node is determined probabilistically.

We speak of a Skip List node having levels, one level per forward reference. The number of levels in a node is called the *size* of the node. In an ordinary sorted list, insert, remove, and find operations require sequential traversal of the list. This results in O($n$) performance per operation. Skip Lists allow intermediate nodes in the list to be skipped during a traversal - resulting in an expected performance of O($logn$) per operation.

## Implementation

```
#include <stdio.h>
#include <stdlib.h>
#define MAXSKIPLEVEL 5
struct ListNode {
    int data;
    struct ListNode *next[1];
};
struct SkipList {
    struct ListNode *header;
    int listLevel;              //current level of list */
};
struct SkipList list;
struct ListNode *insertElement(int data) {
    int i, newLevel;
    struct ListNode *update[MAXSKIPLEVEL+1];
    struct ListNode *temp;
    temp = list.header;
    for (i = list.listLevel; i >= 0; i--) {
        while (temp→next[i] !=list.header && temp→next[i]→data < data)
            temp = temp→next[i];
        update[i] = temp;
    }
    temp = temp→next[0];
    if (temp != list.header && temp→data == data)
        return(temp);
    //determine level
    for (newLevel = 0; rand() < RAND_MAX/2 && newLevel < MAXSKIPLEVEL; newLevel++);
    if (newLevel > list.listLevel) {
        for (i = list.listLevel + 1; i <= newLevel; i++)
            update[i] = list.header;
        list.listLevel = newLevel;
    }
    // make new node
    if ((temp = malloc(sizeof(Node) +
      newLevel*sizeof(Node *))) == 0) {
        printf ("insufficient memory (insertElement)\n");
        exit(1);
    }
    temp→data = data;
    for (i = 0; i <= newLevel; i++) {   // update next links
        temp→next[i] = update[i]→next[i];
        update[i]→next[i] = temp;
    }
    return(temp);
}
// delete node containing data
void deleteElement(int data) {
    int i;
    struct ListNode *update[MAXSKIPLEVEL+1], *temp;
    temp = list.header;
    for (i = list.listLevel; i >= 0; i--) {
        while (temp→next[i] != list.header && temp→next[i]→data < data)
            temp = temp→next[i];
        update[i] = temp;
    }
    temp = temp→next[0];
    if (temp == list.header || !(temp→data == data) return;
    //adjust next pointers
    for (i = 0; i <= list.listLevel; i++) {
```

```
            if (update[i]→next[i] != temp) break;
            update[i]→next[i] = temp→next[i];
        }
        free (temp);
        //adjust header level
        while ((list.listLevel > 0) && (list.header→next[list.listLevel] == list.header))
            list.listLevel--;
    }
    // find node containing data
    struct ListNode *findElement(int data) {
        struct ListNode *temp = list.header;
        for (int i = list.listLevel; i >= 0; i--) {
            while (temp→next[i] != list.header
              && temp→next[i]→data < data)
                temp = temp→next[i];
        }
        temp = temp→next[0];
        if (temp != list.header && temp→data == data) return (temp);
        return(0);
    }
    // initialize skip list
    void initList() {
        int i;
        if ((list.header = malloc(sizeof(struct ListNode) + MAXSKIPLEVEL*sizeof(struct ListNode *))) == 0) {
            printf ("Memory Error\n");
            exit(1);
        }
        for (i = 0; i <= MAXSKIPLEVEL; i++)
            list.header→next[i] = list.header;
        list.listLevel = 0;
    }
    /* command-line: skipList maxnum skipList 2000: process 2000 sequential records */
    int main(int argc, char **argv) {
        int i, *a, maxnum = atoi(argv[1]);
        initList();
        if ((a = malloc(maxnum * sizeof(*a))) == 0) {
            fprintf (stderr, "insufficient memory (a)\n");
            exit(1);
        }
        for (i = 0; i < maxnum; i++) a[i] = rand();
            printf ("Random, %d items\n", maxnum);
        for (i = 0; i < maxnum; i++) {
            insertElement(a[i]);
        }
        for (i = maxnum-1; i >= 0; i--) {
            findElement(a[i]);
        }
        for (i = maxnum-1; i >= 0; i--) {
            deleteElement(a[i]);
        }
        return 0;
    }
```

## 3.12 Linked Lists: Problems & Solutions

**Problem-1** Which of the following operations is the most time-efficient for a singly linked list?

A. Adding a new node to the beginning of the list
B. Adding a new node to the end of the list
C. Removing a node from the beginning of the list
D. Removing a node from the end of the list

**Solution**: The correct answer is: A. Adding a new node to the beginning of the list.

This operation has a time complexity of O(1), meaning that it takes constant time, regardless of the size of the list. In contrast, adding a node to the end of the list (option B) requires traversing the entire list, resulting in a time complexity of O(n), where n is the number of nodes in the list. Similarly, removing a node from the end of the list (option D) also requires traversing the entire list, making it an O(n) operation. Removing a node from the beginning of the list (option C) is also an O(1) operation, but it requires updating the head pointer, which can be more complicated than simply adding a new node to the beginning of the list.

**Problem-2** Which of the following best describes the advantages of a doubly linked list over a singly linked list?

A. Doubly linked lists have faster insertion and deletion operations.
B. Doubly linked lists require less memory than singly linked lists.
C. Doubly linked lists provide more efficient traversal of the list in reverse order.
D. Doubly linked lists are less prone to pointer errors than singly linked lists.

**Solution**: The correct answer is: C. Doubly linked lists provide more efficient traversal of the list in reverse order.

While doubly linked lists do allow for faster deletion and insertion operations at certain points in the list, this is not a universal advantage over singly linked lists. Additionally, doubly linked lists require more memory than singly linked lists due to the extra pointer for each node. The claim that doubly linked lists are less prone to pointer errors is also false - both types of linked lists require careful management of pointers to prevent errors.

The primary advantage of a doubly linked list is its ability to efficiently traverse the list in both directions, due to the presence of a previous pointer in each node. This is not possible in a singly linked list, where traversal is only possible in the forward direction.

**Problem-3** Which of the following is a disadvantage of a circular linked list compared to a singly linked list?

A. Circular linked lists require more memory than singly linked lists.
B. Circular linked lists can be more difficult to implement than singly linked lists.
C. Circular linked lists cannot be traversed in reverse order.
D. Circular linked lists can result in an infinite loop if not implemented carefully.

**Solution**: The correct answer is: D. Circular linked lists can result in an infinite loop if not implemented carefully.

While circular linked lists do require an extra pointer to point back to the head of the list, this does not necessarily make them more memory-intensive than singly linked lists. Additionally, while they may be slightly more complex to implement, this is not a universal disadvantage over singly linked lists.

One potential disadvantage of circular linked lists is that they cannot be traversed in reverse order, as the nodes only have pointers to the next node, not the previous one. However, this is not always a critical concern for all use cases.

The most significant disadvantage of circular linked lists is that if the pointers are not managed carefully, they can result in an infinite loop that can cause the program to crash or hang. For example, if the next pointer of the last node is not set to NULL, or if the same node is inserted into the list multiple times, an infinite loop can occur.

**Problem-4** Implement Stack using Linked List.

**Solution:** Refer to *Stacks* chapter.

**Problem-5** True or False: A linked list can contain cycles, where a node points back to an earlier node in the list, creating a loop.

**Solution**: True. A linked list is a data structure that consists of a sequence of nodes, each containing a value and a reference (or pointer) to the next node in the sequence. In a singly-linked list, each node only has a reference to the next node in the list. In a doubly-linked list, each node has references to both the next and previous nodes in the list.

In a linked list, it's possible for a node to have a reference that points back to an earlier node in the list, creating a loop or cycle. This can happen when two or more nodes in the list have the same reference to the next node. For example, if we have a linked list with nodes A, B, C, and D, and node D has a reference back to node B, then the linked list will contain a cycle. Here's an example of a linked list with a cycle:

```
A -> B -> C -> D -> B (cycle)
```

In this example, node D points back to node B, creating a cycle in the linked list. So, to sum up: a linked list can contain cycles, where a node points back to an earlier node in the list, creating a loop. Therefore, the answer to the true/false question "A linked list can contain cycles" is true.

**Problem-6** Find $k^{th}$ node from the end of a Linked List.

**Solution: Brute-Force Method:** Start with the first node and count the number of nodes present after that node. If the number of nodes is $< k - 1$ then return saying "fewer number of nodes in the list". If the number of nodes is $> k - 1$ then go to next node. Continue this until the numbers of nodes after current node are $k - 1$.

Time Complexity: $O(n^2)$, for scanning the remaining list (from current node) for each node. Space Complexity: O(1).

**Problem-7** Can we improve the complexity of Problem-6?

**Solution: Yes**, using hash table. As an example, consider the following list.

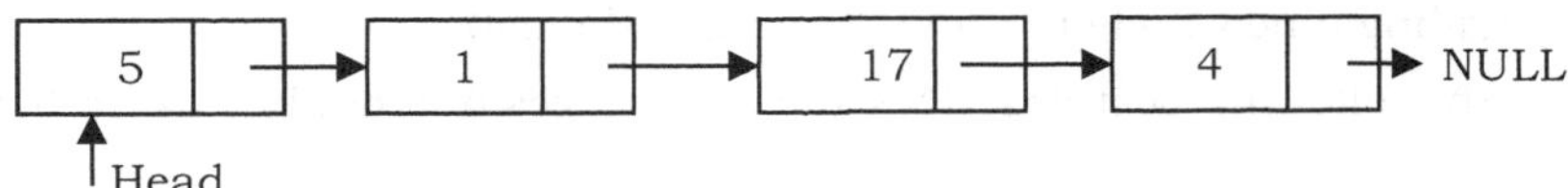


In this approach, create a hash table whose entries are < *position of node, node address* >. That means, key is the position of the node in the list and value is the address of that node.

| Position in List | Address of Node |
|---|---|
| 1 | Address of 5 node |
| 2 | Address of 1 node |
| 3 | Address of 17 node |
| 4 | Address of 4 node |

By the time we traverse the complete list (for creating the hash table), we can find the list length. Let us say the list length is $M$. To find $n^{th}$ from the end of linked list, we can convert this to $M$- $n + 1^{th}$ from the beginning. Since we already know the length of the list, it is just a matter of returning $M$- $n + 1^{th}$ key value from the hash table.

Time Complexity: Time for creating the hash table, $T(m) = O(m)$. Space Complexity: Since we need to create a hash table of size $m$, $O(m)$.

**Problem-8** Can we solve Problem-5 without creating the hash table?

**Solution: Yes**. Upon examining the previous solution, it becomes apparent that we are determining the size of the linked list. This involves utilizing a hash table to accomplish this task. However, we could also find the length of the linked list by starting at the head node and traversing the list. Therefore, we do not necessarily need to create a hash table to determine the length of the list. After finding the length, compute $n - k + 1$ and with one more scan we can get the $(n - k + 1)^{th}$ node from the beginning. This solution needs two scans: one for finding the length of the list and the other for finding $(n - k + 1)^{th}$ node from the beginning.

Time Complexity: Time for finding the length + Time for finding the $(n - k + 1)^{th}$ node from the beginning. Therefore, $T(n) = O(n) + O(n) \approx O(n)$. Space Complexity: $O(1)$. Hence, no need to create the hash table.

**Problem-9** Can we solve Problem-5 in one scan?

**Solution: Yes. Efficient Approach**: Use two pointers *kthNode* and *pTemp*. Initially, both point to head node of the list. *kthNode* starts moving only after *pTemp* has made $k - 1$ moves. From there both move forward until *pTemp* reaches the end of the list. As a result *kthNode* points to $k^{th}$ node from the end of the linked list.

**Note:** Both pointers move one node at a time.

```
struct ListNode* kthNodeFromEnd(struct ListNode* head, int k){
    struct ListNode *pTemp, *kthNode;
    int i;
    pTemp = kthNode = head;
    /* k should be less than length of linked list */
    if(k > getLength(head)){
        printf("Error: k is greater than length of linked list\n");
        return NULL;
    }
    /* Move pTemp pointer k-1 ListNodes. This will create a difference of k-1 ListNodes
        between pTemp and kthNode */
    for(i = 0; i < k-1; i++){
        pTemp = pTemp->next;
    }
    /* Now, move both pointers together till pTemp reaches last ListNode of linked list.
        when pTemp reaches last ListNode kthNode pointer will be pointing to Nth last ListNode*/
    while(pTemp->next != NULL){
        pTemp = pTemp->next;
        kthNode = kthNode->next;
    }
    return kthNode;
}
```

Time Complexity: $O(n)$. Space Complexity: $O(1)$.

**Problem-10** Check whether the given linked list is either NULL-terminated or ends in a cycle (cyclic).

**Solution: Brute-Force Approach. To** check whether a linked list is NULL-terminated or not, we can simply traverse the linked list from the head node to the tail node, following each node's next pointer until we reach the end of the list. If the last node's next pointer is NULL, then the linked list is NULL-terminated. If the last node's next pointer is not NULL, then the linked list contains a cycle.

As an example, consider the following linked list which has a loop in it. The difference between this list and the regular list is that, in this list, there are two nodes whose next pointers are the same. In regular singly linked lists (without a loop) each node's next pointer is unique. That means the repetition of next pointers indicates the existence of a loop.

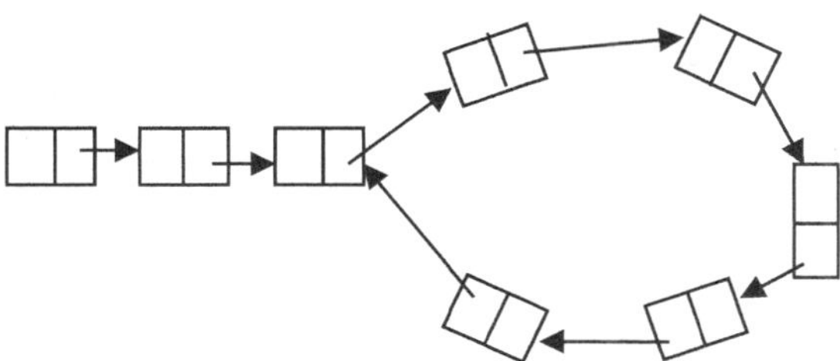

One simple and brute force way of solving this is, start with the first node and see whether there is any node whose next pointer is the current node's address. If there is a node with the same address, then that indicates that some other node is pointing to the current node and we can say a loop exists. Continue this process for all the nodes of the linked list.

**Does this method work?** As per the algorithm, we are checking for the next pointer addresses, but how do we find the end of the linked list (otherwise we will end up in an infinite loop)?

**Note:** If we start with a node in a loop, this method may work depending on the size of the loop.

**Problem-11** Can we use the hashing technique for solving Problem-10?

**Solution: Yes**. Using Hash Tables, we can solve this problem.

**Algorithm:**

- Traverse the linked list nodes one by one.
- Check if the address of the node is available in the hash table or not.
- If it is already available in the hash table, that indicates that we are visiting the node that was already visited. This is possible only if the given linked list has a loop in it.
- If the address of the node is not available in the hash table, insert that node's address into the hash table.
- Continue this process until we reach the end of the linked list *or* we find the loop.

Time Complexity: $O(n)$ for scanning the linked list. Note that we are doing a scan of only the input.
Space Complexity: $O(n)$ for hash table.

**Problem-12** Can we solve Problem-10 using the sorting technique?

**Solution: No**. Consider the following algorithm which is based on sorting. Then we see why this algorithm fails.

**Algorithm:**

- Traverse the linked list nodes one by one and take all the next pointer values into an array.
- Sort the array that has the next node pointers.
- If there is a loop in the linked list, definitely two next node pointers will be pointing to the same node.
- After sorting if there is a loop in the list, the nodes whose next pointers are the same will end up adjacent in the sorted list.
- If any such pair exists in the sorted list then we say the linked list has a loop in it.

Time Complexity: $O(nlogn)$ for sorting the next pointers array. Space Complexity: $O(n)$ for the next pointers array.

**Problem with the above algorithm:** The above algorithm works only if we can find the length of the list. But if the list has a loop then we may end up in an infinite loop. Due to this reason the algorithm fails.

**Problem-13** Can we solve the Problem-10 in $O(n)$?

**Solution: Yes. Efficient Approach (Memoryless Approach)**: The space complexity can be reduced to O(1) by considering two pointers at different speed - a slow pointer and a fast pointer. The slow pointer moves one step at a time while the fast pointer moves two steps at a time. This problem was solved by *Floyd*. The solution is named the Floyd cycle finding algorithm (also known as the "tortoise and hare" algorithm). It uses *two* pointers moving at different speeds to walk the linked list. If there is no cycle in the list, the fast pointer will eventually reach the end and we can return false in this case. Now consider a cyclic list and imagine the slow and fast pointers are two runners racing around a circle track. Once they enter the loop they are expected to meet, which denotes that there is a loop.

This works because the only way a faster moving pointer would point to the same location as a slower moving pointer is if somehow the entire list or a part of it is circular. Think of a tortoise and a hare running on a track. The faster running hare will catch up with the tortoise if they are running in a loop. As an example, consider the following example and trace out the Floyd algorithm. From the diagrams below we can see that after the final step they are meeting at some point in the loop which may not be the starting point of the loop.

**Note:** *slowPtr* (*tortoise*) moves one pointer at a time and *fastPtr* (*hare*) moves two pointers at a time.

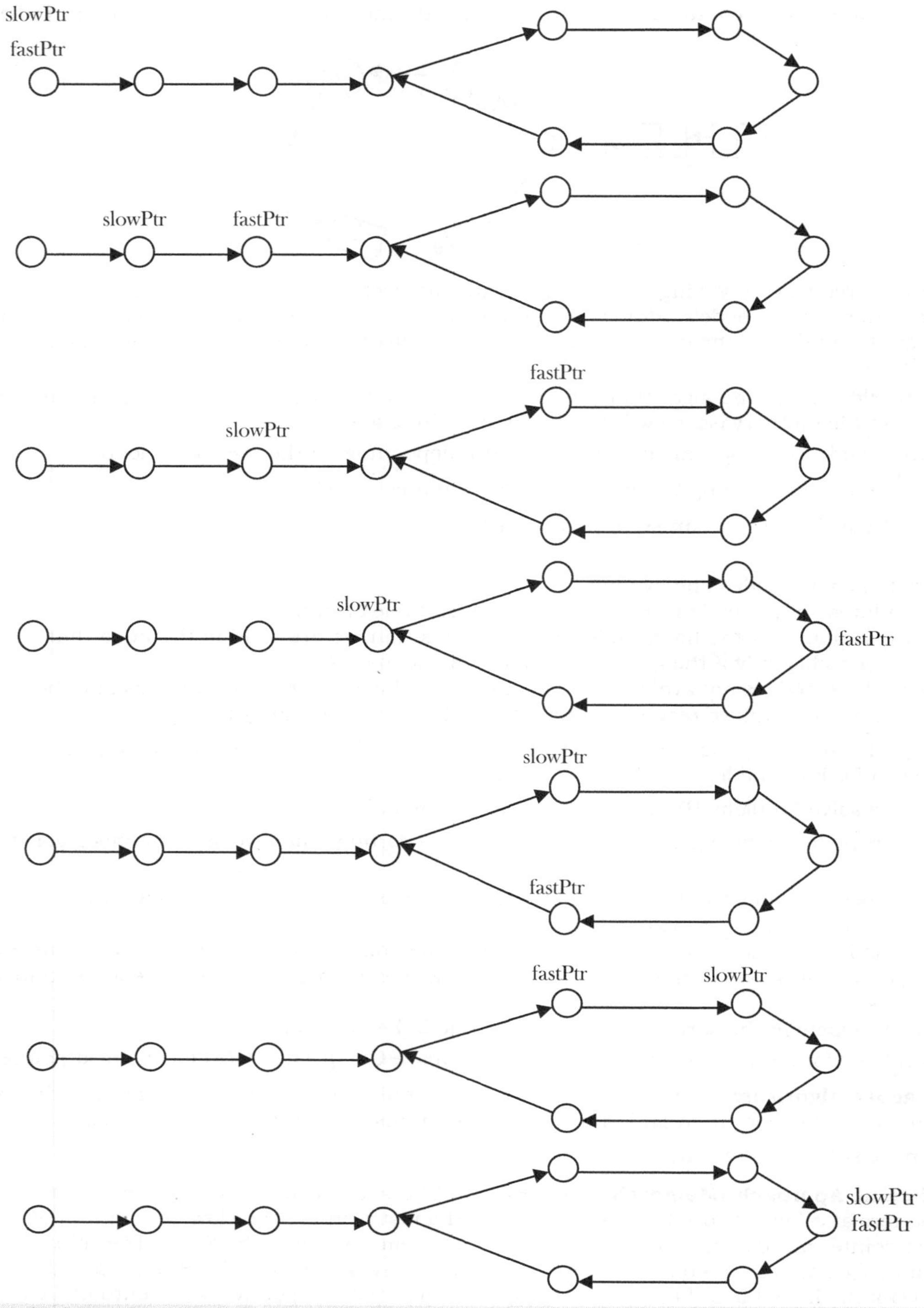


```
int checkLoop(struct ListNode *head) {
    struct ListNode *slow, *fast;
    slow = fast = head;
     while(fast && fast->next) {
        /* Slow pointer will move one node per iteration whereas fast node will move two nodes per iteration */
        slow = slow->next;
        fast = fast->next->next;
```

```
        if (slow == fast) {
            printf("\n Linked list contains a loop\n");
            return 1;
        }
    }
    printf("\n No loop in linked list\n");
    return 0;
}
```

Time Complexity: O($n$). Space Complexity: O(1).

**Problem-14** We are given a pointer to the first element of a linked list $L$. There are two possibilities for $L$: it either ends (snake) or its last element points back to one of the earlier elements in the list (snail). Give an algorithm that tests whether a given list $L$ is a snake or a snail.

**Solution:** It is the same as Problem-10.

**Problem-15** Check whether the given linked list is NULL-terminated or not. If there is a cycle, find the start node of the loop.

**Solution:** This solution builds upon the approach used in Problem-10. Once a loop is detected in the linked list, we set the slow pointer to the head of the linked list. We then move both the slow and fast pointers one node at a time until they meet again at the start of the loop. This approach is commonly used for removing loops in a linked list.

```
struct ListNode* findLoopBeginning(struct ListNode * head) {
    struct ListNode *slow = head, *fast = head;
    int loopExists = 0;
    while (fast && fast->next) {
        slow = slow->next;
        fast = fast->next->next;
        if (slow == fast){
            loopExists = 1;
            break;
        }
    }
    if(loopExists) {
      slow = head;
      while(slow != fast) {
        fast = fast->next;
        slow = slow->next;
      }
      return slow;
    }
    return NULL;
}
```

Time Complexity: O($n$). Space Complexity: O(1).

**Problem-16** From the previous discussion and problems, we understand that the meeting of tortoise and hare concludes the existence of the loop, but how does moving the tortoise to the beginning of the linked list while keeping the hare at the meeting place, followed by moving both one step at a time, make them meet at the starting point of the cycle?

**Solution:** This problem is at the heart of the number theory. In the Floyd cycle finding algorithm, notice that the tortoise and the hare will meet when they are $n \times L$, where $L$ is the loop length. Furthermore, the tortoise is at the midpoint between the hare and the beginning of the sequence because of the way they move. Therefore, the tortoise is $n \times L$ away from the beginning of the sequence as well. If we move both one step at a time, from the position of the tortoise and from the start of the sequence, we know that they will meet as soon as both are in the loop, since they are $n \times L$, a multiple of the loop length, apart. One of them is already in the loop, so we just move the other one in single step until it enters the loop, keeping the other $n \times L$ away from it at all times.

**Problem-17** In the Floyd cycle finding algorithm, does it work if we use steps 2 and 3 instead of 1 and 2?

**Solution: Yes**, but the complexity might be high. Trace out an example.

**Problem-18** Check whether the given linked list is NULL-terminated. If there is a cycle, find the length of the loop.

**Solution:** This solution is also an extension of the basic cycle detection problem. After finding the loop in the linked list, keep the *slow* as it is. The *fast* keeps on moving until it again comes back to *slow*. While moving *fast*, use a counter variable which increments at the rate of 1.

```
int loopLength(struct ListNode * head) {
```

```
    struct ListNode *slow = head, *fast = head;
    int loopExists = 0, counter = 0;
    while (fast && fast->next) {
        slow = slow->next;
        fast = fast->next->next;
        if (slow == fast){
            loopExists = 1;
            break;
        }
    }
    if(loopExists) {
        counter = 1;
        fast = fast->next;
        while(slow != fast) {
            fast = fast->next;
            counter++;
        }
        return counter;
    }
    return 0;
}
```

Time Complexity: O($n$). Space Complexity: O(1).

**Problem-19** Insert a node in a sorted linked list.

**Solution:** Traverse the list and find a position for the element and insert it.

```
// Insert the given node into the correct sorted position in the given list sorted in increasing order
void sortedInsert(struct ListNode** head, int data){
    /* Create a new ListNode */
    struct ListNode* newNode = (struct ListNode*) malloc(sizeof(struct ListNode));
    newNode->data = data;
    // Special case for the head end
    if (*head == NULL || (*head)->data >= newNode->data){
        newNode->next = *head;
        *head = newNode;
        return;
    }
    // Locate the node before the point of insertion
    struct ListNode* current = *head;
    while(current->next != NULL && current->next->data < newNode->data)
        current = current->next;
    newNode->next = current->next;
    current->next = newNode;
}
```

Time Complexity: O($n$). Space Complexity: O(1).

**Problem-20** Reverse a singly linked list.

**Solution:** While traversing the list, change the current node's next pointer to point to its previous element. Since a node does not have reference to its previous node, we must store its previous element beforehand. We also need another pointer to store the next node before changing the reference. We will use three pointers "previous", "current" and "next" to keep track of previous, current and next node during linked list reversal.

```
/* Iterative version: Reverses a given linked list, and return the head pointer of reversed linked list */
struct ListNode* reverseLinkedList(struct ListNode *head) {
    struct ListNode *previous, *current, *next;
    previous = NULL;
    current = head;
    while (current != NULL) {
        next = current->next;
        current->next = previous;
        previous = current;
        current = next;
    }
    return previous;
```

```
}
```

Time Complexity: O($n$). Space Complexity: O(1).

**Recursive version**: The recursive version is slightly trickier, and the key is to work backwards. We will find it easier to start from the bottom up, by asking and answering tiny questions:

- What is the reverse of NULL (the empty list)? NULL.
- What is the reverse of a one element list? The element itself.
- What is the reverse of an $n$ element list? The reverse of the second element followed by the first element.

```
struct ListNode* reverseLinkedListRecursive(struct ListNode *head) {
    if (head == NULL || head->next == NULL)
        return head;
    struct ListNode *secondElem = head->next;
    // unlink list from the rest or you will get a cycle
    head->next = NULL;
    // reverse everything from the second element on
    struct ListNode *reverseRest = reverseLinkedListRecursive(secondElem);
    secondElem->next = head;        // then we join the two lists
    return reverseRest;
}
```

Time Complexity: O($n$).
Space Complexity: O($n$). The extra space comes from implicit stack space due to recursion. The recursion could go up to $n$ levels deep.

**Problem-21** Suppose there are two singly linked lists both of which intersect at some point and become a single linked list. The head or start pointers of both the lists are known, but the intersecting node is not known. Also, the number of nodes in each of the lists before they intersect is unknown and may be different in each list. *List*1 may have $n$ nodes before it reaches the intersection point, and *List*2 might have $m$ nodes before it reaches the intersection point where $m$ and $n$ may be $m = n, m < n$ or $m > n$. Give an algorithm for finding the merging point.

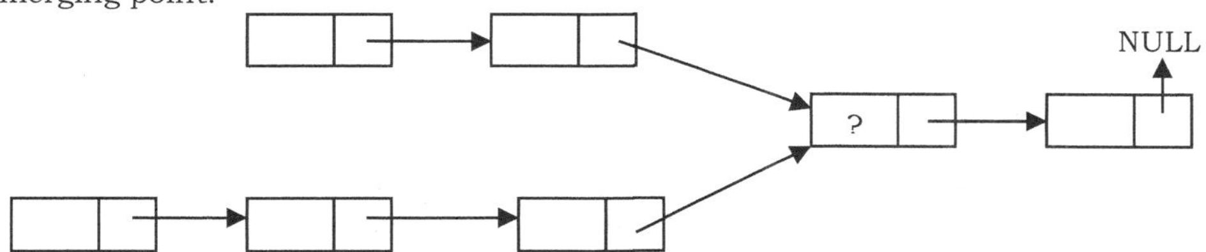


**Solution: Brute-Force Approach:** One easy solution is to compare every node pointer in the first list with every other node pointer in the second list by which the matching node pointers will lead us to the intersecting node. But, the time complexity in this case will be O($mn$) which will be high.

```
struct ListNode * intersectingNodeBruteForce(struct ListNode *head1, struct ListNode *head2){
    // stores the result, if no ListNode is intersecting we return NULL
    struct ListNode *temp;
    while(head1 != NULL){
        temp = head2;
        while(temp != NULL){
            if(temp == head1){
                // found a matching node
                return head1;
            }
            temp = temp -> next;
        }
        head1 = head1 -> next;
    }
    return NULL;
}
```

Time Complexity: O($mn$). Space Complexity: O(1).

**Problem-22** Can we solve Problem-21 using the sorting technique?

**Solution: No.** Consider the following algorithm which is based on sorting and see why this algorithm fails.

**Algorithm:**

- Take first list node pointers and keep them in some array and sort them.

- Take second list node pointers and keep them in some array and sort them.
- After sorting, use two indexes: one for the first sorted array and the other for the second sorted array.
- Start comparing values at the indexes and increment the index according to whichever has the lower value (increment only if the values are not equal).
- At any point, if we are able to find two indexes whose values are the same, then that indicates that those two nodes are pointing to the same node and we return that node.

Time Complexity: Time for sorting lists + Time for scanning (for comparing)
$= O(mlogm) + O(nlogn) + O(m+n)$ We need to consider the one that gives the maximum value.

Space Complexity: O(1).

**Any problem with the above algorithm? Yes**. In the algorithm, we are storing all the node pointers of both the lists and sorting. But we are forgetting the fact that there can be many repeated elements. This is because after the merging point, all node pointers are the same for both the lists. The algorithm works fine only in one case and it is when both lists have the ending node at their merge point.

**Problem-23** Can we solve Problem-21 using hash tables?

**Solution: Yes.**

**Algorithm:**

- Select a list which has a smaller number of nodes (If we do not know the lengths beforehand then select one list randomly).
- Now, traverse the other list and for each node pointer of this list check whether the same node pointer exists in the hash table.
- If there is a merge point for the given lists, then we will definitely encounter the node pointer in the hash table.

Time Complexity: Time for creating the hash table + Time for scanning the second list = $O(m) + O(n)$ (or $O(n) + O(m)$, depending on which list we select for creating the hash table. But in both cases the time complexity is the same. Space Complexity: $O(n)$ or $O(m)$.

**Problem-24** Can we use stacks for solving the Problem-21?

**Solution: Yes.**

**Algorithm:**

- Create two stacks: one for the first list and one for the second list.
- Traverse the first list and push all the node addresses onto the first stack.
- Traverse the second list and push all the node addresses onto the second stack.
- Now both stacks contain the node address of the corresponding lists.
- Now compare the top node address of both stacks.
- If they are the same, take the top elements from both the stacks and keep them in some temporary variable (since both node addresses are node, it is enough if we use one temporary variable).
- Continue this process until the top node addresses of the stacks are not the same.
- This point is the one where the lists merge into a single list.
- Return the value of the temporary variable.

Time Complexity: $O(m+n)$, for scanning both the lists. Space Complexity: $O(m+n)$, for creating two stacks for both the lists.

**Problem-25** Is there any other way of solving Problem-21?

**Solution**: **Yes**. Using "finding the first repeating number" approach in an array (for algorithm refer to *Searching* chapter).

**Algorithm:**

- Create an array $A$ and keep all the next pointers of both the lists in the array.
- In the array find the first repeating element [Refer to *Searching* chapter for algorithm].
- The first repeating number indicates the merging point of both the lists.

Time Complexity: $O(m+n)$. Space Complexity: $O(m+n)$.

**Problem-26** Can we still think of finding an alternative solution for Problem-21?

**Solution: Yes**. By combining sorting and search techniques we can reduce the complexity.

**Algorithm:**

- Create an array $A$ and keep all the next pointers of the first list in the array.
- Sort these array elements.
- Then, for each of the second list elements, search in the sorted array (let us assume that we are using binary search which gives $O(logn)$).

- Since we are scanning the second list one by one, the first repeating element that appears in the array is nothing but the merging point.

Time Complexity: Time for sorting + Time for searching = $O(Max(mlogm, nlogn))$. Space Complexity: $O(Max(m, n))$.

**Problem-27** Can we improve the complexity for Problem-21?

**Solution: Yes**. Maintain two pointers head1 and head2 initialized at the head of list1 and list2, respectively. Then let them both traverse through the lists, one node at a time. First calculate the length of two lists and find the difference. Then start from the longer list at the diff offset, iterate though 2 lists and find the node.

**Efficient Approach:**

- Find lengths (L1 and L2) of both lists -- $O(n) + O(m) = O(max(m, n))$.
- Take the difference $d$ of the lengths -- $O(1)$.
- Make $d$ steps in longer list -- $O(d)$.
- Step in both lists in parallel until links to next node match -- $O(min(m, n))$.
- Total time complexity = $O(max(m, n))$.
- Space Complexity = $O(1)$.

```
struct ListNode * intersectingListNode(struct ListNode * head1, struct ListNode * head2){
    // get lengths of both the lists
    int m = getLength(head1);
    int n = getLength(head2);
    struct ListNode * mergePoint = NULL; // to store the merge point
    // finding the value of d based on the longer list
    int diff = (m > n) ? (m-n) : (n-m);
    //traverse the smaller longer list for 'diff' steps
    if(m > n){
        while(diff--)
            head1 = head1 -> next;
    }
    else{
        while(diff--)
            head2 = head2 -> next;
    }
    // now both lists have equal nodes till the end.
    while(head1 && head2){
        if(head1 -> next == head2 -> next){
            mergePoint = head1 -> next;
            break;
        }
        head1 = head1 -> next;
        head2 = head2 -> next;
    }
    return mergePoint;
}
```

**Problem-28** How will you find the middle of the linked list?

**Solution: Brute-Force Approach:** For each of the node, count how many nodes are there in the list, and see whether it is the middle node of the list.

Time Complexity: $O(n^2)$. Space Complexity: $O(1)$.

**Problem-29** Can we improve the complexity of Problem-28?

**Solution: Yes.**

**Algorithm:**

- Traverse the list and find the length of the list.
- After finding the length, again scan the list and locate $n/2$ node from the beginning.

Time Complexity: Time for finding the length of the list + Time for locating middle node = $O(n) + O(n) \approx O(n)$. Space Complexity: $O(1)$.

**Problem-30** Can we use the hash table for solving Problem-28?

**Solution: Yes.** The reasoning is the same as that of Problem-7.

Time Complexity: Time for creating the hash table. Therefore, $T(n) = O(n)$.
Space Complexity: $O(n)$. Since we need to create a hash table of size $n$.

**Problem-31** Can we solve Problem-28 just in one scan?

**Solution: Efficient Approach:** Use two pointers. Move one pointer at twice the speed of the second. When the first pointer reaches the end of the list, the second pointer will be pointing to the middle node. When traversing the list with a pointer *slow*, make another pointer *fast* that traverses twice as fast. When *fast* reaches the end of the list, *slow* must be in the middle.

**Note:** If the list has an even number of nodes, the middle node will be of $\lfloor n/2 \rfloor$.

```
struct ListNode * middleNode(struct ListNode *head){
    if(head == NULL){
        printf("Error: List is empty!\n");
        return NULL;
    }
    struct ListNode *slow, *fast;
    slow = fast = head;
    /* In every iteration, slow pointer will move one node whereas fast pointer will move two ListNodes.
     When fast pointer reaches last ListNode then slow pointer will be pointing to middle ListNode */
    while(fast != NULL && fast->next != NULL) {
        fast = fast->next->next;
        slow = slow->next;
    }
    return slow;
}
```

Time Complexity: O($n$). Space Complexity: O(1).

**Problem-32** How will you display a Linked List from the end (in reverse)?

**Solution:** Traverse recursively till the end of the linked list. While coming back, start printing the elements.

```
void printListInReverse(struct ListNode *head) {
    if(!head)
        return;
    printListInReverse(head->next);
    printf("%d-->", head->data);
}
```

Time Complexity: O($n$). Space Complexity: O($n$)→ for Stack.

**Problem-33** Check whether the given Linked List length is even or odd?

**Solution:** Use a $2x$ pointer. Take a pointer that moves at $2x$ [two nodes at a time]. At the end, if the length is even, then the pointer will be NULL; otherwise, it will point to the last node.

```
int isLinkedListLengthEven(struct ListNode * listHead) {
    while(listHead && listHead->next)
        listHead = listHead->next->next;
    if(listHead)
        return 0;
    return 1;
}
```

Time Complexity: O($\lfloor n/2 \rfloor$) ≈O($n$). Space Complexity: O(1).

**Problem-34** If the head of a Linked List is pointing to *kth* element, then how will you get the elements before *kth* element?

**Solution:** Use Memory Efficient Linked Lists [XOR Linked Lists].

**Problem-35** Given two sorted Linked Lists, how to merge them into the third list in sorted order?

**Solution:** To merge two sorted linked lists into a third list, follow the steps below:

- Create an empty result linked list to store the merged elements.
- Traverse both the input linked lists simultaneously using two pointers, starting from their respective heads.
- Compare the values of the nodes pointed to by the two pointers. Select the smaller value and append it to the result linked list.
- Move the pointer of the linked list from which the smaller value was selected to the next node.
- Repeat steps 3 and 4 until all the nodes of one of the input linked lists have been added to the result linked list.
- Once one of the input linked lists is exhausted, append the remaining nodes of the other linked list to the result linked list.

- Return the head of the result linked list.

```
struct ListNode *mergeSortedListIterative(struct ListNode *head1, struct ListNode *head2){
    struct ListNode * newNode = (struct ListNode*) (malloc(sizeof(struct ListNode)));
    struct ListNode *temp = newNode;
    newNode = new Node;
    newNode→next = NULL;
    while (head1!=NULL and head2!=NULL){
        if (head1→data<=head2→data){
            temp→next = head1;
            temp = temp→next;
            head1 = head1→next;
        }else{
            temp→next = head2;
            temp = temp→next;
            head2 = head2→next;
        }
    }
    if (head1!=NULL)
        temp→next = head1;
    else
        temp→next = head2;
    temp = newNode→next;
    free(newNode);
    return temp;
}
```

The time complexity of the function is O(n+m), where n and m are the lengths of the input linked lists l1 and l2, respectively. This is because we traverse each linked list exactly once and compare each node at most once. The space complexity is O(1), because we are only using a constant amount of extra space for the pointers dummy, curr, and the merged linked list itself.

**Problem-36** Reverse the linked list in pairs. If you have a linked list that holds $1 \rightarrow 2 \rightarrow 3 \rightarrow 4 \rightarrow X$, then after the function has been called the linked list would hold $2 \rightarrow 1 \rightarrow 4 \rightarrow 3 \rightarrow X$.

**Solution:**

**Recursive:**

```
struct ListNode *reversePairRecursive(struct ListNode *head) {
    struct ListNode *temp;
    if(head ==NULL || head→next ==NULL)
        return;         //base case for empty or 1 element list
    else {
        //Reverse first pair
        temp = head→next;
        head→next = temp→next;
        temp→next = head;
        head = temp;
        //Call the method recursively for the rest of the list
        head→next→next = reversePairRecursive(head→next→next);
        return head;
    }
}
```

**Iterative:**

```
struct ListNode *reversePairIterative(struct ListNode *head) {
    struct ListNode *temp1=NULL, *temp2=NULL, *current = head;
    while(current != NULL && current→next != NULL) {
        if (temp1 != null) {
            temp1→next→next = current→next;
        }
        temp1 = current→next;
        current→next = current→next→next;
        temp1.next = current;
        if (temp2 == null)
```

```
            temp2 = temp1;
        current = current→next;
    }
    return temp2;
}
```

Time Complexity: O($n$). Space Complexity: O(1).

**Problem-37** Given a binary search tree convert it to a doubly linked list.

**Solution:** Refer *Binary Search Trees* section of *Trees* chapter.

**Problem-38** How do we sort the Linked Lists?

**Solution:** Refer *Sorting* chapter.

**Problem-39** Split a Circular Linked List into two equal parts. If the number of nodes in the list are odd, then make first list one node extra than second list.

**Alternative problem statement:** Given a linked list, split it into two sublists — one for the front half, and one for the back half. If the number of elements is odd, the extra element should go in the front list. So the algorithm on the list {2, 3, 5, 7, 11} should yield the two lists {2, 3, 5} and {7, 11}.

**Solution:**

**Algorithm:**

- Store the mid and last pointers of the circular linked list using Floyd cycle finding algorithm.
- Make the second half circular.
- Make the first half circular.
- Set head pointers of the two linked lists.

As an example, consider the following circular list.

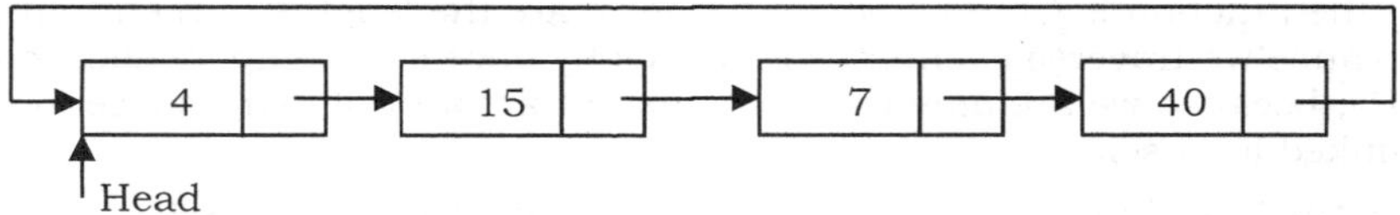


After the split, the above list will look like:

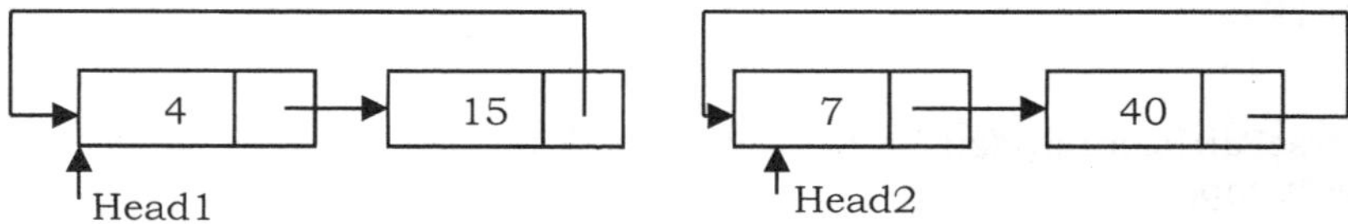


```
// structure for a node
struct ListNode {
    int data;
    struct ListNode *next;
};
// Uses the fast/slow pointer strategy
void splitList(struct ListNode* head, struct ListNode** head1, struct ListNode** head2) {
    struct ListNode* fast;
    struct ListNode* slow;
    if (head==NULL || head->next==NULL) { // length < 2 cases
        *head1 = head;
        *head2 = NULL;
    }
    else {
        slow = head;
        fast = head->next;
        // Advance 'fast' two nodes, and advance 'slow' one ListNode
        while (fast != NULL) {
            fast = fast->next;
            if (fast != NULL) {
                slow = slow->next;
                fast = fast->next;
            }
        }
        // 'slow' is before the midpoint in the list, so split it in two at that point.
```

```
        *head1 = head;
        *head2 = slow->next;
        slow->next = NULL;
    }
}
```

Time Complexity: O($n$). Space Complexity: O(1).

**Problem-40** If we want to concatenate two linked lists which of the following gives O(1) complexity?
1) Singly linked lists 2) Doubly linked lists 3) Circular doubly linked lists

**Solution:** Circular Doubly Linked Lists. This is because for singly and doubly linked lists, we need to traverse the first list till the end and append the second list. But in the case of circular doubly linked lists we don't have to traverse the lists.

**Problem-41** How will you check if the linked list is palindrome or not?

**Solution:**

**Algorithm:**
1. Get the middle of the linked list.
2. Reverse the second half of the linked list.
3. Compare the first half and second half.
4. Construct the original linked list by reversing the second half again and attaching it back to the first half.

Time Complexity: O($n$). Space Complexity: O(1).

**Problem-42** For a given $K$ value ($K > 0$) reverse blocks of $K$ nodes in a list.
**Example**: Input: 1 2 3 4 5 6 7 8 9 10. Output for different $K$ values:
For $K = 2$: 2 1 4 3 6 5 8 7 10 9 For $K = 3$: 3 2 1 6 5 4 9 8 7 10 For $K = 4$: 4 3 2 1 8 7 6 5 9 10

**Solution:**

**Algorithm:** This is an extension of swapping nodes in a linked list.
1) Check if the remaining list has $K$ nodes.
   a. If yes get the pointer of $K + 1^{th}$ node.
   b. Else return.
2) Reverse first $K$ nodes.
3) Set next of last node (after reversal) to $K + 1^{th}$ node.
4) Move to $K + 1^{th}$ node.
5) Go to step 1.
6) $K - 1^{th}$ node of first $K$ nodes become the new head if available. Otherwise, we can return the head.

```
struct ListNode * getKPlusOneThNode(int K, struct ListNode *head) {
    struct ListNode *Kth;
    int i = 0;
    if(!head)
        return head;
    for (i = 0, Kth = head; Kth && (i < K); i++, Kth = Kth→next);
    if(i == K && Kth != NULL)
            return Kth;
    return head→next;
}
int hasKnodes(struct ListNode *head, int K) {
    int i =0;
    for(i = 0; head && (i < K); i++, head = head→next);
    if(i == K)
        return 1;
    return 0;
}
struct ListNode *reverseBlockOfK-nodesInLinkedList(struct ListNode *head, int K) {
    struct ListNode *cur = head, *temp, *next, newHead;
    int i;
    if(K==0 || K==1)
        return head;
    if(HasKnodes(cur, K-1))
        newHead = getKPlusOneThNode(K-1, cur);
    else
        newHead = head;
```

```
        while(cur && hasKnodes(cur, K)) {
                temp = getKPlusOneThNode(K, cur);
                i=0;
                while(i < K) {
                        next = cur→next;
                        cur→next=temp;
                        temp = cur;
                        cur = next;
                        i++;
                }
        }
        return newHead;
}
```

**Problem-43** Is it possible to get O(1) access time for Linked Lists?

**Solution: Yes**. Create a linked list and at the same time keep it in a hash table. For $n$ elements we have to keep all the elements in a hash table which gives a preprocessing time of $O(n)$. To read any element we require only constant time O(1) and to read $n$ elements we require $n * 1$ unit of time $= n$ units. Hence by using amortized analysis we can say that element access can be performed within O(1) time.

Time Complexity – O(1) [Amortized]. Space Complexity - $O(n)$ for Hash Table.

**Problem-44** **Josephus Circle:** $N$ people have decided to elect a leader by arranging themselves in a circle and eliminating every $M^{th}$ person around the circle, closing ranks as each person drops out. Find which person will be the last one remaining (with rank 1).

**Solution:** Assume the input is a circular linked list with $N$ nodes and each node have a number (range 1 to $N$) associated with it. The head node has number 1 as data.

```
struct ListNode *getJosephusPosition(){
        struct ListNode *p, *q;
        printf("Enter N (number of players): ");
        scanf("%d", &N);
        printf("Enter M (every M-th payer gets eliminated): ");
        scanf("%d", &M);
        // Create circular linked list containing all the players:
        p = q = malloc(sizeof(struct node));
        p→data = 1;
        for (int i = 2; i <= N; ++i) {
                p→next = malloc(sizeof(struct node));
                p = p→next;
                p→data = i;
        }
        // Close the circular linked list by having the last node point to the first.
        p→next = q;
        // Eliminate every M-th player as long as more than one player remains:
        for (int count = N; count > 1; --count) {
                for (int i = 0; i < M - 1; i++)
                        p = p→next;
                p→next = p→next→next; // Remove the eliminated player from the circular linked list.
        }
        printf("Last player left standing (Josephus Position) is %d\n.", p→data);
}
```

**Problem-45** Given a linked list consists of data, a next pointer and also a random pointer which points to a random node of the list. Give an algorithm for cloning the list.

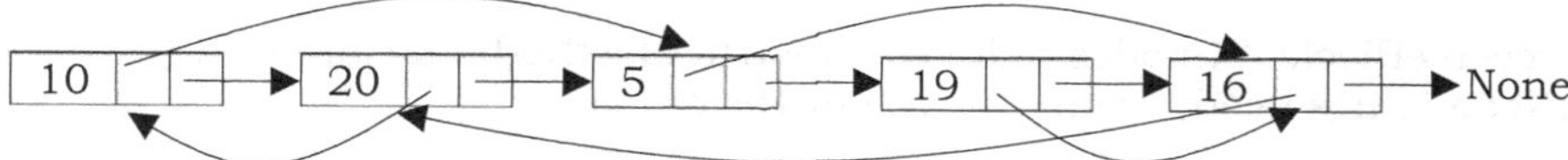


**Solution:** To clone a linked list with random pointers, the idea is to maintain a hash table for storing the mappings from a original linked list node to its clone. For each node in the original linked list, we create a new node with the same data and set its next pointers. While doing so, we also create a mapping from the original node to the duplicate node in the hash table. Finally, we traverse the original linked list again and update random pointers of the duplicate nodes using the hash table.

**Algorithm:**

- Scan the original list and for each node $X$, create a new node $Y$ with data of $X$, then store the pair $(X, Y)$ in hash table using $X$ as a key. Note that during this scan set $Y \rightarrow next$ with $X \rightarrow next$ and $Y \rightarrow random$ to $NULL$ and we will fix it in the next scan. Now for each node $X$ in the original list we have a copy $Y$ stored in our hash table.
- To update the random pointers, read random pointer of node $X$ from original linked list and get the corresponding random node in cloned list from hash table created in previous step. Assign random pointer of node $X$ from cloned list to corresponding node we got.

```
struct ListNode *clone(struct ListNode *head){
    struct ListNode *X, *Y;
    struct HashTable *HT = createHashTable();
    X = head;
    while (X != NULL) {
        Y = (struct ListNode *)malloc(sizeof(struct ListNode *));
        Y→data = X→data;
        Y→next = NULL;
        Y→random = NULL;
        HT.insert(X, Y);
        X = X→next;
    }
    X = head;
    while (X != NULL) {
        // get the node Y corresponding to X from the hash table
        Y = HT.get(X);
        Y→next = HT.get(X→next);
        Y→random = HT.get(X→random);
        X = X→next;
    }
    // Return the head of the new list, that is the Node Y
    return HT.get(head);
}
```

Time Complexity: O($n$). Space Complexity: O($n$).

**Problem-46** Can we solve Problem-45 without any extra space?

**Solution: Yes**. First, a new node is inserted after each node in the original linked list. The content of the new node is the same as the previous node. For example, in the figure, insert 10 after 10, insert 20 after 20, and so on.

Second, how does the random pointer in the original linked list map? For example, in the figure above, the random pointer of 10 node points to 5, and the random pointer of 19 nodes points to 16. For every node X in the original list, the statement: X→next→random = X→random→next this problem can be solved. This works because $X \rightarrow next$ is nothing but copy of original and $X \rightarrow random \rightarrow next$ is nothing but copy of random.

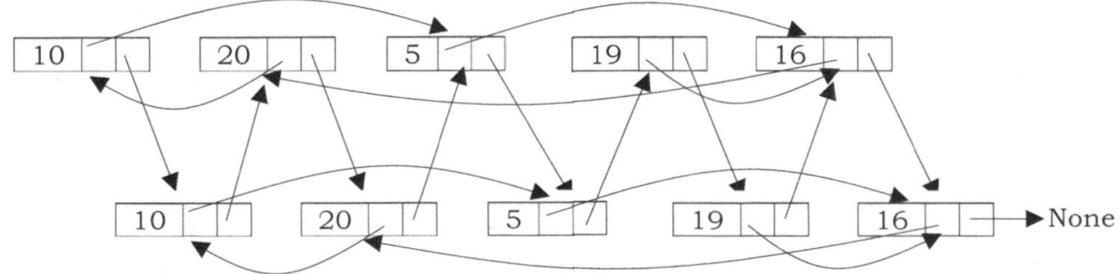


The third step is to split the new linked list from the linked list.

```
void clone(struct ListNode *head){
    struct ListNode *X, *Y;
    //Step1: put X→random in Y→next, so that we can reuse the X→random field to point to Y.
    X = head;
    while (X != NULL) {
        Y = (struct ListNode *)malloc(sizeof(struct ListNode *));
        Y→data = X→data;
        Y→next = X→random;
        X→random = Y;
        X = X→next;
    }
```

```
        //Step2: Setting Y→random.  Y→next is the old copy of the node that
        // Y→random should point to, so X→next→random is the new copy.
        X = head;
        while (X != NULL) {
          Y = X→random;
          Y→random = X→next→random;
          X = X→next;
        }
        //Step3: Repair damage to old list and fill in next pointer in new list.
        X = head;
        while (X != NULL) {
        Y = X→random;
        X→random = Y→next;
        Y→next = X→next→random;
        X = X→next;
        }
}
```

Time Complexity: $O(3n) \approx O(n)$. Space Complexity: O(1).

**Problem-47** We are given a pointer to a node (not the tail node) in a singly linked list. Delete that node from the linked list.

**Solution:** To remove a node, the next pointer of the previous node must be adjusted to point to the following node instead of the current one. However, if we don't have access to a pointer for the previous node, we cannot redirect its next pointer. In such a scenario, we can simply transfer the data from the next node into the current node, and then delete the next node to circumvent the issue.

```
void deleteNodeinLinkedList( struct ListNode * node ){
    struct ListNode * temp = node->next;
    node->data = node->next->data;
    node->next = temp->next;
    free(temp);
}
```

Time Complexity: O(1). Space Complexity: O(1).

**Problem-48** Given a linked list with even and odd numbers, create an algorithm for making changes to the list in such a way that all even numbers appear at the beginning.

**Solution**: One approach to resolve this issue is to utilize a splitting logic. During the linked list traversal, the list can be split into two parts: one consisting of all even nodes, and the other comprising all odd nodes. After this, to obtain the final list, we can concatenate the odd node linked list to the even node linked list.

To accomplish the splitting of the linked list, we can iterate through the original linked list and transfer all odd nodes to a separate linked list dedicated to odd nodes. Upon completion of the loop, the original list will contain only the even nodes, and the odd node list will include all the odd nodes. To maintain the original ordering of all nodes, we must insert all odd nodes at the end of the odd node list.

Time Complexity: $O(n)$. Space Complexity: O(1).

**Problem-49** In a linked list with $n$ nodes, the time taken to insert an element after an element pointed by some pointer is

(A) O(1) (B) $O(logn)$ (C) $O(n)$ (D) $O(n1ogn)$

**Solution**: A.

**Problem-50** **Find modular node:** Given a singly linked list, write a function to find the last element from the beginning whose $n\%k == 0$, where $n$ is the number of elements in the list and $k$ is an integer constant. For example, if $n = 19$ and $k = 3$ then we should return $18^{th}$node.

**Solution:** For this problem the value of $n$ is not known in advance.

```
struct ListNode *modularNodeFromBegin(struct ListNode *head, int k){
    struct ListNode * modularNode;
    int i=0;
    if(k<=0)
        return NULL;
    for (;head != NULL; head = head→next){
        if(i%k == 0){
            modularNode = head;
        } else { modularNode = modularNode→next}
```

```
        i++;
    }
    return modularNode;
}
```

Time Complexity: O($n$). Space Complexity: O(1).

**Problem-51** **Find modular node from the end:** Given a singly linked list, write a function to find the first from the end whose $n\%k == 0$, where $n$ is the number of elements in the list and $k$ is an integer constant. If $n = 19$ and $k = 3$ then we should return $16^{th}$ node.

**Solution:** For this problem the value of $n$ is not known in advance. To solve this problem, we are going to combine the solutions of finding the $k^{th}$element from the end of the linked list and finding the modular node from the beginning. Everytime, whenever *current position mod k* becomes zero, we reinitialize the modular node to point to $k^{th}$ node behind the current location.

```
struct ListNode * modularNodeFromEnd(struct ListNode * head, int k) {
  struct ListNode * modularNode = NULL;
  int i = 0, j;
  if (k <= 0)
    return NULL;
  for (i = 0; i < k; i++) {      // Move the head pointer for k steps so that,
    if (head)                    // we get a difference of k nodes between the pointers
      head = head→ next;
    else
      break;
  }
  while (head != NULL) {   // Maintain the k distance between the pointers, and move till the end
    modularNode = modularNode→ next;
    head = head→ next;
    i++
  }
  j: = k - (i % k);
  while (j > 0 && modularNode != NULL) { // Now, adjust the modularNode to point to the correct node
    modularNode = modularNode→ next;
    j--;
  }
  return modularNode;
}
```

Time Complexity: O($n$). Space Complexity: O(1).

**Problem-52** **Find fractional node:** Given a singly linked list, write a function to find the $\frac{n}{k}th$ element, where $n$ is the number of elements in the list.

**Solution:** For this problem the value of $n$ is not known in advance.

```
struct ListNode *fractionalNodes(struct ListNode *head, int k){
  struct ListNode *fractionalNode = NULL;
  int i=0;
  if(k<=0)
     return NULL;
  for (;head != NULL; head = head→next){
     if(i%k == 0){
        if(fractionalNode == NULL)
            fractionalNode = head;
        else fractionalNode = fractionalNode→next;
     }
     i++;
  }
  return fractionalNode;
}
```

Time Complexity: O($n$). Space Complexity: O(1).

**Problem-53** **Find $\sqrt{n}^{th}$ node:** Given a singly linked list, write a function to find the $\sqrt{n}^{th}$ element, where $n$ is the number of elements in the list. Assume the value of $n$ is not known in advance.

**Solution:** For this problem the value of $n$ is not known in advance. Hence, we would increase the second pointer for every perfect square position.

```
struct ListNode *sqrtNode(struct ListNode *head){
    struct ListNode *sqrtN = NULL;
    int i=1, j=1;
    for (;head != NULL; head = head→next){
        if(i == j*j){
            if(sqrtN == NULL)
                sqrtN = head;
            else
                sqrtN = sqrtN→next;
            j++;
        }
        i++;
    }
    return sqrtN;
}
```

Time Complexity: O($n$). Space Complexity: O(1).

**Problem-54** Given two lists List1 = $\{A_1, A_2, \ldots, A_n\}$ and List2 = $\{B_1, B_2, \ldots, B_m\}$ with data (both lists) in ascending order. Merge them into the third list in ascending order so that the merged list will be:

$$\{A_1, B_1, A_2, B_2 \ldots.. A_m, B_m, A_{m+1} \ldots. A_n\} \text{ if } n >= m$$
$$\{A_1, B_1, A_2, B_2 \ldots.. A_n, B_n, B_{n+1} \ldots. B_m\} \text{ if } m >= n$$

**Solution**: To merge two sorted linked lists, we need to pay attention to the order of their values. We iterate both lists at the same time, but go to next only on the list that has a current node value smaller than the one in the other current list. We have to handle the cases when one or the other list are empty.

```
struct ListNode*alternateMerge(struct ListNode *List1, struct ListNode *List2){
    struct ListNode *newNode = (struct ListNode*) (malloc(sizeof(struct ListNode)));
    struct ListNode *temp;
    newNode→next = NULL;
    temp = newNode;
    while (List1!=NULL and List2!=NULL){
        temp→next = List1;
        temp = temp→next;
        List1 = List1→next;
        temp→next = List2;
        List2 = List2→next;
        temp = temp→next;
    }
    if (List1!=NULL)
        temp→next = List1;
    else
        temp→next = List2;
    temp = newNode→next;
    free(newNode);
    return temp;
}
```

Time Complexity: The *while* loop takes O($min(n, m)$) time as it will run for $min(n, m)$ times. The other steps run in O(1). Therefore the total time complexity is O($min(n, m)$). Space Complexity: O(1).

**Problem-55** Find median in an infinite series of integers.

**Solution:** Median is the middle number in a sorted list of numbers (if we have an odd number of elements). If we have an even number of elements, the median is the average of two middle numbers in a sorted list of numbers. We can solve this problem with linked lists (with both sorted and unsorted linked lists).

*First*, let us try with an *unsorted* linked list. In an unsorted linked list, we can insert the element either at the head or at the tail. The disadvantage with this approach is that finding the median takes O($n$). Also, the insertion operation takes O(1).

Now, let us try with a *sorted* linked list. We can find the median in O(1) time if we keep track of the middle elements. Insertion to a particular location is also O(1) in any linked list. But, finding the right location to insert is not O($logn$) as in a sorted array, it is instead O($n$) because we can't perform binary search in a linked list even if it is sorted. So, using a sorted linked list isn't worth the effort as insertion is O($n$) and finding median is O(1), the same as the sorted array. In the sorted array the insertion is linear due to shifting, but here it's linear because we can't do a binary search in a linked list.

**Note**: For an efficient algorithm refer to the *Priority Queues and Heaps* chapter.

Problem-56 Given a linked list, how do you modify it such that all the even numbers appear before all the odd numbers in the modified linked list?

**Solution**:

```
struct ListNode *exchangeEvenOddList(struct ListNode *head){
    // initializing the odd and even list headers
    struct ListNode *oddList = NULL, *evenList =NULL;
    // creating tail variables for both the list
    struct ListNode *oddListEnd = NULL, *evenListEnd = NULL;
    struct ListNode *itr=head;
    if( head == NULL ){
        return;
    }
    else{
        while( itr != NULL ){
            if( itr→data % 2 == 0 ){
                if( evenList == NULL ){
                    // first even node
                    evenList = evenListEnd = itr;
                }
                else{
                    // inserting the node at the end of linked list
                    evenListEnd→next = itr;
                    evenListEnd = itr;
                }
            }
            else{
                if( oddList == NULL ){
                    // first odd node
                    oddList = oddListEnd = itr;
                }
                else{
                    // inserting the node at the end of linked list
                    oddListEnd→next = itr;
                    oddListEnd = itr;
                }
            }
            itr = itr→next;
        }
        evenListEnd→next = oddList;
        return head;
    }
}
```

Time Complexity: O($n$). Space Complexity: O(1).

Problem-57 Given two linked lists, each list node with one integer digit, add these two linked lists. The result should be stored in the third linked list. Also note that the head node contains the most significant digit of the number.

**Solution**: Since the integer addition starts from the least significant digit, we first need to visit the last node of both lists and add them up, create a new node to store the result, take care of the carry if any, and link the resulting node to the node which will be added to the second least significant node and continue.

First of all, we need to take into account the difference in the number of digits in the two numbers. So before starting recursion, we need to do some calculation and move the longer list pointer to the appropriate place so that we need the last node of both lists at the same time. The other thing we need to take care of is *carry*. If two digits add up to more than 10, we need to forward the *carry* to the next node and add it. If the most significant digit addition results in a *carry*, we need to create an extra node to store the *carry*.

The function below is actually a wrapper function which does all the housekeeping like calculating lengths of lists, calling recursive implementation, creating an extra node for the *carry* in the most significant digit, and adding any remaining nodes left in the longer list.

```
void addListNumbersWrapper(struct ListNode *list1, struct ListNode *list2, int *carry, struct ListNode **result){
```

```
    int list1Length = 0, list2Length = 0, diff =0;
    struct ListNode *current = list1;
    while(current){
        current = current→next;
        list1Length++;
    }
    current = list2;
    while(current){
        current = current→next;
        list2Length++;
    }
    if(list1Length < list2Length){
        current = list1;
        list1 = list2;
        list2 = current;
    }
    diff = abs(list1Length-list2Length);
    current = list1;
    while(diff--)
        current = current→next;
    addListNumbers(current, list2, carry, result);
    diff = abs(list1Length-list2Length);
    addRemainingNumbers(list1, carry, result, diff);
   if(*carry){
        struct ListNode * temp = (struct ListNode *)malloc(sizeof(struct ListNode ));
        temp→next = (*result);
        *result = temp;
    }
    return;
}
void addListNumbers(struct ListNode *list1, struct ListNode *list2, int *carry, struct ListNode **result){
    int sum;
    if(!list1) return;
    addListNumbers(list1→next, list2→next, carry, result);
    //End of both lists, add them
    struct ListNode * temp = (struct ListNode *)malloc(sizeof(struct ListNode ));
    sum = list1→data + list2→data + (*carry);
    // Store carry
    *carry = sum/10;
    sum = sum%10;
    temp→data = sum;
    temp→next = (*result);
    *result = temp;
    return;
}
void addRemainingNumbers(struct ListNode * list1, int *carry, struct ListNode **result, int diff){
    int sum =0;
    if(!list1 || diff == 0)
        return;
    addRemainingNumbers(list1→next, carry, result, diff-1);
    struct ListNode * temp = (struct ListNode *)malloc(sizeof(struct ListNode ));
    sum = list1->data + (*carry);
    *carry = sum/10;
    sum = sum%10;
    temp→data = sum;
    temp→next = (*result);
    *result = temp;
    return;
}
```

Time Complexity: O($max\ (List1\ length, List2\ length)$). Space Complexity: O($min\ (List1\ length, List2\ length)$) for recursive stack.

**Note:** It can be solved using stacks as well.

**Problem-58** Which sorting algorithm is easily adaptable to singly linked lists?

**Solution:** Simple Insertion sort is easily adaptable to singly linked lists. To insert an element, the linked list is traversed until the proper position is found, or until the end of the list is reached. It is inserted into the list by merely adjusting the pointers without shifting any elements, unlike in the array. This reduces the time required for insertion but not the time required for searching for the proper position.

**Problem-59** Given a list, List1 = $\{A_1, A_2, \ldots A_{n-1}, A_n\}$ with data, reorder it to $\{A_1, A_n, A_2, A_{n-1} \ldots\ldots\}$ without using any extra space.

**Solution:** To reorder a list in the desired way without using any extra space, follow the steps below:

- Find the middle point of the input list using the slow and fast pointer technique. If the length of the list is even, the middle point will be the second of the two middle nodes.
- Reverse the second half of the list starting from the node after the middle point.
- Merge the first half of the list with the reversed second half of the list by alternating the nodes from each half.
- Set the next pointer of the last node in the merged list to NULL to terminate the list.

The time complexity of the function is O(n), where n is the length of the input linked list. This is because we traverse each node in the list exactly once and perform constant time operations on each node. The space complexity is O(1), because we are only using a constant amount of extra space for the temporary pointers.

**Problem-60** Given two sorted linked lists, given an algorithm to return the common elements of them.

**Solution**: The easiest way to build up a list with common elements is by adding nodes at the beginning. The disadvantage is that the elements will appear in the list in the reverse order that they are added.

```
// Solution to give common elements in the reverse
struct ListNode * intersection1(struct ListNode *list1, struct ListNode *list2) {
    struct ListNode *head = NULL;
    while (list1 != NULL && list2 != NULL) {
        if (list1->data == list2->data) {
            push(&head, list1->data); // Copy common element.
            list1 = list1->next;
            list2 = list2->next;
        } else if (list1->data > list2->data) {
            list2 = list2->next;
        } else { // list1->data < list2->data
            list1 = list1->next;
        }
    }
    return head;
}
```

Time complexity $O(m + n)$, where $m$ is the lengh of list1 and $n$ is the length of list2. Space Complexity: O(1).

What if we want to get the common elements in the increasing order (or in the same order of their appearance)? i.e., What about adding nodes at the "tail end" of the list? Adding a node at the tail of a list most often involves locating the last node in the list, and then changing its .next field from NULL to point to the new node, such as the tail variable in the following example of adding a "3" node to the end of the list {1, 2}...

This is just a special case of the general rule: to insert or delete a node inside a list, you need a pointer to the node just before that position, so you can change its .next field. Many list problems include the sub-problem of advancing a pointer to the node before the point of insertion or deletion. The one exception is if the operation falls on the first node in the list — in that case the head pointer itself must be changed.

Consider the problem of building up the list {1, 2, 3, 4, 5} by appending the nodes to the tail end. The difficulty is that the very first node must be added at the head pointer, but all the other nodes are inserted after the last node using a tail pointer. The simplest way to deal with both cases is to just have two separate cases in the code. Special case code first adds the head node {1}. Then there is a separate loop that uses a tail pointer to add all the other nodes. The tail pointer is kept pointing at the last node, and each new node is added at tail->next. The only "problem" with this solution is that writing separate special case code for the first node is a little unsatisfying. Nonetheless, this approach is a solid one for production code — it is simple and runs fast.

```
struct ListNode * intersection(struct ListNode *list1, struct ListNode *list2) {
    struct ListNode *head = NULL;
    struct ListNode* tail;
    while (list1 != NULL && list2 != NULL) {
        if (list1->data == list2->data) {
            if (head == NULL) {
                push(&head, list1->data);
                tail = head;
```

```
            }
            else{
                push(&tail->next, list1->data);
                tail = tail->next;
            }
            list1 = list1->next;
            list2 = list2->next;
        } else if (list1->data > list2->data) {
            list2 = list2->next;
        } else { // list1->data < list2->data
            list1 = list1->next;
        }
    }
    return head;
}
```

There is a slightly unusual technique that can be used to shorten the code: The strategy here uses a temporary dummy node as the start of the result list. The trick is that with the dummy, every node appears to be added after the next field of some other node. That way the code for the first node is the same as for the other nodes. The tail pointer plays the same role as in the previous example. The difference is that now it also handles the first node as well.

The pointer tail always points to the last node in the result list, so appending new nodes is easy. The dummy node gives tail something to point to initially when the result list is empty. This dummy node is efficient, since it is only temporary, and it is allocated in the stack. The loop proceeds, removing one node from either 'list1' or 'list2', and adding it to tail. When we are done, the result is in dummy.next.

```
// Solution uses the temporary dummy node to build up the result list
struct ListNode * intersection(struct ListNode *list1, struct ListNode *list2) {
    struct ListNode dummy;
    struct ListNode *tail = &dummy;
    dummy.next = NULL;
    while (list1 != NULL && list2 != NULL) {
        if (list1->data == list2->data) {
            push((&tail->next), list1->data); // Copy common element.
            list1 = list1->next;
            list2 = list2->next;
            tail = tail->next;
        } else if (list1->data > list2->data) {
            list2 = list2->next;
        } else { // list1->data < list2->data
            list1 = list1->next;
        }
    }
    return dummy.next;
}
```

**Problem-61** Sort the linked list elements in O($n$), where $n$ is the number of elements in the linked list.

**Solution**: Refer *Sorting* chapter.

**Problem-62** **Partition list**: Given a linked list and a value X, partition it such that all nodes less than X come before nodes greater than or equal to X. Notice that, you should preserve the original relative order of the nodes in each of the two partitions.

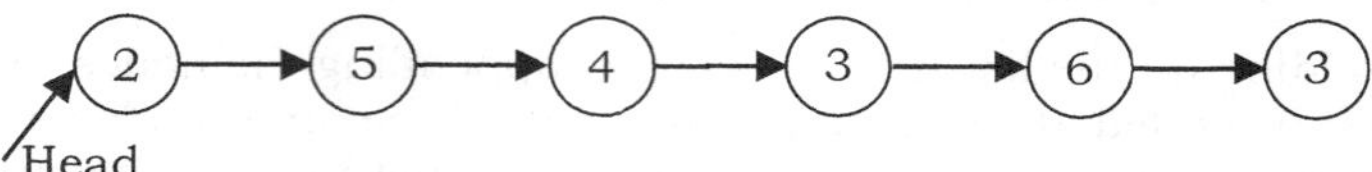


For example, the above linked list with X = 4 should return the following linked list.

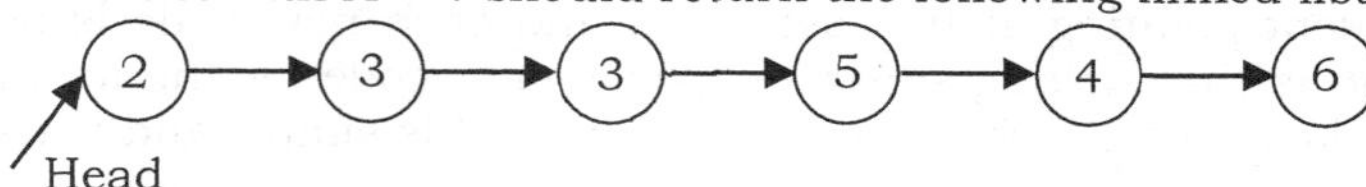


**Solution**: The problem wants us to rearrange the linked list elements, such that the elements lesser than value X, come before the elements greater or equal to X. This essentially means in this rearranged list, there would be a point in the linked list before which all the elements would be smaller than X and after which all the elements would be greater or equal to X. Let's call this point as the *pivot*. Careful observation tells us that if we break the rearranged list at the *pivot*, we will get two smaller linked lists, one with lesser elements and the other with elements greater or equal to X. In the solution, our main aim is to create these two linked lists and join them.

We can take two pointers lesser and greater to keep track of the two linked lists as described above. These two pointers could be used two create two separate lists and then these lists could be combined to form the desired rearranged list. We will traverse the original linked list as usual, and depending upon a node's value, we will append it into one of the partitions.

**Algorithm**:

1. Initialize two pointers lesser and greater with None.
2. Iterate the original linked list, using the head pointer. If the node's value pointed by head is lesser than X, the node should be part of the lesser list. So, we move it to lesser list. Else, the node should be part of greater list. So, we move it to greater list.
3. Once we are done with all the nodes in the original linked list, we would have two list lesser and greater. The original list nodes are either part of lesser list or greater list, depending on its value.
4. Now, these two lists lesser and greater can be combined to form the reformed list.

Since we traverse the original linked list from left to right, at no point would the order of nodes change relatively in the two lists. Another important thing to note here is that we show the original linked list intact in the above diagrams. However, in the implementation, we remove the nodes from the original linked list and attach them in the lesser or greater list. We don't utilize any additional space. We simply move the nodes from the original list around.

```
struct ListNode {
  int data;
  ListNode * next;
  ListNode( int d ) : data{ d }, next{ NULL } {}
};
 /* Start with a new list. Elements bigger than the pivot element are put at the greater list
    and elements smaller are put at the lesser list*/
ListNode * partition( ListNode * head , int X ) {
   ListNode * lesser = NULL;
   ListNode * lesserHead = NULL;   /*The initial node of list lesser*/
   ListNode * greater = NULL;
   ListNode * greaterHead = NULL;   /*The initial node of list greater*/
   while( head != NULL ) {
     ListNode * nextNode = head->next;
     if ( head->data < X ) {
            if (lesser == NULL) {
                lesser = head;
                lesserHead = lesser;
            }
            //insert head node to lesser list
            lesser->next = head;
            lesser = head;
     } else {
            if (greater == NULL) {
                greater = head;
                greaterHead = greater;
            }
        // insert head node to greater list
        greater->next = head;
        greater = head;
     }
     head = nextNode;
   }
   lesser->next = greaterHead;  /*Now, we connect the lesser list to greater list.*/
   greater->next = NULL;
   return lesserHead;
}
```

Time complexity: $O(n)$, where $n$ is the number of nodes in the original linked list and we iterate the original list.
Space complexity: $O(1)$, we have not utilized any extra space, the point to note is that we are reforming the original list, by moving the original nodes, we have not used any extra space as such.

**Problem-63** Give an algorithm to delete duplicate nodes from the sorted linked list. Ideally, the list should only be traversed once.

**Solution**: Since the list is sorted, to remove duplicates from a sorted linked list, we can simply traverse the list and keep track of the last unique node we encountered. When we encounter a new node, we check if it is equal to the last unique node. If it is, we skip it and continue to the next node. If it is not, we set the last unique node to the current node and continue.

```
struct ListNode {
    int data;
    struct ListNode *next;
};
struct ListNode* deleteDuplicates(struct ListNode* head) {
    if (head == NULL) {
        return NULL;
    }
    struct ListNode *last_unique = head;
    struct ListNode *node = head->next;
    while (node != NULL) {
        if (node->data == last_unique->data) {
            last_unique->next = node->next;
        } else {
            last_unique = node;
        }
        node = node->next;
    }
    return head;
}
```

The time complexity of the algorithm to remove duplicates from a sorted linked list is O(n), where n is the number of nodes in the list. This is because we need to visit each node in the list exactly once in the worst case.

The space complexity of the algorithm is O(1), because we are modifying the existing linked list in place and not using any additional data structures. We only need to store a constant number of pointers to keep track of the last unique node and the current node. Therefore, the space used by the algorithm is independent of the size of the input list.

**Problem-64** Give an algorithm that takes a list and divides up its nodes to make two smaller lists. The sublists should be made from alternating elements in the original list. So if the original list is {1, 2, 3, 4, 5}, then one sublist should be {1, 3, 5} and the other should be {2, 4}.

**Solution**: The simplest approach iterates over the given linked list and pull nodes off the list and alternately put them on lists 'a' and b'. The only strange part is that the nodes will be in the reverse order that they occurred in the source list.

```
void alternatingSplit(struct ListNode* head, struct ListNode** head1, struct ListNode** head2) {
    struct ListNode* a = NULL; // Split the nodes to these 'a' and 'b' lists
    struct ListNode* b = NULL;
    struct ListNode* current = head;
    while (current != NULL) {
        // Move a ListNode to 'a'
        struct ListNode* newNode  = current; // the front current node
        current = newNode->next; // Advance the current pointer
        newNode->next = a; // Link the node with the head of list a
        a = newNode;

        // Move a ListNode to 'b'
        if (current != NULL) {
            struct ListNode* newNode = current; // the front source node
            current = newNode->next; // Advance the source pointer
            newNode->next = b; // Link the node with the head of list b
            b = newNode;
        }
    }
    *head1 = a;
    *head2 = b;
}
```

Time Complexity: $O(n)$. Space Complexity: $O(1)$.

**Problem-65** We are given head, the head node of a linked list containing unique integer values. We are also given the list S, a subset of the values in the linked list. Return the number of connected components in S, where two values are connected if they appear consecutively in the linked list.

**Solution**: Scanning through the list, if node.data is in S and node.next.data isn't (including if node.next is null), then this must be the end of a connected component. For example, if the list is 0 -> 1 -> 2 -> 3 -> 4 -> 5 -> 6 -> 7, and S = [0, 2, 3, 5, 7], then when scanning through the list, we fulfill the above condition at 0, 3, 5, 7, for a total answer of 4.

```
class Solution {
public:
    int numComponents(ListNode* head, vector<int>& S) {
        // set of all the subset elements which are considered unvisited initially
        unordered_set<int> unvisited(begin(S), end(S));
        int connComponents = 0;
        ListNode* iter = head;
        // As we traverse through the list, we find all the nodes connected in S
        // from the current node and remove them unvisited set
        while (iter) {
            // check if current node is in S or not
            if (unvisited.find(iter->data) != unvisited.end()) {
                ++connComponents;
                // now find all the nodes connected via current node
                // and remove them from unvisited set
                while (iter && unvisited.find(iter->data) != unvisited.end()) {
                    // remove the current from list of unvisited
                    unvisited.erase(iter->data);
                    iter = iter->next;
                }
            }
            if (iter)
                iter = iter->next;
        }
        return connComponents;
    }
};
```

**Problem-66** Given a pointer to head of a linked list, give an algorithm to repeatedly delete consecutive sequences of nodes that sum to 0 until there are no such sequences. **Input**: 1->2->-3->3->1 **Output**: 3->1

**Solution**: The basic idea of this problem is to record an accumulated sum from head to current position. If we define sum(i) = summation from index 0 to index i and we find sum(i) == sum(j) when i != j, then we can imply that the sum within index (i, j] is 0. So, we can use a map to record the first time this accumulated sum appears, and if we find the same accumulated sum, we discard all nodes between these two nodes. Although we may modify some discarded nodes' next pointer value, it has no impact on our answer.

```
class RemoveZeroSumSublists {
public:
    // Deletes a linked list
    void deleteList(ListNode* head) {
        ListNode *nextptr= nullptr;
        while(head) {
            nextptr = head->next;
            //delete head;
            head = nextptr;
        }
    }
    ListNode* removeZeroSumSublists(ListNode* head) {
        // (sum: pos): cumulative sum till a given node
        unordered_map<int, ListNode*> sum_pos;
        ListNode *start = nullptr, *end = nullptr,
              *after_start = nullptr, *after_end = nullptr;
        long long sum = 0;
        // dummy head for easier head ops
        ListNode *dummy = new ListNode(0);
        dummy->next = head;
        // initial sum 0 for position before head
        sum_pos[0] = dummy;
```

```
        // Store the cumulative sum till each node, for the same cumulative sum we store the latest position
        ListNode *curr = head;
        while(curr) {
            sum += curr->data;
            sum_pos[sum] = curr;
            curr = curr->next;
        }
        // We compute the cumulative sum again, this time for each sum we check that farthest
        // position where it is found again and delete the list till that position
        sum = 0;
        curr = dummy;
        while(curr) {
            sum += curr->data;
            // check the position this sum is last seen
            ListNode *last_seen_pos = sum_pos[sum];
            // delete the sublist to avoid memory leaks
            after_start = curr->next;
            after_end = last_seen_pos->next;
            // when it is not the same node and trhere is somethign to delete
            if(last_seen_pos != curr) {
                last_seen_pos->next = nullptr;
                deleteList(after_start);
            }
            curr->next = after_end;
            curr = curr->next;
        }
        head = dummy->next;
        delete dummy;
        return head;
    }
};
```

Time Complexity: O($n$). Space Complexity: O($n$).

**Problem-67** How do you determine whether a singly linked list is a palindrome?

**Solution**: To determine whether a singly linked list is a palindrome or not, we can follow these steps:

- Traverse the linked list and push each node's value into a stack.
- Traverse the linked list again and compare each node's value with the value at the top of the stack. If they match, pop the value from the stack and continue. If they don't match, return false.
- If we have traversed the entire linked list and all values have matched, return true.

Time Complexity: O($n$). Space Complexity: O($n$), for stack.

For code, refer *Stacks* chapter.

**Problem-68** Can we solve the above problem without using stacks?

**Solution**: As an alternative, we can use the following approach:

- Traverse the list and create a new list in reverse order.
- Traverse the original list and the new list in parallel, comparing each node to see if they are equal.
- If all nodes are equal, the list is a palindrome; otherwise, it is not.

```
struct ListNode {
    int val;
    struct ListNode *next;
};
bool isPalindrome(struct ListNode* head) {
    // Step 1: Traverse the list and create a new list in reverse order.
    struct ListNode *reversed_list = NULL;
    struct ListNode *current_node = head;
    while (current_node != NULL) {
        struct ListNode *new_node = (struct ListNode*) malloc(sizeof(struct ListNode));
        new_node->val = current_node->val;
        new_node->next = reversed_list;
```

```
        reversed_list = new_node;
        current_node = current_node->next;
    }
    // Step 2: Traverse the original list and the new list in parallel, comparing each node to see if they are equal.
    current_node = head;
    while (current_node != NULL) {
        if (current_node->val != reversed_list->val) {
            return false;
        }
        current_node = current_node->next;
        reversed_list = reversed_list->next;
    }

    // Step 3: If all nodes are equal, the list is a palindrome; otherwise, it is not.
    return true;
}
```

The time complexity of the above code is O(n), where n is the number of nodes in the linked list. This is because we traverse the linked list twice - once to reverse it and once to compare it with the original list. Both traversals take O(n) time.

The space complexity of the above code is also O(n), because we create a new linked list to store the reversed nodes of the original linked list. The space required for the reversed linked list is the same as the space required for the original linked list, which is O(n).

**Problem-69** Can we solve the above problem without extra space?

**Solution**: To improve the algorithm for determining whether a linked list is a palindrome, consider using the following alternative approach:

- Find the middle of the linked list using the slow and fast pointer technique.
- Reverse the second half of the linked list.
- Compare the first half of the linked list with the reversed second half.
- If the two halves are equal, then the linked list is a palindrome. Otherwise, it is not.

```
struct ListNode {
    int val;
    struct ListNode *next;
};
bool isPalindrome(struct ListNode* head) {
    // Find the middle of the linked list
    struct ListNode *slow = head, *fast = head;
    while (fast && fast->next) {
        slow = slow->next;
        fast = fast->next->next;
    }
    // Reverse the second half of the linked list
    struct ListNode *prev = NULL, *curr = slow;
    while (curr) {
        struct ListNode *next = curr->next;
        curr->next = prev;
        prev = curr;
        curr = next;
    }
    // Traverse both halves and compare the nodes' values
    struct ListNode *first_half = head, *second_half = prev;
    while (second_half) {
        if (first_half->val != second_half->val) {
            return false;
        }
        first_half = first_half->next;
        second_half = second_half->next;
    }
    return true;
```

```
    }
```

This solution has a time complexity of O(n) and a space complexity of O(1), since we're only using constant space for the slow and fast pointers, and the reversing of the second half of the linked list is done in place.

**Problem-70** **Add Two Numbers**: We are given two non-empty linked lists representing two non-negative integers. The most significant digit comes first and each of their nodes contains a single digit. Add the two numbers and return the sum as a linked list.

**Solution**: To solve this problem, we can traverse both linked lists simultaneously and add the corresponding digits, starting from the least significant digit. We can keep track of a carry variable that will be added to the sum of the next pair of digits. We will create a new linked list to store the sum and keep adding new nodes to the front of the list as we compute the sum. At the end, if there is a carry, we add it to the front of the list as well. The steps are:

1. Initialize a carry variable to 0.
2. Reverse both linked lists.
3. Traverse the linked lists simultaneously until both are empty:
    a. If one linked list is longer than the other, treat the missing nodes as having a value of 0.
    b. Add the values of the current nodes, along with the carry, and update the carry if necessary.
    c. Create a new node for the sum, with a value equal to the sum mod 10.
    d. Update the carry to be the sum divided by 10.
    e. Add the new node to the front of the result linked list.
    f. Move to the next nodes in both linked lists.
4. If there is a remaining carry, create a new node for it and add it to the front of the result linked list.
5. Reverse the result linked list.
6. Return the head of the result linked list.

```
struct ListNode* addTwoNumbers(struct ListNode* l1, struct ListNode* l2) {
    // Reverse the input linked lists
    struct ListNode *prev1 = NULL, *curr1 = l1;
    while (curr1 != NULL) {
        struct ListNode *next = curr1->next;
        curr1->next = prev1;
        prev1 = curr1;
        curr1 = next;
    }
    l1 = prev1;
    struct ListNode *prev2 = NULL, *curr2 = l2;
    while (curr2 != NULL) {
        struct ListNode *next = curr2->next;
        curr2->next = prev2;
        prev2 = curr2;
        curr2 = next;
    }
    l2 = prev2;
    // Add the two linked lists
    int carry = 0;
    struct ListNode *head = NULL;
    while (l1 != NULL || l2 != NULL || carry > 0) {
        int val1 = (l1 != NULL) ? l1->data : 0;
        int val2 = (l2 != NULL) ? l2->data : 0;
        int sum = val1 + val2 + carry;
        carry = sum / 10;
        sum = sum % 10;
        struct ListNode *newNode = (struct ListNode*) malloc(sizeof(struct ListNode));
        newNode->data = sum;
        newNode->next = head;
        head = newNode;
        if (l1 != NULL) {
            l1 = l1->next;
        }
        if (l2 != NULL) {
            l2 = l2->next;
        }
```

```
    }
    // Reverse the result linked list
    struct ListNode *prev = NULL, *curr = head;
    while (curr != NULL) {
        struct ListNode *next = curr->next;
        curr->next = prev;
        prev = curr;
        curr = next;
    }
    return prev;
}
```

The time complexity of this algorithm is O(max(m, n)), where m and n are the lengths of the two input linked lists, since we need to traverse both lists once. The space complexity is also O(max(m, n)), since we are creating a new linked list to store the result.

**Problem-71** **Plus One Linked List**: Given a non-negative integer represented as a linked list of digits, plus one to the integer.

**Solution**: To solve this problem, we can use a modified version of the typical "adding two numbers" linked list algorithm. Instead of adding two numbers, we just need to add 1 to the given linked list. We can follow the following algorithm:

1. Traverse the linked list and find the last node that is not 9.
2. If all nodes are 9, create a new node with a value of 1 and add it to the front of the list.
3. Otherwise, add 1 to the value of the last non-9 node.
4. Set all subsequent nodes to 0.
5. Return the head of the updated linked list.

```
struct ListNode* plusOneLinkedList(struct ListNode* head) {
    // Step 1: Traverse the linked list and find the last non-9 node
    struct ListNode* curr = head;
    struct ListNode* lastNonNineNode = NULL;
    while (curr != NULL) {
        if (curr->data != 9) {
            lastNonNineNode = curr;
        }
        curr = curr->next;
    }
    // Step 2: If all nodes are 9, create a new node with value 1 and add it to the front of the list
    if (lastNonNineNode == NULL) {
        struct ListNode* newHead = malloc(sizeof(struct ListNode));
        newHead->data = 1;
        newHead->next = head;
        curr = head;
        while (curr != NULL) {
            curr->data = 0;
            curr = curr->next;
        }
        return newHead;
    }
    // Step 3: Add 1 to the value of the last non-9 node
    lastNonNineNode->data += 1;
    // Step 4: Set all subsequent nodes to 0
    curr = lastNonNineNode->next;
    while (curr != NULL) {
        curr->data = 0;
        curr = curr->next;
    }
    // Step 5: Return the head of the updated linked list
    return head;
}
```

This algorithm has a time complexity of O(n), where n is the length of the linked list, and a space complexity of O(1), as we are only using constant space to store pointers to nodes in the linked list.

**Problem-72** **Delete N Nodes After M Nodes of a Linked List**: We are given the head of a linked list and two integers m and n. Traverse the linked list and remove some nodes in the following way:

- Start with the head as the current node.
- Keep the first m nodes starting with the current node.
- Remove the next n nodes.
- Keep repeating steps 2 and 3 until you reach the end of the list.
- Return the head of the modified list after removing the mentioned nodes.

**Solution**: To solve this problem, we can simply traverse the linked list and keep track of two pointers - one pointing to the current node and the other pointing to the previous node. We can use these pointers to skip over the nodes that need to be removed. Here is the step-by-step algorithm:

1. Initialize two pointers curr and prev to point to the head of the list.
2. Traverse the list using a loop that runs until the end of the list is reached.
3. Inside the loop, skip over the first m nodes by moving the prev pointer m times and the curr pointer m + n times.
4. If the curr pointer becomes NULL after skipping over m nodes, we have reached the end of the list and we can return the head of the modified list.
5. Otherwise, skip over the next n nodes by moving the curr pointer n times.
6. Set the next pointer of the node pointed to by the prev pointer to the node pointed to by the curr pointer.
7. Set the prev pointer to the node pointed to by the curr pointer.
8. Repeat steps 3-7 until the end of the list is reached.

```
struct ListNode {
    int val;
    struct ListNode* next;
};
struct ListNode* deleteNodes(struct ListNode* head, int m, int n) {
    struct ListNode* curr = head;
    struct ListNode* prev = NULL;
    while (curr != NULL) {
        for (int i = 0; i < m && curr != NULL; i++) {
            prev = curr;
            curr = curr->next;
        }
        for (int i = 0; i < n && curr != NULL; i++) {
            curr = curr->next;
        }
        if (curr == NULL) {
            prev->next = NULL;
            break;
        }
        prev->next = curr;
        prev = curr;
    }
    return head;
}
```

The time complexity of this algorithm is O(n), where n is the number of nodes in the list, because we traverse the list once and perform constant-time operations on each node. The space complexity of the algorithm is O(1), because we use a constant amount of extra space to store the curr and prev pointers.

# CHAPTER 4

# STACKS

## 4.1 What is a Stack DataStructure?

A stack is a simple data structure used for storing data (similar to Linked Lists). In a stack, the order in which the data arrives is important. A stack data structure is an abstract data type that represents a collection of elements with two main operations: push and pop. It is a Last-In-First-Out (LIFO) data structure, meaning that the last element added to the stack will be the first one to be removed.

A stack can be thought of as a physical stack of plates, where you can add a new plate on top of the stack (push operation) and remove the topmost plate from the stack (pop operation). You can only access the top element of the stack, and you cannot access or modify the elements below it until the top element is removed.

**Definition:** A *stack* is an ordered list in which insertion and deletion are done at one end, called *top*. The last element inserted is the first one to be deleted. Hence, it is called the Last in First out (LIFO) or First in Last out (FILO) list.

Special names are given to the two changes that can be made to a stack. When an element is inserted in a stack, the concept is called *push*, and when an element is removed from the stack, the concept is called *pop*. Trying to pop out an empty stack is called *underflow* and trying to push an element in a full stack is called *overflow*. Generally, we treat them as exceptions. As an example, consider the snapshots of the stack.

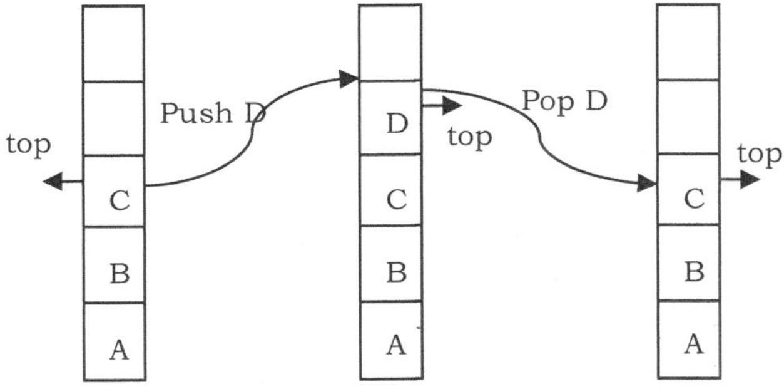


## 4.2 How Stacks are used

Consider a working day in the office. Let us assume a developer is working on a long-term project. The manager then gives the developer a new task which is more important. The developer puts the long-term project aside and begins work on the new task. The phone rings, and this is the highest priority as it must be answered immediately. The developer pushes the present task into the pending tray and answers the phone.

When the call is complete the task that was abandoned to answer the phone is retrieved from the pending tray and work progresses. To take another call, it may have to be handled in the same manner, but eventually the new task will be finished, and the developer can draw the long-term project from the pending tray and continue with that.

## 4.3 Stack ADT

The following operations make a stack an ADT. For simplicity, assume the data is an integer type.

### Main stack operations

- void push (int data): Inserts *data* onto stack.
- int pop(): Removes and returns the last inserted element from the stack.

## Auxiliary stack operations

- int top(): Returns the last inserted element without removing it.
- int size(): Returns the number of elements stored in the stack.
- int isEmpty(): Indicates whether any elements are stored in the stack or not.
- int isFull(): Indicates whether the stack is full or not.

## Exceptions

Attempting the execution of an operation may sometimes cause an error condition, called an exception. Exceptions are said to be "thrown" by an operation that cannot be executed. In the Stack ADT, operations pop and top cannot be performed if the stack is empty. Attempting the execution of pop (top) on an empty stack throws an exception. Trying to push an element in a full stack throws an exception.

## 4.4 Applications

Following are some of the applications in which stacks play an important role.

## Direct applications

- Balancing of symbols
- Infix-to-postfix conversion
- Evaluation of postfix expression
- Implementing function calls (including recursion)
- Finding of spans (finding spans in stock markets, refer to *Problems* section)
- Page-visited history in a Web browser [Back Buttons]
- Undo sequence in a text editor
- Matching Tags in HTML and XML

## Indirect applications

- Auxiliary data structure for other algorithms (Example: Tree traversal algorithms)
- Component of other data structures (Example: Simulating queues, refer *Queues* chapter)

## 4.5 Implementation

There are many ways of implementing stack ADT; below are the commonly used methods.

- Simple array based implementation
- Dynamic array based implementation
- Linked lists implementation

## Simple Array Implementation

This implementation of stack ADT uses an array. In the array, we add elements from left to right and use a variable to keep track of the index of the top element.

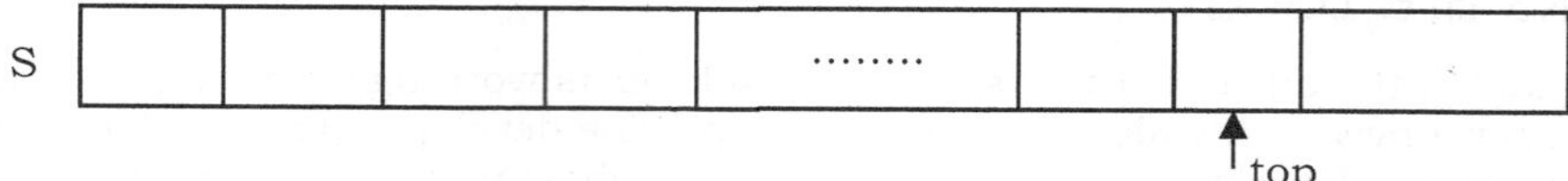


The array storing the stack elements may become full. A push operation will then throw a *full stack exception*. Similarly, if we try deleting an element from an empty stack it will throw *stack empty exception*.

```
#include<stdio.h>
#include <stdlib.h>
#include <limits.h>
struct Stack {
    int top;
    int capacity;
    int *array;
};
struct Stack *createStack(int capacity) {
    struct Stack *S = malloc(sizeof(struct Stack));
    if(!S)
        return NULL;
```

```
        S->capacity = capacity;
        S->top = -1;
        S->array= malloc(S->capacity * sizeof(int));
        if(!S->array)
            return NULL;
        return S;
    }
    int isEmpty(struct Stack *S) {
        return (S->top == -1);  // if the condition is true then 1 is returned else 0 is returned
    }
    int size(struct Stack *S) {
        return (S->top + 1);
    }
    int isFull(struct Stack *S){
        //if the condition is true then 1 is returned else 0 is returned
        return (S->top == S->capacity - 1);
    }
    void push(struct Stack *S, int data){
        /* S->top == capacity -1 indicates that the stack is full*/
        if(isFull(S))
            printf( "Stack Overflow\n");
        else    /*Increasing the 'top' by 1 and storing the value at 'top' position*/
            S->array[++S->top] = data;
    }
    int pop(struct Stack *S){
        /* S->top == - 1 indicates empty stack*/
        if(isEmpty(S)){
            printf("Stack is Empty\n");
            return INT_MIN;
        }
        else /* Removing element from  'top' of the array and reducing 'top' by 1*/
            return (S->array[S->top--]);
    }
    int peek(struct Stack *S){
        /* S->top == - 1 indicates empty stack*/
        if(isEmpty(S)){
            printf("Stack is Empty");
            return INT_MIN;;
        }
        else
            return (S->array[S->top]);
    }
    void deleteStack(struct Stack *S){
        if(S) {
            if(S->array)
                free(S->array);
                    free(S);
        }
    }
    int main(){
        int i = 0, capacity = 15;
        // create a stack of capacity 15
        struct Stack *stk = createStack(capacity);
        for(i = 0; i <= capacity; i++){
            push(stk, i);
        }
        printf("Top element is %d\n", peek(stk));
        printf("Stack size is %d\n", size(stk));
        for (i = 0; i <= capacity; i++){
            printf("Popped element is %d\n", pop(stk));
        }
```

```
        if (isEmpty(stk))
            printf("Stack is empty");
        else
            printf("Stack is not empty");
        deleteStack(stk);
        return 0;
}
```

## Performance & Limitations

### Performance

Let $n$ be the number of elements in the stack. The complexities of stack operations with this representation can be given as:

| | |
|---|---|
| Space complexity (for $n$ push operations) | $O(n)$ |
| Time complexity of push() | O(1) |
| Time complexity of pop() | O(1) |
| Time complexity of size() | O(1) |
| Time complexity of isEmpty() | O(1) |
| Time complexity of isFull() | O(1) |
| Time complexity of deleteStack() | O(1) |

### Limitations

The maximum size of the stack must first be defined, and it cannot be changed. Trying to push a new element into a full stack causes an implementation-specific exception.

## Dynamic Array Implementation

First, let's consider how we implemented a simple array-based stack. We took one index variable *top* which points to the index of the most recently inserted element in the stack. To insert (or push) an element, we increment *top* index and then place the new element at that index.

Similarly, to delete (or pop) an element we take the element at *top* index and then decrement the *top* index. We represent an empty queue with *top* value equal to $-1$. The issue that still needs to be resolved is what we do when all the slots in the fixed size array stack are occupied?

First try: What if we increment the size of the array by 1 every time the stack is full?

- push(): increase size of S[] by 1
- pop(): decrease size of S[] by 1

### Issues with this approach?

This way of incrementing the array size is too expensive. Let us see the reason for this. For example, at $n = 1$, to push an element create a new array of size 2 and copy all the old array elements to the new array, and at the end add the new element. At $n = 2$, to push an element create a new array of size 3 and copy all the old array elements to the new array, and at the end add the new element.

Similarly, at $n = n - 1$, if we want to push an element create a new array of size $n$ and copy all the old array elements to the new array and at the end add the new element. After $n$ push operations the total time $T(n)$ (number of copy operations) is proportional to $1 + 2 + ... + n \approx O(n^2)$.

### Alternative Approach: Repeated Doubling

Let us improve the complexity by using the array *doubling* technique. If the array is full, create a new array of twice the size, and copy the items. With this approach, pushing $n$ items takes time proportional to $n$ (not $n^2$).

For simplicity, let us assume that initially we started with $n = 1$ and moved up to $n = 32$. That means, we do the doubling at $1, 2, 4, 8, 16$. The other way of analyzing the same approach is: at $n = 1$, if we want to add (push) an element, double the current size of the array and copy all the elements of the old array to the new array.

At $n = 1$, we do 1 copy operation, at $n = 2$, we do 2 copy operations, and at $n = 4$, we do 4 copy operations and so on. By the time we reach $n = 32$, the total number of copy operations is $1 + 2 + 4 + 8 + 16 = 31$ which is approximately equal to $2n$ value (32). If we observe carefully, we are doing the doubling operation $logn$ times. Now, let us generalize the discussion. For $n$ push operations we double the array size $logn$ times. That means, we will have $logn$ terms in the expression below. The total time $T(n)$ of a series of $n$ push operations is proportional to

$$1 + 2 + 4 + 8 \ldots + \frac{n}{4} + \frac{n}{2} + n = n + \frac{n}{2} + \frac{n}{4} + \frac{n}{8} \ldots + 4 + 2 + 1$$
$$= n\left(1 + \frac{1}{2} + \frac{1}{4} + \frac{1}{8} \ldots + \frac{4}{n} + \frac{2}{n} + \frac{1}{n}\right)$$
$$= n(2) \approx 2n = O(n)$$

$T(n)$ is $O(n)$ and the amortized time of a push operation is $O(1)$.

```
#includ e<stdio.h>
#include <stdlib.h>
#include <limits.h>
struct Stack {
    int top;
    int capacity;
    int *array;
};
struct Stack *createStack(int capacity) {
    struct Stack *S = malloc(sizeof(struct Stack));
    if(!S)
        return NULL;
    S->capacity = capacity;
    S->top = -1;
    S->array= malloc(S->capacity * sizeof(int));
    if(!S->array)
        return NULL;
    return S;
}
int isEmpty(struct Stack *S) {
    return (S->top == -1);   // if the condition is true then 1 is returned else 0 is returned
}
int size(struct Stack *S) {
    return (S->top + 1);
}
int isFull(struct Stack *S){
    //if the condition is true then 1 is returned else 0 is returned
    return (S->top == S->capacity - 1);
}
void doubleStack(struct Stack *S){
    S->capacity *= 2;
    S->array = realloc(S->array, S->capacity * sizeof(int));
}

void push(struct Stack *S, int data){
    if(isFull(S))
        doubleStack(S);
    S->array[++S->top] = data;
}
int pop(struct Stack *S){
    /* S->top == - 1 indicates empty stack*/
    if(isEmpty(S)){
        printf("Stack is Empty\n");
        return INT_MIN;
    }
    else /* Removing element from 'top' of the array and reducing 'top' by 1*/
        return (S->array[S->top--]);
}
int peek(struct Stack *S){
    /* S->top == - 1 indicates empty stack*/
    if(isEmpty(S)){
        printf("Stack is Empty");
        return INT_MIN;;
    }
    else
        return (S->array[S->top]);
```

```
}
void deleteStack(struct Stack *S){
    if(S) {
        if(S->array)
            free(S->array);
            free(S);
    }
}
int main(){
    int i = 0, capacity = 5;
    // create a stack of capacity 5
    struct Stack *stk = createStack(capacity);
    for(i = 0; i <= 2 * capacity; i++){
        push(stk, i);
    }
    printf("Top element is %d\n", peek(stk));
    printf("Stack size is %d\n", size(stk));
    for (i = 0; i <= capacity; i++){
        printf("Popped element is %d\n", pop(stk));
    }
    if (isEmpty(stk))
        printf("Stack is empty");
    else
        printf("Stack is not empty");
    deleteStack(stk);
    return 0;
}
```

## Performance

Let $n$ be the number of elements in the stack. The complexities for operations with this representation can be given as:

| | |
|---|---|
| Space complexity (for $n$ push operations) | $O(n)$ |
| Time complexity of createStack() | O(1) |
| Time complexity of push() | O(1) (Average) |
| Time complexity of pop() | O(1) |
| Time complexity of top() | O(1) |
| Time complexity of isEmpty() | O(1)) |
| Time complexity of isFull() | O(1) |
| Time complexity of deleteStack() | O(1) |

**Note:** Too many doublings may cause memory overflow exception.

## Linked List Implementation

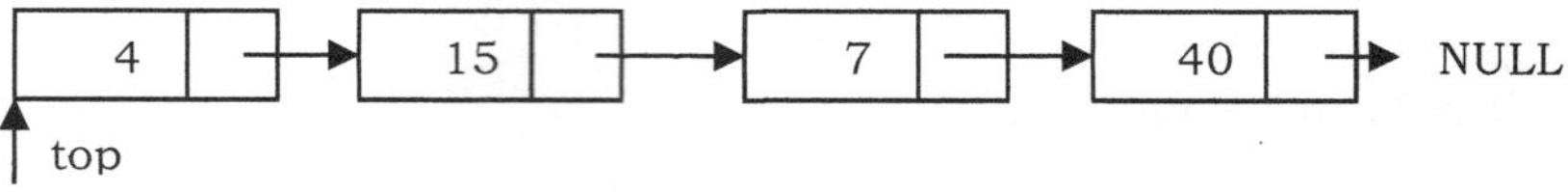


The other way of implementing stacks is by using Linked lists. Push operation is implemented by inserting element at the beginning of the list. Pop operation is implemented by deleting the node from the beginning (the header/top node).

```
#include <stdio.h>
#include <stdlib.h>
#include <limits.h>
struct ListNode{
    int data;
    struct ListNode *next;
};
struct Stack{
    struct ListNode *top;
};
```

```
struct Stack *createStack(){
    struct Stack *stk;
    stk = malloc(sizeof(struct Stack));
    stk->top = NULL;
    return stk;
}
void push(struct Stack *stk, int data){
    struct ListNode *temp;
    temp = malloc(sizeof(struct ListNode));
    if(!temp){
        printf("\nStack/Heap overflow");
        return;
    }
    temp->data = data;
    temp->next = stk->top;
    stk->top = temp;
}
int size(struct Stack *stk){
    // we can improve the size function by adding extra size variable in stack structure
    // and update it while push/pop operations
    int count = 0;
    struct ListNode *temp;
    if(isEmpty(stk))
        return 0;
    temp = stk->top;
    while (temp){
        count++;
        temp = temp->next;
    }
    return count;
}
int isEmpty(struct Stack *stk){
    return stk->top == NULL;
}
int pop(struct Stack *stk){
    int data;
    struct ListNode *temp;
    if(isEmpty(stk))
        return INT_MIN;
    temp = stk->top;
    stk->top = stk->top->next;
    data = temp->data;
    free(temp);
    return data;
}
int peek(struct Stack * stk){
    if(isEmpty(stk))
        return INT_MIN;
    return stk->top->data;
}
void deleteStack(struct Stack *stk){
    struct ListNode *temp, *p;
    p = stk->top;
    while( p) {
        temp = p->next;
        p = p->next;
        free(temp);
    }
    free(stk);
}
int main(){
    int i = 0;
```

```
    struct Stack *stk = createStack();
    for(i = 0; i <= 10; i++){
        push(stk, i);
    }
    printf("Top element is %d\n", peek(stk));
    printf("Stack size is %d\n", size(stk));
    for (i = 0; i <= 10; i++){
        printf("Popped element is %d\n", pop(stk));
    }
    if (isEmpty(stk))
        printf("Stack is empty");
    else
        printf("Stack is not empty");
    deleteStack(stk);
    return 0;
}
```

## Performance

Let $n$ be the number of elements in the stack. The complexities for operations with this representation can be given as:

| Space complexity (for $n$ push operations) | $O(n)$ |
|---|---|
| Time complexity of createStack() | O(1) |
| Time complexity of push() | O(1) (Average) |
| Time complexity of pop() | O(1) |
| Time complexity of top() | O(1) |
| Time complexity of isEmpty() | O(1) |
| Time complexity of deleteStack() | $O(n)$ |

# 4.6 Comparison of Implementations

## Comparing Incremental Strategy and Doubling Strategy

We compare the incremental strategy and doubling strategy by analyzing the total time $T(n)$ needed to perform a series of $n$ push operations. We start with an empty stack represented by an array of size 1. We call *amortized* time of a push operation is the average time taken by a push over the series of operations, that is, $\frac{T(n)}{n}$.

### Incremental Strategy

The amortized time (average time per operation) of a push operation is $O(n)$ $[O(n^2)/n]$.

### Doubling Strategy

In this method, the amortized time of a push operation is O(1) $[O(n)/n]$.

**Note**: For analysis, refer to the *Implementation* section.

## Comparing Array Implementation and Linked List Implementation

### Array Implementation

- Operations take constant time.
- Expensive doubling operation every once in a while.
- Any sequence of $n$ operations (starting from empty stack) – "*amortized*" bound takes time proportional to $n$.

### Linked List Implementation

- Grows and shrinks gracefully.
- Every operation takes constant time O(1).
- Every operation uses extra space and time to deal with references.

# 4.7 Stacks: Problems & Solutions

**Problem-1** Discuss how stacks can be used for checking balancing of symbols/parentheses.

**Solution:** Stacks can be used to check whether the given expression has balanced symbols. This algorithm is very useful in compilers. Each time the parser reads one character at a time. If the character is an opening delimiter such as (, {, or [- then it is written to the stack. When a closing delimiter is encountered like ), }, or ]- the stack is popped.

The opening and closing delimiters are then compared. If they match, the parsing of the string continues. If they do not match, the parser indicates that there is an error on the line. A linear-time $O(n)$ algorithm based on stack can be given as:

**Algorithm:**

a) Create a stack.

b) while (end of input is not reached) {

  1) If the character read is not a symbol to be balanced, ignore it.
  2) If the character is an opening symbol like (, [, {, push it onto the stack
  3) If it is a closing symbol like ),],}, then if the stack is empty report an error. Otherwise pop the stack.
  4) If the symbol popped is not the corresponding opening symbol, report an error.

}

c) At end of input, if the stack is not empty report an error.

**Examples:**

| Example | Valid? | Description |
|---|---|---|
| (A+B)+(C-D) | Yes | The expression has a balanced symbol |
| ((A+B)+(C-D) | No | One closing brace is missing |
| ((A+B)+[C-D]) | Yes | Opening and immediate closing braces correspond |
| ((A+B)+[C-D]} | No | The last closing brace does not correspond with the first opening parenthesis |

For tracing the algorithm let us assume that the input is: () (() [()])

| Input Symbol, A[i] | Operation | Stack | Output |
|---|---|---|---|
| ( | Push ( | ( | |
| ) | Pop (<br>Test if ( and A[i] match? YES | | |
| ( | Push ( | ( | |
| ( | Push ( | (( | |
| ) | Pop (<br>Test if ( and A[i] match? YES | ( | |
| [ | Push [ | ([ | |
| ( | Push ( | ([( | |
| ) | Pop (<br>Test if( and A[i] match? YES | ([ | |
| ] | Pop [<br>Test if [ and A[i] match? YES | ( | |
| ) | Pop (<br>Test if( and A[i] match? YES | | |
| | Test if stack is Empty? YES | | TRUE |

```
#include <stdio.h>
#include <stdlib.h>
#include <string.h>
struct Stack {
    int top;
    int capacity;
    int *array;
};
struct Stack *createStack(int capacity) {
    struct Stack *S = malloc(sizeof(struct Stack));
    if(!S)
        return NULL;
    S->capacity = capacity;
    S->top = -1;
```

```
    S->array= malloc(S->capacity * sizeof(int));
    if(!S->array)
        return NULL;
    return S;
}
int isEmpty(struct Stack *S) {
    return (S->top == -1);  // if the condition is true then 1 is returned else 0 is returned
}
int isFull(struct Stack *S){
    return (S->top == S->capacity - 1);    //if the condition is true then 1 is returned else 0 is returned
}
void doubleStack(struct Stack *S){
    S->capacity *= 2;
    S->array = realloc(S->array, S->capacity * sizeof(int));
}
void push(struct Stack *S, char data){
    if(isFull(S))
        doubleStack(S);
    S->array[++S->top] = data;
}
char pop(struct Stack *S){
    if(isEmpty(S)){
        printf("Stack is Empty\n");
        return '\0';
    }
    else /* Removing element from 'top' of the array and reducing 'top' by 1*/
        return (S->array[S->top--]);
}
void deleteStack(struct Stack *S){
    if(S) {
        if(S->array)
            free(S->array);
                free(S);
    }
}
int matchSymbol(char a, char b){
    if(a == '[' && b == ']'){
        return 1;
    }
    else if(a == '{' && b == '}'){
        return 1;
    }
    else if(a == '(' && b == ')'){
        return 1;
    }
    return 0;
}
int checkExpression(char expression[]){
    int count;
    char temp;
    // create a stack of capacity 5
    struct Stack *stk = createStack(5);
    for(count = 0; count < strlen(expression); count++){
        if(expression[count] == '(' || expression[count] == '{' || expression[count] == '['){
            push(stk, expression[count]);
        }
        if(expression[count] == ')' || expression[count] == '}' || expression[count] == ']'){
            if(isEmpty(stk)){
                printf("The right symbols are more than the Left symbols\n");
                return 0;
```

```
                }
                else{
                    temp = pop(stk);
                    if(!matchSymbol(temp, expression[count])){
                        printf("The mismatched symbols are:\t%c and %c\n", temp, expression[count]);
                        return 0;
                    }
                }
            }
        }
        if(isEmpty(stk)){
            printf("\nThe Expression has Balanced Parentheses\n");
            return 1;
        }
        else{
            printf("The Expression has unbalanced parentheses\n");
            return 0;
        }
    }
    int main(){ // test code
        int validity;
        validity = checkExpression("[a+(b*{d+2})]");
        if(validity == 1){
            printf("The expression is valid\n");
        }
        else{
            printf("The expression is invalid\n");
        }
        return 0;
    }
```

Time Complexity: O($n$). Since we are scanning the input only once. Space Complexity: O($n$) [for stack].

Problem-2 Discuss infix to postfix conversion algorithm using stack.

**Solution:** Before discussing the algorithm, first let us see the definitions of infix, prefix and postfix expressions.

**Infix:** An infix expression is a single letter, or an operator, proceeded by one infix string and followed by another Infix string.

A
A+B
(A+B)+ (C-D)

**Prefix:** A prefix expression is a single letter, or an operator, followed by two prefix strings. Every prefix string longer than a single variable contains an operator, first operand and second operand.

A
+AB
++AB-CD

**Postfix**: A postfix expression (also called Reverse Polish Notation) is a single letter or an operator, preceded by two postfix strings. Every postfix string longer than a single variable contains first and second operands followed by an operator.

A
AB+
AB+CD-+

Prefix and postfix notions are methods of writing mathematical expressions without parenthesis. Time to evaluate a postfix and prefix expression is O($n$), where $n$ is the number of elements in the array.

| Infix | Prefix | Postfix |
|---|---|---|
| A+B | +AB | AB+ |
| A+B-C | -+ABC | AB+C- |
| (A+B)*C-D | -*+ABCD | AB+C*D- |

Now, let us focus on the algorithm. In infix expressions, the operator precedence is implicit unless we use parentheses. Therefore, for the infix to postfix conversion algorithm we have to define the operator precedence (or priority) inside the algorithm.

The table shows the precedence and their associativity (order of evaluation) among operators.

| Token | Operator | Precedence | Associativity |
|---|---|---|---|
| ( )<br>[ ]<br>→ . | function call<br>array element<br>struct or union member | 17 | left-to-right |
| -- ++ | increment, decrement | 16 | left-to-right |
| -- ++<br>!<br>-<br>- +<br>& *<br>sizeof | decrement, increment<br>logical not<br>one's complement<br>unary minus or plus<br>address or indirection<br>size (in bytes) | 15 | right-to-left |
| (type) | type cast | 14 | right-to-left |
| * / % | multiplicative | 13 | Left-to-right |
| + - | binary add or subtract | 12 | left-to-right |
| << >> | shift | 11 | left-to-right |
| > >=<br>< <= | relational | 10 | left-to-right |
| == != | equality | 9 | left-to-right |
| & | bitwise and | 8 | left-to-right |
| ^ | bitwise exclusive or | 7 | left-to-right |
| \| | bitwise or | 6 | left-to-right |
| && | logical and | 5 | left-to-right |
| \|\| | logical or | 4 | left-to-right |
| ?: | conditional | 3 | right-to-left |
| = += -= /= *= %=<br><<= >>=<br>&= ^= | assignment | 2 | right-to-left |
| , | comma | 1 | left-to-right |

## Important Properties

- Let us consider the infix expression 2 + 3 * 4 and its postfix equivalent 2 3 4 * +. Notice that between infix and postfix the order of the numbers (or operands) is unchanged. It is 2 3 4 in both cases. But the order of the operators * and + is affected in the two expressions.
- Only one stack is enough to convert an infix expression to postfix expression. The stack that we use in the algorithm will be used to change the order of operators from infix to postfix. The stack we use will only contain operators and the open parentheses symbol '('.
  Postfix expressions do not contain parentheses. We shall not output the parentheses in the postfix output.

**Algorithm:**

```
a) Create a stack
b) for each character t in the input stream{
       if(t is an operand)
              output t
       else if(t is a right parenthesis){
              Pop and output tokens until a left parenthesis is popped (but not output)
       }
       else // t is an operator or left parenthesis{
              pop and output tokens until one of lower priority than t is encountered or a left parenthesis
              is encountered or the stack is empty
              Push t
       }
   }
c) pop and output tokens until the stack is empty.
```

For better understanding let us trace out an example: A * B- (C + D) + E

| Input Character | Operation on Stack | Stack | Postfix Expression |
|---|---|---|---|
| A | | Empty | A |
| * | Push | * | A |
| B | | * | AB |
| - | Check and Push | - | AB* |

| ( | Push | -( | AB* |
|---|---|---|---|
| C | | -( | AB*C |
| + | Check and Push | -(+ | AB*C |
| D | | | AB*CD |
| ) | Pop and append to postfix till '(' | - | AB*CD+ |
| + | Check and Push | + | AB*CD+- |
| E | | + | AB*CD+-E |
| End of input | Pop till empty | | AB*CD+-E+ |

```
// Refer stack implementation from previous section
int priority(char x){
    if(x == '(')
        return 0;
    if(x == '+' || x == '-')
        return 1;
    if(x == '*' || x == '/')
        return 2;
}
int infixToPostfix(char expression[]){
    char *e, x;
    // create a stack of capacity 5
    struct Stack *stk = createStack(5);
    e = expression;
    while(*e != '\0'){
        if(isalnum(*e))
            printf("%c",*e);
        else if(*e == '(')
            push(stk, *e);
        else if(*e == ')'){
            while((x = pop(stk)) != '(')
                printf("%c", x);
        }
        else{
            while(priority(peek(stk)) >= priority(*e))
                printf("%c",pop(stk));
            push(stk, *e);
        }
        e++;
    }
    while(!isEmpty(stk)){
        printf("%c",pop(stk));
    }
}
int main(){ // test code
    infixToPostfix("(a+(b*(d+2)))");
}
```

**Problem-3** Discuss postfix evaluation using stacks?

**Solution:**

**Algorithm:**

1. Scan the Postfix string from left to right.
2. Initialize an empty stack.
3. Repeat steps 4 and 5 till all the characters are scanned.
4. If the scanned character is an operand, push it onto the stack.
5. If the scanned character is an operator, and if the operator is a unary operator, then pop an element from the stack. If the operator is a binary operator, then pop two elements from the stack. After popping the elements, apply the operator to those popped elements. Let the result of this operation be retVal onto the stack.
6. After all characters are scanned, we will have only one element in the stack.
7. Return top of the stack as result.

**Example:** Let us see how the above-mentioned algorithm works using an example. Assume that the postfix string is 123*+5-.

Initially the stack is empty. Now, the first three characters scanned are 1, 2 and 3, which are operands. They will be pushed into the stack in that order.

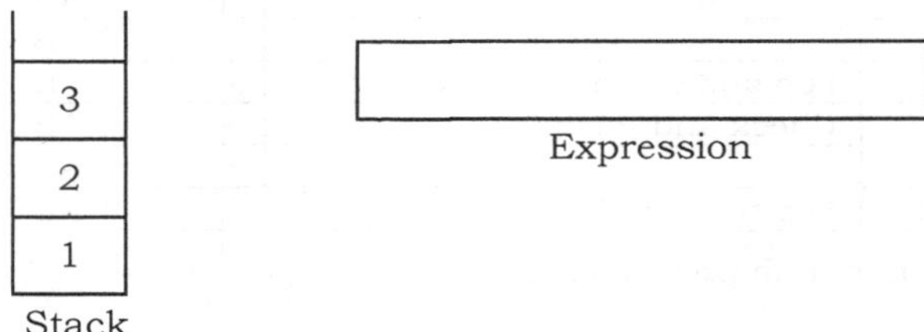


The next character scanned is "*", which is an operator. Thus, we pop the top two elements from the stack and perform the "*" operation with the two operands. The second operand will be the first element that is popped.

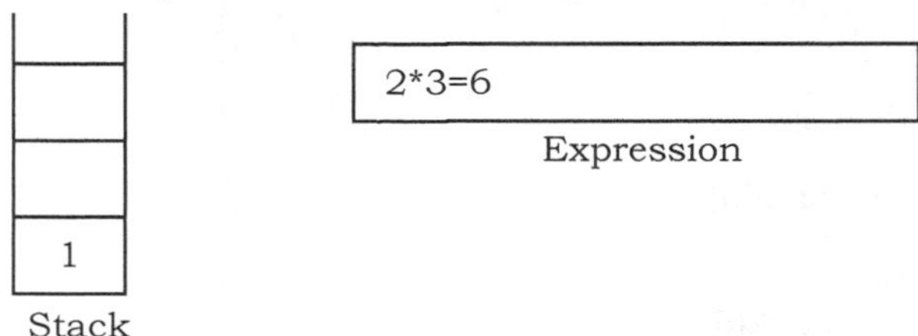


The value of the expression (2*3) that has been evaluated (6) is pushed into the stack.

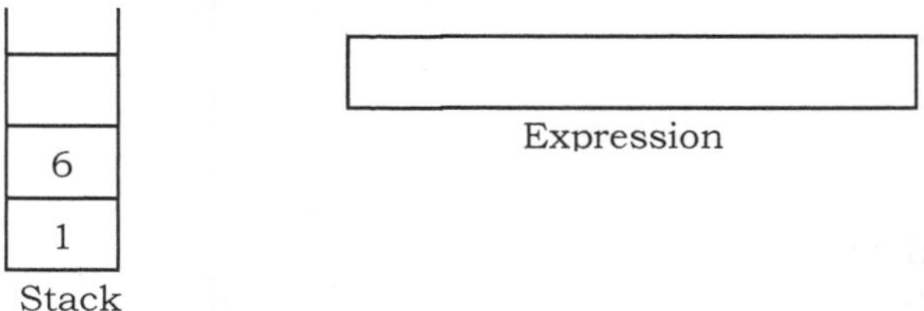


The next character scanned is "+", which is an operator. Thus, we pop the top two elements from the stack and perform the "+" operation with the two operands. The second operand will be the first element that is popped.

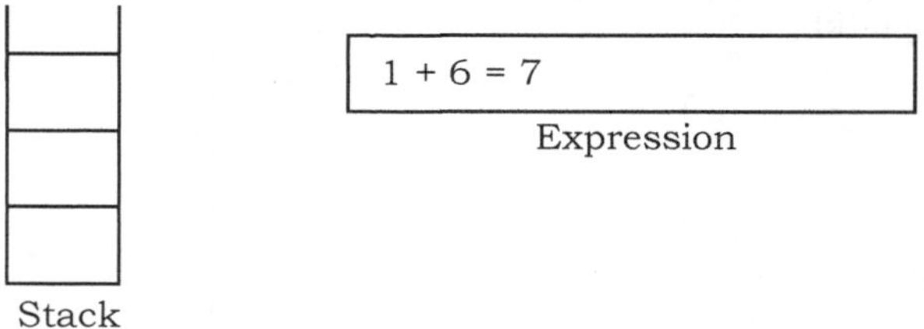


The value of the expression (1+6) that has been evaluated (7) is pushed into the stack.

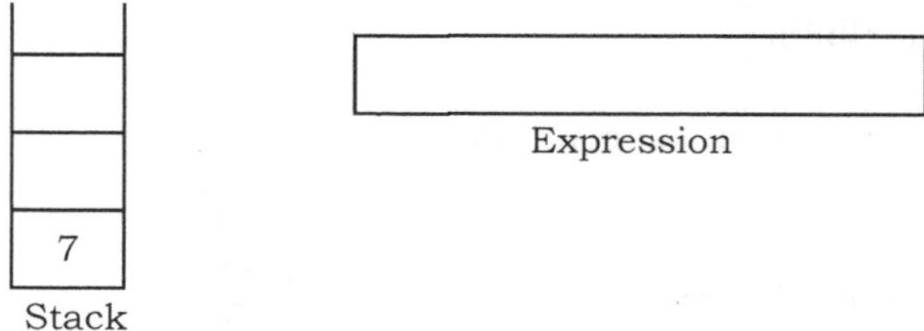


The next character scanned is "5", which is added to the stack.

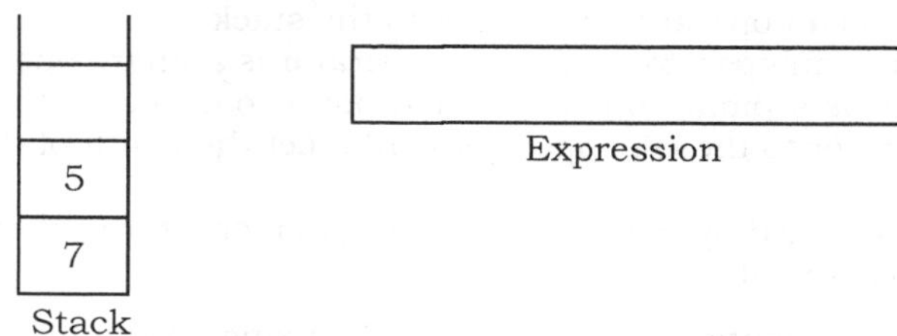


The next character scanned is "-", which is an operator. Thus, we pop the top two elements from the stack and perform the "-" operation with the two operands. The second operand will be the first element that is popped.

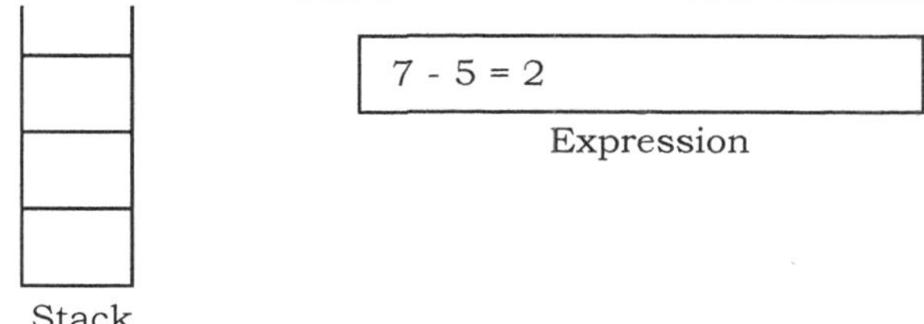


The value of the expression(7-5) that has been evaluated(23) is pushed into the stack.

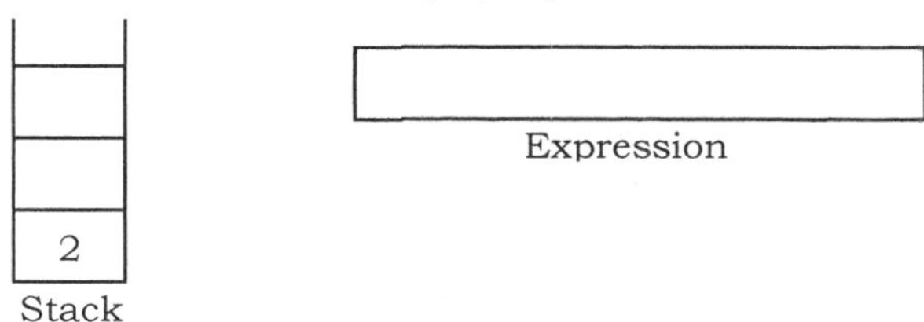


Now, since all the characters are scanned, the remaining element in the stack (there will be only one element in the stack) will be returned. End result:

- Postfix String : 123*+5-
- Result : 2

```
// Refer stack implementation from previous section
int postfixEvaluation(char expression[]){
    // Create a stack of capacity equal to expression size
    struct Stack* stk = createStack(strlen(expression));
    int i;
    // Scan all characters one by one
    for (i = 0; expression[i]; ++i){
        // If the scanned character is an operand (number here),
        // push it to the Stack.
        if (isdigit(expression[i]))
            push(stk, expression[i] - '0');
        // If the scanned character is an operator, pop top two
        // elements from stack apply the operator
        else{
            int topElement = pop(stk);
            int secondTopElement = pop(stk);
            switch (expression[i]){
                case '+': push(stk, secondTopElement + topElement); break;
                case '-': push(stk, secondTopElement - topElement); break;
                case '*': push(stk, secondTopElement * topElement); break;
                case '/': push(stk, secondTopElement/topElement); break;
            }
        }
    }
    return pop(stk);
}
// test code
int main() {
    printf ("postfix evaluation: %d", postfixEvaluation("123*+5-"));
    return 0;
}
```

**Problem-4** Can we evaluate the infix expression with stacks in one pass?

**Solution:** Using 2 stacks we can evaluate an infix expression in 1 pass without converting to postfix.

**Algorithm:**

1) Create an empty operator stack.
2) Create an empty operand stack.
3) For each token in the input string
    a. Get the next token in the infix string.
    b. If next token is an operand, place it on the operand stack.
    c. If next token is an operator

i. Evaluate the operator (next op)

4) While the operator stack is not empty, pop operator and operands (left and right), evaluate left operator right and push result onto operand stack.
5) Pop result from operator stack

**Problem-5** How to design a stack such that getMinimum( ) should be O(1)?

**Solution:** Take an auxiliary stack that maintains the minimum of all values in the stack. Also, assume that each element of the stack is less than its below elements. For simplicity let us call the auxiliary stack *min stack*.

When we *pop* the main stack, *pop* the min stack too. When we push the main stack, push either the new element or the current minimum, whichever is lower. At any point, if we want to get the minimum, then we just need to return the top element from the min stack. Let us take an example and trace it out. Initially let us assume that we have pushed 2, 6, 4, 1 and 5. Based on the above-mentioned algorithm the *min stack* will look like:

| Main stack | Min stack |
|---|---|
| 5 → top | 1 → top |
| 1 | 1 |
| 4 | 2 |
| 6 | 2 |
| 2 | 2 |

After popping twice we get:

| Main stack | Min stack |
|---|---|
| 4 -→ top | 2 → top |
| 6 | 2 |
| 2 | 2 |

Based on the discussion above, now let us code the push, pop and getMinimum() operations.

```
// Refer basic stack implementation from previous section
struct AdvancedStack {
    struct Stack *elementStack;
    struct Stack *minStack;
};
int isEmptyA(struct AdvancedStack *S) {
   return (S->elementStack->top == -1);   // if the condition is true then 1 is returned else 0 is returned
}
int sizeA(struct AdvancedStack *S) {
   return (S->elementStack->top + 1);
}
int isFullA(struct AdvancedStack *S){
   //if the condition is true then 1 is returned else 0 is returned
   return (S->elementStack->top == S->elementStack->capacity - 1);
}
void pushA(struct AdvancedStack *S, int data){
   push(S->elementStack, data);
   if(isEmpty(S->minStack) || peek(S->minStack) >= data)
      push (S->minStack, data);
   else push (S->minStack, peek(S->minStack));
}
int popA(struct AdvancedStack *S ){
   int temp;
   if(isEmpty(S->elementStack))
      return INT_MIN;
   temp = peek(S->elementStack);
   if(peek(S->minStack) == pop(S->elementStack))
      pop (S->minStack);
   return temp;
}
int peekA(struct AdvancedStack *S ){
   return peek(S->elementStack);
}
int getMinimum(struct AdvancedStack *S){
```

```
        return peek(S->minStack);
}
struct AdvancedStack * createAdvancedStack(int capacity){
        struct AdvancedStack *S = malloc (sizeof (struct AdvancedStack));
        if(!S)
                return NULL;
        S->elementStack = createStack(capacity);
        S->minStack = createStack(capacity);
        return S;
}
void deleteStackA(struct AdvancedStack *S){
        if(S) {
                deleteStackA(S->elementStack);
                deleteStackA(S->minStack);
                free(S);
        }
}
int main(){
        int i = 0, capacity = 5;
        // create a stack of capacity 5
        struct AdvancedStack *stk = createAdvancedStack(capacity);
        for(i = 0; i <= 2 * capacity; i++){
                pushA(stk, (7*i)%4);
        }
        printf("Top element is %d\n", peekA(stk));
        printf("Stack size is %d\n", sizeA(stk));
        for (i = 0; i <= capacity; i++){
                printf("Popped element is %d\n", popA(stk));
                printf("Minimum element is %d\n", getMinimum(stk));
        }
        if (isEmptyA(stk))
                printf("Stack is empty");
        else
                printf("Stack is not empty");
        deleteStackA(stk);
        return 0;
}
```

Time complexity: O(1).
Space complexity: O($n$) [for Min stack]. This algorithm has much better space usage if we rarely get a "new minimum or equal".

**Problem-6** For Problem-5 is it possible to improve the space complexity?

**Solution: Yes.** The main problem of the previous approach is, for each push operation we are pushing the element on to min stack also (either the new element or existing minimum element). That means, we are pushing the duplicate minimum elements on to the stack.

Now, let us change the algorithm to improve the space complexity. We still have the min stack, but we only pop from it when the value we pop from the main stack is equal to the one on the min stack. We only *push* to the min stack when the value being pushed onto the main stack is less than *or equal* to the current min value. In this modified algorithm also, if we want to get the minimum then we just need to return the top element from the min stack. For example, taking the original version and pushing 1 again, we'd get:

| Main stack | Min stack |
|---|---|
| 1 → top | |
| 5 | |
| 1 | |
| 4 | 1 → top |
| 6 | 1 |
| 2 | 2 |

Popping from the above pops from both stacks because 1 == 1, leaving:

| Main stack | Min stack |
|---|---|
| 5 → top | |
| 1 | |
| 4 | |
| 6 | 1 → top |
| 2 | 2 |

Popping again *only* pops from the main stack, because 5 > 1:

| Main stack | Min stack |
|---|---|
| 1 → top | |
| 4 | |
| 6 | 1 → top |
| 2 | 2 |

Popping again pops both stacks because 1 == 1:

| Main stack | Min stack |
|---|---|
| 4 → top | |
| 6 | |
| 2 | 2 → top |

**Note**: The difference is only in push & pop operations.

```
// No change in other functions
void pushA(struct AdvancedStack *S, int data){
    push(S->elementStack, data);

    if(isEmpty(S->minStack) || peek(S->minStack) >= data)
        push(S->minStack, data);
}
int popA(struct AdvancedStack *S ){
    int temp;
    if(isEmpty(S->elementStack))
        return -1;
    temp = peek(S->elementStack);
    if(peek(S->minStack) == pop(S->elementStack))
        pop(S->minStack);
    return temp;
}
```

Time complexity: O(1).
Space complexity: O($n$) [for Min stack]. But this algorithm has much better space usage if we rarely get a "new minimum or equal".

**Problem-7** For a given array with $n$ symbols how many stack permutations are possible?

**Solution:** The number of stack permutations with n symbols is represented by Catalan number and we will discuss this in the *Dynamic Programming* chapter.

**Problem-8** Given an array of characters formed with a's and b's. The string is marked with special character X which represents the middle of the list (for example: ababa...ababXbabab.....baaa). Check whether the string is palindrome.

**Solution:** This is one of the simplest algorithms. What we do is, start two indexes, one at the beginning of the string and the other at the end of the string. Each time compare whether the values at both the indexes are the same or not. If the values are not the same then we say that the given string is not a palindrome.

If the values are the same then increment the left index and decrement the right index. Continue this process until both the indexes meet at the middle (at X) or if the string is not palindrome.

```
#include<stdio.h>
#include<stdlib.h>
int isPalindrome(char str[]){
    //the first index
    int i = 0;
    //the last index
    int j = strlen(str)-1;
    while(i < j && str[i] == str[j]){
        //increment start index and decrement last index
        i++;
```

```
            j--;
        }
        if(i < j){
            //did not reach the center
            printf("Not a palindrome\n");
            return 0;
        }
        else{
            //reached the center
            printf("Palindrome\n");
            return 1;
        }
    }
    int main(void){
        isPalindrome("ababaXababa");
        isPalindrome("ababababXbababbbbabba");
        return 0;
    }
```

Time Complexity: O($n$). Space Complexity: O(1).

**Problem-9** For Problem-8, if the input is in singly linked list then how do we check whether the list elements form a palindrome (That means, moving backward is not possible).

**Solution:** Refer Linked Lists chapter.

**Problem-10** Can we solve Problem-8 using stacks?

**Solution: Yes.**

**Algorithm:**

- Traverse the list till we encounter X as input element.
- During the traversal push all the elements (until X) on to the stack.
- For the second half of the list, compare each element's content with top of the stack. If they are the same then pop the stack and go to the next element in the input list.
- If they are not the same then the given string is not a palindrome.
- Continue this process until the stack is empty or the string is not a palindrome.

```
    // Refer basic stack implementation from previous section
    int isPalindrome(char A[]){
        int i=0;
        struct Stack *stk = createStack(strlen(A));
        while(A[i] && A[i] != 'X') {
            push(stk, A[i]);
            i++;
        }
        i++;
        while(A[i]) {
            if(isEmpty(stk) || A[i] != pop(stk)) {
                printf("Not a palindrome\n");
                return 0;
            }
            i++;
        }
        printf("Palindrome\n");
        return 1;
    }
    int main(void){
        isPalindrome("ababaXababa");
        isPalindrome("ababababXbababbbbabba");
        return 0;
    }
```

Time Complexity: O($n$). Space Complexity: O($n/2$) $\approx$O($n$).

**Problem-11** Given a stack, how to reverse the elements of the stack using only stack operations (push & pop)?

**Solution:**

**Algorithm:**

- First pop all the elements of the stack till it becomes empty.
- For each upward step in recursion, insert the element at the bottom of the stack.

```
// Refer basic stack implementation from previous section
void reverseStack(struct Stack *S){
    char data;
    if(isEmpty(S))
        return;
    data = pop(S);
    reverseStack(S);
    insertAtBottom(S, data);
}
void insertAtBottom(struct Stack *S, char data){
    char temp;
    if(isEmpty(S)) {
        push(S, data);
        return;
    }
    temp = pop(S);
    insertAtBottom(S, data);
    push(S, temp);
}
int main(void){
    int i = 0, capacity = 2;
    // create a stack of capacity 2
    struct Stack *stk = createStack(capacity);
    for(i = 0; i <= capacity; i++){
        push(stk, i);
    }
    reverseStack(stk);
    printf("Top element is %d\n", peek(stk));
    printf("Stack size is %d\n", size(stk));
    for (i = 0; i <= capacity; i++){
        printf("Popped element is %d\n", pop(stk));
    }
    deleteStack(stk);
    return 0;
}
```

Time Complexity: $O(n^2)$. Space Complexity: $O(n)$, for recursive stack.

**Problem-12** Show how to implement one queue efficiently using two stacks. Analyze the running time of the queue operations.

**Solution:** Refer Queues chapter.

**Problem-13** Show how to implement one stack efficiently using two queues. Analyze the running time of the stack operations.

**Solution:** Refer Queues chapter.

**Problem-14** How do we implement *two* stacks using only one array? Our stack routines should not indicate an exception unless every slot in the array is used?

**Solution:**

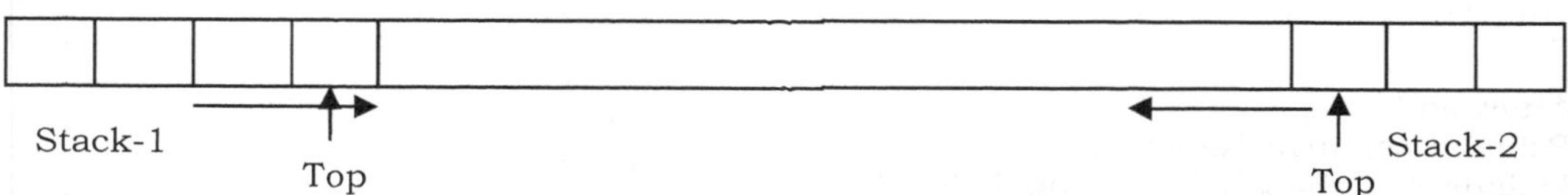


**Algorithm:**

- Start two indexes one at the left end and the other at the right end.
- The left index simulates the first stack and the right index simulates the second stack.
- If we want to push an element into the first stack then put the element at the left index.
- Similarly, if we want to push an element into the second stack then put the element at the right index.
- The first stack grows towards the right, and the second stack grows towards the left.

```
#include <stdio.h>
#include <stdlib.h>
#include <string.h>
#include <limits.h>
struct MultiStacks {
    int top1, top2;
    int capacity;
    char *array;
};
struct MultiStacks *createStack(int capacity) {
    struct MultiStacks *twoStacks = malloc(sizeof(struct MultiStacks));
    if(!twoStacks)
        return NULL;
    twoStacks->capacity = capacity;
    twoStacks->top1 = -1;
    twoStacks->top2 = capacity;
    twoStacks->array= malloc(twoStacks->capacity * sizeof(int));
    if(!twoStacks->array)
        return NULL;
    return twoStacks;
}
int isEmpty(struct MultiStacks *twoStacks, int stackNumber) {
    if (stackNumber == 1){
        return (twoStacks->top1 == -1);
    } else {
        return (twoStacks->top2 == twoStacks->capacity);
    }
}
int size(struct MultiStacks *twoStacks, int stackNumber) {
    if (stackNumber == 1){
        return (twoStacks->top1 + 1);
    } else {
        return (twoStacks->capacity - twoStacks->top2);
    }
}
int isFull(struct MultiStacks *twoStacks){
    return (size(twoStacks, 1) + size(twoStacks, 2) == twoStacks->capacity);
}
void push(struct MultiStacks *twoStacks, int stackNumber, char data){
    if(isFull(twoStacks)){
        printf("Stack overflow\n");
        return;
    }
    if (stackNumber == 1){
        twoStacks->array[++twoStacks->top1] = data;
    } else {
        twoStacks->array[--twoStacks->top2] = data;
    }
}
char pop(struct MultiStacks *twoStacks, int stackNumber){
    /* twoStacks->top == - 1 indicates empty stack*/
    if(isEmpty(twoStacks, stackNumber)){
        printf("Stack is Empty\n");
        return '\0';
    }
    if (stackNumber == 1){
        return (twoStacks->array[twoStacks->top1--]);
    } else {
        return (twoStacks->array[twoStacks->top2++]);
    }
}
```

```
int peek(struct MultiStacks *twoStacks, int stackNumber){
    if(isEmpty(twoStacks, stackNumber)){
        printf("Stack is Empty");
        return INT_MIN;;
    }
    if (stackNumber == 1){
        return (twoStacks->array[twoStacks->top1]);
    } else {
        return (twoStacks->array[twoStacks->top2]);
    }
}
void deleteStack(struct MultiStacks *twoStacks){
    if(twoStacks) {
        if(twoStacks->array)
            free(twoStacks->array);
                free(twoStacks);
    }
}
int main(void){
    int i = 0, capacity = 15;
    // create a stack of capacity 15
    struct MultiStacks *stk = createStack(capacity);
    for(i = 0; i <= capacity; i++){
        printf("Pushing %d to %d\n", i, i%2+1);
        push(stk, i%2+1, i);
    }
    printf("Top element in first stack is %d\n", peek(stk, 1));
    printf("Top element in second stack is %d\n", peek(stk, 2));
    printf("Size of first stack is %d\n", size(stk,1));
    printf("Size of second stack is %d\n", size(stk,2));
    for (i = 0; i <= capacity; i++){
        printf("Popped element from stack %d is %d\n", i%2+1, pop(stk, i%2+1));
    }
    deleteStack(stk);
    return 0;
}
```

Time Complexity of push and pop for both stacks is O(1). Space Complexity is O(1).

**Problem-15** 3 stacks in one array: How to implement 3 stacks in one array?

**Solution:** For this problem, there could be other ways of solving it. Given below is one possibility and it works as long as there is an empty space in the array.

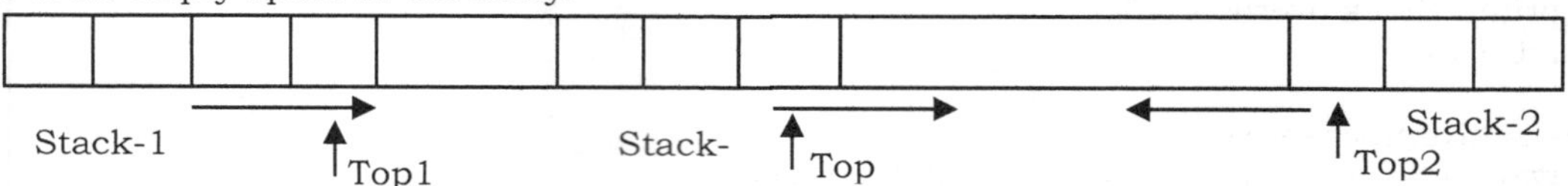


To implement 3 stacks we keep the following information.

- The index of the first stack (Top1): this indicates the size of the first stack.
- The index of the second stack (Top2): this indicates the size of the second stack.
- Starting index of the third stack (base address of third stack).
- Top index of the third stack.

Now, let us define the push and pop operations for this implementation.

**Pushing:**

- For pushing on to the first stack, we need to see if adding a new element causes it to bump into the third stack. If so, try to shift the third stack upwards. Insert the new element at (start1 + Top1).
- For pushing to the second stack, we need to see if adding a new element causes it to bump into the third stack. If so, try to shift the third stack downward. Insert the new element at (start2 – Top2).
- When pushing to the third stack, see if it bumps into the second stack. If so, try to shift the third stack downward and try pushing again. Insert the new element at (start3 + Top3).

Time Complexity: $O(n)$. Since we may need to adjust the third stack. Space Complexity: O(1).

**Popping:** For popping, we don't need to shift, just decrement the size of the appropriate stack.

Time Complexity: O(1). Space Complexity: O(1).

**Problem-16** For Problem-15, is there any other way implementing the middle stack?

**Solution: Yes.** When either the left stack (which grows to the right) or the right stack (which grows to the left) bumps into the middle stack, we need to shift the entire middle stack to make room. The same happens if a push on the middle stack causes it to bump into the right stack.

To solve the above-mentioned problem (number of shifts) what we can do is: alternating pushes can be added at alternating sides of the middle list (For example, even elements are pushed to the left, odd elements are pushed to the right). This would keep the middle stack balanced in the center of the array but it would still need to be shifted when it bumps into the left or right stack, whether by growing on its own or by the growth of a neighboring stack. We can optimize the initial locations of the three stacks if they grow/shrink at different rates and if they have different average sizes. For example, suppose one stack doesn't change much. If we put it at the left, then the middle stack will eventually get pushed against it and leave a gap between the middle and right stacks, which grow toward each other. If they collide, then it's likely we've run out of space in the array. There is no change in the time complexity but the average number of shifts will get reduced.

**Problem-17** Multiple ($m$) stacks in one array: Similar to Problem-15, what if we want to implement $m$ stacks in one array?

**Solution:** Let us assume that array indexes are from 1 to n. Similar to the discussion in Problem-15, to implement $m$ stacks in one array, we divide the array into $m$ parts (as shown below). The size of each part is $\frac{n}{m}$.

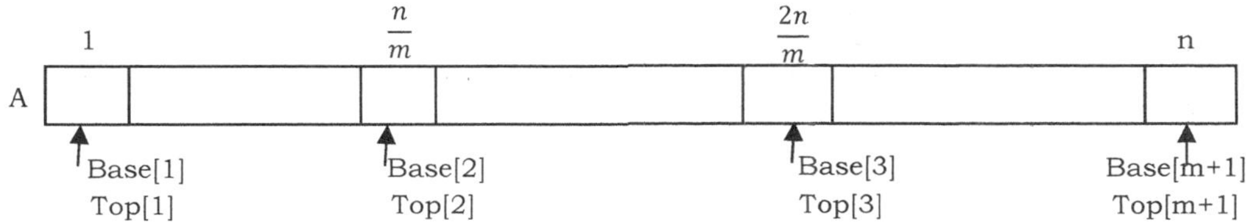


From the above representation we can see that, first stack is starting at index 1 (starting index is stored in Base[1]), second stack is starting at index $\frac{n}{m}$ (starting index is stored in Base[2]), third stack is starting at index $\frac{2n}{m}$ (starting index is stored in Base[3]), and so on. Similar to *Base* array, let us assume that *Top* array stores the top indexes for each of the stack. Consider the following terminology for the discussion.

- Top[i], for $1 \leq i \leq m$ will point to the topmost element of the stack $i$.
- If Base[i] == Top[i], then we can say the stack $i$ is empty.
- If Top[i] == Base[i+1], then we can say the stack i is full.
  Initially Base[i] = Top[i] = $\frac{n}{m}(i-1)$, for $1 \leq i \leq m$.
- The $i^{th}$stack grows from Base[i]+1 to Base[i+1].

**Pushing on to $i^{th}$ stack:**

1) For pushing on to the $i^{th}$ stack, we check whether the top of $i^{th}$ stack is pointing to Base[i+1] (this case defines that $i^{th}$ stack is full). That means, we need to see if adding a new element causes it to bump into the $i+1^{th}$ stack. If so, try to shift the stacks from $i+1^{th}$ stack to $m^{th}$ stack toward the right. Insert the new element at (Base[i] + Top[i]).
2) If right shifting is not possible then try shifting the stacks from 1 to $i-1^{th}$ stack toward the left.
3) If both of them are not possible then we can say that all stacks are full.

```
void push(int stackID, int data) {
    if(top[i] == base[i+1])
        Print ith Stack is full and does the necessary action (shifting);
    top[i] = top[i]+1;
    A[top[i]] = data;
}
```

Time Complexity: O($n$). Since we may need to adjust the stacks. Space Complexity: O(1).

**Popping from $i^{th}$ stack:** For popping, we don't need to shift, just decrement the size of the appropriate stack. The only case to check is stack empty case.

```
int pop(int stackID) {
    if(top[i] == base[i])
        Print ith Stack is empty;
    return A[top[i]--];
}
```

Time Complexity: O(1). Space Complexity: O(1).

**Problem-18** Consider an empty stack of integers. Let the numbers 1, 2, 3, 4, 5, 6 be pushed on to this stack in the order they appear from left to right. Let $S$ indicate a push and $X$ indicate a pop operation. Can they be permuted in to the order 325641(output) and order 154623?

**Solution:** SSSXXSSXSXXX outputs 325641. 154623 cannot be output as 2 is pushed much before 3 so can appear only after 3 is output.

**Problem-19** Earlier in this chapter, we discussed that for dynamic array implementation of stacks, the 'repeated doubling' approach is used. For the same problem, what is the complexity if we create a new array whose size is $n + K$ instead of doubling?

**Solution:** Let us assume that the initial stack size is 0. For simplicity let us assume that $K = 10$. For inserting the element we create a new array whose size is $0 + 10 = 10$. Similarly, after 10 elements we again create a new array whose size is $10 + 10 = 20$ and this process continues at values: 30, 40 ... That means, for a given $n$ value, we are creating the new arrays at: $\frac{n}{10}, \frac{n}{20}, \frac{n}{30}, \frac{n}{40}$ ... The total number of copy operations is:

$$= \frac{n}{10} + \frac{n}{20} + \frac{n}{30} + \cdots 1 = \frac{n}{10}\left(\frac{1}{1} + \frac{1}{2} + \frac{1}{3} + \cdots \frac{1}{n}\right) = \frac{n}{10} logn \approx O(nlogn)$$

If we are performing $n$ push operations, the cost per operation is $O(logn)$.

**Problem-20** Given a string containing $n$ $S's$ and $n$ $X's$ where $S$ indicates a push operation and $X$ indicates a pop operation, and with the stack initially empty, formulate a rule to check whether a given string $S$ of operations is admissible or not?

**Solution:** Given a string of length $2n$, we wish to check whether the given string of operations is permissible or not with respect to its functioning on a stack. The only restricted operation is pop whose prior requirement is that the stack should not be empty. So while traversing the string from left to right, prior to any pop the stack shouldn't be empty, which means the number of $S's$ is always greater than or equal to that of $X's$. Hence the condition is at any stage of processing of the string, the number of push operations ($S$) should be greater than the number of pop operations ($X$).

**Problem-21** **Finding Spans:** Given an array $A$, the span $S[i]$ of $A[i]$ is the maximum number of consecutive elements $A[j]$ immediately preceding $A[i]$ and such that $A[j] \leq A[i]$?

**Other way of asking**: Given an array $A$ of integers, find the maximum of $j - i$ subjected to the constraint of $A[i] < A[j]$.

**Solution:**

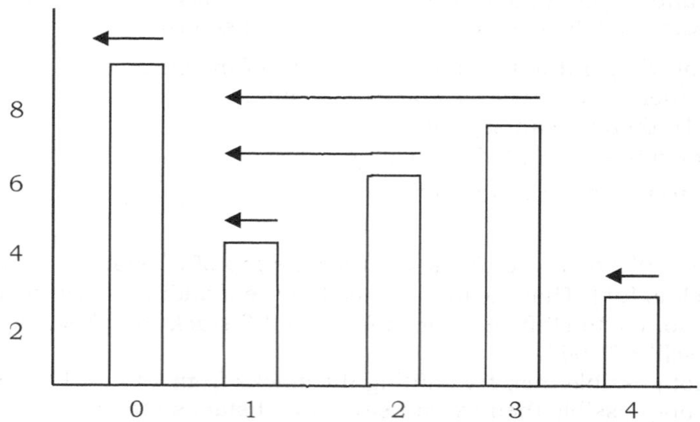


| Day: Index i | Input Array A[i] | S[i]: Span of A[i] |
|---|---|---|
| 0 | 6 | 1 |
| 1 | 3 | 1 |
| 2 | 4 | 2 |
| 3 | 5 | 3 |
| 4 | 2 | 1 |

This is a very common problem in stock markets to find the peaks. Spans are used in financial analysis (E.g., stock at 52-week high). The span of a stock price on a certain day, $i$, is the maximum number of consecutive days (up to the current day) the price of the stock has been less than or equal to its price on $i$.

As an example, let us consider the table and the corresponding spans diagram. In the figure the arrows indicate the length of the spans. Now, let us concentrate on the algorithm for finding the spans. One simple way is, each day, check how many contiguous days have a stock price that is less than the current price.

```
int* find_spans(int A[], int n) {
    int* spans = (int*) malloc(n * sizeof(int));
    spans[0] = 1;
    for (int i = 1; i < n; i++) {
        int j = i - 1;
        while (j >= 0 && A[j] <= A[i])
            j = j - spans[j];
        spans[i] = i - j;
    }

    return spans;
}
```

The algorithm works by starting from the first element and computing its span as 1. Then, for each subsequent element, we iterate backwards through the array, starting from the previous element, and subtracting the spans of the elements we encounter until we find an element that is greater than the current element. The span of the current element is then the difference between its index and the index of the last element we encountered that was greater than it.

Time Complexity: $O(n^2)$. Space Complexity: O(1).

**Problem-22** Can we improve the complexity of Problem-21?

**Solution:** Alternative way to solve this problem is to use a stack. From the example above, we can see that span $S[i]$ on day $i$ can be easily calculated if we know the closest day preceding $i$, such that the price is greater on that day than the price on day $i$. Let us call such a day as $P$. If such a day exists then the span is now defined as $spans[i] = i - P$.

We can iterate through the array from left to right, and for each element A[i], we pop elements from the stack as long as they are less than or equal to A[i]. The stack will contain the indices of the elements that are larger than A[i] and that have been seen so far. The span of A[i] is then the difference between i and the index of the top element of the stack.

```
int* find_spans(int A[], int n) {
    int* spans = (int*) malloc(n * sizeof(int));
    int* stack = (int*) malloc(n * sizeof(int));
    int top = -1;
    for (int i = 0; i < n; i++) {
        while (top >= 0 && A[stack[top]] <= A[i])
            top--;
        spans[i] = (top >= 0) ? (i - stack[top]) : (i + 1);
        stack[++top] = i;
    }
    free(stack);
    return spans;
}
```

Time Complexity: Each index of the array is pushed into the stack exactly once and also popped from the stack at most once. The statements in the while loop are executed at most $n$ times. Even though the algorithm has nested loops, the complexity is $O(n)$ as the inner loop is executing only $n$ times during the course of the algorithm (trace out an example and see how many times the inner loop becomes successful). Space Complexity: $O(n)$ [for stack].

**Problem-23** **Largest rectangle under histogram:** A histogram is a polygon composed of a sequence of rectangles aligned at a common base line. For simplicity, assume that the rectangles have equal widths but may have different heights. For example, the figure on the left shows a histogram that consists of rectangles with the heights 3, 2, 5, 6, 1, 4, 4, measured in units where 1 is the width of the rectangles. Here our problem is: given an array with heights of rectangles (assuming width is 1), we need to find the largest rectangle possible. For the given example, the largest rectangle is the shared part.

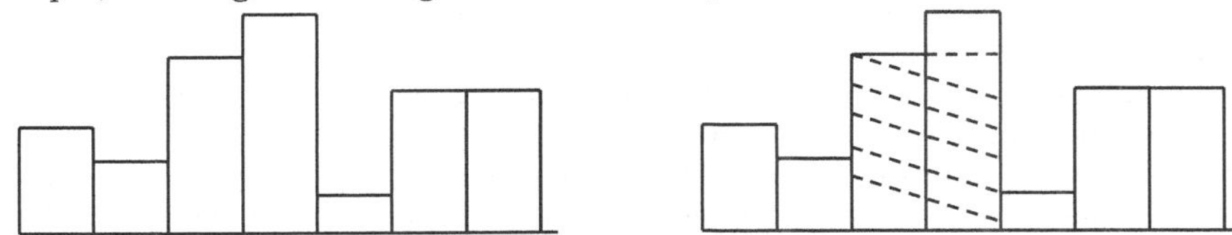

**Solution:** The first insight is to identify which rectangles to be considered for the solution: those which cover a contiguous range of the input histogram and whose height equals the minimum bar height in the range (rectangle height cannot exceed the minimum height in the range and there's no point in considering a height less than the minimum height because we can just increase the height to the minimum height in the range and get a better solution). This greatly constrains the set of rectangles we need to consider. Formally, we need to consider only those rectangles with $width = j - i + 1$ $(0 = i = j < n)$ and $height = min(A[i..j])$.

At this point, we can directly implement this solution.

```
int findMin(vector<int> &A, int i, int j){
    int min = A[i];
    while(i <= j){
        if (min > A[i])
            min = A[i];
            i++;
    }
    return min;
}
int largestHistrogram(vector<int> &A) {
    int maxArea = 0;
    for (int i = 0; i < A.size(); i++) {
        for (int j = i, minimum_height = A[i]; j < A.size(); j++) {
            minimum_height = findMin(A, i, j);
            maxArea = max(maxArea, (j-i+1) * minimum_height);
        }
    }
    return maxArea;
}
```

There are only $n^2$ choices for i and j. If we naively calculate the minimum height in the range [i..j], this will have time complexity O($n^3$).

Instead, we can keep track of the minimum height in the inner loop for j, leading to the following implementation with O($n^2$) time complexity and O(1) auxiliary space complexity.

```
int largestHistogram(vector<int> &A) {
    int maxArea = 0;
    for (int i = 0; i < A.size(); i++) {
        for (int j = i, minimum_height = A[i]; j < A.size(); j++) {
            minimum_height = min(minimum_height, A[j]);
            maxArea = max(maxArea, (j-i+1) * minimum_height);
        }
    }
    return maxArea;
}
```

**Problem-24** For Problem-23, can we improve the time complexity?

**Solution:** We are still doing a lot of repeated work by considering all $n^2$ rectangles. There are only $n$ possible heights. For each position j, we need to consider only 1 rectangle: the one with height = A[j] and width = k-i+1, where 0=i<=j<=k<n, A[i..k] >= A[j], A[i-1] < A[j] and A[k+1] < A[j].

**Linear search using a stack of incomplete sub problems:** There are many ways of solving this problem. *Judge* has given a nice algorithm for this problem which is based on stack. Process the elements in left-to-right order and maintain a stack of information about started but unfinished sub histograms. The idea is to traverse the histogram from left to right, maintaining a stack of heights in non-decreasing order. Whenever a new height is encountered that is smaller than the top of the stack, the rectangles that can be formed with the heights in the stack are computed and the maximum area is recorded.

Here are the steps:

1. Create an empty stack to store the indices of the rectangles.
2. Traverse the array of heights, and for each height, do the following:
    a. If the stack is empty or the current height is greater than or equal to the height at the index on the top of the stack, push the current index onto the stack.
    b. Otherwise, keep popping indices from the stack until you find an index whose corresponding height is less than the current height. For each popped index, calculate the area of the rectangle with the height at the popped index as the height and the width as the difference between the

current index and the index at the top of the stack (or -1 if the stack is empty). Update the maximum area seen so far accordingly.

3. After traversing the entire array, if there are any indices remaining in the stack, repeat step 2b for each index until the stack is empty.

The maximum area seen during the traversal is the answer to the problem.

```
// Calculate the area of the rectangle with given height and width
int getArea(int height, int width) {
    return height * width;
}
// Find the largest rectangle under the histogram
int findLargestRectangle(int* heights, int n) {
    struct Stack* stack = createStack(n);
    int maxArea = INT_MIN;
    int i = 0;
    while (i < n) {
        if (isEmpty(stack) || heights[i] >= heights[peek(stack)]) {
            push(stack, i++);
        }
        else {
            int topIndex = pop(stack);
            int width = isEmpty(stack) ? i : i - peek(stack) - 1;
            int area = getArea(heights[topIndex], width);
            if (area > maxArea) {
                maxArea = area;
            }
        }
    }
    while (!isEmpty(stack)) {
        int topIndex = pop(stack);
        int width = isEmpty(stack) ? i : i - peek(stack) - 1;
        int area = getArea(heights[topIndex], width);
        if (area > maxArea) {
            maxArea = area;
        }
    }
    free(stack->array);
    free(stack);
    return maxArea;
}
```

At the first impression, this solution seems to be having $O(n^2)$ complexity. But if we look carefully, every element is pushed and popped at most once, and in every step of the function at least one element is pushed or popped. Therefore, the number of iterations is proportional to the number of elements in the input array, which gives a time complexity of $O(n)$. Space Complexity: $O(n)$ [for stack].

**Problem-25** On a given machine, how do you check whether the stack grows up or down?

**Solution**: Try noting down the address of a local variable. Call another function with a local variable declared in it and check the address of that local variable and compare.

```
int testStackGrowth() {
    int temporary;
    stackGrowth(&temporary);
    exit(0);
}
void stackGrowth(int *temp){
    int temp2;
    printf("\nAddress of first local valuable: %u", temp);
    printf("\nAddress of second local: %u", &temp2);
    if(temp < &temp2)
        printf("\n Stack is growing downwards");
    else
        printf("\n Stack is growing upwards");
}
```

Time Complexity: O(1). Space Complexity: O(1).

**Problem-26** Suppose there are two singly linked lists which intersect at some point and become a single linked list. The head or start pointers of both the lists are known, but the intersecting node is not known. Also, the number of nodes in each of the lists before they intersect are unknown and both lists may have a different number. *List*1 may have $n$ nodes before it reaches the intersection point and *List*2 may have $m$ nodes before it reaches the intersection point where $m$ and $n$ may be $m = n, m < n$ or $m > n$. Can we find the merging point using stacks?

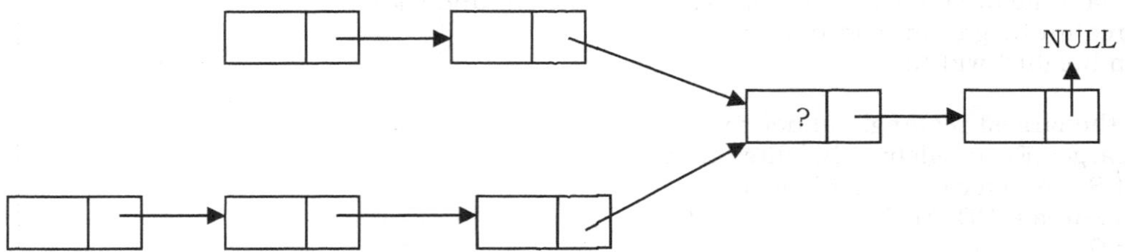


**Solution: Yes**. For algorithm refer to *Linked Lists* chapter.

**Problem-27** Given a stack of integers, how do you check whether each successive pair of numbers in the stack is consecutive or not. The pairs can be increasing or decreasing, and if the stack has an odd number of elements, the element at the top is left out of a pair. For example, if the stack of elements are [4, 5, -2, -3, 11, 10, 5, 6, 20], then the output should be true because each of the pairs (4, 5), (-2, -3), (11, 10), and (5, 6) consists of consecutive numbers.

**Solution**: Refer to *Queues* chapter.

**Problem-28** Recursively remove all adjacent duplicates: Given a string of characters, recursively remove adjacent duplicate characters from string. The output string should not have any adjacent duplicates.

| *Input*: careermonk | *Input*: mississippi |
|---|---|
| *Output*: camonk | *Output*: m |

**Solution:** This solution runs with the concept of in-place stack. When the element on stack doesn't match the current character, we add it to stack. When it matches to stack top, we skip characters until the element matches the top of stack and remove the element from stack.

```
void removeAdjacentDuplicates(char *str){
    int stkptr=-1;
    int i=0;
    int len=strlen(str);
    while (i<len){
        if (stkptr == -1 || str[stkptr]!=str[i]){
            stkptr++;
            str[stkptr]=str[i];
            i++;
        }else {
            while(i < len&& str[stkptr]==str[i])
                i++;
            stkptr--;
        }
    }
    str[stkptr+1]='\0';
}
```

Time Complexity: O($n$). Space Complexity: O(1) as the stack simulation is done in place.

**Problem-29** Given an array of elements, replace every element with nearest greater element on the right of that element.

**Solution**: One simple approach would involve scanning the array elements and for each of the elements, scan the remaining elements and find the nearest greater element.

```
void replaceWithNearestGreaterElement(int A[], int n){
    int nextNearestGreater = INT_MIN;
    int i = 0, j = 0;
    for (i=0; i<n; i++){
        nextNearestGreater = -INT_MIN;
        for (j = i+1; j<n; j++){
            if (A[i] < A[j]){
                nextNearestGreater = A[j];
```

```
                break;
            }
        }
        printf("For the element %d, %d is the nearest greater element\n", A[i], nextNearestGreater);
    }
}
```

Time Complexity: $O(n^2)$. Space Complexity: O(1).

**Problem-30** For Problem-29, can we improve the complexity?

**Solution**: The approach is pretty much similar to Problem-21. Create a stack and push the first element. For the rest of the elements, mark the current element as *nextNearestGreater*. If stack is not empty, then pop an element from stack and compare it with *nextNearestGreater*. If *nextNearestGreater* is greater than the popped element, then *nextNearestGreater* is the next greater element for the popped element. Keep popping from the stack while the popped element is smaller than *nextNearestGreater*. *nextNearestGreater* becomes the next greater element for all such popped elements. If *nextNearestGreater* is smaller than the popped element, then push the popped element back.

```
void replaceWithNearestGreaterElement(int A[], int n){
    int i = 0;
    struct Stack *S = createStack();
    int element, nextNearestGreater;
    push(S, A[0]);
    for (i=1; i<n; i++){
        nextNearestGreater = A[i];
        if (!isEmpty(S)){
        element = pop(S);
            while (element < nextNearestGreater){
                printf("For the element %d, %d is the nearest greater element\n", A[i], nextNearestGreater);
                if(isEmpty(S))
                    break;
                element = pop(S);
            }
            if (element > nextNearestGreater)
                push(S, element);
        }
        push(S, nextNearestGreater);
    }
    while (!isEmpty(S)){
        element = pop(S);
        nextNearestGreater = -INT_MIN;
        printf("For the element %d, %d is the nearest greater element\n", A[i], nextNearestGreater);
    }
}
```

Time Complexity: $O(n)$. Space Complexity: $O(n)$.

**Problem-31** How to implement a stack which will support following operations in O(1) time complexity?

- Push which adds an element to the top of stack.
- Pop which removes an element from top of stack.
- Find middle which will return middle element of the stack.
- Delete middle which will delete the middle element.

**Solution:** We can use a LinkedList data structure with an extra pointer to the middle element. Also, we need another variable to store whether the LinkedList has an even or odd number of elements.

- *Push*: Add the element to the head of the LinkedList. Update the pointer to the middle element according to variable.
- *Pop*: Remove the head of the LinkedList. Update the pointer to the middle element according to variable.
- *Find middle*: Find middle which will return middle element of the stack.
- *Delete middle*: Delete middle which will delete the middle element use the logic of Problem-43 from *Linked Lists* chapter.

**Problem-32** How do you determine whether a singly linked list is a palindrome?

**Solution**: To determine whether a singly linked list is a palindrome or not, we can follow these steps:

- Traverse the linked list and push each node's value into a stack.
- Traverse the linked list again and compare each node's value with the value at the top of the stack. If they match, pop the value from the stack and continue. If they don't match, return false.
- If we have traversed the entire linked list and all values have matched, return true.

```
// Definition for singly-linked list.
struct ListNode {
    int val;
    struct ListNode *next;
};
bool isPalindrome(struct ListNode* head){
    // Step 1: Create an empty stack and a pointer to the head of the linked list
    int stack[100000]; // Assuming maximum of 100000 nodes in the linked list
    int top = -1;
    struct ListNode* cur = head;
    // Step 2: Traverse the linked list, pushing each node's value onto the stack
    while (cur != NULL) {
        stack[++top] = cur->val;
        cur = cur->next;
    }
    // Step 3: Pop values from the stack and compare them with the corresponding values in the linked list
    cur = head;
    while (cur != NULL && top >= 0) {
        if (cur->val != stack[top--]) {
            // If the values don't match, the linked list is not a palindrome
            return false;
        }
        cur = cur->next;
    }
    // If we reach this point, all values in the linked list matched their corresponding values in the stack,
    // so the linked list is a palindrome
    return true;
}
```

The time complexity of the code is O(n), where n is the number of nodes in the linked list. This is because we iterate through the entire linked list once to push all the values onto the stack, and then we iterate through the first half of the stack to compare each value with its corresponding value in the linked list. The time complexity of both iterations is O(n/2), which is asymptotically equivalent to O(n).

The space complexity of the algorithm is also O(n) because we need to create a stack of size n to store all the values in the linked list. This is because the worst-case scenario is when the linked list is a palindrome, so we need to store all n values in the stack. For alternative solutions, refer *Linked Lists* chapter.

**Problem-33** **Remove All Adjacent Duplicates in String**: We are given a string s consisting of lowercase English letters. A duplicate removal consists of choosing two adjacent and equal letters and removing them.

**Solution**: One way to solve this problem is to use a stack data structure. We can iterate through each character in the string and push it onto the stack. If the current character is equal to the top of the stack, we pop the top element of the stack and continue. If not, we continue pushing elements onto the stack. At the end, we concatenate the elements left in the stack and return the result.

Let's walk through an example to see how this algorithm works. Suppose we have the input string "abbaca". Here are the steps of the algorithm:

1. Initialize an empty stack.
2. Iterate through each character in the string:
    - Push 'a' onto the stack.
    - Push 'b' onto the stack.
    - Pop 'b' from the stack (since it's equal to the top of the stack, which is 'b').
    - Pop 'a' from the stack (since it's equal to the top of the stack, which is 'a').
    - Push 'c' onto the stack.
    - Pop 'c' from the stack (since it's equal to the top of the stack, which is 'c').
3. Concatenate the remaining elements in the stack, which are 'a' and 'a', and return the result "aa".

So, the output for the input "abbaca" is "aa", which is the expected result after removing all adjacent duplicates.

```
char* removeDuplicates(char* s) {
    int len = strlen(s);
    char* stack = (char*)malloc(sizeof(char) * (len + 1)); // add 1 for null terminator
    int top = -1; // initialize stack top to -1
    for (int i = 0; i < len; i++) {
        if (top >= 0 && s[i] == stack[top]) {
            top--; // remove top element from stack
        } else {
            top++; // add element to stack
            stack[top] = s[i];
        }
    }
    stack[top + 1] = '\0'; // add null terminator
    return stack;
}
```

The time complexity of the algorithm is O(n), where n is the length of the input string. This is because we iterate through each character in the string once, and each character is pushed and popped from the stack at most once. The space complexity of the algorithm is also O(n), since the stack can contain at most n/2 characters (if all characters in the string are the same). Therefore, the algorithm is both time and space efficient.

Problem-34 **Minimum Number of Swaps to Make the String Balanced**: We are given a 0-indexed string s of even length n. The string consists of exactly n / 2 opening brackets '[' and n / 2 closing brackets ']'. A string is called balanced if and only if:

- It is the empty string, or
- It can be written as AB, where both A and B are balanced strings, or
- It can be written as [C], where C is a balanced string.
- You may swap the brackets at any two indices any number of times.

Return the minimum number of swaps to make s balanced.

**Solution**: We can solve this problem using a stack. We can iterate through the string s and maintain a count of opening brackets that we have seen so far. When we see a closing bracket, we can check if we have an opening bracket on the top of the stack. If we do, we can pop the opening bracket from the stack, since it has been paired with the current closing bracket. If we don't have an opening bracket on the stack, we need to swap the current closing bracket with an opening bracket that we have not yet used.

```
int min_swaps(char* s) {
    int n = strlen(s);
    int stack[n/2];
    int top = -1;
    int swaps = 0;
    for (int i = 0; i < n; i++) {
        if (s[i] == '[') {
            stack[++top] = i;
        } else {
            if (top >= 0 && s[stack[top]] == '[') {
                top--;
            } else {
                swaps++;
            }
        }
    }
    return swaps;
}
```

The time complexity of the min_swaps function is O(n), where n is the length of the input string s. This is because we iterate through each character in the string exactly once.

The space complexity of the function is also O(n), since the maximum size of the stack is n/2 (since the input string has n/2 opening and n/2 closing brackets) and we may need to store additional opening brackets that we have not yet used in the stack.

Problem-35 Given a stack of integers, how do you check whether each successive pair of numbers in the stack is consecutive or not. The pairs can be increasing or decreasing, and if the stack has an odd number of elements, the element at the top is left out of a pair. For example, if the stack of elements are [4, 5, -2, -3, 11, 10, 5, 6, 20], then the output should be true because each of the pairs (4, 5), (-2, -3), (11, 10), and (5, 6) consists of consecutive numbers.

**Solution**: To solve this problem, we can use a stack and iterate over the stack to check if each successive pair of elements is consecutive or not.

Here is the algorithm:

1. Pop the first two elements from the stack.
2. Check if the absolute difference between the two elements is 1. If it is not, return false.
3. If the difference is 1, remember the sign of the difference.
4. Repeat steps 1-3 until there are no more pairs to check.
5. If all pairs have been checked and passed the consecutive test, return true. Otherwise, return false.

```
#include <stdio.h>
#include <stdlib.h>
#include <stdbool.h>
#define STACK_SIZE 100
struct Stack {
    int items[STACK_SIZE];
    int top;
};
void push(struct Stack *s, int value) {
    if (s->top == STACK_SIZE - 1) {
        printf("Stack is full\n");
    } else {
        s->top++;
        s->items[s->top] = value;
    }
}
int pop(struct Stack *s) {
    if (s->top == -1) {
        printf("Stack is empty\n");
        return -1;
    } else {
        int value = s->items[s->top];
        s->top--;
        return value;
    }
}
bool isConsecutivePair(struct Stack *s) {
    if (s->top < 1) {
        return true;
    }
    int prev, curr;
    prev = pop(s);
    while (s->top > 0) {
        curr = pop(s);
        if (abs(prev - curr) != 1) {
            return false;
        }
        prev = pop(s);
    }
    return true;
}
```

The time complexity of the given algorithm is O(n), where n is the number of elements in the stack. This is because we are iterating over each pair of elements in the stack exactly once. The space complexity of the algorithm is also O(n), as we are using a stack to store the elements. However, the actual space used by the stack may be less than n, as elements are popped off as soon as we compare them. Therefore, the space used by the algorithm depends on the size of the largest consecutive sequence in the stack.

# QUEUES

## 5.1 What is a Queue Data Structure?

A queue is a data structure used for storing data (similar to Linked Lists and Stacks). In queue, the order in which data arrives is important. In general, a queue is a line of people or things waiting to be served in sequential order starting at the beginning of the line or sequence.

**Definition:** A *queue* is an ordered list in which insertions are done at one end (*rear*) and deletions are done at other end (*front*). The first element to be inserted is the first one to be deleted. Hence, it is called First in First out (FIFO) or Last in Last out (LILO) list.

Similar to *Stacks*, special names are given to the two changes that can be made to a queue. When an element is inserted in a queue, the concept is called *EnQueue*, and when an element is removed from the queue, the concept is called *DeQueue*.

*DeQueueing* an empty queue is called *underflow* and *EnQueuing* an element in a full queue is called *overflow*. Generally, we treat them as exceptions. As an example, consider the snapshot of the queue.

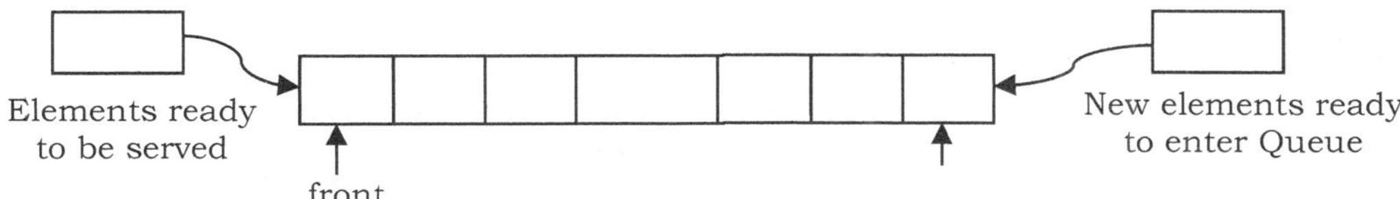


## 5.2 How are Queues Used?

The concept of a queue can be explained by observing a line at a reservation counter. When we enter the line we stand at the end of the line and the person who is at the front of the line is the one who will be served next. He will exit the queue and be served.

As this happens, the next person will come at the head of the line, will exit the queue and will be served. As each person at the head of the line keeps exiting the queue, we move towards the head of the line. Finally we will reach the head of the line and we will exit the queue and be served. This behavior is very useful in cases where there is a need to maintain the order of arrival.

## 5.3 Queue ADT

The following operations make a queue an ADT. Insertions and deletions in the queue must follow the FIFO scheme. For simplicity we assume the elements are integers.

### Main Queue Operations

- void enQueue(int data): Inserts an element at the end of the queue (at rear)
- int deQueue(): Removes and returns the element from the front of the queue

### Auxiliary Queue Operations

- int front(): Returns the element at the front without removing it
- int rear(): Returns the element at the rear without removing it
- int size(): Returns the number of elements stored in the queue
- int isEmpty (): Indicates whether no elements are stored in the queue or not

## 5.4 Exceptions

Similar to other ADTs, executing *DeQueue* on an empty queue throws an *"Empty Queue Exception"* and executing *EnQueue* on a full queue throws *"Full Queue Exception"*.

## 5.5 Applications

Following are some of the applications that use queues.

### Direct Applications

- Operating systems schedule jobs (with equal priority) in the order of arrival (e.g., a print queue).
- Simulation of real-world queues such as lines at a ticket counter or any other first-come first-served scenario requires a queue.
- Multiprogramming.
- Asynchronous data transfer (file IO, pipes, sockets).
- Waiting times of customers at call center.
- Determining number of cashiers to have at a supermarket.

### Indirect Applications

- Auxiliary data structure for algorithms
- Component of other data structures

## 5.6 Implementation

There are many ways (similar to Stacks) of implementing queue operations and some of the commonly used methods are listed below.

- Simple circular array based implementation
- Dynamic circular array based implementation
- Linked list implementation

### Why Circular Arrays?

First, let us see whether we can use simple arrays for implementing queues as we have done for stacks. We know that, in queues, the insertions are performed at one end and deletions are performed at the other end. After performing some insertions and deletions the process becomes easy to understand.

In the example shown below, it can be seen clearly that the initial slots of the array are getting wasted. So, simple array implementation for queue is not efficient. To solve this problem we assume the arrays as circular arrays. That means, we treat the last element and the first array elements as contiguous. With this representation, if there are any free slots at the beginning, the rear pointer can easily go to its next free slot.

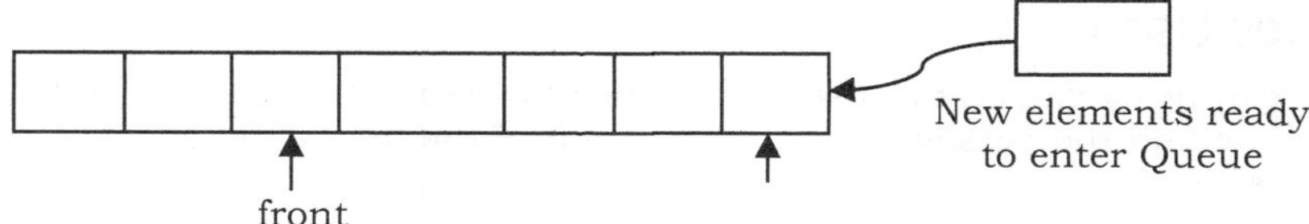


**Note:** The simple circular array and dynamic circular array implementations are very similar to stack array implementations. Refer to *Stacks* chapter for analysis of these implementations.

### Simple Circular Array Implementation

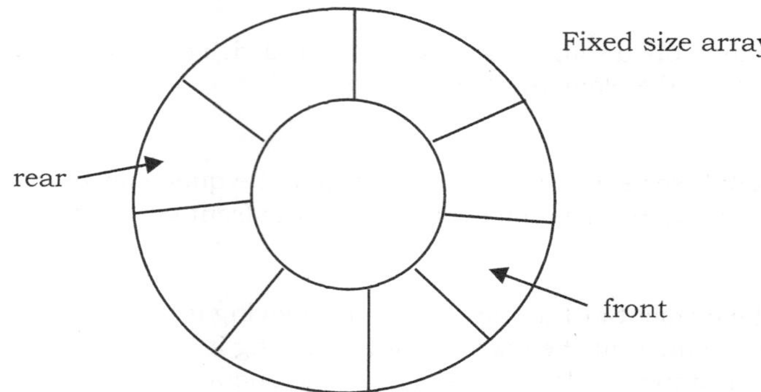


This simple implementation of Queue ADT uses an array. In the array, we add elements circularly and use two variables to keep track of the start element and end element. Generally, *front* is used to indicate the start element and *rear* is used to indicate the end element in the queue. The array storing the queue elements may become full. An *EnQueue* operation will then throw a *full queue exception*. Similarly, if we try deleting an element from an empty queue it will throw *empty queue exception*.

With stacks, the push method caused the single index field count to be increased by one, while the method pop caused it to be decreased by one. With queues, however, the two index fields, *front* and *rear*, can each only be increased by one. The field *front* is increased by one by the deQueue method, while the field rear is increased by one by the *enQueue* method. So as items leave and join the queue, the section of the array used to store the queue items will gradually shift along the array and will eventually reach its end. This is different from stacks, where the section of the array used to store the items in a stack only reaches the end of the array if the size of the stack goes beyond the size of the array.

To deal with this problem, a "wraparound" technique is used with queues implemented with arrays. When either the front or rear field is increased to the point where it would index past the end of the array, it is set *rear* to 0. Thus the state is reached where the front section of the queue is in the higher indexed section of the array and the rear section of the queue in the lower indexed section of the array.

**Note:** Initially, both front and rear points to -1 which indicates that the queue is empty.

```
#include <stdio.h>
#include <stdlib.h>
#include <limits.h>
struct Queue {
    int front, rear;
    int capacity;
    int size;
    int *array;
};
// Create an empty queue
struct Queue *createQueue(int capacity) {
    struct Queue *Q = malloc(sizeof(struct Queue));
    if(!Q)
        return NULL;
    Q->capacity = capacity;
    Q->front = Q->rear = -1;
    Q->size = 0;
    Q->array= malloc(Q->capacity * sizeof(int));
    if(!Q->array)
        return NULL;
    return Q;
}
// Returns queue size
int size(struct Queue *Q) {
    return Q->size;
}
// Returns Frnt Element of the Queue
int frontElement(struct Queue *Q) {
    return Q->array[Q->front];
}
// Returns the Rear Element of the Queue
int rearElement(struct Queue *Q) {
    return Q->array[Q->rear];
}
// Check's if Queue is empty or not
int isEmpty(struct Queue *Q) {
    // if the condition is true then 1 is returned else 0 is returned
    return (Q->size == 0);
}
// Check's if Queue is full or not
int isFull(struct Queue *Q) {
    // if the condition is true then 1 is returned else 0 is returned
    return (Q->size == Q->capacity);
}
// Adding elements in Queue
void enQueue(struct Queue *Q, int data) {
    if(isFull(Q))
        printf("Queue overflow\n");
```

```
        else {
            Q->rear = (Q->rear+1) % Q->capacity;
            Q->array[Q->rear]= data;
            if(Q->front == -1)
                Q->front = Q->rear;
            Q->size += 1;
        }
    }
    // Removes an element from front of the queue
    int deQueue(struct Queue *Q) {
        int data = INT_MIN; //or element which does not exist in Queue
        if(isEmpty(Q)){
            printf("Queue is empty\n");
            return data;
        }
        data = Q->array[Q->front];
        if(Q->front == Q->rear) {
            Q->front = Q->rear = -1;
            Q->size = 0;
        } else {
            Q->front = (Q->front+1) % Q->capacity;
            Q->size -= 1;
        }
        return data;
    }
    void deleteQueue(struct Queue *Q) {
        if(Q) {
            if(Q->array)
                free(Q->array);
            free(Q);
        }
    }
    int main() {
        // Initializing Queue
        struct Queue *Q;
        Q = createQueue(4);
        // Adding elements in Queue
        enQueue(Q, 1);
        enQueue(Q, 3);
        enQueue(Q, 7);
        enQueue(Q, 5);
        enQueue(Q, 10);
        // Printing size of Queue
        printf("\nSize of queue : %d\n", size(Q));
        // Printing front and rear element of Queue */
        printf("Front element : %d\n", frontElement(Q));
        printf("Rear element : %d\n", rearElement(Q));
        // Removing Element from Queue
        printf("\nDequeued element : %d\n", deQueue(Q));
        printf("Dequeued element : %d\n", deQueue(Q));
        printf("Dequeued element : %d\n", deQueue(Q));
        printf("Dequeued element : %d\n", deQueue(Q));
        printf("Dequeued element : %d\n", deQueue(Q));
        printf("Dequeued element : %d\n", deQueue(Q));
        enQueue(Q, 15);
        enQueue(Q, 100);
        // Printing size of Queue
        printf("\nSize of queue : %d\n", size(Q));
        // Printing front and rear element of Queue
        printf("Front element : %d\n", frontElement(Q));
        printf("Rear element : %d\n", rearElement(Q));
```

```
    // Removing Queue
    deleteQueue(Q);
    return 0;
}
```

## Performance and Limitations

**Performance:** Let $n$ be the number of elements in the queue:

| Space Complexity (for $n$ enQueue operations) | $O(n)$ |
|---|---|
| Time Complexity of enQueue() | O(1) |
| Time Complexity of deQueue() | O(1) |
| Time Complexity of isEmpty() | O(1) |
| Time Complexity of isFull() | O(1) |
| Time Complexity of size() | O(1) |
| Time Complexity of deleteQueue() | O(1) |

**Limitations:** The maximum size of the queue must be defined as prior and cannot be changed. Trying to *EnQueue* a new element into a full queue causes an implementation-specific exception.

## Dynamic Circular Array Implementation

```
#include <stdio.h>
#include <stdlib.h>
#include <limits.h>
struct Queue {
    int front, rear;
    int capacity;
    int size;
    int *array;
};
// Create an empty queue
struct Queue *createQueue(int capacity) {
    struct Queue *Q = malloc(sizeof(struct Queue));
    if(!Q)
        return NULL;
    Q->capacity = capacity;
    Q->front = Q->rear = -1;
    Q->size = 0;
    Q->array= malloc(Q->capacity * sizeof(int));
    if(!Q->array)
        return NULL;
    return Q;
}
// Returns queue size
int size(struct Queue *Q) {
    return Q->size;
}
// Returns Frnt Element of the Queue
int frontElement(struct Queue *Q) {
    return Q->array[Q->front];
}
// Returns the Rear Element of the Queue
int rearElement(struct Queue *Q) {
    return Q->array[Q->rear];
}
// Check's if Queue is empty or not
int isEmpty(struct Queue *Q) {
    // if the condition is true then 1 is returned else 0 is returned
    return (Q->size == 0);
}
// Check's if Queue is full or not
int isFull(struct Queue *Q) {
```

```
        // if the condition is true then 1 is returned else 0 is returned
        return (Q->size == Q->capacity);
    }
    void resizeQueue(struct Queue *Q) {
        int size = Q->capacity;
        Q->capacity = Q->capacity*2;
        Q->array = realloc (Q->array, sizeof(int) * Q->capacity);
        if(!Q->array) {
            printf("Memory Error");
            return;
        }
        if(Q->front > Q->rear ) {
            for(int i=0; i < Q->front; i++) {
                Q->array[i+size] =Q->array[i];
            }
            Q->rear = Q->rear + size;
        }
    }
    // Adding elements in Queue
    void enQueue(struct Queue *Q, int data) {
        if(isFull(Q))
            resizeQueue(Q);
        Q->rear = (Q->rear+1) % Q->capacity;
        Q->array[Q->rear]= data;
        if(Q->front == -1)
            Q->front = Q->rear;
        Q->size += 1;
    }
    // Removes an element from front of the queue
    int deQueue(struct Queue *Q) {
        int data = INT_MIN; //or element which does not exist in Queue
        if(isEmpty(Q)){
            printf("Queue is empty\n");
            return data;
        }
        data = Q->array[Q->front];
        if(Q->front == Q->rear) {
            Q->front = Q->rear = -1;
            Q->size = 0;
        } else {
            Q->front = (Q->front+1) % Q->capacity;
            Q->size -= 1;
        }
        return data;
    }
    void deleteQueue(struct Queue *Q) {
        if(Q) {
            if(Q->array)
                free(Q->array);
            free(Q);
        }
    }
    int main() {
        struct Queue *Q;        // Initializing Queue
        Q = createQueue(3);
        // Adding elements in Queue
        enQueue(Q, 1);
        enQueue(Q, 3);
        enQueue(Q, 7);
        enQueue(Q, 5);
        enQueue(Q, 10);
        enQueue(Q, 19);
        // Printing size of Queue
        printf("\nSize of queue : %d\n", size(Q));
```

```
    // Printing front and rear element of Queue */
    printf("Front element : %d\n", frontElement(Q));
    printf("Rear element : %d\n", rearElement(Q));
    // Removing Element from Queue
    printf("\nDequeued element : %d\n", deQueue(Q));
    printf("Dequeued element : %d\n", deQueue(Q));
    printf("Dequeued element : %d\n", deQueue(Q));
    printf("Dequeued element : %d\n", deQueue(Q));
    printf("Dequeued element : %d\n", deQueue(Q));
    printf("Dequeued element : %d\n", deQueue(Q));
    enQueue(Q, 15);
    enQueue(Q, 100);
    // Printing size of Queue
    printf("\nSize of queue : %d\n", size(Q));
    // Printing front and rear element of Queue
    printf("Front element : %d\n", frontElement(Q));
    printf("Rear element : %d\n", rearElement(Q));
    // Removing Queue
    deleteQueue(Q);
    return 0;
}
```

## Performance

Let $n$ be the number of elements in the queue.

| | |
|---|---|
| Space Complexity (for $n$ enQueue operations) | O($n$) |
| Time Complexity of enQueue() | O(1) (Average) |
| Time Complexity of deQueue() | O(1) |
| Time Complexity of QueueSize() | O(1) |
| Time Complexity of isEmpty() | O(1) |
| Time Complexity of IsFullQueue() | O(1) |
| Time Complexity of QueueSize() | O(1) |
| Time Complexity of deleteQueue() | O(1) |

## Linked List Implementation

Another way of implementing queues is by using Linked lists. *EnQueue* operation is implemented by inserting an element at the end of the list. *DeQueue* operation is implemented by deleting an element from the beginning of the list.

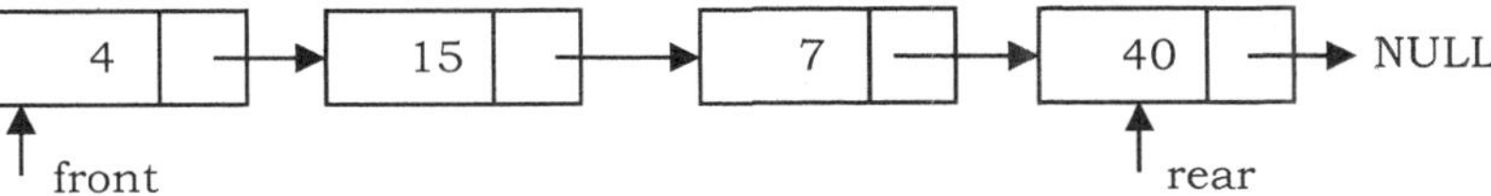


```
#include <stdio.h>
#include <stdlib.h>
struct ListNode {
    int data;
    struct ListNode *next;
};
struct Queue {
    struct ListNode *front;
    struct ListNode *rear;
};
// Create an empty queue
struct Queue *createQueue() {
    struct Queue *Q;
    struct ListNode *temp;
    Q = malloc(sizeof(struct Queue));
    if(!Q)
        return NULL;
    temp = malloc(sizeof(struct ListNode));
    Q->front = Q->rear = NULL;
    return Q;
```

```
}
// Returns queue size
int size(struct Queue *Q) {
    struct ListNode *temp = Q->front;
    int count = 0;
    if(Q->front == NULL && Q->rear == NULL)
        return 0;
    while(temp != Q->rear){
        count++;
        temp = temp->next;
    }
    if(temp == Q->rear)
        count++;
    return count;
}
// Returns Frnt Element of the Queue
int frontElement(struct Queue *Q) {
    return Q->front->data;
}
// Returns the Rear Element of the Queue
int rearElement(struct Queue *Q) {
    return Q->rear->data;
}
// Check's if Queue is empty or not
void isEmpty(struct Queue *Q) {
    if (Q->front == NULL && Q->rear == NULL)
        printf("Empty Queue\n");
    else
        printf("Queue is not Empty\n");
}
// Adding elements in Queue
void enQueue(struct Queue *Q, int num) {
    struct ListNode *temp;
    temp = (struct ListNode *)malloc(sizeof(struct ListNode));
    temp->data = num;
    temp->next = NULL;
    if (Q->rear == NULL) {
        Q->front = Q->rear = temp;
    } else {
        Q->rear->next = temp;
        Q->rear = temp;
    }
}
// Removes an element from front of the queue
void deQueue(struct Queue *Q) {
    struct ListNode *temp;
    if (Q->front == NULL) {
        printf("\nQueue is Empty \n");
        return;
    } else {
        temp = Q->front;
        Q->front = Q->front->next;
        if(Q->front == NULL){
            Q->rear = NULL;
        }
        printf("Removed Element : %d\n", temp->data);
        free(temp);
    }
}
// Print's Queue
void printQueue(struct Queue *Q) {
```

```
    struct ListNode *temp = Q->front;
    if ((Q->front == NULL) && (Q->rear == NULL)) {
        printf("Queue is Empty\n");
        return;
    }
    while (temp != NULL) {
        printf("%d", temp->data);
        temp = temp->next;
        if(temp != NULL)
            printf("-->");
    }
}
void deleteQueue(struct Queue *Q) {
    struct ListNode *temp;
    while(Q->front) {
        temp = Q->front;
        printf("Element being deleted: %d\n", temp->data);
        Q->front = Q->front->next;
        free(temp);
    }
    free(Q);
}
int main() {
    // Initializing Queue
    struct Queue *Q;
    Q = createQueue();
    // Adding elements in Queue
    enQueue(Q, 1);
    enQueue(Q, 3);
    enQueue(Q, 7);
    enQueue(Q, 5);
    enQueue(Q, 10);
    // Printing Queue
    printQueue(Q);
    // Printing size of Queue
    printf("\nSize of Queue : %d\n", size(Q));
    // Printing front and rear element of Queue
    printf("Front Element : %d\n", frontElement(Q));
    printf("Rear Element : %d\n", rearElement(Q));
    // Removing Element from Queue
    deQueue(Q);
    deQueue(Q);
    deQueue(Q);
    deQueue(Q);
    deQueue(Q);
    deQueue(Q);
    enQueue(Q, 15);
    enQueue(Q, 100);
    // Printing Queue
    printQueue(Q);
    // Printing size of Queue
    printf("\nSize of Queue : %d\n", size(Q));
    // Printing front and rear element of Queue
    printf("Front Element : %d\n", frontElement(Q));
    printf("Rear Element : %d\n", rearElement(Q));
    // Removing Queue
    deleteQueue(Q);
    return 0;
}
```

## Performance

Let $n$ be the number of elements in the queue, then

| Space Complexity (for $n$ enQueue operations) | O($n$) |
|---|---|
| Time Complexity of enQueue() | O(1) (Average) |
| Time Complexity of deQueue() | O(1) |
| Time Complexity of isEmpty() | O(1) |
| Time Complexity of deleteQueue() | O(1) |

### Comparison of Implementations

**Note**: Comparison is very similar to stack implementations and *Stacks* chapter.

## 5.7 Queues: Problems & Solutions

**Problem-1** Give an algorithm for reversing a queue $Q$. To access the queue, we are only allowed to use the methods of queue ADT.

**Solution:** To solve this question will take the help of an auxiliary stack. The steps involved will be:-

- Create an auxiliary stack S.
- Until the queue Q is not empty, deQueue all the elements of the queue Q and push on to the stack S.
- Now we have a stack in which the last element of the queue Q is at the top in the stack S.
- Until the stack is empty pop(S), pop all the elements of the stack S and enQueue to the queue Q.

```
void reverseQueue(struct Queue *Q) {
    struct Stack *S = createStack(5);
    while (!isEmptyQueue(Q))
        push(S, deQueue(Q));
    while (!isEmptyStack(S))
        enQueue(Q, pop(S));
}
```

Time Complexity: O($n$).

**Problem-2** How can you implement a queue using two stacks?

**Solution**: Let S1 and S2 be the two stacks to be used in the implementation of queue. All we have to do is to define the enQueue and deQueue operations for the queue.

```
struct Queue {
    struct Stack *S1;       // for enQueue
    struct Stack *S2;       // for deQueue
};
```

**EnQueue Algorithm**

- Just push on to stack S1

```
void enQueue(struct Queue *Q, int data) {
    push(Q→S1, data);
}
```

Time Complexity: O(1).

**DeQueue Algorithm**

- If stack S2 is not empty then pop from S2 and return that element.
- If stack is empty, then transfer all elements from S1 to S2 and pop the top element from S2 and return that popped element [we can optimize the code a little by transferring only $n-1$ elements from S1 to S2 and pop the $n^{th}$ element from S1 and return that popped element].
- If stack S1 is also empty then throw error.

```
int deQueue(struct Queue *Q) {
    if(!isEmpty(Q->S2))
        return pop(Q->S2);
    else {
        while( !isEmpty(Q->S1) )
            push(Q->S2, pop(Q->S1));
        return pop(Q->S2);
    }
}
```

Time Complexity: From the algorithm, if the stack S2 is not empty then the complexity is O(1). If the stack S2 is empty, then we need to transfer the elements from S1 to S2. But if we carefully observe, the number of transferred elements and the number of popped elements from S2 are equal. Due to this the average complexity of pop operation in this case is O(1). The amortized complexity of pop operation is O(1).

**Problem-3** Show how you can efficiently implement one stack using two queues. Analyze the running time of the stack operations.

**Solution:** Yes, it is possible to implement the Stack ADT using 2 implementations of the Queue ADT. One of the queues will be used to store the elements and the other to hold them temporarily during the *pop* and *top* methods. The *push* method would *enqueue* the given element onto the storage queue. The *top* method would transfer all but the last element from the storage queue onto the temporary queue, save the front element of the storage queue to be returned, transfer the last element to the temporary queue, then transfer all elements back to the storage queue. The *pop* method would do the same as top, except instead of transferring the last element onto the temporary queue after saving it for return, that last element would be discarded. Let Q1 and Q2 be the two queues to be used in the implementation of stack. All we have to do is to define the *push* and *pop* operations for the stack.

```
struct Stack {
    struct Queue *Q1;
    struct Queue *Q2;
};
```

In the algorithms below, we make sure that one queue is always empty.

**Push Operation Algorithm:** Insert the element in whichever queue is not empty.

- Check whether queue Q1 is empty or not. If Q1 is empty then Enqueue the element into Q2.
- Otherwise enQueue the element into Q1.

```
void push(struct Stack *S, int data) {
  if(isEmpty(S→Q1))
     enQueue(S→Q2, data);
  else
     enQueue(S→Q1, data);
}
```

Time Complexity: O(1).

**Pop Operation Algorithm:** Transfer $n - 1$ elements to the other queue and delete last from queue for performing pop operation.

- If queue Q1 is not empty then transfer $n - 1$ elements from Q1 to Q2 and then, deQueue the last element of Q1 and return it.
- If queue Q2 is not empty then transfer $n - 1$ elements from Q2 to Q1 and then, deQueue the last element of Q2 and return it.

```
int pop(struct Stack *S) {
  int i, size;
  if(isEmpty(S→Q2)) {
        size = size(S→Q1);
        i = 0;
          while(i < size-1) {
          enQueue(S→Q2, deQueue(S→Q1));
          i++;
          }
        return deQueue(S→Q1);
  }
  else {
        size = size(S→Q2);
        while(i < size-1) {
          enQueue(S→Q1, deQueue(S→Q2));
          i++;
        }
     return deQueue(S→Q2);
  }
}
```

Time Complexity: Running time of pop operation is $O(n)$ as each time pop is called, we are transferring all the elements from one queue to the other.

**Problem-4** **Maximum sum in sliding window:** Given array A[] with sliding window of size $w$ which is moving from the very left of the array to the very right. Assume that we can only see the $w$ numbers in the window. Each time the sliding window moves rightwards by one position. For example: The array is [1 3 -1 -3 5 3 6 7], and $w$ is 3.

| Window position | Max |
|---|---|
| [1 3 -1] -3 5 3 6 7 | 3 |
| 1 [3 -1 -3] 5 3 6 7 | 3 |
| 1 3 [-1 -3 5] 3 6 7 | 5 |
| 1 3 -1 [-3 5 3] 6 7 | 5 |
| 1 3 -1 -3 [5 3 6] 7 | 6 |
| 1 3 -1 -3 5 [3 6 7] | 7 |

**Input**: A long array A[], and a window width $w$. **Output**: An array B[], B[i] is the maximum value from A[i] to A[i+w-1].
**Requirement**: Find a good optimal way to get B[i]

**Solution:** This problem can be solved with doubly ended queue (which supports insertion and deletion at both ends). Refer *Priority Queues* chapter for algorithms.

**Problem-5** Given a queue Q containing $n$ elements, transfer these items on to a stack S (initially empty) so that front element of Q appears at the top of the stack and the order of all other items is preserved. Using enQueue and deQueue operations for the queue, and push and pop operations for the stack, outline an efficient O($n$) algorithm to accomplish the above task, using only a constant amount of additional storage.

**Solution**: Assume the elements of queue Q are $a_1, a_2 \ldots a_n$. Dequeuing all elements and pushing them onto the stack will result in a stack with $a_n$ at the top and $a_1$ at the bottom. This is done in O($n$) time as deQueue and each push require constant time per operation. The queue is now empty. By popping all elements and pushing them on the queue we will get $a_1$ at the top of the stack. This is done again in O($n$) time.

As in big-oh arithmetic we can ignore constant factors. The process is carried out in O($n$) time. The amount of additional storage needed here has to be big enough to temporarily hold one item.

**Problem-6** A queue is set up in a circular array A[0..n - 1] with front and rear defined as usual. Assume that $n - 1$ locations in the array are available for storing the elements (with the other element being used to detect full/empty condition). Give a formula for the number of elements in the queue in terms of *rear, front*, and $n$.

**Solution**: Consider the following figure to get a clear idea of the queue.

- Rear of the queue is somewhere clockwise from the front.
- To enQueue an element, we move *rear* one position clockwise and write the element in that position.
- To deQueue, we simply move *front* one position clockwise.
- Queue migrates in a clockwise direction as we enQueue and deQueue.
- Emptiness and fullness to be checked carefully.
- Analyze the possible situations (make some drawings to see where *front* and *rear* are when the queue is empty, and partially and totally filled). We will get this:

$$Number\ Of\ Elements = \begin{cases} rear - front + 1 & \text{if rear == front} \\ rear - front + n & \text{otherwise} \end{cases}$$

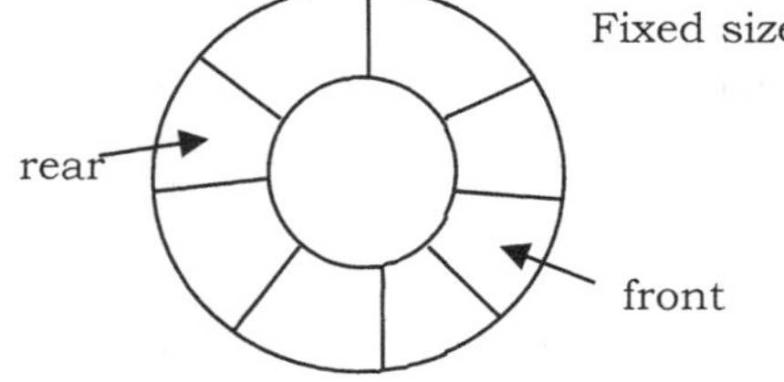


**Problem-7** What is the most appropriate data structure to print elements of queue in reverse order?

**Solution**: Stack.

**Problem-8** Implement doubly ended queues. A double-ended queue is an abstract data structure that implements a queue for which elements can only be added to or removed from the front (head) or back (tail). It is also often called a head-tail linked list.

**Solution:**

```
void pushBackDEQ(struct ListNode **head, int data){
    struct ListNode *newNode = (struct ListNode*) malloc(sizeof(struct ListNode));
    newNode→data = data;
```

```
    if(*head == NULL){
        *head = newNode;
        (*head)→next = *head;
        (*head)→prev = *head;
    }
    else{
        newNode→prev = (*head)→prev;
        newNode→next = *head;
        (*head)→prev→next = newNode;
        (*head)→prev = newNode;
    }
}
void pushFrontDEQ(struct ListNode **head, int data){
    pushBackDEQ(head,data);
    *head = (*head)→prev;
}
int popBackDEQ(struct ListNode **head){
    int data;
    if( (*head)→prev == *head ){
        data = (*head)→data;
        free(*head);
        *head = NULL;
    }
    else{
        struct ListNode *newTail = (*head)→prev→prev;
        data = (*head)→prev→data;
        newTail→next = *head;
        free((*head)→prev);
        (*head) →prev = newTail;
    }
    return data;
}
int popFront(struct ListNode **head){
    int data;
    *head = (*head)→next;
    data = popBackDEQ(head);
    return data;
}
```

**Problem-9** Given a stack of integers, how do you check whether each successive pair of numbers in the stack is consecutive or not. The pairs can be increasing or decreasing, and if the stack has an odd number of elements, the element at the top is left out of a pair. For example, if the stack of elements are [4, 5, -2, -3, 11, 10, 5, 6, 20], then the output should be true because each of the pairs (4, 5), (-2, -3), (11, 10), and (5, 6) consists of consecutive numbers.

**Solution**:

```
int checkStackPairwiseOrder(struct Stack *s) {
    struct Queue *q = createQueue();
    int pairwiseOrdered = 1;
    while (!isEmptyStack(s))
        enQueue (q, pop(s));
    while (!isEmptyQueue(q))
        push(s, deQueue(q));
    while (!isEmptyStack(s)) {
        int n = pop(s);
        enQueue(q, n);
        if (!isEmptyStack(s)) {
            int m = pop(s);
            enQueue(q, m);
            if (abs(n - m) != 1) {
                pairwiseOrdered = 0;
            }
        }
```

```
    }
    while (!isEmptyQueue(q))
        push(s, DdequeueeQueue(q));
    return pairwiseOrdered;
}
```

Time Complexity: O(*n*). Space Complexity: O(*n*).

**Problem-10** Given a queue of integers, rearrange the elements by interleaving the first half of the list with the second half of the list. For example, suppose a queue stores the following sequence of values: [11, 12, 13, 14, 15, 16, 17, 18, 19, 20]. Consider the two halves of this list: first half: [11, 12, 13, 14, 15] second half: [16, 17, 18, 19, 20]. These are combined in an alternating fashion to form a sequence of interleave pairs: the first values from each half (11 and 16), then the second values from each half (12 and 17), then the third values from each half (13 and 18), and so on. In each pair, the value from the first half appears before the value from the second half. Thus, after the call, the queue stores the following values: [11, 16, 12, 17, 13, 18, 14, 19, 15, 20].

**Solution**: To solve this problem, we can use a temporary queue and two pointers to keep track of the halves of the original queue. Here is the algorithm:

- Find the midpoint of the queue by dividing the size of the queue by 2.
- Create two queues, one for the first half and one for the second half of the original queue.
- Enqueue the first half of the original queue into the first half queue and the second half of the original queue into the second half queue.
- Create a temporary queue to hold the interleaved elements.
- Use a loop to iterate over the size of the original queue, and in each iteration, alternate between dequeuing from the first half queue and the second half queue, and enqueue the dequeued element into the temporary queue.

Set the original queue to be the temporary queue.

```
void interLeavingQueue(struct Queue *q) {
    if (size(q) % 2 != 0)  return;
    struct Stack *s = createStack();
    int halfSize = size(q) / 2;
    for (int i = 0; i < halfSize; i++)
        push(s, deQueue(q));
    while (!isEmptyStack(s))
        enQueue (q, pop(s));
    for (int i = 0; i < halfSize; i++)
        enQueue (q, deQueue(q));
    for (int i = 0; i < halfSize; i++)
        push(s, deQueue(q));
    while (!isEmptyStack(s)) {
        enQueue (q, pop(s));
        enQueue (q, deQueue(q));
    }
}
```

Time Complexity: O(*n*). Space Complexity: O(*n*).

**Problem-11** Given an integer *k* and a queue of integers, how do you reverse the order of the first *k* elements of the queue, leaving the other elements in the same relative order? For example, if *k*=4 and queue has the elements [10, 20, 30, 40, 50, 60, 70, 80, 90]; the output should be [40, 30, 20, 10, 50, 60, 70, 80, 90].

**Solution**: To reverse the order of the first k elements of the queue, we can follow the following algorithm:

- Initialize an empty stack.
- Dequeue the first k elements from the queue and push them onto the stack.
- Enqueue the elements from the stack back into the queue.
- Dequeue the remaining elements from the queue and enqueue them back into the queue.

```
void reverseQueueFirstKElements(int k, struct Queue *q) {
    if (q == Null || k > size(q)) {
        return;
    }
    else if (k > 0) {
        struct Stack *s = createStack();
        for (int i = 0; i < k; i++) {
            push(s, deQueue(q));
        }
        while (!isEmptyStack(s)) {
            enQueue(q, pop(s));
```

```
        }
        for (int i = 0; i < size(q) - k; i++) { // wrap around rest of elements
            enQueue (q, deQueue(q));
        }
    }
}
```

Time Complexity: O(*n*). Space Complexity: O(*n*).

**Problem-12** **Number of Recent Calls**: We have a RecentCounter class which counts the number of recent requests within a certain time frame. Implement the RecentCounter class:

- RecentCounter() Initializes the counter with zero recent requests.
- int ping(int t) Adds a new request at time t, where t represents some time in milliseconds, and returns the number of requests that has happened in the past 3000 milliseconds (including the new request). Specifically, return the number of requests that have happened in the inclusive range [t - 3000, t].

**Solution**: The RecentCounter class can be implemented using a queue data structure. When a new request is made, it is added to the end of the queue. Then, we iterate through the queue from the front, removing any elements that are older than 3000 milliseconds from the current time t. Finally, we return the size of the queue, which represents the number of requests made in the past 3000 milliseconds.

```
#include <stdio.h>
#define MAX_QUEUE_SIZE 10000
typedef struct {
    int queue[MAX_QUEUE_SIZE];
    int front;
    int rear;
} RecentCounter;
RecentCounter* recentCounterCreate() {
    RecentCounter* obj = (RecentCounter*)malloc(sizeof(RecentCounter));
    obj->front = 0;
    obj->rear = -1;
    return obj;
}
int ping(RecentCounter* obj, int t) {
    obj->rear++;
    obj->queue[obj->rear] = t;
    while (obj->queue[obj->front] < t - 3000) {
        obj->front++;
    }
    return obj->rear - obj->front + 1;
}
void recentCounterFree(RecentCounter* obj) {
    free(obj);
}
int main() {
    RecentCounter* obj = recentCounterCreate();
    printf("%d\n", ping(obj, 100)); // expected output: 1
    printf("%d\n", ping(obj, 3001)); // expected output: 0
    printf("%d\n", ping(obj, 3002)); // expected output: 1
    printf("%d\n", ping(obj, 7000)); // expected output: 0
    recentCounterFree(obj);
    return 0;
}
```

The time complexity of the ping() function in the RecentCounter class implementation is O(n), where n is the number of requests in the queue. This is because in the worst case, we may need to remove all requests from the front of the queue that are older than 3000ms, which can take up to n iterations of the while loop. However, since the maximum size of the queue is limited to 10000 in this implementation, the worst-case time complexity is also limited.

The space complexity of the RecentCounter class implementation is O(n), where n is the number of requests in the queue. This is because we need to store all requests in the queue. However, since the maximum size of the queue is limited to 10000 in this implementation, the worst-case space complexity is also limited.

**Problem-13** **Design Hit Counter:** Design a hit counter which counts the number of hits received in the past 5 minutes (i.e., the past 300 seconds). Your system should accept a timestamp parameter (in seconds granularity), and you may assume that calls are being made to the system in chronological order (i.e., timestamp is monotonically increasing). Several hits may arrive roughly at the same time. mplement the HitCounter class:

- HitCounter() Initializes the object of the hit counter system.
- void hit(int timestamp) Records a hit that happened at timestamp (in seconds). Several hits may happen at the same timestamp.
- int getHits(int timestamp) Returns the number of hits in the past 5 minutes from timestamp (i.e., the past 300 seconds).

**Solution**: Here's the algorithm for designing a hit counter:

- Create a data structure to store the timestamps of the hits, such as a queue or a circular buffer.
- When a hit occurs, add its timestamp to the data structure.
- When getHits() is called, iterate through the data structure and count the number of timestamps that fall within the past 5 minutes from the given timestamp.

Here's a high-level algorithm for designing a hit counter class that counts the number of hits received in the past 5 minutes:

- Create a circular buffer of size 300 to store the timestamps of the hits.
- Initialize the head index of the buffer to 0, the tail index to -1, and the size to 0.
- Implement a hit method that takes a timestamp parameter and records a hit that happened at that timestamp. If the timestamp is the same as the tail timestamp in the buffer, increment its frequency. Otherwise, add the timestamp to the buffer and set its frequency to 1. If the buffer size exceeds 300, remove the oldest timestamp by incrementing the head index and decrementing the size.
- Implement a getHits method that takes a timestamp parameter and returns the number of hits in the past 5 minutes from that timestamp. Iterate over the timestamps in the buffer starting from the head index and count the number of timestamps that fall within the 5-minute window from the given timestamp. If a timestamp is outside of the 5-minute window, stop iterating since the buffer is in chronological order.

This algorithm should provide an efficient solution to the problem of counting the number of hits received in the past 5 minutes, assuming that the calls are being made to the system in chronological order.

```
#include <stdlib.h>
typedef struct {
    int *timestamps;
    int head;
    int tail;
    int size;
} HitCounter;
/** Initialize your data structure here. */
HitCounter* hitCounterCreate() {
    HitCounter *hc = (HitCounter *) malloc(sizeof(HitCounter));
    hc->timestamps = (int *) calloc(300, sizeof(int));
    hc->head = 0;
    hc->tail = 0;
    hc->size = 0;
    return hc;
}
/** Record a hit.
    @param timestamp - The current timestamp (in seconds granularity). */
void hitCounterHit(HitCounter* obj, int timestamp) {
    if (obj->size > 0 && timestamp == obj->timestamps[obj->tail]) {
        // If the current timestamp is the same as the tail timestamp,
        // increment the frequency of the tail timestamp
        obj->timestamps[obj->tail]++;
    } else {
        // Otherwise, add the current timestamp to the buffer and set its frequency to 1
        obj->tail = (obj->tail + 1) % 300;
        obj->timestamps[obj->tail] = timestamp;
        obj->size++;
        if (obj->size > 300) {
            obj->size = 300;
            obj->head = (obj->head + 1) % 300;
```

```
        }
      }
    }
    /** Return the number of hits in the past 5 minutes.
       @param timestamp - The current timestamp (in seconds granularity). */
    int hitCounterGetHits(HitCounter* obj, int timestamp) {
       int count = 0;
       for (int i = 0; i < obj->size; i++) {
          int j = (obj->head + i) % 300;
          if (timestamp - obj->timestamps[j] < 300) {
             count++;
          } else {
             // If the timestamp at position j is outside of the 5-minute window,
             // we can stop iterating since the buffer is in chronological order
             break;
          }
       }
       return count;
    }
    /** Deallocates memory previously allocated for the hit counter. */
    void hitCounterFree(HitCounter* obj) {
       free(obj->timestamps);
       free(obj);
    }
```

The hit method has O(1) time complexity since it only involves adding or updating a timestamp in the circular buffer, which has a fixed size of 300.

The getHits method has O(min(n, 300)) time complexity, where n is the number of hits in the buffer. The method iterates over the timestamps in the buffer starting from the head index and counting the number of timestamps that fall within the 5-minute window from the given timestamp. The worst-case scenario is when all the hits in the buffer fall within the 5-minute window, which would result in iterating over all n hits in the buffer. However, since the buffer has a fixed size of 300, the number of hits that are older than 5 minutes is limited to 300, so the worst-case time complexity is O(min(n, 300)).

CHAPTER

# TREES

## 6.1 What is a Tree?

A *tree* is a data structure similar to a linked list but instead of each node pointing simply to the next node in a linear fashion, each node points to a number of nodes. Tree is an example of a non-linear data structure. A *tree* structure is a way of representing the hierarchical nature of a structure in a graphical form.

In trees ADT (Abstract Data Type), the order of the elements is not important. If we need ordering information, linear data structures like linked lists, stacks, queues, etc. can be used.

## 6.2 Glossary

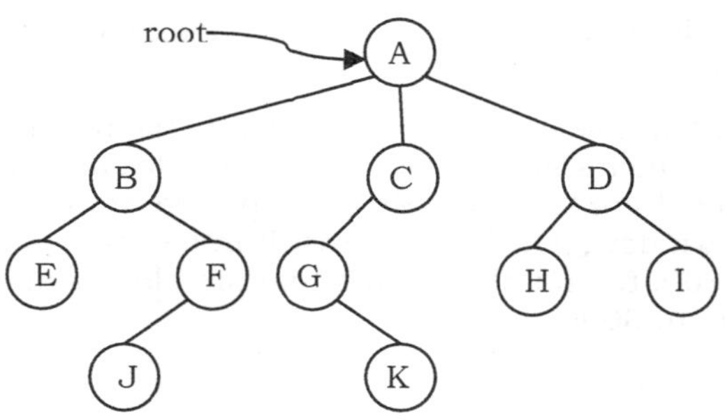


- The *root* of a tree is the node with no parents. There can be at most one root node in a tree (node $A$ in the above example).
- An *edge* refers to the link from parent to child (all links in the figure).
- A node with no children is called *leaf* node ($E, J, K, H$ and $I$).
- Children of same parent are called *siblings* ($B, C, D$ are siblings of $A$, and $E, F$ are the siblings of $B$).
- A node $p$ is an *ancestor* of node $q$ if there exists a path from *root* to $q$ and $p$ appears on the path. The node $q$ is called a *descendant* of $p$. For example, $A, C$ and $G$ are the ancestors of $K$.
- The set of all nodes at a given depth is called the *level* of the tree ($B, C$ and $D$ are the same level). The root node is at level zero.

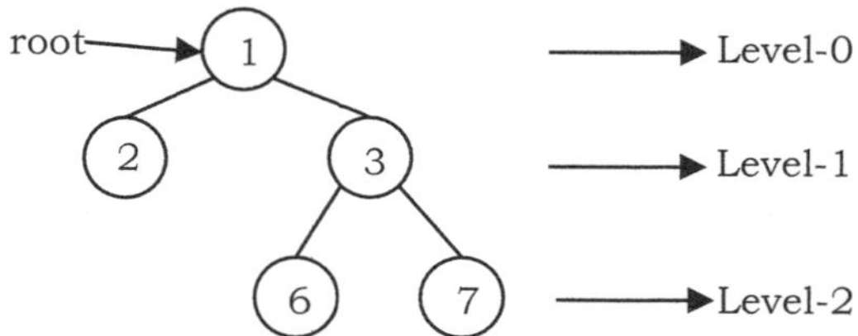


- The *depth* of a node is the length of the path from the root to the node (depth of $G$ is 2, $A - C - G$).
- The *height* of a node is the length of the path from that node to the deepest node. The height of a tree is the length of the path from the root to the deepest node in the tree. A (rooted) tree with only one node (the root) has a height of zero. In the previous example, the height of $B$ is 2 ($B - F - J$).
- *Height of the tree* is the maximum height among all the nodes in the tree and *depth of the tree* is the maximum depth among all the nodes in the tree. For a given tree, depth and height returns the same value. But for individual nodes we may get different results.

- The size of a node is the number of descendants it has including itself (the size of the subtree $C$ is 3).
- If every node in a tree has only one child (except leaf nodes) then we call such trees *skew trees*. If every node has only left child then we call them *left skew trees*. Similarly, if every node has only right child then we call them *right skew trees*.

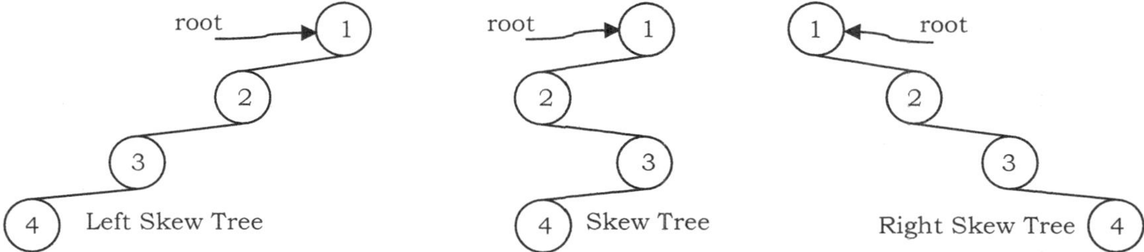


## 6.3 Binary Trees

A tree is called *binary tree* if each node has zero child, one child or two children. Empty tree is also a valid binary tree. We can visualize a binary tree as consisting of a root and two disjoint binary trees, called the left and right subtrees of the root.

**Generic Binary Tree**

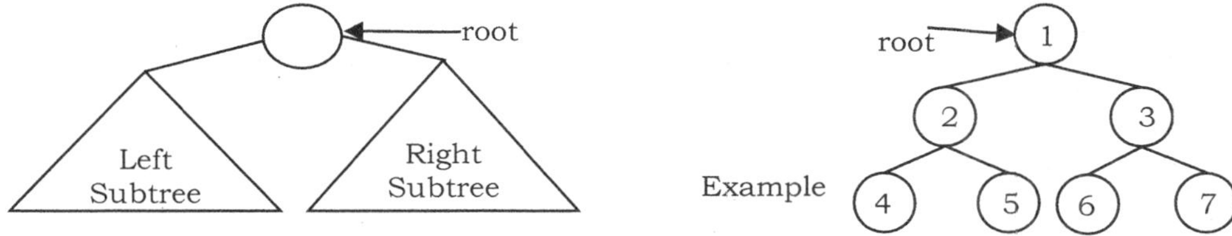


## 6.4 Types of Binary Trees

**Strict Binary Tree:** A binary tree is called *strict binary tree* if each node has exactly two children or no children.

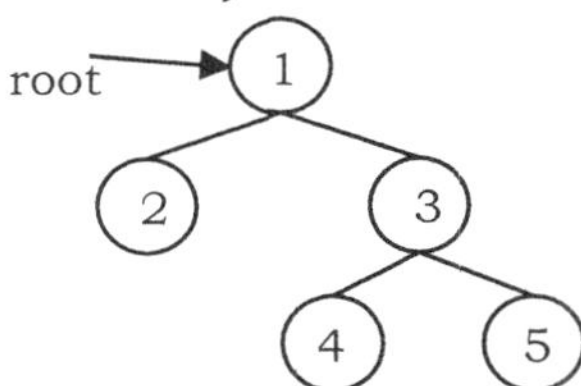


**Full Binary Tree:** A binary tree is called *full binary tree* if each node has exactly two children and all leaf nodes are at the same level.

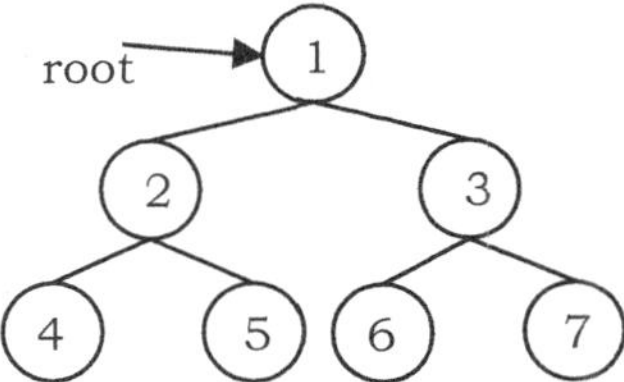


**Complete Binary Tree:** Before defining the *complete binary tree*, let us assume that the height of the binary tree is $h$. In complete binary trees, if we give numbering for the nodes by starting at the root (let us say the root node has 1) then we get a complete sequence from 1 to the number of nodes in the tree. While traversing we should give numbering for NULL pointers also. A binary tree is called *complete binary tree* if all leaf nodes are at height $h$ or $h - 1$ and also without any missing number in the sequence.

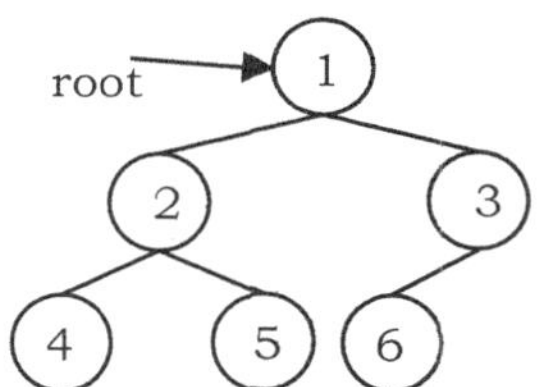

## 6.5 Properties of Binary Trees

For the following properties, let us assume that the height of the tree is $h$. Also, assume that root node is at height zero.

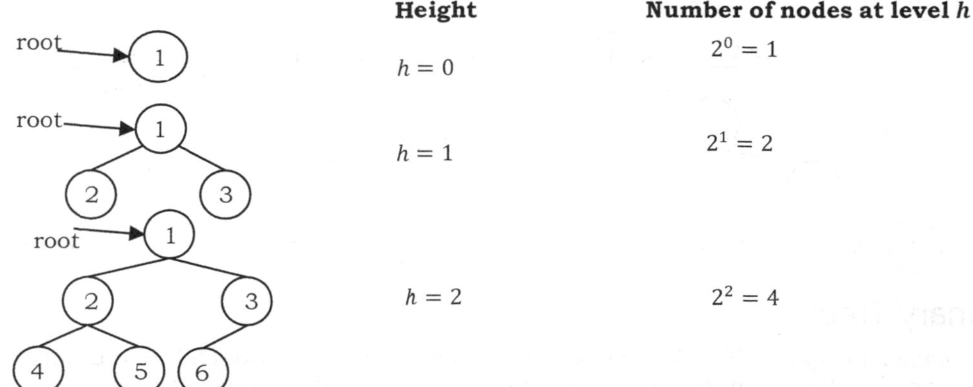


From the diagram we can infer the following properties:

- The number of nodes $n$ in a full binary tree is $2^{h+1} - 1$. Since, there are $h$ levels we need to add all nodes at each level $[2^0 + 2^1 + 2^2 + \cdots + 2^h = 2^{h+1} - 1]$.
- The number of nodes $n$ in a complete binary tree is between $2^h$ (minimum) and $2^{h+1} - 1$ (maximum). For more information on this, refer to *Priority Queues* chapter.
- The number of leaf nodes in a full binary tree is $2^h$.
- The number of None links (wasted pointers) in a complete binary tree of $n$ nodes is $n + 1$.

### Structure of Binary Trees

Now let us define structure of the binary tree. For simplicity, assume that the data of the nodes are integers. One way to represent a node (which contains data) is to have two links which point to left and right children along with data fields as shown below:

```
struct BinaryTreeNode {
    int data;
    struct BinaryTreeNode *left;
    struct BinaryTreeNode *right;
};
```

**Note:** In trees, the default flow is from parent to children and it is not mandatory to show directed branches. For our discussion, we assume both the representations shown below are the same.

### Operations on Binary Trees

**Basic Operations**

- Inserting an element into a tree
- Deleting an element from a tree
- Searching for an element
- Traversing the tree

**Auxiliary Operations**

- Finding the size of the tree
- Finding the height of the tree
- Finding the level which has maximum sum
- Finding the least common ancestor (LCA) for a given pair of nodes, and many more.

## Applications of Binary Trees

Following are the some of the applications where *binary trees* play an important role:

- Expression trees are used in compilers.
- Huffman coding trees that are used in data compression algorithms.
- Binary Search Tree (BST), which supports search, insertion and deletion on a collection of items in $O(logn)$ (average).
- Priority Queue (PQ), which supports search and deletion of minimum (or maximum) on a collection of items in logarithmic time (in worst case).

# 6.6 Binary Tree Traversals

In order to process trees, we need a mechanism for traversing them, and that forms the subject of this section. The process of visiting all nodes of a tree is called *tree traversal*. Each node is processed only once but it may be visited more than once. As we have already seen in linear data structures (like linked lists, stacks, queues, etc.), the elements are visited in sequential order. But, in tree structures there are many different ways.

Tree traversal is like searching the tree, except that in traversal the goal is to move through the tree in a particular order. In addition, all nodes are processed in the *traversal but searching* stops when the required node is found.

## Traversal Possibilities

Starting at the root of a binary tree, there are three main steps that can be performed and the order in which they are performed defines the traversal type. These steps are: performing an action on the current node (referred to as "visiting" the node and denoted with "$D$"), traversing to the left child node (denoted with "$L$"), and traversing to the right child node (denoted with "$R$"). This process can be easily described through recursion. Based on the above definition there are 6 possibilities:

1. $LDR$: Process left subtree, process the current node data and then process right subtree
2. $LRD$: Process left subtree, process right subtree and then process the current node data
3. $DLR$: Process the current node data, process left subtree and then process right subtree
4. $DRL$: Process the current node data, process right subtree and then process left subtree
5. $RDL$: Process right subtree, process the current node data and then process left subtree
6. $RLD$: Process right subtree, process left subtree and then process the current node data

## Classifying the Traversals

The sequence in which these entities (nodes) are processed defines a particular traversal method. The classification is based on the order in which current node is processed. That means, if we are classifying based on current node ($D$) and if $D$ comes in the middle then it does not matter whether $L$ is on left side of $D$ or $R$ is on left side of $D$.

Similarly, it does not matter whether $L$ is on right side of $D$ or $R$ is on right side of $D$. Due to this, the total 6 possibilities are reduced to 3 and these are:

- Preorder ($DLR$) Traversal
- Inorder ($LDR$) Traversal
- Postorder ($LRD$) Traversal

There is another traversal method which does not depend on the above orders and it is:

- Level Order Traversal: This method is inspired from Breadth First Traversal (BFS of Graph algorithms).

Let us use the diagram below for the remaining discussion.

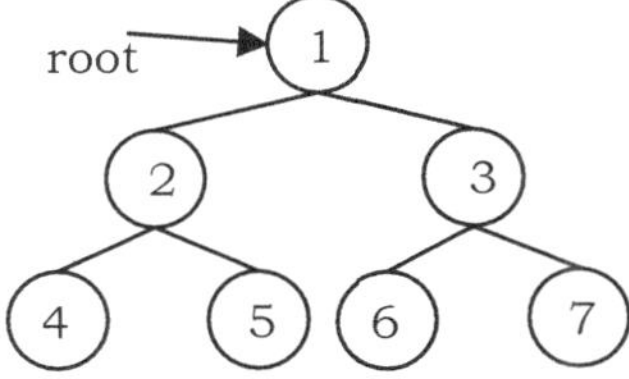


## PreOrder Traversal

In preorder traversal, each node is processed before (pre) either of its subtrees. This is the simplest traversal to understand. However, even though each node is processed before the subtrees, it still requires that some information must be maintained while moving down the tree. In the example above, 1 is processed first, then the left subtree, and this is followed by the right subtree.

Therefore, processing must return to the right subtree after finishing the processing of the left subtree. To move to the right subtree after processing the left subtree, we must maintain the root information. The obvious ADT for such information is a stack. Because of its LIFO structure, it is possible to get the information about the right subtrees back in the reverse order.

Preorder traversal is defined as follows:

- Visit the root.
- Traverse the left subtree in Preorder.
- Traverse the right subtree in Preorder.

The nodes of tree would be visited in the order: 1 2 4 5 3 6 7

```
void preOrder(struct BinaryTreeNode *root){
    if(root) {
        printf("%d",root→data);
        preOrder(root→left);
        preOrder (root→right);
    }
}
```

Time Complexity: $O(n)$. Space Complexity: $O(n)$.

### Non-Recursive Preorder Traversal

In the recursive version, a stack is required as we need to remember the current node so that after completing the left subtree we can go to the right subtree. To simulate the same, first we process the current node and before going to the left subtree, we store the current node on stack. After completing the left subtree processing, *pop* the element and go to its right subtree. Continue this process until stack is nonempty.

```
void preOrderNonRecursive(struct BinaryTreeNode *root){
    struct Stack *S = createStack();
    while(1) {
        while(root) {
            printf("%d",root→data); //Process current node
            push(S,root);
            root = root→left;       //If left subtree exists, add to stack
        }
        if(isEmpty(S))
            break;
        root = pop(S);
        // Completion of left subtree and current node, now go to right subtree
        root = root→right;
    }
    deleteStack(S);
}
```

Time Complexity: $O(n)$. Space Complexity: $O(n)$.

## InOrder Traversal

In Inorder Traversal the root is visited between the subtrees. Inorder traversal is defined as follows:

- Traverse the left subtree in Inorder.
- Visit the root.
- Traverse the right subtree in Inorder.

The nodes of tree would be visited in the order: 4 2 5 1 6 3 7

```
void inOrder(struct BinaryTreeNode *root){
    if(root) {
        inOrder (root→left);
        printf("%d",root→data);
        inOrder (root→right);
    }
}
```

Time Complexity: $O(n)$. Space Complexity: $O(n)$.

### Non-Recursive Inorder Traversal

The Non-recursive version of Inorder traversal is similar to Preorder. The only change is, instead of processing the node before going to left subtree, process it after popping (which is indicated after completion of left subtree processing).

```
void inOrderNonRecursive(struct BinaryTreeNode *root){
    struct Stack *S = createStack();
    while(1) {
        while(root) {
            push(S,root);
            // Got left subtree and keep on adding to stack
            root = root→left;
        }
        if(isEmpty(S))
            break;
        root = pop(S);
        printf("%d", root→data);    //After popping, process the current node
        // Completion of left subtree and current node, now go to right subtree
        root = root→right;
    }
    deleteStack(S);
}
```

Time Complexity: O($n$). Space Complexity: O($n$).

## PostOrder Traversal

In postorder traversal, the root is visited after both subtrees. Postorder traversal is defined as follows:

- Traverse the left subtree in Postorder.
- Traverse the right subtree in Postorder.
- Visit the root.

The nodes of the tree would be visited in the order: 4 5 2 6 7 3 1

```
void postOrder(struct BinaryTreeNode *root){
    if(root)        {
        postOrder(root→left);
        postOrder(root→right);
        printf("%d",root→data);
    }
}
```

Time Complexity: O($n$). Space Complexity: O($n$).

### Non-Recursive Postorder Traversal

In preorder and inorder traversals, after popping the stack element we do not need to visit the same vertex again. But in postorder traversal, each node is visited twice. That means, after processing the left subtree we will visit the current node and after processing the right subtree we will visit the same current node. But we should be processing the node during the second visit. Here the problem is how to differentiate whether we are returning from the left subtree or the right subtree.

We use a *previous* variable to keep track of the earlier traversed node. Let's assume *current* is the current node that is on top of the stack. When *previous* is *current's* parent, we are traversing down the tree. In this case, we try to traverse to *current's* left child if available (i.e., push left child to the stack). If it is not available, we look at *current's* right child. If both left and right child do not exist (ie, *current* is a leaf node), we print *current's* value and pop it off the stack.

If prev is *current's* left child, we are traversing up the tree from the left. We look at *current's* right child. If it is available, then traverse down the right child (i.e., push right child to the stack); otherwise print *current's* value and pop it off the stack. If *previous* is *current's* right child, we are traversing up the tree from the right. In this case, we print *current's* value and pop it off the stack.

```
void postOrderNonRecursive(struct BinaryTreeNode *root) {
    struct SimpleArrayStack *S = createStack();
    struct BinaryTreeNode *previous = NULL;
    do{
        while (root!=NULL){
```

```
            push(S, root);
            root = root->left;
        }
        while(root == NULL && !isEmpty(S)){
            root = top(S);
            if(root->right == NULL || root->right == previous){
                printf("%d ", root->data);
                pop(S);
                previous = root;
                root = NULL;
            }
            else
                root = root->right;
        }
    } while(!isEmpty(S));  // End of do-while
}
```

Time Complexity: O($n$). Space Complexity: O($n$).

## Level Order Traversal

Level order traversal is defined as follows:

- Visit the root.
- While traversing level $l$, keep all the elements at level $l + 1$ in queue.
- Go to the next level and visit all the nodes at that level.
- Repeat this until all levels are completed.

The nodes of the tree are visited in the order: 1 2 3 4 5 6 7

```
void levelOrder(struct BinaryTreeNode *root){
    struct BinaryTreeNode *temp;
    struct Queue *Q = createQueue();
    if(!root)
        return;
    enQueue(Q, root);
    while(!isEmpty(Q)){
        temp = deQueue(Q);
        //Process current node
        printf("\n %d", temp->data);
        if(temp->left)
            enQueue(Q, temp->left);
        if(temp->right)
            enQueue(Q, temp->right);
    }
    deleteQueue(Q);
}
```

Time Complexity: O($n$).
Space Complexity: O($n$). Since, in the worst case, all the nodes on the entire last level could be in the queue simultaneously.

## Binary Trees: Problems & Solutions

**Problem-1** Give an algorithm for finding maximum element in binary tree.

**Solution:** One simple way of solving this problem is: find the maximum element in left subtree, find the maximum element in right sub tree, compare them with root data and select the one which is giving the maximum value. This approach can be easily implemented with recursion.

```
int findMax(struct BinaryTreeNode *root) {
    int root_val, left, right, max = INT_MIN;
    if(root !=NULL) {
        root_val = root→data;
        left = findMax(root→left);
        right = findMax(root→right);
        // Find the largest of the three values.
        if(left > right)
```

```
            max = left;
        else max = right;
        if(root_val > max)
            max = root_val;
    }
    return max;
}
```

Time Complexity: O($n$). Space Complexity: O($n$).

**Problem-2** Give an algorithm for finding the maximum element in binary tree without recursion.

**Solution:** Using level order traversal: just observe the element's data while deleting.

```
int findMaxUsingLevelOrder(struct BinaryTreeNode *root){
    struct BinaryTreeNode *temp;
    int max = INT_MIN;
    struct Queue *Q = createQueue();
    enQueue(Q,root);
    while(!isEmpty(Q)) {
        temp = deQueue(Q);
        // largest of the three values
        if(max < temp->data)
            max = temp->data;
        if(temp->left)
            enQueue (Q, temp->left);
        if(temp->right)
            enQueue (Q, temp->right);
    }
    deleteQueue(Q);
    return max;
}
```

Time Complexity: O($n$). Space Complexity: O($n$).

**Problem-3** Give an algorithm for searching an element in binary tree.

**Solution:** Given a binary tree, return true if a node with data is found in the tree. Recurse down the tree, choose the left or right branch by comparing data with each node's data.

```
int findInBinaryTreeUsingRecursion(struct BinaryTreeNode *root, int data) {
    int temp;
    // Base case == empty tree, in that case, the data is not found so return false
    if(root == NULL)
        return 0;
    else {
        //see if found here
        if(data == root→data)
            return 1;
        else {
            // otherwise recur down the correct subtree
            temp = findInBinaryTreeUsingRecursion (root→left, data)
            if(temp != 0)
                return temp;
            else return(findInBinaryTreeUsingRecursion(root→right, data));
        }
    }
    return 0;
}
```

Time Complexity: O($n$). Space Complexity: O($n$).

**Problem-4** Give an algorithm for searching an element in binary tree without recursion.

**Solution:** We can use level order traversal for solving this problem. The only change required in level order traversal is, instead of printing the data, we just need to check whether the root data is equal to the element we want to search.

```
int searchUsingLevelOrder(struct BinaryTreeNode *root, int data){
```

```
        struct BinaryTreeNode *temp;
        struct Queue *Q = createQueue();
        enQueue(Q,root);
        while(!isEmpty(Q)) {
           temp = deQueue(Q);
           // foujnd the element
           if(data == temp->data){
              deleteQueue(Q);
              return 1;
           }
           if(temp->left)
              enQueue (Q, temp->left);
           if(temp->right)
              enQueue (Q, temp->right);
        }
        deleteQueue(Q);
        return 0;
    }
```

Time Complexity: O($n$). Space Complexity: O($n$).

**Problem-5** Give an algorithm for inserting an element into binary tree.

**Solution:** Since the given tree is a binary tree, we can insert the element wherever we want. To insert an element, we can use the level order traversal and insert the element wherever we find the node whose left or right child is NULL.

```
    void insertInBinaryTree(struct BinaryTreeNode *root, int data){
        struct Queue *Q;
        struct BinaryTreeNode *temp;
        struct BinaryTreeNode *newNode;
        newNode = (struct BinaryTreeNode *) malloc(sizeof(struct BinaryTreeNode));
        newNode→left = newNode→right = NULL;
        if(!newNode) {
           printf("Memory Error"); return;
        }
        if(!root) {
           root = newNode;
           return;
        }
        Q = createQueue();
        enQueue(Q,root);
        while(!isEmpty(Q)) {
           temp = deQueue(Q);
           if(temp→left)
              enQueue(Q, temp→left);
           else {
              temp→left=newNode;
              deleteQueue(Q);
              return;
           }
           if(temp→right)
              enQueue(Q, temp→right);
           else {
              temp→right=newNode;
              deleteQueue(Q);
              return;
           }
        }
        deleteQueue(Q);
    }
```

Time Complexity: O($n$). Space Complexity: O($n$).

**Problem-6** Give an algorithm for finding the size of binary tree.

**Solution:** Calculate the size of left and right subtrees recursively, add 1 (current node) and return to its parent.

```
// Compute the number of nodes in a tree.
int sizeOfBinaryTree(struct BinaryTreeNode *root) {
    if(root==NULL)
        return 0;
    else
        return(sizeOfBinaryTree(root→left) + 1 + sizeOfBinaryTree(root→right));
}
```

Time Complexity: $O(n)$. Space Complexity: $O(n)$.

**Problem-7** Can we solve Problem-6 without recursion?

**Solution: Yes,** using level order traversal.

```
int sizeofBTUsingLevelOrder(struct BinaryTreeNode *root){
    struct BinaryTreeNode *temp;
    if(!root)
        return 0;
    struct Queue *Q = createQueue();;
    int count = 0;
    enQueue(Q,root);
    while(!isEmpty(Q)) {
        temp = deQueue(Q);
        count++;
        if(temp→left)
            enQueue (Q, temp→left);
        if(temp→right)
            enQueue (Q, temp→right);
    }
    deleteQueue(Q);
    return count;
}
```

Time Complexity: $O(n)$. Space Complexity: $O(n)$.

**Problem-8** Give an algorithm for printing the level order data in reverse order. For example, the output for the below tree should be: 4 5 6 7 2 3 1

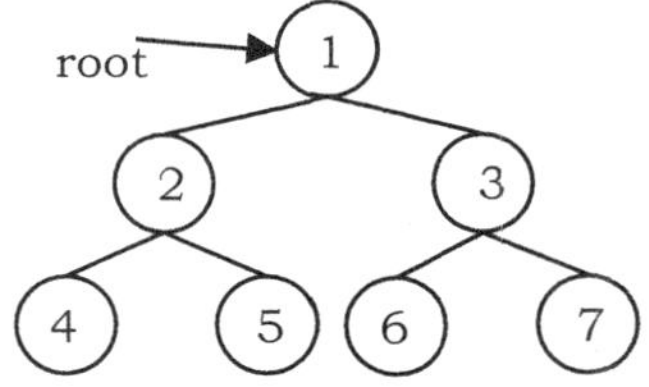


**Solution:**

```
void levelOrderTraversalInReverse(struct BinaryTreeNode *root){
    if(!root)
        return;
    struct Queue *Q = createQueue();
    struct Stack *S = createStack();
    struct BinaryTreeNode *temp;
    enQueue(Q, root);
    while(!isEmptyQueue(Q)) {
        temp = deQueue(Q);
        if(temp->right)
            enQueue(Q, temp->right);
        if(temp->left)
            enQueue (Q, temp->left);
        push(S, temp);
    }
    while(!isEmptyStack(S))
        printf("%d",pop(S)->data);
}
```

Time Complexity: $O(n)$. Space Complexity: $O(n)$.

**Problem-9** Give an algorithm for deleting the tree.

**Solution:**

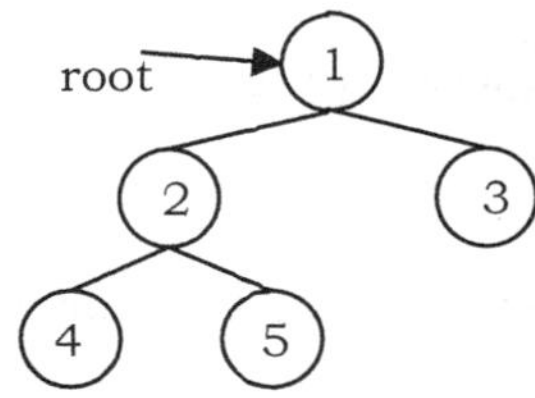


To delete a tree, we must traverse all the nodes of the tree and delete them one by one. So which traversal should we use: Inorder, Preorder, Postorder or Level order Traversal?

Before deleting the parent node we should delete its children nodes first. We can use postorder traversal as it does the work without storing anything. We can delete tree with other traversals also with extra space complexity. For the following, tree nodes are deleted in order – 4, 5, 2, 3, 1.

```
void deleteBinaryTree(struct BinaryTreeNode *root){
    if(root == NULL)
        return;
    /* first delete both subtrees */
    deleteBinaryTree(root→left);
    deleteBinaryTree(root→right);
    //Delete current node only after deleting subtrees
    free(root);
}
```

Time Complexity: $O(n)$. Space Complexity: $O(n)$.

**Problem-10** Give an algorithm for finding the height (or depth) of the binary tree.

**Solution:** Recursively calculate height of left and right subtrees of a node and assign height to the node as max of the heights of two children plus 1. This is similar to *PreOrder* tree traversal (and *DFS* of Graph algorithms).

```
int heightOfBinaryTree(struct BinaryTreeNode    *root){
    int leftheight, rightheight;
    if(root == NULL)
        return 0;
    else {
        /* compute the depth of each subtree */
        leftheight = heightOfBinaryTree(root→left);
        rightheight = heightOfBinaryTree(root→right);
        if(leftheight > rightheight)
            return(leftheight + 1);
        else
                return(rightheight + 1);
    }
}
```

Time Complexity: $O(n)$. Space Complexity: $O(n)$.

**Problem-11** Can we solve Problem-10 without recursion?

**Solution: Yes,** using level order traversal. This is similar to *BFS* of Graph algorithms. End of level is identified with NULL.

```
int findHeightofBinaryTree(struct BinaryTreeNode *root){
    if(!root)
        return 0;
    int level = 0;
    struct Queue *Q = createQueue();
    // End of first level
    enQueue(Q,NULL);
    while(!isEmpty(Q)) {
        root=deQueue(Q);
        // Completion of current level.
        if(root==NULL) {
            // Put another marker for next level.
            if(!isEmpty(Q))
```

```
                enQueue(Q, NULL);
            level++;
        }
        else {
            if(root->left)
                enQueue(Q, root->left);
            if(root->right)
                enQueue(Q, root->right);
        }
    }
    return level;
}
```

Time Complexity: $O(n)$. Space Complexity: $O(n)$.

**Problem-12** Give an algorithm for finding the deepest node of the binary tree.

**Solution:**

```
struct BinaryTreeNode *deepestNodeinBinaryTree(struct BinaryTreeNode *root){
    if(!root)
        return NULL;
    struct BinaryTreeNode *temp;
    struct Queue *Q = createQueue();
    enQueue(Q,root);
    while(!isEmpty(Q)) {
        temp = deQueue(Q);
        if(temp->left)
            enQueue(Q, temp->left);
        if(temp->right)
            enQueue(Q, temp->right);
    }
    deleteQueue(Q);
    return temp;
}
```

Time Complexity: $O(n)$. Space Complexity: $O(n)$.

**Problem-13** Give an algorithm for deleting an element (assuming data is given) from binary tree.

**Solution:** The deletion of a node in binary tree can be implemented as

- Starting at root, find the node which we want to delete.
- Find the deepest node in the tree.
- Replace the deepest node's data with node to be deleted.
- Then delete the deepest node.

**Problem-14** Give an algorithm for finding the number of leaves in the binary tree without using recursion.

**Solution:** The set of nodes whose both left and right children are NULL are called leaf nodes.

```
int numberOfLeavesInBTusingLevelOrder(struct BinaryTreeNode *root){
    if(!root)
        return 0;
    struct BinaryTreeNode *temp;
    struct Queue *Q = createQueue();
    enQueue(Q,root);
    while(!isEmpty(Q)) {
        temp = deQueue(Q);
        if(!temp->left && !temp->right)
            count++;
        else {
            if(temp->left)
                enQueue(Q, temp->left);
            if(temp->right)
                enQueue(Q, temp->right);
        }
    }
    deleteQueue(Q);
```

```
    return count;
}
```

Time Complexity: O($n$). Space Complexity: O($n$).

**Problem-15** Give an algorithm for finding the number of full nodes in the binary tree without using recursion.

**Solution:** The set of all nodes with both left and right children are called full nodes.

```
int numberOfFullNodesInBTusingLevelOrder(struct BinaryTreeNode *root){
    if(!root)
        return 0;
    struct BinaryTreeNode *temp;
    struct Queue *Q = createQueue();
    int count = 0;
    enQueue(Q,root);
    while(!isEmpty(Q)) {
        temp = deQueue(Q);
        if(temp→left && temp→right)
            count++;
        if(temp→left)
            enQueue (Q, temp→left);
        if(temp→right)
            enQueue (Q, temp→right);
    }
    deleteQueue(Q);
    return count;
}
```

Time Complexity: O($n$). Space Complexity: O($n$).

**Problem-16** Give an algorithm for finding the number of half nodes (nodes with only one child) in the binary tree without using recursion.

**Solution:** The set of all nodes with either left or right child (but not both) are called half nodes.

```
int numberOfHalfNodesInBTusingLevelOrder(struct BinaryTreeNode *root){
    if(!root)
        return 0;
    struct BinaryTreeNode *temp;
    struct Queue *Q = createQueue();
    int count = 0;
    enQueue(Q,root);
    while(!isEmpty(Q)) {
        temp = deQueue(Q);
        //we can use this condition also instead of two temp->left ^ temp->right
        if(!temp->left && temp->right || temp->left && !temp->right)
            count++;
        if(temp->left)
            enQueue (Q, temp->left);
        if(temp->right)
            enQueue (Q, temp->right);
    }
    deleteQueue(Q);
    return count;
}
```

Time Complexity: O($n$). Space Complexity: O($n$).

**Problem-17** Given two binary trees, return true if they are structurally identical.

**Solution:**

**Algorithm:**

- If both trees are NULL then return true.
- If both trees are not NULL, then compare data and recursively check left and right subtree structures.

```
//Return true if they are structurally identical.
int areStructurullySameTrees(struct BinaryTreeNode *root1, struct BinaryTreeNode *root2) {
    // both empty->1
    if(root1==NULL && root2==NULL)
```

```
        return 1;
    if(root1==NULL || root2==NULL)
        return 0;
    // both non-empty->compare them
    return(root1->data == root2->data && areStructurullySameTrees(root1->left, root2->left)
                    && areStructurullySameTrees(root1->right, root2->right));
}
```

Time Complexity: $O(n)$. Space Complexity: $O(n)$, for recursive stack.

**Problem-18** Give an algorithm for finding the diameter of the binary tree. The diameter of a tree (sometimes called the *width*) is the number of nodes on the longest path between two leaves in the tree.

**Solution:** To find the diameter of a tree, first calculate the diameter of left subtree and right subtrees recursively. Among these two values, we need to send maximum value along with current level (+1).

```
int diameterOfTree(struct BinaryTreeNode *root, int *ptr){
    int left, right;
    if(!root)
        return 0;
    left = diameterOfTree(root→left, ptr);
    right = diameterOfTree(root→right, ptr);
    if(left + right > *ptr)
        *ptr = left + right;
    return max(left, right)+1;
}
//Alternative Coding
static int diameter(struct BinaryTreeNode *root) {
    if (root == NULL)
        return 0;
    int lHeight = height(root->eft);
    int rHeight = height(root-right);
    int lDiameter = diameter(root-left);
    int rDiameter = diameter(root-right);
    return max(lHeight + rHeight + 1, max(lDiameter, rDiameter));
}
/* The function Compute the "height" of a tree. Height is the number of nodes along
the longest path from the root node down to the farthest leaf node.*/
static int height(Node root) {
    if (root == null)
        return 0;
    return 1 + max(height(root.left), height(root.right));
}
```

There is another solution and the complexity is O(n). The main idea of this approach is that the node stores its left child's and right child's maximum diameter if the node's child is the "root", therefore, there is no need to recursively call the height method. The drawback is we need to add two extra variables in the node structure.

```
int findMaxLen(Node root) {
    int nMaxLen = 0;
    if (root == null)
        return 0;
    if (root.left == null)
        root.nMaxLeft = 0;
    if (root.right == null)
        root.nMaxRight = 0;
    if (root.left != null)
        findMaxLen(root.left);
    if (root.right != null)
        findMaxLen(root.right);
    if (root.left != null) {
        int nTempMaxLen = 0;
        nTempMaxLen = (root.left.nMaxLeft > root.left.nMaxRight) ? root.left.nMaxLeft : root.left.nMaxRight;
```

```
            root.nMaxLeft = nTempMaxLen + 1;
        }
        if (root.right != null) {
            int nTempMaxLen = 0;
            nTempMaxLen = (root.right.nMaxLeft > root.right.nMaxRight) ?
                                                root.right.nMaxLeft : root.right.nMaxRight;
            root.nMaxRight = nTempMaxLen + 1;
        }
        if (root.nMaxLeft + root.nMaxRight > nMaxLen) nMaxLen = root.nMaxLeft + root.nMaxRight;
            return nMaxLen;
}
```

Time Complexity: O($n$). Space Complexity: O($n$).

**Problem-19** Give an algorithm for finding the level that has the maximum sum in the binary tree.

**Solution:** The logic is very much similar to finding the number of levels. The only change is, we need to keep track of the sums as well.

```
int findLevelwithMaxSum(struct BinaryTreeNode *root){
    if(!root)
        return 0;
    struct BinaryTreeNode *temp;
    struct Queue *Q = createQueue();
    int level=0, maxLevel=0, currentSum = 0, maxSum = 0;
    enQueue(Q,root);
    enQueue(Q,NULL);                        // End of first level.
    while(!isEmpty(Q)) {
        temp =deQueue(Q);
        // If the current level is completed then compare sums
        if(temp == NULL) {
            if(currentSum> maxSum) {
                maxSum = currentSum;
                maxLevel = level;
            }
            currentSum = 0;
            //place the indicator for end of next level at the end of queue
            if(!isEmpty(Q))
                enQueue(Q,NULL);
            level++;
        }
        else {
            currentSum += temp->data;
            if(temp->left)
                enQueue(temp, temp->left);
            if(root->right)
                enQueue(temp, temp->right);
        }
    }
    return maxLevel;
}
```

Time Complexity: O($n$). Space Complexity: O($n$).

**Problem-20** Given a binary tree, print out all its root-to-leaf paths.

**Solution:** Refer to comments in functions.

```
void printPathsRecur(struct BinaryTreeNode *root, int path[], int pathLen) {
    if(root ==NULL)
        return;
    // append this node to the path array
    path[pathLen] = root→data;
    pathLen++;
    // it's a leaf, so print the path that led to here
    if(root→left==NULL && root→right==NULL)
        printArray(path, pathLen);
    else {
```

```
            // otherwise try both subtrees
            printPathsRecur(root→left, path, pathLen);
            printPathsRecur(root→right, path, pathLen);
        }
    }
    // Function that prints out an array on a line.
    void printArray(int ints[], int len) {
        for (int i=0; i<len; i++)
            printf("%d",ints[i]);
    }
```

Time Complexity: O($n$). Space Complexity: O($n$), for recursive stack.

**Problem-21** Give an algorithm for checking the existence of path with given sum. That means, given a sum, check whether there exists a path from root to any of the nodes.

**Solution:** For this problem, the strategy is: subtract the node value from the sum before calling its children recursively, and check to see if the sum is 0 when we run out of tree.

```
int hasPathSum(struct BinaryTreeNode * root, int sum) {
    // return true if we run out of tree and sum==0
    if(root == NULL)
        return(sum == 0);
    else {
        // otherwise check both subtrees
        int remainingSum = sum - root→data;
        if((root→left && root→right) | | (!root→left && !root→right))
            return(hasPathSum(root→left, remainingSum) | | hasPathSum(root→right, remainingSum));
        else if(root→left)
            return hasPathSum(root→left, remainingSum);
        else
            return hasPathSum(root→right, remainingSum);
    }
}
```

Time Complexity: O($n$). Space Complexity: O($n$).

**Problem-22** Give an algorithm for finding the sum of all elements in binary tree.

**Solution:** Recursively, call left subtree sum, right subtree sum and add their values to current nodes data.

```
int add(struct BinaryTreeNode *root) {
    if(root == NULL)
        return 0;
    else return (root→data + add(root→left) + add(root→right));
}
```

Time Complexity: O($n$). Space Complexity: O($n$).

**Problem-23** Can we solve Problem-22 without recursion?

**Solution:** We can use level order traversal with simple change. Every time after deleting an element from queue, add the nodes data value to *sum* variable.

```
int sumofBTusingLevelOrder(struct BinaryTreeNode *root){
    if(!root)
        return 0;
    struct BinaryTreeNode *temp;
    struct Queue *Q = createQueue();
    int sum = 0;
    enQueue(Q,root);
    while(!isEmpty(Q)) {
        temp = deQueue(Q);
        sum += temp->data;
        if(temp->left)
            enQueue (Q, temp→left);
        if(temp->right)
            enQueue (Q, temp->right);
    }
    deleteQueue(Q);
```

```
    return sum;
}
```

Time Complexity: O($n$). Space Complexity: O($n$).

**Problem-24** Give an algorithm for converting a tree to its mirror. Mirror of a tree is another tree with left and right children of all non-leaf nodes interchanged. The trees below are mirrors to each other.

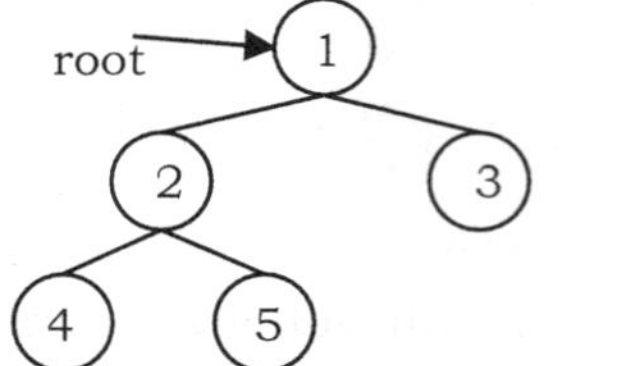

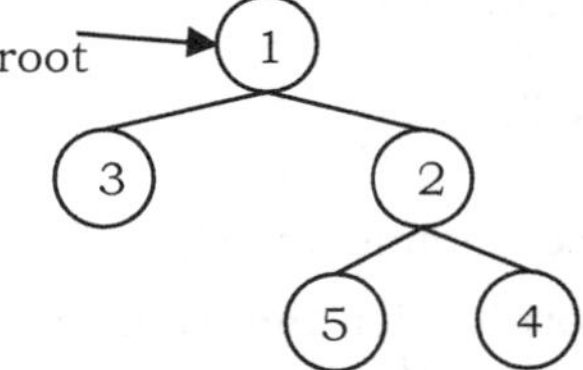


**Solution:**

```
struct BinaryTreeNode *mirrorOfBinaryTree(struct BinaryTreeNode *root){
    struct BinaryTreeNode * temp;
    if(root) {
        mirrorOfBinaryTree(root->left);
        mirrorOfBinaryTree(root->right);
        /* swap the pointers in this node */
        temp = root->left;
        root->left = root->right;
        root->right = temp;
    }
    return root;
}
```

Time Complexity: O($n$). Space Complexity: O($n$).

**Problem-25** Given two trees, give an algorithm for checking whether they are mirrors of each other.

**Solution:**

```
int areMirrors(struct BinaryTreeNode * root1, struct BinaryTreeNode * root2) {
    if(root1 == NULL && root2 == NULL) return 1;
    if(root1 == NULL || root2 == NULL) return 0;
    if(root1->data != root2->data)
        return 0;
    else
        return areMirrors(root1->left, root2->right) && areMirrors(root1->right, root2->left);
}
```

Time Complexity: O($n$). Space Complexity: O($n$).

**Problem-26** Give an algorithm for finding LCA (Least Common Ancestor) of two nodes in a Binary Tree.

**Solution:**

```
struct BinaryTreeNode *LCA(struct BinaryTreeNode *root, struct BinaryTreeNode *α, struct BinaryTreeNode
                                        *β){
    struct BinaryTreeNode *left, *right;
    if(root == NULL)
        return root;
    if(root == α || root == β)
        return root;
    left = LCA (root→left, α, β );
    right = LCA (root→right, α, β );
    if(left && right)
        return root;
    else return (left? left: right)
}
```

Time Complexity: O($n$). Space Complexity: O($n$) for recursion.

**Problem-27** Give an algorithm for constructing binary tree from given Inorder and Preorder traversals.

**Solution:** Let us consider the traversals below:

```
Inorder sequence:  D B E A F C
Preorder sequence: A B D E C F
```

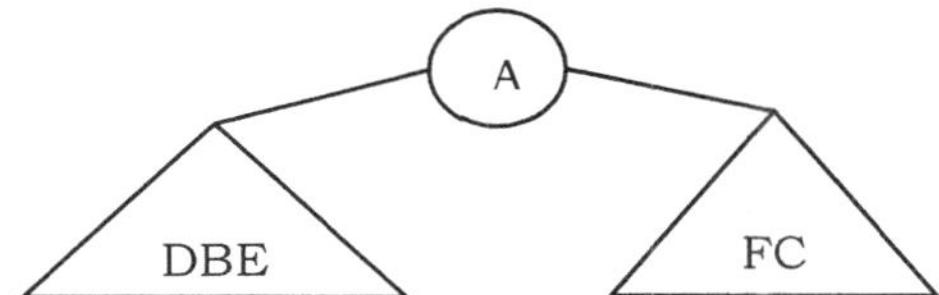


In a Preorder sequence, leftmost element denotes the root of the tree. So we know '*A*' is the root for given sequences. By searching '*A*' in Inorder sequence we can find out all elements on the left side of '*A*', which come under the left subtree, and elements on the right side of '*A*', which come under the right subtree. So we get the structure as seen below.

We recursively follow the above steps and get the following tree.

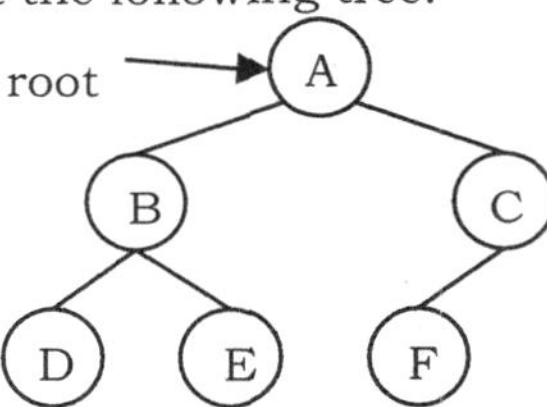


**Algorithm:** buildTree()

1 Select an element from *Preorder*. Increment a *Preorder* index variable (*preOrderIndex* in code below) to pick next element in next recursive call.
2 Create a new tree node (*newNode*) from heap with the data as selected element.
3 Find the selected element's index in Inorder. Let the index be *inOrderIndex*.
4 Call BuildBinaryTree for elements before *inOrderIndex* and make the built tree as left subtree of *newNode*.
5 Call BuildBinaryTree for elements after *inOrderIndex* and make the built tree as right subtree of *newNode*.
6 return *newNode*.

```
struct BinaryTreeNode *buildBinaryTree(int inOrder[], int preOrder[], int inOrderStart, int inOrderEnd){
    static int preOrderIndex = 0;
    struct BinaryTreeNode *newNode;
    if(inOrderStart > inOrderEnd) return NULL;
    newNode = (struct BinaryTreeNode *) malloc (sizeof(struct BinaryTreeNode));
    if(!newNode) {
      printf("Memory Error");
      return NULL;
    }
    // Select current node from Preorder traversal using preOrderIndex
    newNode→data = preOrder[preOrderIndex];
    preOrderIndex++;
    if(inOrderStart == inOrderEnd)
        return newNode;
    // find the index of this node in Inorder traversal
    int inOrderIndex = search(inOrder, inOrderStart, inOrderEnd, newNode→data);
    //Fill the left and right subtrees using index in Inorder traversal
    newNode→left = buildBinaryTree(inOrder, preOrder, inOrderStart, inOrderIndex -1);
    newNode→right = buildBinaryTree(inOrder, preOrder, inOrderIndex +1, inOrderEnd);
    return newNode;
}
```

Time Complexity: $O(n)$. Space Complexity: $O(n)$.

**Problem-28** If we are given two traversal sequences, can we construct the binary tree uniquely?

**Solution:** It depends on what traversals are given. If one of the traversal methods is *Inorder* then the tree can be constructed uniquely, otherwise not.

Therefore, the following combinations can uniquely identify a tree:

- Inorder and Preorder
- Inorder and Postorder
- Inorder and Level-order

The following combinations do not uniquely identify a tree.

- Postorder and Preorder
- Preorder and Level-order
- Postorder and Level-order

For example, Preorder, Level-order and Postorder traversals are the same for the above trees:

Preorder Traversal = AB Postorder Traversal = BA Level-order Traversal = AB

So, even if three of them (PreOrder, Level-Order and PostOrder) are given, the tree cannot be constructed uniquely.

**Problem-29** Give an algorithm for printing all the ancestors of a node in a Binary tree. For the tree below, for 7 the ancestors are 1 3 7.

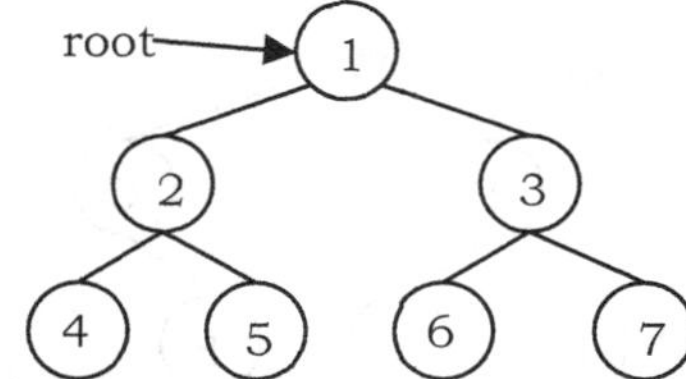


**Solution:** Apart from the Depth First Search of this tree, we can use the following recursive way to print the ancestors.

```
int printAllAncestors(struct BinaryTreeNode *root, struct BinaryTreeNode *node){
    if(root == NULL) return 0;
    if(root→left == node || root→right == node ||
        printAllAncestors(root→left, node) || printAllAncestors(root→right, node)) {
            printf("%d",root→data);
            return 1;
    }
    return 0;
}
```

Time Complexity: O($n$). Space Complexity: O($n$) for recursion.

**Problem-30** **Zigzag Tree Traversal:** Give an algorithm to traverse a binary tree in Zigzag order. For example, the output for the tree below should be: 1 3 2 4 5 6 7

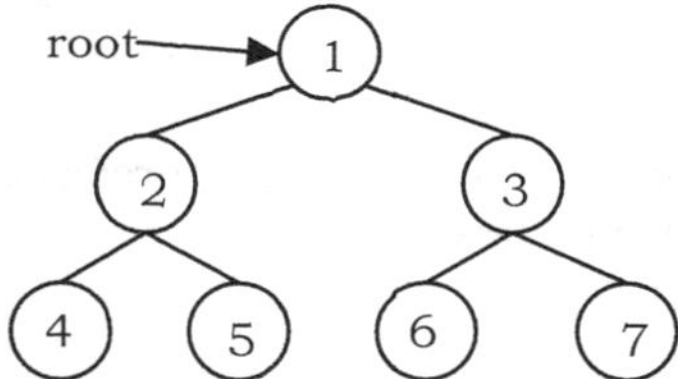


**Solution:** This problem can be solved easily using two stacks. Assume the two stacks are: *currentLevel* and *nextLevel*. We would also need a variable to keep track of the current level order (whether it is left to right or right to left). We pop from *currentLevel* stack and print the node's value. Whenever the current level order is from left to right, push the node's left child, then its right child, to stack *nextLevel*. Since a stack is a Last In First Out (*LIFO*) structure, the next time that nodes are popped off nextLevel, it will be in the reverse order.

On the other hand, when the current level order is from right to left, we would push the node's right child first, then its left child. Finally, don't forget to swap those two stacks at the end of each level (*i.e.*, when *currentLevel* is empty).

```
void zigZagTraversal(struct BinaryTreeNode *root){
    struct BinaryTreeNode *temp;
    int leftToRight = 1;
    if(!root)
        return;
    struct Stack *currentLevel = createStack(), *nextLevel = createStack();
    push(currentLevel, root);
    while(!isEmpty(currentLevel)) {
            temp = pop(currentLevel);
            if(temp) {
                    printf("%d",temp→data);
                    if(leftToRight) {
                        if(temp→left)
                            push(nextLevel, temp→left);
```

```
                    if(temp→right)
                        push(nextLevel, temp→right);
                }
                else {
                    if(temp→right)
                        push(nextLevel, temp→right);
                    if(temp→left)
                        push(nextLevel, temp→left);
                }
            }
            if(isEmpty(currentLevel)) {
                leftToRight = 1-leftToRight;
                swap(currentLevel, nextLevel);
            }
        }
    }
```

Time Complexity: $O(n)$. Space Complexity: Space for two stacks = $O(n) + O(n) = O(n)$.

**Problem-31** Give an algorithm for finding the vertical sum of a binary tree. For example,

The tree has 5 vertical lines

Vertical-1: nodes-4 => vertical sum is 4

Vertical-2: nodes-2 => vertical sum is 2

Vertical-3: nodes-1,5,6 => vertical sum is 1 + 5 + 6 = 12

Vertical-4: nodes-3 => vertical sum is 3

Vertical-5: nodes-7 => vertical sum is 7

We need to output: 4 2 12 3 7

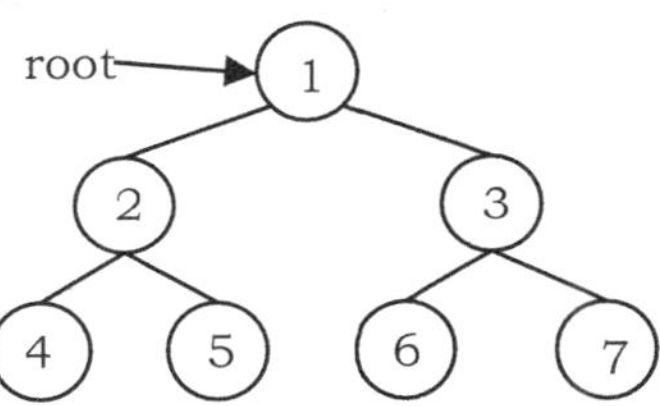


**Solution:** This problem can be easily solved with the help of hashing tables. The idea is to create an empty map where each key represents the relative horizontal distance of a node from the root node and value in the map maintains sum of all nodes present at same horizontal distance. Then we do a pre-order traversal of the tree and we update the sum for current horizontal distance in the map. For each node, we recur for its left subtree by decreasing horizontal distance by 1 and recur for right subtree by increasing horizontal distance by 1.

```
void verticalSumInBinaryTree (struct BinaryTreeNode *root, int column){
    if(root==NULL)
        return;
    verticalSumInBinaryTree(root→left, column-1);
    //Refer Hashing chapter for implementation of hash table
    Hash[column] += root→data;
    verticalSumInBinaryTree(root→right, column+1);
}
verticalSumInBinaryTree(root, 0);
Print Hash;
```

**Problem-32** How many different binary trees are possible with $n$ nodes?

**Solution:** For example, consider a tree with 3 nodes ($n = 3$). It will have the maximum combination of 5 different (i.e., $2^3 - 3 = 5$) trees.

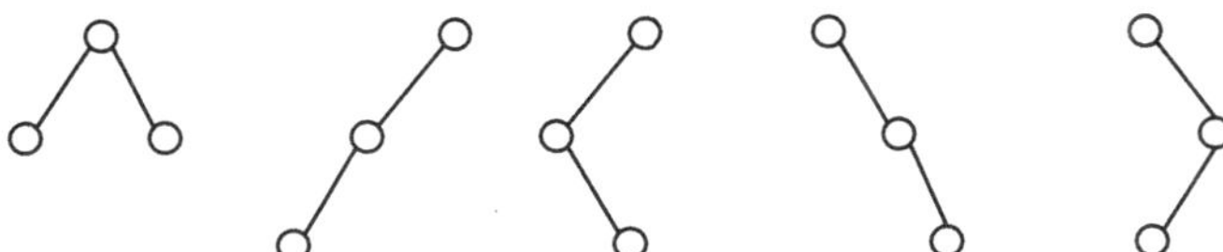

In general, if there are $n$ nodes, there exist $2^n - n$ different trees.

**Problem-33** Given a tree with a special property where leaves are represented with 'L' and internal node with 'I'. Also, assume that each node has either 0 or 2 children. Given preorder traversal of this tree, construct the tree.

**Example**: Given preorder string => ILILL

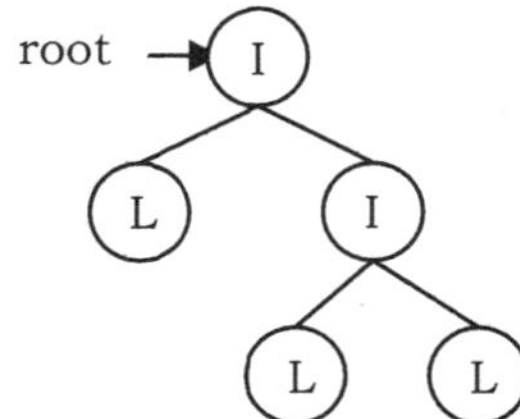


**Solution**: First, we should see how preorder traversal is arranged. Pre-order traversal means first put root node, then pre-order traversal of left subtree and then pre-order traversal of right subtree. In a normal scenario, it's not possible to detect where left subtree ends and right subtree starts using only pre-order traversal. Since every node has either 2 children or no child, we can surely say that if a node exists then its sibling also exists. So every time when we are computing a subtree, we need to compute its sibling subtree as well.

Secondly, whenever we get 'L' in the input string, that is a leaf and we can stop for a particular subtree at that point. After this 'L' node (left child of its parent 'L'), its sibling starts. If 'L' node is right child of its parent, then we need to go up in the hierarchy to find the next subtree to compute.

Keeping the above invariant in mind, we can easily determine when a subtree ends and the next one starts. It means that we can give any start node to our method and it can easily complete the subtree it generates going outside of its nodes. We just need to take care of passing the correct start nodes to different sub-trees.

```
struct BinaryTreeNode *buildTreeFromPreOrder(char* A, int *i){
    struct BinaryTreeNode *newNode;
    newNode = (struct BinaryTreeNode *) malloc(sizeof(struct BinaryTreeNode));
    newNode→data = A[*i];
    newNode→left = newNode→right = NULL;
    if(A == NULL){                              //Boundary Condition
        free(newNode);
        return NULL;
    }
    if(A[*i] == 'L')                            //On reaching leaf node, return
        return newNode;
    *i = *i + 1;                                //populate left sub tree
    newNode→left = buildTreeFromPreOrder(A, i);
    *i = *i + 1;                                //populate right sub tree
    newNode→right = buildTreeFromPreOrder(A, i);
    return newNode;
}
```

Time Complexity: $O(n)$.

**Problem-34** Given a binary tree with three pointers (left, right and nextSibling), give an algorithm for filling the *nextSibling* pointers assuming they are NULL initially.

**Solution:** We can use simple queue (similar to the solution of Problem-11). Let us assume that the structure of binary tree is:

```
struct BinaryTreeNode {
    struct BinaryTreeNode* left;
    struct BinaryTreeNode* right;
    struct BinaryTreeNode* nextSibling;
};
int fillNextSiblings(struct BinaryTreeNode *root){
    if(!root)
        return 0;
    struct BinaryTreeNode *temp;
    struct Queue *Q = createQueue();
    enQueue(Q,root);
    enQueue(Q,NULL);
    while(!isEmpty(Q)) {
        temp =deQueue(Q);
        // Completion of current level.
        if(temp ==NULL) { //Put another marker for next level.
            if(!isEmpty(Q))
                enQueue(Q,NULL);
        }
```

```
            else {
                temp->nextSibling = QueueFront(Q);
                if(root->left)
                    enQueue(Q, temp->left);
                if(root->right)
                    enQueue(Q, temp->right);
            }
        }
    }
```

Time Complexity: O(*n*). Space Complexity: O(*n*).

Problem-35 Is there any other way of solving Problem-34?

**Solution:** The trick is to re-use the populated *nextSibling* pointers. As mentioned earlier, we just need one more step for it to work. Before we pass the *left* and *right* to the recursion function itself, we connect the right child's *nextSibling* to the current node's nextSibling left child. In order for this to work, the current node *nextSibling* pointer must be populated, which is true in this case.

```
void fillNextSiblings(struct BinaryTreeNode* root) {
    if (!root) return;
    if (root→left) root→left→nextSibling = root→right;
    if (root→right) root→right→nextSibling = (root→nextSibling) ? root→nextSibling→left: NULL;
    fillNextSiblings(root→left);
    fillNextSiblings(root→right);
}
```

Time Complexity: O(*n*).

Problem-36 Given a binary tree, find its minimum depth. The minimum depth of a binary tree is the number of nodes along the shortest path from the root node down to the nearest leaf node. For example, minimum depth of the following binary tree is 3.

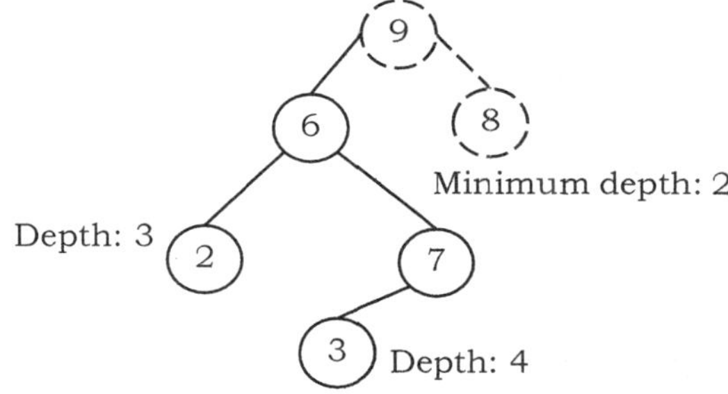


**Solution**: The algorithm is similar to the algorithm of finding depth (or height) of a binary tree, except here we are finding minimum depth. One simplest approach to solve this problem would be by using recursion. But the question is when do we stop it? We stop the recursive calls when it is a leaf node or *None*.

**Algorithm**:

Let *root* be the pointer to the root node of a subtree.

- If the *root* is equal to *NULL*, then the minimum depth of the binary tree would be 0.
- If the *root* is a leaf node, then the minimum depth of the binary tree would be 1.
- If the *root* is not a leaf node and if left subtree of the *root* is *NULL*, then find the minimum depth in the right subtree. Otherwise, find the minimum depth in the left subtree.
- If the *root* is not a leaf node and both left subtree and right subtree of the *root* are not *NULL*, then recursively find the minimum depth of left and right subtree. Let it be *leftSubtreeMinDepth* and *rightSubtreeMinDepth* respectively.
- To get the minimum height of the binary tree rooted at root, we will take minimum of *leftSubtreeMinDepth* and *rightSubtreeMinDepth* and 1 for the *root* node.

```
class Solution {
 public:
    int minDepth(BinaryTreeNode * root) {
        // If root (tree) is empty, minimum depth would be 0
        if(!root)
            return 0;
```

```
        // If root is a leaf node, minimum depth would be 1
        if(!root->left && !root->right)
           return 1;
        // If left subtree is NULL, find minimum depth in right subtree
        if(!root->left) {
           return minDepth(root->right) + 1;
        }
        // If right subtree is NULL, find minimum depth in left subtree
        if(!root->right) {
           return minDepth(root->left) + 1;
        }
        // Get the minimum depths of left and right subtrees and add 1 for current level.
        return min(minDepth(root->left), minDepth(root->right)) + 1;
      }
};
# Approach two
class Solution {
  public:
    int minDepth(BinaryTreeNode * root) {
        if(!root) {
           return 0;
        }
       if (root.left == NULL or root.right == NULL)
           return minDepth (root.left) + minDepth (root.right) + 1
        int left = minDepth(root->left) + 1;
        int right = minDepth(root->right) + 1;
        return (left < right ? left : right);
      }
};
```

Time complexity: O($n$), as we are doing pre order traversal of tree only once.
Space complexity: O($n$), for recursive stack space.

**Solution with level order traversal:** The above recursive approach may end up with complete traversal of the binary tree even when the minimum depth leaf is close to the root node. A better approach is to use level order traversal. In this algorithm, we will traverse the binary tree by keeping track of the levels of the node and closest leaf node found till now.

**Algorithm**:

Let *root* be the pointer to the root node of a subtree at level L.

- If root is equal to *NULL*, then the minimum depth of the binary tree would be 0.
- If root is a leaf node, then check if its level(L) is less than the level of closest leaf node found till now. If yes, then update closest leaf node to current node and return.
- Recursively traverse left and right subtree of node at level L + 1.

```
// A binary tree BinaryTreeNode declaration
struct BinaryTreeNode {
    int data;
    struct BinaryTreeNode *left;
    struct BinaryTreeNode *right;
};
// A queue item (stores pointer to BinaryTreeNode and its depth)
struct QueueElement {
    BinaryTreeNode *btNode;
    int depth;
};
// Iterative method to find minimum depth of Bianry Tree
int minDepth(BinaryTreeNode *root) {
    // If root (tree) is empty, minimum depth would be 0
    if (root == NULL)
       return 0;
    // Create an empty queue for level order traversal
    queue<QueueElement> q;
```

```
        // Enqueue root and initialize depth as 1
        QueueElement queueElement = {root, 1};
        q.push(queueElement);
        // Do level order traversal
        while (q.empty() == false){
            // Remove the front queue item
            queueElement = q.front();
            q.pop();
            // Get details of the remove item
            BinaryTreeNode *btNode = queueElement.btNode;
            int depth = queueElement.depth;
            // If this is the first leaf btNode seen so far then return its depth as answer
            if (btNode->left == NULL && btNode->right == NULL)
                return depth;
            // If left subtree is not NULL, add it to queue
            if (btNode->left != NULL) {
                queueElement.btNode = btNode->left;
                queueElement.depth = depth + 1;
                q.push(queueElement);
            }
            // If right subtree is not NULL, add it to queue
            if (btNode->right != NULL) {
                queueElement.btNode = btNode->right;
                queueElement.depth = depth+1;
                q.push(queueElement);
            }
        }
        return 0;
    }
```

Time complexity: O($n$), as we are doing lever order traversal of the tree only once.Space complexity: O($n$), for queue.

**Symmetric question: Maximum depth of a binary tree**: Given a binary tree, find its maximum depth. The maximum depth of a binary tree is the number of nodes along the path from the root node down to the farthest leaf node. For example, maximum depth of following binary tree is 4. Careful observation tells us that it is exactly same as finding the depth (or height) of the tree.

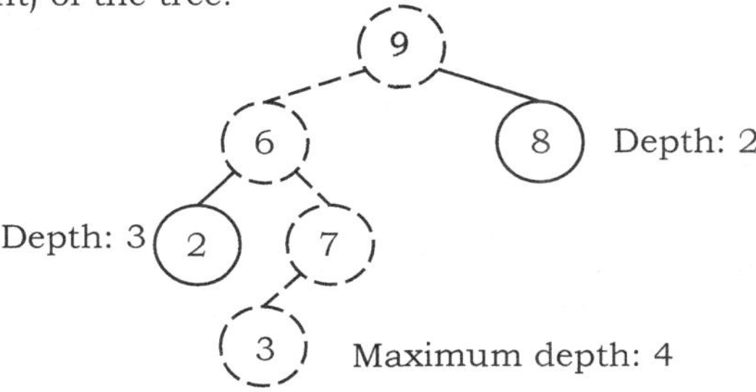


Problem-37 Given a binary tree, how do we check whether it is a complete binary tree?

**Solution**: A complete binary tree is a binary tree in which all the levels are completely filled except possibly the lowest one, which is filled from the left. A complete binary tree is a binary tree in which every level, except possibly the last, is completely filled, and all nodes are as far left as possible. Whereas, a full binary tree (sometimes proper binary tree or 2-tree) is a tree in which every node other than the leaves has two children.

If we have say, 4 nodes in a row with depth 3 and positions 0, 1, 2, 3; and we want 8 new nodes in a row with depth 4 and positions 0, 1, 2, 3, 4, 5, 6, 7; then we can see that the rule for going from a node to its left child is (depth, position) -> (depth + 1, position * 2), and the rule for going from a node to its right child is (depth, position) -> (depth + 1, position * 2 + 1). Then, our row at depth dd is completely filled if it has $2^{d-1}$ nodes, and all the nodes in the last level are left-justified when their positions take the form 0, 1, ... in sequence with no gaps.

```
bool isCompleteBinaryTree(BinaryTreeNode* root){
    if (root == NULL)
        return true;
    BinaryTreeNode *p, *r;
    std::queue<BinaryTreeNode*> q{};       // Queue is created
    q.push(root);
```

```
        int count = 0;
        while (!q.empty()){                              // while q is empty it will run
            int z = q.size();
            for (int i = 0; i < z; i++) {
                p = q.front();
                q.pop();
                if (p == NULL){                          // If null is recived all the next elements must be
                    count++;                             // null in order to be a complete binary tree
                    while (!q.empty()) {
                        r = q.front();
                        q.pop();
                        if (r != NULL)
                            return false;
                    }
                    break;
                }
                q.push(p->left);
                q.push(p->right);
            }
        }
        return true;                                     // If all nodes after first null are null, it returns true;
    }
```

## 6.7 Generic Trees (N-ary Trees)

In the previous section we discussed binary trees where each node can have a maximum of two children and these are represented easily with two pointers. But suppose if we have a tree with many children at every node and also if we do not know how many children a node can have, how do we represent them?

For example, consider the tree shown below.

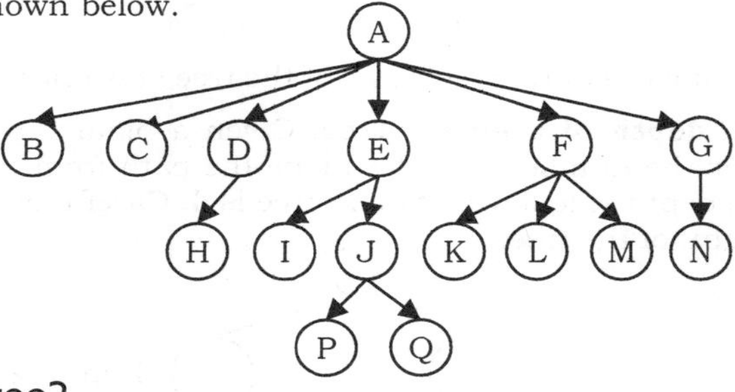


### How do we represent the tree?

In the above tree, there are nodes with 6 children, with 3 children, with 2 children, with 1 child, and with zero children (leaves). To present this tree we have to consider the worst case (6 children) and allocate that many child pointers for each node. Based on this, the node representation can be given as:

```
    struct TreeNode{
        int data;
        struct TreeNode *firstChild;
        struct TreeNode *secondChild;
        struct TreeNode *thirdChild;
        struct TreeNode *fourthChild;
        struct TreeNode *fifthChild;
        struct TreeNode *sixthChild;
    };
```

Since we are not using all the pointers in all the cases, there is a lot of memory wastage. Another problem is that we do not know the number of children for each node in advance. In order to solve this problem we need a representation that minimizes the wastage and also accepts nodes with any number of children.

### Representation of Generic Trees

Since our objective is to reach all nodes of the tree, a possible solution to this is as follows:

- At each node link children of same parent (siblings) from left to right.
- Remove the links from parent to all children except the first child.

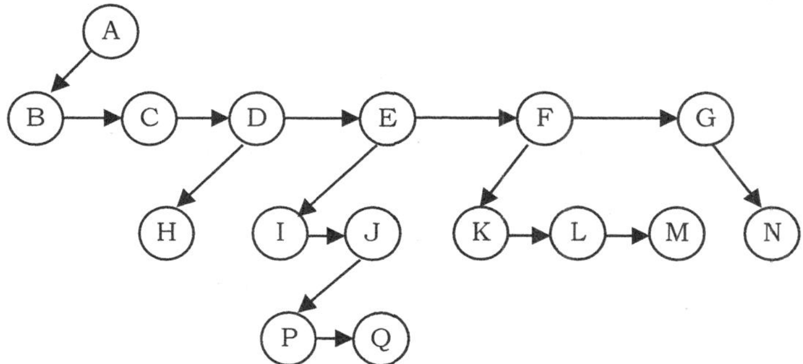


What these above statements say is if we have a link between children then we do not need extra links from parent to all children. This is because we can traverse all the elements by starting at the first child of the parent. So if we have a link between parent and first child and also links between all children of same parent then it solves our problem.

This representation is sometimes called first child/next sibling representation. First child/next sibling representation of the generic tree is shown above. The actual representation for this tree is:

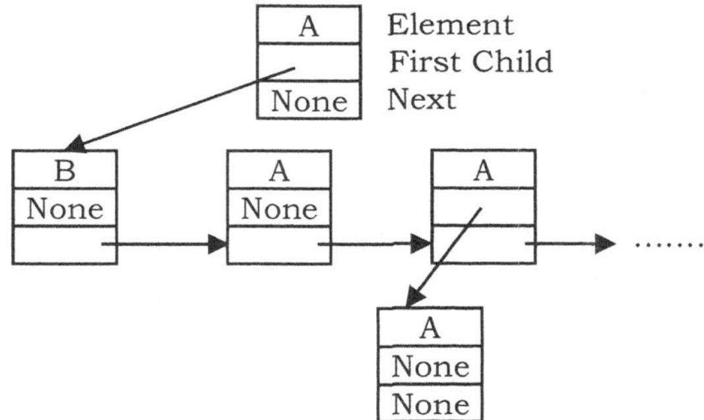


Based on this discussion, the tree node declaration for general tree can be given as:

```
struct TreeNode {
    int data;
    struct TreeNode *firstChild;
    struct TreeNode *nextSibling;
};
```

**Note:** Since we are able to convert any generic tree to binary representation; in practice we use binary trees. We can treat all generic trees with a first child/next sibling representation as binary trees.

## Generic Trees: Problems & Solutions

Problem-38 Given a tree, give an algorithm for finding the sum of all the elements of the tree.

**Solution:** The solution is similar to what we have done for simple binary trees. That means, traverse the complete list and keep on adding the values. We can either use level order traversal or simple recursion.

```
int findSum(struct TreeNode *root){
    if(!root) return 0;
    return root→data + findSum(root→firstChild) + findSum(root→nextSibling);
}
```

Time Complexity: $O(n)$. Space Complexity: $O(1)$ (if we do not consider stack space), otherwise $O(n)$.

**Note:** All problems which we have discussed for binary trees are applicable for generic trees also. Instead of left and right pointers we just need to use firstChild and nextSibling.

Problem-39 For a 4-ary tree (each node can contain maximum of 4 children), what is the maximum possible height with 100 nodes? Assume height of a single node is 0.

**Solution:** In 4-ary tree each node can contain 0 to 4 children, and to get maximum height, we need to keep only one child for each parent. With 100 nodes, the maximum possible height we can get is 99.

If we have a restriction that at least one node has 4 children, then we keep one node with 4 children and the remaining nodes with 1 child. In this case, the maximum possible height is 96. Similarly, with $n$ nodes the maximum possible height is $n - 4$.

Problem-40 For a 4-ary tree (each node can contain maximum of 4 children), what is the minimum possible height with $n$ nodes?

**Solution:** Similar to the above discussion, if we want to get minimum height, then we need to fill all nodes with maximum children (in this case 4). Now let's see the following table, which indicates the maximum number of nodes for a given height.

| Height, h | Maximum Nodes at height, $h = 4^h$ | Total Nodes height $h = \frac{4^{h+1}-1}{3}$ |
|---|---|---|
| 0 | 1 | 1 |
| 1 | 4 | 1+4 |
| 2 | 4 × 4 | 1+ 4 × 4 |
| 3 | 4 × 4 × 4 | 1+ 4 × 4 + 4 × 4 × 4 |

For a given height $h$ the maximum possible nodes are: $\frac{4^{h+1}-1}{3}$. To get minimum height, take logarithm on both sides:

$$n = \frac{4^{h+1}-1}{3} \Rightarrow 4^{h+1} = 3n + 1 \Rightarrow (h + 1)log4 = \log(3n + 1) \Rightarrow h + 1 = \log_4(3n + 1) \Rightarrow h = \log_4(3n + 1) - 1$$

Problem-41 Given a node in the generic tree, give an algorithm for counting the number of siblings for that node.

**Solution:** Since tree is represented with the first child/next sibling method, the tree structure can be given as:

```
struct TreeNode{
    int data;
    struct TreeNode *firstChild;
    struct TreeNode *nextSibling;
};
```

For a given node in the tree, we just need to traverse all its next siblings.

```
int SiblingsCount(struct TreeNode *current){
    int count = 0;
    while(current) {
        count++;
        current = current→nextSibling;
    }
    return count;
}
```

Time Complexity: O($n$). Space Complexity: O(1).

Problem-42 Given a node in the generic tree, give an algorithm for counting the number of children for that node.

**Solution:** Since the tree is represented as first child/next sibling method, the tree structure can be given as:

```
struct TreeNode {
    int data;
    struct TreeNode * firstChild;
    struct TreeNode * nextSibling;
};
```

For a given node in the tree, we just need to point to its first child and keep traversing all its next siblings.

```
int ChildCount(struct TreeNode * current) {
    int count = 0;
    current = current→ firstChild;
    while (current) {
        count++;
        current = current→ nextSibling;
    }
    return count;
}
```

Time Complexity: O($n$). Space Complexity: O(1).

Problem-43 Given two trees how do we check whether the trees are isomorphic to each other or not?

**Solution:** Two binary trees *root*1 and *root*2 are isomorphic if they have the same structure. The values of the nodes does not affect whether two trees are isomorphic or not. In the diagram below, the tree in the middle is not isomorphic to the other trees, but the tree on the right is isomorphic to the tree on the left.

```
int isIsomorphic(struct TreeNode *root1, struct TreeNode *root2){
    if(!root1 && !root2)
        return 1;
```

```
    if((!root1 && root2) || (root1 && !root2))
        return 0;
    return (isIsomorphic(root1→left, root2→left) && isIsomorphic(root1→right, root2→right));
}
```

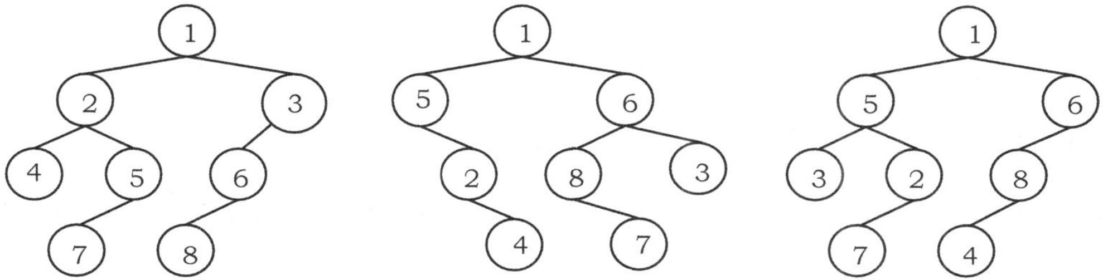

Time Complexity: $O(n)$. Space Complexity: $O(n)$.

Problem-44 Given two trees how do we check whether they are quasi-isomorphic to each other or not?

**Solution:**

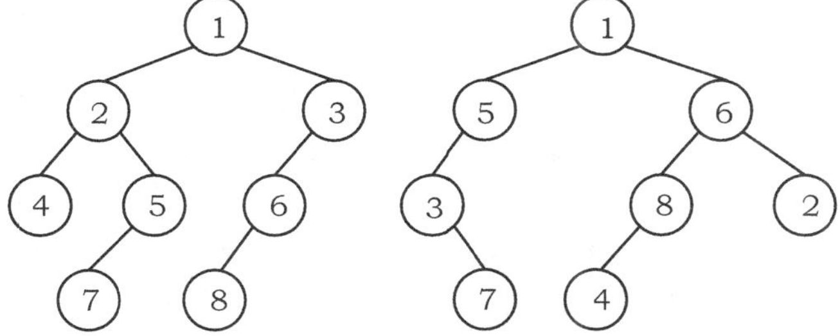

Two trees *root*1 and *root*2 are quasi-isomorphic if *root*1 can be transformed into *root*2 by swapping the left and right children of some of the nodes of *root*1. Data in the nodes are not important in determining quasi-isomorphism; only the shape is important. The trees below are quasi-isomorphic because if the children of the nodes on the left are swapped, the tree on the right is obtained.

```
int quasiIsomorphic(struct TreeNode * root1, struct TreeNode * root2) {
  if (!root1 && !root2) return 1;
  if ((!root1 && root2) || (root1 && !root2))
    return 0;
  return (quasiIsomorphic(root1→ left, root2→ left) && quasiIsomorphic(root1→ right, root2→ right) ||
    quasiIsomorphic(root1→ right, root2→ left) && quasiIsomorphic(root1→ left, root2→ right));
}
```

Time Complexity: $O(n)$. Space Complexity: $O(n)$.

Problem-45 Given a parent array $P$, where $P[i]$ indicates the parent of $i^{th}$ node in the tree (assume parent of root node is indicated with $-1$). Give an algorithm for finding the height or depth of the tree.

**Solution:** For example: if the P is

| -1 | 0 | 1 | 6 | 6 | 0 | 0 | 2 | 7 |
|---|---|---|---|---|---|---|---|---|
| 0 | 1 | 2 | 3 | 4 | 5 | 6 | 7 | 8 |

Its corresponding tree is:

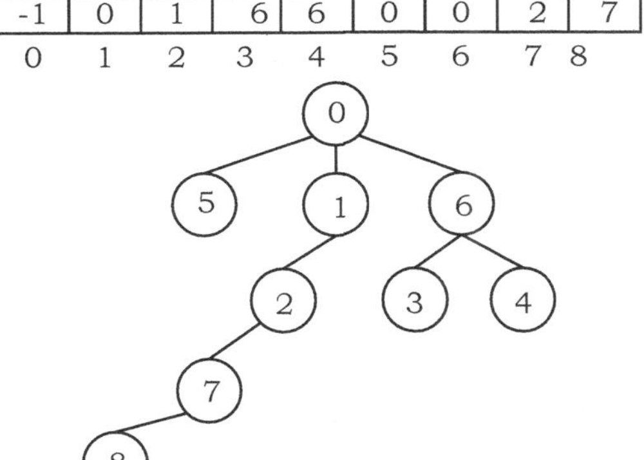

From the problem definition, the given array represents the parent array. That means, we need to consider the tree for that array and find the depth of the tree. The depth of this given tree is 4. If we carefully observe, we just need to start at every node and keep going to its parent until we reach $-1$ and also keep track of the maximum depth among all nodes.

```
int findDepthInGenericTree(int P[], int n){
    int maxDepth =-1, currentDepth =-1, j;
```

```
        for (int i = 0; i < n; i++)  {
            currentDepth = 0; j = i;
            while(P[j] != -1) {
                currentDepth++; j = P[j];
            }
            if(currentDepth > maxDepth)
                maxDepth = currentDepth;
        }
        return maxDepth;
}
```

Time Complexity: $O(n^2)$. For skew trees we will be re-calculating the same values. Space Complexity: O(1).

**Note:** We can optimize the code by storing the previous calculated nodes' depth in some hash table or other array. This reduces the time complexity but uses extra space.

Problem-46 A full $k$ –ary tree is a tree where each node has either 0 or $k$ children. Given an array which contains the preorder traversal of full $k$ –ary tree, give an algorithm for constructing the full $k$ –ary tree.

**Solution:** In $k$ –ary tree, for a node at $i^{th}$ position its children will be at $k * i + 1$ to $k * i + k$. For example, the example below is for full 3-ary tree.

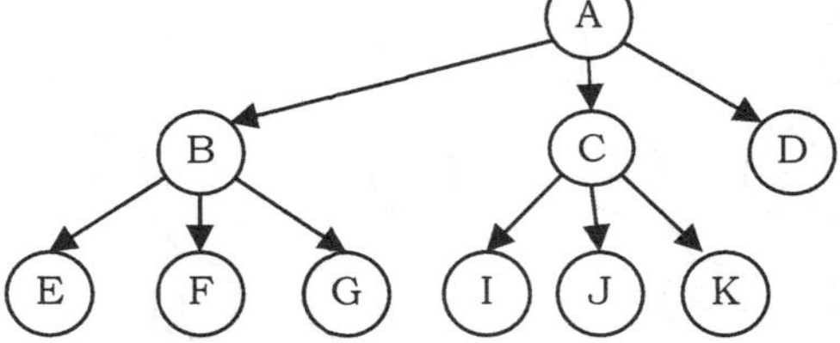


As we have seen, in preorder traversal first left subtree is processed then followed by root node and right subtree. Because of this, to construct a full $k$-ary, we just need to keep on creating the nodes without bothering about the previous constructed nodes. We can use this trick to build the tree recursively by using one global index. The declaration for $k$-ary tree can be given as:

```
struct K - aryTreeNode {
    char data;
    struct K - aryTreeNode * child[];
};
int * Ind = 0;
struct K - aryTreeNode * buildK - aryTree(char A[], int n, int k) {
    if (n <= 0)
        return NULL;
    struct K - aryTreeNode * newNode = (struct K - aryTreeNode * ) malloc(sizeof(struct K - aryTreeNode));
    if (!newNode) {
        printf("Memory Error");
        return;
    }
    newNode→child = (struct K - aryTreeNode * ) malloc(k * sizeof(struct K - aryTreeNode));
    if (!newNode→child) {
        printf("Memory Error");
        return;
    }
    newNode→ data = A[Ind];
    for (int i = 0; i < k; i++) {
        if (k * Ind + i < n) {
            Ind++;
            newNode→child[i] = buildK - aryTree(A, n, k, Ind);
        } else newNode→child[i] = NULL;
    }
    return newNode;
}
```

Time Complexity: $O(n)$, where $n$ is the size of the pre-order array. This is because we are moving sequentially and not visiting the already constructed nodes.

## 6.8 Threaded Binary Tree Traversals (Stack or Queue-less Traversals)

In earlier sections we have seen that, *preorder, inorder and postorder* binary tree traversals used stacks and *level order* traversals used queues as an auxiliary data structure. In this section we will discuss new traversal algorithms which do not need both stacks and queues. Such traversal algorithms are called *threaded binary tree traversals* or *stack/queue – less traversals*.

### Issues with Regular Binary Tree Traversals

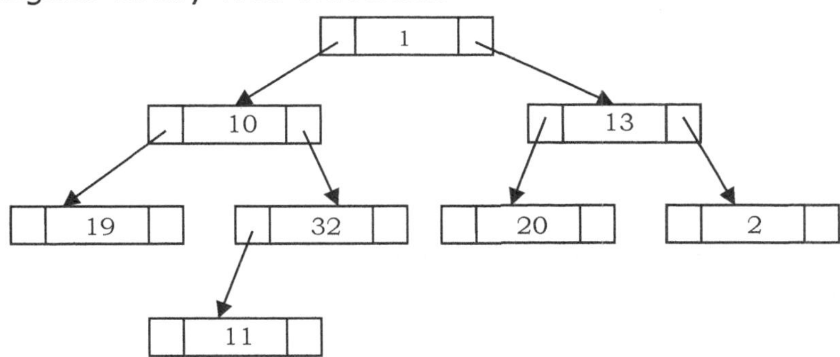


- The storage space required for the stack and queue is large.
- The majority of pointers in any binary tree are NULL. For example, a binary tree with $n$ nodes has $n + 1$ NULL pointers and these were wasted.
- It is difficult to find successor node (preorder, inorder and postorder successors) for a given node.

### Motivation for Threaded Binary Trees

To solve these problems, one idea is to store some useful information in NULL pointers. If we observe the previous traversals carefully, stack/queue is required because we have to record the current position in order to move to the right subtree after processing the left subtree. If we store the useful information in NULL pointers, then we don't have to store such information in stack/queue.

The binary trees which store such information in NULL pointers are called *threaded binary trees*. From the above discussion, let us assume that we want to store some useful information in NULL pointers. The next question is what to store?

The common convention is to put predecessor/successor information. That means, if we are dealing with preorder traversals, then for a given node, NULL left pointer will contain preorder predecessor information and NULL right pointer will contain preorder successor information. These special pointers are called *threads*.

### Classifying Threaded Binary Trees

The classification is based on whether we are storing useful information in both NULL pointers or only in one of them.

- If we store predecessor information in NULL left pointers only, then we can call such binary trees *left threaded binary trees*.
- If we store successor information in NULL right pointers only, then we can call such binary trees *right threaded binary trees*.
- If we store predecessor information in NULL left pointers and successor information in NULL right pointers, then we can call such binary trees *fully threaded binary trees* or simply *threaded binary trees*.

**Note:** For the remaining discussion we consider only (*fully*) *threaded binary trees*.

### Types of Threaded Binary Trees

Based on above discussion we get three representations for threaded binary trees.

- *Preorder Threaded Binary Trees*: NULL left pointer will contain PreOrder predecessor information and NULL right pointer will contain PreOrder successor information.
- *Inorder Threaded Binary Trees*: NULL left pointer will contain InOrder predecessor information and NULL right pointer will contain InOrder successor information.
- *Postorder Threaded Binary Trees*: NULL left pointer will contain PostOrder predecessor information and NULL right pointer will contain PostOrder successor information.

**Note:** As the representations are similar, for the remaining discussion we will use InOrder threaded binary trees.

### Threaded Binary Tree structure

Any program examining the tree must be able to differentiate between a regular *left/right* pointer and a *thread*. To do this, we use two additional fields in each node, giving us, for threaded trees, nodes of the following form:

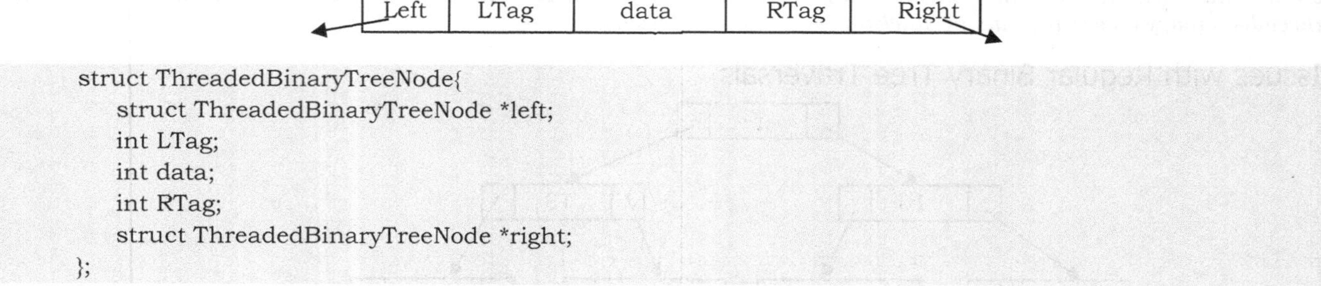


```
struct ThreadedBinaryTreeNode{
    struct ThreadedBinaryTreeNode *left;
    int LTag;
    int data;
    int RTag;
    struct ThreadedBinaryTreeNode *right;
};
```

### Difference between Binary Tree and Threaded Binary Tree Structures

| | Regular Binary Trees | Threaded Binary Trees |
|---|---|---|
| if LTag == 0 | NULL | left points to the in-order predecessor |
| if LTag == 1 | left points to the left child | left points to left child |
| if RTag == 0 | NULL | right points to the in-order successor |
| if RTag == 1 | right points to the right child | right points to the right child |

**Note:** Similarly, we can define preorder/postorder differences as well.

As an example, let us try representing a tree in inorder threaded binary tree form. The tree below shows what an inorder threaded binary tree will look like. The dotted arrows indicate the threads. If we observe, the left pointer of left most node (2) and right pointer of right most node (31) are hanging.

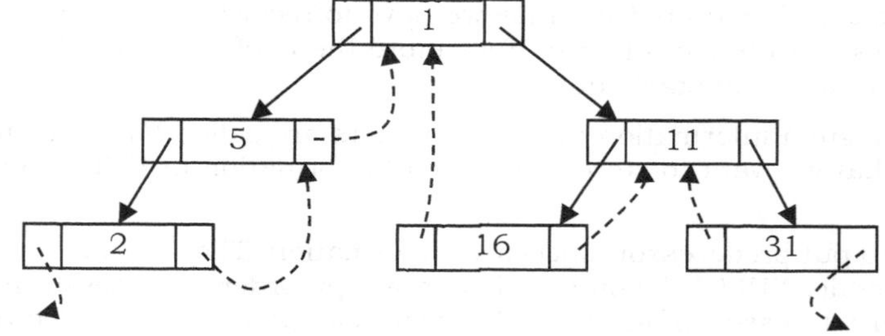


**What should leftmost and rightmost pointers point to?**

In the representation of a threaded binary tree, it is convenient to use a special node *Dummy* which is always present even for an empty tree. Note that right tag of Dummy node is 1 and its right child points to itself.

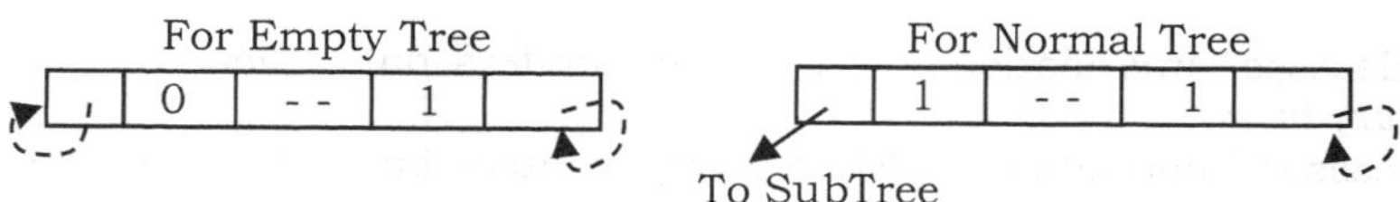


With this convention the above tree can be represented as:

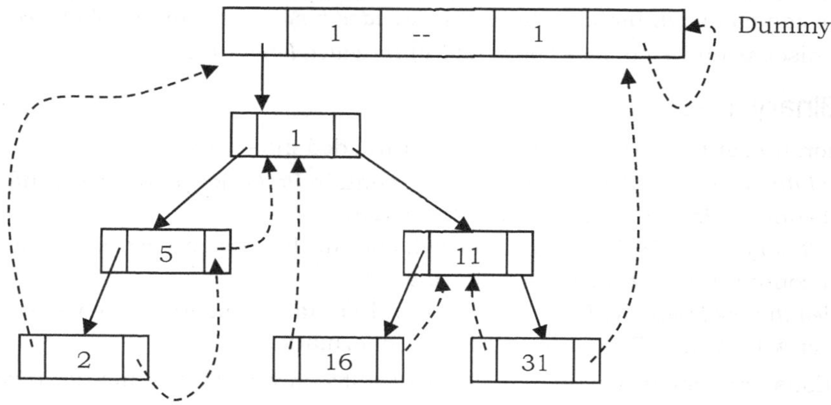

## Finding Inorder Successor in Inorder Threaded Binary Tree

To find inorder successor of a given node without using a stack, assume that the node for which we want to find the inorder successor is *P*.

**Strategy:** If *P* has a no right subtree, then return the right child of *P*. If *P* has right subtree, then return the left of the nearest node whose left subtree contains *P*.

```
struct ThreadedBinaryTreeNode* inorderSuccessor(struct ThreadedBinaryTreeNode *P){
    struct ThreadedBinaryTreeNode *Position;
    if(P→RTag == 0)
        return P→right;
    else {
        Position = P→right;
        while(Position→LTag == 1)
            Position = Position→left;
        return Position;
    }
}
```

Time Complexity: O(*n*). Space Complexity: O(1).

## Inorder Traversal in Inorder Threaded Binary Tree

We can start with *dummy* node and call inorderSuccessor() to visit each node until we reach *dummy* node.

```
void InorderTraversal(struct ThreadedBinaryTreeNode *root){
        struct ThreadedBinaryTreeNode *P = inorderSuccessor(root);
        while(P != root) {
                P = inorderSuccessor(P);
            printf("%d",P→data);
        }
}
```

**Alternative coding:**

```
void inorderTraversal(struct ThreadedBinaryTreeNode *root){
        struct ThreadedBinaryTreeNode *P = root;
        while(1) {
                P = inorderSuccessor(P);
            if(P == root)
                return;
            printf("%d",P→data);
        }
}
```

Time Complexity: O(*n*). Space Complexity: O(1).

## Finding PreOrder Successor in InOrder Threaded Binary Tree

**Strategy:** If *P* has a left subtree, then return the left child of *P*. If *P* has no left subtree, then return the right child of the nearest node whose right subtree contains *P*.

```
struct ThreadedBinaryTreeNode* preorderSuccessor(struct ThreadedBinaryTreeNode *P){
        struct ThreadedBinaryTreeNode *Position;
        if(P→LTag == 1)
                return P→left;
        else {
                Position = P;
                while(Position→RTag == 0)
                    Position = Position→right;
                return Position→right;
        }
}
```

Time Complexity: O(*n*). Space Complexity: O(1).

## PreOrder Traversal of InOrder Threaded Binary Tree

As in inorder traversal, start with *dummy* node and call preorderSuccessor() to visit each node until we get *dummy* node again.

```
void PreorderTraversal(struct ThreadedBinaryTreeNode *root){
    struct ThreadedBinaryTreeNode *P;
    P = preorderSuccessor(root);
    while(P != root) {
            P = preorderSuccessor(P);
            printf("%d",P→data);
    }
}
```

**Alternative coding:**

```
void PreorderTraversal(struct ThreadedBinaryTreeNode *root) {
    struct ThreadedBinaryTreeNode *P = root;
    while(1){
            P = preorderSuccessor(P);
            if(P == root)
                return;
            printf("%d",P→data);
    }
}
```

Time Complexity: O($n$). Space Complexity: O(1).

**Note:** From the above discussion, it should be clear that inorder and preorder successor finding is easy with threaded binary trees. But finding postorder successor is very difficult if we do not use stack.

## Insertion of Nodes in InOrder Threaded Binary Trees

For simplicity, let us assume that there are two nodes $P$ and $Q$ and we want to attach $Q$ to right of $P$. For this we will have two cases.

- Node $P$ does not have right child: In this case we just need to attach $Q$ to $P$ and change its left and right pointers.

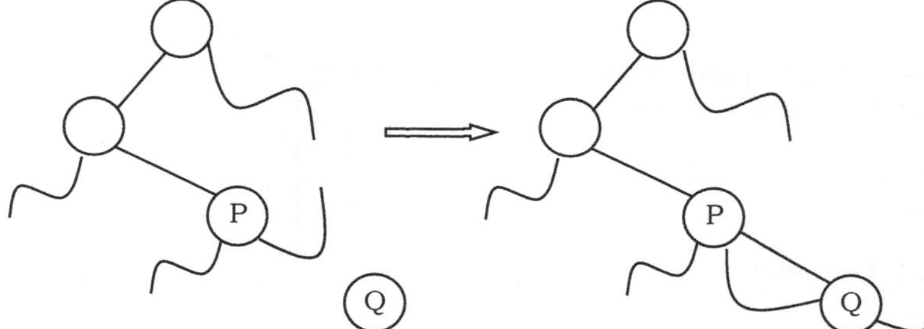


- Node $P$ has right child (say, $R$): In this case we need to traverse $R's$ left subtree and find the left most node and then update the left and right pointer of that node (as shown below).

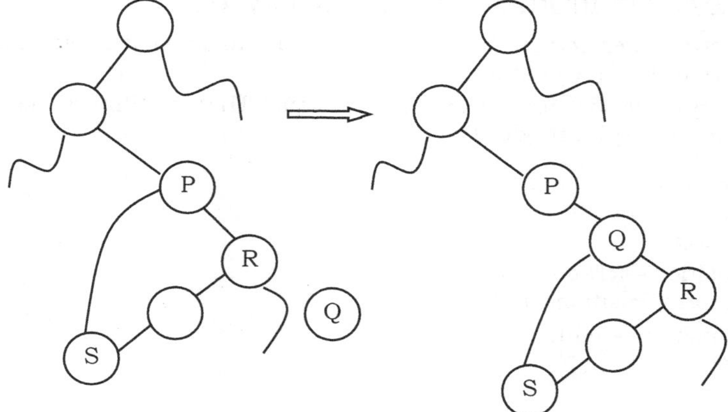


```
void insertRightInInorderTBT(struct ThreadedBinaryTreeNode *P,  struct ThreadedBinaryTreeNode *Q){
    struct ThreadedBinaryTreeNode *Temp;
    Q→right = P→right;
    Q→RTag = P→RTag;
    Q→left = P;
    Q→LTag = 0;
```

```
        P→right = Q;
        P→RTag = 1;
        if(Q→RTag == 1) {                          //Case-2
            Temp = Q→right;
            while(Temp→LTag)
                Temp = Temp→left;
            Temp→left = Q;
        }
    }
```

Time Complexity: $O(n)$. Space Complexity: $O(1)$.

## Threaded Binary Trees: Problems & Solutions

Problem-47 For a given binary tree (not threaded) how do we find the preorder successor?

**Solution:** For solving this problem, we need to use an auxiliary stack *S*. On the first call, the parameter node is a pointer to the head of the tree, and thereafter its value is NULL. Since we are simply asking for the successor of the node we got the last time we called the function. It is necessary that the contents of the stack *S* and the pointer *P* to the last node "visited" are preserved from one call of the function to the next; they are defined as static variables.

```
// pre-order successor for an unthreaded binary tree
struct BinaryTreeNode *preorderSuccessor(struct BinaryTreeNode *node){
    static struct BinaryTreeNode *P;
    static Stack *S = createStack();
    if(node != NULL)
        P = node;
    if(P→left != NULL) {
        push(S,P);
        P = P→left;
    }
    else {
        while (P→right == NULL)
            P = pop(S);
        P = P→right;
    }
    return P;
}
```

Problem-48 For a given binary tree (not threaded) how do we find the inorder successor?

**Solution:** Similar to the above discussion, we can find the inorder successor of a node as:

```
// In-order successor for an unthreaded binary tree
struct BinaryTreeNode *inorderSuccessor(struct BinaryTreeNode *node){
    static struct BinaryTreeNode *P;
    static Stack *S = createStack();
    if(node != NULL)
        P = node;
    if(P→right == NULL)
        P = pop(S);
    else {
        P = P→right;
        while (P→left != NULL)
            push(S, P);
        P = P→left;
    }
    return P;
}
```

## 6.9 Expression Trees

A tree representing an expression is called an *expression tree*. In expression trees, leaf nodes are operands and non-leaf nodes are operators. That means, an expression tree is a binary tree where internal nodes are operators and leaves are operands. An expression tree consists of binary expression. But for a u-nary operator, one subtree will be empty. The figure below shows a simple expression tree for (A + B * C) / D.

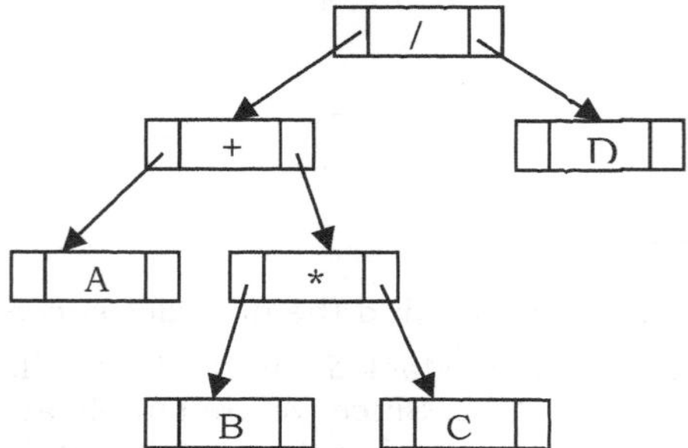


**Algorithm for Building Expression Tree from Postfix Expression**

```
struct BinaryTreeNode *buildExprTree(char postfixExpr[], int size){
    struct Stack *S = Stack(size);
    for (int i = 0; i< size; i++) {
        if(postfixExpr[i] is an operand) {
            struct BinaryTreeNode newNode = (struct BinaryTreeNode*) malloc( sizeof (struct BinaryTreeNode));
            if(!newNode) {
                printf("Memory Error");
                return NULL;
            }
            newNode→data =postfixExpr[i];
            newNode→left = newNode→right = NULL;
            push(S, newNode);
        }
        else {
            struct BinaryTreeNode *T2 = pop(S), *T1 = pop(S);
            struct BinaryTreeNode newNode = (struct BinaryTreeNode*) malloc(sizeof(struct BinaryTreeNode));
            if(!newNode) {
                printf("Memory Error");
                return NULL;
            }
            newNode→data = postfixExpr[i];
            newNode→left = T1;
            newNode→right = T2;
            push(S, newNode);
        }
    }
    return S;
}
```

**Example**: Assume that one symbol is read at a time. If the symbol is an operand, we create a tree node and push a pointer to it onto a stack. If the symbol is an operator, pop pointers to two trees $T_1$ and $T_2$ from the stack ($T_1$ is popped first) and form a new tree whose root is the operator and whose left and right children point to $T_2$ and $T_1$ respectively. A pointer to this new tree is then pushed onto the stack.

As an example, assume the input is A B C * + D /. The first three symbols are operands, so create tree nodes and push pointers to them onto a stack as shown below.

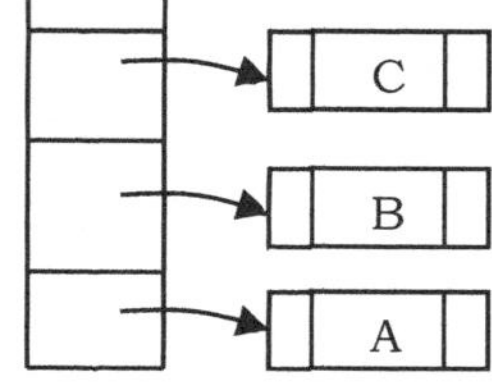


Next, an operator '*' is read, so two pointers to trees are popped, a new tree is formed and a pointer to it is pushed onto the stack.

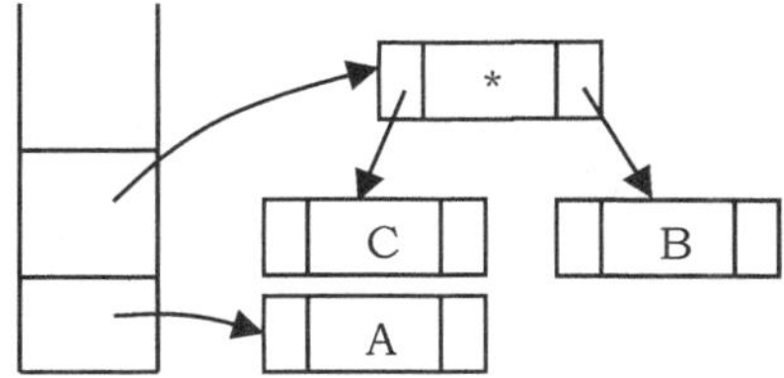


Next, an operator '+' is read, so two pointers to trees are popped, a new tree is formed and a pointer to it is pushed onto the stack.

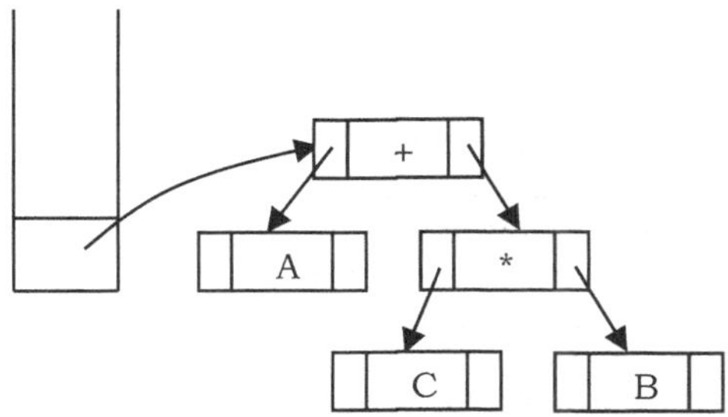


Next, an operand 'D' is read, a one-node tree is created and a pointer to the corresponding tree is pushed onto the stack.

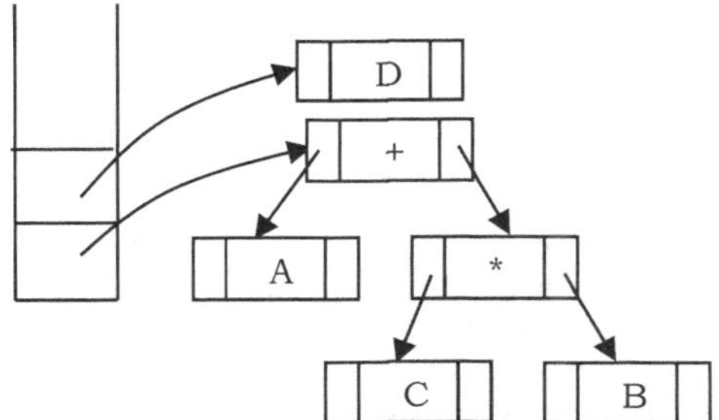


Finally, the last symbol ('/') is read, two trees are merged and a pointer to the final tree is left on the stack.

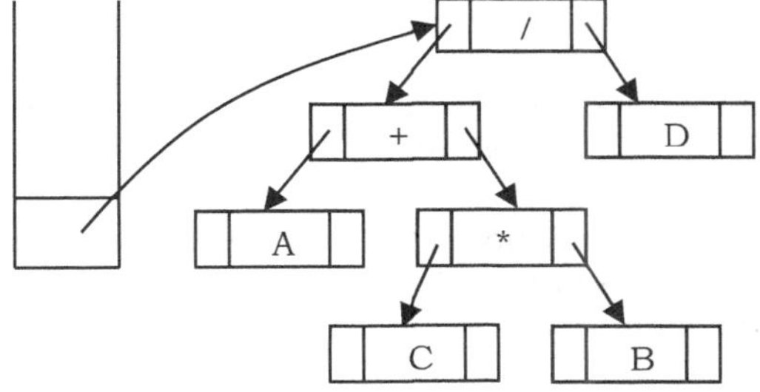


## 6.10 XOR Trees

This concept is similar to *memory efficient doubly linked lists* of *Linked Lists* chapter. Also, like threaded binary trees this representation does not need stacks or queues for traversing the trees. This representation is used for traversing back (to parent) and forth (to children) using ⊕ operation. To represent the same in XOR trees, for each node below are the rules used for representation:

- Each nodes left will have the ⊕ of its parent and its left children.
- Each nodes right will have the ⊕ of its parent and its right children.
- The root nodes parent is NULL and also leaf nodes children are NULL nodes.

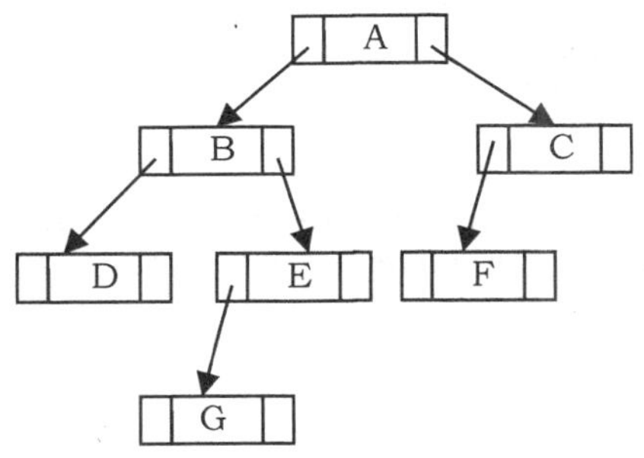

Based on the above rules and discussion, the tree can be represented as:

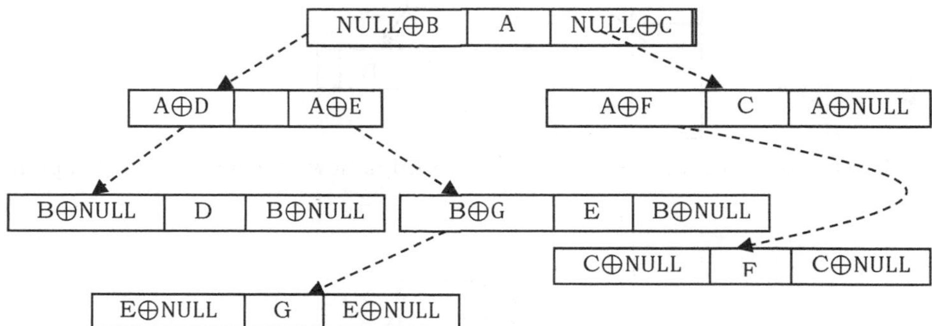


The major objective of this presentation is the ability to move to parent as well to children. Now, let us see how to use this representation for traversing the tree. For example, if we are at node B and want to move to its parent node A, then we just need to perform ⊕ on its left content with its left child address (we can use right child also for going to parent node). Similarly, if we want to move to its child (say, left child D) then we have to perform ⊕ on its left content with its parent node address. One important point that we need to understand about this representation is: When we are at node B, how do we know the address of its children D? Since the traversal starts at node root node, we can apply ⊕ on root's left content with NULL. As a result we get its left child, B. When we are at B, we can apply ⊕ on its left content with A address.

## 6.11 Binary Search Trees (BSTs)

### Why Binary Search Trees?

In previous sections we have discussed different tree representations and in all of them we did not impose any restriction on the nodes data. As a result, to search for an element we need to check both in left subtree and in right subtree. Due to this, the worst case complexity of search operation is $O(n)$. In this section, we will discuss another variant of binary trees: Binary Search Trees (BSTs). As the name suggests, the main use of this representation is for *searching*. In this representation we impose restriction on the kind of data a node can contain. As a result, it reduces the worst case average search operation to $O(logn)$.

### Binary Search Tree Property

In binary search trees, all the left subtree elements should be less than root data and all the right subtree elements should be greater than root data. This is called binary search tree property. Note that, this property should be satisfied at every node in the tree.

- The left subtree of a node contains only nodes with keys less than the nodes key.
- The right subtree of a node contains only nodes with keys greater than the nodes key.
- Both the left and right subtrees must also be binary search trees.

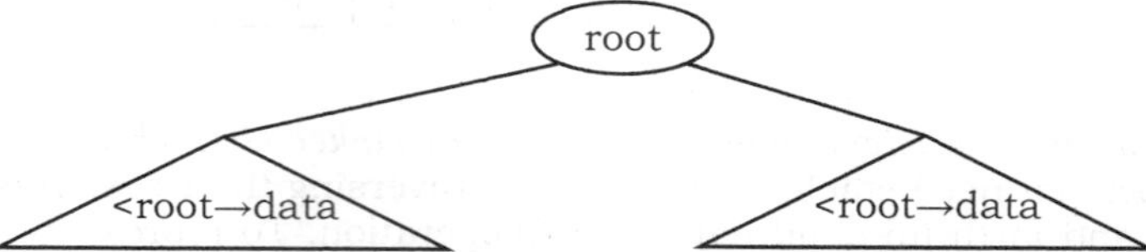


**Example:** The left tree is a binary search tree and the right tree is not a binary search tree (at node 6 it's not satisfying the binary search tree property).

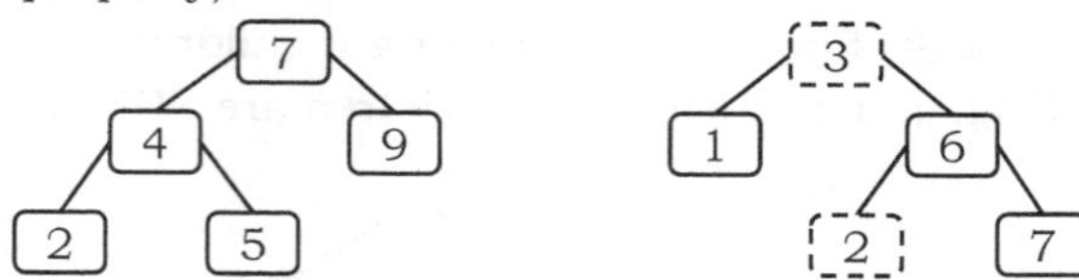


### Binary Search Tree Declaration

There is no difference between regular binary tree declaration and binary search tree declaration. The difference is only in data but not in structure. But for our convenience we change the structure name as:

```
struct BinarySearchTreeNode{
    int data;
    struct BinarySearchTreeNode *left;
    struct BinarySearchTreeNode *right;
};
```

## Operations on Binary Search Trees

**Main operations:** Following are the main operations that are supported by binary search trees:

- Find/ Find Minimum / Find Maximum element in binary search trees
- Inserting an element in binary search trees
- Deleting an element from binary search trees

**Auxiliary operations:** Checking whether the given tree is a binary search tree or not

- Finding $k^{th}$-smallest element in tree
- Sorting the elements of binary search tree and many more

## Important Notes on Binary Search Trees

- Since root data is always between left subtree data and right subtree data, performing inorder traversal on binary search tree produces a sorted list.
- While solving problems on binary search trees, first we process left subtree, then root data, and finally we process right subtree. This means, depending on the problem, only the intermediate step (processing root data) changes and we do not touch the first and third steps.
- If we are searching for an element and if the left subtree root data is less than the element we want to search, then skip it. The same is the case with the right subtree.. Because of this, binary search trees take less time for searching an element than regular binary trees. In other words, the binary search trees consider either left or right subtrees for searching an element but not both.
- The basic operations that can be performed on binary search tree (BST) are insertion of element, deletion of element, and searching for an element. While performing these operations on BST the height of the tree gets changed each time. Hence there exists variations in time complexities of best case, average case, and worst case.
- The basic operations on a binary search tree take time proportional to the height of the tree. For a complete binary tree with node n, such operations runs in O(lgn) worst-case time. If the tree is a linear chain of n nodes (skew-tree), however, the same operations takes O($n$) worst-case time.

## Finding an Element in Binary Search Trees

Find operation is straightforward in a BST. Start with the root and keep moving left or right using the BST property. If the data we are searching is same as nodes data then we return current node. If the data we are searching is less than nodes data then search left subtree of current node; otherwise search right subtree of current node. If the data is not present, we end up in a NULL link.

```
struct BinarySearchTreeNode *find(struct BinarySearchTreeNode *root, int data ){
    if( root == NULL )
        return NULL;
    if( data < root→data )
        return find(root→left, data);
    else if( data > root→data )
        return( find( root→right, data );
    return root;
}
```

Time Complexity: O($n$), in worst case (when BST is a skew tree). Space Complexity: O($n$), for recursive stack.

*Non recursive* version of the above algorithm can be given as:

```
struct BinarySearchTreeNode *find(struct BinarySearchTreeNode *root, int data ){
    if( root == NULL )
        return NULL;
    while (root) {
        if(data == root→data)
            return root;
        else if(data > root→data)
            root = root→right;
        else root = root→left;
    }
    return NULL;
}
```

Time Complexity: O($n$). Space Complexity: O(1).

## Finding Minimum Element in Binary Search Trees

In BSTs, the minimum element is the left-most node, which does not has left child. In the BST below, the minimum element is **4**.

```
struct BinarySearchTreeNode *findMin(struct BinarySearchTreeNode *root){
    if(root == NULL)
        return NULL;
    else if( root→left == NULL )
        return root;
    else
        return findMin( root→left );
}
```

Time Complexity: O($n$), in worst case (when BST is a *left skew* tree). Space Complexity: O($n$), for recursive stack.

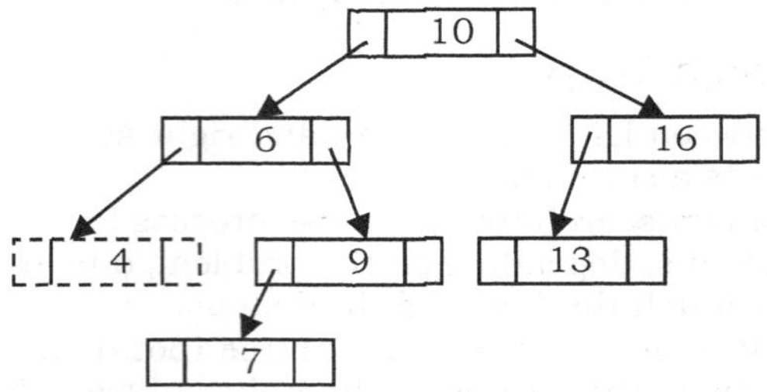


*Non recursive* version of the above algorithm can be given as:

```
struct BinarySearchTreeNode *findMin(struct BinarySearchTreeNode * root ) {
    if( root == NULL )
        return NULL;
    while( root→left != NULL )
        root = root→left;
    return root;
}
```

Time Complexity: O($n$). Space Complexity: O(1).

## Finding Maximum Element in Binary Search Trees

In BSTs, the maximum element is the right-most node, which does not have right child. In the BST below, the maximum element is **16**.

```
struct BinarySearchTreeNode *findMax(struct BinarySearchTreeNode *root) {
    if(root == NULL)
        return NULL;
    else if( root→right == NULL )
        return root;
    else
        return findMax( root→right );
}
```

Time Complexity: O($n$), in worst case (when BST is a *right skew* tree). Space Complexity: O($n$), for recursive stack.

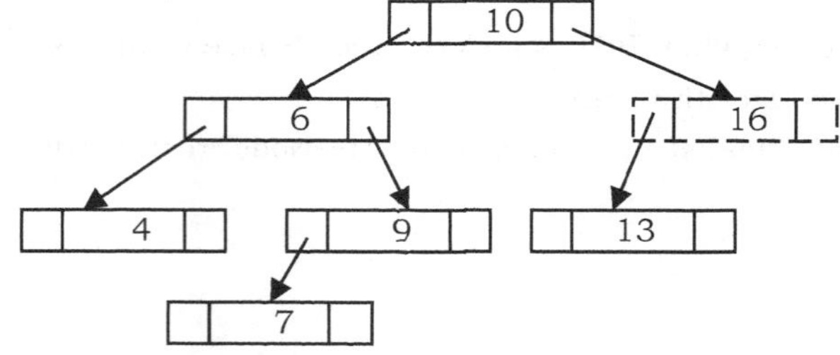


*Non recursive* version of the above algorithm can be given as:

```
struct BinarySearchTreeNode *findMax(struct BinarySearchTreeNode * root ) {
    if( root == NULL )
        return NULL;
    while( root→right != NULL )
        root = root→right;
    return root;
}
```

Time Complexity: O($n$). Space Complexity: O(1).

## Where is Inorder Predecessor and Successor?

Where is the inorder predecessor and successor of node $X$ in a binary search tree assuming all keys are distinct?

If $X$ has two children then its inorder predecessor is the maximum value in its left subtree and its inorder successor the minimum value in its right subtree.

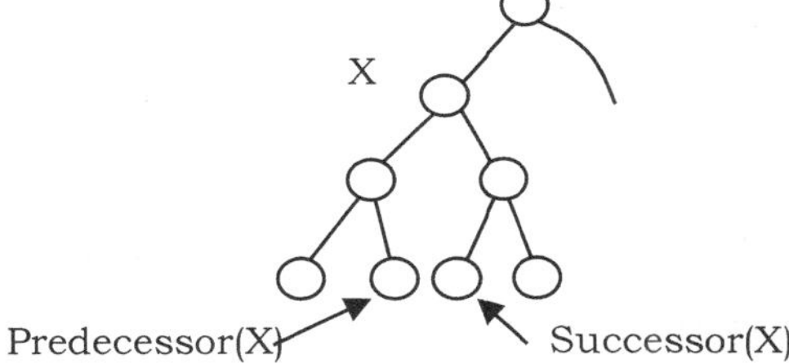


If it does not have a left child, then a node's inorder predecessor is its first left ancestor.

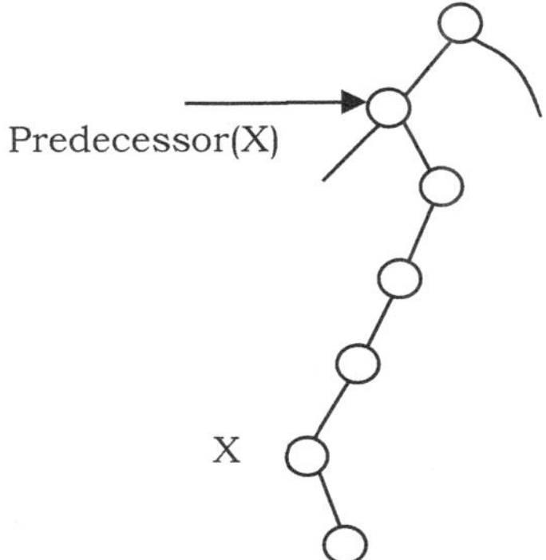


## Inserting an Element from Binary Search Tree

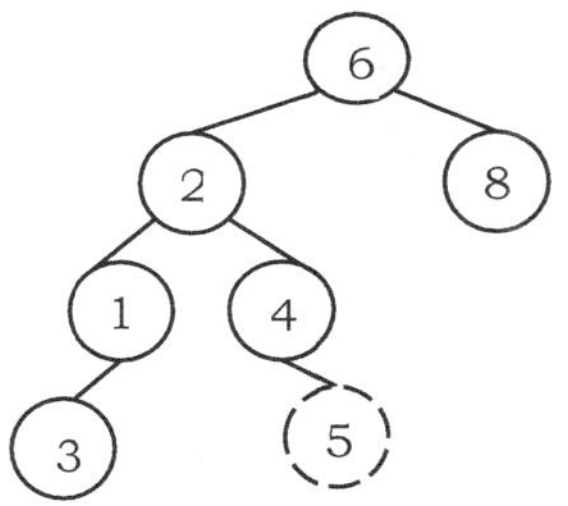


To insert *data* into binary search tree, first we need to find the location for that element. We can find the location of insertion by following the same mechanism as that of *find* operation. While finding the location, if the *data* is already there then we can simply neglect and come out. Otherwise, insert *data* at the last location on the path traversed.

As an example let us consider the following tree. The dotted node indicates the element (5) to be inserted. To insert 5, traverse the tree using *find* function. At node with key 4, we need to go right, but there is no subtree, so 5 is not in the tree, and this is the correct location for insertion.

```
struct BinarySearchTreeNode *insert(struct BinarySearchTreeNode *root, int data) {
   if( root == NULL ) {
      root = (struct BinarySearchTreeNode *) malloc(sizeof(struct  BinarySearchTreeNode));
      if( root == NULL ) {
         printf("Memory Error");
         return;
      }
      else {
         root→data = data;
         root→left = root→right = NULL;
      }
   }
   else {
      if( data < root→data )
```

```
            root→left = insert(root→left, data);
        else if( data > root→data )
            root→right = insert(root→right, data);
    }
    return root;
}
```

**Note:** In the above code, after inserting an element in subtrees, the tree is returned to its parent. As a result, the complete tree will get updated.

Time Complexity:O($n$).
Space Complexity:O($n$), for recursive stack. For iterative version, space complexity is O(1).

## Deleting an Element from Binary Search Tree

The delete operation is more complicated than other operations. This is because the element to be deleted may not be the leaf node. In this operation also, first we need to find the location of the element which we want to delete.

Once we have found the node to be deleted, consider the following cases:

- If the element to be deleted is a leaf node: return NULL to its parent. That means make the corresponding child pointer NULL. In the tree below to delete 5, set NULL to its parent node 2.

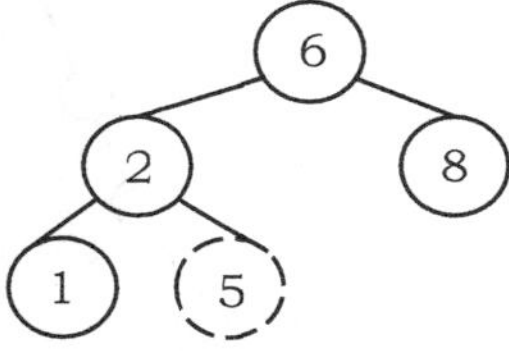


- If the element to be deleted has one child: In this case we just need to send the current node's child to its parent. In the tree below, to delete 4, 4 left subtree is set to its parent node 2.

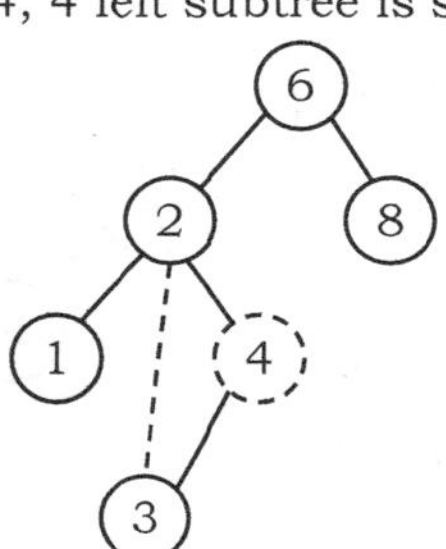


- If the element to be deleted has both children: The general strategy is to replace the key of this node with the largest element of the left subtree and recursively delete that node (which is now empty). The largest node in the left subtree cannot have a right child, so the second *delete* is an easy one. As an example, let us consider the following tree. In the tree below, to delete 8, it is the right child of the root. The key value is 8. It is replaced with the largest key in its left subtree (7), and then that node is deleted as before (second case).

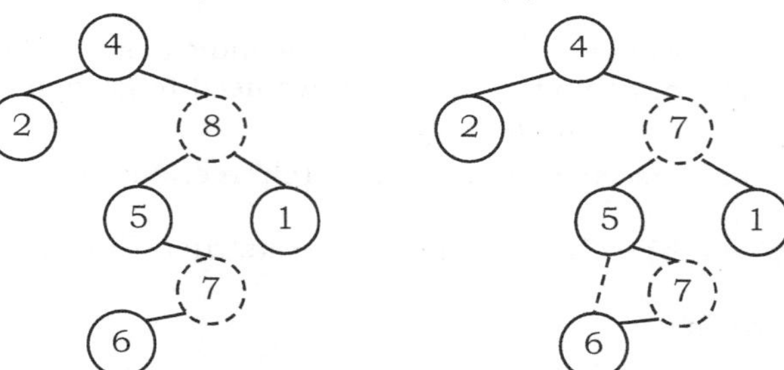


**Note:** We can replace with minimum element in right subtree also.

```
struct BinarySearchTreeNode *delete(struct BinarySearchTreeNode *root, int data) {
    struct BinarySearchTreeNode *temp;
    if( root == NULL )
        printf("Element not there in tree");
    else if(data < root→data)
        root→left = delete(root→left, data);
```

```
        else if(data > root→data )
            root→right = delete(root→right, data);
        else {
            // Found element
            if( root→left && root→right ) {
                /* Replace with largest in left subtree */
                temp = findMax( root→left );
                root→data = temp→data;
                root→left = delete(root→left, root→data);
            }
            else {
                /* One child */
                temp = root;
                if( root→left == NULL )
                    root = root→right;
                if( root→right == NULL )
                    root = root→left;
                free( temp );
            }
        }
        return root;
    }
```

Time Complexity: $O(n)$. Space Complexity: $O(n)$ for recursive stack. For iterative version, space complexity is $O(1)$.

## Binary Search Trees: Problems & Solutions

**Note**: For ordering related problems with binary search trees and balanced binary search trees, Inorder traversal has advantages over others as it gives the sorted order.

Problem-49 Given pointers to two nodes in a binary search tree, find the lowest common ancestor (*LCA*). Assume that both values already exist in the tree.

**Solution:**

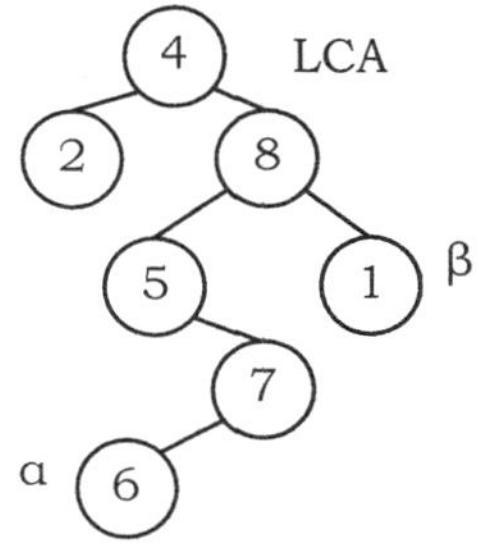


The main idea of the solution is: while traversing BST from root to bottom, the first node we encounter with value between $\alpha$ and $\beta$, i.e., $\alpha < node \rightarrow data < \beta$, is the Least Common Ancestor(LCA) of $\alpha$ and $\beta$ (where $\alpha < \beta$). So just traverse the BST in pre-order, and if we find a node with value in between $\alpha$ and $\beta$, then that node is the LCA. If its value is greater than both $\alpha$ and $\beta$, then the LCA lies on the left side of the node, and if its value is smaller than both α and β, then the LCA lies on the right side.

```
struct BinarySearchTreeNode *findLCA(struct BinarySearchTreeNode *root, struct BinarySearchTreeNode *α,
                                                        struct BinarySearchTreeNode * β) {
    while(1) {
        if((α→data < root→data && β→data > root→data) ||
                                            (α→data > root→data && β→data < root→data))
            return root;
        if(α→data < root→data)
            root = root→left;
        else root = root→right;
    }
}
```

Time Complexity: $O(n)$. Space Complexity: $O(n)$, for skew trees.

Problem-50 Give an algorithm for finding the shortest path between two nodes in a BST.

**Solution:** It's nothing but finding the LCA of two nodes in BST.

Problem-51 Give an algorithm for counting the number of BSTs possible with $n$ nodes.

**Solution:** This is a DP problem. Refer to chapter on *Dynamic Programming* for the algorithm.

Problem-52 Give an algorithm to check whether the given binary tree is a BST or not.

**Solution:**

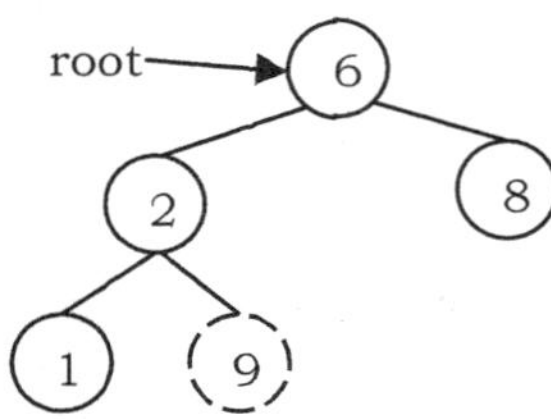


Consider the following simple program. For each node, check if the node on its left is smaller and check if the node on its right is greater. This approach is wrong as this will return true for binary tree below. Checking only at current node is not enough.

```
int isBST(struct BinaryTreeNode* root) {
    if(root == NULL)
        return 1;
    // false if left is > than root
    if(root→left != NULL && root→left→data > root→data)
        return 0;
    // false if right is < than root
    if(root→right != NULL && root→right→data < root→data)
        return 0;
    // false if, recursively, the left or right is not a BST
    if(!isBST(root→left) || !isBST(root→right))
        return 0;
    // passing all that, it's a BST
    return 1;
}
```

Problem-53 Can we think of getting the correct algorithm?

**Solution:** For each node, check if max value in left subtree is smaller than the current node data and min value in right subtree greater than the node data. It is assumed that we have helper functions *FindMin*() and *FindMax*() that return the min or max integer value from a non-empty tree.

```
/* Returns true if a binary tree is a binary search tree */
int isBST(struct BinaryTreeNode* root) {
    if(root == NULL)
        return 1;
    /* false if the max of the left is > than root */
    if(root→left != NULL && findMax(root→left) > root→data)
        return 0;
    /* false if the min of the right is <= than root */
    if(root→right != NULL && findMin(root→right) < root→data)
        return 0;
    /* false if, recursively, the left or right is not a BST */
    if(!isBST(root→left) || !isBST(root→right))
        return 0;
    /* passing all that, it's a BST */
    return 1;
}
```

Time Complexity: $O(n^2)$. Space Complexity: $O(n)$.

Problem-54 Can we improve the complexity of Problem-53?

**Solution: Yes.** A better solution is to look at each node only once. The trick is to write a utility helper function isBSTUtil(struct BinaryTreeNode* root, int min, int max) that traverses down the tree keeping track of the narrowing min and max allowed values as it goes, looking at each node only once. The initial values for min and max should be INT_MIN and INT_MAX — they narrow from there.

```
Initial call: isBST(root, INT_MIN, INT_MAX);
int isBST(struct BinaryTreeNode *root, int min, int max) {
    if(!root)
        return 1;
```

```
        return (root->data >min && root->data < max && isBST(root->left, min, root->data) && isBST(root->right,
root->data, max));
    }
```

Time Complexity: $O(n)$. Space Complexity: $O(n)$, for stack space.

Problem-55 Can we further improve the complexity of Problem-53?

**Solution: Yes,** by using inorder traversal. The idea behind this solution is that inorder traversal of BST produces sorted lists. While traversing the BST in inorder, at each node check the condition that its key value should be greater than the key value of its previous visited node. Also, we need to initialize the prev with possible minimum integer value (say, INT_MIN).

```
int prev = INT_MIN;
int isBST(struct BinaryTreeNode *root, int *prev) {
    if(!root) return 1;
    if(!isBST(root→left, prev))
        return 0;
    if(root→data < *prev)
        return 0;
    *prev = root→data;
    return isBST(root→right, prev);
}
```

Time Complexity: $O(n)$. Space Complexity: $O(n)$, for stack space.

Problem-56 Give an algorithm for converting BST to circular DLL with space complexity O(1).

**Solution:** Convert left and right subtrees to DLLs and maintain end of those lists. Then, adjust the pointers.

```
struct BinarySearchTreeNode *BST2DLL(struct BinarySearchTreeNode *root, struct BinarySearchTreeNode
**Ltail) {
    struct BinarySearchTreeNode *left, *ltail, *right, *rtail;
    if(!root) {
        *ltail = NULL;
            return NULL;
    }
    left = BST2DLL(root→left, &ltail);
    right = BST2DLL(root→right, &rtail);
    root→left = ltail;
    root→right = right;
    if(!right)
        * ltail = root;
    else {
        right→left = root;
        *ltail = rtail;
    }
    if(!left)
        return root;
    else {
        ltail→right = root;
        return left;
    }
}
```

Time Complexity: $O(n)$.

Problem-57 For Problem-56, is there any other way of solving it?

**Solution: Yes.** There is an alternative solution based on the divide and conquer method which is quite neat.

```
struct BinarySearchTreeNode *Append(struct BinarySearchTreeNode *a, struct BinarySearchTreeNode *b) {
    struct BinarySearchTreeNode *aLast, *bLast;
    if (a==NULL) return b;
    if (b==NULL) return a;
    aLast = a→left;
    bLast = b→left;
    aLast→right = b;
    b→left = aLast;
    bLast→right = a;
```

```
        a→left = bLast;
        return a;
    }
    struct BinarySearchTreeNode* TreeToList(struct BinarySearchTreeNode *root) {
        struct BinarySearchTreeNode *aList, *bList;
        if (root==NULL)
          return NULL;
        aList = TreeToList(root→left);
        bList = TreeToList(root→right);
        root→left = root;
        root→right = root;
        aList = Append(aList, root);
        aList = Append(aList, bList);
        return(aList);
    }
```

Time Complexity: $O(n)$.

Problem-58 Given a sorted doubly linked list, give an algorithm for converting it into balanced binary search tree.

**Solution:** Find the middle node and adjust the pointers.

```
    struct DLLNode * DLLtoBalancedBST(struct DLLNode *head) {
        struct DLLNode *temp, *p, *q;
        if( !head || !head→next)
            return head;
        temp = findMiddleNode(head);
        p = head;
        while(p→next != temp)
            p = p→next;
        p→next = NULL;
        q = temp→next;
        temp→next = NULL;
        temp→prev = DLLtoBalancedBST(head);
        temp→next = DLLtoBalancedBST(q);
        return temp;
    }
```

Time Complexity: $2T(n/2) + O(n)$ [for finding the middle node] = $O(nlogn)$.

**Note:** For *FindMiddleNode* function refer *Linked Lists* chapter.

Problem-59 Given a sorted array, give an algorithm for converting the array to BST.

**Solution:** If we have to choose an array element to be the root of a balanced BST, which element should we pick? The root of a balanced BST should be the middle element from the sorted array. We would pick the middle element from the sorted array in each iteration. We then create a node in the tree initialized with this element. After the element is chosen, what is left? Could you identify the sub-problems within the problem?

There are two arrays left — the one on its left and the one on its right. These two arrays are the sub-problems of the original problem, since both of them are sorted. Furthermore, they are subtrees of the current node's left and right child.

The code below creates a balanced BST from the sorted array in $O(n)$ time ($n$ is the number of elements in the array). Compare how similar the code is to a binary search algorithm. Both are using the divide and conquer methodology.

```
    struct BinaryTreeNode * buildBST(int A[], int left, int right) {
        struct BinaryTreeNode * newNode;
        int mid;
        if (left > right)
            return NULL;
        newNode = (struct BinaryTreeNode * ) malloc(sizeof(struct BinaryTreeNode));
        if (!newNode) {
            printf("Memory Error");
            return;
        }
        if (left == right) {
            newNode→ data = A[left];
```

```
        newNode→ left = newNode→ right = NULL;
    } else {
        mid = left + (right - left) / 2;
        newNode→ data = A[mid];
        newNode→ left = buildBST(A, left, mid - 1);
        newNode→ right = buildBST(A, mid + 1, right);
    }
    return newNode;
}
```

Time Complexity: O($n$). Space Complexity: O($n$), for stack space.

Problem-60 Given a singly linked list where elements are sorted in ascending order, convert it to a height balanced BST.

**Solution:** A naive way is to apply the Problem-58 solution directly. In each recursive call, we would have to traverse half of the list's length to find the middle element. The run time complexity is clearly O($nlogn$), where $n$ is the total number of elements in the list. This is because each level of recursive call requires a total of $n/2$ traversal steps in the list, and there are a total of $logn$ number of levels (ie, the height of the balanced tree).

Problem-61 For Problem-60, can we improve the complexity?

**Solution: Hint**: How about inserting nodes following the list order? If we can achieve this, we no longer need to find the middle element as we are able to traverse the list while inserting nodes to the tree.

**Best Solution:** As usual, the best solution requires us to think from another perspective. In other words, we no longer create nodes in the tree using the top-down approach. Create nodes bottom-up, and assign them to their parents. The bottom-up approach enables us to access the list in its order while creating nodes [42].

Isn't the bottom-up approach precise? Any time we are stuck with the top-down approach, we can give bottom-up a try. Although the bottom-up approach is not the most natural way we think, it is helpful in some cases. However, we should prefer top-down instead of bottom-up in general, since the latter is more difficult to verify.

Below is the code for converting a singly linked list to a balanced BST. Please note that the algorithm requires the list length to be passed in as the function parameters. The list length can be found in O($n$) time by traversing the entire list once. The recursive calls traverse the list and create tree nodes by the list order, which also takes O($n$) time. Therefore, the overall run time complexity is still O($n$).

```
struct BinaryTreeNode* sortedListToBST(struct ListNode *& list, int start, int end) {
    if(start > end)
        return NULL;
    // same as (start+end)/2, avoids overflow
    int mid = start + (end - start) / 2;
    struct BinaryTreeNode *leftChild = sortedListToBST(list, start, mid-1);
    struct BinaryTreeNode * parent;
    parent = (struct BinaryTreeNode *)malloc(sizeof(struct BinaryTreeNode));
    if(!parent) {
        printf("Memory Error");
        return;
    }
    parent→data=list→data;
    parent→left = leftChild;
    list = list→next;
    parent→right = sortedListToBST(list, mid+1, end);
    return parent;
}
struct BinaryTreeNode * sortedListToBST(struct ListNode *head, int n) {
    return sortedListToBST(head, 0, n-1);
}
```

Problem-62 Give an algorithm for finding the $k^{th}$ smallest element in BST.

**Solution:** The idea behind this solution is that, inorder traversal of BST produces sorted lists. While traversing the BST in inorder, keep track of the number of elements visited.

```
struct BinarySearchTreeNode *kthSmallestInBST(struct BinarySearchTreeNode *root, int k, int *count){
    if(!root)
        return NULL;
    struct BinarySearchTreeNode *left = kthSmallestInBST(root→left, k, count);
    if( left )
```

```
        return left;
    if(++count == k)
        return root;
    return kthSmallestInBST(root→right, k, count);
}
```

Time Complexity: O($n$). Space Complexity: O(1).

Problem-63 **Floor and ceiling:** If a given key is less than the key at the root of a BST then the floor of the key (the largest key in the BST less than or equal to the key) must be in the left subtree. If the key is greater than the key at the root, then the floor of the key could be in the right subtree, but only if there is a key smaller than or equal to the key in the right subtree; if not (or if the key is equal to the key at the root) then the key at the root is the floor of the key. Finding the ceiling is similar, with interchanging right and left. For example, if the sorted with input array is {1, 2, 8, 10, 10, 12, 19}, then

For $x = 0$: floor doesn't exist in array, ceil = 1, For $x = 1$: floor = 1, ceil = 1

For $x = 5$: floor = 2, ceil = 8, For $x = 20$: floor = 19, ceil doesn't exist in array

**Solution:** The idea behind this solution is that, inorder traversal of BST produces sorted lists. While traversing the BST in inorder, keep track of the values being visited. If the roots data is greater than the given value then return the previous value which we have maintained during traversal. If the roots data is equal to the given data then return root data.

```
struct BinaryTreeNode * floorInBST(struct BinaryTreeNode * root, int data) {
    struct BinaryTreeNode * prev = NULL;
    return floorInBSTUtil(root, prev, data);
}
struct BinaryTreeNode * floorInBSTUtil(struct BinaryTreeNode * root, struct BinaryTreeNode * prev, int data) {
    if (!root)
        return NULL;
    if (!floorInBSTUtil(root→ left, prev, data))
        return 0;
    if (root→ data == data)
        return root;
    if (root→ data > data)
        return prev;
    prev = root;
    return floorInBSTUtil(root→ right, prev, data);
}
```

Time Complexity: O($n$). Space Complexity: O($n$), for stack space.

For ceiling, we just need to call the right subtree first, followed by left subtree.

```
struct BinaryTreeNode *ceilingInBST(struct BinaryTreeNode *root, int data){
    struct BinaryTreeNode *prev=NULL;
    return ceilingInBSTUtil(root, prev, data);
}
struct BinaryTreeNode *ceilingInBSTUtil(struct BinaryTreeNode *root,  struct BinaryTreeNode *prev, int data){
    if(!root)
            return NULL;
    if(!ceilingInBSTUtil(root→right, prev, data))
            return 0;
    if(root→data == data)
            return root;
    if(root→data < data)
            return prev;
    prev = root;
    return ceilingInBSTUtil(root→left, prev, data);
}
```

Time Complexity: O($n$). Space Complexity: O($n$), for stack space.

Problem-64 Give an algorithm for finding the union and intersection of BSTs. Assume parent pointers are available (say threaded binary trees). Also, assume the lengths of two BSTs are $m$ and $n$ respectively.

**Solution:** If parent pointers are available then the problem is same as merging of two sorted lists. This is because if we call inorder successor each time we get the next highest element. It's just a matter of which inorderSuccessor to call.

Time Complexity: O($m + n$). Space complexity: O(1).

Problem-65 For Problem-64, what if parent pointers are not available?

**Solution:** If parent pointers are not available, the BSTs can be converted to linked lists and then merged.

1 Convert both the BSTs into sorted doubly linked lists in $O(n + m)$ time. This produces 2 sorted lists.
2 Merge the two double linked lists into one and also maintain the count of total elements in $O(n + m)$ time.
3 Convert the sorted doubly linked list into height balanced tree in $O(n + m)$ time.

Problem-66 For Problem-64, is there any alternative way of solving the problem?

**Solution:** Yes, by using inorder traversal.

- Perform inorder traversal on one of the BSTs.
- While performing the traversal store them in table (hash table).
- After completion of the traversal of first *BST*, start traversal of second *BST* and compare them with hash table contents.

Time Complexity: $O(m + n)$. Space Complexity: $O(Max(m, n))$.

Problem-67 Given a *BST* and two numbers *K*1 and *K*2, give an algorithm for printing all the elements of *BST* in the range *K*1 and *K*2.

**Solution:**

```
void rangePrinter(struct BinarySearchTreeNode * root, int K1, int K2) {
    if (root == NULL) return;
    if (root→ data >= K1) rangePrinter(root→ left, K1, K2);
    if (root→ data >= K1 && root→ data <= K2) printf(" % d", root→ data);
    if (root→ data <= K2) rangePrinter(root→ right, K1, K2);
}
```

Time Complexity: $O(n)$. Space Complexity: $O(n)$, for stack space.

Problem-68 For Problem-67, is there any alternative way of solving the problem?

**Solution:** We can use level order traversal: while adding the elements to queue check for the range.

```
void rangeSeachLevelOrder(struct BinarySearchTreeNode *root, int K1, int K2){
    struct BinarySearchTreeNode *temp;
    struct Queue *Q = createQueue();
    if(!root)
        return NULL;
    Q = enQueue(Q, root);
    while(!isEmpty(Q)) {
            temp=deQueue(Q);
            if(temp→data >= K1 && temp→data <= K2)
                printf("%d",temp→data);
            if(temp→left && temp→data >= K1)
                enQueue(Q, temp→left);
            if(temp→right && temp→data <= K2)
                enQueue(Q, temp→right);
    }
    deleteQueue(Q);
    return NULL;
}
```

Time Complexity: $O(n)$. Space Complexity: $O(n)$, for queue.

Problem-69 For Problem-67, can we still think of an alternative way to solve the problem?

**Solution:** First locate *K*1 with normal binary search and after that use InOrder successor until we encounter *K*2. For algorithm, refer to problems section of threaded binary trees.

Problem-70 Given root of a Binary Search tree, trim the tree, so that all elements returned in the new tree are between the inputs *A* and *B*.

**Solution:** It's just another way of asking Problem-67.

Problem-71 Given two BSTs, check whether the elements of them are the same or not. For example: two BSTs with data 10 5 20 15 30 and 10 20 15 30 5 should return true and the dataset with 10 5 20 15 30 and 10 15 30 20 5 should return false. **Note:** BSTs data can be in any order.

**Solution:** One simple way is performing an inorder traversal on first tree and storing its data in hash table. As a second step, perform inorder traversal on second tree and check whether that data is already there in hash table or not (if it exists in hash table then mark it with -1 or some unique value).

During the traversal of second tree if we find any mismatch return false. After traversal of second tree check whether it has all -1s in the hash table or not (this ensures extra data available in second tree).

Time Complexity: $O(max(m, n))$, where $m$ and $n$ are the number of elements in first and second BST.
Space Complexity: $O(max(m, n))$. This depends on the size of the first tree.

Problem-72 For Problem-71, can we reduce the time complexity?

**Solution:** Instead of performing the traversals one after the other, we can perform $in - order$ traversal of both the trees in parallel. Since the $in - order$ traversal gives the sorted list, we can check whether both the trees are generating the same sequence or not.

Time Complexity: $O(max(m, n))$. Space Complexity: O(1). This depends on the size of the first tree.

Problem-73 For the key values $1 \ldots n$, how many structurally unique BSTs are possible that store those keys.

**Solution:** Strategy: consider that each value could be the root. Recursively find the size of the left and right subtrees.

```
int countTrees(int n) {
    if (n <= 1)
        return 1;
    else {
        // there will be one value at the root, with whatever remains on the left and right
        // each forming their own subtrees. Iterate through all the values that could be the root...
        int sum = 0;
        int left, right, root;
        for (root=1; root<=n; root++) {
            left = countTrees(root - 1);
            right = countTrees(n - root);
            // number of possible trees with this root == left*right
            sum += left*right;
        }
        return(sum);
    }
}
```

Problem-72 Given a BST of size $n$, in which each node r has an additional field $r \rightarrow size$, the number of the keys in the sub-tree rooted at $r$ (including the root node $r$). Give an $O(h)$ algorithm $GreaterthanConstant(r, k)$ to find the number of keys that are strictly greater than $k$ ($h$ is the height of the binary search tree).

**Solution**:

```
int greaterthanConstant (struct BinarySearchTreeNode *r, int k){
    keysCount = 0
    while (r != Null ){
        if (k < r→data){
            keysCount = keysCount + r→right→size + 1;
            r = r→left;
        }
        else if (k > r→data)
            r = r→right;
        else{ // k = r→data
            keysCount = keysCount + r→right→size;
            break;
        }
    }
    return keysCount;
}
```

The suggested algorithm works well if the key is a unique value for each node. Otherwise when reaching $k{=}r{\rightarrow}data$, we should start a process of moving to the right until reaching a node $y$ with a key that is bigger then $k$, and then we should return $keysCount + y{\rightarrow}size$. Time Complexity: $O(h)$ where $h{=}O(n)$ in the worst case and $O(logn)$ in the average case.

## 6.12 Balanced Binary Search Trees

In earlier sections we have seen different trees whose worst case complexity is $O(n)$, where $n$ is the number of nodes in the tree. This happens when the trees are skew trees. In this section we will try to reduce this worst case complexity to $O(logn)$ by imposing restrictions on the heights.

In general, the height balanced trees are represented with $HB(k)$, where $k$ is the difference between left subtree height and right subtree height. Sometimes $k$ is called balance factor.

## Full Balanced Binary Search Trees

In $HB(k)$, if $k = 0$ (if balance factor is zero), then we call such binary search trees as *full* balanced binary search trees. That means, in $HB(0)$ binary search tree, the difference between left subtree height and right subtree height should be at most zero. This ensures that the tree is a full binary tree. For example,

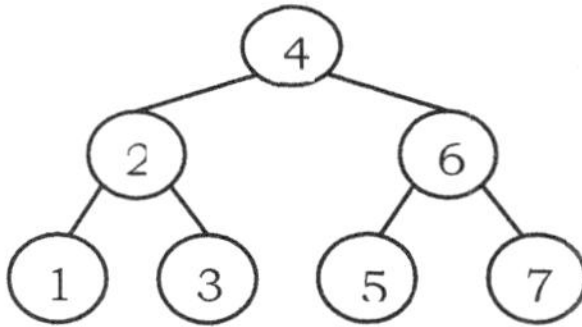


**Note:** For constructing $HB(0)$ tree refer to *Problems* section.

## 6.13 AVL (Adelson-Velskii and Landis) Trees

In $HB(k)$, if $k = 1$ (if balance factor is one), such a binary search tree is called an *AVL tree*. That means an AVL tree is a binary search tree with a *balance* condition: the difference between left subtree height and right subtree height is at most 1.

## Properties of AVL Trees

A binary tree is said to be an AVL tree, if:

- It is a binary search tree, and
- For any node $X$, the height of left subtree of $X$ and height of right subtree of $X$ differ by at most 1.

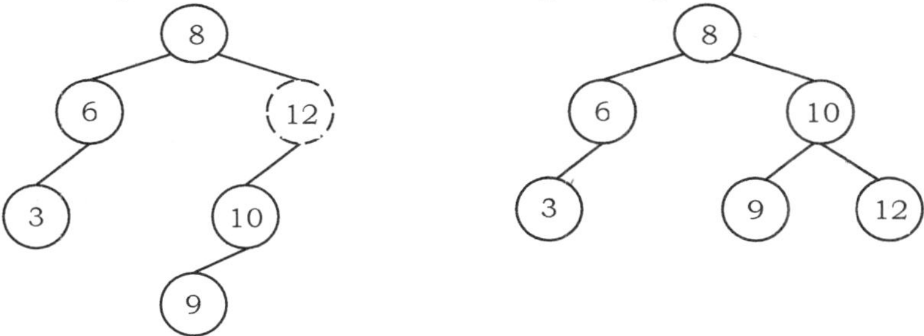


As an example, among the above binary search trees, the left one is not an AVL tree, whereas the right binary search tree is an AVL tree.

## Minimum/Maximum Number of Nodes in AVL Tree

For simplicity let us assume that the height of an AVL tree is $h$ and $N(h)$ indicates the number of nodes in AVL tree with height $h$. To get the minimum number of nodes with height $h$, we should fill the tree with the minimum number of nodes possible. That means if we fill the left subtree with height $h-1$ then we should fill the right subtree with height $h-2$. As a result, the minimum number of nodes with height $h$ is:

$$N(h) = N(h-1) + N(h-2) + 1$$

In the above equation:

- $N(h-1)$ indicates the minimum number of nodes with height $h-1$.
- $N(h-2)$ indicates the minimum number of nodes with height $h-2$.
- In the above expression, "1" indicates the current node.

We can give $N(h-1)$ either for left subtree or right subtree. Solving the above recurrence gives:

$$N(h) = O(1.618^h) \Longrightarrow h = 1.44logn \approx O(logn)$$

Where $n$ is the number of nodes in AVL tree. Also, the above derivation says that the maximum height in AVL trees is $O(logn)$. Similarly, to get maximum number of nodes, we need to fill both left and right subtrees with height $h-1$. As a result, we get:

$$N(h) = N(h-1) + N(h-1) + 1 = 2N(h-1) + 1$$

The above expression defines the case of full binary tree. Solving the recurrence we get:

$$N(h) = O(2^h) \Longrightarrow h = logn \approx O(logn)$$

$\therefore$ In both the cases, AVL tree property is ensuring that the height of an AVL tree with $n$ nodes is $O(logn)$.

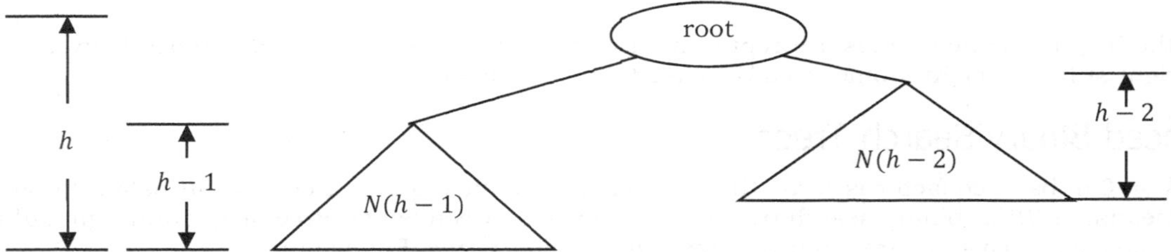


## AVL Tree Declaration

Since AVL tree is a BST, the declaration of AVL is similar to that of BST. But just to simplify the operations, we also include the height as part of the declaration.

```
struct AVLTreeNode{
    struct AVLTreeNode *left;
    int data;
    struct AVLTreeNode *right;
    int height;
};
```

## Finding the Height of an AVL tree

```
int height(struct AVLTreeNode *root ){
    if( !root)
        return -1;
    else
        return root→height;
}
```

Time Complexity: O(1).

## Rotations

When the tree structure changes (e.g., with insertion or deletion), we need to modify the tree to restore the AVL tree property. This can be done using single rotations or double rotations. Since an insertion/deletion involves adding/deleting a single node, this can only increase/decrease the height of a subtree by 1.

So, if the AVL tree property is violated at a node $X$, it means that the heights of left($X$) and right($X$) differ by exactly 2. This is because, if we balance the AVL tree every time, then at any point, the difference in heights of left($X$) and right($X$) differ by exactly 2. Rotations is the technique used for restoring the AVL tree property. This means, we need to apply the rotations for the node $X$.

**Observation:** One important observation is that, after an insertion, only nodes that are on the path from the insertion point to the root might have their balances altered, because only those nodes have their subtrees altered. To restore the AVL tree property, we start at the insertion point and keep going to the root of the tree.

While moving to the root, we need to consider the first node that is not satisfying the AVL property. From that node onwards, every node on the path to the root will have the issue.

Also, if we fix the issue for that first node, then all other nodes on the path to the root will automatically satisfy the AVL tree property. That means we always need to care for the first node that is not satisfying the AVL property on the path from the insertion point to the root and fix it.

## Types of Violations

Let us assume the node that must be rebalanced is $X$. Since any node has at most two children, and a height imbalance requires that $X$'s two subtree heights differ by two, we can observe that a violation might occur in four cases:

1. An insertion into the left subtree of the left child of $X$.
2. An insertion into the right subtree of the left child of $X$.
3. An insertion into the left subtree of the right child of $X$.
4. An insertion into the right subtree of the right child of $X$.

Cases 1 and 4 are symmetric and easily solved with single rotations. Similarly, cases 2 and 3 are also symmetric and can be solved with double rotations (needs two single rotations).

## Single Rotations

**Left Left Rotation (LL Rotation) [Case-1]:** In the case below, node *X* is not satisfying the AVL tree property. As discussed earlier, the rotation does not have to be done at the root of a tree. In general, we start at the node inserted and travel up the tree, updating the balance information at every node on the path.

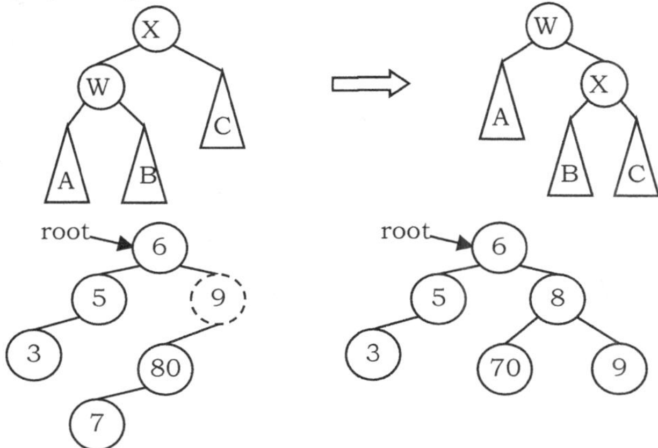


For example, in the figure above, after the insertion of 7 in the original AVL tree on the left, node 9 becomes unbalanced. So, we do a single left-left rotation at 9. As a result we get the tree on the right.

```
struct AVLTreeNode *singleRotateLeft(struct AVLTreeNode *X ){
    struct AVLTreeNode *W = X→left;
    X→left = W→right;
    W→right = X;
    X→height = max( height(X→left), height(X→right) ) + 1;
    W→height = max( height(W→left), X→height ) + 1;
    return W;  /* New root */
}
```

Time Complexity: O(1). Space Complexity: O(1).

**Right Right Rotation (RR Rotation) [Case-4]:** In this case, node *X* is not satisfying the AVL tree property.

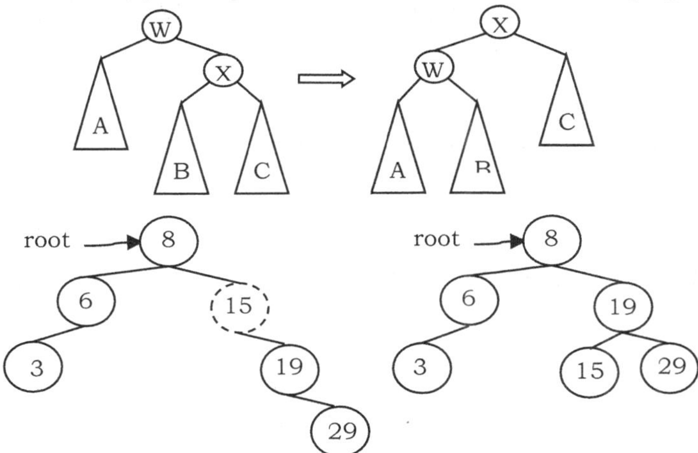


For example, in the above figure, after the insertion of 29 in the original AVL tree on the left, node 15 becomes unbalanced. So, we do a single right-right rotation at 15. As a result we get the tree on the right.

```
struct AVLTreeNode *singleRotateRight(struct AVLTreeNode *W ) {
    struct AVLTreeNode *X  = W→right;
    W→right = X→left;
    X→left = W;
    W→height = max( height(W→right), height(W→left) ) + 1;
    X→height = max( height(X→right), W→height) + 1;
    return X;
}
```

Time Complexity: O(1). Space Complexity: O(1).

## Double Rotations

**Left Right Rotation (LR Rotation) [Case-2]:** For case-2 and case-3 single rotation does not fix the problem. We need to perform two rotations.

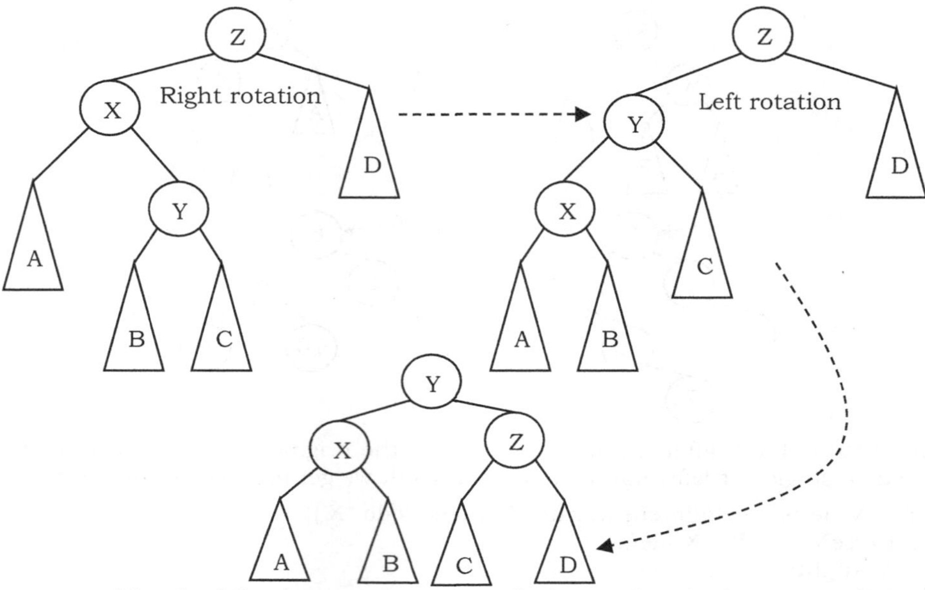


As an example, let us consider the following tree: Insertion of 7 is creating the case-2 scenario and right side tree is the one after double rotation.

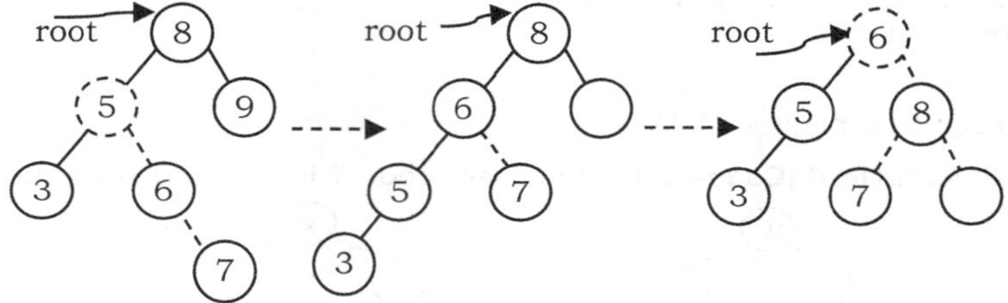


Code for left-right double rotation can be given as:

```
struct AVLTreeNode *doubleRotatewithLeft( struct AVLTreeNode *Z ){
    Z→left = singleRotateRight( Z→left );
    return singleRotateLeft(Z);
}
```

**Right Left Rotation (RL Rotation) [Case-3]:** Similar to case-2, we need to perform two rotations to fix this scenario.

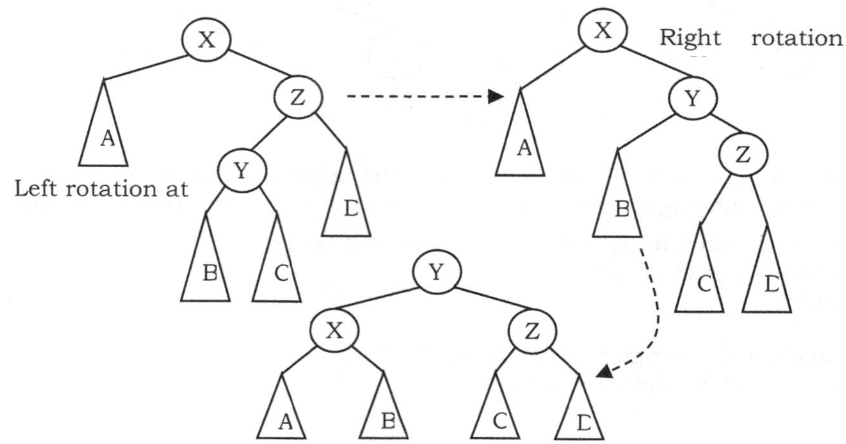

As an example, let us consider the following tree: The insertion of 6 is creating the case-3 scenario and the right side tree is the one after the double rotation.

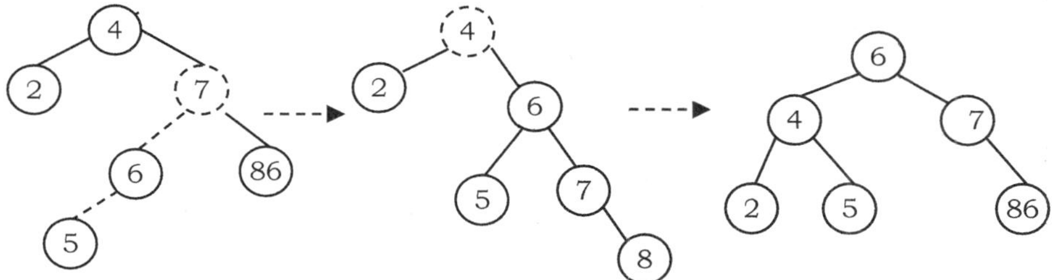


## Insertion into an AVL tree

Insertion into an AVL tree is similar to a BST insertion. After inserting the element, we just need to check whether there is any height imbalance. If there is an imbalance, call the appropriate rotation functions.

```
struct AVLTreeNode *insert( struct AVLTreeNode *root, struct AVLTreeNode *parent, int data){
    if( !root) {
        root = (struct AVLTreeNode*) malloc(sizeof (struct AVLTreeNode*) );
        if(!root) {
            printf("Memory Error");
            return NULL;
        }
        else {
            root→data = data;
            root→height = 0;
            root→left = root→right = NULL;
        }
    }
    else if( data < root→data ) {
        root→left = insert( root→left, root, data );
        if( ( height( root→left ) - height( root→right ) ) == 2 ) {
            if( data < root→left→data )
                root = singleRotateLeft( root );
            else        root = doubleRotateLeft( root );
        }
    }
    else if( data > root→data ) {
        root→right = insert( root→right, root, data );
        if( ( height( root→right ) - height( root→left ) ) == 2 ) {
            if( data < root→right→data )
                root = singleRotateRight( root );
            else  root = doubleRotateRight( root );
        }
    }
    /* Else data is in the tree already. We'll do nothing */
    root→height = max( height(root→left), height(root→right) ) + 1;
    return root;
}
```

Time Complexity: $O(logn)$. Space Complexity: $O(logn)$.

## AVL Trees: Problems & Solutions

**Problem-73** Given a height $h$, give an algorithm for generating the $HB(0)$.

**Solution:** As we have discussed, $HB(0)$ is nothing but generating full binary tree. In full binary tree the number of nodes with height $h$ is: $2^{h+1} - 1$ (let us assume that the height of a tree with one node is 0). As a result the nodes can be numbered as: 1 to $2^{h+1} - 1$.

```
struct BinarySearchTreeNode *buildHB0(int h){
    struct BinarySearchTreeNode *temp;
    if(h == 0)
        return NULL;
    temp = (struct BinarySearchTreeNode *) malloc (sizeof(struct BinarySearchTreeNode));
    temp→left = buildHB0 (h-1);
```

```
        temp→data = count++;      //assume count is a global variable
        temp→right = buildHB0 (h-1);
        return temp;
    }
```

Time Complexity: O($n$). Space Complexity: O($logn$), where $logn$ indicates the maximum stack size which is equal to height of tree.

**Problem-74** Is there any alternative way of solving Problem-73?

**Solution: Yes**, we can solve it following Mergesort logic. That means, instead of working with height, we can take the range. With this approach we do not need any global counter to be maintained.

```
    struct BinarySearchTreeNode *buildHB0(int l, int r){
        struct BinarySearchTreeNode *temp;
        int mid = l + (r-l)/2;
        if( l > r)
            return NULL;
        temp = (struct BinarySearchTreeNode *) malloc (sizeof(struct BinarySearchTreeNode));
        temp→data = mid;
        temp→left = buildHB0(l, mid-1);
        temp→right = buildHB0(mid+1, r);
        return temp;
    }
```

The initial call to the $BuildHB0$ function could be: $BuildHB0(1,\ 1 \ll h)$. $1 \ll h$ does the shift operation for calculating the $2^{h+1} - 1$.

Time Complexity: O($n$). Space Complexity: O($logn$). Where $logn$ indicates maximum stack size which is equal to the height of the tree.

**Problem-75** Construct minimal AVL trees of height 0, 1, 2, 3, 4, and 5. What is the number of nodes in a minimal AVL tree of height 6?

**Solution** Let $N(h)$ be the number of nodes in a minimal AVL tree with height $h$.

$N(0) = 1$

$N(1) = 2$

$N(h) = 1 + N(h-1) + N(h-2)$

$N(2) = 1 + N(1) + N(0)$
$= 1 + 2 + 1 = 4$

$N(3) = 1 + N(2) + N(1)$
$= 1 + 4 + 2 = 7$

$N(4) = 1 + N(3) + N(2)$
$= 1 + 7 + 4 = 12$

$N(5) = 1 + N(4) + N(3)$
$= 1 + 12 + 7 = 20$

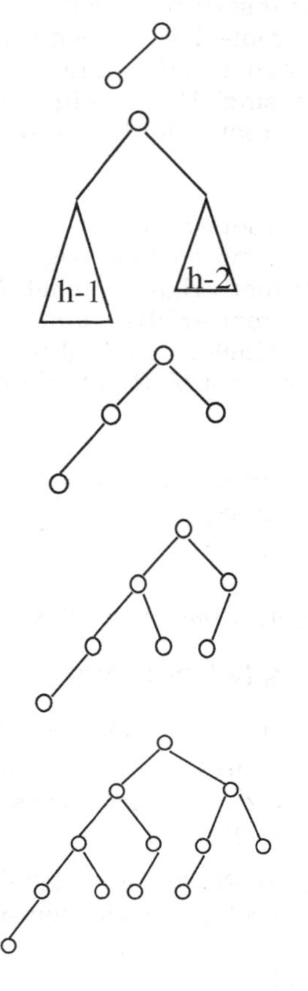

**Problem-76** For Problem-73, how many different shapes can there be of a minimal AVL tree of height $h$?

**Solution:** Let $NS(h)$ be the number of different shapes of a minimal AVL tree of height $h$.

$$NS(0) = 1$$

$$NS(1) = 2$$

$$NS(2) = 2 * NS(1) * NS(0) = 2 * 2 * 1 = 4$$

$$NS(3) = 2 * NS(2) * NS(1) = 2 * 4 * 1 = 8$$

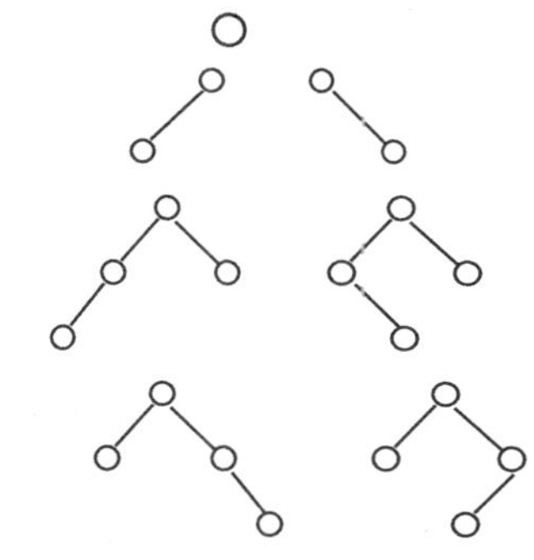

...

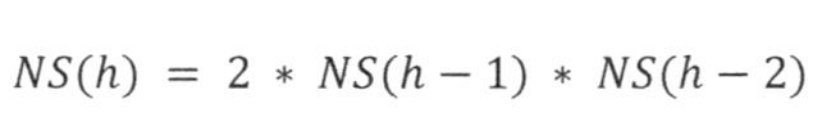

$$NS(h) = 2 * NS(h-1) * NS(h-2)$$

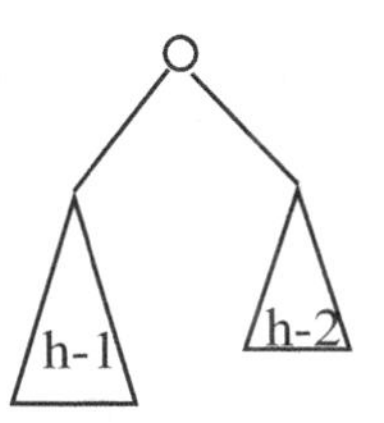


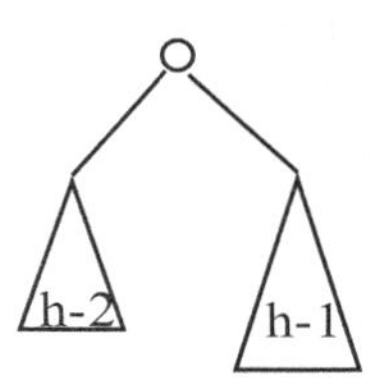


**Problem-77** Given a binary search tree, check whether it is an AVL tree or not?

**Alternative problem statement**: Given a binary tree, determine if it is height-balanced. For this problem, a height-balanced binary tree is defined as: a binary tree in which the left and right subtrees of every node differ in height by no more than 1.

**Solution:** Simple solution would be to calculate the height of left subtree and right subtree for each node in the tree. If for any node, the absolute difference between the height of its left and right subtree is more than 1, the tree is unbalanced. The time complexity of this solution is $O(n^2)$ as there are n nodes in the tree and for every node we are calculating height of its left subtree and right subtree that takes $O(n)$ time.

We can solve this problem in linear time by doing post-order traversal of the tree. Instead of calculating height of left subtree and right subtree for every node in the tree, we can get the height in constant time. The idea is to start from the bottom of the tree and return height of subtree rooted at given node to its parent node. The height of subtree rooted at any node is equal to 1 plus maximum height of the left subtree or right subtree.

```
int isBalanced(struct BinarySearchTreeNode * root) {
  if (root == nullptr)
    return 1;
  return checkHeight(root) != -1;
}
int checkHeight(struct BinarySearchTreeNode * root) {
  int leftHeight, rightHeight;
  if (root == nullptr) {
    return 0;
  }
  leftHeight = checkHeight(root -> left);
  rightHeight = checkHeight(root -> right);
  if (leftHeight == -1 || rightHeight == -1 || abs(leftHeight - rightHeight) > 1) {
    return -1;
  }
  return 1 + max(leftHeight, rightHeight);
}
```

Time Complexity: $O(n)$. Space Complexity: $O(n)$.

**Problem-78** Given a height $h$, give an algorithm to generate an AVL tree with minimum number of nodes.

**Solution:** To get minimum number of nodes, fill one level with $h-1$ and the other with $h-2$.

```
struct AVLTreeNode *GenerateAVLTree(int h){
    struct AVLTreeNode *temp;
    if(h == 0)
        return NULL;
    temp = (struct AVLTreeNode *)malloc (sizeof(struct AVLTreeNode));
    temp→left = GenerateAVLTree(h-1);
```

```
        temp→data = count++; //assume count is a global variable
        temp→right = GenerateAVLTree(h-2);
        temp→height = temp→left→height+1; // or temp→height = h;
        return temp;
}
```

**Problem-79** Given an AVL tree with $n$ integer items and two integers $a$ and $b$, where $a$ and $b$ can be any integers with $a <= b$. Implement an algorithm to count the number of nodes in the range $[a, b]$.

**Solution:**

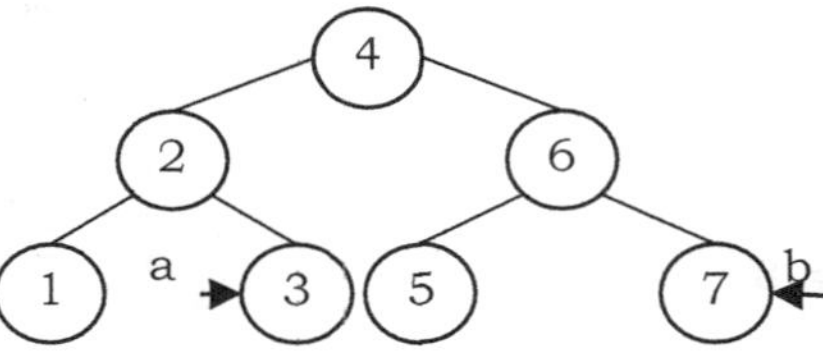


The idea is to make use of the recursive property of binary search trees. There are three cases to consider: whether the current node is in the range $[a, b]$, on the left side of the range $[a, b]$, or on the right side of the range $[a, b]$. Only subtrees that possibly contain the nodes will be processed under each of the three cases.

```
int rangeCount(struct AVLNode *root, int a, int b) {
        if(root == NULL)
                return 0;
        else if(root→data > b)
                return rangeCount(root→left, a, b);
        else if(root→data < a)
                return rangeCount(root→right, a, b);
        else if(root→data >= a && root→data <= b)
                return rangeCount(root→left, a, b) + rangeCount(root→right, a, b) + 1;
}
```

The complexity is similar to *in – order* traversal of the tree but skipping left or right sub-trees when they do not contain any answers. So in the worst case, if the range covers all the nodes in the tree, we need to traverse all the $n$ nodes to get the answer. The worst time complexity is therefore $O(n)$.

If the range is small, which only covers a few elements in a small subtree at the bottom of the tree, the time complexity will be $O(h) = O(logn)$, where $h$ is the height of the tree. This is because only a single path is traversed to reach the small subtree at the bottom and many higher level subtrees have been pruned along the way.

**Note:** Refer similar problem in BST.

**Problem-80** Given a BST (applicable to AVL trees as well) where each node contains two data elements (its data and also the number of nodes in its subtrees) as shown below. Convert the tree to another BST by replacing the second data element (number of nodes in its subtrees) with previous node data in inorder traversal. Note that each node is merged with *inorder* previous node data. Also make sure that conversion happens in-place.

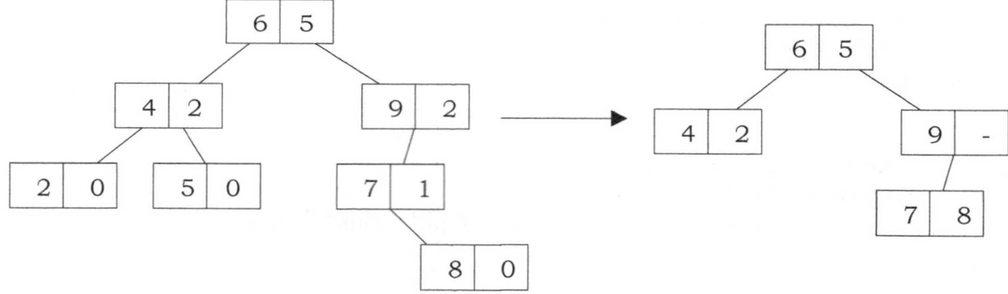


**Solution:** The simplest way is to use level order traversal. If the number of elements in the left subtree is greater than the number of elements in the right subtree, find the maximum element in the left subtree and replace the current node second data element with it. Similarly, if the number of elements in the left subtree is less than the number of elements in the right subtree, find the minimum element in the right subtree and replace the current node *second* data element with it.

```
struct BST *treeCompression (struct BST *root){
        struct BST *temp, *temp2;
        struct Queue *Q = createQueue();
        if(!root)
                return NULL;
        enQueue(Q, root);
        while(!isEmpty(Q)) {
```

```
            temp = deQueue(Q);
            if(temp→left && temp→right && temp→left→data2 > temp→right→data2)
                temp2 = findMax(temp);
            else temp2 = findMin(temp);
            temp→data2 = temp2→data2;     //Process current node
                //Remember to delete this node.
            deleteNodeInBST(temp2);
            if(temp→left)
                enQueue(Q, temp→left);
            if(temp→right)
                enQueue(Q, temp→right);
        }
        deleteQueue(Q);
}
```

Time Complexity: O(*nlogn*) on average since BST takes O(*logn*) on average to find the maximum or minimum element. Space Complexity: O(*n*). Since, in the worst case, all the nodes on the entire last level could be in the queue simultaneously.

**Problem-81** Can we reduce time complexity for the previous problem?

**Solution:** Let us try using an approach that is similar to what we followed in Problem-62. The idea behind this solution is that inorder traversal of BST produces sorted lists. While traversing the BST in inorder, keep track of the elements visited and merge them.

```
struct BinarySearchTreeNode * treeCompression(struct BinarySearchTreeNode *root, int *previousNodeData){
    if(!root) return NULL;
        treeCompression(root→left, previousNode);
    if(*previousNodeData == INT_MIN){
        *previousNodeData = root→data;
        free(root);
    }
    if(*previousNodeData != INT_MIN){                          // Process current node
        root→data2 = previousNodeData;
        *previousNodeData = INT_MIN;
    }
    return treeCompression(root→right, previousNode);
}
```

Time Complexity: O(*n*).
Space Complexity: O(1). Note that, we are still having recursive stack space for inorder traversal.

**Problem-82** Given a BST and a key, find the element in the BST which is closest to the given key.

**Solution:** As a simple solution, we can use level-order traversal and for every element compute the difference between the given key and the element's value. If that difference is less than the previous maintained difference, then update the difference with this new minimum value. With this approach, at the end of the traversal we will get the element which is closest to the given key.

```
int closestInBST(struct BinaryTreeNode *root, int key){
    struct BinaryTreeNode *temp, *element;
    struct Queue *Q;
    int difference = INT_MAX;
    if(!root)
        return 0;
    Q = createQueue();
    enQueue(Q,root);
    while(!isEmpty(Q)) {
        temp = deQueue(Q);
        if(difference > (abs(temp→data-key))){
                difference = abs(temp→data-key);
                element = temp;
        }
        if(temp→left)
            enQueue (Q, temp→left);
        if(temp→right)
            enQueue (Q, temp→right);
    }
    deleteQueue(Q);
```

```
        return element→data;
}
```

Time Complexity: O($n$). Space Complexity: O($n$).

**Problem-83** For Problem-82, can we solve it using the recursive approach?

**Solution:** The approach is similar to Problem-18. Following is a simple algorithm for finding the closest Value in BST.

1. If the root is NULL, then the closest value is zero (or NULL).
2. If the root's data matches the given key, then the closest is the root.
3. Else, consider the root as the closest and do the following:
    a. If the key is smaller than the root data, find the closest on the left side tree of the root recursively and call it temp.
    b. If the key is larger than the root data, find the closest on the right side tree of the root recursively and call it temp.
4. Return the root or temp depending on whichever is nearer to the given key.

```
struct BinaryTreeNode * closestInBST(struct BinaryTreeNode *root, int key){
    struct BinaryTreeNode *temp;
    if(root == NULL)
            return root;
    if(root→data == key)
            return root;
    if(key < root→data){
        if(!root→left)
            return root;
        temp = closestInBST(root→left, key);
        return abs(temp→data-key) > abs(root→data-key) ? root : temp;
    }else{
        if(!root→right)
            return root;
        temp = closestInBST(root→right, key);
        return abs(temp→data-key) > abs(root→data-key) ? root : temp;
    }
    return NULL;
}
```

Time Complexity: O($n$) in worst case, and in average case it is O($logn$). Space Complexity: O($n$).

**Problem-84** Median in an infinite series of integers

**Solution:** Median is the middle number in a sorted list of numbers (if we have odd number of elements). If we have even number of elements, median is the average of two middle numbers in a sorted list of numbers.

For solving this problem we can use a binary search tree with additional information at each node, and the number of children on the left and right subtrees. We also keep the number of total nodes in the tree. Using this additional information we can find the median in O($logn$) time, taking the appropriate branch in the tree based on the number of children on the left and right of the current node. But, the insertion complexity is O($n$) because a standard binary search tree can degenerate into a linked list if we happen to receive the numbers in sorted order.

So, let's use a balanced binary search tree to avoid worst case behavior of standard binary search trees. For this problem, the balance factor is the number of nodes in the left subtree minus the number of nodes in the right subtree. And only the nodes with a balance factor of +1 or 0 are considered to be balanced.

So, the number of nodes on the left subtree is either equal to or 1 more than the number of nodes on the right subtree, but not less.

If we ensure this balance factor on every node in the tree, then the root of the tree is the median, if the number of elements is odd. In the number of elements is even, the median is the average of the root and its inorder successor, which is the leftmost descendent of its right subtree. So, the complexity of insertion maintaining a balanced condition is O($logn$) and finding a median operation is O(1) assuming we calculate the inorder successor of the root at every insertion if the number of nodes is even.

Insertion and balancing is very similar to AVL trees. Instead of updating the heights, we update the number of nodes information. Balanced binary search trees seem to be the most optimal solution, insertion is O($logn$) and find median is O(1).

**Note**: For an efficient algorithm refer to the *Priority Queues and Heaps* chapter.

**Problem-85** Given a binary tree, how do you remove all the half nodes (which have only one child)? Note that we should not touch leaves.

**Solution**: By using post-order traversal we can solve this problem efficiently. We first process the left children, then the right children, and finally the node itself. So we form the new tree bottom up, starting from the leaves towards the root. By the time we process the current node, both its left and right subtrees have already been processed.

```
struct BinaryTreeNode *removeHalfNodes(struct BinaryTreeNode *root){
    if (!root)
            return NULL;
    root→left=removeHalfNodes(root→left);
    root→right=removeHalfNodes(root→right);
    if (root→left == NULL && root→right == NULL)
        return root;
    if (root→left == NULL)
        return root→right;
    if (root→right == NULL)
        return root→left;
    return root;
}
```

Time Complexity: O(*n*).

**Problem-86** Given a binary tree, how do you remove its leaves?

**Solution**: By using post-order traversal we can solve this problem (other traversals would also work).

```
struct BinaryTreeNode* removeLeaves(struct BinaryTreeNode* root) {
    if (root != NULL) {
        if (root→left == NULL && root→right == NULL) {
            free(root);
            return NULL;
        } else {
            root→left = removeLeaves(root→left);
            root→right = removeLeaves(root→right);
        }
    }
    return root;
}
```

Time Complexity: O(*n*).

**Problem-87** Given a BST and two integers (minimum and maximum integers) as parameters, how do you remove (prune) elements that are not within that range?

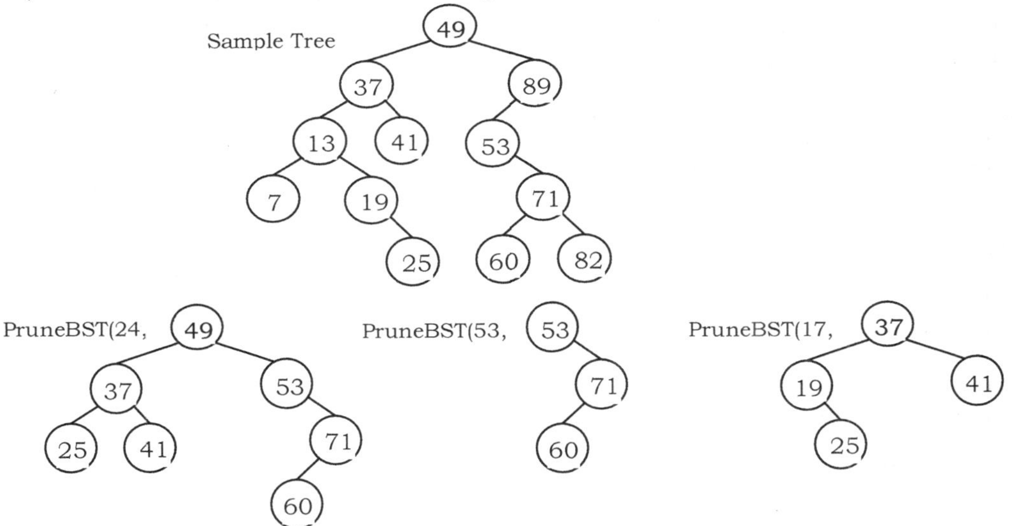


**Solution: Observation**: Since we need to check each and every element in the tree, and the subtree changes should be reflected in the parent, we can think about using post order traversal. So we process the nodes starting from the leaves towards the root. As a result, while processing the node itself, both its left and right subtrees are valid pruned BSTs. At each node we will return a pointer based on its value, which will then be assigned to its parent's left or right child pointer, depending on whether the current node is the left or right child of the parent.

If the current node's value is between $A$ and $B$ ($A <= node's\ data <= B$) then no action needs to be taken, so we return the reference to the node itself.

If the current node's value is less than $A$, then we return the reference to its right subtree and discard the left subtree. Because if a node's value is less than $A$, then its left children are definitely less than A since this is a binary search tree. But its right children may or may not be less than A; we can't be sure, so we return the reference to it. Since we're performing bottom-up post-order traversal, its right subtree is already a trimmed valid binary search tree (possibly NULL), and its left subtree is definitely NULL because those nodes were surely less than A and they were eliminated during the post-order traversal.

A similar situation occurs when the node's value is greater than $B$, so we now return the reference to its left subtree. Because if a node's value is greater than $B$, then its right children are definitely greater than $B$. But its left children may or may not be greater than $B$; So we discard the right subtree and return the reference to the already valid left subtree.

```
struct BinarySearchTreeNode* pruneBST(struct BinarySearchTreeNode *root, int A, int B){
    if(!root) return NULL;
    root→left= pruneBST(root→left,A,B);
    root→right= pruneBST(root→right,A,B);
    if(A<=root→data && root→data<=B)
        return root;
    if(root→data<A)
        return root→right;
    if(root→data>B)
        return root→left;
}
```

Time Complexity: O($n$) in worst case and in average case it is O($logn$).

**Note**: If the given BST is an AVL tree then O($n$) is the average time complexity.

**Problem-88** Given a binary tree, how do you connect all the adjacent nodes at the same level? Assume that given binary tree has next pointer along with left and right pointers as shown below.

```
struct BinaryTreeNode {
    int data;
    struct BinaryTreeNode *left;
    struct BinaryTreeNode *right;
    struct BinaryTreeNode *next;
};
```

**Solution**: One simple approach is to use level-order traversal and keep updating the next pointers. While traversing, we will link the nodes on the next level. If the node has left and right node, we will link left to right. If node has next node, then link rightmost child of current node to leftmost child of next node.

```
void linkingNodesOfSameLevel(struct BinaryTreeNode *root){
    struct Queue *Q = createQueue();
    struct BinaryTreeNode *prev=NULL;    // Pointer to the previous node of the current level
    struct BinaryTreeNode *temp;
    int currentLevelNodeCount, nextLevelNodeCount;
    if(!root) return;
    enQueue(Q, root);
    currentLevelNodeCount = 1;
    nextLevelNodeCount = 0;
    while (!isEmpty(Q)) {
        temp = deQueue(Q);
        if (temp→left){
            enQueue(Q, temp→left);
            nextLevelNodeCount++;
        }
        if (temp→right){
            enQueue(Q, temp→right);
            nextLevelNodeCount++;
        }
        // Link the previous node of the current level to this node
        if (prev)
            prev→next = temp;
        // Set the previous node to the current
        prev = temp;
        currentLevelNodeCount--;
```

```
        if (currentLevelNodeCount == 0) {  // if this is the last node of the current level
            currentLevelNodeCount = nextLevelNodeCount;
            nextLevelNodeCount = 0;
            prev = NULL;
        }
    }
}
```

Time Complexity: O($n$). Space Complexity: O($n$).

**Problem-89** Can we improve space complexity for Problem-88?

**Solution**: We can process the tree level by level, but without a queue. The logical part is that when we process the nodes of the next level, we make sure that the current level has already been linked.

```
void linkingNodesOfSameLevel(struct BinaryTreeNode *root) {
    if(!root) return;
    struct BinaryTreeNode *rightMostNode = NULL, *nextHead = NULL, *temp = root;
    while(temp!= NULL){  //connect next level of current root node level
        if(temp→left!= NULL)
            if(rightMostNode== NULL){
                rightMostNode=temp->left;
                nextHead=temp→left;
            }
            else{
                rightMostNode→next = temp→left;
                rightMostNode = rightMostNode→next;
            }
        if(temp→right!= NULL)
            if(rightMostNode== NULL){
                rightMostNode=temp→right;
                nextHead=temp→right;
            }
            else{
                rightMostNode→next = temp→right;
                rightMostNode = rightMostNode→next;
            }
        temp=temp→next;
    }
    linkingNodesOfSameLevel(nextHead);
}
```

Time Complexity: O($n$). Space Complexity: O($depth\ of\ tree$) for stack space.

**Problem-90** Assume that a set $S$ of $n$ numbers are stored in some form of balanced binary search tree; i.e. the depth of the tree is O($logn$). In addition to the key value and the pointers to children, assume that every node contains the number of nodes in its subtree. Specify a reason(s) why a balanced binary tree can be a better option than a complete binary tree for storing the set S.

**Solution**: Implementation of a balanced binary tree requires less RAM space as we do not need to keep the complete tree in RAM (since they use pointers).

**Problem-91** For the Problem-90, specify a reason (s) why a complete binary tree can be a better option than a balanced binary tree for storing the set S.

**Solution**: A complete binary tree is more space efficient as we do not need any extra flags. A balanced binary tree usually takes more space since we need to store some flags. For example, in a Red-Black tree we need to store a bit for the color. Also, a complete binary tree can be stored in a RAM as an array without using pointers.

**Problem-92** Given a binary tree, find the maximum path sum. The path may start and end at any node in the tree.

**Solution**:

```
int maxPathSum(struct BinaryTreeNode *root){
        int maxValue = INT_MIN;
        return maxPathSumRec(root);
}
int max(int a, int b){
        if (a>b)   return a;
        else return b;
}
```

```
int maxPathSumRec(struct BinaryTreeNode *root){
    if (root == NULL)
        return 0;
    int leftSum = maxPathSumRec(root→left);
    int rightSum = maxPathSumRec(root→right);
    if (leftSum < 0 && rightSum < 0){
        maxValue = max(maxValue, root→data);
        return root→data;
    }
    if (leftSum>0 && rightSum>0)
        maxValue = max(maxValue, root→data + leftSum + rightSum);
    maxValueUp = max(leftSum, rightSum) + root→data;
    maxValue = max(maxValue, maxValueUp);
    return maxValueUp;
}
```

**Problem-93** Let T be a proper binary tree with root r. Consider the following algorithm.

```
Algorithm TreeTraversal(r):
    if (!r) return 1;
    else {
        a = TreeTraversal(r→left);
        b = TreeTraversal(r→right);
        return a + b;
    }
```

What does the algorithm do?

A. It always returns the value 1.
B. It computes the number of nodes in the tree.
C. It computes the depth of the nodes.
D. It computes the height of the tree.
E. It computes the number of leaves in the tree.

**Solution**: E.

**Problem-94** Convert Binary Search Tree to Sorted Doubly Linked List.

**Solution**: To convert a binary search tree (BST) to a sorted doubly linked list, we can perform an in-order traversal of the BST, which visits the nodes in sorted order. During the traversal, we can keep track of the previously visited node and update the pointers to create the doubly linked list.

**Algorithm**:

- Perform an in-order traversal of the BST, visiting the nodes in sorted order.
- During the traversal, keep track of the previously visited node and update the pointers to create the doubly linked list.
- Return the head of the doubly linked list.

```
struct Node {
    int data;
    struct Node* left;
    struct Node* right;
};

struct Node* prev = NULL;
struct Node* head = NULL;

void bstToDoublyList(struct Node* root) {
    if (root == NULL) {
        return;
    }
    bstToDoublyList(root->left);
    if (prev == NULL) {
        head = root;
    } else {
        root->left = prev;
        prev->right = root;
    }
    prev = root;
    bstToDoublyList(root->right);
}
```

## 6.14 Other Variations on Trees

In this section, let us enumerate the other possible representations of trees. In the earlier sections, we have looked at AVL trees, which is a binary search tree (BST) with balancing property. Now, let us look at a few more balanced binary search trees: Red-black Trees and Splay Trees.

### 6.14.1 Red-Black Trees

In Red-black trees each node is associated with an extra attribute: the color, which is either red or black. To get logarithmic complexity we impose the following restrictions.

**Definition:** A Red-black tree is a binary search tree that satisfies the following properties:

- Root Property: the root is black
- External Property: every leaf is black
- Internal Property: the children of a red node are black
- Depth Property: all the leaves have the same black

Similar to AVL trees, if the Red-black tree becomes imbalanced, then we perform rotations to reinforce the balancing property. With Red-black trees, we can perform the following operations in $O(logn)$ in worst case, where $n$ is the number of nodes in the trees.

- Insertion, Deletion
- Finding predecessor, successor
- Finding minimum, maximum

### 6.14.2 Splay Trees

Splay-trees are BSTs with a self-adjusting property. Another interesting property of splay-trees is: starting with an empty tree, any sequence of $K$ operations with maximum of $n$ nodes takes $O(Klogn)$ time complexity in worst case. Splay trees are easier to program and ensure faster access to recently accessed items. Like $AVL$ and Red-Black trees, at any point that the splay tree becomes imbalanced, we can perform rotations to reinforce the balancing property.

Splay-trees cannot guarantee the $O(logn)$ complexity in the worst case. But it gives amortized $O(logn)$ complexity. Even though individual operations can be expensive, any sequence of operations gets the complexity of logarithmic behavior. One operation may take more time (a single operation may take $O(n)$ time) but the subsequent operations may not take worst case complexity and on the average *per operation* complexity is $O(logn)$.

### 6.14.3 B-Trees

B-Tree is like other self-balancing trees such as AVL and Red-black tree such that it maintains its balance of nodes while operations are performed against it. B-Tree has the following properties:

- Minimum degree "$t$" where, except root node, all other nodes must have no less than $t - 1$ keys
- Each node with $n$ keys has $n + 1$ children
- Keys in each node are lined up where $k_1 < k_2 < .. k_n$
- Each node cannot have more than 2t-1 keys, thus 2t children
- Root node at least must contain one key. There is no root node if the tree is empty.
- Tree grows in depth only when root node is split.

Unlike a binary-tree, each node of a b-tree may have a variable number of keys and children. The keys are stored in non-decreasing order. Each key has an associated child that is the root of a subtree containing all nodes with keys less than or equal to the key but greater than the preceding key. A node also has an additional rightmost child that is the root for a subtree containing all keys greater than any keys in the node.

A b-tree has a minimum number of allowable children for each node known as the *minimization factor*. If $t$ is this *minimization factor*, every node must have at least $t - 1$ keys. Under certain circumstances, the root node is allowed to violate this property by having fewer than $t - 1$ keys. Every node may have at most $2t - 1$ keys or, equivalently, $2t$ children.

Since each node tends to have a large branching factor (a large number of children), it is typically necessary to traverse relatively few nodes before locating the desired key. If access to each node requires a disk access, then a B-tree will minimize the number of disk accesses required. The minimization factor is usually chosen so that the total size of each node corresponds to a multiple of the block size of the underlying storage device. This choice simplifies and optimizes disk access. Consequently, a B-tree is an ideal data structure for situations where all data cannot reside in primary storage and accesses to secondary storage are comparatively expensive (or time consuming).

To *search* the tree, it is similar to binary tree except that the key is compared multiple times in a given node because the node contains more than 1 key. If the key is found in the node, the search terminates. Otherwise, it moves down where at child pointed by ci where key $k < k_i$.

Key *insertions* of a B-tree happens from the bottom fashion. This means that it walks down the tree from root to the target child node first. If the child is not full, the key is simply inserted. If it is full, the child node is split in the middle, the median key moves up to the parent, then the new key is inserted. When inserting and walking down the tree, if the root node is found to be full, it's split first and we have a new root node. Then the normal insertion operation is performed.

Key *deletion* is more complicated as it needs to maintain the number of keys in each node to meet the constraint. If a key is found in leaf node and deleting it keeps the number of keys in the nodes not too low, it's simply done right away. If it's done to the inner node, the predecessor of the key in the corresponding child node is moved to replace the key in the inner node. If moving the predecessor will cause the child node to violate the node count constraint, the sibling child nodes are combined and the key in the inner node is deleted.

## 6.14.4 Augmented Trees

In earlier sections, we have seen various problems like finding the $K^{th}$ – smallest – element in the tree and other similar ones. Of all the problems the worst complexity is $O(n)$, where $n$ is the number of nodes in the tree. To perform such operations in $O(logn)$, augmented trees are useful. In these trees, extra information is added to each node and that extra data depends on the problem we are trying to solve.

For example, to find the $K^{th}$element in a binary search tree, let us see how augmented trees solve the problem. Let us assume that we are using Red-Black trees as balanced BST (or any balanced BST) and augmenting the size information in the nodes data. For a given node $X$ in Red-Black tree with a field $size(X)$ equal to the number of nodes in the subtree and can be calculated as:

$$size(X) = size(X \to left) + size(X \to right)) + 1$$

$K^{th}$ – smallest – operation can be defined as:

```
struct BinarySearcTreeNode *kthSmallest (struct BinarySearcTreeNode *X, int K) {
    int r = size(X→left) + 1;
    if(K == r)
        return X;
    if(K < r)
        return kthSmallest (X→left, K);
    if(K > r)
        return kthSmallest (X→right, K-r);
}
```

Time Complexity: $O(logn)$. Space Complexity: $O(logn)$.

**Example:** With the extra size information, the augmented tree will look like:

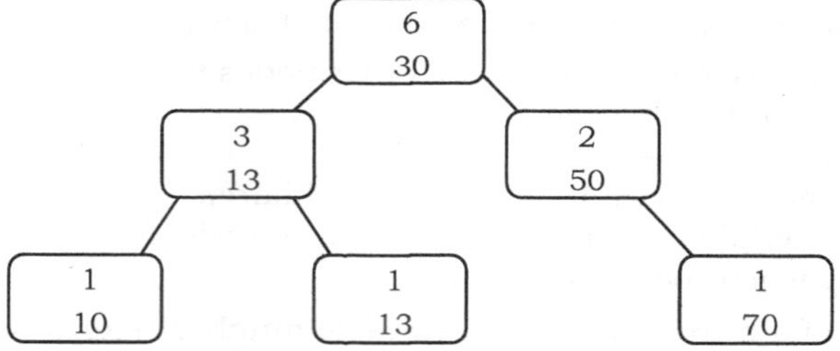


## 6.14.5 Interval Trees [Segment Trees]

We often face questions that involve queries made in an array based on range. For example, for a given array of integers, what is the maximum number in the range $\alpha$ to $\beta$, where $\alpha$ and $\beta$ are of course within array limits. To iterate over those entries with intervals containing a particular value, we can use a simple array. But if we need more efficient access, we need a more sophisticated data structure.

An array-based storage scheme and a brute-force search through the entire array is acceptable only if a single search is to be performed, or if the number of elements is small. For example, if you know all the array values of interest in advance, you need to make only one pass through the array. However, if you can interactively specify different search operations at different times, the brute-force search becomes impractical because every element in the array must be examined during each search operation.

If you sort the array in ascending order of the array values, you can terminate the sequential search when you reach the object whose low value is greater than the element we are searching. Unfortunately, this technique becomes increasingly ineffective as the low value increases because fewer search operations are eliminated. That means, what if we must answer a large number of queries like this? – is brute force still a good option?

Another example is when we need to return a sum in a given range. We can brute force this too, but the problem for a large number of queries still remains. So, what can we do? With a bit of thinking we can come up with an approach like maintaining a separate array of $n$ elements, where $n$ is the size of the original array, where each index stores the sum of all elements from 0 to that index. So essentially we have with a bit of preprocessing brought down the query time from a worst case O($n$) to O(1). Now this is great as far as static arrays are concerned, but what if we are required to perform updates on the array too?

The first approach gives us an O($n$) query time, but an O(1) update time. The second approach, on the other hand, gives us O(1) query time, but an O($n$) update time. So, which one do we choose?

Interval trees are also binary search trees, and they store interval information in the node structure. That means, we maintain a set of $n$ intervals $[i_1, i_2]$ such that one of the intervals containing a query point $Q$ (if any) can be found efficiently. Interval trees are used for performing range queries efficiently.

A segment tree is a heap-like data structure that can be used for making update/query operations upon array intervals in logarithmical time. We define the segment tree for the interval $[i,j]$ in the following recursive manner:

- The root (first node in the array) node will hold the information for the interval $[i,j]$
- If $i < j$ the left and right children will hold the information for the intervals $[i, \frac{i+j}{2}]$ and $[\frac{i+j}{2}+1, j]$

Segment trees (also called *segtrees* and *interval trees*) is a cool data structure, primarily used for range queries. It is a height balanced binary tree with a static structure. The nodes of a segment tree correspond to various intervals and can be augmented with appropriate information pertaining to those intervals. It is somewhat less powerful than a balanced binary tree because of its static structure, but due to the recursive nature of operations on the segtree, it is incredibly easy to think about and code.

We can use segment trees to solve a range of minimum/maximum query problems. The time complexity is T($nlogn$) where O($n$) is the time required to build the tree and each query takes O($logn$) time.

**Example:** Given a set of intervals: $S$ = {[2-5], [6-7], [6-10], [8-9], [12-15], [15-23], [25-30]}. A query with $Q$ = 9 returns [6, 10] or [8, 9] (assume these are the intervals which contain 9 among all the intervals). A query with $Q$ = 23 returns [15, 23].

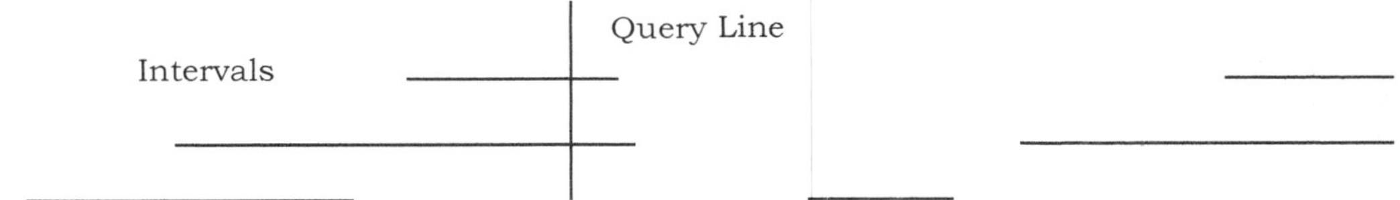


**Construction of Interval Trees:** Let us assume that we are given a set $S$ of $n$ intervals (called *segments*). These $n$ intervals will have $2n$ endpoints. Now, let us see how to construct the interval tree.

**Algorithm: Recursively** build tree on interval set $S$ as follows:

- Sort the $2n$ endpoints
- Let $X_{mid}$ be the median point

Time Complexity for building interval trees: O($nlogn$). Since we are choosing the median, Interval Trees will be approximately balanced. This ensures that we split the set of end points up in half each time. The depth of the tree is O($logn$). To simplify the search process, generally $X_{mid}$ is stored with each node.

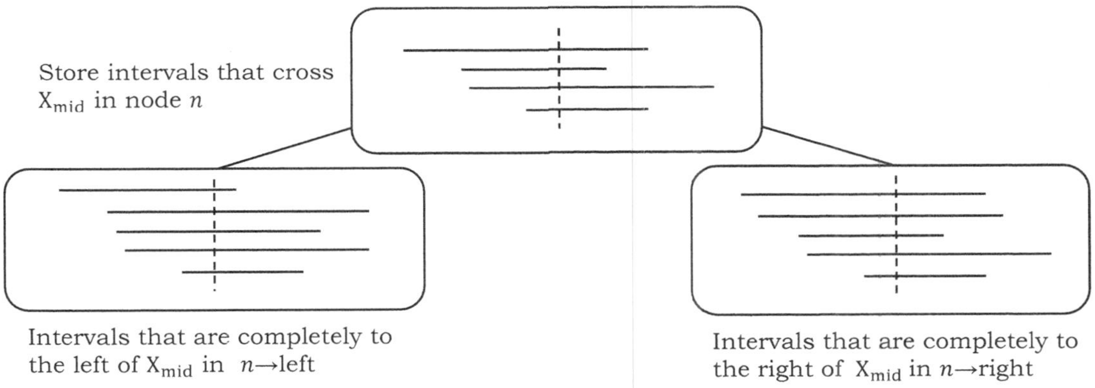


## 6.14.6 Scapegoat Trees

Scapegoat tree is a self-balancing binary search tree, discovered by Arne Andersson. It provides worst-case O($logn$) search time, and O($logn$) amortized (average) insertion and deletion time.

AVL trees rebalance whenever the height of two sibling subtrees differ by more than one; scapegoat trees rebalance whenever the size of a child exceeds a certain ratio of its parents, a ratio known as a. After inserting the element, we traverse back up the tree. If we find an imbalance where a child's size exceeds the parent's size times alpha, we must rebuild the subtree at the parent, the *scapegoat*.

There might be more than one possible scapegoat, but we only have to pick one. The most optimal scapegoat is determined by height balance. When removing it, we see if the total size of the tree is less than alpha of the largest size since the last rebuilding of the tree. If so, we rebuild the entire tree. The alpha for a scapegoat tree can be any number between 0.5 and 1.0. The value 0.5 will force perfect balance, while 1.0 will cause rebalancing to never occur, effectively turning it into a BST.

## 6.15 Supplementary Questions

**Problem-95** A binary tree is univalued if every node in the tree has the same value. Give an algorithm to check whether the given binary tree is univalued or not.

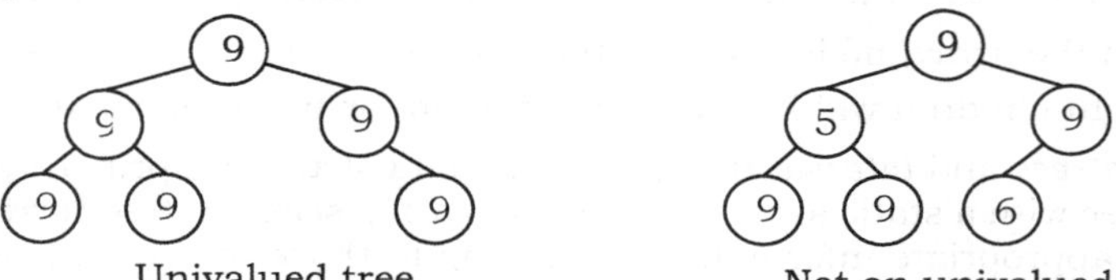

Univalued tree Not an univalued

**Solution**: A tree is univalued if both its children are univalued, plus the root node has the same value as the child nodes. We can write our function recursively. *isLeftUnivalTree* will represent that the left subtree is correct: ie., that it is univalued, and the root value is equal to the left child's value. *isRightUnivalTree* will represent the same thing for the right subtree. We need both properties to be true.

```
class Solution {
  public:
    bool isUnivalueTree(BinaryTreeNode* root) {
        if (root->left != NULL) {
            if (root->data != root->left->data || !isUnidataTree(root->left)) {
                return false;
            }
        }
        if (root->right != NULL) {
            if (root->data != root->right->data || !isUnidataTree(root->right)) {
                return false;
            }
        }
        return true;
    }
};
```

Time complexity: O($n$), where $n$ is the number of nodes in the given tree.
Space complexity: O($h$), where $h$ is the height of the given tree.

# Priority Queues and Heaps

## 7.1 What is a Priority Queue?

In some situations, we may need to find the minimum/maximum element among a collection of elements. We can do this with the help of Priority Queue ADT. A priority queue ADT is a data structure that supports the operations *Insert* and *DeleteMin* (which returns and removes the minimum element) or *DeleteMax* (which returns and removes the maximum element).

These operations are equivalent to *EnQueue* and *DeQueue* operations of a queue. The difference is that, in priority queues, the order in which the elements enter the queue may not be the same in which they were processed. An example application of a priority queue is job scheduling, which is prioritized instead of serving in first come first serve.

A priority queue is called an *ascending – priority* queue, if the item with the smallest key has the highest priority (that means, delete the smallest element always). Similarly, a priority queue is said to be a *descending – priority* queue if the item with the largest key has the highest priority (delete the maximum element always). Since these two types are symmetric we will be concentrating on one of them: ascending-priority queue.

## 7.2 Priority Queue ADT

The following operations make priority queues an ADT.

### Main Priority Queues Operations

A priority queue is a container of elements, each having an associated key.

- insert (key, data): Inserts data with *key* to the priority queue. Elements are ordered based on key.
- deleteMin/deleteMax: Remove and return the element with the smallest/largest key.
- GetMinimum/getMaximum: Return the element with the smallest/largest key without deleting it.

### Auxiliary Priority Queues Operations

- $k^{th}$ – Smallest/$k^{th}$ – Largest: Returns the $k^{th}$ –Smallest/$k^{th}$ –Largest key in priority queue.
- Size: Returns number of elements in priority queue.
- Heap Sort: Sorts the elements in the priority queue based on priority (key).

## 7.3 Priority Queue Applications

Priority queues have many applications – a few of them are listed below:

- Data compression: Huffman Coding algorithm
- Shortest path algorithms: Dijkstra's algorithm
- Minimum spanning tree algorithms: Prim's algorithm
- Event-driven simulation: customers in a line
- Selection problem: Finding $k^{th}$- smallest element

## 7.4 Priority Queue Implementations

Before discussing the actual implementation, let us enumerate the possible options.

### Unordered Array Implementation

Elements are inserted into the array without bothering about the order. Deletions (deleteMax) are performed by searching the key and then deleting.

Insertions complexity: O(1). deleteMin complexity: O($n$).

### Unordered List Implementation

It is very similar to array implementation, but instead of using arrays, linked lists are used.

Insertions complexity: O(1). deleteMin complexity: O($n$).

### Ordered Array Implementation

Elements are inserted into the array in sorted order based on key field. Deletions are performed at only one end.

Insertions complexity: O($n$). deleteMin complexity: O(1).

### Ordered List Implementation

Elements are inserted into the list in sorted order based on key field. Deletions are performed at only one end, hence preserving the status of the priority queue. All other functionalities associated with a linked list ADT are performed without modification.

Insertions complexity: O($n$). deleteMin complexity: O(1).

### Binary Search Trees Implementation

Both insertions and deletions take O($logn$) on average if insertions are random (refer to *Trees* chapter).

### Balanced Binary Search Trees Implementation

Both insertions and deletion take O($logn$) in the worst case (refer to *Trees* chapter).

### Binary Heap Implementation

In subsequent sections we will discuss this in full detail. For now, assume that binary heap implementation gives O($logn$) complexity for search, insertions and deletions and O(1) for finding the maximum or minimum element.

### Comparing Implementations

| Implementation | Insertion | Deletion (deleteMax) | Find Min |
|---|---|---|---|
| Unordered array | 1 | $n$ | $n$ |
| Unordered list | 1 | $n$ | $n$ |
| Ordered array | $n$ | 1 | 1 |
| Ordered list | $n$ | 1 | 1 |
| Binary Search Trees | $logn$ (average) | $logn$ (average) | $logn$ (average) |
| Balanced Binary Search Trees | $logn$ | $logn$ | $logn$ |
| Binary Heaps | $logn$ | $logn$ | 1 |

## 7.5 Heaps and Binary Heaps

### What is a Heap?

A heap is a tree with some special properties. The basic requirement of a heap is that the value of a node must be ≥ (or ≤) than the values of its children. This is called *heap property*. A heap also has the additional property that all leaves should be at $h$ or $h - 1$ levels (where $h$ is the height of the tree) for some $h > 0$ (*complete binary trees*). That means heap should form a *complete binary tree* (as shown below).

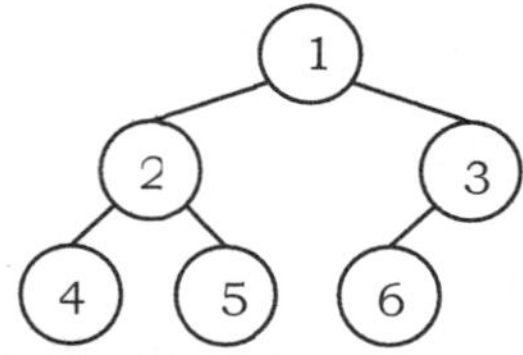


In the examples below, the left tree is a heap (each element is greater than its children) and the right tree is not a heap (since 11 is greater than 2).

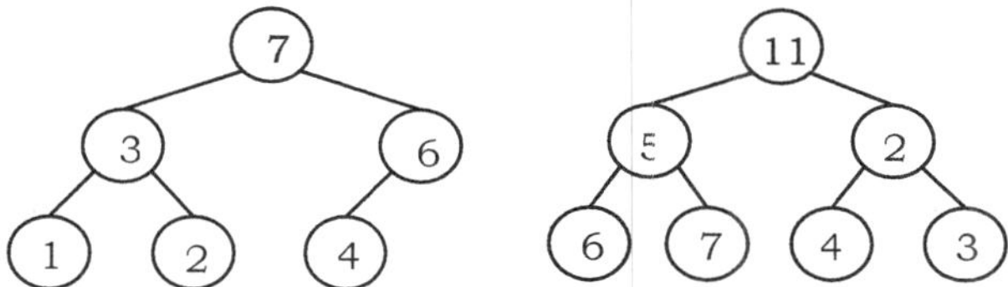


## Types of Heaps?

Based on the property of a heap we can classify heaps into two types:

- **Min heap:** The value of a node must be less than or equal to the values of its children.

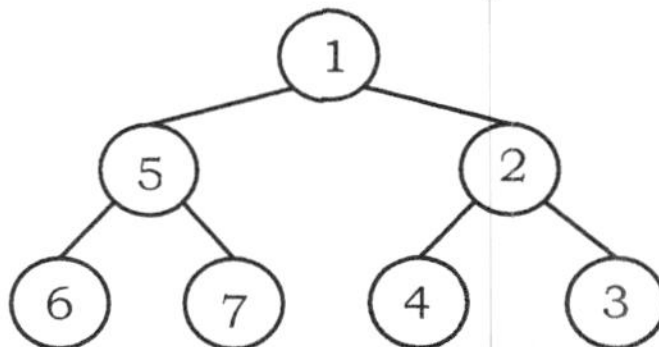


- **Max heap:** The value of a node must be greater than or equal to the values of its children.

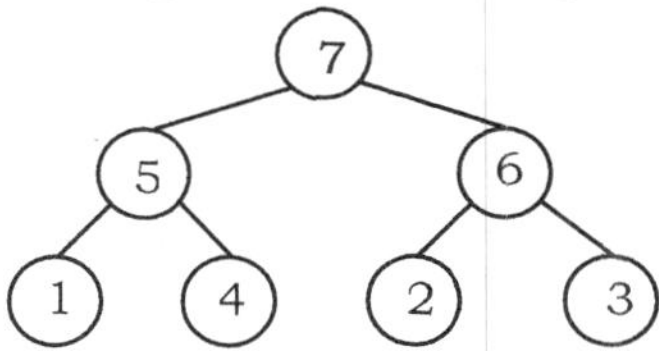


## 7.6 Binary Heaps

In binary heap each node may have up to two children. In practice, binary heaps are enough, and we concentrate on binary min heaps and binary max heaps for the remaining discussion.

**Representing Heaps:** Before looking at heap operations, let us see how heaps can be represented. One possibility is using arrays. Since heaps are forming complete binary trees, there will not be any wastage of locations. For the discussion below let us assume that elements are stored in arrays, which starts at index 0. The previous max heap can be represented as:

| 7 | 5 | 6 | 1 | 4 | 2 | 3 |
|---|---|---|---|---|---|---|
| 0 | 1 | 2 | 3 | 4 | 5 | 6 |

**Note:** For the remaining discussion let us assume that we are doing manipulations in max heap.

### Declaration of Heap

```
struct Heap {
    int *array;
    int count;      // Number of elements in Heap
    int capacity;   // Size of the heap
    int heap_type;          // Min Heap or Max Heap
};
```

### Creating Heap

```
struct Heap * createHeap(int capacity, int heap_type) {
    struct Heap * h = (struct Heap *)malloc(sizeof(struct Heap));
    if(h == NULL) {
        printf("Memory Error");
        return;
    }
    h→heap_type = heap_type;
    h→count = 0;
    h→capacity = capacity;
    h→array = (int *) malloc(sizeof(int) * h→capacity);
    if(h→array == NULL) {
        printf("Memory Error");
        return;
    }
    return h;
}
```

Time Complexity: O(1).

## Parent of a Node

For a node at $i^{th}$ location, its parent is at $\frac{i-1}{2}$ location. In the previous example, the element 6 is at second location and its parent is at $0^{th}$ location.

```
int parent (struct Heap * h, int i) {
    if(i <= 0 || i >= h→count)
        return -1;
    return i-1/2;
}
```

Time Complexity: O(1).

## Children of a Node

Similar to the above discussion, for a node at $i^{th}$ location, its children are at $2 * i + 1$ and $2 * i + 2$ locations. For example, in the above tree the element 6 is at second location and its children 2 and 5 are at 5 $(2 * i + 1 = 2 * 2 + 1)$ and 6 $(2 * i + 2 = 2 * 2 + 2)$ locations.

```
int leftChild(struct Heap *h, int i) {
    int left = 2 * i + 1;
    if(left >= h→count)
        return -1;
    return left;
}
```

Time Complexity: O(1).

```
int rightChild(struct Heap *h, int i) {
    int right = 2 * i + 2;
    if(right >= h→count)
        return -1;
    return right;
}
```

Time Complexity: O(1).

## Getting the Maximum Element

Since the maximum element in max heap is always at root, it will be stored at h→array[0].

```
int getMaximum(Heap * h) {
    if(h→count == 0)
        return -1;
    return h→array[0];
}
```

Time Complexity: O(1).

## Heapifying an Element

After inserting an element into heap, it may not satisfy the heap property. In that case we need to adjust the locations of the heap to make it heap again. This process is called *heapifying*. In max-heap, to heapify an element, we have to find the maximum of its children and swap it with the current element and continue this process until the heap property is satisfied at every node.

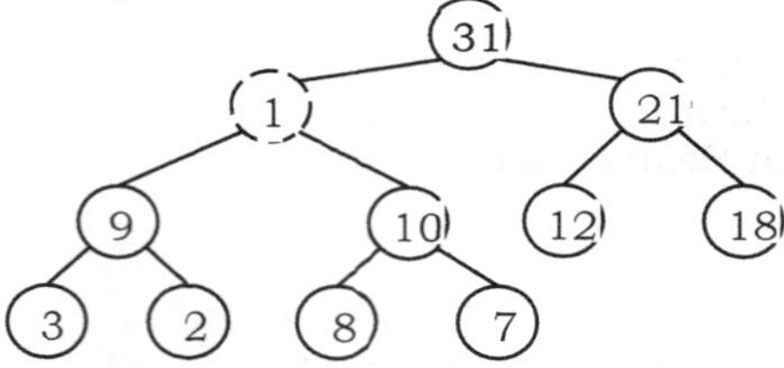


**Observation:** One important property of heap is that, if an element is not satisfying the heap property, then all the elements from that element to the root will have the same problem. In the example below, element 1 is not satisfying the heap property and its parent 31 is also having the issue.

Similarly, if we heapify an element, then all the elements from that element to the root will also satisfy the heap property automatically. Let us go through an example. In the above heap, the element 1 is not satisfying the heap property. Let us try heapifying this element.

To heapify 1, find the maximum of its children and swap with that.

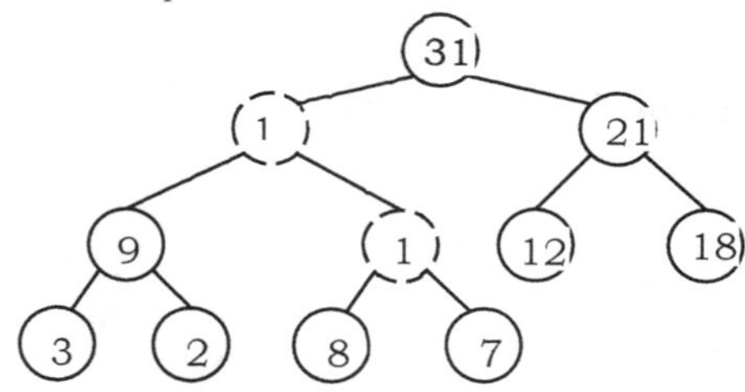

We need to continue this process until the element satisfies the heap properties. Now, swap 1 with 8.

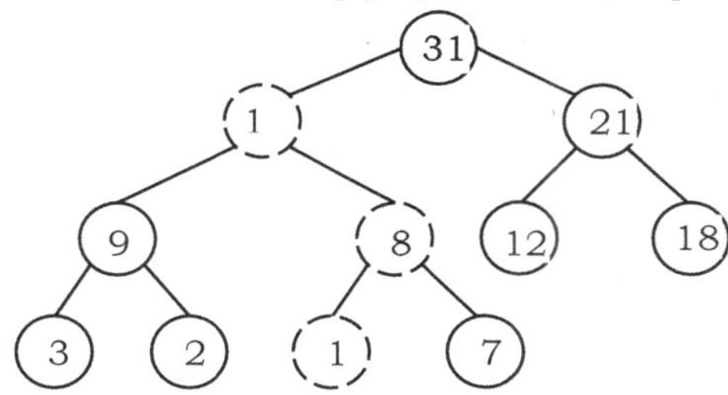


Now the tree is satisfying the heap property. In the above heapifying process, since we are moving from top to bottom, this process is sometimes called *percolate down*. Similarly, if we start heapifying from any other node to root, we can that process *percolate up* as move from bottom to top.

```
//Heapifying the element at location i.
void percolateDown(struct Heap *h, int i) {
    int l, r, max, temp;
    l = leftChild(h, i);
    r = rightChild(h, i);
if(l != -1 && h→array[l] > h→array[i])
        max = l;
    else
        max = i;
    if(r != -1&& h→array[r] > h→array[max])
        max = r;
    if(max != i) {
        //Swap h→array[i] and  h→array[max];
        temp = h→array[i];
        h→array[i] = h→array[max];
        h→array[max] = temp;
        percolateDown(h, max);
    }
}
```

Time Complexity: $O(logn)$. Heap is a complete binary tree and in the worst case we start at the root and come down to the leaf. This is equal to the height of the complete binary tree. Space Complexity: $O(1)$.

## Deleting an Element

To delete an element from heap, we just need to delete the element from the root. This is the only operation (maximum element) supported by standard heap. After deleting the root element, copy the last element of the heap (tree) and delete that last element. After replacing the last element, the tree may not satisfy the heap property. To make it heap again, call the *PercolateDown* function.

- Copy the first element into some variable
- Copy the last element into first element location
- *PercolateDown* the first element

```
int deleteMax(struct Heap *h) {
    int data;
    if(h→count == 0)
        return -1;
    data = h→array[0];
    h→array[0] = h→array[h→count-1];
    h→count--; //reducing the heap size
    percolateDown(h, 0);
    return data;
}
```

**Note:** Deleting an element uses *PercolateDown*, and inserting an element uses *PercolateUp*.

Time Complexity: same as *Heapify* function and it is $O(logn)$.

## Inserting an Element

Insertion of an element is similar to the heapify and deletion process.

- Increase the heap size

- Keep the new element at the end of the heap (tree)
- Heapify the element from bottom to top (root)

Before going through code, let us look at an example. We have inserted the element 19 at the end of the heap and this is not satisfying the heap property.

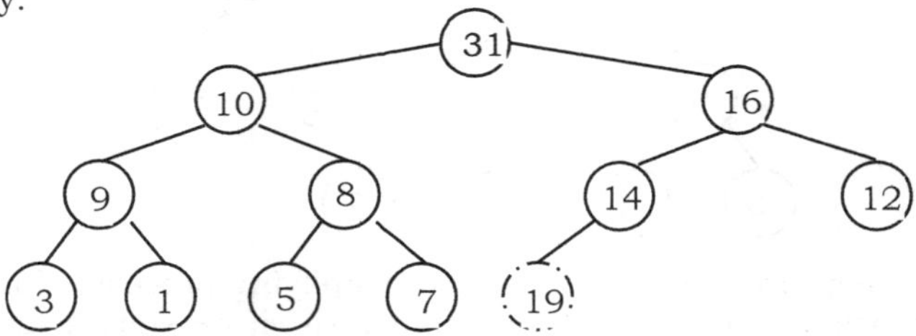

In order to heapify this element (19), we need to compare it with its parent and adjust them. Swapping 19 and 14 gives:

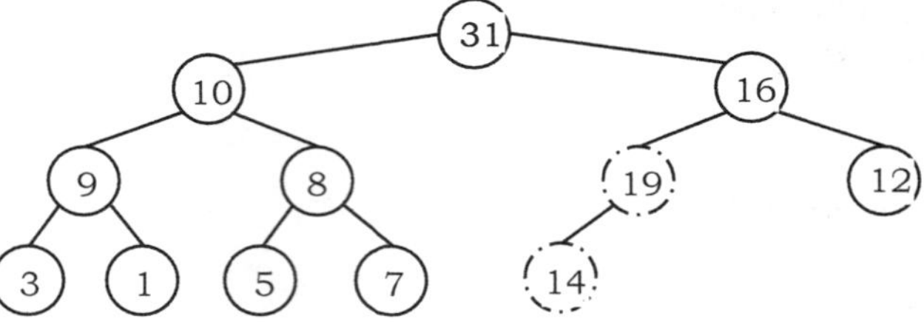

Again, swap 19 and16:

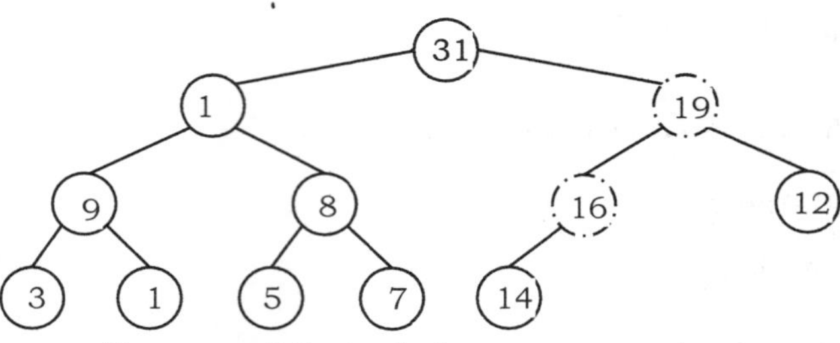

Now the tree is satisfying the heap property. Since we are following the bottom-up approach we sometimes call this process *percolate up*.

```
int insert(struct Heap *h, int data) {
    int i;
    if(h→count == h→capacity)
        resizeHeap(h);
    h→count++;          //increasing the heap size to hold this new item
    i = h→count-1;
    while(i>=0 && data > h→array[(i-1)/2]) {
        h→array[i] = h→array[(i-1)/2];
        i = i-1/2;
    }
    h→array[i] = data;
}
void resizeHeap(struct Heap * h) {
    int *array_old = h→array;
    h→array = (int *) malloc(sizeof(int) * h→capacity * 2);
    if(h→array == NULL) {
        printf("Memory Error");
        return;
    }
    for (int i = 0; i < h→capacity; i ++)
        h→array[i] = array_old[i];
    h→capacity *= 2;
    free(array_old);
}
```

Time Complexity: $O(logn)$. The explanation is the same as that of the *Heapify* function.

## Destroying Heap

```
void DestroyHeap (struct Heap *h) {
    if(h == NULL)
```

```
        return;
    free(h→array);
    free(h);
    h = NULL;
}
```

## Heapifying the Array

One simple approach for building the heap is, take $n$ input items and place them into an empty heap. This can be done with $n$ successive inserts and takes $O(nlogn)$ in the worst case. This is due to the fact that each insert operation takes $O(logn)$.

To finish our discussion of binary heaps, we will look at a method to build an entire heap from a list of keys. The first method you might think of may be like the following. Given a list of keys, you could easily build a heap by inserting each key one at a time. Since you are starting with a list of one item, the list is sorted and you could use binary search to find the right position to insert the next key at a cost of approximately $O(logn)$ operations. However, remember that inserting an item in the middle of the list may require $O(n)$ operations to shift the rest of the list over to make room for the new key. Therefore, to insert $n$ keys into the heap would require a total of $O(nlogn)$ operations. However, if we start with an entire list then we can build the whole heap in $O(n)$ operations.

**Observation**: Leaf nodes always satisfy the heap property and do not need to care for them. The leaf elements are always at the end and to heapify the given array it should be enough if we heapify the non-leaf nodes. Now let us concentrate on finding the first non-leaf node. The last element of the heap is at location $h \rightarrow count - 1$, and to find the first non-leaf node it is enough to find the parent of the last element.

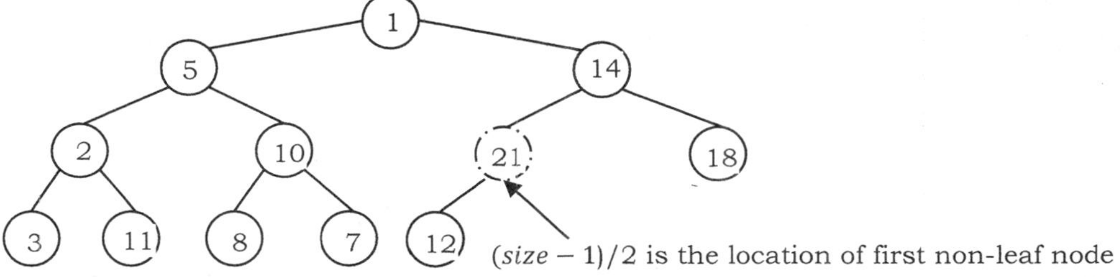


```
void buildHeap(struct Heap *h, int A[], int n) {
    if(h == NULL)
        return;
    while (n > h→capacity)
        ResizeHeap(h);
    for (int i = 0; i < n; i ++)
        h→array[i] = A[i];
    h→count = n;
    for (int i = (n-1)/2; i >=0; i --)
        percolateDown(h, i);
}
```

Time Complexity: The linear time bound of building heap can be shown by computing the sum of the heights of all the nodes. For a complete binary tree of height $h$ containing $n = 2^{h+1} - 1$ nodes, the sum of the heights of the nodes is $n - h - 1 = n - logn - 1$ (for proof refer to *Problems Section*). That means, building the heap operation can be done in linear time ($O(n)$) by applying a *PercolateDown* function to the nodes in reverse level order.

## 7.7 Heapsort

One main application of heap ADT is sorting (heap sort). The heap sort algorithm inserts all elements (from an unsorted array) into a heap, then removes them from the root of a heap until the heap is empty. Note that heap sort can be done in place with the array to be sorted. Instead of deleting an element, exchange the first element (maximum) with the last element and reduce the heap size (array size). Then, we heapify the first element. Continue this process until the number of remaining elements is one.

```
void Heapsort(int A[], in n) {
    struct Heap *h = createHeap(n);
    int old_size, i, temp;
    buildHeap(h, A, n);
    old_size = h→count;
    for(i = n-1; i > 0; i--) {
        //h→array [0] is the largest element
```

```
        temp = h→array[0];
        h→array[0] = h→array[h→count-1];
        h→array[0] = temp;
        h→count--;
        percolateDown(h, 0);
    }
    h→count = old_size;
}
```

Time complexity: As we remove the elements from the heap, the values become sorted (since maximum elements are always *root* only). Since the time complexity of both the insertion algorithm and deletion algorithm is O($logn$) (where $n$ is the number of items in the heap), the time complexity of the heap sort algorithm is O($nlogn$).

## 7.8 Priority Queues [Heaps]: Problems & Solutions

**Problem-1** What are the minimum and maximum number of elements in a heap of height $h$?

**Solution:** Since heap is a complete binary tree (all levels contain full nodes except possibly the lowest level), it has at most $2^{h+1} - 1$ elements (if it is complete). This is because, to get maximum nodes, we need to fill all the $h$ levels completely and the maximum number of nodes is nothing but the sum of all nodes at all $h$ levels.

To get minimum nodes, we should fill the $h - 1$ levels fully and the last level with only one element. As a result, the minimum number of nodes is nothing but the sum of all nodes from $h - 1$ levels plus 1 (for the last level) and we get $2^h - 1 + 1 = 2^h$ elements (if the lowest level has just 1 element and all the other levels are complete).

**Problem-2** Is there a min-heap with seven distinct elements so that the preorder traversal of it gives the elements in sorted order?

**Solution**: **Yes**. For the tree below, preorder traversal produces ascending order.

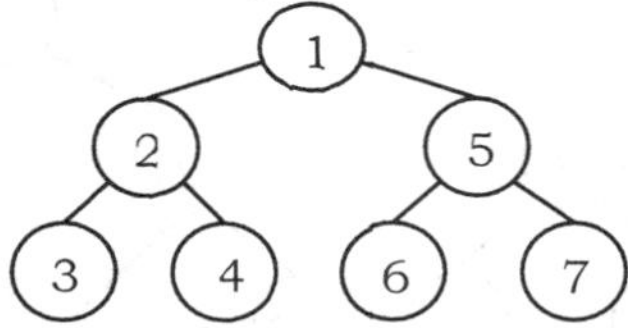


**Problem-3** Is there a max-heap with seven distinct elements so that the preorder traversal of it gives the elements in sorted order?

**Solution: Yes**. For the tree below, preorder traversal produces descending order.

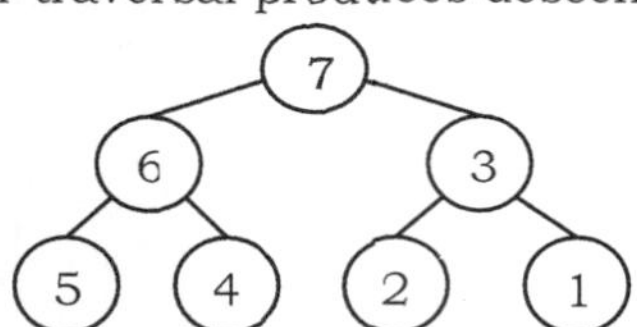


**Problem-4** Is there a min-heap/max-heap with seven distinct elements so that the inorder traversal of it gives the elements in sorted order?

**Solution: No.** Since a heap must be either a min-heap or a max-heap, the root will hold the smallest element or the largest. An inorder traversal will visit the root of the tree as its second step, which is not the appropriate place if the tree's root contains the smallest or largest element.

**Problem-5** Is there a min-heap/max-heap with seven distinct elements so that the postorder traversal of it gives the elements in sorted order?

**Solution:**

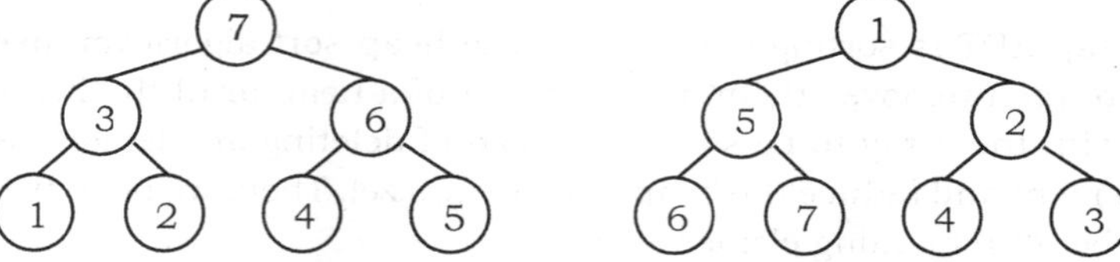


**Yes**, if the tree is a max-heap and we want descending order (below left), or if the tree is a min-heap and we want ascending order (below right).

**Problem-6** Show that the height of a heap with $n$ elements is $logn$?

**Solution:** A heap is a complete binary tree. All the levels, except the lowest, are completely full. A heap has at least $2^h$ elements and at most elements $2^h \leq n \leq 2^{h+1} - 1$. This implies, $h \leq logn \leq h + 1$. Since $h$ is an integer, $h = logn$.

**Problem-7** Given a min-heap, give an algorithm for finding the maximum element.

**Solution:** For a given min heap, the maximum element will always be at leaf only. Now, the next question is how to find the leaf nodes in the tree.

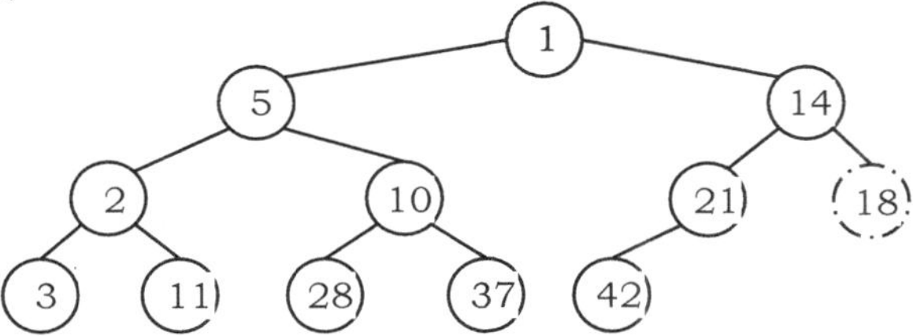


If we carefully observe, the next node of the last element's parent is the first leaf node. Since the last element is always at the $size - 1^{th}$ location, the next node of its parent (parent at location $\frac{size-1}{2}$) can be calculated as:

$$\frac{size - 1}{2} + 1 \approx \frac{size + 1}{2}$$

Now, the only step remaining is scanning the leaf nodes and finding the maximum among them.

```
int findMaxInMinHeap(struct Heap *h) {
    int Max = -1;
    for(int i = (h→count+1)/2; i < h→count; i++)
        if(h→array[i] > Max)
            Max = h→array[i];
}
```

Time Complexity: $O(\frac{n}{2}) \approx O(n)$.

**Problem-8** Give an algorithm for deleting an arbitrary element from min heap.

**Solution:** To delete an element, first we need to search for an element. Let us assume that we are using level order traversal for finding the element. After finding the element we need to follow the deleteMin process.

Time Complexity = Time for finding the element + Time for deleting an element
$= O(n) + O(logn) \approx O(n)$. //Time for searching is dominated.

**Problem-9** Give an algorithm for deleting the $i^{th}$ indexed element in a given min-heap.

**Solution:**

```
int delete(struct Heap *h, int i) {
    int key;
    if(i > h→count) {
        printf("Wrong position");
        return;
    }
    key = h→array[i];
    h→array[i]= h→array[h→count-1];
    h→count--;
    percolateDown(h, i);
    return key;
}
```

Time Complexity = $O(logn)$.

**Problem-10** Prove that, for a complete binary tree of height $h$ the sum of the height of all nodes is $O(n - h)$.

**Solution:** A complete binary tree has $2^i$ nodes on level $i$. Also, a node on level $i$ has depth $i$ and height $h - i$. Let us assume that $S$ denotes the sum of the heights of all these nodes and $S$ can be calculated as:

$$S = \sum_{i=0}^{h} 2^i(h - i)$$
$$S = h + 2(h - 1) + 4(h - 2) + \cdots + 2^{h-1}(1)$$

Multiplying with 2 on both sides gives: $2S = 2h + 4(h - 1) + 8(h - 2) + \cdots + 2^h(1)$

Now, subtract $S$ from $2S$: $2S - S = -h + 2 + 4 + \cdots + 2^h \Rightarrow S = (2^{h+1} - 1) - (h - 1)$

But, we already know that the total number of nodes $n$ in a complete binary tree with height $h$ is $n = 2^{h+1} - 1$. This gives us: $h = \log(n + 1)$.

Finally, replacing $2^{h+1} - 1$ with $n$, gives: $S = n - (h - 1) = O(n - logn) = O(n - h)$.

**Problem-11** Give an algorithm to find all elements less than some value of $k$ in a binary heap.

**Solution:** Start from the root of the heap. If the value of the root is smaller than $k$ then print its value and call recursively once for its left child and once for its right child. If the value of a node is greater or equal than $k$ then the function stops without printing that value.

The complexity of this algorithm is $O(n)$, where $n$ is the total number of nodes in the heap. This bound takes place in the worst case, where the value of every node in the heap will be smaller than $k$, so the function has to call each node of the heap.

**Problem-12** Give an algorithm for merging two binary max-heaps. Let us assume that the size of the first heap is $m+n$ and the size of the second heap is $n$.

**Solution:** One simple way of solving this problem is:

- Assume that the elements of the first array (with size $m+n$) are at the beginning. That means, first $m$ cells are filled and remaining $n$ cells are empty.
- Without changing the first heap, just append the second heap and heapify the array.
- Since the total number of elements in the new array is $m+n$, each heapify operation takes $O(log(m+n))$.

The complexity of this algorithm is : $O((m+n)log(m+n))$.

**Problem-13** Can we improve the complexity of Problem-12?

**Solution:** Instead of heapifying all the elements of the $m+n$ array, we can use the technique of "building heap with an array of elements (heapifying array)". We can start with non-leaf nodes and heapify them. The algorithm can be given as:

- Assume that the elements of the first array (with size $m+n$) are at the beginning. That means, the first $m$ cells are filled and the remaining $n$ cells are empty.
- Without changing the first heap, just append the second heap.
- Now, find the first non-leaf node and start heapifying from that element.

In the theory section, we have already seen that building a heap with $n$ elements takes $O(n)$ complexity. The complexity of merging with this technique is: $O(m+n)$.

**Problem-14** Is there an efficient algorithm for merging 2 max-heaps (stored as an array)? Assume both arrays have $n$ elements.

**Solution:** The alternative solution for this problem depends on what type of heap it is. If it's a standard heap where every node has up to two children and which gets filled up so that the leaves are on a maximum of two different rows, we cannot get better than $O(n)$ for the merge.

There is an $O(logm \times logn)$ algorithm for merging two binary heaps with sizes $m$ and $n$. For $m = n$, this algorithm takes $O(log^2 n)$ time complexity. We will be skipping it due to its difficulty and scope.

For better merging performance, we can use another variant of binary heap like a *Fibonacci-Heap* which can merge in O(1) on average (amortized).

**Problem-15** Give an algorithm for finding the $k^{th}$ smallest element in min-heap.

**Solution:** One simple solution to this problem is: perform deletion $k$ times from min-heap.

```
int findKthLargestEle(struct Heap *h, int k) {
    //Just delete first k-1 elements and return the k-th element.
     for(int i=0;i<k-1;i++)
         deleteMin(h);
     return deleteMin(h);
}
```

Time Complexity: $O(klogn)$. Since we are performing deletion operation $k$ times and each deletion takes $O(logn)$.

**Problem-16** For Problem-15, can we improve the time complexity?

**Solution:** Assume that the original min-heap is called *HOrig* and the auxiliary min-heap is named *HAux*. Initially, the element at the top of *HOrig*, the minimum one, is inserted into *HAux*. Here we don't do the operation of deleteMin with *HOrig*.

```
Heap HOrig;
Heap HAux;
int findKthLargestEle( int k ) {
    int heapElement;//Assuming heap data is of integers
    int count=1;
    HAux.insert(HOrig.min());
    while( true ) {
```

```
            //return the minimum element and delete it from the HA heap
            heapElement = HAux.deleteMin();
            if(++count == k ) {
                    return heapElement;
            }
            else {    //insert the left and right children in HO into the HA
                    HAux.insert(heapElement.leftChild());
                    HAux.insert(heapElement.rightChild());
            }
        }
    }
```

Every while-loop iteration gives the $k^{th}$ smallest element and we need $k$ loops to get the $k^{th}$ smallest elements. Because the size of the auxiliary heap is always less than $k$, every while-loop iteration the size of the auxiliary heap increases by one, and the original heap $HOrig$ has no operation during the finding, the running time is O($klogk$).

**Note**: The above algorithm is useful if the $k$ value is too small compared to $n$. If the $k$ value is approximately equal to $n$, then we can simply sort the array (let's say, using *couting* sort or any other linear sorting algorithm) and return $k^{th}$ smallest element from the sorted array. This gives O($n$) solution.

**Problem-17** Find $k$ max elements from max heap.

**Solution:** One simple solution to this problem is: build max-heap and perform deletion $k$ times.

$$T(n) = \text{deleteMin from heap } k \text{ times} = \Theta(klogn).$$

**Problem-18** For Problem-17, is there any alternative solution?

**Solution:** We can use the Problem-16 solution. At the end, the auxiliary heap contains the k-largest elements. Without deleting the elements we should keep on adding elements to $HAux$.

**Problem-19** How do we implement stack using heap?

**Solution:** To implement a stack using a priority queue PQ (using min heap), let us assume that we are using one extra integer variable $c$. Also, assume that $c$ is initialized equal to any known value (e.g., 0). The implementation of the stack ADT is given below. Here $c$ is used as the priority while inserting/deleting the elements from PQ.

```
void push(int element) {
    PQ.insert(c, element);
    c--;
}
int pop() {
    return PQ.deleteMin();
}
int top() {
    return PQ.min();
}
int size() {
    return PQ.size();
}
int isEmpty() {
    return PQ.isEmpty();
}
```

We could also increment $c$ back when popping.

**Observation:** We could use the negative of the current system time instead of $c$ (to avoid overflow). The implementation based on this can be given as:

```
void push(int element) {
    PQ.insert(-gettime(),element);
}
```

**Problem-20** How do we implement Queue using heap?

**Solution:** To implement a queue using a priority queue PQ (using min heap), as similar to stacks simulation, let us assume that we are using one extra integer variable, $c$. Also, assume that $c$ is initialized equal to any known value (e.g., 0). The implementation of the queue ADT is given below. Here the $c$ is used as the priority while inserting/deleting the elements from PQ.

```
void enQueue(int element) {
    PQ.insert(c, element);
```

```
        c++;
    }
    int deQueue() {
        return PQ.deleteMin();
    }
    int Front() {
        return PQ.min();
    }
    int size() {
        return PQ.size();
    }
    int isEmpty() {
        return PQ.isEmpty();
    }
```

**Note:** We could also decrement $c$ when popping.

**Observation:** We could use just the current system time instead of $c$ (to avoid overflow). The implementation based on this can be given as:

```
    void enQueue(int element) {
        PQ.insert(gettime(),element);
    }
```

**Note:** The only change is that we need to take a positive $c$ value instead of negative.

**Problem-21** Given a big file containing billions of numbers, how can you find the 10 maximum numbers from that file?

**Solution:** Always remember that when you need to find max $n$ elements, the best data structure to use is priority queues.

One solution for this problem is to divide the data in sets of 1000 elements (let's say 1000) and make a heap of them, and then take 10 elements from each heap one by one. Finally heap sort all the sets of 10 elements and take the top 10 among those. But the problem in this approach is where to store 10 elements from each heap. That may require a large amount of memory as we have billions of numbers.

Reusing the top 10 elements (from the earlier heap) in subsequent elements can solve this problem. That means take the first block of 1000 elements and subsequent blocks of 990 elements each. Initially, Heapsort the first set of 1000 numbers, take max 10 elements, and mix them with 990 elements of the $2^{nd}$ set. Again, Heapsort these 1000 numbers (10 from the first set and 990 from the $2^{nd}$ set), take 10 max elements, and mix them with 990 elements of the $3^{rd}$ set. Repeat till the last set of 990 (or less) elements and take max 10 elements from the final heap. These 10 elements will be your answer.

Time Complexity: $O(n) = n/1000 \times$(complexity of Heapsort 1000 elements) Since complexity of heap sorting 1000 elements will be a constant so the $O(n) = n$ i.e. linear complexity.

**Problem-22** **Merge $k$ sorted lists with total of $n$ elements:** We are given $k$ sorted lists with total $n$ inputs in all the lists. Give an algorithm to merge them into one single sorted list.

**Solution:** Since there are $k$ equal size lists with a total of $n$ elements, the size of each list is $\frac{n}{k}$. One simple way of solving this problem is:

- Take the first list and merge it with the second list. Since the size of each list is $\frac{n}{k}$, this step produces a sorted list with size $\frac{2n}{k}$. This is similar to merge sort logic. The time complexity of this step is: $\frac{2n}{k}$. This is because we need to scan all the elements of both the lists.
- Then, merge the second list output with the third list. As a result, this step produces a sorted list with size $\frac{3n}{k}$. The time complexity of this step is: $\frac{3n}{k}$. This is because we need to scan all the elements of both lists (one with size $\frac{2n}{k}$ and the other with size $\frac{n}{k}$).
- Continue this process until all the lists are merged to one list.

Total time complexity: $= \frac{2n}{k} + \frac{3n}{k} + \frac{4n}{k} + \cdots . \frac{kn}{k} = \sum_{i=2}^{n} \frac{in}{k} = \frac{n}{k}\sum_{i=2}^{n} i \approx \frac{n(k^2)}{k} \approx O(nk)$.
Space Complexity: $O(1)$.

**Problem-23** For Problem-22, can we improve the time complexity?

**Solution:**

1 Divide the lists into pairs and merge them. That means, first take two lists at a time and merge them so that the total elements parsed for all lists is $O(n)$. This operation gives $k/2$ lists.
2 Repeat step-1 until the number of lists becomes one.

Time complexity: Step-1 executes $logk$ times and each operation parses all $n$ elements in all the lists for making $k/2$ lists. For example, if we have 8 lists, then the first pass would make 4 lists by parsing all $n$ elements. The second pass would make 2 lists by again parsing $n$ elements and the third pass would give 1 list by again parsing $n$ elements. As a result the total time complexity is $O(nlogn)$.
Space Complexity: $O(n)$.

**Problem-24** For Problem-23, can we improve the space complexity?

**Solution:** Let us use heaps for reducing the space complexity.

1. Build the max-heap with all the first elements from each list in $O(k)$.
2. In each step, extract the maximum element of the heap and add it at the end of the output.
3. Add the next element from the list of the one extracted. That means we need to select the next element of the list which contains the extracted element of the previous step.
4. Repeat step-2 and step-3 until all the elements are completed from all the lists.

Time Complexity = $O(nlogk)$. At a time we have $k$ elements max-heap and for all $n$ elements we have to read just the heap in $logk$ time, so total time = $O(nlogk)$. Space Complexity: $O(k)$ [for Max-heap].

**Problem-25** Given 2 arrays $A$ and $B$ each with $n$ elements. Give an algorithm for finding largest $n$ pairs $(A[i], B[j])$.

**Solution:**

**Algorithm:**

- Heapify $A$ and $B$. This step takes $O(2n) \approx O(n)$.
- Then keep on deleting the elements from both the heaps. Each step takes $O(2logn) \approx O(logn)$.

Total Time complexity: $O(nlogn)$.

**Problem-26** **Min-Max heap:** Give an algorithm that supports min and max in $O(1)$ time, insert, delete min, and delete max in $O(logn)$ time. That means, design a data structure which supports the following operations:

| Operation | Complexity |
|---|---|
| init | $O(n)$ |
| insert | $O(logn)$ |
| findMin | $O(1)$ |
| findMax | $O(1)$ |
| deleteMin | $O(logn)$ |
| deleteMax | $O(logn)$ |

**Solution:** This problem can be solved using two heaps. Let us say two heaps are: Minimum-Heap $H_{min}$ and Maximum-Heap $H_{max}$. Also, assume that elements in both the arrays have mutual pointers. That means, an element in $H_{min}$ will have a pointer to the same element in $H_{max}$ and an element in $H_{max}$ will have a pointer to the same element in $H_{min}$.

| | |
|---|---|
| init | Build $H_{min}$ in $O(n)$ and $H_{max}$ in $O(n)$ |
| insert(x) | Insert x to $H_{min}$ in $O(logn)$. Insert x to $H_{max}$ in $O(logn)$. Update the pointers in $O(1)$ |
| findMin() | Return root($H_{min}$) in $O(1)$ |
| findMax | Return root($H_{max}$) in $O(1)$ |
| deleteMin | Delete the minimum from $H_{min}$ in $O(logn)$. Delete the same element from $H_{max}$ by using the mutual pointer in $O(logn)$ |
| deleteMax | Delete the maximum from $H_{max}$ in $O(logn)$. Delete the same element from $H_{min}$ by using the mutual pointer in $O(logn)$ |

**Problem-27** Dynamic median finding. Design a heap data structure that supports finding the median.

**Solution:** In a set of $n$ elements, median is the middle element, such that the number of elements lesser than the median is equal to the number of elements larger than the median. If $n$ is odd, we can find the median by sorting the set and taking the middle element. If $n$ is even, the median is usually defined as the average of the two middle elements. This algorithm works even when some of the elements in the list are equal. For example, the median of the multiset {1, 1, 2, 3, 5} is 2, and the median of the multiset {1, 1, 2, 3, 5, 8} is 2.5.

"*Median heaps*" are the variant of heaps that give access to the median element. A median heap can be implemented using two heaps, each containing half the elements. One is a max-heap, containing the smallest elements; the other is a min-heap, containing the largest elements. The size of the max-heap may be equal to the size of the min-heap, if the total number of elements is even. In this case, the median is the average of the maximum element of the max-heap and the minimum element of the min-heap. If there is an odd number of elements, the max-heap will contain one more element than the min-heap. The median in this case is simply the maximum element of the max-heap.

**Problem-28** **Maximum sum in sliding window:** Given array A[] with sliding window of size $w$ which is moving from the very left of the array to the very right. Assume that we can only see the $w$ numbers in the window.

Each time the sliding window moves rightwards by one position. For example: The array is [1 3 -1 -3 5 3 6 7], and *w* is 3.

| Window position | Max |
|---|---|
| [1 3 -1] -3 5 3 6 7 | 3 |
| 1 [3 -1 -3] 5 3 6 7 | 3 |
| 1 3 [-1 -3 5] 3 6 7 | 5 |
| 1 3 -1 [-3 5 3] 6 7 | 5 |
| 1 3 -1 -3 [5 3 6] 7 | 6 |
| 1 3 -1 -3 5 [3 6 7] | 7 |

**Input**: A long array A[], and a window width *w*. **Output**: An array B[], B[i] is the maximum value of from A[i] to A[i+w-1]
**Requirement**: Find a good optimal way to get B[i]

**Solution:** Brute force solution is, every time the window is moved we can search for a total of *w* elements in the window.

Time complexity: O(*nw*).

**Problem-29** For Problem-28, can we reduce the complexity?

**Solution: Yes,** we can use heap data structure. This reduces the time complexity to O(*nlogw*). Insert operation takes O(*logw*) time, where *w* is the size of the heap. However, getting the maximum value is cheap; it merely takes constant time as the maximum value is always kept in the root (head) of the heap. As the window slides to the right, some elements in the heap might not be valid anymore (range is outside of the current window). How should we remove them? We would need to be somewhat careful here. Since we only remove elements that are out of the window's range, we would need to keep track of the elements' indices too.

**Problem-30** For Problem-28, can we further reduce the complexity?

**Solution: Yes,** The double-ended queue is the perfect data structure for this problem. It supports insertion/deletion from the front and back. The trick is to find a way such that the largest element in the window would always appear in the front of the queue. How would you maintain this requirement as you push and pop elements in and out of the queue?

Besides, you will notice that there are some redundant elements in the queue that we shouldn't even consider. For example, if the current queue has the elements: [10 5 3], and a new element in the window has the element 11. Now, we could have emptied the queue without considering elements 10, 5, and 3, and insert only element 11 into the queue.

Typically, most people try to maintain the queue size the same as the window's size. Try to break away from this thought and think out of the box. Removing redundant elements and storing only elements that need to be considered in the queue is the key to achieving the efficient O(*n*) solution below. This is because each element in the list is being inserted and removed at most once. Therefore, the total number of insert + delete operations is 2*n*.

```
void maxSlidingWindow(int A[], int n, int w, int B[]) {
    struct DoubleEndQueue *Q = createDoubleEndQueue();
    for (int i = 0; i < w; i++) {
            while (!isEmptyQueue(Q) && A[i] >= A[QBack(Q)])
                    popBack(Q);
            pushBack(Q, i);
    }
    for (int i = w; i < n; i++) {
            B[i-w] = A[QFront(Q)];
            while (!isEmptyQueue(Q) && A[i] >= A[QBack(Q)])
                    popBack(Q);
            while (!isEmptyQueue(Q) && QFront(Q) <= i-w)
                    popFront(Q);
            pushBack(Q, i);
    }
    B[n-w] = A[QFront(Q)];
}
```

**Problem-31** A priority queue is a list of items in which each item has associated with it a priority. Items are withdrawn from a priority queue in order of their priorities starting with the highest priority item first. If the maximum priority item is required, then a heap is constructed such than priority of every node is greater than the priority of its children.

Design such a heap where the item with the middle priority is withdrawn first. If there are n items in the heap, then the number of items with the priority smaller than the middle priority is $\frac{n}{2}$ if $n$ is odd, else $\frac{n}{2} \mp 1$.

Explain how withdraw and insert operations work, calculate their complexity, and how the data structure is constructed.

**Solution**: We can use one min heap and one max heap such that root of the min heap is larger than the root of the max heap. The size of the min heap should be equal or one less than the size of the max heap. So the middle element is always the root of the max heap.

For the insert operation, if the new item is less than the root of max heap, then insert it into the max heap; else insert it into the min heap. After the withdraw or insert operation, if the size of heaps are not as specified above than transfer the root element of the max heap to min heap or vice-versa. With this implementation, insert and withdraw operation will be in O($logn$) time.

**Problem-32** Given two heaps, how do you merge (union) them?

**Solution**: Binary heap supports various operations quickly: Find-min, insert, decrease-key. If we have two min-heaps, H1 and H2, there is no efficient way to combine them into a single min-heap.

For solving this problem efficiently, we can use mergeable heaps. Mergeable heaps support efficient union operation. It is a data structure that supports the following operations:

- create-Heap(): creates an empty heap
- insert(H,X,K) : insert an item x with key K into a heap H
- find-Min(H) : return item with min key
- delete-Min(H) : return and remove
- Union(H1, H2) : merge heaps H1 and H2

Examples of mergeable heaps are:

- Binomial Heaps
- Fibonacci Heaps

Both heaps also support:

- decrease-Key(H,X,K): assign item Y with a smaller key K
- delete(H,X) : remove item X

**Binomial Heaps:** Unlike binary heap which consists of a single tree, a *binomial* heap consists of a small set of component trees and no need to rebuild everything when union is performed. Each component tree is in a special format, called a *binomial tree*.

A binomial tree of order $k$, denoted by $B_k$ is defined recursively as follows:

- $B_0$ is a tree with a single node
- For $k \geq 1$, $B_k$ is formed by joining two $B_{k-1}$, such that the root of one tree becomes the leftmost child of the root of the other.

**Example**:

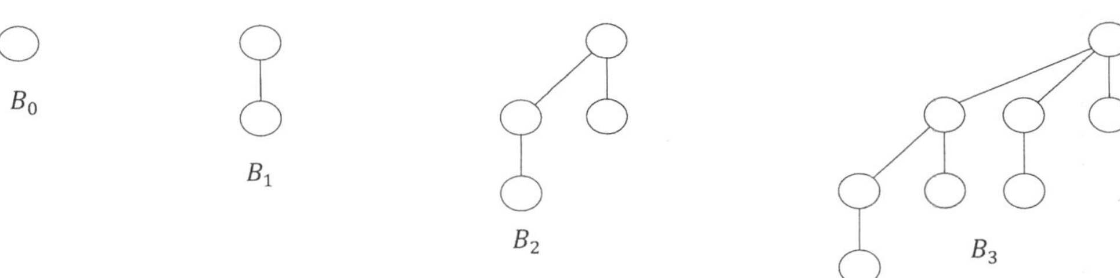


**Fibonacci Heaps:** Fibonacci heap is another example of mergeable heap. It has no good worst-case guarantee for any operation (except insert/create-Heap). Fibonacci Heaps have excellent amortized cost to perform each operation. Like *binomial* heap, *fibonacci* heap consists of a set of min-heap ordered component trees. However, unlike binomial heap, it has

- No limit on number of trees (up to O($n$)), and
- No limit on height of a tree (up to O($n$))

Also, *Find-Min, Delete-Min, Union, Decrease-Key, Delete* all have worst-case O($n$) running time. However, in the amortized sense, each operation performs very quickly.

| Operation | Binary Heap | Binomial Heap | Fibonacci Heap |
|---|---|---|---|
| create-Heap | $\Theta(1)$ | $\Theta(1)$ | $\Theta(1)$ |
| find-Min | $\Theta(1)$ | $\Theta(logn)$ | $\Theta(1)$ |
| delete-Min | $\Theta(logn)$ | $\Theta(logn)$ | $\Theta(logn)$ |

| insert | $\Theta(logn)$ | $\Theta(logn)$ | $\Theta(1)$ |
|---|---|---|---|
| delete | $\Theta(logn)$ | $\Theta(logn)$ | $\Theta(logn)$ |
| decrease-Key | $\Theta(logn)$ | $\Theta(logn)$ | $\Theta(1)$ |
| Union | $\Theta(n)$ | $\Theta(logn)$ | $\Theta(1)$ |

**Problem-33** Median in an infinite series of integers.

**Solution**: Median is the middle number in a sorted list of numbers (if we have odd number of elements). If we have even number of elements, median is the average of two middle numbers in a sorted list of numbers.

We can solve this problem efficiently by using 2 heaps: One MaxHeap and one MinHeap.

1. MaxHeap contains the smallest half of the received integers
2. MinHeap contains the largest half of the received integers

The integers in MaxHeap are always less than or equal to the integers in MinHeap. Also, the number of elements in MaxHeap is either equal to or 1 more than the number of elements in the MinHeap.

In the stream if we get $2n$ elements (at any point of time), MaxHeap and MinHeap will both contain equal number of elements (in this case, $n$ elements in each heap). Otherwise, if we have received $2n + 1$ elements, MaxHeap will contain $n + 1$ and MinHeap $n$.

Let us find the Median: If we have $2n + 1$ elements (odd), the Median of received elements will be the largest element in the MaxHeap (nothing but the root of MaxHeap). Otherwise, the Median of received elements will be the average of largest element in the MaxHeap (nothing but the root of MaxHeap) and smallest element in the MinHeap (nothing but the root of MinHeap). This can be calculated in O(1).

Inserting an element into heap can be done in O($logn$). Note that, any heap containing $n + 1$ elements might need one delete operation (and insertion to other heap) as well.

**Example**:

Insert 1: Insert to MaxHeap.
MaxHeap: {1}, MinHeap:{}
Insert 9: Insert to MinHeap. Since 9 is greater than 1 and MinHeap maintains the maximum elements.
MaxHeap: {1}, MinHeap:{9}
Insert 2: Insert MinHeap. Since 2 is less than all elements of MinHeap.
MaxHeap: {1,2}, MinHeap:{9}
Insert 0: Since MaxHeap already has more than half; we have to drop the max element from MaxHeap and insert it to MinHeap. So, we have to remove 2 and insert into MinHeap. With that it becomes:
MaxHeap: {1}, MinHeap:{2,9}
Now, insert 0 to MaxHeap.

Total Time Complexity: O($logn$).

**Problem-34** Suppose the elements 7, 2, 10 and 4 are inserted, in that order, into the valid 3-ary max heap found in the above question, Which one of the following is the sequence of items in the array representing the resultant heap?

(A) 10, 7, 9, 8, 3, 1, 5, 2, 6, 4
(B) 10, 9, 8, 7, 6, 5, 4, 3, 2, 1
(C) 10, 9, 4, 5, 7, 6, 8, 2, 1, 3
(D) 10, 8, 6, 9, 7, 2, 3, 4, 1, 5

**Solution**: The 3-ary max heap with elements 9, 5, 6, 8, 3, 1 is:

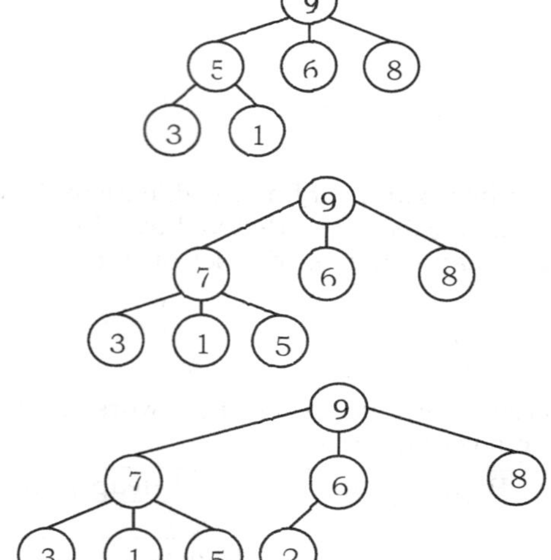

After Insertion of 7:

After Insertion of 2:

After Insertion of 10:

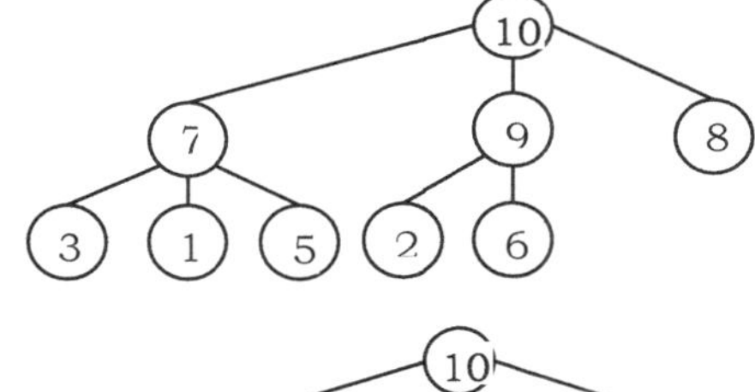


After Insertion of 4:

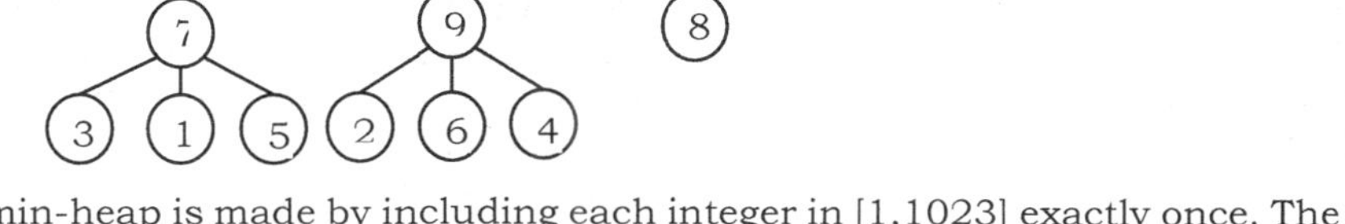


**Problem-35** A complete binary min-heap is made by including each integer in [1,1023] exactly once. The depth of a node in the heap is the length of the path from the root of the heap to that node. Thus, the root is at depth 0. The maximum depth at which integer 9 can appear is___.

**Solution**: As shown in the figure below, for a given number $i$, we can fix the element $i$ at $i^{th}$ level and arrange the numbers 1 to $i-1$ to the levels above. Since the root is at depth *zero*, the maximum depth of the $i^{th}$ element in a min-heap is $i-1$. Hence, the maximum depth at which integer 9 can appear is 8.

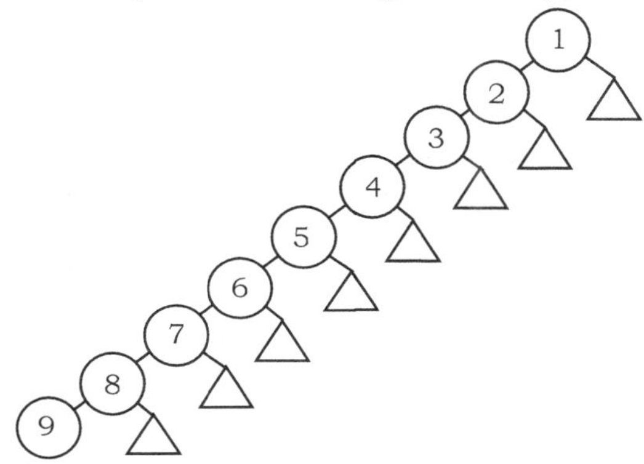


**Problem-36** A $d$-ary heap is like a binary heap, but instead of 2 children, nodes have $d$ children. How would you represent a $d$-ary heap with $n$ elements in an array? What are the expressions for determining the parent of a given element, $Parent(i)$, and a $j^{th}$ child of a given element, $Child(i,j)$, where $1 \leq j \leq d$?

**Solution**: The following expressions determine the parent and $j^{th}$ child of element i (where $1 \leq j \leq d$):

$$Parent(i) = \left\lfloor \frac{i+d-2}{d} \right\rfloor$$

$$Child(i,j) = (i-1).d+j+1$$

**Problem-37** Given an integer array, sort the integers in the array in ascending order by the number of 1's in their binary representation and in case of two or more integers have the same number of 1's you have to sort them in ascending order.

**Solution**: The very basic approach to solve this problem is to count the number of 1's (set bits) in each element of the array and then use a comparator function to sort the array. The comparator function compares two elements. If both elements contain a different number of set bits then the number which contains less number of set bits comes first else smaller number comes first. We can use a min-heap for solving this problem. In the min-heap, by storing pair<count of ones, number> as the values the pair with minimum number of ones will be at the top.

```
vector<int> sortByBits(vector<int>& A) {
    priority_queue<pair<int,int>, vector<pair<int,int>>, greater<pair<int,int>>> pq;
    for(auto element: A){
        int counterSetBits = 0;
        int t = element;
        while(element){
            element = (element&(element-1));
            counterSetBits++;
        }
        pq.push({counterSetBits, t});
    }
```

```
        vector<int> v;
        while(pq.size()){
            v.push_back(pq.top().second);
            pq.pop();
        }
        return v;
    }
```

Time Complexity: O($nlogn$).

Problem-38 **The K Weakest Rows in a Matrix:** We are given an m x n binary matrix mat of 1's (representing soldiers) and 0's (representing civilians). The soldiers are positioned in front of the civilians. That is, all the 1's will appear to the left of all the 0's in each row. A row i is weaker than a row j if one of the following is true:

- The number of soldiers in row i is less than the number of soldiers in row j.
- Both rows have the same number of soldiers and i < j.
- Return the indices of the k weakest rows in the matrix ordered from weakest to strongest.

**Solution**: We can solve this problem using a combination of priority queues and binary search. The idea is to use a priority queue to keep track of the k weakest rows seen so far. We can maintain the size of the priority queue at k by popping the strongest row from the queue whenever its size exceeds k.

To determine the number of soldiers in each row, we can use binary search to find the index of the first zero in each row. The number of soldiers in a row will be equal to the index of the first zero.

Here is the algorithm in more detail:

- Create an empty priority queue called "pq".
- Iterate through each row i in the matrix mat.
- Use binary search to find the index of the first zero in row i. Let this index be "j".
- Add a tuple (number of soldiers, row index) = (j, i) to the priority queue "pq".
- If the size of "pq" exceeds k, pop the strongest row (i.e., the row with the largest number of soldiers) from "pq".
- After iterating through all rows, extract the row indices from "pq" and return them in a list.

```
#include <stdio.h>
#include <stdlib.h>
typedef struct {
    int numSoldiers;
    int rowIndex;
} Row;
int binarySearch(int *row, int n) {
    int lo = 0, hi = n - 1;
    while (lo <= hi) {
        int mid = (lo + hi) / 2;
        if (row[mid] == 1) {
            lo = mid + 1;
        } else {
            hi = mid - 1;
        }
    }
    return lo;
}
int cmp(const void *a, const void *b) {
    Row *rowA = (Row *)a;
    Row *rowB = (Row *)b;
    if (rowA->numSoldiers == rowB->numSoldiers) {
        return rowA->rowIndex - rowB->rowIndex;
    }
    return rowA->numSoldiers - rowB->numSoldiers;
}
int *kWeakestRows(int **mat, int matSize, int *matColSize, int k, int *returnSize) {
    Row *rows = (Row *)malloc(matSize * sizeof(Row));
    for (int i = 0; i < matSize; i++) {
        rows[i].numSoldiers = binarySearch(mat[i], matColSize[i]);
        rows[i].rowIndex = i;
```

```
    }
    qsort(rows, matSize, sizeof(Row), cmp);
    *returnSize = k;
    int *result = (int *)malloc(k * sizeof(int));
    for (int i = 0; i < k; i++) {
        result[i] = rows[i].rowIndex;
    }
    free(rows);
    return result;
}
```

The time complexity of this algorithm is O(mn log k), where m is the number of rows and n is the number of columns in the matrix. The binary search takes O(log n) time for each row, and we iterate through m rows, so the total time complexity of the binary search step is O(m log n). The priority queue has a maximum size of k, so each push and pop operation takes O(log k) time, and we perform at most mn such operations, leading to a total time complexity of O(mn log k). The space complexity of this algorithm is O(k), which is the space required to store the priority queue.

# DISJOINT SETS ADT

## 8.1 Introduction

In this chapter, we will represent an important mathematics concept: *sets*. This means how to represent a group of elements which do not need any order. The disjoint sets ADT is the one used for this purpose. It is used for solving the equivalence problem. It is very simple to implement. A simple array can be used for the implementation and each function takes only a few lines of code. Disjoint sets ADT acts as an auxiliary data structure for many other algorithms (for example, *Kruskal's* algorithm in graph theory). Before starting our discussion on disjoint sets ADT, let us look at some basic properties of sets.

## 8.2 Equivalence Relations and Equivalence Classes

For the discussion below let us assume that $S$ is a set containing the elements and a relation $R$ is defined on it. That means for every pair of elements in $a, b \in S$, $a\ R\ b$ is either true or false. If $a\ R\ b$ is true, then we say $a$ is related to $b$, otherwise $a$ is not related to $b$. A relation $R$ is called an *equivalence relation* if it satisfies the following properties:

- *Reflexive*: For every element $a \in S, a\ R\ a$ is true.
- *Symmetric*: For any two elements $a, b \in S$, if $a\ R\ b$ is true then $b\ R\ a$ is true.
- *Transitive*: For any three elements a, b, c ∈ S, if a R b and $b\ R\ c$ are true then $a\ R\ c$ is true.

As an example, relations $\leq$ (less than or equal to) and $\geq$ (greater than or equal to) on a set of integers are not equivalence relations. They are reflexive (since $a \leq a$) and transitive ($a \leq b$ and $b \leq c$ implies $a \leq c$) but not symmetric ($a \leq b$ does not imply $b \leq a$).

Similarly, *rail connectivity* is an equivalence relation. This relation is reflexive because any location is connected to itself. If there is connectivity from city $a$ to city $b$, then city $b$ also has connectivity to city $a$, so the relation is symmetric. Finally, if city $a$ is connected to city $b$ and city $b$ is connected to city $c$, then city $a$ is also connected to city $c$.

The *equivalence class* of an element $a \in S$ is a subset of $S$ that contains all the elements that are related to $a$. Equivalence classes create a *partition* of $S$. Every member of $S$ appears in exactly one equivalence class. To decide if $a\ R\ b$, we just need to check whether $a$ and $b$ are in the same equivalence class (group) or not.

In the above example, two cities will be in same equivalence class if they have rail connectivity. If they do not have connectivity then they will be part of different equivalence classes.

Since the intersection of any two equivalence classes is empty ($\phi$), the equivalence classes are sometimes called *disjoint sets*. In the subsequent sections, we will try to see the operations that can be performed on equivalence classes. The possible operations are:

- Creating an equivalence class (making a set)
- Finding the equivalence class name (Find)
- Combining the equivalence classes (Union)

## 8.3 Disjoint Sets ADT

To manipulate the set elements we need basic operations defined on sets. In this chapter, we concentrate on the following set operations:

- MAKESET($X$): Creates a new set containing a single element $X$.
- UNION($X$, $Y$): Creates a new set containing the elements $X$ and $Y$ in their union and deletes the sets containing the elements $X$ and $Y$.
- FIND($X$): Returns the name of the set containing the element $X$.

## 8.4 Applications

Disjoint sets ADT have many applications and a few of them are:

- To represent network connectivity
- Image processing
- To find least common ancestor
- To define equivalence of finite state automata
- Kruskal's minimum spanning tree algorithm (graph theory)
- In game algorithms

## 8.5 Tradeoffs in Implementing Disjoint Sets ADT

Let us see the possibilities for implementing disjoint set operations. Initially, assume the input elements are a collection of $n$ sets, each with one element. That means, initial representation assumes all relations (except reflexive relations) are false. Each set has a different element, so that $S_i \cap S_j = \phi$. This makes the sets *disjoint*.

To add the relation $a\ R\ b$ (UNION), we first need to check whether $a$ and $b$ are already related or not. This can be verified by performing FINDs on both $a$ and $b$ and checking whether they are in the same equivalence class (set) or not.

If they are not, then we apply UNION. This operation merges the two equivalence classes containing $a$ and $b$ into a new equivalence class by creating a new set $S_k = S_i \cup S_j$ and deletes $S_i$ and $S_j$. Basically there are two ways to implement the above FIND/UNION operations:

- Fast FIND implementation (also called Quick FIND)
- Fast UNION operation implementation (also called Quick UNION)

## 8.6 Fast FIND Implementation (Quick FIND)

In this method, we use an array. As an example, in the representation below the array contains the set name for each element. For simplicity, let us assume that all the elements are numbered sequentially from 0 to $n-1$. In the example below, element 0 has the set name 3, element 1 has the set name 5, and so on. With this representation FIND takes only O(1) since for any element we can find the set name by accessing its array location in constant time.

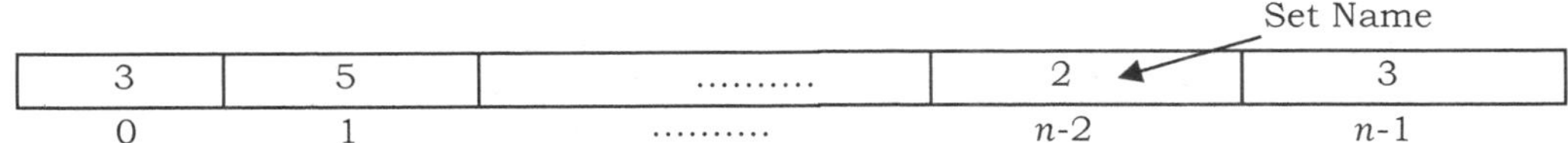


In this representation, to perform UNION($a, b$) [assuming that $a$ is in set $i$ and $b$ is in set $j$] we need to scan the complete array and change all $i$'s to $j$. This takes O($n$).

A sequence of $n-1$ unions take O($n^2$) time in the worst case. If there are O($n^2$) FIND operations, this performance is fine, as the average time complexity is O(1) for each UNION or FIND operation. If there are fewer FINDs, this complexity is not acceptable.

## 8.7 Fast UNION Implementation (Quick UNION)

In this and subsequent sections, we will discuss the faster *UNION* implementations and its variants. There are different ways of implementing this approach and the following is a list of a few of them.

- Fast UNION implementations (Slow FIND)
- Fast UNION implementations (Quick FIND)
- Fast UNION implementations with path compression

## 8.8 Fast UNION Implementation (Slow FIND)

As we have discussed, FIND operation returns the same answer (set name) if and only if they are in the same set. In representing disjoint sets, our main objective is to give a different set name for each group. In general we do not care about the name of the set. One possibility for implementing the set is *tree* as each element has only one *root* and we can use it as the set name.

**How are these represented?** One possibility is using an array: for each element keep the *root* as its set name. But with this representation, we will have the same problem as that of FIND array implementation. To solve this problem, instead of storing the *root* we can keep the parent of the element. Therefore, using an array which stores the parent of each element solves our problem.

To differentiate the root node, let us assume its parent is the same as that of the element in the array. Based on this representation, MAKESET, FIND, UNION operations can be defined as:

- $(X)$: Creates a new set containing a single element $X$ and in the array update the parent of $X$ as $X$. That means root (set name) of $X$ is $X$.

- UNION($X$, $Y$): Replaces the two sets containing $X$ and $Y$ by their union and in the array updates the parent of $X$ as $Y$.

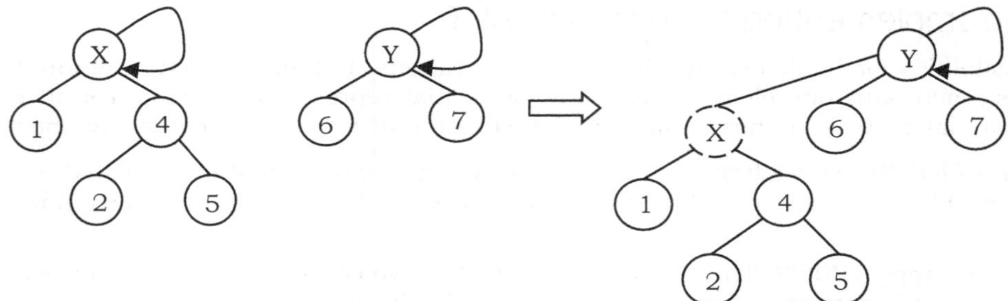


- FIND(X): Returns the name of the set containing the element $X$. We keep on searching for $X$'s set name until we come to the root of the tree.

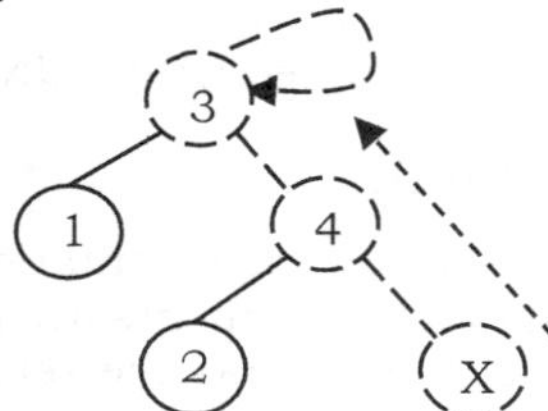


For the elements 0 to $n - 1$ the initial representation is:

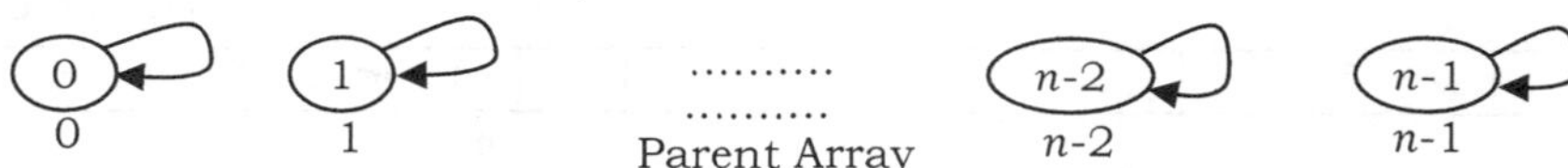


To perform a UNION on two sets, we merge the two trees by making the root of one tree point to the root of the other.

Initial Configuration for the elements 0 to 6

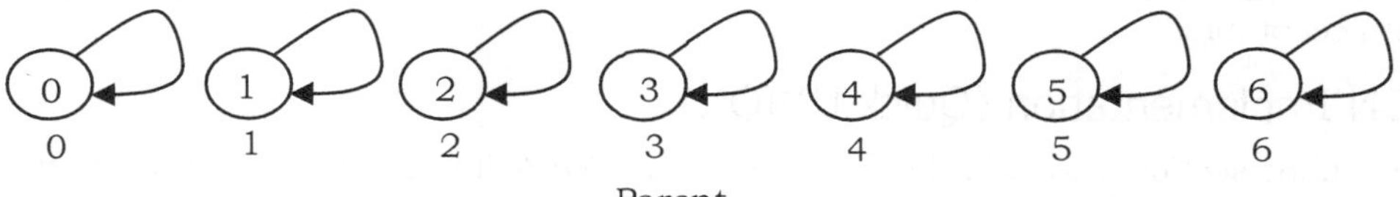


After UNION(5,6)

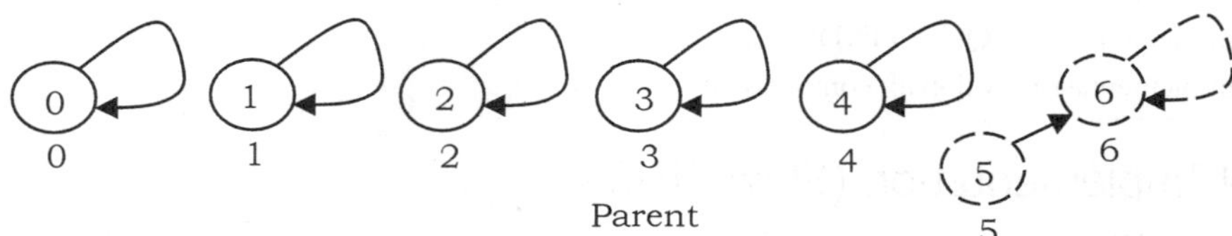


After UNION(1,2)

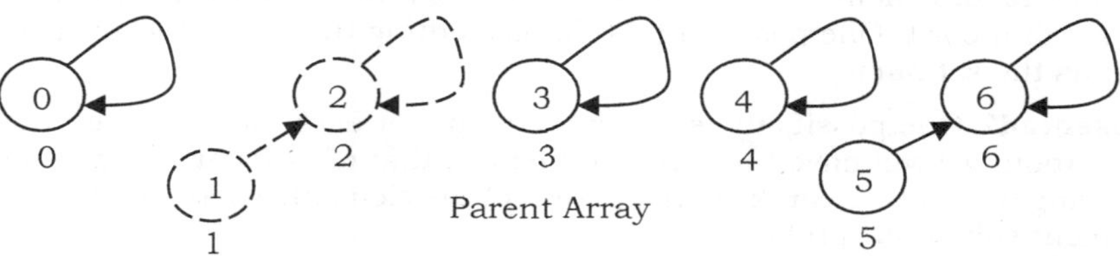

After UNION(0,2)

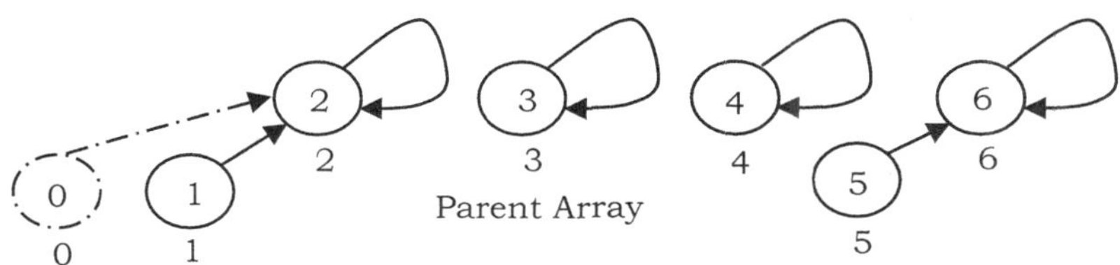


One important thing to observe here is, UNION operation is changing the root's parent only, but not for all the elements in the sets. Due to this, the time complexity of UNION operation is O(1). A FIND($X$) on element $X$ is performed by returning the root of the tree containing $X$.

The time to perform this operation is proportional to the depth of the node representing $X$. Using this method, it is possible to create a tree of depth $n - 1$ (Skew Trees). The worst-case running time of a FIND is O($n$) and $m$ consecutive FIND operations take O($mn$) time in the worst case.

### MAKESET

```
void MAKESET( int S[], int size) {
    for(int i = size-1; i >=0; i-- )
        S[i] = i;
}
```

### FIND

```
int FIND(int S[], int size, int X) {
    if(!(X >= 0 && X < size))
        return -1;
    if( S[X] == X )
        return X;
    else    return FIND(S, S[X]);
}
```

### UNION

```
void UNION( int S[], int size, int root1, int root2 ) {
    if(FIND(S, size, root1) == FIND(S, size, root2))
        return;
    if(!((root1 >= 0 && root1 < size) && (root2 >= 0 && root2 < size)))
        return;
    S[root1] = root2;
}
```

## 8.9 Fast UNION Implementations (Quick FIND)

The main problem with the previous approach is that, in the worst case we are getting the skew trees and as a result the FIND operation is taking O($n$) time complexity. There are two ways to improve it:

- UNION by Size (also called UNION by Weight): Make the smaller tree a subtree of the larger tree
- UNION by Height (also called UNION by Rank): Make the tree with less height a subtree of the tree with more height

### UNION by Size

In the earlier representation, for each element $i$ we have stored $i$ (in the parent array) for the root element and for other elements we have stored the parent of $i$. But in this approach we store negative of the size of the tree (that means, if the size of the tree is 3 then store −3 in the parent array for the root element). For the previous example (after UNION(0,2)), the new representation will look like:

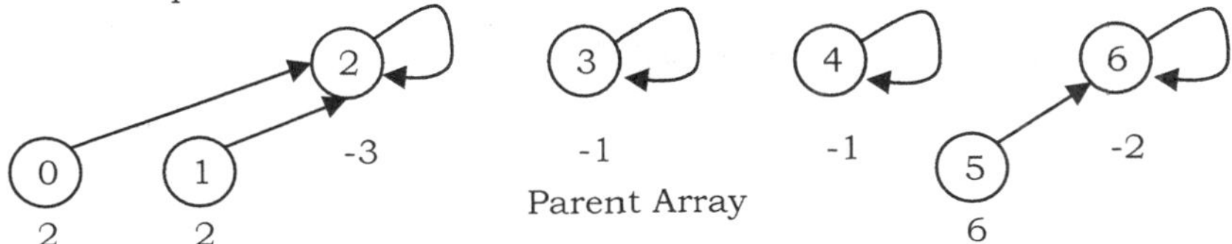


Assume that the size of one element set is 1 and store −1. Other than this there is no change.

MAKESET

```
void MAKESET( int S[], int size) {
    for(int  i = size-1; i >= 0; i-- )
        S[i] = -1;
}
```

FIND

```
int FIND(int S[], int size, int X) {
    if(!(X >= 0 && X < size))
        return -1;
    if( S[X] == -1 )
        return X;
    else return FIND(S, S[X]);
}
```

UNION by Size

```
void UNIONBySize(int S[], int size, int root1, int root2) {
    if((FIND(S, size, root1) == FIND(S, size, root2)) && FIND(S, size, root1) != -1)
        return;
    if( S[root2] < S[root1] ) {
        S[root1] = root2;
        S[root2] += S[root1];
    }
    else {
        S[root2] = root1;
        S[root1] += S[root2];
    }
}
```

**Note:** There is no change in FIND operation implementation.

## UNION by Height (UNION by Rank)

As in UNION by size, in this method we store negative of height of the tree (that means, if the height of the tree is 3 then we store $-3$ in the parent array for the root element). We assume the height of a tree with one element set is 1. For the previous example (after UNION(0,2)), the new representation will look like:

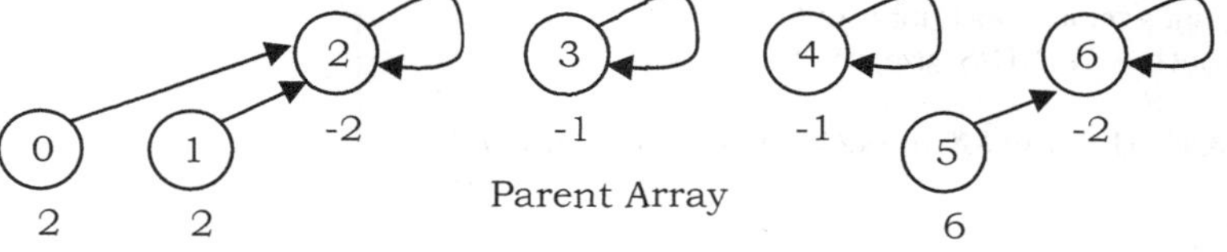


UNION by Height

```
void UNIONByHeight(int S[], int size, int root1, int root2) {
    if((FIND(S, size, root1) == FIND(S, size, root2)) && FIND(S, size, root1) != -1)
        return;
    if( S[root2] < S[root1] )
        S[root1] = root2;
    else {
        if( S[root2] == S[root1] ){
            S[root1]--;
            S[root2] = root1;
        }
    }
}
```

**Note:** For FIND operation there is no change in the implementation.

## Comparing UNION by Size and UNION by Height

With UNION by size, the depth of any node is never more than $logn$. This is because a node is initially at depth 0. When its depth increases as a result of a UNION, it is placed in a tree that is at least twice as large as before. That means its depth can be increased at most $logn$ times. This means that the running time for a FIND operation is O($logn$), and a sequence of $m$ operations takes O($m$ $logn$).

Similarly with UNION by height, if we take the UNION of two trees of the same height, the height of the UNION is one larger than the common height, and otherwise equal to the max of the two heights. This will keep the height of tree of $n$ nodes from growing past $O(logn)$. A sequence of $m$ UNIONs and FINDs can then still cost $O(m\ logn)$.

## Path Compression

FIND operation traverses a list of nodes on the way to the root. We can make later FIND operations efficient by making each of these vertices point directly to the root. This process is called *path compression*. For example, in the FIND($X$) operation, we travel from $X$ to the root of the tree. The effect of path compression is that every node on the path from $X$ to the root has its parent changed to the root.

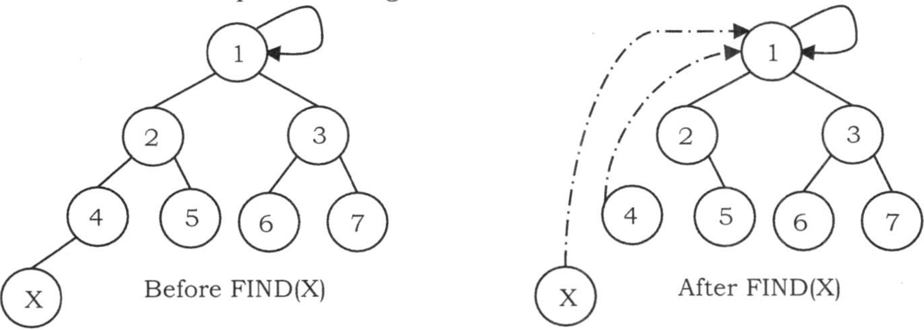


With path compression the only change to the FIND function is that $S[X]$ is made equal to the value returned by FIND. That means, after the root of the set is found recursively, $X$ is made to point directly to it. This happen recursively to every node on the path to the root.

## FIND with path compression

```
int FIND(int S[], int size, int X) {
    if(!(X >= 0 && X < size))
        return INT_MIN;
    if( S[X] <= 0 )
        return X;
    else return(S[X] = FIND( S, S[X]));
}
// Iterative approach
int find (int S[], int size, int X) {
    int i, temp;
    /* Find root of class (class-representative) of 'X'
      At the end of this process, 'i' points to the root */
    for (i = X; S[i] > 0; i = S[i]);
    /* Perform "path compression": point all members along the just-found
      path directly to the root so future find operations are faster */
    while (S[X] > 0) {
        temp = X;
        X = S[X];
        S[temp] = i;
    }
    // return the class representative found above
    return i;
}
```

**Note:** Path compression is compatible with UNION by size but not with UNION by height as there is no efficient way to change the height of the tree.

## 8.10 Summary

Performing $m$ union-find operations on a set of $n$ objects.

| Algorithm | Worst-case time |
|---|---|
| Quick-Find | $mn$ |
| Quick-Union | $mn$ |
| Quick-Union by Size/Height | $n + m\ logn$ |
| Path compression | $n + m\ logn$ |
| Quick-Union by Size/Height + Path Compression | $(m + n)\ logn$ |

## 8.11 Disjoint Sets: Problems & Solutions

**Problem-1** Consider a list of cities $c_1, c_2, \ldots, c_n$. Assume that we have a relation $R$ such that, for any $i, j$, $R(c_i, c_j)$ is 1 if cities $c_i$ and $c_j$ are in the same state, and 0 otherwise. If $R$ is stored as a table, how much space does it require?

**Solution:** $R$ must have an entry for every pair of cities. There are $\Theta(n^2)$ of these.

**Problem-2** For Problem-1, using a Disjoint sets ADT, give an algorithm that puts each city in a set such that $c_i$ and $c_j$ are in the same set if and only if they are in the same state.

**Solution:**

```
for (i = 1; i<= n; i++) {
    MAKESET(ci);
    for (j = 1; j <= i-1; j++) {
        if(R(cj, ci)) {
            UNION(cj, ci);
            break;
        }
    }
}
```

**Problem-3** For Problem-1, when the cities are stored in the Disjoint sets ADT, if we are given two cities $c_i$ and $c_j$, how do we check if they are in the same state?

**Solution:** Cities $c_i$ and $c_j$ are in the same state if and only if FIND($c_i$) = FIND($c_j$).

**Problem-4** For Problem-1, if we use linked-lists with UNION by size to implement the union-find ADT, how much space do we use to store the cities?

**Solution:** There is one node per city, so the space is $\Theta(n)$.

**Problem-5** For Problem-1, if we use trees with UNION by rank, what is the worst-case running time of the algorithm from Problem-2?

**Solution:** Whenever we do a UNION in the algorithm from Problem-2, the second argument is a tree of size 1. Therefore, all trees have height 1, so each union takes time O(1). The worst-case running time is then $\Theta(n^2)$.

**Problem-6** If we use trees without union-by-rank, what is the worst-case running time of the algorithm from Problem-2? Are there more worst-case scenarios than Problem-5?

**Solution:** Because of the special case of the unions, union-by-rank does not make a difference for our algorithm. Hence, everything is the same as in Problem-5.

**Problem-7** With the quick-union algorithm we know that a sequence of $n$ operations ($unions$ and $finds$) can take slightly more than linear time in the worst case. Explain why if all the $finds$ are done before all the $unions$, a sequence of $n$ operations is guaranteed to take O($n$) time.

**Solution:** If the $find$ operations are performed first, then the $find$ operations take O(1) time each because every item is the root of its own tree. No item has a parent, so finding the set an item is in takes a fixed number of operations. Union operations always take O(1) time. Hence, a sequence of $n$ operations with all the $finds$ before the $unions$ takes O($n$) time.

**Problem-8** With reference to Problem-7, explain why if all the unions are done before all the finds, a sequence of $n$ operations is guaranteed to take O($n$) time.

**Solution:** This problem requires amortized analysis. *Find* operations can be expensive, but this expensive $find$ operation is balanced out by lots of cheap $union$ operations.

The accounting is as follows. *Union* operations always take O(1) time, so let's say they have an actual cost of ₹1. Assign each $union$ operation an amortized cost of ₹2, so every $union$ operation puts ₹1 in the account. Each $union$ operation creates a new child. (Some node that was not a child of any other node before is a child now.) When all the union operations are done, there is $1 in the account for every child, or in other words, for every node with a depth of one or greater. Let's say that a $find(u)$ operation costs ₹1 if $u$ is a root. For any other node, the $find$ operation costs an additional ₹1 for each parent pointer the $find$ operation traverses. So the actual cost is ₹$(1 + d)$, where $d$ is the depth of $u$. Assign each $find$ operation an amortized cost of ₹2. This covers the case where $u$ is a root or a child of a root. For each additional parent pointer traversed, ₹1 is withdrawn from the account to pay for it.

Fortunately, path compression changes the parent pointers of all the nodes we pay ₹1 to traverse, so these nodes become children of the root. All of the traversed nodes whose depths are 2 or greater move up, so their depths are now 1. We will never have to pay to traverse these nodes again. Say that a node is a grandchild if its depth is 2 or greater.

Every time $find(u)$ visits a grandchild, ₹1 is withdrawn from the account, but the grandchild is no longer a grandchild. So the maximum number of dollars that can ever be withdrawn from the account is the number of grandchildren. But we initially put $1 in the bank for every child, and every grandchild is a child, so the bank balance will never drop below zero. Therefore, the amortization works out. *Union* and $find$ operations both have amortized costs of ₹2, so any sequence of $n$ operations where all the unions are done first takes O($n$) time.

# GRAPH ALGORITHMS

CHAPTER

## 9.1 Introduction

In the real world, many problems are represented in terms of objects and connections between them. For example, in an airline route map, we might be interested in questions like: "What's the fastest way to go from Hyderabad to New York?" *or* "What is the cheapest way to go from Hyderabad to New York?" To answer these questions we need information about connections (airline routes) between objects (towns). Graphs are data structures used for solving these kinds of problems.

As part of this chapter, you will learn several ways to traverse graphs and how you can do useful things while traversing the graph in some order. We will also talk about shortest paths algorithms. We will finish with minimum spanning trees, which are used to plan road, telephone and computer networks and also find applications in clustering and approximate algorithms.

## 9.2 Glossary

**Graph:** A graph G is simply a way of encoding pairwise relationships among a set of objects: it consists of a collection V of nodes and a collection E of edges, each of which "joins" two of the nodes. We thus represent an edge e in E as a two-element subset of V: e = {u, v} for some u, v in V, where we call u and v the ends of e.

Edges in a graph indicate a symmetric relationship between their ends. Often we want to encode asymmetric relationships, and for this, we use the closely related notion of a directed graph. A directed graph G' consists of a set of nodes V and a set of directed edges E'. Each e' in E' is an ordered pair (u, v); in other words, the roles of u and v are not interchangeable, and we call u the tail of the edge and v the head. We will also say that edge e' leaves node u and enters node v.

When we want to emphasize that the graph we are considering is *not directed*, we will call it an *undirected graph*; by default, however, the term "graph" will mean an undirected graph. It is also worth mentioning two warnings in our use of graph terminology. First, although an edge e in an undirected graph should properly be written as a set of nodes {u, u}, one will more often see it written in the notation used for ordered pairs: e = (u, v). Second, a node in a graph is also frequently called a vertex; in this context, the two words have exactly the same meaning.

- *Vertices* and *edges* are positions and store elements
- Definitions that we use:
  - *Directed edge*:
    - Ordered pair of vertices $(u, v)$
    - First vertex $u$ is the origin
    - Second vertex $v$ is the destination
    - Example: one-way road traffic

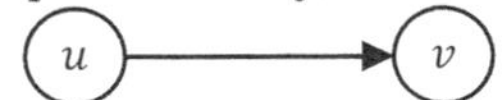


  - *Undirected edge*:
    - Unordered pair of vertices $(u, v)$
    - Example: railway lines

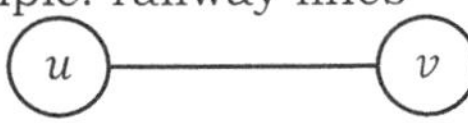


  - *Directed graph*:
    - All the edges are directed
    - Example: route network

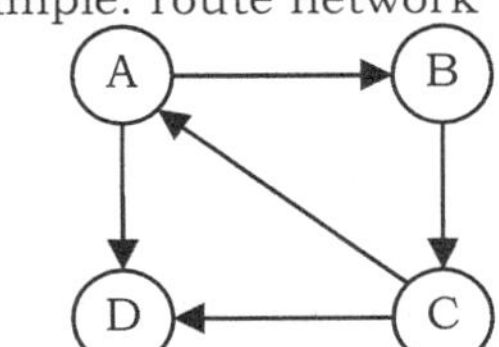

- *Undirected graph*:
  - All the edges are undirected
  - Example: flight network

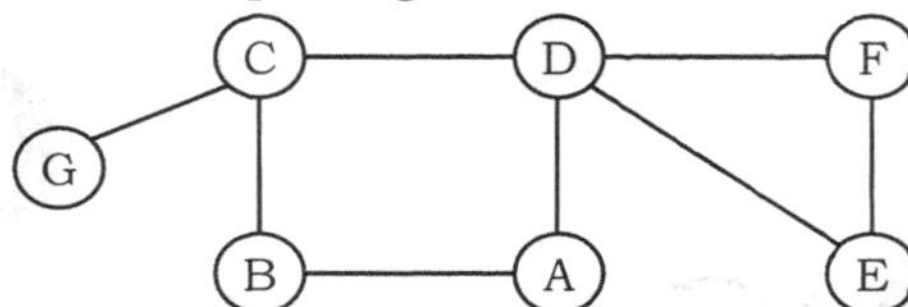


- When an edge connects two vertices, the vertices are said to be adjacent to each other and the edge is incident on both vertices.
- A graph with no cycles is called a *tree*. A tree is an acyclic connected graph.

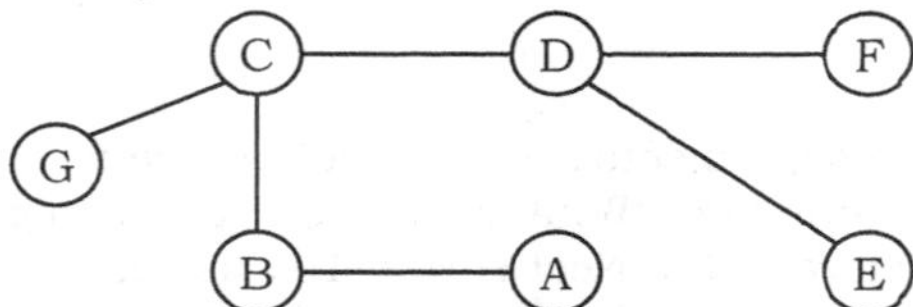


- A self loop is an edge that connects a vertex to itself.

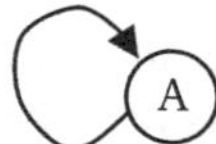


- Two edges are parallel if they connect the same pair of vertices.

- The *d*egree of a vertex is the number of edges incident on it.
- A subgraph is a subset of a graph's edges (with associated vertices) that form a graph.

One of the fundamental operations in a graph is that of traversing a sequence of nodes connected by edges. We define a path in an undirected graph G = (V, E) to be a sequence P of nodes $v_1$, $v_2$, ..., $v_{k-1}$, $v_k$ with the property that each consecutive pair $v_i$, $v_{i+1}$ is ioined by an edge in G. P is often called a path from $v_1$ to $v_k$, or a $v_1$-$v_k$ path. A path is called *simple* if all its vertices are distinct from one another. A cycle is a path $v_1$, $v_2$, ..., $v_{k-1}$, $v_k$ in which $k > 2$, the first $k - 1$ nodes are all distinct, and $v_1 = v_k$. In other words, the sequence of nodes "cycles back" to where it began. All of these definitions carry over naturally to directed graphs, with the following change: in a directed path or cycle, each pair of consecutive nodes has the property that ($v_i$, $v_{i+1}$) is an edge. In other words, the sequence of nodes in the path or cycle must respect the directionality of edges.

- A path in a graph is a sequence of adjacent vertices. Simple path is a path with no repeated vertices. In the graph below, the dotted lines represent a path from *G* to *E*.

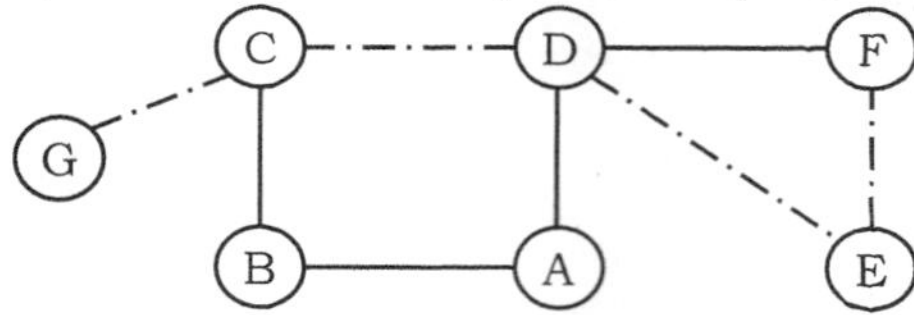


- A cycle is a path where the first and last vertices are the same. A simple cycle is a cycle with no repeated vertices or edges (except the first and last vertices).

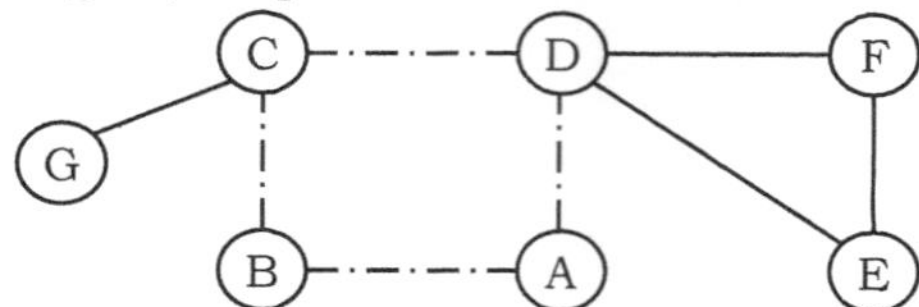


We say that an undirected graph is connected if, for every pair of nodes u and v, there is a path from u to v. Choosing how to define connectivity of a directed graph is a bit more subtle, since it's possible for u to have a path to v while v has no path to u. We say that a directed graph is strongly connected if, for every two nodes u and v, there is a path from u to v and a path from v to u.

- We say that one vertex is connected to another if there is a path that contains both of them.
- A graph is connected if there is a path from *every* vertex to every other vertex.
- If a graph is not connected then it consists of a set of connected components.

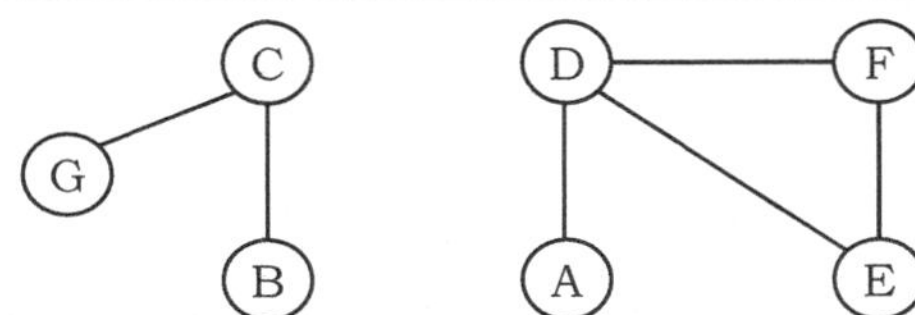


- A *directed acyclic graph* [DAG] is a directed graph with no cycles.

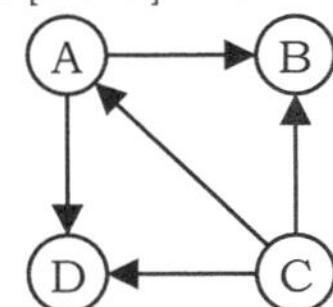


- In *weighted graphs* integers (*weights*) are assigned to each edge to represent (distances or costs).

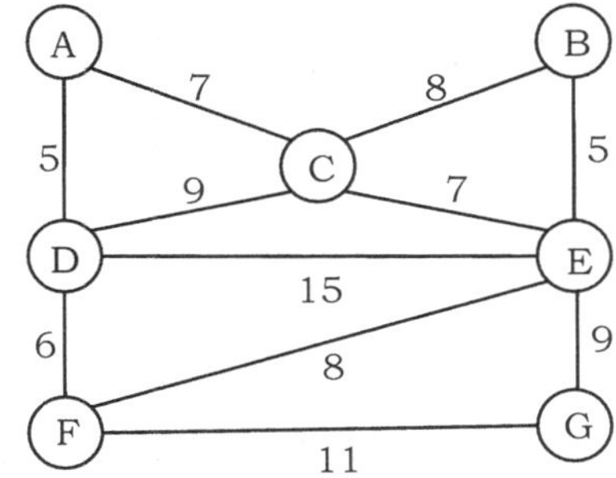


- In addition to simply knowing about the existence of a path between some pair of nodes u and v, we may also want to know whether there is a short path. Thus we define the distance between two nodes u and v to be the minimum number of edges in a u-v path.
- A forest is a disjoint set of trees.
- A spanning tree of a connected graph is a subgraph that contains all of that graph's vertices and is a single tree. A spanning forest of a graph is the union of spanning trees of its connected components.
- A bipartite graph is a graph whose vertices can be divided into two sets such that all edges connect a vertex in one set with a vertex in the other set.

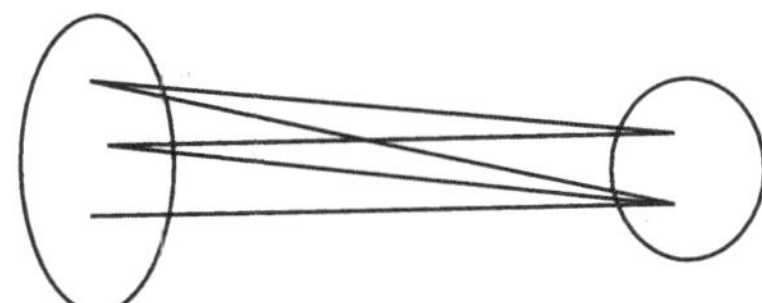

- Graphs with all edges present are called *complete* graphs.

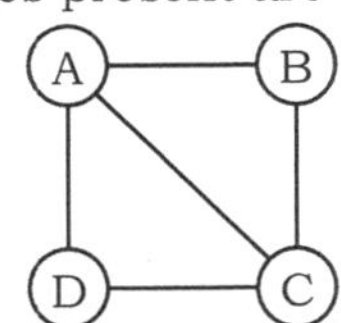


- Graphs with relatively few edges (generally if it edges $< |V| \log |V|$) are called *sparse graphs*.
- Graphs with relatively few of the possible edges missing are called *dense* graphs.
- Directed weighted graphs are sometimes called *network*.
- We will denote the number of vertices in a given graph by $|V|$, and the number of edges by $|E|$. Note that $E$ can range anywhere from 0 to $\frac{|V|(|V|-1)}{2}$ (in undirected graph). This is because each node can connect to every other node.

## 9.3 Applications of Graphs

- Representing relationships between components in electronic circuits
- Transportation networks: Highway network, Flight network
- Computer networks: Local area network, Internet, Web
- Databases: For representing ER (Entity Relationship) diagrams in databases, for representing dependency of tables in databases

## 9.4 Graph Representation

As in other ADTs, to manipulate graphs we need to represent them in some useful form. There are several ways to represent graphs, each with its advantages and disadvantages. Some situations, or algorithms that we want to run with graphs as input, call for one representation, and others call for a different representation. Here, we'll see three ways to represent graphs.

- Adjacency Matrix
- Adjacency List
- Adjacency Set

### Adjacency Matrix

#### Graph Declaration for Adjacency Matrix

First, let us look at the components of the graph data structure. To represent graphs, we need the number of vertices, the number of edges and also their interconnections. So, the graph can be declared as:

```
struct Graph {
  int V;
  int E;
  int **adjMatrix; // we need two dimensional matrix
};
```

#### Description

The adjacency matrix of a graph is a square matrix of size $V \times V$. The $V$ is the number of vertices of the graph G. The values of matrix are boolean. Let us assume the matrix is $adjMatrix$. The value $adjMatrix[u, v]$ is set to 1 if there is an edge from vertex u to vertex v and 0 otherwise. In the matrix, each edge is represented by two bits for undirected graphs. That means, an edge from u to v is represented by 1 value in both $adjMatrix$[u,v] and $adjMatrix[u, v]$. To save time, we can process only half of this symmetric matrix. Also, we can assume that there is an "edge" from each vertex to itself. So, $adjMatrix$[u, u] is set to 1 for all vertices.

If the graph is a directed graph then we need to mark only one entry in the adjacency matrix. As an example, consider the directed graph below.

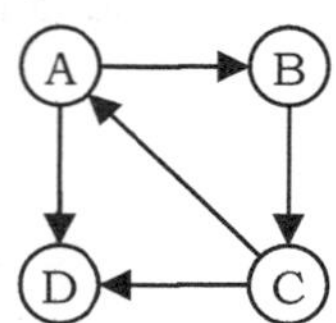


The adjacency matrix for this graph can be given as:

| | A | B | C | D |
|---|---|---|---|---|
| A | 0 | 1 | 0 | 1 |
| B | 0 | 0 | 1 | 0 |
| C | 1 | 0 | 0 | 1 |
| D | 0 | 0 | 0 | 0 |

Now, let us concentrate on the implementation. To read a graph, one way is to first read the vertex names and then read pairs of vertex names (edges). The code below reads an undirected graph.

```
// This code creates a graph with adj matrix representation
#include <stdio.h>
#include <stdlib.h>
#include <time.h>
#include <assert.h>
#define MAX_VERTICES 50   // max number of vertices for our graph
#define MAX_DEGREE 50     // max degree for a vertex
struct graph{
    int V;            // number of vertices
    int E;            // number of edges
    int **adjMatrix;          // adjacency matrix
};
struct edge{
    int source;
    int destination;
};
```

```
void rand_init(void){    // Initializes the random generator rand()
   time_t t;
   srand((unsigned) time(&t));
}
struct graph* createGraph(const int numVertices){
    assert(numVertices >= 0);
   // Create an empty graph with numVertices
   int i, j;
   struct graph* G =  (struct graph *) malloc(sizeof( struct graph));
   G->V = numVertices;
   G->E = 0;
   // allocate memory for each row
   G->adjMatrix = malloc(numVertices * sizeof(int *));
   assert(G != NULL);
   // allocate memory for each column and initialise with 0
   for (i = 0; i < numVertices; i++) {
      G->adjMatrix[i] = calloc(numVertices, sizeof(int));
      assert(G->adjMatrix[i] != NULL);
   }
   return G;
}
void displayGraph(const struct graph* G){
   // Display the graph (adjMatrix)
   int i, j, v;
   v = G->V;
   printf("%d vertices; %d edges.\n", G->V, G->E);
   for(i=0; i< v; i++){
      for(j=0; j < v; j++) printf("%3d ",(G->adjMatrix)[i][j]);
      printf("\n");
   }
}
void displayEdges(const struct graph* G){
   int v,i,j;
   v = G->V;
   for(i=0; i < v; i++){
      for(j=i+1; j < v; j++){
         if(G->adjMatrix[i][j]==1) printf("%d-%d ",i,j);
      }
   }
}
void insertEdge(struct graph* G, const struct edge E){
   int v, x, y;
   v = G->V;
   x = E.source;  y = E.destination;
   if(x >= v || y >= v) {
      printf("Error when adding edge.");
      exit(EXIT_FAILURE);
   }
   if (G->adjMatrix[x][y] == 0){ // For undirected graphs set both the bits
      G->adjMatrix[x][y] = 1;
      G->adjMatrix[y][x] = 1;
      (G->E)++;
   }
}
void removeEdge(struct graph* G, const struct edge E){
   int v, x, y;
   v = G->V;
   x = E.source;
   y = E.destination;
   if(x >= v || y >= v) {
      printf("Error when deleting edge.");
      exit(EXIT_FAILURE);
   }
```

```
        if (G->adjMatrix[x][y] == 1){
            G->adjMatrix[x][y] = 0;
            G->adjMatrix[y][x] = 0;
            (G->E)--;
        }
    }
    void destroyGraph(struct graph* G){ // to free memory
        if (G){
          if (G->adjMatrix){
              int i;
              for (i = 0; i < G->V; i++)
                 free(G->adjMatrix[i]);
              free(G->adjMatrix);
          }
          free(G);
        }
    }
    struct edge newEdge(int x, int y){
        // return an edge with ends x and y
        struct edge e;
        e.source = x;
        e.destination = y;
        return e;
    }
    struct graph* randomGraph(const int N, const float p){
        // A random graph with N vertices and probability p for each edge
        int i, j;
        struct edge E;
        struct graph* G = createGraph(N);
        rand_init();
        for (i=0; i < N; i++) for(j=i+1; j < N; j++) {
            if (rand() < p * RAND_MAX) {  // rand() returns an integer between 0 and RAND_MAX
                E = newEdge(i,j);
                insertEdge(G, E);
            }
        }
        return G;
    }
    void main(void){   // Test code
        struct edge E;
        struct graph* G = randomGraph(10, 0.15);
        displayGraph(G);
        E = newEdge(5,6);
        insertEdge(G, E);
        displayGraph(G);
        printf("\n");
        displayEdges(G);
        removeEdge(G, E);
        displayGraph(G);
        printf("\n");
        displayEdges(G);
        destroyGraph(G);
    }
```

The adjacency matrix representation is good if the graphs are dense. The matrix requires $O(V^2)$ bits of storage and $O(V^2)$ time for initialization. If the number of edges is proportional to $V^2$, then there is no problem because $V^2$ steps are required to read the edges. If the graph is sparse, the initialization of the matrix dominates the running time of the algorithm as it takes takes $O(V^2)$.

The downsides of adjacency matrices are that enumerating the outgoing edges from a vertex takes $O(n)$ time even if there aren't very many, and the $O(V^2)$ space cost is high for sparse graphs, those with much fewer than $V^2$ edges. The adjacency matrix representation takes $O(V^2)$ amount of space while it is computed. When graph has maximum number of edges or minimum number of edges, in both cases the required space will be same.

## Adjacency List

### Graph Declaration for Adjacency List

In this representation all the vertices connected to a vertex $v$ are listed on an adjacency list for that vertex $v$. This can be easily implemented with linked lists. That means, for each vertex $v$ we use a linked list and list nodes represents the connections between $v$ and other vertices to which $v$ has an edge.

The total number of linked lists is equal to the number of vertices in the graph. The graph ADT can be declared as:

```
struct Graph {
    int V;
    int E;
    int *Adj; // head pointer        s to linked list
};
```

### Description

Considering the same example as that of the adjacency matrix, the adjacency list representation can be given as:

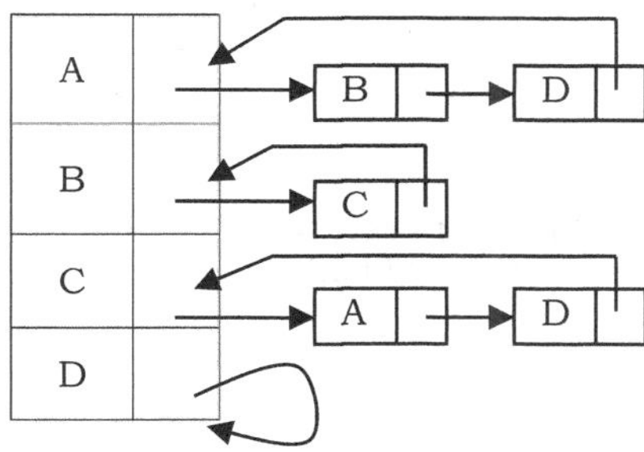


Since vertex A has an edge for B and D, we have added them in the adjacency list for A. The same is the case with other vertices as well.

```
#include <stdio.h>
#include <stdlib.h>
#include <malloc.h>
#include <assert.h>
#include <time.h>
struct ListNode {
  int vertex;
  struct ListNode *next;
};
struct edge{
    int source;
    int destination;
};
struct graph{
    int V;                    // number of vertices
    int E;                    // number of edges
    struct ListNode *adjList[];   // adjacency matrix
};
void rand_init(void){
    // Initializes the random generator rand()
    time_t t;
    srand((unsigned) time(&t));
}
int insertEdge(struct graph* G, const struct edge E) {
  int n, from, to;
  n = G->V;
  from = E.source;
  to = E.destination;
  if (0 > from || from > n || 0 > to || to > n) return -1;
  struct ListNode *prev = NULL, *ptr = G->adjList[from];
  while (ptr != NULL) {
    if (ptr->vertex == to) return 0;
```

```
        else {
            prev = ptr;
            ptr = ptr->next;
        }
    }
    if (ptr==NULL) {
        struct ListNode *newNode = (struct ListNode *) malloc(sizeof(struct ListNode));
        newNode->vertex = to;
        newNode->next = NULL;
        if (prev == NULL) {
            G->adjList[from] = newNode;
        } else {
            prev->next = newNode;
        }
    }
    return 1;
}
int removeEdge(struct graph* G, const struct edge E) {
    int n, from, to;
    n = G->V;
    from = E.source;
    to = E.destination;
    if (0 > from || from > n || 0 > to || to > n) return -1;
    struct ListNode *prev = NULL, *ptr = G->adjList[from];
    while (ptr != NULL) {
        if (ptr->vertex == to) {
            if (prev == NULL) {
                G->adjList[from] = ptr->next;
                free(ptr);
            } else {
                prev->next = ptr->next;
                free(ptr);
            }
            return 1;
        } else {
            prev = ptr;
            ptr = ptr->next;
        }
    }
    return 0;
}
struct graph* createGraph(const int numVertices) {
    assert(numVertices >= 0);
    // Create an empty graph with numVertices
    int i, j;
    struct graph* G =  (struct graph *) malloc(sizeof( struct graph));
    assert(G != NULL);
    G->V = numVertices;
    G->E = 0;

    // allocate memory for each column and initialise with 0
    struct ListNode *newNode, *last;
    for (int i = 0; i < G->V; i++) {
        G->adjList[i] = (struct ListNode *) malloc(sizeof(struct ListNode));
        assert(G->adjList[i] != NULL);
        G->adjList[i]->vertex = i;
        G->adjList[i]->next = NULL;
    }
    return G;
}
struct edge newEdge(int x, int y){     // return an edge with ends x and y
    struct edge e;
    e.source = x;
```

```
        e.destination = y;
        return e;
    }
    struct graph* randomGraph(const int N, const float p){
        // A random graph with N vertices and probability p for each edge
        int i, j;
        struct edge E;
        struct graph* G = createGraph(N);
        rand_init();
        for (i=0; i < N; i++) for(j=i+1; j < N; j++) {
            if (rand() < p * RAND_MAX) { // rand() returns an integer between 0 and RAND_MAX
                E = newEdge(i,j);
                insertEdge(G, E);
            }
        }
        return G;
    }
    void displayGraph(struct graph* G) {
      struct ListNode *ptr;
      int i;
      for (i = 0; i < G->V; i++) {
        ptr = G->adjList[i];
        printf("\nnode %d neighbors:", i);
        while (ptr != NULL) {
          printf(" %d", ptr->vertex);
          ptr = ptr->next;
        }
      }
    }
    void destroyGraph(struct graph* G) {
      int i;
      struct ListNode *temp, *ptr;
      for (i = 0; i < G->V; i++) {
        ptr = G->adjList[i];
        while (ptr != NULL) {
          temp = ptr;
          ptr = ptr->next;
          free(temp);
        }
        G->adjList[i] = NULL;
      }
      printf("\nGraph is deleted");
    }
    int main(int argc, char *args[]) { // Test code
        struct edge E;
        struct graph* G = randomGraph(10, 0.15);
        displayGraph(G);
        E = newEdge(5,6);
        insertEdge(G, E);
        displayGraph(G);
        printf("\n");
        removeEdge(G, E);
        displayGraph(G);
        printf("\n");
        destroyGraph(G);
        return 0;
    }
```

For this representation, the order of edges in the input is *important*. This is because they determine the order of the vertices on the adjacency lists. The same graph can be represented in many different ways in an adjacency list. The order in which edges appear on the adjacency list affects the order in which edges are processed by algorithms.

### Disadvantages of Adjacency Lists

Using adjacency list representation we cannot perform some operations efficiently. As an example, consider the case of deleting a node. . In adjacency list representation, it is not enough if we simply delete a node from the list representation. if we delete a node from the adjacency list then that is enough. For each node on the adjacency list of that node specifies another vertex. We need to search other nodes linked list also for deleting it. This problem can be solved by linking the two list nodes that correspond to a particular edge and making the adjacency lists doubly linked. But all these extra links are risky to process.

### Adjacency Set

It is very much similar to adjacency list but instead of using Linked lists, Disjoint Sets [Union-Find] are used. For more details refer to the *Disjoint Sets ADT* chapter.

## 9.5 Graph Traversals

To solve problems on graphs, we need a mechanism for traversing the graphs. Graph traversal algorithms are also called *graph search* algorithms. Like trees traversal algorithms (Inorder, Preorder, Postorder and Level-Order traversals), graph search algorithms can be thought of as starting at some source vertex in a graph and "searching" the graph by going through the edges and marking the vertices. Now, we will discuss two such algorithms for traversing the graphs.

- Depth First Search [DFS]
- Breadth First Search [BFS]

A graph can contain cycles, which may bring you to the same node again while traversing the graph. To avoid processing of same node again, use a boolean array which marks the node after it is processed. While visiting the nodes in the layer of a graph, store them in a manner such that you can traverse the corresponding child nodes in a similar order.

### Comparison of Graph Representations

Directed and undirected graphs are represented with the same structures. For directed graphs, everything is the same, except that each edge is represented just once. An edge from $x$ to $y$ is represented by a 1 value in $Adj[x][y]$ in the adjacency matrix, or by adding $y$ on $x's$ adjacency list. For weighted graphs, everything is the same, except fill the adjacency matrix with weights instead of boolean values.

| Representation | Space | Checking edge between $v$ and $w$? | Iterate over edges incident to $v$? |
|---|---|---|---|
| List of edges | E | $E$ | $E$ |
| Adj Matrix | $V^2$ | 1 | $V$ |
| Adj List | $E+V$ | $Degree(v)$ | $Degree(v)$ |
| Adj Set | $E+V$ | $log(Degree(v))$ | $Degree(v)$ |

### Depth First Search [DFS]

Depth-first search (DFS) is a method for exploring a tree or graph. In a DFS, you go as deep as possible down one path before backing up and trying a different one. DFS algorithm works in a manner similar to preorder traversal of the trees. Like preorder traversal, internally this algorithm also uses stack. Let us consider the following example. Suppose a person is trapped inside a maze. To come out from that maze, the person visits each path and each intersection (in the worst case). Let us say the person uses two colors of paint to mark the intersections already passed. When discovering a new intersection, it is marked grey, and he continues to go deeper.

After reaching a "dead end" the person knows that there is no more unexplored path from the grey intersection, which now is completed, and he marks it with black. This "dead end" is either an intersection which has already been marked grey or black, or simply a path that does not lead to an intersection.

The intersections of the maze are the vertices and the paths between the intersections are the edges of the graph. The process of returning from the "dead end" is called *backtracking*. We are trying to go away from the starting vertex into the graph as deep as possible, until we have to backtrack to the preceding grey vertex. In DFS algorithm, we encounter the following types of edges.

| *Tree edge*: encounter new vertex |
|---|
| *Back edge*: from descendent to ancestor |
| *Forward edge*: from ancestor to descendent |
| *Cross edge*: between a tree or subtrees |

For most algorithms boolean classification, unvisited/visited is enough (for three color implementation refer to problems section). That means, for some problems we need to use three colors, but for our discussion two colors are enough.

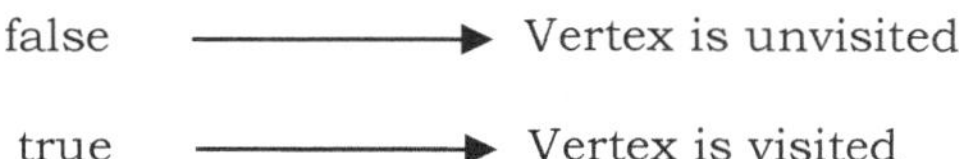


Initially all vertices are marked unvisited (false). The DFS algorithm starts at a vertex $u$ in the graph. By starting at vertex $u$ it considers the edges from $u$ to other vertices. If the edge leads to an already visited vertex, then backtrack to current vertex $u$. If an edge leads to an unvisited vertex, then go to that vertex and start processing from that vertex. That means the new vertex becomes the current vertex. Follow this process until we reach the dead-end. At this point start *backtracking*. The process terminates when backtracking leads back to the start vertex.

As an example, consider the following graph. We can see that sometimes an edge leads to an already discovered vertex. These edges are called *back edges,* and the other edges are called *tree edges* because deleting the back edges from the graph generates a tree.

The final generated tree is called the DFS tree and the order in which the vertices are processed is called *DFS numbers* of the vertices. In the graph below, the gray color indicates that the vertex is visited (there is no other significance). We need to see when the visited table is being updated. In the following example, DFS algorithm traverses from A to B to C to D first, then to E, F, and G and lastly to H. It employs the following rules.

1. Visit the adjacent unvisited vertex. Mark it as visited. Display it (processing). Push it onto a stack.
2. If no adjacent vertex is found, pop up a vertex from the stack. (It will pop up all the vertices from the stack, which do not have adjacent vertices.)
3. Repeat step 1 and step 2 until the stack is empty.

Mark A as visited and put it onto the stack. Explore any unvisited adjacent node from A. We have only one adjacent node B and we can pick that. For this example, we shall take the node in an alphabetical order. Then, mark B as visited and put it onto the stack.

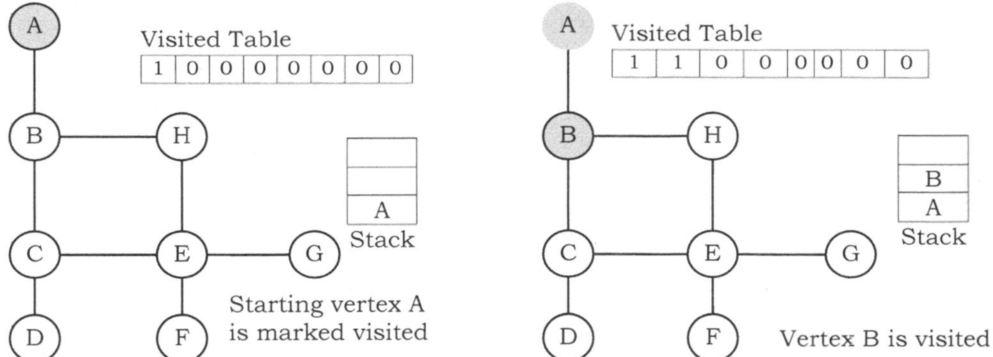


Explore any unvisited adjacent node from B. Both C and H are adjacent to B but we are concerned for unvisited nodes only. Visit C and mark it as visited and put onto the stack. Here, we have B, D, and E nodes, which are adjacent to C and nodes D and E are unvisited. Let us choose one of them; say, D.

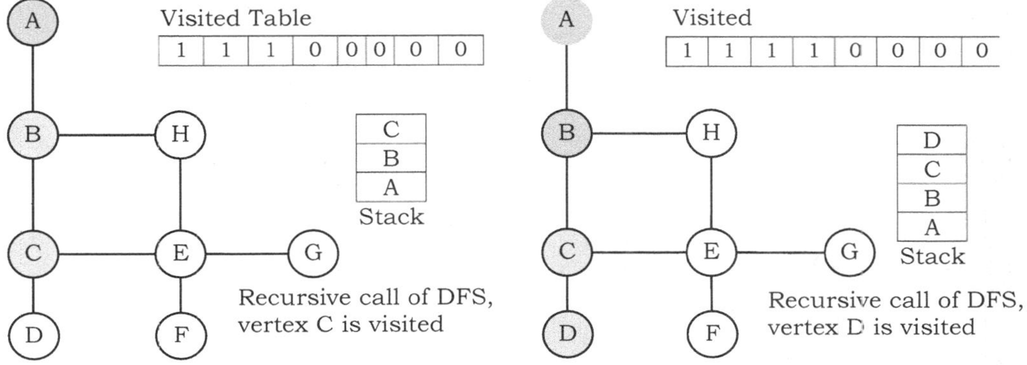


Here D does not have any unvisited adjacent node. So, we pop D from the stack. We check the stack top for return to the previous node and check if it has any unvisited nodes. Here, we find C to be on the top of the stack. Here, we have B, D, and E nodes which are adjacent to C and node E is unvisited.

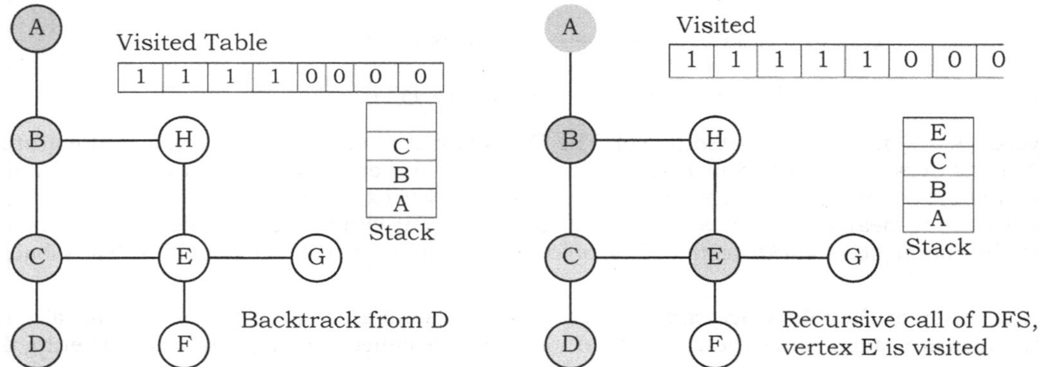


Here, we find E to be on the top of the stack. Here, we have C, F, G, and H nodes which are adjacent to E and nodes F, G, and H are unvisited. Let us choose one of them; say, F. Here node F does not have any unvisited adjacent node. So, we pop F from the stack.

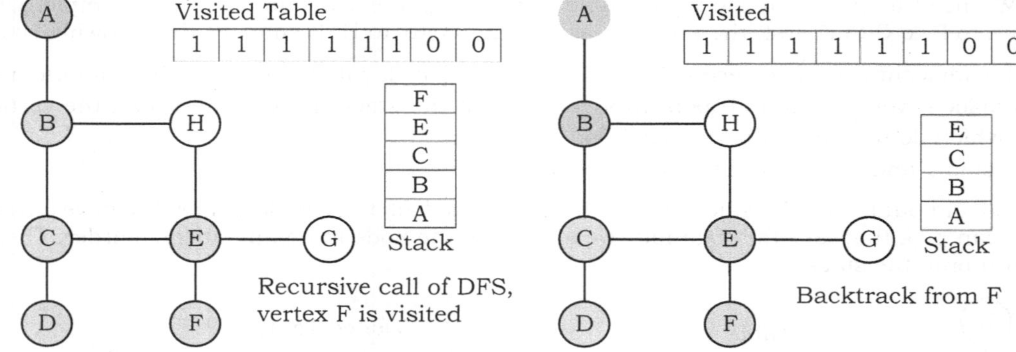


Here, we find E to be on the top of the stack. Here, we have C, F, G, and H nodes which are adjacent to E and nodes G, and H are unvisited. Let us choose one of them; say, G. Here node G does not have any unvisited adjacent node. So, we pop G from the stack.

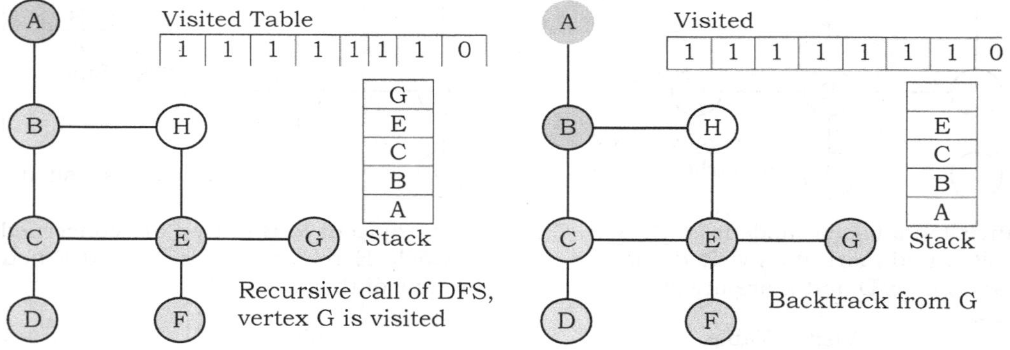


Here, we find E to be on the top of the stack. Here, we have C, F, G, and H nodes which are adjacent to E and node H is unvisited. Let us choose that remaining node H. Here node H does not have any unvisited adjacent node. So, we pop H from the stack.

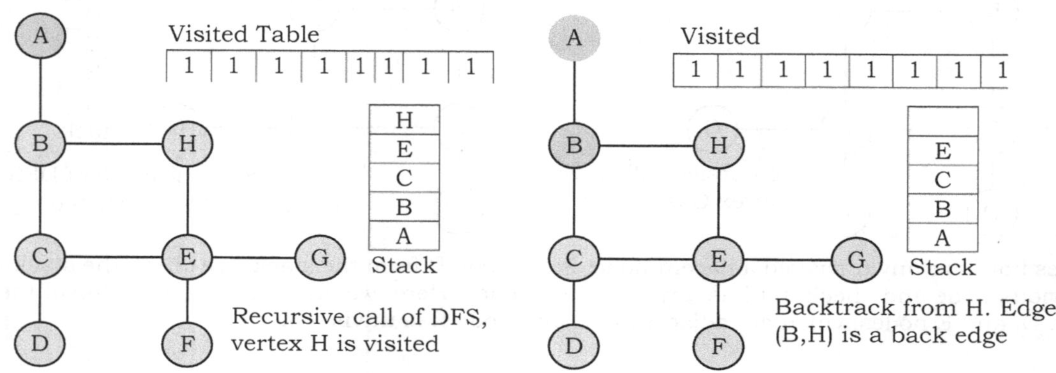

Now, we find E to be on the top of the stack with no unvisited nodes adjacent to it. So, we pop E from the stack. Then, node C becomes the top of the stack. For node C too, there were no adjacent unvisited nodes. Hence, pop node C from the stack.

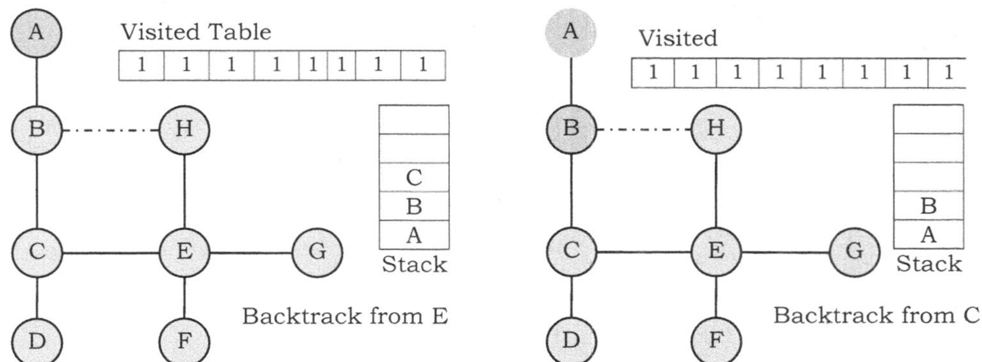


Similarly, we find B to be on the top of the stack with no unvisited nodes adjacent to it. So, we pop B from the stack. Then, node A becomes the top of the stack. For node A too, there were no adjacent unvisited nodes. Hence, pop node A from the stack. With this, the stack is empty.

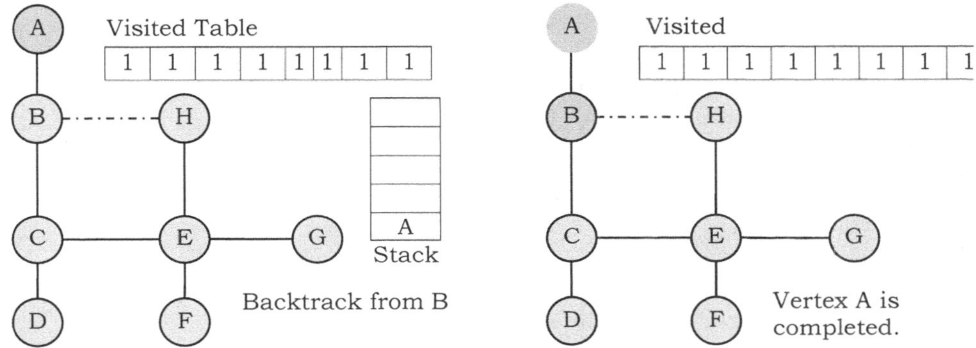


From the above diagrams, it can be seen that the DFS traversal creates a tree (without back edges) and we call such tree a *DFS tree*. In DFS, if we start from a start node it will mark all the nodes connected to the start node as visited. Therefore, if we choose any node in a connected component and run DFS on that node it will mark the whole connected component as visited. The above algorithm works even if the given graph has connected components.

We can see that sometimes an edge leads to an already discovered vertex. These edges are called *back edges*, and the other edges are called *tree edges* because deleting the back edges from the graph generates a tree.

The final generated tree is called the DFS tree and the order in which the vertices are processed is called *DFS numbers* of the vertices. In the graph below, the gray color indicates that the vertex is visited (there is no other significance). We need to see when the visited table is updated.

### Advantages

- Depth-first search on a binary tree generally requires less memory than breadth-first.
- Depth-first search can be easily implemented with recursion.

### Disadvantages

- A DFS doesn't necessarily find the shortest path to a node, while breadth-first search does.

## Applications of DFS

- Topological sorting
- Finding connected components
- Finding articulation points (cut vertices) of the graph
- Finding strongly connected components
- Solving puzzles such as mazes

For algorithms refer to *Problems Section*.

### Implementation

The algorithm based on this mechanism is given below: assume visited[] is a global array.

```
// Refer graph implementation from previous section
void DFS_iterative(struct graph* G, int visited[], int start){
  int stack[G->V];
  int top = -1, i;
  visited[start] = 1;
  stack[++top] = start;
  struct ListNode *p = NULL;
  while (top != -1) {
    start = stack[top--];
    printf("%d ", start);
    p = G->adjList[start];
    while (p) {
      i = p->vertex;
      if (visited[i] == 0) {
        stack[++top] = i;
        visited[i] = 1;
      }
      p = p->next;
    }
  }
}
void DFS_recursive(struct graph* G, int visited[], int start){
  int i;
  struct ListNode *p = NULL;
  visited[start] = 1;
  printf("%d ", start);
  p = G->adjList[start];
  while (p) {
    i = p->vertex;
    if (visited[i] == 0) {
      DFS_recursive(G, visited, i);
    }
    p = p->next;
  }
}
int main(int argc, char *args[]) {
    // Test code
    struct edge E;
    int n = 10;
    struct graph* G = randomGraph(n, 0.15);
    displayGraph(G);
    int i;                                          // initialization of visited array
    int visited[n];
    for (i = 0; i < n; i++) visited[i] = 0;
    printf("\nDFS recursive order:\n");
    DFS_recursive(G, visited, 0);                   // DFS start from 0
    printf("\nvisited by DFS:\n");
    for (i=0; i<n; i++) {
      if (visited[i] == 1) printf("%d ", i);
    }
    for (i = 0; i < n; i++) visited[i] = 0;         // initialization of visited array
    printf("\nDFS iterative order:\n");
    DFS_iterative(G, visited, 0);                   // DFS start from 0
    printf("\nvisited by DFS:\n");
    for (i=0; i<n; i++) {
      if (visited[i] == 1) printf("%d ", i);
    }
    return 0;
}
```

The time complexity of DFS is $O(V + E)$, if we use adjacency lists for representing the graphs. This is because we are starting at a vertex and processing the adjacent nodes only if they are not visited. Similarly, if an adjacency matrix is used for a graph representation, then all edges adjacent to a vertex can't be found efficiently, and this gives $O(V^2)$ complexity.

## Breadth First Search [BFS]

Breadth-first search (BFS) is a method for exploring a tree or graph. In a BFS, you first explore all the nodes one step away, then all the nodes two steps away, etc. Breadth-first search is like throwing a stone in the center of a pond. The nodes you explore "ripple out" from the starting point.

The BFS algorithm works similar to *level – order* traversal of the trees. Like *level – order* traversal, BFS also uses queues. In fact, *level – order* traversal got inspired from BFS. BFS works level by level. Initially, BFS starts at a given vertex, which is at level 0. In the first stage it visits all vertices at level 1 (that means, vertices whose distance is 1 from the start vertex of the graph). In the second stage, it visits all vertices at the second level. These new vertices are the ones which are adjacent to level 1 vertices. BFS continues this process until all the levels of the graph are completed.

To make this process easy, use a queue to store the node and mark it as 'visited' once all its neighbors (vertices that are directly connected to it) are marked or added to the queue. The queue follows the First In First Out (FIFO) queuing method, and therefore, the neighbor's of the node will be visited in the order in which they were inserted in the node i.e. the node that was inserted first will be visited first, and so on. Generally *queue* data structure is used for storing the vertices of a level.

BFS employs the following rules:

1. Visit the adjacent unvisited vertex. Mark it as visited. Display it. Insert it in a queue.
2. If no adjacent vertex is found, remove the first vertex from the queue.
3. Repeat step 1 and step 2 until the queue is empty.

As similar to DFS, assume that initially all vertices are marked *unvisited* (*false*). Vertices that have been processed and removed from the queue are marked *visited* (*true*). We use a queue to represent the visited set as it will keep the vertices in the order of when they were first visited. As an example, let us consider the same graph as that of the DFS example.

We start from node A (starting node), and add it to the queue. The only element in queue is A. Dequeue the element A and mark it as visited. We then see an unvisited adjacent node B from A. So, enqueue the element B to the queue.

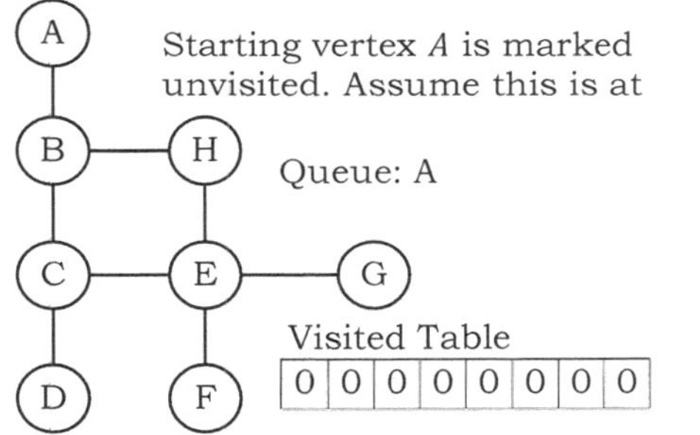


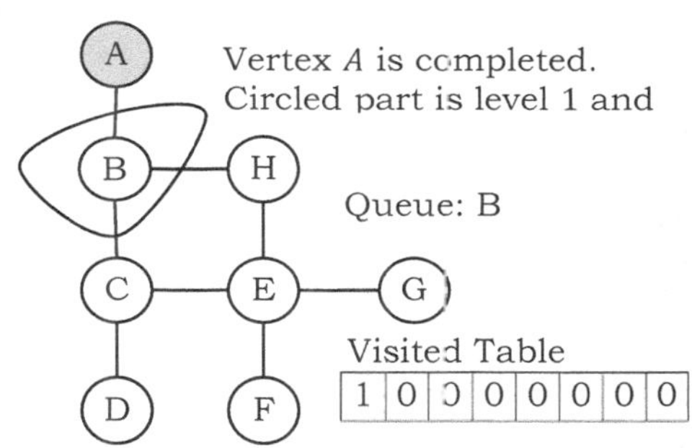


Next, dequeue the element B and mark it as visited. We then see an unvisited adjacent nodes C and H from node B, and enqueue them. Then dequeue the element C, mark it as visited, and enqueue its unvisited adjacent nodes D and E to the queue. Next, dequeue the element H, and mark it as visited. Observe that, node H does not have any unvisited adjacent nodes.

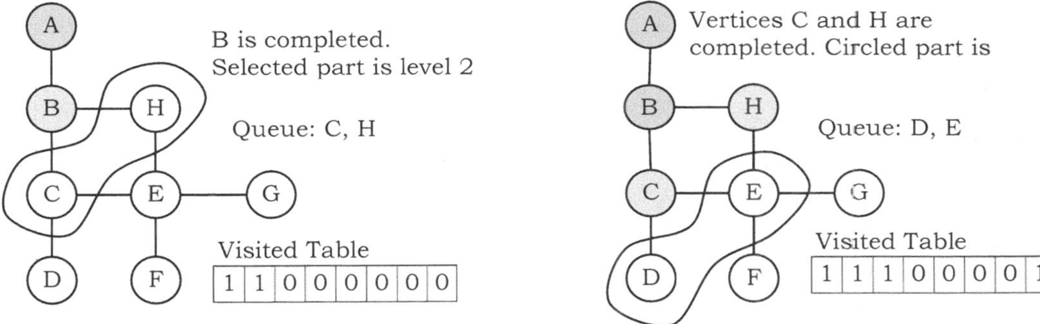


Next, dequeue the element D, and mark it as visited. We see no unvisited adjacent nodes from node D. Then dequeue the element E, mark it as visited, and enqueue its unvisited adjacent nodes F and G to the queue. Next, dequeue the element F, and mark it as visited. Observe that, node G does not have any unvisited adjacent nodes. At this point, queue has only one element G. Dequeue the element and mark it visited. Notice that, node G too does not have any unvisited adjacent nodes.

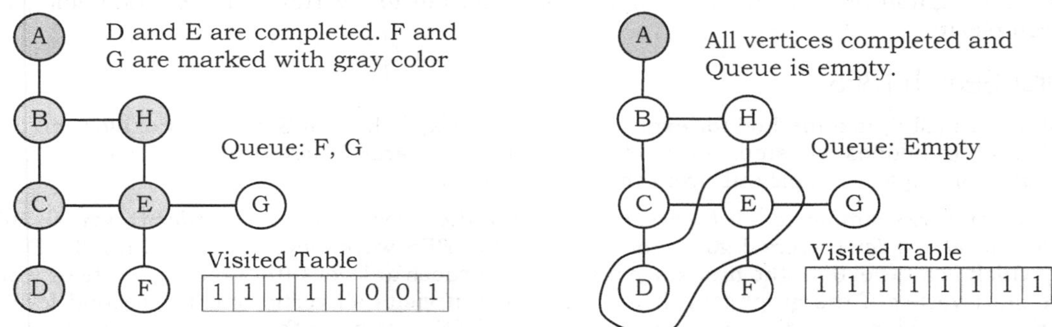


Time complexity of BFS is $O(V + E)$, if we use adjacency lists for representing the graphs, and $O(V^2)$ for adjacency matrix representation.

### Advantages

- A BFS will find the shortest path between the starting point and any other reachable node. A depth-first search will not necessarily find the shortest path.

### Disadvantages

- A BFS on a binary tree generally requires more memory than a DFS.

### Applications of BFS

- Finding all connected components in a graph
- Finding all nodes within one connected component
- Finding the shortest path between two nodes
- Testing a graph for bipartiteness

### Implementation

The implementation for the above discussion can be given as:

```
#include <stdio.h>
#include <stdlib.h>
#define SIZE 40
struct Queue {
   int items[SIZE];
   int front;
   int rear;
};
struct ListNode{
   int vertex;
   struct ListNode* next;
};
struct ListNode* createNode(int);
struct Graph{
   int V;
   struct ListNode** adjLists;
   int* visited;
};
struct ListNode* createNode(int v){
   struct ListNode* newNode = malloc(sizeof(struct ListNode));
   newNode->vertex = v;
   newNode->next = NULL;
   return newNode;
}
struct Graph* createGraph(int vertices){
   struct Graph* graph = malloc(sizeof(struct Graph));
   graph->V = vertices;
   graph->adjLists = malloc(vertices * sizeof(struct ListNode*));
```

```
        graph->visited = malloc(vertices * sizeof(int));
        int i;
        for (i = 0; i < vertices; i++) {
            graph->adjLists[i] = NULL;
            graph->visited[i] = 0;
        }
        return graph;
    }
    void addEdge(struct Graph* graph, int src, int dest){
        // Add edge from src to dest
        struct ListNode* newNode = createNode(dest);
        newNode->next = graph->adjLists[src];
        graph->adjLists[src] = newNode;
        // Add edge from dest to src
        newNode = createNode(src);
        newNode->next = graph->adjLists[dest];
        graph->adjLists[dest] = newNode;
    }
    struct Queue* createQueue() {
        struct Queue* q = malloc(sizeof(struct Queue));
        q->front = -1;
        q->rear = -1;
        return q;
    }
    int isEmpty(struct Queue* q) {
        if(q->rear == -1)
            return 1;
        else
            return 0;
    }
    void enQueue(struct Queue* q, int value){
        if(q->rear == SIZE-1)
            printf("\nQueue is Full!!");
        else {
            if(q->front == -1)
                q->front = 0;
            q->rear++;
            q->items[q->rear] = value;
        }
    }
    int deQueue(struct Queue* q){
        int item;
        if(isEmpty(q)){
            printf("Queue is empty");
            item = -1;
        }
        else{
            item = q->items[q->front];
            q->front++;
            if(q->front > q->rear){
                printf("Resetting Queue");
                q->front = q->rear = -1;
            }
        }
        return item;
    }
    void printQueue(struct Queue *q) {
        int i = q->front;
        if(isEmpty(q)) {
            printf("Queue is empty");
        } else {
            printf("\nQueue contents: \n");
            for(i = q->front; i < q->rear + 1; i++) {
                    printf("%d ", q->items[i]);
```

```
        }
    }
}
void displayGraph(struct Graph* graph) {
  struct ListNode *ptr;
  int i;
  for (i = 0; i < graph->V; i++) {
    ptr = graph->adjLists[i];
    printf("\nnode %d neighbors:", i);
    while (ptr != NULL) {
      printf(" %d", ptr->vertex);
      ptr = ptr->next;
    }
  }
}
void BFS(struct Graph* graph, int startVertex) {
    struct Queue* q = createQueue();
    enQueue(q, startVertex);
    while(!isEmpty(q)){
        //printQueue(q);
        int currentVertex = deQueue(q);
        printf("\nVisited %d\n", currentVertex);
        graph->visited[currentVertex] = 1;
        struct ListNode* temp = graph->adjLists[currentVertex];
       while(temp) {
            int adjVertex = temp->vertex;
            if(graph->visited[adjVertex] == 0){
                graph->visited[adjVertex] = 1;
                enQueue(q, adjVertex);
            }
            temp = temp->next;
       }
    }
}
int main(){
    struct Graph* graph = createGraph(8);
    addEdge(graph, 0, 1);
    addEdge(graph, 1, 2);
    addEdge(graph, 1, 7);
    addEdge(graph, 2, 3);
    addEdge(graph, 2, 5);
    addEdge(graph, 4, 5);
    addEdge(graph, 4, 6);
    addEdge(graph, 4, 7);
    displayGraph(graph);
    BFS(graph, 0);
    return 0;
}
```

## Comparing DFS and BFS

Comparing BFS and DFS, the big advantage of DFS is that it has much lower memory requirements than BFS because it's not required to store all of the child pointers at each level. Depending on the data and what we are looking for, either DFS or BFS can be advantageous. For example, in a family tree if we are looking for someone who's still alive and if we assume that person would be at the bottom of the tree, then DFS is a better choice. BFS would take a very long time to reach that last level.

The DFS algorithm finds the goal faster. Now, if we were looking for a family member who died a very long time ago, then that person would be closer to the top of the tree. In this case, BFS finds faster than DFS. So, the advantages of either vary depending on the data and what we are looking for.

DFS is related to preorder traversal of a tree. Like *preorder* traversal, DFS visits each node before its children. The BFS algorithm works similar to *level – order* traversal of the trees.

If someone asks whether DFS is better or BFS is better, the answer depends on the type of the problem that we are trying to solve. BFS visits each level one at a time, and if we know the solution we are searching for is at a low depth, then BFS is good. DFS is a better choice if the solution is at maximum depth. The below table shows the differences between DFS and BFS in terms of their applications.

| Applications | DFS | BFS |
|---|---|---|
| Spanning forest, connected components, paths, cycles | Yes | Yes |
| Shortest paths | | Yes |
| Minimal use of memory space | Yes | |

## 9.6 Topological Sort

Assume that we need to schedule a series of tasks, such as classes or construction jobs, where we cannot start one task until after its prerequisites are completed. We wish to organize the tasks into a linear order that allows us to complete them one at a time without violating any prerequisites. We can model the problem using a DAG. The graph is directed because one task is a prerequisite of another -- the vertices have a directed relationship. It is acyclic because a cycle would indicate a conflicting series of prerequisites that could not be completed without violating at least one prerequisite. The process of laying out the vertices of a DAG in a linear order to meet the prerequisite rules is called a topological sort.

*Topological sort* is an ordering of vertices in a directed acyclic graph [DAG] in which each node comes before all nodes to which it has outgoing edges. As an example, consider the course prerequisite structure at universities. A directed *edge* $(v, w)$ indicates that course $v$ must be completed before course $w$. Topological ordering for this example is the sequence which does not violate the prerequisite requirement. Every DAG may have one or more topological orderings. Topological sort is not possible if the graph has a cycle, since for two vertices $v$ and $w$ on the cycle, $v$ precedes $w$ and $w$ precedes $v$.

Topological sort has an interesting property. All pairs of consecutive vertices in the sorted order are connected by edges; then these edges form a directed Hamiltonian path [refer to *Problems Section*] in the DAG. If a Hamiltonian path exists, the topological sort order is unique. If a topological sort does not form a Hamiltonian path, DAG can have two or more topological orderings. In the graph below: 7, 5, 3, 11, 8, 2, 9, 10 and 3, 5, 7, 8, 11, 2, 9, 10 are both topological orderings.

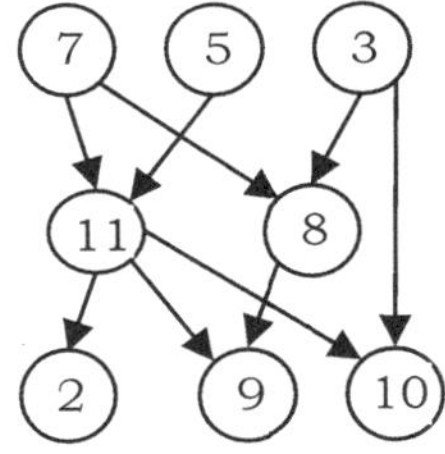


We can implement topological sort using a queue. First visit all edges, counting the number of edges that lead to each vertex (i.e., count the number of prerequisites for each vertex). Initially, *indegree* is computed for all vertices, starting with the vertices which are having indegree 0. That means consider the vertices which do not have any prerequisite. To keep track of vertices with indegree zero we can use a queue.

All vertices with no prerequisites (indegree 0) are placed on the queue. We then begin processing the queue. While the queue is not empty, a vertex $v$ is removed, and all edges adjacent to $v$ have their indegrees decremented. A vertex is put on the queue as soon as its indegree falls to 0. The topological ordering is the order in which the vertices deQueue. If the queue becomes empty without printing all of the vertices, then the graph contains a cycle (i.e., there is no possible ordering for the tasks that does not violate some prerequisite).

```
// Refer adjacent graph representation code from previous sections.
int queue[MAX_VERTICES], front = -1, rear = -1;
int findIndegree(struct graph* G, int node) {
    int i, indegree = 0;
    for (i = 0; i < G->V; i++) {
        if (G->adjMatrix[i][node] == 1)
            indegree++;
    }
    return indegree;
}
void insertQueue(int node) {
    if (rear == MAX_VERTICES)
        printf("\nOVERFLOW ");
    else {
        if (front == -1) /*If queue is initially empty */
            front = 0;
```

```
            queue[++rear] = node;
        }
    }
    int deleteQueue() {
        int del_node;
        if (front == -1 || front > rear) {
            printf("\nUNDERFLOW %d %d", front, rear);
            return -1;
        } else {
            del_node = queue[front++];
            return del_node;
        }
    }
    void topologicalSort( struct graph *G ) {
        int topsort[G->V], indeg[G->V];
        int i;
        for (i = 0; i < G->V; i++) {      /*Find the in-degree of each node*/
            indeg[i] = findIndegree(G, i);
            if (indeg[i] == 0)
                insertQueue(i);
        }
        int j=0;
        int del_node;
        while (front <= rear){ /*Continue loop until queue is empty */
            del_node = deleteQueue();
            topsort[j] = del_node; /*Add the deleted node to topsort*/
            j++;
            for (i = 0; i < G->V; i++) {        /*Delete the del_node edges */
                if (G->adjMatrix[del_node][i] == 1) {
                    G->adjMatrix[del_node][i] = 0;
                    indeg[i] = indeg[i] - 1;
                    if (indeg[i] == 0)
                        insertQueue(i);
                }
            }
        }
        printf("The topological sorting can be given as:\n");
        for (i=0; i<j; i++)
            printf("%d ", topsort[i]);
    }
    void main(void){                 // Test code
        struct edge E;
        struct graph* G = randomGraph(10, 0.15);
        displayGraph(G);
        topologicalSort(G);
    }
```

The time complexity of this algorithm is $O(|E| + |V|)$ if adjacency lists are used.

**Note:** The Topological sorting problem can be solved with DFS. Refer to the *Problems Section* for the algorithm.

### Applications of Topological Sorting

- Representing course prerequisites
- Detecting deadlocks
- Pipeline of computing jobs
- Checking for symbolic link loop
- Evaluating formulae in spreadsheet

## 9.7 Shortest Path Algorithms

Shortest path algorithms are a family of algorithms designed to solve the shortest path problem. The shortest path problem is something most people have some intuitive familiarity with: given two points, A and B, what is the shortest path between them? Given a graph $G = (V, E)$ and a distinguished vertex s, we need to find the shortest path from $s$ to every other vertex in $G$. There are variations in the shortest path algorithms which depends on the type of the input graph and are given below.

## Variations of Shortest Path Algorithms

If the edges have weights, the graph is called a weighted graph. Sometimes these edges are bidirectional and the graph is called undirected. Sometimes there can be even be cycles in the graph. Each of these subtle differences are what makes one algorithm work better than another for certain graph type.

There are also different types of shortest path algorithms. Maybe you need to find the shortest path between point A and B, but maybe you need to shortest path between point A and all other points in the graph.

| Shortest path in unweighted graph |
|---|
| Shortest path in weighted graph |
| Shortest path in weighted graph with negative edges |

## Applications of Shortest Path Algorithms

Shortest path algorithms have many applications. As noted earlier, mapping software like Google or Apple maps makes use of shortest path algorithms. They are also important for road network, operations, and logistics research. Shortest path algorithms are also very important for computer networks, like the Internet.

Any software that helps you choose a route uses some form of a shortest path algorithm. Google Maps, for instance, has you put in a starting point and an ending point and will solve the shortest path problem for you.

- Finding fastest way to go from one place to another
- Finding cheapest way to fly/send data from one city to another

## Types of Shortest Path Algorithms

- *Single source shortest path problem*: In a Single Source Shortest Paths Problem, we are given a Graph G = (V, E), we want to find the shortest path from a given source vertex s ∈ V to every vertex v ∈ V.
- *Single destination shortest path problem*: Find the shortest path to a given destination vertex t from every vertex v. By shift the direction of each edge in the graph, we can shorten this problem to a single - source problem.
- *Single pair shortest path problem*: Find the shortest path from u to v for given vertices u and v. If we determine the single - source problem with source vertex u, we clarify this problem also. Furthermore, no algorithms for this problem are known that run asymptotically faster than the best single - source algorithms in the worst case.
- *All pairs shortest path problem*: Find the shortest path from u to v for every pair of vertices u and v. Running a single - source algorithm once from each vertex can clarify this problem; but it can generally be solved faster, and its structure is of interest in the own right.

All these types have algorithms that perform best in their own way. All-pairs algorithms take longer to run because of the added complexity. All shortest path algorithms return values that can be used to find the shortest path, even if those return values vary in type or form from algorithm to algorithm. The most common algorithm for the all-pairs problem is the floyd-warshall algorithm.

## Shortest Path in Unweighted Graph

Let $s$ be the input vertex from which we want to find the shortest path to all other vertices. Unweighted graph is a special case of the weighted shortest-path problem, with all edges a weight of 1. The algorithm is similar to BFS and we need to use the following data structures:

- A distance table with three columns (each row corresponds to a vertex):
  - Distance from source vertex.
  - Path - contains the name of the vertex through which we get the shortest distance.
- A queue is used to implement breadth-first search. It contains vertices whose distance from the source node has been computed and their adjacent vertices are to be examined.

As an example, consider the following graph and its adjacency list representation.

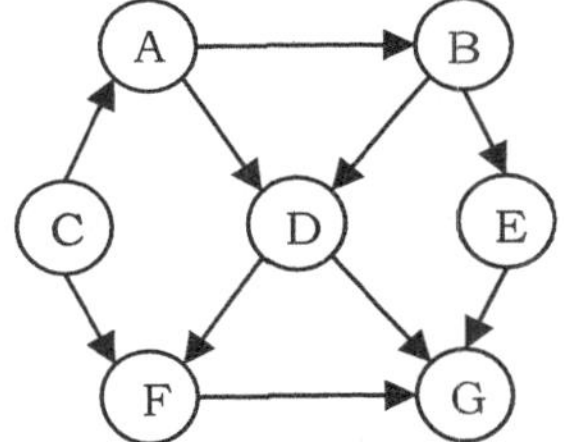

The adjacency list for this graph is:

$A: B \rightarrow D$
$B: D \rightarrow E$
$C: A \rightarrow F$
$D: F \rightarrow G$
$E: G$
$F: -$
$G: F$

Let $s = C$. The distance from $C$ to $C$ is 0. Initially, distances to all other nodes are not computed, and we initialize the second column in the distance table for all vertices (except $C$) with -1 as below.

| Vertex | Distance[v] | Previous vertex which gave Distance[v] |
|---|---|---|
| $A$ | -1 | - |
| $B$ | -1 | - |
| $C$ | 0 | - |
| $D$ | -1 | - |
| $E$ | -1 | - |
| $F$ | -1 | - |
| $G$ | -1 | - |

## Algorithm

```
void UnweightedShortestPath(struct Graph *G, int s) {
    struct Queue *Q = createQueue();
    int v, w;
    enQueue(Q, s);
    for (int i = 0; i< G→V;i++)
        Distance[i]=-1;
    Distance[s]= 0;
    while (!isEmpty(Q)) {
        v = deQueue(Q);
        for each w adjacent to v          ← Each vertex examined at most once
            if(Distance[w] == -1) {
                Distance[w] = Distance[v] + 1;
                Path[w] = v;
                enQueue(Q, w);            ← Each vertex EnQueue'd at most once
            }
    }
    deleteQueue(Q);
}
```

Running time: $O(|E| + |V|)$, if adjacency lists are used. In for loop, we are checking the outgoing edges for a given vertex and the sum of all examined edges in the while loop is equal to the number of edges which gives $O(|E|)$.

If we use matrix representation the complexity is $O(|V|^2)$, because we need to read an entire row in the matrix of length $|V|$ in order to find the adjacent vertices for a given vertex.

## Shortest path in Weighted Graph without Negative Edge Weights [Dijkstra's Algorithm]

A famous solution for the shortest path problem was developed by *Dijkstra*. *Dijkstra's* algorithm is a generalization of the BFS algorithm. The regular BFS algorithm cannot solve the shortest path problem as it cannot guarantee that the vertex at the front of the queue is the vertex closest to source $s$.

Dijkstra's algorithm makes use of breadth-first search (which is not a single source shortest path algorithm) to solve the single-source problem. It does place one constraint on the graph: there can be no negative weight edges. Dijkstra's algorithm is also sometimes used to solve the all-pairs shortest path problem by simply running it on all vertices in V. Again, this requires all edge weights to be positive.

Before going to code let us understand how the algorithm works. As in unweighted shortest path algorithm, here too we use the distance table. The algorithm works by keeping the shortest distance of vertex $v$ from the source in the *Distance* table. The value *Distance*[$v$] holds the distance from s to v. The shortest distance of the source to itself is zero. The *Distance* table for all other vertices is set to $-1$ to indicate that those vertices are not already processed.

| Vertex | Distance[v] | Previous vertex which gave Distance[v] |
|---|---|---|
| $A$ | -1 | - |
| $B$ | -1 | - |
| $C$ | 0 | - |

| D | -1 | - |
|---|---|---|
| E | -1 | - |
| F | -1 | - |
| G | -1 | - |

After the algorithm finishes, the *Distance* table will have the shortest distance from source $s$ to each other vertex $v$. To simplify the understanding of *Dijkstra's* algorithm, let us assume that the given vertices are maintained in two sets. Initially the first set contains only the source element and the second set contains all the remaining elements. After the $k^{th}$ iteration, the first set contains $k$ vertices which are closest to the source. These $k$ vertices are the ones for which we have already computed the shortest distances from source.

The *Dijkstra's* algorithm can be better understood through an example, which will explain each step that is taken and how *Distance* is calculated. The weighted graph below has 5 vertices from $A - E$.

The value between the two vertices is known as the edge cost between two vertices. For example, the edge cost between $A$ and $C$ is 1. Dijkstra's algorithm can be used to find the shortest path from source $A$ to the remaining vertices in the graph.

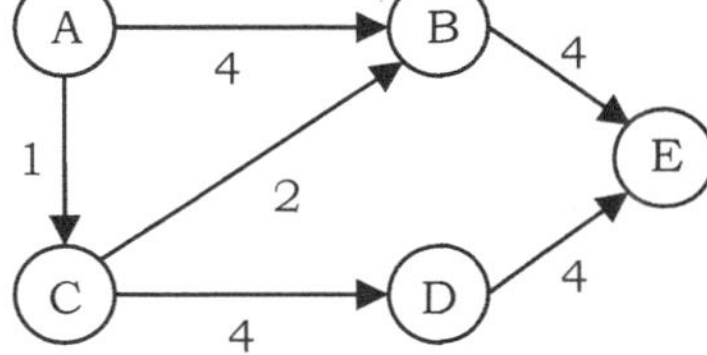


Initially the *Distance* table is:

| Vertex | Distance[v] | Previous vertex which gave Distance[v] |
|---|---|---|
| A | 0 | - |
| B | -1 | - |
| C | -1 | - |
| D | -1 | - |
| E | -1 | - |

After the first step, from vertex $A$, we can reach $B$ and $C$. So, in the *Distance* table we update the reachability of $B$ and $C$ with their costs and the same is shown below.

| A | 0 | - |
|---|---|---|
| B | 4 | A |
| C | 1 | A |
| D | -1 | - |
| E | -1 | - |

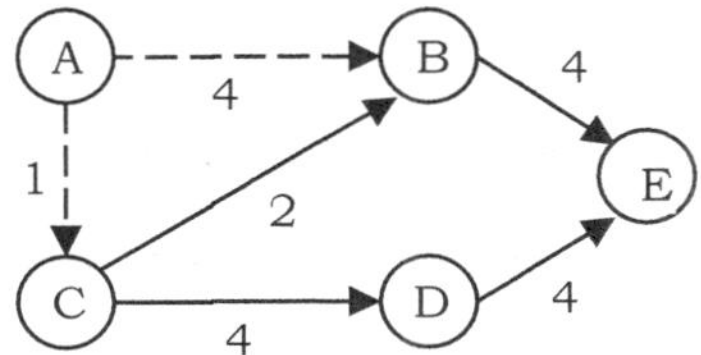


*Shortest path from B, C from A*

Now, let us select the minimum distance among all. The minimum distance vertex is $C$. That means, we have to reach other vertices from these two vertices ($A$ and $C$). For example, $B$ can be reached from $A$ and also from $C$. In this case we have to select the one which gives the lowest cost. Since reaching $B$ through $C$ is giving the minimum cost $(1 + 2)$, we update the *Distance* table for vertex $B$ with cost 3 and the vertex from which we got this cost as $C$.

| A | 0 | - |
|---|---|---|
| B | 3 | C |
| C | 1 | A |
| D | 5 | C |
| E | -1 | - |

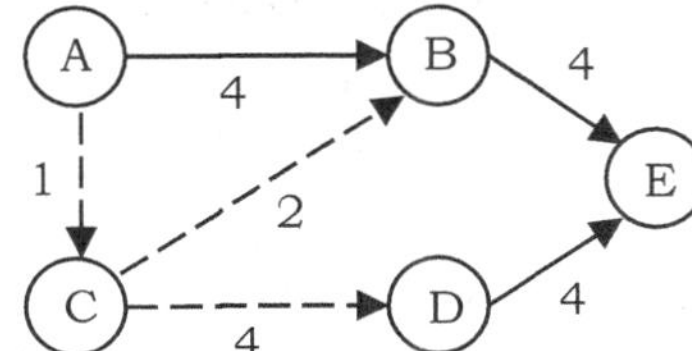


*Shortest path to B, D using C as intermediate vertex*

The only vertex remaining is $E$. To reach $E$, we have to see all the paths through which we can reach $E$ and select the one which gives the minimum cost. We can see that if we use $B$ as the intermediate vertex through $C$ we get the minimum cost.

| A | 0 | - |
|---|---|---|
| B | 3 | C |
| C | 1 | A |
| D | 5 | C |
| E | 7 | B |

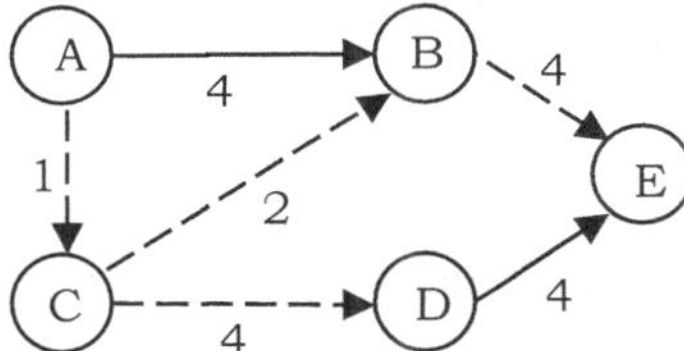


The final minimum cost tree which Dijkstra's algorithm generates is:

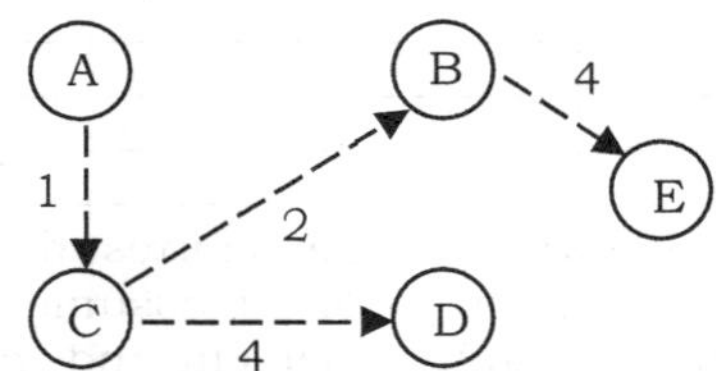


```
void Dijkstra(struct Graph *G, int s) {
    struct PriorityQueue *PQ = createPriorityQueue();
    int v, w;
    enQueue(PQ, s);
    for (int i = 0; i< G→V;i++)
        Distance[i]=-1;
    Distance[s] = 0;
    while ((!isEmpty(PQ)) {
        v = deleteMin(PQ);
        for all adjacent vertices w of v {
            Compute new distance d= Distance[v] + weight[v][w];
            if(Distance[w] == -1) {
                Distance[w] = new distance d;
                Insert w in the priority queue with priority d
                Path[w] = v;
            }
            if(Distance[w]  > new distance d) {
                Distance[w] = new distance d;
                Update priority of vertex w to be d;
                Path[w] = v;
            }
        }
    }
}
```

### Performance

In Dijkstra's algorithm, the efficiency depends on the number of deleteMins ($V$ deleteMins) and updates for priority queues ($E$ updates) that are used. If a *standard binary heap* is used then the complexity is O($ElogV$). The term $ElogV$ comes from $E$ updates (each update takes $logV$) for the standard heap. If the set used is an array then the complexity is O($E + V^2$).

### Notes on Dijkstra's Algorithm

- It uses greedy method: Always pick the next closest vertex to the source.
- It uses priority queue to store unvisited vertices by distance from $s$.
- It does not work with negative weights.

### Difference between Unweighted Shortest Path and Dijkstra's Algorithm

1) To represent weights in the adjacency list, each vertex contains the weights of the edges (in addition to their identifier).
2) Instead of ordinary queue we use priority queue [distances are the priorities] and the vertex with the smallest distance is selected for processing.
3) The distance to a vertex is calculated by the sum of the weights of the edges on the path from the source to that vertex.
4) We update the distances in case the newly computed distance is smaller than the old distance which we have already computed.

### Disadvantages of Dijkstra's Algorithm

- As discussed above, the major disadvantage of the algorithm is that it does a blind search, thereby wasting time and necessary resources.
- Another disadvantage is that it cannot handle negative edges. This leads to acyclic graphs and most often cannot obtain the right shortest path.

### Relatives of Dijkstra's Algorithm

- The *Bellman- Ford* algorithm computes single-source shortest paths in a weighted digraph. It uses the same concept as that of *Dijkstra's* algorithm but can handle negative edges as well. It has more running time than *Dijkstra's* algorithm.
- Prim's algorithm finds a minimum spanning tree for a connected weighted graph. It implies that a subset of edges that form a tree where the total weight of all the edges in the tree is minimized.

## Bellman-Ford Algorithm

The Bellman-Ford algorithm is a graph search algorithm that finds the shortest path between a given source vertex and all other vertices in the graph. This algorithm can be used on both weighted and unweighted graphs. Like Dijkstra's shortest path algorithm, the Bellman-Ford algorithm is guaranteed to find the shortest path in a graph. If the graph has negative edge costs, then *Dijkstra's* algorithm does not work.

Though it is slower than Dijkstra's algorithm, Bellman-Ford is capable of handling graphs that contain negative edge weights, so it is more versatile. It is worth noting that if there exists a negative cycle in the graph, then there is no shortest path. Going around the negative cycle an infinite number of times would continue to decrease the cost of the path (even though the path length is increasing). Because of this, Bellman-Ford can also detect negative cycles which is a useful feature.

The Bellman-Ford algorithm operates on an input graph, G, with |V| vertices and |E| edges. A single source vertex, s, must be provided as well, as the Bellman-Ford algorithm is a single-source shortest path algorithm. No destination vertex needs to be supplied, however, because Bellman-Ford calculates the shortest distance to all vertices in the graph from the source vertex.

The Bellman-Ford algorithm, like Dijkstra's algorithm, uses the principle of relaxation to find increasingly accurate path length. Bellman-Ford, though, tackles two main issues with this process:

1. If there are negative weight cycles, the search for a shortest path will go on forever.
2. Choosing a bad ordering for relaxations leads to exponential relaxations.

The detection of negative cycles is important, but the main contribution of this algorithm is in its ordering of relaxations. Relaxation is the most important step in Bellman-Ford. It is what increases the accuracy of the distance to any given vertex. Relaxation works by continuously shortening the calculated distance between vertices comparing that distance with other known distances.

Bellman Ford algorithm works by overestimating the length of the path from the starting vertex to all other vertices. Then it iteratively relaxes those estimates by finding new paths that are shorter than the previously overestimated paths. Take the baseball example. Let's say I think the distance to the baseball stadium is 30 miles. However, I know that the distance to the corner right before the stadium is 15 miles, and I know that from the corner to the stadium, the distance is 1 mile. Clearly, the distance from me to the stadium is at most 16 miles. So, I can update my belief to reflect that. That is one cycle of relaxation, and it's done over and over until the shortest paths are found.

The problem with *Dijkstra's* algorithm is that once a vertex $u$ is declared known, it is possible that from some other, unknown vertex $v$ there is a path back to $u$ that is very negative. In such case, taking a path from $s$ to $v$ back to $u$ is better than going from $s$ to $u$ without using $v$. A combination of Dijkstra's algorithm and unweighted algorithms will solve the problem. Initialize the queue with $s$. Then, at each stage, we *DeQueue* a vertex $v$. We find all vertices $w$ adjacent to $v$ such that,

$$distance\ to\ v\ +\ weight(v,w) < \text{old distance to w}$$

We update w old distance and path, and place $w$ on a queue if it is not already there. A bit can be set for each vertex to indicate presence in the queue. We repeat the process until the queue is empty.

```
void BellmanFordAlgorithm(struct graph *G, int s) {
    struct Queue *Q = createQueue();
    int v, w;
    enQueue(Q, s);
    Distance[s] = 0;                    // assume the Distance table is filled with INT_MAX
    while ( !isEmpty(Q) ){
        v = deQueue(Q);
        for all adjacent vertices w of v {
            Compute new distance d= Distance[v] + weight[v][w];
            if(old distance to w > new distance d ) {
                Distance[v] = (distance to v) + weight[v][w]);
                Path[w] = v;
                if(w is there in queue)
                    enQueue(Q, w)
            }
        }
    }
}
```

This algorithm works if there are no negative-cost cycles. Each vertex can deQueue at most $|V|$ times, so the running time is $O(|E| . |V|)$ if adjacency lists are used.

## Overview of Shortest Path Algorithms

| | |
|---|---|
| Shortest path in unweighted graph [*Modified BFS*] | $O(\|E\| + \|V\|)$ |
| Shortest path in weighted graph [*Dijkstra's*] | $O(\|E\| \log \|V\|)$ |
| Shortest path in weighted graph with negative edges [*Bellman – Ford*] | $O(\|E\|.\|V\|)$ |
| Shortest path in weighted acyclic graph | $O(\|E\| + \|V\|)$ |

# 9.8 Minimal Spanning Tree

The *spanning tree* of a graph is a subgraph that contains all the vertices and is also a tree. A graph may have many spanning trees. As an example, consider a graph with 4 vertices as shown below. Let us assume that the corners of the graph are vertices.

For this simple graph, we can have multiple spanning trees as shown below.

The cost of the spanning tree is the sum of the weights of all the edges in the tree. There can be many spanning trees. Minimum spanning tree is the spanning tree where the cost is minimum among all the spanning trees. There also can be many minimum spanning trees.

The algorithm we will discuss now is *minimum spanning tree* in an undirected graph. We assume that the given graphs are weighted graphs. If the graphs are unweighted graphs then we can still use the weighted graph algorithms by treating all weights as equal. A *minimum spanning tree* of an undirected graph $G$ is a tree formed from graph edges that connect all the vertices of $G$ with minimum total cost (weights). A minimum spanning tree exists only if the graph is connected. There are two famous algorithms for this problem:

- *Prim's* Algorithm
- *Kruskal's* Algorithm

## Prim's Algorithm

Prim's algorithm also use *greedy* approach to find the minimum spanning tree. Prim's algorithm shares a similarity with the shortest path first algorithms. In Prim's algorithm we grow the spanning tree from a starting position. Prim's algorithm is almost same as Dijkstra's algorithm. Like in Dijkstra's algorithm, in Prim's algorithm also we keep values *distance* and *paths* in distance table. The only exception is that since the definition of *distance* is different and as a result the updating statement also changes little. The update statement is simpler than before.

In Prim's algorithm, we will start with an arbitrary node (it doesn't matter which one) and mark it. In each iteration we will mark a new vertex that is adjacent to the one that we have already marked. As a greedy algorithm, Prim's algorithm will select the cheapest edge and mark the vertex.

### Algorithm

- Maintain two disjoint sets of vertices. One containing vertices that are in the growing spanning tree and other that are not in the growing spanning tree.
- Select the cheapest vertex that is connected to the growing spanning tree and is not in the growing spanning tree and add it into the growing spanning tree. This can be done using priority queues. Insert the vertices, that are connected to growing spanning tree, into the priority queue.
- Check for cycles. To do that, mark the nodes which have been already selected and insert only those nodes in the priority queue that are not marked.

```
void Prims(struct Graph *G, int s) {
    struct PriorityQueue *PQ = createPriorityQueue();
    int v, w;
    enQueue(PQ, s);
    Distance[s] = 0;                    // assume the Distance table is filled with -1
    while ((!isEmpty(PQ)) {
        v = deleteMin(PQ);
        for all adjacent vertices w of v {
            Compute new distance d= Distance[v] + weight[v][w];
            if(Distance[w] == -1) {
                Distance[w] = weight[v][w];
                Insert w in the priority queue with priority d
```

```
                Path[w] = v;
            }
            if(Distance[w] > new distance d) {
                Distance[w] = weight[v][w];
                Update priority of vertex w to be d;
                Path[w] = v;
            }
        }
    }
}
```

The time complexity of the Prim's algorithm is $O((V+E)logV)$ because each vertex is inserted in the priority queue only once and insertion in priority queue take logarithmic time. The entire implementation of this algorithm is identical to that of Dijkstra's algorithm. The running time is $O(|V|^2)$ without heaps [good for dense graphs], and $O(ElogV)$ using binary heaps [good for sparse graphs].

## Kruskal's Algorithm

Kruskal's algorithm is a minimum spanning tree algorithm that uses the *greedy* approach. This algorithm treats the graph as a forest and every node it has as an individual tree. A tree connects to another only and only if, it has the least cost among all available options and does not violate MST properties. Kruskal's Algorithm builds the spanning tree by adding edges one by one into a growing spanning tree.

The algorithm starts with V different trees (V is the vertices in the graph). While constructing the minimum spanning tree, every time Kruskal's algorithm selects an edge that has minimum weight and then adds that edge if it doesn't create a cycle. So, initially, there are |V| single-node trees in the forest. Adding an edge merges two trees into one. When the algorithm is completed, there will be only one tree, and that is the minimum spanning tree.

### Algorithm

- Sort the graph edges with respect to their weights.
- Start adding edges to the minimum snapping tree from the edge with the smallest weight until the edge of the largest weight.
- Only add edges which doesn't form a cycle, edges which connect only disconnected components.

The greedy Choice is to put the smallest weight edge that does not because a cycle in the MST constructed so far.

There are two ways of implementing Kruskal's algorithm:

- By using disjoint sets: Using UNION and FIND operations
- By using priority queues: Maintains weights in priority queue

So now the question is how to check if vertices are connected or not ?

This could be done using DFS which starts from the first vertex, then check if the second vertex is visited or not. But DFS will make time complexity large as it has an order of O(E+V) where V is the number of vertices, E is the number of edges. Disjoint sets are sets whose intersection is the empty set so it means that they don't have any element in common.

The appropriate data structure is the UNION/FIND algorithm [for implementing forests]. Two vertices belong to the same set if and only if they are connected in the current spanning forest. Each vertex is initially in its own set. If $u$ and $v$ are in the same set, the edge is rejected because it forms a cycle. Otherwise, the edge is accepted, and a UNION is performed on the two sets containing $u$ and $v$.

As an example, consider the following graph (the edges show the weights).

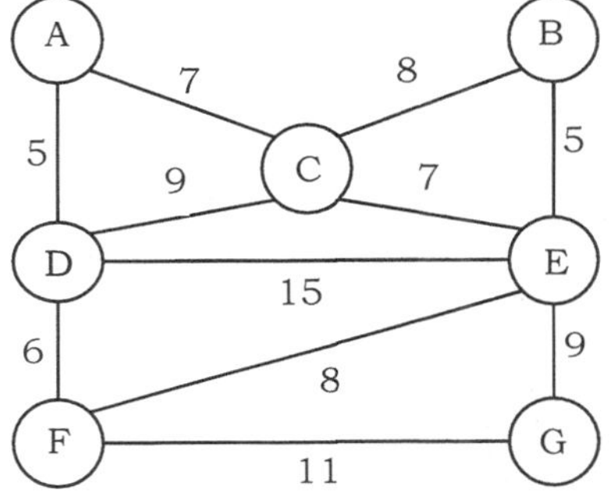

Now let us perform Kruskal's algorithm on this graph. We always select the edge which has minimum weight.

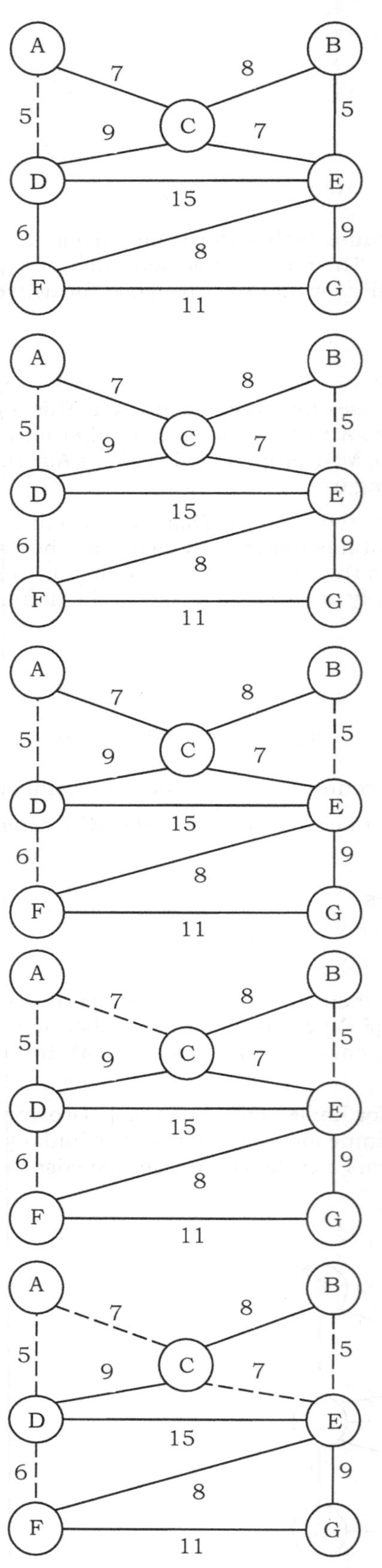


From the above graph, the edges which have minimum weight (cost) are: AD and BE. From these two we can select one of them and let us assume that we select AD (dotted line).

BE now has the lowest cost and we select it (dotted lines indicate selected edges).

DF is the next edge that has the lowest cost (6).

Next, AC and CE have the low cost of 7 and we select AC.

Then we select CE as its cost is 7 and it does not form a cycle.

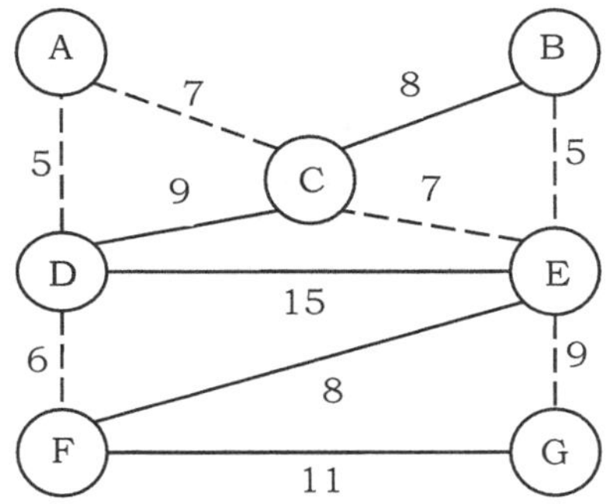


The next lowest cost edges are CB and EF. But if we select CB, then it forms a cycle. So, we discard it. This is also the case with EF. So, we should not select those two. And the next low cost is 9 (DC and EG). Selecting DC forms a cycle so we discard it. Adding EG will not form a cycle and therefore with this edge we complete all vertices of the graph.

```
// Refer Disjoin Sets chapter for implementation of sets
void Kruskals(struct Graph *G) {
    S = ϕ;   // At the end S will contains the edges of minimum spanning trees
    for (int v = 0; v< G→V; v++)
        MakeSet (v);
    Sort edges of E by increasing weights w;
    for each edge (u, v) in E { //from sorted list
        if(FIND (u) ≠ FIND (v)) {
            S = S ∪ {(u, v)};
            UNION (u, v);
        }
    }
    return S;
}
```

**Note:** For implementation of UNION and FIND operations, refer to the *Disjoint Sets ADT* chapter.

The worst-case running time of this algorithm is $O(ElogE)$, which is dominated by the heap operations. That means, since we are constructing the heap with E edges, we need $O(ElogE)$ time to do that.

## 9.9 Graph Algorithms: Problems & Solutions

**Problem-1** In an undirected simple graph with $n$ vertices, what is the maximum number of edges? Self-loops are not allowed.

**Solution:** Since every node can connect to all other nodes, the first node can connect to $n-1$ nodes. The second node can connect to $n-2$ nodes [since one edge is already there from the first node]. The total number of edges is: $1 + 2 + 3 + \cdots + n - 1 = \frac{n(n-1)}{2}$ edges.

**Problem-2** How many different adjacency matrices does a graph with $n$ vertices and $E$ edges have?

**Solution:** It's equal to the number of permutations of $n$ elements. i.e., $n!$.

**Problem-3** How many different adjacency lists does a graph with $n$ vertices have?

**Solution:** It's equal to the number of permutations of edges. i.e., $E!$.

**Problem-4** Which undirected graph representation is most appropriate for determining whether or not a vertex is isolated (is not connected to any other vertex)?

**Solution: Adjacency List**. If we use the adjacency matrix, then we need to check the complete row to determine whether that vertex has edges or not. By using the adjacency list, it is very easy to check, and it can be done just by checking whether that vertex has NULL for next pointer or not [NULL indicates that the vertex is not connected to any other vertex].

**Problem-5** For checking whether there is a path from source $s$ to target $t$, which one is best between disjoint sets and DFS?

**Solution:** The table below shows the comparison between disjoint sets and DFS. The entries in the table represent the case for any pair of nodes (for $s$ and $t$).

| Method | Processing Time | Query Time | Space |
|---|---|---|---|
| Union-Find | $V + E\,logV$ | $logV$ | $V$ |
| DFS | $E + V$ | 1 | $E + V$ |

**Problem-6** What is the maximum number of edges a directed graph with $n$ vertices can have and still not contain a directed cycle?

**Solution:** The number is V (V − 1)/2. Any directed graph can have at most $n^2$ edges. However, since the graph has no cycles it cannot contain a self loop, and for any pair $x, y$ of vertices, at most one edge from $(x,y)$ and $(y,x)$ can be included. Therefore the number of edges can be at most $(V^2 - V)/2$ as desired. It is possible to achieve V(V − 1)/2 edges. Label $n$ nodes $1, 2 \ldots n$ and add an edge (x, y) if and only if $x < y$. This graph has the appropriate number of edges and cannot contain a cycle (any path visits an increasing sequence of nodes).

**Problem-7** How many simple directed graphs with no parallel edges and self-loops are possible in terms of $V$?

**Solution:** (V) × (V − 1). Since, each *vertex can connect to* V − 1 *vertices without* self-loops.

**Problem-8** What are the differences between DFS and BFS?

**Solution:**

| DFS | BFS |
|---|---|
| Backtracking is possible from a dead end. | Backtracking is not possible. |
| Vertices from which exploration is incomplete are processed in a LIFO order | The vertices to be explored are organized as a FIFO queue. |
| The search is done in one particular direction | The vertices at the same level are maintained in parallel. |

**Problem-9** Earlier in this chapter, we discussed minimum spanning tree algorithms. Now, give an algorithm for finding the maximum-weight spanning tree in a graph.

**Solution:**

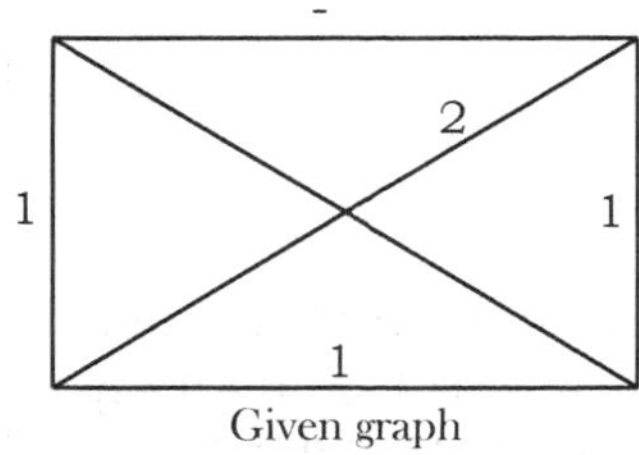

Given graph

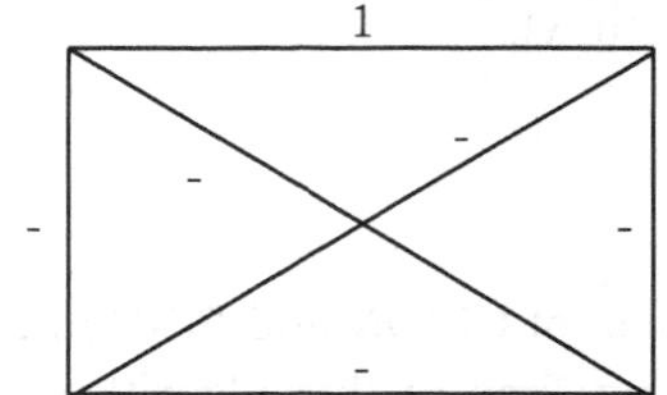

Transformed graph with negative edge

Using the given graph, construct a new graph with the same nodes and edges. But instead of using the same weights, take the negative of their weights. That means, weight of an edge = negative of weight of the corresponding edge in the given graph. Now, we can use existing *minimum spanning tree* algorithms on this new graph. As a result, we will get the maximum-weight spanning tree in the original one.

**Problem-10** Give an algorithm for checking whether a given graph $G$ has simple path from source $s$ to destination $d$. Assume the graph $G$ is represented using the adjacent matrix.

**Solution:** Let us assume that the structure for the graph is:

```
struct Graph {
    int V;              //Number of vertices
    int E;              //Number of edges
    int ** adjMatrix;   //Two dimensional array for storing the connections
};
```

For each vertex call *DFS* and check whether the current vertex is the same as the destination vertex or not. If they are the same, then return 1. Otherwise, call the *DFS* on its unvisited neighbors. One important thing to note here is that, we are calling the DFS algorithm on vertices which are not yet visited.

```
void HasSimplePath(struct Graph *G, int s, int d) {
    int t;
    Viisited[s] = 1;
    if(s == d)
        return 1;
    for(t = 0; t < G→V; t++) {
        if(G→adjMatrix[s][t] && !Viisited[t])
            if(DFS(G, t, d))
                return 1;
    }
    return 0;
}
```

Time Complexity: O($E$). In the above algorithm, for each node, since we are not calling *DFS* on all of its neighbors (discarding through *if* condition). Space Complexity: O($V$).

**Problem-11** Count simple paths for a given graph $G$ has simple path from source s to destination d? Assume the graph is represented using the adjacent matrix.

**Solution:** Similar to the discussion in Problem-10, start at one node and call DFS on that node. As a result of this call, it visits all the nodes that it can reach in the given graph. That means it visits all the nodes of the connected component of that node. If there are any nodes that have not been visited, then again start at one of those nodes and call DFS.

Before the first DFS in each connected component, increment the connected components *count*. Continue this process until all of the graph nodes are visited. As a result, at the end we will get the total number of connected components. The implementation based on this logic is given below.

```
void CountSimplePaths(struct Graph * G, int s, int d) {
    int t;
    Viisited[s] = 1;
    if(s == d) {
        count++;
        Visited[s] = 0;
        return;
    }
    for(t = 0; t < G→V; t++) {
        if(G→adjMatrix[s][t] && !Viisited[t]) {
            DFS(G, t, d);
            Visited[t] = 0;
        }
    }
}
```

**Problem-12** **All pairs shortest path problem:** Find the shortest graph distances between every pair of vertices in a given graph. Let us assume that the given graph does not have negative edges.

**Solution:** The problem can be solved using $n$ applications of *Dijkstra's* algorithm. That means we apply *Dijkstra's* algorithm on each vertex of the given graph. This algorithm does not work if the graph has edges with negative weights.

**Problem-13** In Problem-12, how do we solve the all pairs shortest path problem if the graph has edges with negative weights?

**Solution:** This can be solved by using the *Floyd – Warshall algorithm.* This algorithm also works in the case of a weighted graph where the edges have negative weights. This algorithm is an example of Dynamic Programming - refer to the *Dynamic Programming* chapter.

**Problem-14** **DFS Application:** *Cut Vertex* or *Articulation Points.*

**Solution:** In an undirected graph, a *cut vertex* (or articulation point) is a vertex, and if we remove it, then the graph splits into two disconnected components. As an example, consider the following figure. Removal of the "$D$" vertex divides the graph into two connected components ($\{E, F\}$ and $\{A, B, C, G\}$).

Similarly, removal of the "$C$" vertex divides the graph into ($\{G\}$ and $\{A, B, D, E, F\}$). For this graph, $A$ and $C$ are the cut vertices.

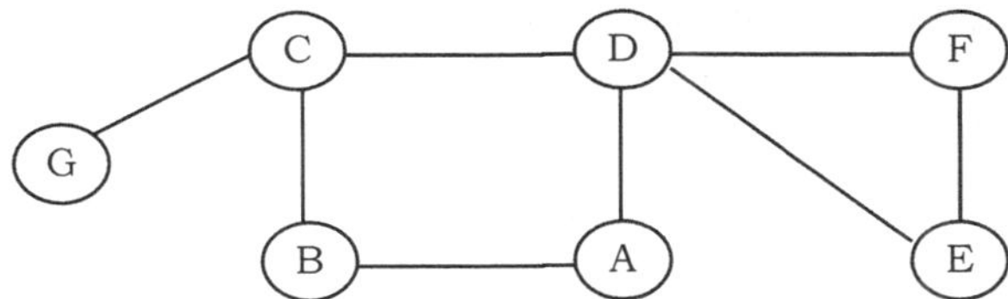


**Note:** A connected, undirected graph is called *bi – connected* if the graph is still connected after removing any vertex.

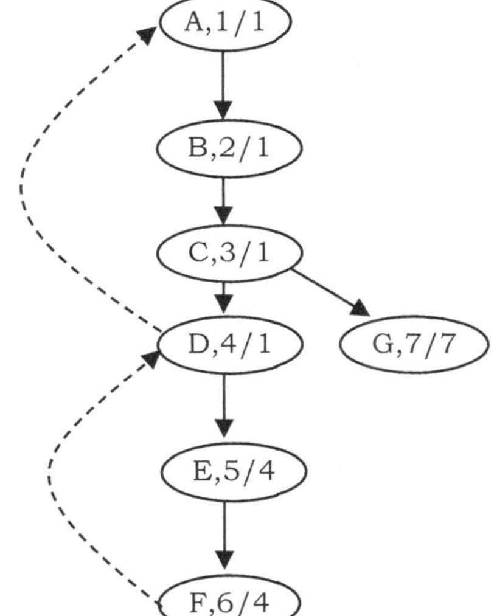

$DFS$ provides a linear-time algorithm ($O(n)$) to find all cut vertices in a connected graph. Starting at any vertex, call a $DFS$ and number the nodes as they are visited. For each vertex $v$, we call this DFS number $dfsnum$(v). The tree generated with DFS traversal is called $DFS$ $spanning$ $tree$. Then, for every vertex $v$ in the $DFS$ spanning tree, we compute the lowest-numbered vertex, which we call $low(v)$, that is reachable from $v$ by taking zero or more tree edges and then possibly one back edge (in that order).

Based on the above discussion, we need the following information for this algorithm: the $dfsnum$ of each vertex in the $DFS$ tree (once it gets visited), and for each vertex $v$, the lowest depth of neighbors of all descendants of $v$ in the $DFS$ tree, called the $low$.

The $dfsnum$ can be computed during DFS. The low of $v$ can be computed after visiting all descendants of $v$ (i.e., just before $v$ gets popped off the $DFS$ stack) as the minimum of the $dfsnum$ of all neighbors of $v$ (other than the parent of $v$ in the $DFS$ tree) and the $low$ of all children of $v$ in the $DFS$ tree.

The root vertex is a cut vertex if and only if it has at least two children. A non-root vertex u is a cut vertex if and only if there is a son $v$ of $u$ such that $low(v) \geq dfsnum(u)$. This property can be tested once the $DFS$ is returned from every child of $u$ (that means, just before u gets popped off the DFS stack), and if true, $u$ separates the graph into different bi-connected components. This can be represented by computing one bi-connected component out of every such $v$ (a component which contains $v$ will contain the sub-tree of $v$, plus $u$), and then erasing the sub-tree of $v$ from the tree.

For the given graph, the $DFS$ tree with $dfsnum/low$ can be given as shown in the figure below. The implementation for the above discussion is:

```
int adjMatrix [256] [256] ;
int dfsnum [256], num = 0, low [256];
void CutVertices( int u ) {
    low[u] = dfsnum[u] = num++;
    for (int v = 0 ; v < 256; ++v ) {
        if(adjMatrix[u][v] && dfsnum[v] == -1) {
            CutVertices( v ) ;
            if(low[v] > dfsnum[u])
                printf("Cut Vetex:%d",u);
            low[u] = min ( low[u] , low[v] ) ;
        }
        else    // (u,v) is a back edge
            low[u ] = min(low[u] , dfsnum[v]) ;
    }
}
```

**Problem-15** Let $G$ be a connected graph of order $n$. What is the maximum number of cut-vertices that $G$ can contain?

**Solution:** $n - 2$. As an example, consider the following graph. In the graph below, except for the vertices 1 and $n$, all the remaining vertices are cut vertices. This is because removing 1 and $n$ vertices does not split the graph into two. This is a case where we can get the maximum number of cut vertices.

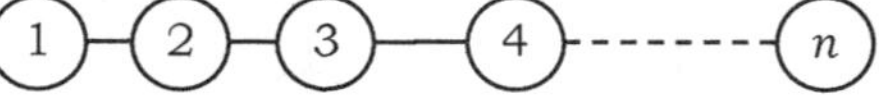


**Problem-16** **DFS Application:** *Cut Bridges* or *Cut Edges*

**Solution: Definition:** Let $G$ be a connected graph. An edge $uv$ in $G$ is called a *bridge* of $G$ if $G - uv$ is disconnected. As an example, consider the following graph.

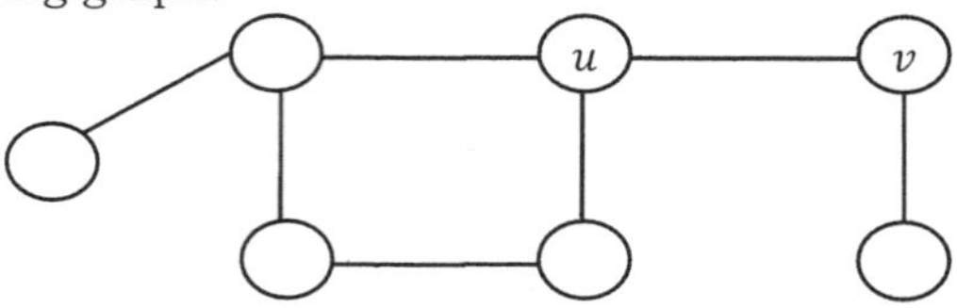


In the above graph, if we remove the edge $uv$ then the graph splits into two components. For this graph, $uv$ is a bridge. The discussion we had for cut vertices holds good for bridges also. The only change is, instead of printing the vertex, we give the edge. The main observation is that an edge $(u, v)$ cannot be a bridge if it is part of a cycle. If $(u, v)$ is not part of a cycle, then it is a bridge.

We can detect cycles in $DFS$ by the presence of back edges. $(u, v)$ is a bridge if and only if none of v or $v's$ children has a back edge to $u$ or any of $u's$ ancestors. To detect whether any of $v's$ children has a back edge to $u's$ parent, we can use a similar idea as above to see what is the smallest $dfsnum$ reachable from the subtree rooted at $v$.

```
int dfsnum[256], num = 0, low [256];
void Bridges( struct Graph *G, int u ) {
    low[u] = dfsnum[u] = num++;
    for (int v = 0 ; G→V; ++v ) {
```

```
                if(G→adjMatrix[u][v] && dfsnum[v] == -1) {
                        Bridges( v ) ;

                        if(low[v] > dfsnum[u])
                                print (u,v)  as a bridge

                        low[u] = min ( low[u] , low[v] ) ;
                }
                else    // (u,v) is a back edge
                        low[u ] = min(low[u] , dfsnum[v]) ;
        }
}
```

**Problem-17** **DFS Application:** Discuss *Euler* Circuits

**Solution:** Before discussing this problem let us see the terminology:

- *Eulerian tour* – a path that contains all edges without repetition.
- *Eulerian circuit* – a path that contains all edges without repetition and starts and ends in the same vertex.
- *Eulerian graph* – a graph that contains an Eulerian circuit.
- *Even vertex*: a vertex that has an even number of incident edges.
- *Odd vertex*: a vertex that has an odd number of incident edges.

*Euler* circuit: For a given graph we have to reconstruct the circuits using a pen, drawing each line exactly once. We should not lift the pen from the paper while drawing. That means, we must find a path in the graph that visits every edge exactly once and this problem is called an *Euler path* (also called *Euler tour*) or *Euler circuit problem*. This puzzle has a simple solution based on DFS.

An *Euler* circuit exists if and only if the graph is connected and the number of neighbors of each vertex is even. Start with any node, select any untraversed outgoing edge, and follow it. Repeat until there are no more remaining unselected outgoing edges. For example, consider the following graph: A legal Euler Circuit of this graph is 0 1 3 4 1 2 3 5 4 2 0.

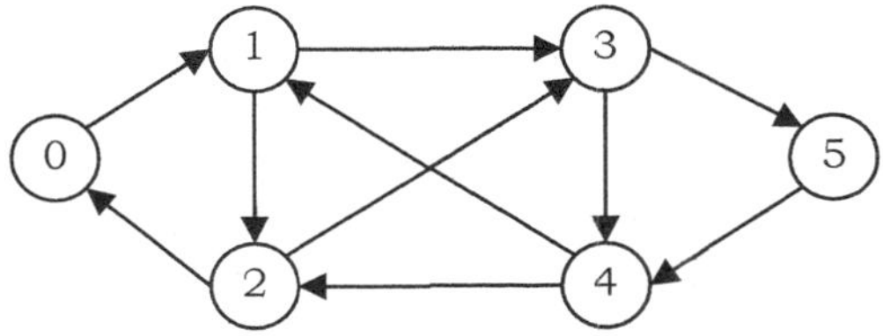


If we start at vertex 0, we can select the edge to vertex 1, then select the edge to vertex 2, then select the edge to vertex 0. There are now no remaining unchosen edges from vertex 0:

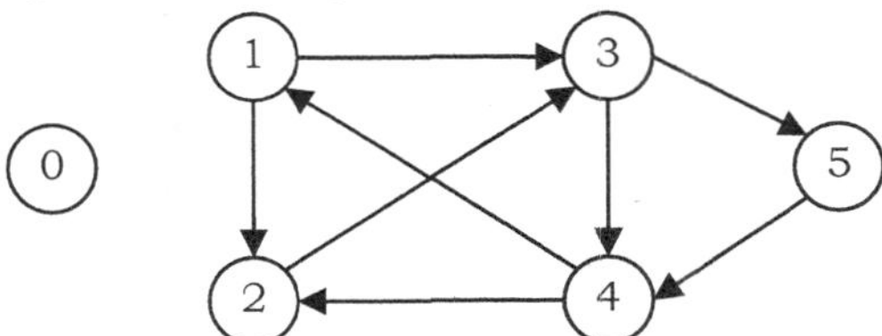


We now have a circuit 0,1,2,0 that does not traverse every edge. So, we pick some other vertex that is on that circuit, say vertex 1. We then do another depth first search of the remaining edges. Say we choose the edge to node 3, then 4, then 1. Again we are stuck. There are no more unchosen edges from node 1. We now splice this path 1,3,4,1 into the old path 0,1,2,0 to get: 0,1,3,4,1,2,0. The unchosen edges now look like this:

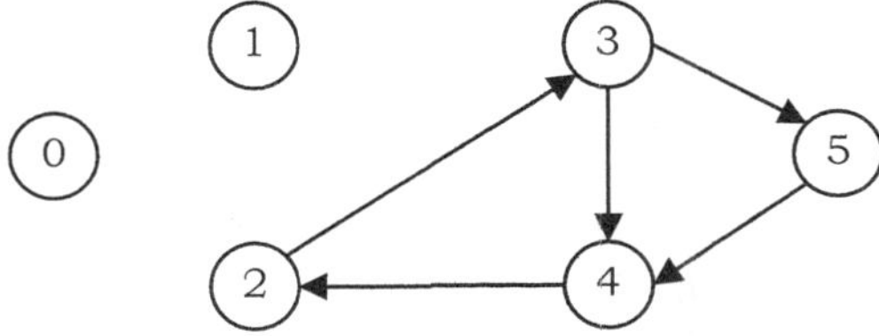


We can pick yet another vertex to start another DFS. If we pick vertex 2, and splice the path 2,3,5,4,2, then we get the final circuit 0,1,3,4,1,2,3,5,4,2,0.

A similar problem is to find a simple cycle in an undirected graph that visits every vertex. This is known as the *Hamiltonian cycle problem*. Although it seems almost identical to the *Euler* circuit problem, no efficient algorithm for it is known.

**Notes:**

- A connected undirected graph is *Eulerian* if and only if every graph vertex has an even degree, or exactly two vertices with an odd degree.
- A directed graph is *Eulerian* if it is strongly connected and every vertex has an equal *in* and *out* degree.

**Application:** A postman has to visit a set of streets in order to deliver mails and packages. He needs to find a path that starts and ends at the post-office, and that passes through each street (edge) exactly once. This way the postman will deliver mails and packages to all the necessary streets, and at the same time will spend minimum time/effort on the road.

**Problem-18** **DFS Application:** Finding Strongly Connected Components.

**Solution:** This is another application of DFS. In a directed graph, two vertices $u$ and $v$ are strongly connected if and only if there exists a path from $u$ to $v$ and there exists a path from $v$ to $u$. The strong connectedness is an equivalence relation.

- A vertex is strongly connected with itself
- If a vertex $u$ is strongly connected to a vertex $v$, then $v$ is strongly connected to $u$
- If a vertex $u$ is strongly connected to a vertex $v$, and $v$ is strongly connected to a vertex $x$, then $u$ is strongly connected to $x$

What this says is, for a given directed graph we can divide it into strongly connected components. This problem can be solved by performing two depth-first searches. With two DFS searches we can test whether a given directed graph is strongly connected or not. We can also produce the subsets of vertices that are strongly connected.

**Algorithm**

- Perform DFS on given graph $G$.
- Number vertices of given graph $G$ according to a post-order traversal of depth-first spanning forest.
- Construct graph $G_r$ by reversing all edges in $G$.
- Perform DFS on $G_r$: Always start a new DFS (initial call to Visit) at the highest-numbered vertex.
- Each tree in the resulting depth-first spanning forest corresponds to a strongly-connected component.

**Why this algorithm works?**

Let us consider two vertices, $v$ and $w$. If they are in the same strongly connected component, then there are paths from $v$ to $w$ and from $w$ to $v$ in the original graph $G$, and hence also in $G_r$. If two vertices $v$ and $w$ are not in the same depth-first spanning tree of $G_r$, clearly they cannot be in the same strongly connected component. As an example, consider the graph shown below on the left. Let us assume this graph is $G$.

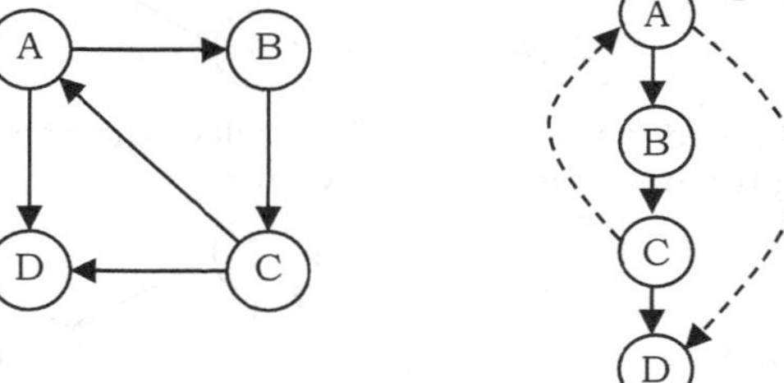


Now, as per the algorithm, performing *DFS* on this *G* graph gives the following diagram. The dotted line from $C$ to $A$ indicates a back edge.

Now, performing post order traversal on this tree gives: $D, C, B$ and $A$.

| Vertex | Post Order Number |
|---|---|
| A | 4 |
| B | 3 |
| C | 2 |
| D | 1 |

Now reverse the given graph $G$ and call it $G_r$ and at the same time assign postorder numbers to the vertices. The reversed graph $G_r$ will look like:

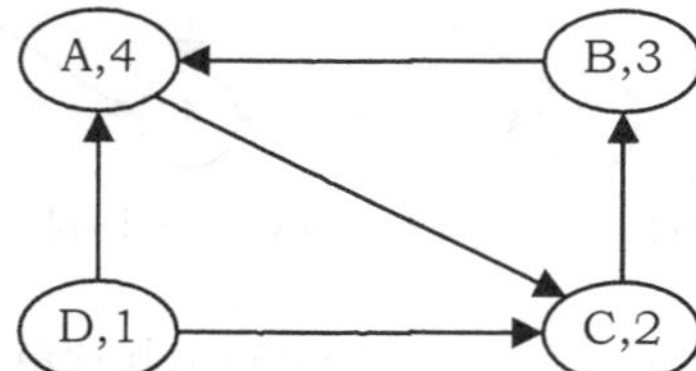


The last step is performing DFS on this reversed graph $G_r$. While doing *DFS*, we need to consider the vertex which has the largest DFS number. So, first we start at $A$ and with *DFS* we go to $C$ and then $B$. At B, we cannot move further. This says that $\{A, B, C\}$ is a strongly connected component. Now the only remaining element is $D$ and we end our second $DFS$ at $D$. So the connected components are: $\{A, B, C\}$ and $\{D\}$.

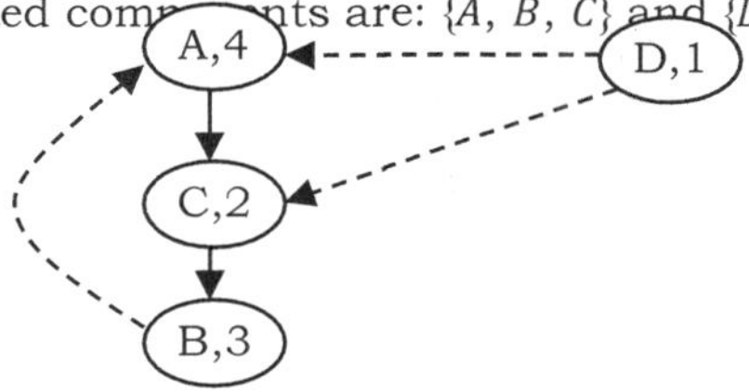


The implementation based on this discussion can be shown as:

```
//Graph represented in adj matrix.
int adjMatrix [256][256], table[256];
vector <int> st ;
int counter = 0 ;
//This table contains the DFS Search number
int dfsnum [256], num = 0, low[256] ;
void StronglyConnectedComponents( int u ) {
        low[u] = dfsnum[ u ] = num++;
        push(st, u) ;
        for( int v = 0 ; v < 256; ++v ) {
                if(graph[u][v] && table[v] == -1) {
                        if( dfsnum[v] == -1)
                        StronglyConnectedComponents(v) ;
                    low[u] = min(low[u] , low[v]) ;
                }
        }
        if(low[u] == dfsnum[u]) {
                while( table[u] != counter) {
                        table[st.back()] = counter;
                        push(st) ;
                }
                ++ counter;
        }
}
```

**Problem-19** Count the number of connected components of Graph $G$ which is represented in the adjacent matrix.

**Solution:** This problem can be solved with one extra counter in $DFS$.

```
//Visited[] is a global array.
int Visited[G→V];
void DFS(struct Graph *G, int u) {
    Visited[u] = 1;
    for( int v = 0; v < G→V; v++ ) {
        /* For example, if the adjacency matrix is used for representing the
            graph, then the condition to be used for finding unvisited adjacent
            vertex of u  is: if( !Visited[v] && G→Adj[u][v] ) */
        for each unvisited adjacent node v of u {
            DFS(G, v);
        }
    }
}
void DFSTraversal(struct Graph *G) {
    int count = 0;
    for (int i = 0; i< G→V;i++)
            Visited[i]=0;
    //This loop is required if the graph has more than one component
    for (int i = 0; i< G→V;i++)
            if(!Visited[i]) {
                    DFS(G, i);
                    count++;
            }
    return count;
```

```
}
```

Time Complexity: Same as that of DFS and it depends on implementation. With adjacency matrix the complexity is O($|E| + |V|$) and with adjacency matrix the complexity is O($|V|^2$).

**Problem-20** Can we solve the Problem-19, using BFS?

**Solution: Yes.** This problem can be solved with one extra counter in BFS.

```
void BFS(struct Graph *G, int u) {
    int v,
    Queue Q = createQueue();
    enQueue(Q, u);
    while(!isEmpty(Q)) {
          u = deQueue(Q);
          Process u; //For example, print
          Visited[s]=1;
          /* For example, if the adjacency matrix is used for representing the
                graph, then the condition be used for finding unvisited adjacent
                vertex of u  is: if( !Visited[v] && G→Adj[u][v] ) */
         for each unvisited adjacent node v of u {
              enQueue(Q, v);
         }
    }
}
void BFSTraversal(struct Graph *G) {
      for (int i = 0; i< G→V;i++)
              Visited[i]=0;
      //This loop is required if the graph has more than one component
      for (int i = 0; i< G→V; i++)
              if(!Visited[i])
                        BFS(G, i);
}
```

Time Complexity: Same as that of $BFS$ and it depends on implementation. With adjacency matrix the complexity is O($|E| + |V|$) and with adjacency matrix the complexity is O($|V|^2$).

**Problem-21** Let us assume that $G(V, E)$ is an undirected graph. Give an algorithm for finding a spanning tree which takes O($|E|$) time complexity (not necessarily a minimum spanning tree).

**Solution:** The test for a cycle can be done in constant time, by marking vertices that have been added to the set $S$. An edge will introduce a cycle, if both its vertices have already been marked.

**Algorithm:**

```
S = {}; //Assume S is a set
for each edge e ∈ E {
      if(adding e to S doesn't form a cycle) {
            add e to S;
            mark e;
      }
}
```

**Problem-22** Is there any other way of solving Problem-20?

**Solution:** Yes. We can run $BFS$ and find the $BFS$ tree for the graph (level order tree of the graph). Then start at the root element and keep moving to the next levels and at the same time we have to consider the nodes in the next level only once. That means, if we have a node with multiple input edges then we should consider only one of them; otherwise they will form a cycle.

**Problem-23** Detecting a cycle in an undirected graph

**Solution:** An undirected graph is acyclic if and only if a $DFS$ yields no back edges, edges $(u, v)$ where $v$ has already been discovered and is an ancestor of $u$.

- Execute $DFS$ on the graph.
- If there is a back edge - the graph has a cycle.

If the graph does not contain a cycle, then $|E| < |V|$ and $DFS$ cost O($|V|$). If the graph contains a cycle, then a back edge is discovered after $2|V|$ steps at most.

**Problem-24** Detecting a cycle in DAG

**Solution:**

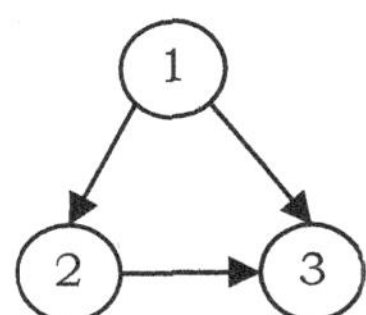


Cycle detection on a graph is different than on a tree. This is because in a graph, a node can have multiple parents. In a tree, the algorithm for detecting a cycle is to do a depth first search, marking nodes as they are encountered. If a previously marked node is seen again, then a cycle exists. This won't work on a graph. Let us consider the graph shown in the figure below. If we use a tree cycle detection algorithm, then it will report the wrong result. That means that this graph has a cycle in it. But the given graph does not have a cycle in it. This is because node 3 will be seen twice in a *DFS* starting at node 1.

The cycle detection algorithm for trees can easily be modified to work for graphs. The key is that in a *DFS* of an acyclic graph, a node whose descendants have all been visited can be seen again without implying a cycle. But, if a node is seen for the second time before all its descendants have been visited, then there must be a cycle. Can you see why this is? Suppose there is a cycle containing node A. This means that A must be reachable from one of its descendants. So when the *DFS* is visiting that descendant, it will see *A* again, before it has finished visiting all of *A's* descendants. So there is a cycle. In order to detect cycles, we can modify the depth first search.

```
int DetectCycle(struct Graph *G) {
	for (int i = 0; i< G→V; i++) {
		Visited[s]=0;
		Predecessor[i] = 0;
	}
	for (int i = 0; i < G→V;i++) {
		if(!Visited[i] && HasCycle(G, i))
			return 1;
	}
	return 0;
}
int HasCycle(struct Graph *G, int u) {
	Visited[u]=1;
	for (int i = 0; i< G→V; i++) {
	  if(G→Adj[s][i]) {
		if(Predecessor[i] != u && Visited[i])
			return 1;
		else {
			Predecessor[i] = u;
			return  HasCycle(G, i);
		}
	  }
	}
	return 0;
}
```

Time Complexity: $O(V + E)$.

**Problem-25** Given a directed acyclic graph, give an algorithm for finding its depth.

**Solution:** If it is an undirected graph, we can use the simple unweighted shortest path algorithm (check *Shortest Path Algorithms* section). We just need to return the highest number among all distances. For directed acyclic graph, we can solve by following the similar approach which we used for finding the depth in trees. In trees, we have solved this problem using level order traversal (with one extra special symbol to indicate the end of the level).

```
//Assuming the given  graph is a DAG
int DepthInDAG( struct Graph *G ) {
	struct Queue *Q;
	int counter;
	int v, w;
	Q = createQueue();
	counter =  0;
	for (v = 0; v< G→V; v++)
		if( indegree[v] ==  0 )
			enQueue( Q , v );
```

```
        enQueue( Q, '$' );
        while( !isEmpty( Q )) {
                v = deQueue( Q );
                if(v == '$') {
                        counter++;
                        if(!isEmpty( Q ))
                                enQueue( Q , '$' );
                }
            for each w adjacent to v
                if( --indegree[w] == 0 )
                        enQueue ( Q , w );
        }
        deleteQueue( Q );
        return counter;
}
```

Total running time is $O(V + E)$ .

**Problem-26** How many topological sorts of the following dag are there?

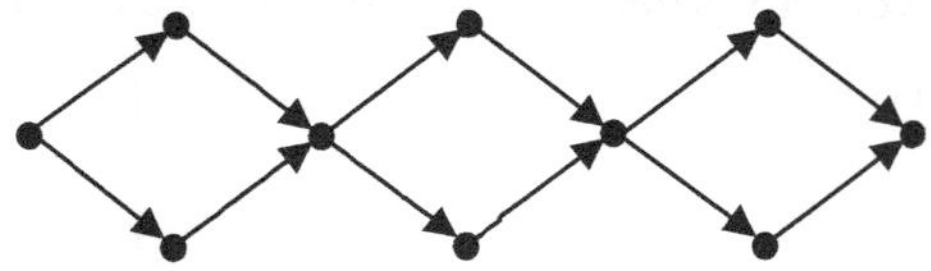

**Solution:** If we observe the above graph there are three stages with 2 vertices. In the early discussion of this chapter, we saw that topological sort picks the elements with zero indegree at any point of time. At each of the two vertices stages, we can first process either the top vertex or the bottom vertex. As a result, at each of these stages we have two possibilities. So the total number of possibilities is the multiplication of possibilities at each stage and that is, $2 \times 2 \times 2 = 8$.

**Problem-27** **Unique topological ordering:** Design an algorithm to determine whether a directed graph has a unique topological ordering.

**Solution:** A directed graph has a unique topological ordering if and only if there is a directed edge between each pair of consecutive vertices in the topological order. This can also be defined as: a directed graph has a unique topological ordering if and only if it has a Hamiltonian path. If the digraph has multiple topological orderings, then a second topological order can be obtained by swapping a pair of consecutive vertices.

**Problem-28** Let us consider the prerequisites for courses at *IIT Bombay*. Suppose that all prerequisites are mandatory, every course is offered every semester, and there is no limit to the number of courses we can take in one semester. We would like to know the minimum number of semesters required to complete the major. Describe the data structure we would use to represent this problem, and outline a linear time algorithm for solving it.

**Solution:** Use a directed acyclic graph (DAG). The vertices represent courses and the edges represent the prerequisite relation between courses at *IIT Bombay*. It is a DAG, because the prerequisite relation has no cycles.

The number of semesters required to complete the major is one more than the longest path in the dag. This can be calculated on the DFS tree recursively in linear time. The longest path out of a vertex $x$ is $0$ if $x$ has outdegree $0$, otherwise it is $1 + max$ $\{longest\ path\ out\ of\ y \mid (x, y)\ is\ an\ edge\ of\ G\}$.

**Problem-29** At a university let's say *IIT Bombay*), there is a list of courses along with their prerequisites. That means, two lists are given:

$A$ - Courses list

$B$ – Prerequisites: B contains couples $(x, y)$ where $x, y \in A$ indicating that course $x$ can't be taken before course $y$.

Let us consider a student who wants to take only one course in a semester. Design a schedule for this student.

**Example:** A = {C-Lang, Data Structures, OS, CO, Algorithms, Design Patterns, Programming }. B = { (C-Lang, CO), (OS, CO), (Data Structures, Algorithms), (Design Patterns, Programming) }. *One possible schedule could be*:

Semester 1: Data Structures
Semester 2: Algorithms
Semester 3: C-Lang
Semester 4: OS
Semester 5: CO
Semester 6: Design Patterns

Semester 7: Programming

**Solution:** The solution to this problem is exactly the same as that of topological sort. Assume that the courses names are integers in the range $[1..n]$, $n$ is known ($n$ is not constant). The relations between the courses will be represented by a directed graph $G = (V, E)$, where $V$ are the set of courses and if course $i$ is prerequisite of course $j$, $E$ will contain the edge $(i, j)$. Let us assume that the graph will be represented as an Adjacency list.

First, let's observe another algorithm to topologically sort a DAG in $O(|V| + |E|)$.

- Find in-degree of all the vertices - $O(|V| + |E|)$
- Repeat:
  Find a vertex v with in-degree=0 - $O(|V|)$
  Output v and remove it from G, along with its edges - $O(|V|)$
  Reduce the in-degree of each node u such as $(v, u)$ was an edge in G and keep a list of vertices with in-degree=0 - $O(degree(v))$
  Repeat the process until all the vertices are removed

The time complexity of this algorithm is also the same as that of the topological sort and it is $O(|V| + |E|)$.

**Problem-30** In Problem-29, a student wants to take all the courses in $A$, in the minimal number of semesters. That means the student is ready to take any number of courses in a semester. Design a schedule for this scenario. *One possible schedule is*:
*Semester* 1: C-Lang, OS, Design Patterns
*Semester* 2: Data Structures, CO, Programming
*Semester* 3: Algorithms

**Solution:** A variation of the above topological sort algorithm with a slight change: In each semester, instead of taking one subject, take all the subjects with zero indegree. That means, execute the algorithm on all the nodes with degree 0 (instead of dealing with one source in each stage, all the sources will be dealt and printed).

Time Complexity: $O(|V| + |E|)$.

**Problem-31** **LCA of a DAG:** Given a DAG and two vertices $v$ and $w$, find the *lowest common ancestor* (LCA) of $v$ and $w$. The LCA of $v$ and $w$ is an ancestor of $v$ and $w$ that has no descendants that are also ancestors of $v$ and $w$.

**Hint**: Define the height of a vertex $v$ in a DAG to be the length of the longest path from *root* to $v$. Among the vertices that are ancestors of both $v$ and $w$, the one with the greatest height is an LCA of $v$ and $w$.

**Problem-32** **Shortest ancestral path:** Given a DAG and two vertices $v$ and $w$, find the *shortest ancestral path* between $v$ and $w$. An ancestral path between $v$ and $w$ is a common ancestor $x$ along with a shortest path from $v$ to $x$ and a shortest path from $w$ to $x$. The shortest ancestral path is the ancestral path whose total length is minimized.

**Hint**: Run BFS two times. First run from $v$ and second time from $w$. Find a DAG where the shortest ancestral path goes to a common ancestor $x$ that is not an LCA.

**Problem-33** Let us assume that we have two graphs $G_1$ and $G_2$. How do we check whether they are isomorphic or not?

**Solution:** There are many ways of representing the same graph. As an example, consider the following simple graph. It can be seen that all the representations below have the same number of vertices and the same number of edges.

**Definition:** Graphs $G_1 = \{V_1, E_1\}$ and $G_2 = \{V_2, E_2\}$ are isomorphic if
1) There is a one-to-one correspondence from $V_1$ to $V_2$ and
2) There is a one-to-one correspondence from $E_1$ to $E_2$ that map each edge of $G_1$ to $G_2$.

Now, for the given graphs how do we check whether they are isomorphic or not?

In general, it is not a simple task to prove that two graphs are isomorphic. For that reason we must consider some properties of isomorphic graphs. That means those properties must be satisfied if the graphs are isomorphic. If the given graph does not satisfy these properties then we say they are not isomorphic graphs.

*Property*: Two graphs are isomorphic if and only if for some ordering of their vertices their adjacency matrices are equal.

Based on the above property we decide whether the given graphs are isomorphic or not. I order to check the property, we need to do some matrix transformation operations.

**Problem-34** How many simple undirected non-isomorphic graphs are there with $n$ vertices?

**Solution:** We will try to answer this question in two steps. First, we count all labeled graphs. Assume all the representations below are labeled with $\{1, 2, 3\}$ as vertices. The set of all such graphs for $n = 3$ are:

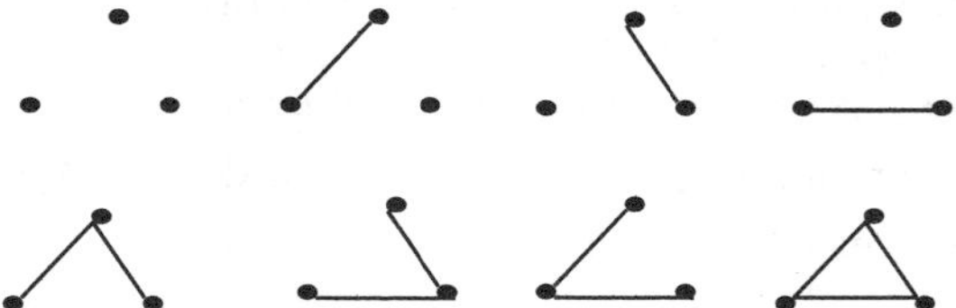

There are only two choices for each edge: it either exists or it does not. Therefore, since the maximum number of edges is $\binom{n}{2}$ *(and since* the maximum number of edges in an undirected graph with $n$ vertices is $\frac{n(n-1)}{2} = n_{c_2} = \binom{n}{2}$*)*, the total number of undirected labeled graphs is $2^{\binom{n}{2}}$.

**Problem-35** **Hamiltonian path in DAGs:** Given a DAG, design a linear time algorithm to determine whether there is a path that visits each vertex exactly once.

**Solution:** The *Hamiltonian* path problem is an NP-Complete problem (for more details ref *Complexity Classes* chapter). To solve this problem, we will try to give the approximation algorithm (which solves the problem, but it may not always produce the optimal solution).

Let us consider the topological sort algorithm for solving this problem. Topological sort has an interesting property: that if all pairs of consecutive vertices in the sorted order are connected by edges, then these edges form a directed *Hamiltonian* path in the DAG. If a *Hamiltonian* path exists, the topological sort order is unique. Also, if a topological sort does not form a *Hamiltonian* path, the DAG will have two or more topological orderings.

*Approximation Algorithm*: Compute a topological sort and check if there is an edge between each consecutive pair of vertices in the topological order.

In an unweighted graph, find a path from **s** to **t** that visits each vertex exactly once. The basic solution based on backtracking is, we start at $s$ and try all of its neighbors recursively, making sure we never visit the same vertex twice. The algorithm based on this implementation can be given as:

```
bool seenTable[32];
void HamiltonianPath( struct Graph *G, int u ) {
    if( u == t )
        /* Check that we have seen all vertices. */
    else {
        for( int v = 0; v < n; v++ )
            if( !seenTable[v] && G→Adj[u][v] ) {
                seenTable[v] = true;
                HamiltonianPath( v );
                seenTable[v] = false;
            }
    }
}
```

Note that if we have a partial path from s to u using vertices $s = v_1, v_2, \ldots, v_k = u$, then we don't care about the order in which we visited these vertices so as to figure out which vertex to visit next. All that we need to know is the set of vertices we have seen (the seenTable[] array) and which vertex we are at right now (u).

There are $2^n$ possible sets of vertices and n choices for u. In other words, there are $2^n$ possible *seenTable*[ ] arrays and n different parameters to HamiltonianPath(). What HamiltonianPath() does during any particular recursive call is completely determined by the *seenTable*[ ] array and the parameter u.

**Problem-36** For a given graph $G$ with $n$ vertices how many trees we can construct?

**Solution:** There is a simple formula for this problem and it is named after Arthur Cayley. For a given graph with $n$ labeled vertices the formula for finding number of trees on is $n^{n-2}$. Below, the number of trees with different $n$ values is shown.

| n value | Formula value: $n^{n-2}$ | Number of Trees |
|---|---|---|
| 2 | 1 | 1 ——— 2 |

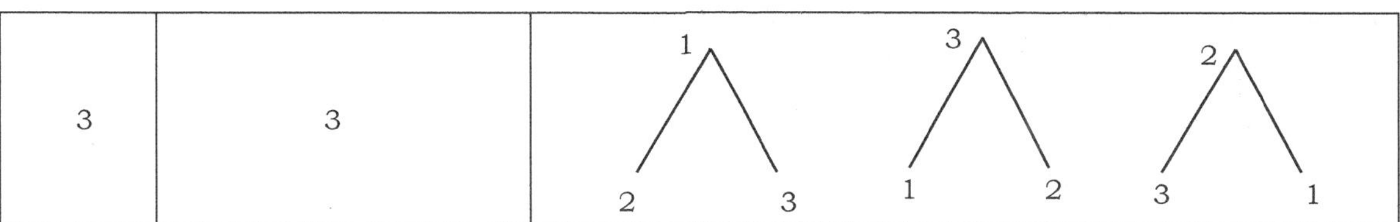


**Problem-37** For a given graph G with $n$ vertices how many spanning trees can we construct?

**Solution:** The solution to this problem is the same as that of Problem-36. It is just another way of asking the same question. Because the number of edges in both regular tree and spanning tree are the same.

**Problem-38** The *Hamiltonian cycle* problem: Is it possible to traverse each of the vertices of a graph exactly once, starting and ending at the same vertex?

**Solution:** Since the *Hamiltonian* path problem is an NP-Complete problem, the *Hamiltonian* cycle problem is an NP-Complete problem. A *Hamiltonian* cycle is a cycle that traverses every vertex of a graph exactly once. There are no known conditions in which are both necessary and sufficient, but there are a few sufficient conditions.

- For a graph to have a *Hamiltonian* cycle the degree of each vertex must be two or more.
- The Petersen graph does not have a *Hamiltonian* cycle and the graph is given below.

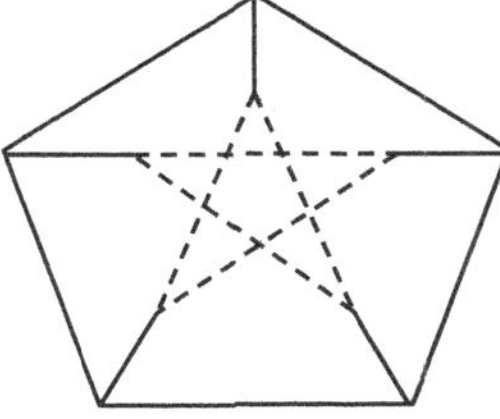

- In general, the more edges a graph has, the more likely it is to have a *Hamiltonian* cycle.
- Let G be a simple graph with $n \geq 3$ vertices. If every vertex has a degree of at least $\frac{n}{2}$, then G has a *Hamiltonian* cycle.
- The best known algorithm for finding a *Hamiltonian* cycle has an exponential worst-case complexity.

**Note**: For the approximation algorithm of *Hamiltonian* path, refer to the *Dynamic Programming* chapter.

**Problem-39** What is the difference between *Dijkstra's* and *Prim's* algorithm?

**Solution:** *Dijkstra's* algorithm is almost identical to that of *Prim's*. The algorithm begins at a specific vertex and extends outward within the graph until all vertices have been reached. The only distinction is that *Prim's* algorithm stores a minimum cost edge whereas *Dijkstra's* algorithm stores the total cost from a source vertex to the current vertex. More simply, *Dijkstra's* algorithm stores a summation of minimum cost edges whereas *Prim's* algorithm stores at most one minimum cost edge.

**Problem-40** **Reversing Graph:** Give an algorithm that returns the reverse of the directed graph (each edge from $v$ to $w$ is replaced by an edge from $w$ to $v$).

**Solution:** In graph theory, the reverse (also called *transpose*) of a directed graph $G$ is another directed graph on the same set of vertices with all the edges reversed. That means, if $G$ contains an edge $(u, v)$ then the reverse of $G$ contains an edge $(v, u)$ and vice versa.

**Algorithm:**

```
Graph ReverseTheDirectedGraph(struct Graph *G) {
        Create new graph with name ReversedGraph and
                let us assume that this will contain the reversed graph.
        // The reversed graph also will contain same number of vertices and edges.
        for each vertex of given graph G {
                for each vertex w adjacent to v {
                    Add the w to v edge in ReversedGraph;
                    // That means we just need to reverse the bits in adjacency matrix.
                }
        }
        return ReversedGraph;
}
```

**Problem-41** **Travelling Sales Person Problem:** Find the shortest path in a graph that visits each vertex at least once, starting and ending at the same vertex.

**Solution:** The Traveling Salesman Problem (*TSP*) is related to finding a Hamiltonian cycle. Given a weighted graph $G$, we want to find the shortest cycle (may be non-simple) that visits all the vertices.

**Approximation algorithm:** This algorithm does not solve the problem but gives a solution which is within a factor of 2 of optimal (in the worst-case).

1) Find a Minimal Spanning Tree (MST).
2) Do a DFS of the MST.

For details, refer to the chapter on *Complexity Classes*.

**Problem-42** Discuss Bipartite matchings?

**Solution:** In Bipartite graphs, we divide the graphs in to two disjoint sets, and each edge connects a vertex from one set to a vertex in another subset (as shown in figure).

**Definition:** A simple graph $G = (V, E)$ is called a *bipartite graph* if its vertices can be divided into two disjoint sets $V = V_1 \cup V_2$, such that every edge has the form $e = (a, b)$ where $a \in V_1$ and $b \in V_2$. One important condition is that no vertices both in $V_1$ or both in $V_2$ are connected.

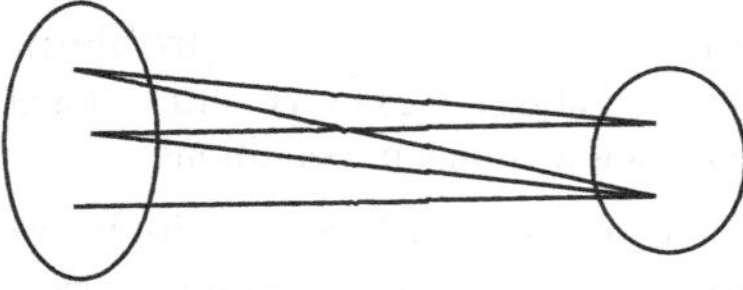

**Properties of Bipartite Graphs**

- A graph is called bipartite if and only if the given graph does not have an odd length cycle.
- A *complete bipartite graph* $K_{m.n}$ is a bipartite graph that has each vertex from one set adjacent to each vertex from another set.

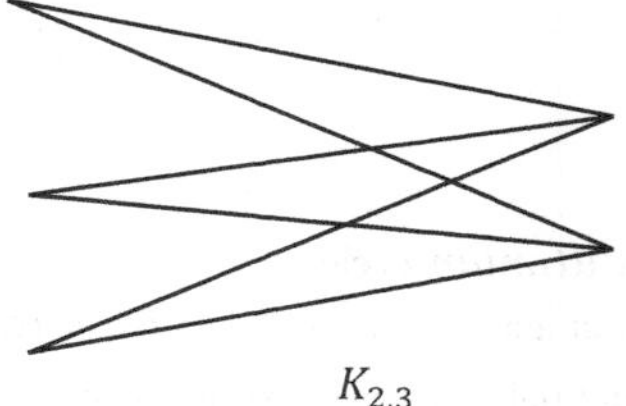

$K_{2,3}$

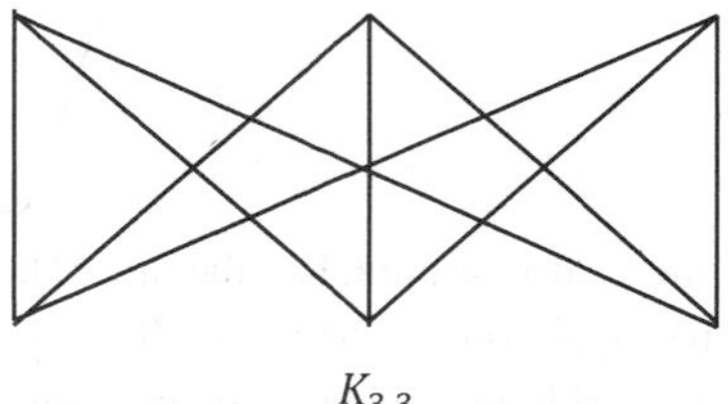

$K_{3,3}$

- A subset of edges $M \subset E$ is a *matching* if no two edges have a common vertex. As an example, matching sets of edges are represented with dotted lines. A matching $M$ is called *maximum* if it has the largest number of possible edges. In the graphs, the dotted edges represent the alternative matching for the given graph.

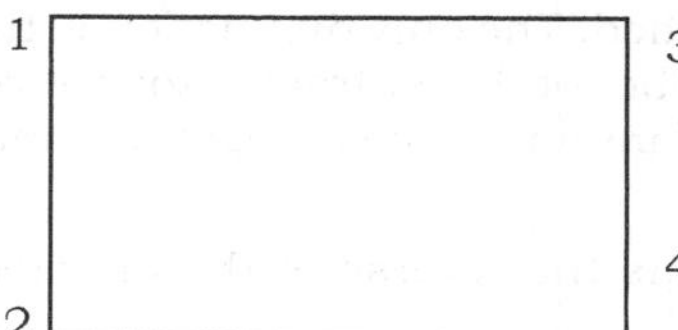


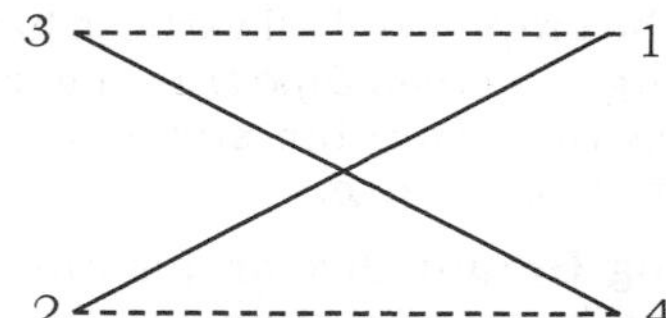


- A matching $M$ is *perfect* if it matches all vertices. We must have $V_1 = V_2$ in order to have perfect matching.
- An *alternating path* is a path whose edges alternate between matched and unmatched edges. If we find an alternating path, then we can improve the matching. This is because an alternating path consists of matched and unmatched edges. The number of unmatched edges exceeds the number of matched edges by one. Therefore, an alternating path always increases the matching by one.

**The next question is, how do we find a perfect matching?** Based on the above theory and definition, we can find the perfect matching with the following approximation algorithm.

**Matching Algorithm (Hungarian algorithm)**

1) Start at unmatched vertex.
2) Find an alternating path.
3) If it exists, change matching edges to no matching edges and conversely. If it does not exist, choose another unmatched vertex.
4) If the number of edges equals $V/2$, stop. Otherwise proceed to step 1 and repeat, as long as all vertices have been examined without finding any alternating paths.

**Time Complexity of the Matching Algorithm:** The number of iterations is in $O(V)$. The complexity of finding an alternating path using BFS is $O(E)$. Therefore, the total time complexity is $O(V \times E)$.

**Problem-43** Marriage and Personnel Problem?

**Marriage Problem:** There are $X$ men and $Y$ women who desire to get married. Participants indicate who among the opposite sex could be a potential spouse for them. Every woman can be married to at most one man, and every man to at most one woman. How can we marry everybody to someone they like?

**Personnel Problem:** You are the boss of a company. The company has $M$ workers and $N$ jobs. Each worker is qualified to do some jobs, but not others. How will you assign jobs to each worker?

**Solution:** These two cases are just another way of asking about bipartite graphs, and the solution is the same as that of Problem-42.

**Problem-44** How many edges will be there in complete bipartite graph $K_{m,n}$?

**Solution**: $m \times n$. This is because each vertex in the first set can connect all vertices in the second set.

**Problem-45** A graph is called regular graph if it has no loops and multiple edges where each vertex has the same number of neighbors; i.e. every vertex has the same degree. Now, if $K_{m,n}$ is a regular graph what is the relation between $m$ and $n$?

**Solution:** Since each vertex should have the same degree, the relation should be $m = n$.

**Problem-46** What is the maximum number of edges in the maximum matching of a bipartite graph with $n$ vertices?

**Solution:** From the definition of *matching*, we should not have edges with common vertices. So in a bipartite graph, each vertex can connect to only one vertex. Since we divide the total vertices into two sets, we can get the maximum number of edges if we divide them in half. Finally the answer is $\frac{n}{2}$.

**Problem-47** Discuss Planar Graphs. *Planar graph*: Is it possible to draw the edges of a graph in such a way that the edges do not cross?

**Solution:** A graph G is said to be planar if it can be drawn in the plane in such a way that no two edges meet each other except at a vertex to which they are incident. Any such drawing is called a plane drawing of G. As an example consider the below graph:

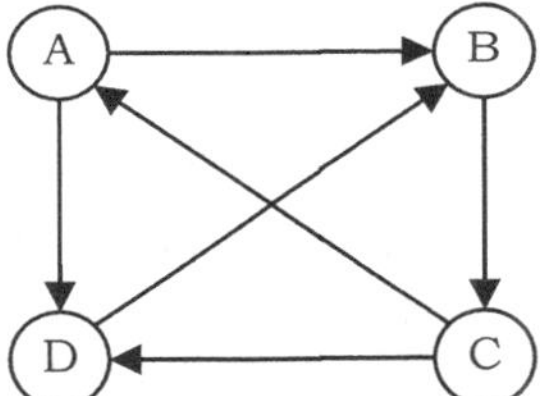


This graph we can easily convert to a planar graph as below (without any crossed edges).

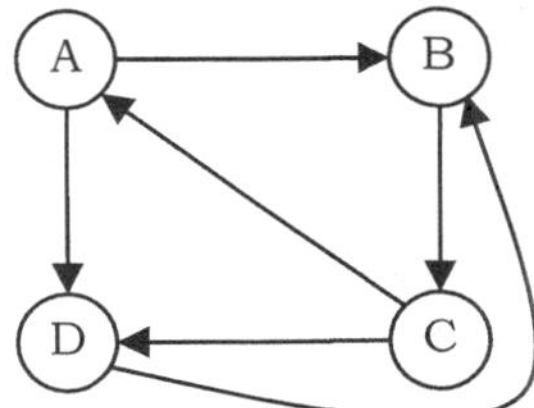


How do we decide whether a given graph is planar or not?

The solution to this problem is not simple, but researchers have found some interesting properties that we can use to decide whether the given graph is a planar graph or not.

**Properties of Planar Graphs**

- If a graph $G$ is a connected planar simple graph with $V$ vertices, where $V = 3$ and $E$ edges, then $E = 3V - 6$.
- $K_5$ is non-planar. [$K_5$ stands for complete graph with 5 vertices].
- If a graph $G$ is a connected planar simple graph with $V$ vertices and $E$ edges, and no triangles, then $E = 2V - 4$.
- $K_{3,3}$ is non-planar. [$K_{3,3}$ stands for bipartite graph with 3 vertices on one side and the other 3 vertices on the other side. $K_{3,3}$ contains 6 vertices].
- If a graph $G$ is a connected planar simple graph, then $G$ contains at least one vertex of 5 degrees or less.
- A graph is planar if and only if it does not contain a subgraph that has $K_5$ and $K_{3,3}$ as a contraction.
- If a graph $G$ contains a nonplanar graph as a subgraph, then $G$ is non-planar.

- If a graph $G$ is a planar graph, then every subgraph of $G$ is planar.
- For any connected planar graph $G = (V, E)$, the following formula should hold: $V + F - E = 2$, where $F$ stands for the number of faces.
- For any planar graph $G = (V, E)$ with $K$ components, the following formula holds: $V + F - E = 1 + K$.

In order to test the planarity of a given graph, we use these properties and decide whether it is a planar graph or not. Note that all the above properties are only the necessary conditions but not sufficient.

**Problem-48** How many faces does $K_{2,3}$ have?

**Solution:** From the above discussion, we know that $V + F - E = 2$, and from an earlier problem we know that $E = m \times n = 2 \times 3 = 6$ and $V = m + n = 5$. $\therefore\ 5 + F - 6 = 2 \Rightarrow F = 3$.

**Problem-49** Discuss Graph Coloring.

**Solution:** A $k$ –coloring of a graph $G$ is an assignment of one color to each vertex of $G$ such that no more than k colors are used and no two adjacent vertices receive the same color. A graph is called $k$ –colorable if and only if it has a $k$ –coloring.

**Applications of Graph Coloring:** The graph coloring problem has many applications such as scheduling, register allocation in compilers, frequency assignment in mobile radios, etc.

**Clique:** A *clique* in a graph $G$ is the maximum complete subgraph and is denoted by $\omega(G)$.

**Chromatic number:** The chromatic number of a graph $G$ is the smallest number k such that $G$ is $k$ –colorable, and it is denoted by $X(G)$.

The lower bound for $X(G)$ is $\omega(G)$, and that means $\omega(G) \le X(G)$.

**Properties of Chromatic number:** Let G be a graph with n vertices and G′ is its complement. Then,

- $X(G) \le \Delta(G) + 1$, where $\Delta$ (G) is the maximum degree of G.
- $X(G)\,\omega(G') \ge n$
- $X(G) + \omega(G') \le n + 1$
- $X(G) + (G') \le n + 1$

**K-colorability problem:** Given a graph $G = (V, E)$ and a positive integer $k \le V$. Check whether $G$ is $k$ –colorable?

This problem is NP-complete and will be discussed in detail in the chapter on *Complexity Classes*.

**Graph coloring algorithm:** As discussed earlier, this problem is *NP*-Complete. So we do not have a polynomial time algorithm to determine $X(G)$. Let us consider the following approximation (no efficient) algorithm.

- Consider a graph G with two non-adjacent vertices $a$ and $b$. The connection $G_1$ is obtained by joining the two non-adjacent vertices $a$ and $b$ with an edge. The contraction $G_2$ is obtained by shrinking $\{a, b\}$ into a single vertex $c(a, b)$ and by joining it to each neighbor in G of vertex $a$ and of vertex $b$ (and eliminating multiple edges).
- A coloring of $G$ in which $a$ and $b$ have the same color yields a coloring of $G_1$. A coloring of $G$ in which $a$ and $b$ have different colors yields a coloring of $G_2$.
- Repeat the operations of connection and contraction in each graph generated, until the resulting graphs are all cliques. If the smallest resulting clique is a $K$ –clique, then $(G) = \text{K}$.

**Important notes on Graph Coloring**

- Any simple planar graph $G$ can be colored with 6 colors.
- Every simple planar graph can be colored with less than or equal to 5 colors.

**Problem-50** What is the *four coloring* problem?

**Solution:** A graph can be constructed from any map. The regions of the map are represented by the vertices of the graph, and two vertices are joined by an edge if the regions corresponding to the vertices are adjacent. The resulting graph is planar. That means it can be drawn in the plane without any edges crossing.

The *Four Color Problem* is whether the vertices of a planar graph can be colored with at most four colors so that no two adjacent vertices use the same color.

**History:** The *Four Color Problem* was first given by *Francis Guthrie*. He was a student at *University College London* where he studied under *Augusts De Morgan*. After graduating from London he studied law, but some years later his brother Frederick Guthrie had become a student of *De Morgan*. One day Francis asked his brother to discuss this problem with *De Morgan*.

**Problem-51** When an adjacency-matrix representation is used, most graph algorithms require time $O(V^2)$. Show that determining whether a directed graph, represented in an adjacency-matrix that contains a sink can be done in time $O(V)$. A sink is a vertex with in-degree $|V| - 1$ and out-degree 0 (Only one can exist in a graph).

**Solution:** A vertex i is a sink if and only if $M[i,j] = 0$ for all j and $M[j,i] = 1$ for all $j \neq i$. For any pair of vertices $i$ and $j$:

$$M[i,j] = 1 \rightarrow \text{vertex i can't be a sink}$$
$$M[i,j] = 0 \rightarrow \text{vertex j can't be a sink}$$

**Algorithm:**

- Start at $i = 1, j = 1$
- If $M[i,j] = 0 \rightarrow i$ wins, $j++$
- If $M[i,j] = 1 \rightarrow j$ wins, $i++$
- Proceed with this process until $j = n$ or $i = n + 1$
- If $i == n + 1$ , the graph does not contain a sink
- Otherwise, check row $i$ – it should be all zeros; and check column $i$ – it should be all but $M[i,i]$ ones; – if so, $i$ is a sink.

Time Complexity: $O(V)$, because at most $2|V|$ cells in the matrix are examined.

**Problem-52** What is the worst – case memory usage of DFS?

**Solution:** It occurs when the O(|V|), which happens if the graph is actually a list. So the algorithm is memory efficient on graphs with small diameter.

**Problem-53** Does DFS find the shortest path from start node to some node w ?

**Solution: No.** In DFS it is not compulsory to select the smallest weight edge.

**Problem-54** True or False: Dijkstra's algorithm does not compute the "all pairs" shortest paths in a directed graph with positive edge weights because, running the algorithm a single time, starting from some single vertex $x$, it will compute only the min distance from $x$ to $y$ for all nodes $y$ in the graph.

**Solution**: True.

**Problem-55** True or False: Prim's and Kruskal's algorithms may compute different minimum spanning trees when run on the same graph.

**Solution**: True.

CHAPTER

# 10

# SORTING

## 10.1 What is Sorting?

*Sorting* is an algorithm that arranges the elements of a list in a certain order [either *ascending* or *descending*]. The output is a permutation or reordering of the input.

## 10.2 Why is Sorting Necessary?

Sorting is one of the important categories of algorithms in computer science and a lot of research has gone into this category. Sorting can significantly reduce the complexity of a problem, and is often used for database algorithms and searches.

## 10.3 Classification of Sorting Algorithms

Sorting algorithms are generally categorized based on the following parameters.

### By Number of Comparisons

In this method, sorting algorithms are classified based on the number of comparisons. For comparison based sorting algorithms, best case behavior is $O(nlogn)$ and worst case behavior is $O(n^2)$. Comparison-based sorting algorithms evaluate the elements of the list by key comparison operation and need at least $O(nlogn)$ comparisons for most inputs.

Later in this chapter we will discuss a few *non − comparison* (*linear*) sorting algorithms like Counting sort, Bucket sort, Radix sort, etc. Linear Sorting algorithms impose few restrictions on the inputs to improve the complexity.

### By Number of Swaps

In this method, sorting algorithms are categorized by the number of *swaps* (also called *inversions*).

### By Memory Usage

Some sorting algorithms are "*in place*" and they need $O(1)$ or $O(logn)$ memory to create auxiliary locations for sorting the data temporarily.

### By Recursion

Sorting algorithms are either recursive [quick sort] or non-recursive [selection sort, and insertion sort], and there are some algorithms which use both (merge sort).

### By Stability

Sorting algorithm is *stable* if for all indices $i$ and $j$ such that the key $A[i]$ equals key $A[j]$, if record $R[i]$ precedes record $R[j]$ in the original file, record $R[i]$ precedes record $R[j]$ in the sorted list. Few sorting algorithms maintain the relative order of elements with equal keys (equivalent elements retain their relative positions even after sorting).

### By Adaptability

With a few sorting algorithms, the complexity changes based on pre-sortedness [quick sort]: pre-sortedness of the input affects the running time. Algorithms that take this into account are known to be adaptive.

## 10.4 Other Classifications

Another method of classifying sorting algorithms is:

- Internal Sort
- External Sort

### Internal Sort

Sort algorithms that use main memory exclusively during the sort are called *internal* sorting algorithms. This kind of algorithm assumes high-speed random access to all memory.

### External Sort

Sorting algorithms that use external memory, such as tape or disk, during the sort come under this category.

## 10.5 Bubble Sort

Bubble sort is the simplest sorting algorithm. Bubble sort, sometimes referred to as sinking sort, is a simple sorting algorithm that repeatedly steps through the list to be sorted, compares each pair of adjacent items and swaps them if they are in the wrong order.

In the bubble sorting, two adjacent elements of a list are first checked and then swapped. In case the adjacent elements are in the incorrect order then the process keeps on repeating until a fully sorted list is obtained. Each pass that goes through the list will place the next largest element value in its proper place. So, in effect, every item bubbles up with an intent of reaching the location wherein it rightfully belongs.

The only significant advantage that bubble sort has over other implementations is that it can detect whether the input list is already sorted or not.

Following table shows the first pass of a bubble sort. The shaded items are being compared to see if they are out of order. If there are $n$ items in the list, then there are $n-1$ pairs of items that need to be compared on the first pass. It is important to note that once the largest value in the list is part of a pair, it will continually be moved along until the pass is complete.

| First pass → | | | | | | | | | Remarks |
|---|---|---|---|---|---|---|---|---|---|
| 10 | 4 | 43 | 5 | 57 | 91 | 45 | 9 | 7 | Swap |
| 4 | 10 | 43 | 5 | 57 | 91 | 45 | 9 | 7 | No swap |
| 4 | 10 | 43 | 5 | 57 | 91 | 45 | 9 | 7 | Swap |
| 4 | 10 | 5 | 43 | 57 | 91 | 45 | 9 | 7 | No swap |
| 4 | 10 | 5 | 43 | 57 | 91 | 45 | 9 | 7 | No swap |
| 4 | 10 | 5 | 43 | 57 | 91 | 45 | 9 | 7 | Swap |
| 4 | 10 | 5 | 43 | 57 | 45 | 91 | 9 | 7 | Swap |
| 4 | 10 | 5 | 43 | 57 | 45 | 9 | 91 | 7 | Swap |
| 4 | 10 | 5 | 43 | 57 | 45 | 9 | 7 | 91 | At the end of first pass, 91 is in correct place |

At the start of the first pass, the largest value is now in place. There are $n-1$ items left to sort, meaning that there will be $n-2$ pairs. Since each pass places the next largest value in place, the total number of passes necessary will be $n-1$. After completing the $n-1$ passes, the smallest item must be in the correct position with no further processing required.

## Implementation

```
void bubbleSort(int data[], int size){
    for(int step=0; step<size-1; ++step){
        for(int i=0; i<size-step-1; ++i){
            // To sort in descending order, change > to <.
            if (data[i]>data[i+1]){
                int temp = data[i];
                data[i] = data[i+1];
                data[i+1]= temp;
            }
        }
    }
}
```

Algorithm takes $O(n^2)$ (even in best case). In the above code, all the comparisons are made even if the array is already sorted at some point. It increases the execution time.

The code can be optimized by introducing an extra variable *swapped*. After every pass, if there is no swapping taking place then, there is no need for performing further loops. Variable *swapped* is false if there is no swapping. Thus, we can prevent further iterations. No more swaps indicate the completion of sorting. If the list is already sorted, we can use this flag to skip the remaining passes.

```
void bubbleSortImproved(int data[], int size) {
    int pass, i, temp, swapped = 1;
    for (pass = size - 1; pass >= 0 && swapped; pass--) {
        swapped = 0;
        for (i = 0; i <= pass - 1 ; i++) {
            if(data[i] > data[i+1]) {
                // swap elements
                temp = data[i];
                data[i] = data[i+1];
                data[i+1] =  temp;
                swapped = 1;
            }
        }
    }
}
```

This modified version improves the best case of bubble sort to $O(n)$.

## Performance

| | |
|---|---|
| Worst case complexity | $O(n^2)$ |
| Best case complexity (Improved version) | $O(n)$ |
| Average case complexity (Basic version) | $O(n^2)$ |
| Worst case space complexity | $O(1)$ auxiliary |

## 10.6 Selection Sort

In selection sort, the smallest element is exchanged with the first element of the unsorted list of elements (the exchanged element takes the place where smallest element is initially placed). Then the second smallest element is exchanged with the second element of the unsorted list of elements and so on until all the elements are sorted.

The selection sort improves on the bubble sort by making only one exchange for every pass through the list. In order to do this, a selection sort looks for the smallest (or largest) value as it makes a pass and, after completing the pass, places it in the proper location. As with a bubble sort, after the first pass, the largest item is in the correct place. After the second pass, the next largest is in place. This process continues and requires $n - 1$ passes to sort $n$ items, since the final item must be in place after the $(n - 1)^{st}$ pass.

Selection sort is an in-place sorting algorithm. Selection sort works well for small files. It is used for sorting the files with very large values and small keys. This is because selection is made based on keys and swaps are made only when required.

Following table shows the entire sorting process. On each pass, the largest remaining item is selected and then placed in its proper location. The first pass places 91, the second pass places 57, the third places 45, and so on.

| → | | | | | | | | | Remarks: Select largest in each pass |
|---|---|---|---|---|---|---|---|---|---|
| 10 | 4 | 43 | 5 | 57 | 91 | 45 | 9 | 7 | Swap 91 and 7 |
| 10 | 4 | 43 | 5 | 57 | 7 | 45 | 9 | 91 | Swap 57 and 9 |
| 10 | 4 | 43 | 5 | 9 | 7 | 45 | 57 | 91 | 45 is the next largest, skip |
| 10 | 4 | 43 | 5 | 9 | 7 | 45 | 57 | 91 | Swap 43 and 7 |
| 10 | 4 | 7 | 5 | 9 | 43 | 45 | 57 | 91 | Swap 10 amd 9 |
| 9 | 4 | 7 | 5 | 10 | 43 | 45 | 57 | 91 | Swap 9 amd 5 |
| 5 | 4 | 7 | 9 | 10 | 43 | 45 | 57 | 91 | 7 is the next largest, skip |
| 5 | 4 | 7 | 9 | 10 | 43 | 45 | 57 | 91 | Swap 5 amd 4 |
| 4 | 5 | 7 | 9 | 10 | 43 | 45 | 57 | 91 | List is ordered |

Alternatively, on each pass, we can select the smallest remaining item and then place in its proper location.

| → | | | | | | | | | Remarks: Select smallest in each pass |
|---|---|---|---|---|---|---|---|---|---|
| 10 | 4 | 43 | 5 | 57 | 91 | 45 | 9 | 7 | Swap 10 and 4 |
| 4 | 10 | 43 | 5 | 57 | 7 | 45 | 9 | 91 | Swap 10 and 5 |
| 4 | 5 | 43 | 10 | 57 | 7 | 45 | 9 | 91 | Swap 43 and 7 |

| 4 | 5 | 7 | 10 | 57 | 43 | 45 | 9 | 91 | Swap 10 and 9 |
|---|---|---|---|---|---|---|---|---|---|
| 4 | 5 | 7 | 9 | 57 | 43 | 45 | 10 | 91 | Swap 57 amd 10 |
| 4 | 5 | 7 | 9 | 10 | 43 | 45 | 57 | 91 | 43 is the next smallest, skip |
| 5 | 4 | 7 | 9 | 10 | 43 | 45 | 57 | 91 | 45 is the next smallest, skip |
| 5 | 4 | 7 | 9 | 10 | 43 | 45 | 57 | 91 | 57 is the next smallest, skip |
| 4 | 5 | 7 | 9 | 10 | 43 | 45 | 57 | 91 | List is ordered |

## Advantages

- Easy to implement
- In-place sort (requires no additional storage space)

## Disadvantages

- Doesn't scale well: $O(n^2)$

## Algorithm

1. Find the minimum value in the list
2. Swap it with the value in the current position
3. Repeat this process for all the elements until the entire array is sorted

This algorithm is called *selection sort* since it repeatedly *selects* the smallest element.

## Implementation

```
void selectionSort(int data[], int size) {
    int i, j, min, temp;
    for (i = 0; i < size - 1; i++) {
        min = i;
        for (j = i+1; j < size; j++) {
            if(data [j] < data [min])
                min = j;
        }
        temp = data[min]; // Swap the elements
        data[min] = data[i];
        data[i] = temp;
    }
}
```

## Performance

| | |
|---|---|
| Worst case complexity | $O(n^2)$ |
| Best case complexity (Improved version) | $O(n^2)$ |
| Average case complexity (Basic version) | $O(n^2)$ |
| Worst case space complexity | O(1) auxiliary |

# 10.7 Insertion Sort

Insertion sort algorithm picks elements one by one and places it to the right position where it belongs in the sorted list of elements. Insertion sort is a simple and efficient comparison sort. In this algorithm, each iteration removes an element from the input list and inserts it into the sorted sublist. The choice of the element being removed from the input list is random and this process is repeated until all input elements have gone through.

It always maintains a sorted sublist in the lower positions of the list. Each new item is then "inserted" back into the previous sublist such that the sorted sublist is one item larger.

We begin by assuming that a list with one item (position 0) is already sorted. On each pass, one for each item 1 through $n - 1$, the current item is checked against those in the already sorted sublist. As we look back into the already sorted sublist, we shift those items that are greater to the right. When we reach a smaller item or the end of the sublist, the current item can be inserted.

## Advantages

- Easy to implement
- Efficient for small data
- Adaptive: If the input list is presorted [may not be completely] then insertions sort takes $O(n + d)$, where $d$ is the number of inversions

- Practically more efficient than selection and bubble sorts, even though all of them have $O(n^2)$ worst case complexity
- Stable: Maintains relative order of input data if the keys are same
- In-place: It requires only a constant amount O(1) of additional memory space
- Online: Insertion sort can sort the list as it receives it

## Algorithm

Every repetition of insertion sort removes an element from the input list, and inserts it into the correct position in the already-sorted list until no input elements remain. Sorting is typically done in-place. The resulting array after $k$ iterations has the property where the first $k + 1$ entries are sorted.

| Sorted partial | | | Unordered |
|---|---|---|---|
| result $\leq x$ | $> x$ | $x$ | elements... |

becomes

| Sorted partial | | | Unordered |
|---|---|---|---|
| result $\leq x$ | $x$ | $> x$ | elements... |

Each element greater than $x$ is copied to the right as it is compared against $x$.

## Implementation

```
void insertionSort(int data[], int size) {
   int i, j, key;
   for (i = 1; i <= size - 1; i++) {
      key = data[i];
      j = i;
      while (data[j-1] > key && j >= 1) {
         data[j] = data[j-1];
         j--;
      }
      data[j] = key;
   }
}
```

## Example

Following table shows the sixth pass in detail. At this point in the algorithm, a sorted sublist of six elements consisting of 4, 5, 10, 43, 57 and 91 exists. We want to insert 45 back into the already sorted items. The first comparison against 91 causes 91 to be shifted to the right. 57 is also shifted. When the item 43 is encountered, the shifting process stops and 45 is placed in the open position. Now we have a sorted sublist of seven elements.

| ⟶ | | | | | | | | | Remarks: Sixth pass |
|---|---|---|---|---|---|---|---|---|---|
| 0 | 1 | 2 | 3 | 4 | 5 | 6 | 7 | 8 | Hold the current element A[6] in a variable |
| 4 | 5 | 10 | 43 | 57 | 91 | 45 | 9 | 7 | Need to insert 45 into the sorted list, copy 91 to A[6] as 91> 45 |
| 4 | 5 | 10 | 43 | 57 | 91 | 91 | 9 | 7 | copy 57 to A[5] as 57> 45 |
| 4 | 5 | 10 | 43 | 57 | 57 | 91 | 9 | 7 | 45 is the next largest, skip |
| 4 | 5 | 10 | 43 | 45 | 57 | 91 | 9 | 7 | 45>43, so we can insert 45 at A[4], and sublist is sorted |

## Analysis

The implementation of insertionSort shows that there are again $n - 1$ passes to sort $n$ items. The iteration starts at position 1 and moves through position $n - 1$, as these are the items that need to be inserted back into the sorted sublists. Notice that this is not a complete swap as was performed in the previous algorithms.

The maximum number of comparisons for an insertion sort is the sum of the first $n - 1$ integers. Again, this is $O(n^2)$. However, in the best case, only one comparison needs to be done on each pass. This would be the case for an already sorted list.

One note about shifting versus exchanging is also important. In general, a shift operation requires approximately a third of the processing work of an exchange since only one assignment is performed. In benchmark studies, insertion sort will show very good performance.

### Worst case analysis

Worst case occurs when for every $i$ the inner loop has to move all elements $A[1], \ldots, A[i - 1]$ (which happens when $A[i]$ = key is smaller than all of them), that takes $\Theta(i - 1)$ time.

$$T(n) = \Theta(1) + \Theta(2) + \Theta(2) + \ldots\ldots + \Theta(n-1)$$
$$= \Theta(1 + 2 + 3 + \ldots\ldots + n - 1) = \Theta\left(\frac{n(n-1)}{2}\right) \approx \Theta(n^2)$$

**Average case analysis**

For the average case, the inner loop will insert $A[i]$ in the middle of $A[1], \ldots, A[i-1]$. This takes $\Theta\left(\frac{i}{2}\right)$ time.

$$T(n) = \sum_{i=1}^{n} \Theta(i/2) \approx \Theta(n^2)$$

## Performance

If every element is greater than or equal to every element to its left, the running time of insertion sort is $\Theta(n)$. This situation occurs if the array starts out already sorted, and so an already-sorted array is the best case for insertion sort.

| | |
|---|---|
| Worst case complexity | $O(n^2)$ |
| Best case complexity (Improved version) | $O(n)$ |
| Average case complexity (Basic version) | $O(n^2)$ |
| Worst case space complexity | $O(n^2)$ total, $O(1)$ auxiliary |

## Comparisons to Other Sorting Algorithms

Insertion sort is one of the elementary sorting algorithms with $O(n^2)$ worst-case time. Insertion sort is used when the data is nearly sorted (due to its adaptiveness) or when the input size is small (due to its low overhead). For these reasons and due to its stability, insertion sort is used as the recursive base case (when the problem size is small) for higher overhead divide-and-conquer sorting algorithms, such as merge sort or quick sort.

**Notes:**

- Bubble sort takes $\frac{n^2}{2}$ comparisons and $\frac{n^2}{2}$ swaps (inversions) in both average case and in worst case.
- Selection sort takes $\frac{n^2}{2}$ comparisons and $n$ swaps.
- Insertion sort takes $\frac{n^2}{4}$ comparisons and $\frac{n^2}{8}$ swaps in average case and in the worst case they are double.
- Insertion sort is almost linear for partially sorted input.
- Selection sort is best suits for elements with bigger values and small keys.

## 10.8 Shell Sort

*Shell sort* (also called *diminishing increment sort*) was invented by *Donald Shell*. This sorting algorithm is a generalization of insertion sort. Insertion sort works efficiently on input that is already almost sorted. Shell sort is also known as $n$-gap insertion sort. Instead of comparing only the adjacent pair, shell sort makes several passes and uses various gaps between adjacent elements (ending with the gap of 1 or classical insertion sort).

In insertion sort, comparisons are made between the adjacent elements. At most 1 inversion is eliminated for each comparison done with insertion sort. The variation used in shell sort is to avoid comparing adjacent elements until the last step of the algorithm. So, the last step of shell sort is effectively the insertion sort algorithm. It improves insertion sort by allowing the comparison and exchange of elements that are far away. This is the first algorithm which got less than quadratic complexity among comparison sort algorithms.

Shellsort is actually a simple extension for insertion sort. The primary difference is its capability of exchanging elements that are far apart, making it considerably faster for elements to get to where they should be. For example, if the smallest element happens to be at the end of an array, with insertion sort it will require the full array of steps to put this element at the beginning of the array. However, with shell sort, this element can jump more than one step a time and reach the proper destination in fewer exchanges.

The basic idea in shellsort is to exchange every hth element in the array. Now this can be confusing so we'll talk more about this. $h$ determines how far apart element exchange can happen, say for example take $h$ as 13, the first element (index-0) is exchanged with the $14^{th}$ element (index-13) if necessary (of course). The second element with the $15^{th}$ element, and so on. Now if we take $h$ as 1, it is exactly the same as a regular insertion sort.

Shellsort works by starting with big enough (but not larger than the array size) $h$ so as to allow eligible element exchanges that are far apart. Once a sort is complete with a particular $h$, the array can be said as $h$-sorted. The next step is to reduce $h$ by a certain sequence, and again perform another complete $h$-sort. Once $h$ is 1 and $h$-sorted, the array is completely sorted. Notice that the last sequence for $h$ is 1 so the last sort is always an insertion sort, except by this time the array is already well-formed and easier to sort.

Shell sort uses a sequence $h1, h2, \ldots, ht$ called the *increment sequence*. Any increment sequence is fine as long as $h1 = 1$, and some choices are better than others. Shell sort makes multiple passes through the input list and sorts a number of equally sized sets using the insertion sort. Shell sort improves the efficiency of insertion sort by *quickly* shifting values to their destination.

## Implementation

```
void ShellSort(int A[], int array_size) {
    int i, j, h, v;
    for (h = 1; h = array_size/9; h = 3*h+1);
    for ( ; h > 0; h = h/3) {
            for (i = h+1; i = array_size; i += 1) {
                    v = A[i];
                    j = i;
                    while (j > h && A[j-h] > v) {
                            A[j] = A[j-h];
                            j -= h;
                    }
                    A[j] = v;
            }
    }
}
```

Note that when $h == 1$, the algorithm makes a pass over the entire list, comparing adjacent elements, but doing very few element exchanges. For $h == 1$, shell sort works just like insertion sort, except the number of inversions that have to be eliminated is greatly reduced by the previous steps of the algorithm with $h > 1$.

## Analysis

Shell sort is efficient for medium size lists. For bigger lists, the algorithm is not the best choice. It is the fastest of all $O(n^2)$ sorting algorithms.

The disadvantage of Shell sort is that it is a complex algorithm and not nearly as efficient as the merge, heap, and quick sorts. Shell sort is significantly slower than the merge, heap, and quick sorts, but is a relatively simple algorithm, which makes it a good choice for sorting lists of less than 5000 items unless speed is important. It is also a good choice for repetitive sorting of smaller lists.

The best case in Shell sort is when the array is already sorted in the right order. The number of comparisons is less. The running time of Shell sort depends on the choice of increment sequence.

## Performance

| | |
|---|---|
| Worst case complexity depends on gap sequence. Best known: | $O(nlog^2n)$ |
| Best case complexity | $O(n)$ |
| Average case complexity depends on gap sequence | |
| Worst case space complexity | $O(n)$ |

# 10.9 Merge Sort

Merge sort is an example of the divide and conquer strategy. Merge sort first divides the array into equal halves and then combines them in a sorted manner. It is a recursive algorithm that continually splits an array in half. If the array is empty or has one element, it is sorted by definition (the base case). If the array has more than one element, we split the array and recursively invoke a merge sort on both halves. Once the two halves are sorted, the fundamental operation, called a merge, is performed. Merging is the process of taking two smaller sorted arrays and combining them together into a single, sorted, new array.

## Algorithm

Because we're using divide-and-conquer to sort, we need to decide what our subproblems are going to look like. The full problem is to sort an entire array. Let's say that a subproblem is to sort a subarray. In particular, we'll think of a subproblem as sorting the subarray starting at index *left* and going through index *right*. It will be convenient to have a notation for a subarray, so let's say that $A[left..right]$ denotes this subarray of array $A$. In terms of our notation, for an array of $n$ elements, we can say that the original problem is to sort A[0..n-1].

**Algorithm Merge-sort(A):**

- *Divide* by finding the number *mid* of the position midway between *left* and *right*. Do this step the same way we found the midpoint in binary search:

$$mid = low + \frac{(high-low)}{2} \ or \ \frac{low+high}{2}.$$

- *Conquer* by recursively sorting the subarrays in each of the two subproblems created by the divide step. That is, recursively sort the subarray $A[left..mid]$ and recursively sort the subarray $A[mid+1..right]$.
- *Combine* by merging the two sorted subarrays back into the single sorted subarray $A[left..right]$.

We need a base case. The base case is a subarray containing fewer than two elements, that is, when $left \geq right$, since a subarray with no elements or just one element is already sorted. So we'll divide-conquer-combine only when $left < right$.

## Example

To understand merge sort, let us walk through an example:

54 | 26 | 93 | 17 | 77 | 31 | 44 | 55

We know that merge sort first divides the whole array iteratively into equal halves unless the atomic values are achieved. We see here that an array of 8 items is divided into two arrays of size 4.

54 | 26 | 93 | 17    77 | 31 | 44 | 55

This does not change the sequence of appearance of items in the original. Now we divide these two arrays into halves.

54 | 26    93 | 17    77 | 31    44 | 55

We further divide these arrays and we achieve atomic value which can no more be divided.

54    26    93    17    77    31    44    55

Now, we combine them in exactly the same manner as they were broken down.

We first compare the element for each array and then combine them into another array in a sorted manner. We see that 54 and 26 and in the target array of 2 values we put 26 first, followed by 54.

Similarly, we compare 93 and 17 and in the target array of 2 values we put 17 first, followed by 93. On the similar lines, we change the order of 77 and 31 whereas 44 and 55 are placed sequentially.

26 | 54    17 | 93    31 | 77    44 | 55

In the next iteration of the combining phase, we compare lists of two data values, and merge them into an array of found data values placing all in a sorted order.

17 | 26 | 54 | 93    31 | 44 | 55 | 77

After the final merging, the array should look like this:

17 | 26 | 31 | 44 | 54 | 55 | 77 | 93

The overall flow of above discussion can be depicted as:

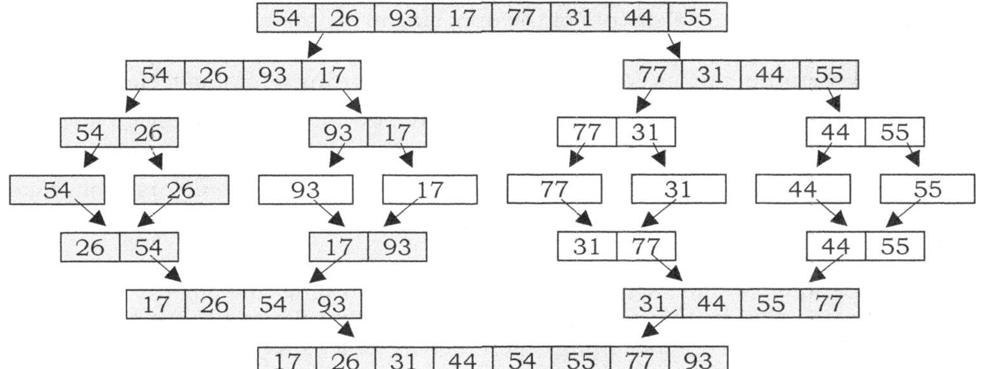

## Implementation

```
void Mergesort(int A[], int temp[], int left, int right) {
    int mid;
    if(right > left) {
            mid = (right + left) / 2;
            Mergesort(A, temp, left, mid);
            Mergesort(A, temp, mid+1, right);
            Merge(A, temp, left, mid+1, right);
    }
}
void Merge(int A[], int temp[], int left, int mid, int right) {
    int i, left_end, size, temp_pos;
    left_end = mid - 1;
    temp_pos = left;
```

```
    size = right - left + 1;
    while ((left <= left_end) && (mid <= right)) {
        if(A[left] <= A[mid]) {
                temp[temp_pos] = A[left];
                temp_pos = temp_pos + 1;
                left = left +1;
        }
        else {
                temp[temp_pos] = A[mid];
                temp_pos = temp_pos + 1;
                mid = mid + 1;
        }
    }
    while (left <= left_end) {
        temp[temp_pos] = A[left];
        left = left + 1;
        temp_pos = temp_pos + 1;
    }
    while (mid <= right) {
        temp[temp_pos] = A[mid];
        mid = mid + 1;
        temp_pos = temp_pos + 1;
    }
    for (i = 0; i <= size; i++) {
        A[right] = temp[right];
        right = right - 1;
    }
}
```

## Analysis

In merge-sort the input array is divided into two parts and these are solved recursively. After solving the subarrays, they are merged by scanning the resultant subarrays. In merge sort, the comparisons occur during the merging step, when two sorted arrays are combined to output a single sorted array. During the merging step, the first available element of each array is compared and the lower value is appended to the output array. When either array runs out of values, the remaining elements of the opposing array are appended to the output array.

How do determine the complexity of merge-sort? We start by thinking about the three parts of divide-and-conquer and how to account for their running times. We assume that we're sorting a total of $n$ elements in the entire array.

The divide step takes constant time, regardless of the subarray size. After all, the divide step just computes the midpoint $mid$ of the indices $left$ and $right$. Recall that in big-Θ notation, we indicate constant time by $\Theta(1)$.

The conquer step, where we recursively sort two subarrays of approximately $\frac{n}{2}$ elements each, takes some amount of time, but we'll account for that time when we consider the subproblems. The combine step merges a total of $n$ elements, taking $\Theta(n)$ time.

If we think about the divide and combine steps together, the $\Theta(1)$ running time for the divide step is a low-order term when compared with the $\Theta(n)$ running time of the combine step. So let's think of the divide and combine steps together as taking $\Theta(n)$ time. To make things more concrete, let's say that the divide and combine steps together take $cn$ time for some constant $c$.

Let us assume $T(n)$ is the complexity of merge-sort with $n$ elements. The recurrence for the merge-sort can be defined as:

$$T(n) = 2T(\frac{n}{2}) + \Theta(n)$$

Using Master theorem, we get, $T(n) = \Theta(nlogn)$.

For merge-sort there is no running time difference between best, average and worse cases as the division of input arrays happen irrespective of the order of the elements. Above merge sort algorithm uses an auxiliary space of $O(n)$ for left and right subarrays together. Merge-sort is a recursive algorithm and each recursive step puts another frame on the run time stack. Sorting 32 items will take one more recursive step than 16 items, and it is in fact the size of the stack that is referred to when the space requirement is said to be $O(logn)$.

| | |
|---|---|
| Worst case complexity | $\Theta(nlogn)$ |
| Best case complexity | $\Theta(nlogn)$ |
| Average case complexity | $\Theta(nlogn)$ |
| Space complexity | $\Theta(logn)$ for runtime stack space and $O(n)$ for the auxiliary space |

## 10.10 Heap Sort

Heapsort is a comparison-based sorting algorithm and is part of the selection sort family. Although somewhat slower in practice on most machines than a good implementation of Quick sort, it has the advantage of a more favorable worst-case $\Theta(nlogn)$ runtime. Heapsort is an in-place algorithm but is not a stable sort.

### Performance

| | |
|---|---|
| Worst case performance | $\Theta(nlogn)$ |
| Best case performance | $\Theta(nlogn)$ |
| Average case performance | $\Theta(nlogn)$ |
| Worst case space complexity | $\Theta(n)$ total, $\Theta(1)$ auxiliary space |

For other details on Heapsort refer to the *Priority Queues* chapter.

## 10.11 Quick Sort

Quick sort is the famous algorithm among comparison-based sorting algorithms. Like merge sort, quick sort uses divide-and-conquer technique, and so it's a recursive algorithm. The way that quick sort uses divide-and-conquer is a little different from how merge sort does. The quick sort uses divide and conquer technique to gain the same advantages as the merge sort, while not using additional storage. As a trade-off, however, it is possible that the list may not be divided into half. When this happens, we will see that the performance is diminished.

It sorts in place and no additional storage is required as well. The slight disadvantage of quick sort is that its worst-case performance is similar to the average performances of the bubble, insertion or selection sorts (i.e., $O(n^2)$).

### Divide and conquer strategy

A quick sort first selects an element from the given list, which is called the *pivot* value. Although there are many different ways to choose the pivot value, we will simply use the *first* item in the list. The role of the pivot value is to assist with splitting the list into two sublists. The actual position where the pivot value belongs in the final sorted list, commonly called the *partition* point, will be used to divide the list for subsequent calls to the quick sort.

All elements in the first sublist are arranged to be smaller than the *pivot*, while all elements in the second sublist are arranged to be larger than the *pivot*. The same partitioning and arranging process is performed repeatedly on the resulting sublists until the whole list of items are sorted.

Let us assume that array $A$ is the list of elements to be sorted, and has the lower and upper bounds *low* and *high* respectively. With this information, we can define the divide and conquer strategy as follows:

*Divide*: The list $A[low ... high]$ is partitioned into two non-empty sublists $A[low ... q]$ and $A[q + 1 ... high]$, such that each element of $A[low ... q]$ is less than or equal to each element of $A[q + 1 ... high]$. The index $q$ is computed as part of partitioning procedure with the first element as *pivot*.

*Conquer*: The two sublists $A[low ... q]$ and $A[q + 1 ... high]$ are sorted by recursive calls to quick sort.

### Algorithm

The recursive algorithm consists of four steps:

1) If there are one or no elements in the list to be sorted, return.
2) Pick an element in the list to serve as the *pivot* point. Usually the first element in the list is used as a *pivot*.
3) Split the list into two parts - one with elements larger than the *pivot* and the other with elements smaller than the *pivot*.
4) Recursively repeat the algorithm for both halves of the original list.

In the above algorithm, the important step is partitioning the list into two sublists. The basic steps to partition a list are:

1. Select the first element as a *pivot* in the list.
2. Start a pointer (the *left* pointer) at the second item in the list.
3. Start a pointer (the *right* pointer) at the last item in the list.
4. While the value at the *left* pointer in the list is lesser than the *pivot* value, move the *left* pointer to the right (add 1). Continue this process until the value at the *left* pointer is greater than or equal to the *pivot* value.
5. While the value at the *right* pointer in the list is greater than the *pivot* value, move the *right* pointer to the left (subtract 1). Continue this process until the value at the *right* pointer is lesser than or equal to the *pivot* value.

6. If the *left* pointer value is greater than or equal to the *right* pointer value, then swap the values at these locations in the list.
7. If the *left* pointer and *right* pointer don't meet, go to step 1.

## Example

Following example shows that 50 will serve as our first pivot value. The partition process will happen next. It will find the ***partition*** point and at the same time move other items to the appropriate side of the list, either lesser than or greater than the ***pivot*** value.

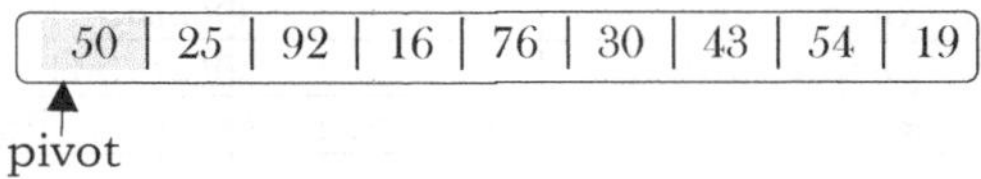

pivot

Partitioning begins by locating two position markers—let's call them ***left*** and ***right***—at the beginning and end of the remaining items in the list (positions 1 and 8 in figure). The goal of the partition process is to move items that are on the wrong side with respect to the pivot value while converging on the split point also. The figure given below shows this process as we locate the position of 50.

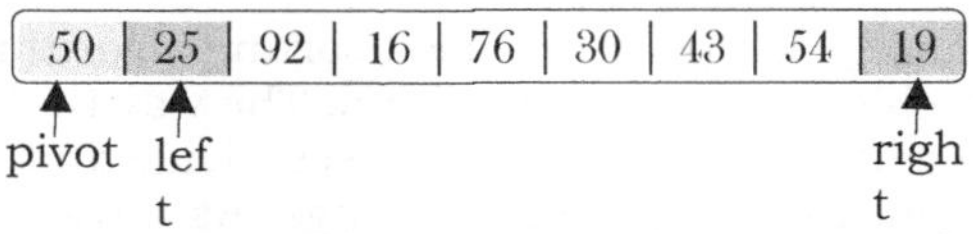

50 | 25 | 92 | 16 | 76 | 30 | 43 | 54 | 19

pivot left right

25 < 50, move ***left*** pointer to right:

50 | 25 | 92 | 16 | 76 | 30 | 43 | 54 | 19

pivot left right

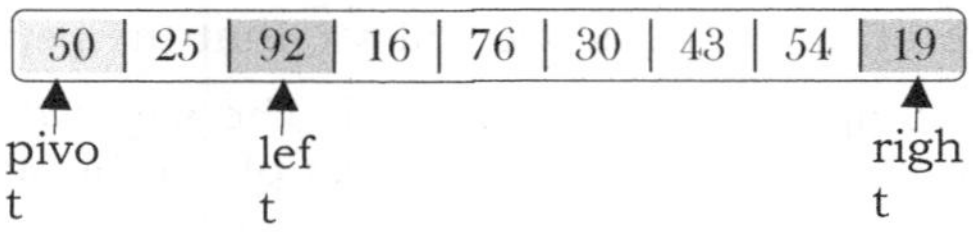

92 > 50, stop from moving ***left*** pointer:

50 | 25 | 92 | 16 | 76 | 30 | 43 | 54 | 19

pivot left right

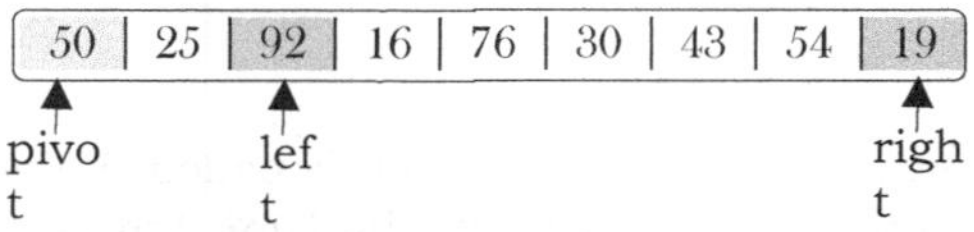

19 < 50, stop from moving ***right*** pointer:

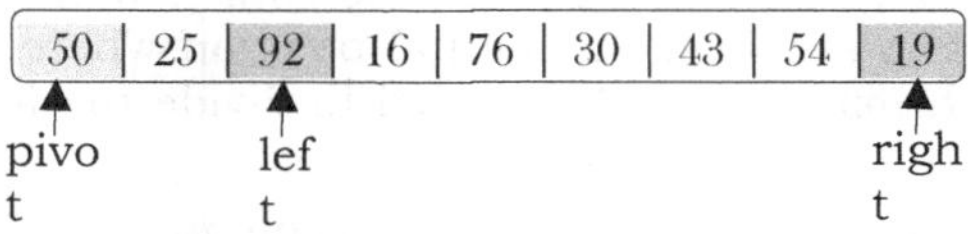

50 | 25 | 92 | 16 | 76 | 30 | 43 | 54 | 19

pivot left right

Swap 19 and 92:

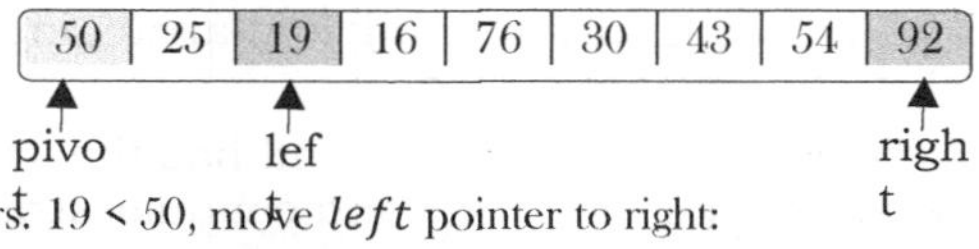

50 | 25 | 19 | 16 | 76 | 30 | 43 | 54 | 92

pivot left right

Now, continue moving left and right pointers. 19 < 50, move ***left*** pointer to right:

50 | 25 | 19 | 16 | 76 | 30 | 43 | 54 | 92

pivot left right

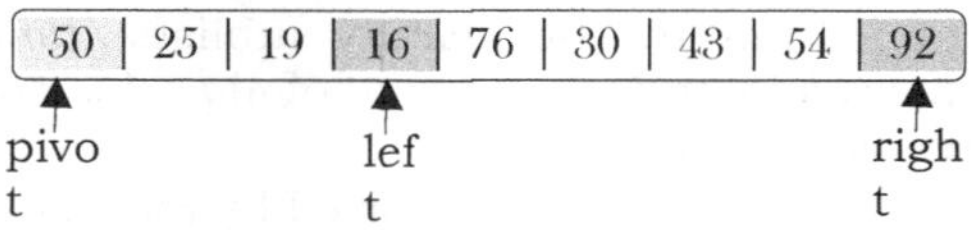

16 < 50, move ***left*** pointer to right:

50 | 25 | 19 | 16 | 76 | 30 | 43 | 54 | 92

pivot left right

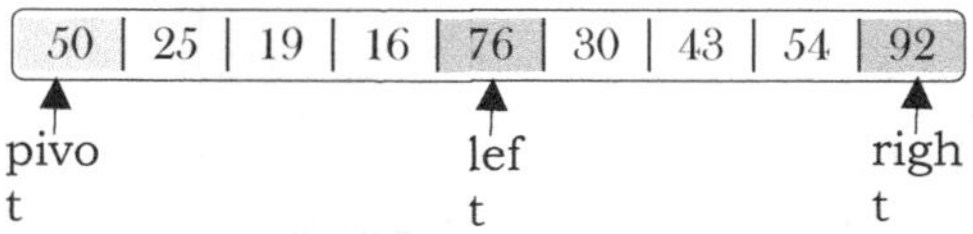

76 > 50, stop from moving ***left*** pointer:

50 | 25 | 19 | 16 | 76 | 30 | 43 | 54 | 92

pivot left right

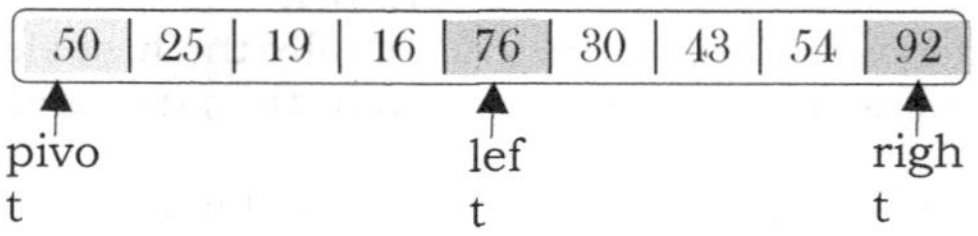

92 > 50, move ***right*** pointer to left:

50 | 25 | 19 | 16 | 76 | 30 | 43 | 54 | 92

pivot left right

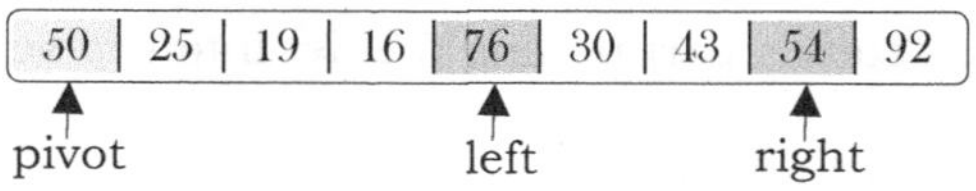

54 > 50, move ***right*** pointer to left:

50 | 25 | 19 | 16 | 76 | 30 | 43 | 54 | 92

pivot left right

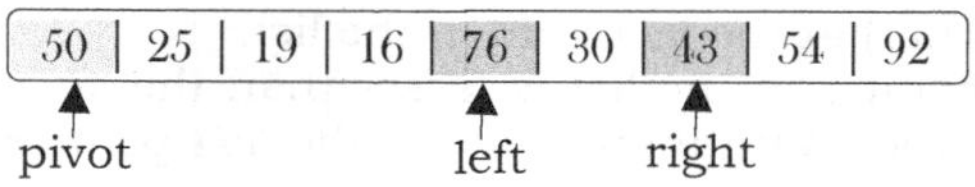

43 < 50, stop from moving ***right*** pointer:

50 | 25 | 19 | 16 | 76 | 30 | 43 | 54 | 92

pivot left right

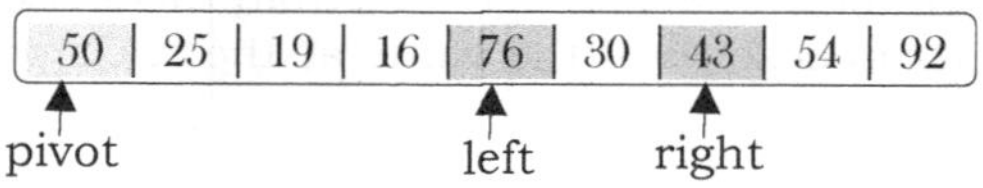

Swap 76 and 43:

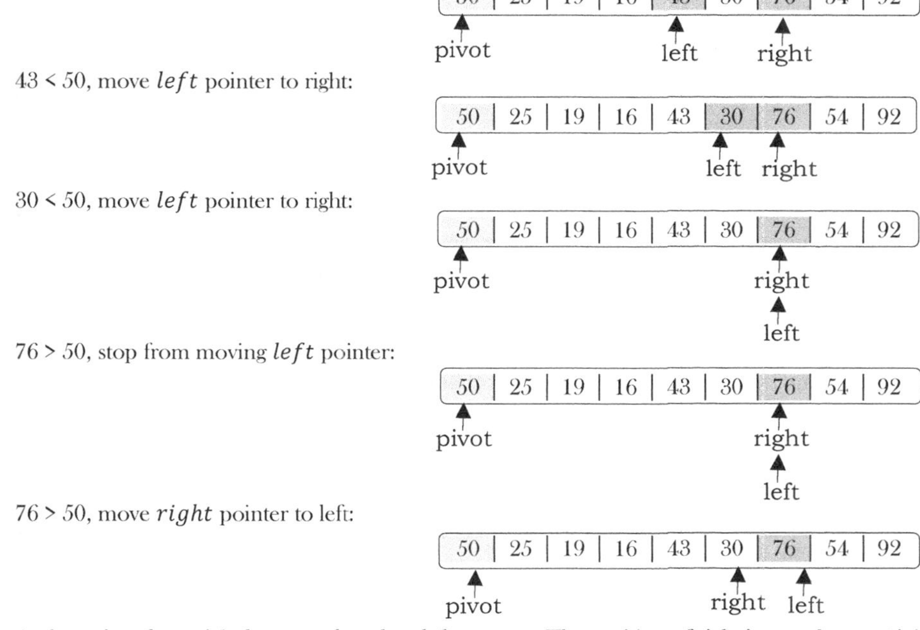


At the point where right becomes less than left, we stop. The position of right is now the *partition* point. The *pivot* value can be exchanged with the contents of the *partition* point. In addition, all the items to the left of the split point are less than the pivot value, and all the items to the right of the split point are greater than the pivot value. Now, we can exchange these two elements 50 and 30. Element 50 is now in correct position.

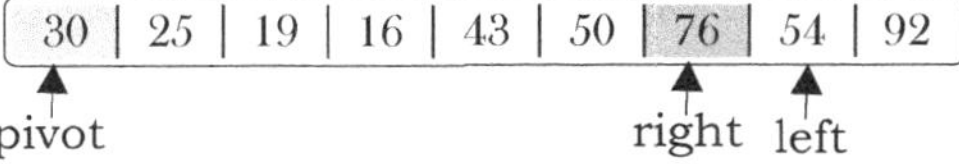


The list can now be divided at the partition point and the quick sort can be invoked recursively on the two halves.

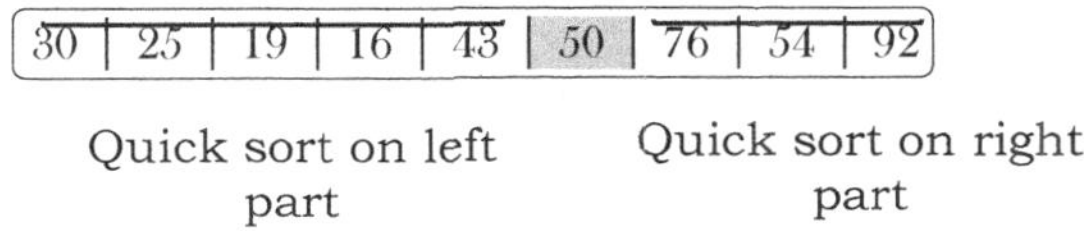


Repeat the process for the two sublists.

## Implementation

```
void quickSort( int A[], int low, int high ) {
    int pivot;
    /* Termination condition! */
    if( high > low ) {
            pivot = partition( A, low, high );
            quickSort ( A, low, pivot-1 );
            quickSort ( A, pivot+1, high );
    }
}
int partition( int A, int low, int high ) {
    int left, right, pivot_item = A[low];
    left = low;
    right = high;
    while ( left < right ) {
            /* Move left while item < pivot */
            while( A[left] <= pivot_item )
                    left++;
            /* Move right while item > pivot */
            while( A[right] > pivot_item )
                    right--;
            if( left < right )
                    swap(A,left,right);
```

```
        }
        /* right is final position for the pivot */
        A[low] = A[right];
        A[right] = pivot_item;
        return right;
}
```

## Analysis

Let us assume that $T(n)$ be the complexity of Quick sort and also assume that all elements are distinct. Recurrence for $T(n)$ depends on two subproblem sizes which depend on partition element. If pivot is $i^{th}$ smallest element then exactly $(i - 1)$ items will be in left part and $(n - i)$ in right part. Let us call it as $i$ −split. Since each element has equal probability of selecting it as pivot the probability of selecting $i^{th}$ element is $\frac{1}{n}$.

**Best Case:** Each partition splits array in halves and gives

$$T(n) = 2T(n/2) + \Theta(n) = \Theta(nlogn), \text{[using } \textit{Divide and Conquer} \text{ master theorem]}$$

**Worst Case:** Each partition gives unbalanced splits and we get

$$T(n) = T(n - 1) + \Theta(n) = \Theta(n^2)[using\ Subtraction\ and\ Conquer\ master\ theorem]$$

The worst-case occurs when the list is already sorted and last element chosen as pivot.

**Average Case:** In the average case of Quick sort, we do not know where the split happens. For this reason, we take all possible values of split locations, add all their complexities and divide with $n$ to get the average case complexity.

$$T(n) = \sum_{i=1}^{n} \frac{1}{n}(runtime\ with\ i - split) + n + 1$$

$$= \frac{1}{n}\sum_{i=1}^{N}\left(T(i-1) + T(n-i)\right) + n + 1$$

//since we are dealing with best case we can assume $T(n - i)$ and $T(i - 1)$ are equal

$$= \frac{2}{n}\sum_{i=1}^{n} T(i-1) + n + 1$$

$$= \frac{2}{n}\sum_{i=0}^{n-1} T(i) + n + 1$$

Multiply both sides by $n$.

$$nT(n) = 2\sum_{i=0}^{n-1} T(i) + n^2 + n$$

Same formula for $n - 1$.

$$(n-1)T(n-1) = 2\sum_{i=0}^{n-2} T(i) + (n-1)^2 + (n-1)$$

Subtract the $n - 1$ formula from $n$.

$$nT(n) - (n-1)T(n-1) = 2\sum_{i=0}^{n-1} T(i) + n^2 + n - (2\sum_{i=0}^{n-2} T(i) + (n-1)^2 + (n-1))$$

$$nT(n) - (n-1)T(n-1) = 2T(n-1) + 2n$$

$$nT(n) = (n+1)T(n-1) + 2n$$

Divide with $n(n + 1)$.

$$\begin{aligned}
\frac{T(n)}{n+1} &= \frac{T(n-1)}{n} + \frac{2}{n+1} \\
&= \frac{T(n-2)}{n-1} + \frac{2}{n} + \frac{2}{n+1} \\
&\ \ \vdots \\
&= O(1) + 2\textstyle\sum_{i=3}^{n}\frac{1}{i} \\
&= O(1) + O\,(2logn) \\
\frac{T(n)}{n+1} &= O\,(logn) \\
T(n) &= O\left((n+1)\,logn\right) = O(nlogn)
\end{aligned}$$

Time Complexity, $T(n) = O(nlogn)$.

### Performance

| | |
|---|---|
| Worst case complexity | $O(n^2)$ |
| Best case complexity | $O(nlogn)$ |
| Average case complexity | $O(nlogn)$ |
| Worst case space complexity | $O(1)$ |

### Randomized Quick sort

In average-case behavior of Quick sort, we assume that all permutations of the input numbers are equally likely. However, we cannot always expect it to hold. We can add randomization to an algorithm in order to reduce the probability of getting worst case in Quick sort. There are two ways of adding randomization in Quick sort: either by randomly placing the input data in the array or by randomly choosing an element in the input data for pivot. The second choice is easier to analyze and implement. The change will only be done at the *partition* algorithm.

In normal Quick sort, *pivot* element was always the leftmost element in the list to be sorted. Instead of always using $A[low]$ as *pivot*, we will use a randomly chosen element from the subarray $A[low..high]$ in the randomized version of Quick sort. It is done by exchanging element $A[low]$ with an element chosen at random from $A[low..high]$. This ensures that the *pivot* element is equally likely to be any of the $high - low + 1$ elements in the subarray.

Since the pivot element is randomly chosen, we can expect the split of the input array to be reasonably well balanced on average. This can help in preventing the worst-case behavior of quick sort which occurs in unbalanced partitioning. Even though the randomized version improves the worst case complexity, its worst case complexity is still $O(n^2)$. One way to improve *Randomized – Quick sort* is to choose the pivot for partitioning more carefully than by picking a random element from the array. One common approach is to choose the pivot as the median of a set of 3 elements randomly selected from the array.

## 10.12 Tree Sort

Tree sort uses a binary search tree. It involves scanning each element of the input and placing it into its proper position in a binary search tree. This has two phases:

- First phase is creating a binary search tree using the given array elements.
- Second phase is traversing the given binary search tree in inorder, thus resulting in a sorted array.

### Performance

The average number of comparisons for this method is $O(nlogn)$. But in worst case, the number of comparisons is reduced by $O(n^2)$, a case which arises when the sort tree is skew tree.

## 10.13 Comparison of Sorting Algorithms

| Name | Average Case | Worst Case | Auxiliary Memory | Is Stable? | Other Notes |
|---|---|---|---|---|---|
| Bubble | $O(n^2)$ | $O(n^2)$ | 1 | yes | Small code |
| Selection | $O(n^2)$ | $O(n^2)$ | 1 | no | Stability depends on the implementation. |
| Insertion | $O(n^2)$ | $O(n^2)$ | 1 | yes | Average case is also $O(n + d)$, where $d$ is the number of inversions. |
| Shell | - | $O(nlog^2n)$ | 1 | no | |
| Merge sort | $O(nlogn)$ | $O(nlogn)$ | depends | yes | |
| Heap sort | $O(nlogn)$ | $O(nlogn)$ | 1 | no | |
| Quick sort | $O(nlogn)$ | $O(n^2)$ | $O(logn)$ | depends | Can be implemented as a stable sort depending on how the pivot is handled. |
| Tree sort | $O(nlogn)$ | $O(n^2)$ | $O(n)$ | depends | Can be implemented as a stable sort. |

**Note:** $n$ denotes the number of elements in the input.

## 10.14 Linear Sorting Algorithms

In earlier sections, we have seen many examples of comparison-based sorting algorithms. Among them, the best comparison-based sorting has the complexity $O(nlogn)$. In this section, we will discuss other types of algorithms: Linear Sorting Algorithms. To improve the time complexity of sorting these algorithms, we make some assumptions about the input. A few examples of Linear Sorting Algorithms are:

- Counting Sort
- Bucket Sort
- Radix Sort

## 10.15 Counting Sort

Counting sort is not a comparison sort algorithm and gives $O(n)$ complexity for sorting. To achieve $O(n)$ complexity, *counting* sort assumes that each of the elements is an integer in the range 1 to $K$, for some integer $K$. When $K = O(n)$, the *counting* sort runs in $O(n)$ time. The basic idea of Counting sort is to determine, for each input element $X$, the number of elements less than $X$. This information can be used to place it directly into its correct position. For example, if 10 elements are less than $X$, then $X$ belongs to position 11 in the output.

In the code below, $A[0..n-1]$ is the input array with length $n$. In Counting sort we need two more arrays: let us assume array $B[0..n-1]$ contains the sorted output and the array $C[0..K-1]$ provides temporary storage.

```
void countingSort (int A[], int n, int B[], int K) {
    int C[K], i, j;
    //Complexity: O(K)
    for (i =0 ; i<K; i++)
        C[i] = 0;
    //Complexity: O(n)
    for (j =0 ; j<n; j++)
        C[A[j]] = C[A[j]] + 1;
    //C[i] now contains the number of elements equal to i
    //Complexity: O(K)
    for (i =1 ; i<K; i++)
        C[i] = C[i] + C[i-1];

    // C[i] now contains the number of elements ≤ i
    //Complexity: O(n)
    for (j = n-1; j>=0; j--) {
        B[C[A[j]]] = A[j];
        C[A[j]] = C[A[j]] - 1;
    }
}
```

Total Complexity: $O(K) + O(n) + O(K) + O(n) = O(n)$ if $K = O(n)$. Space Complexity: $O(n)$ if $K = O(n)$.

**Note**: Counting works well if $K = O(n)$. Otherwise, the complexity will be greater.

## 10.16 Bucket Sort (or Bin Sort)

Like *Counting* sort, *Bucket* sort also imposes restrictions on the input to improve the performance. In other words, Bucket sort works well if the input is drawn from fixed set. *Bucket* sort is the generalization of *Counting* Sort. For example, assume that all the input elements from $\{0, 1, \ldots, K-1\}$, i.e., the set of integers in the interval $[0, K-1]$. That means, $K$ is the number of distant elements in the input. *Bucket* sort uses $K$ counters. The $i^{th}$ counter keeps track of the number of occurrences of the $i^{th}$ element. Bucket sort with two buckets is effectively a version of Quick sort with two buckets.

For bucket sort, the hash function that is used to partition the elements need to be very good and must produce ordered hash: if i < k then hash(i) < hash(k). Second, the elements to be sorted must be uniformly distributed.

The aforementioned aside, bucket sort is actually very good considering that counting sort is reasonably speaking its upper bound. And counting sort is very fast. The particular distinction for bucket sort is that it uses a hash function to partition the keys of the input array, so that multiple keys may hash to the same bucket. Hence each bucket must effectively be a growable list; similar to radix sort.

In the below code Insertionsort is used to sort each bucket. This is to inculcate that the bucket sort algorithm does not specify which sorting technique to use on the buckets. A programmer may choose to continuously use bucket sort on each bucket until the collection is sorted (in the manner of the radix sort program below). Whichever sorting method is used on the , bucket sort still tends toward $O(n)$.

```
#define BUCKETS 10
void bucketSort(int A[], int array_size) {
  int i, j, k;
  int buckets[BUCKETS];
  for(j =0; j < BUCKETS; j++)
          buckets[j] = 0;
  for(i =0; i < array_size; i++)
          ++ buckets[A[i]];
  for(i =0, j=0; j < BUCKETS; j++)
          for(k = buckets[j];k > 0; --k)
```

```
            A[i++] = j;
    }
```

Time Complexity: $O(n)$. Space Complexity: $O(n)$.

## 10.17 Radix Sort

Similar to *Counting* sort and *Bucket* sort, this sorting algorithm also assumes some kind of information about the input elements. Suppose that the input values to be sorted are from base $d$. That means all numbers are $d$-digit numbers.

In Radix sort, first sort the elements based on the last digit [the least significant digit]. These results are again sorted by second digit [the next to least significant digit]. Continue this process for all digits until we reach the most significant digits. Use some stable sort to sort them by last digit. Then stable sort them by the second least significant digit, then by the third, etc. If we use Counting sort as the stable sort, the total time is $O(nd) \approx O(n)$.

**Algorithm**:

1) Take the least significant digit of each element.
2) Sort the list of elements based on that digit, but keep the order of elements with the same digit (this is the definition of a stable sort).
3) Repeat the sort with each more significant digit.

The speed of Radix sort depends on the inner basic operations. If the operations are not efficient enough, Radix sort can be slower than other algorithms such as Quick sort and Merge sort. These operations include the insert and delete functions of the sub-lists and the process of isolating the digit we want. If the numbers are not of equal length then a test is needed to check for additional digits that need sorting. This can be one of the slowest parts of Radix sort and also one of the hardest to make efficient.

Since Radix sort depends on the digits or letters, it is less flexible than other sorts. For every different type of data, Radix sort needs to be rewritten, and if the sorting order changes, the sort needs to be rewritten again. In short, Radix sort takes more time to write, and it is very difficult to write a general purpose Radix sort that can handle all kinds of data.

For many programs that need a fast sort, Radix sort is a good choice. Still, there are faster sorts, which is one reason why Radix sort is not used as much as some other sorts.

Time Complexity: $O(nd) \approx O(n)$, if $d$ is small.

## 10.18 Topological Sort

Refer to *Graph Algorithms* Chapter.

## 10.19 External Sorting

External sorting is a generic term for a class of sorting algorithms that can handle massive amounts of data. These external sorting algorithms are useful when the files are too big and cannot fit into main memory.

As with internal sorting algorithms, there are a number of algorithms for external sorting. One such algorithm is External Mergesort. In practice, these external sorting algorithms are being supplemented by internal sorts.

### Simple External Mergesort

A number of records from each tape are read into main memory, sorted using an internal sort, and then output to the tape. For the sake of clarity, let us assume that 900 megabytes of data needs to be sorted using only 100 megabytes of RAM.

1) Read 100MB of the data into main memory and sort by some conventional method (let us say Quick sort).
2) Write the sorted data to disk.
3) Repeat steps 1 and 2 until all of the data is sorted in chunks of 100MB. Now we need to merge them into one single sorted output file.
4) Read the first 10MB of each sorted chunk (call them input buffers) in main memory (90MB total) and allocate the remaining 10MB for output buffer.
5) Perform a 9-way Mergesort and store the result in the output buffer. If the output buffer is full, write it to the final sorted file. If any of the 9 input buffers gets empty, fill it with the next 10MB of its associated 100MB sorted chunk; or if there is no more data in the sorted chunk, mark it as exhausted and do not use it for merging.

The above algorithm can be generalized by assuming that the amount of data to be sorted exceeds the available memory by a factor of $K$. Then, $K$ chunks of data need to be sorted and a $K$ -way merge has to be completed.

If $X$ is the amount of main memory available, there will be $K$ input buffers and 1 output buffer of size $X/(K+1)$ each. Depending on various factors (how fast is the hard drive?) better performance can be achieved if the output buffer is made larger (for example, twice as large as one input buffer).

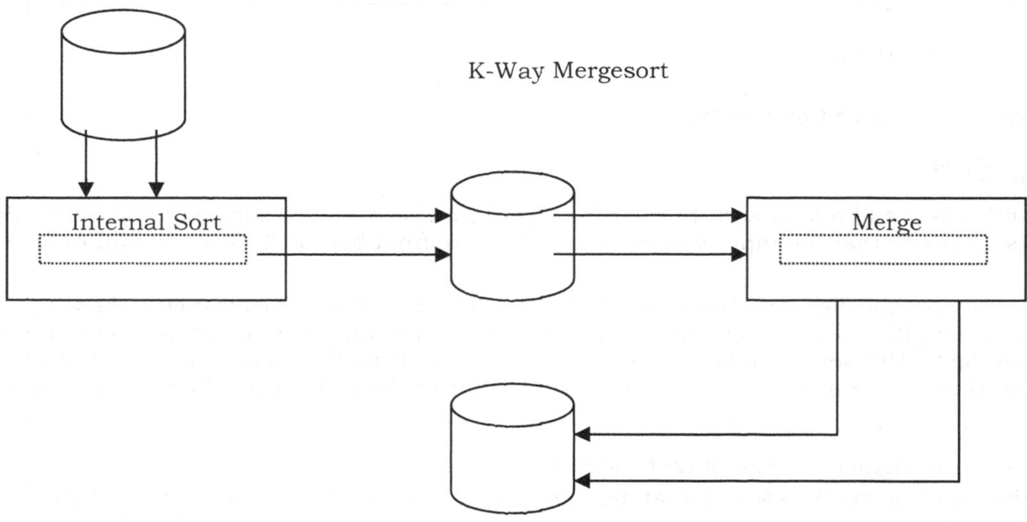


Complexity of the 2-way External Merge sort: In each pass we read + write each page in file. Let us assume that there are $n$ pages in file. That means we need $\lceil logn \rceil + 1$ number of passes. The total cost is $2n(\lceil logn \rceil + 1)$.

## 10.20 Sorting: Problems & Solutions

**Problem-1** Given an array $A[0 \ldots n-1]$ of $n$ numbers containing the repetition of some number. Give an algorithm for checking whether there are repeated elements or not. Assume that we are not allowed to use additional space (i.e., we can use a few temporary variables, O(1) storage).

**Solution**: Since we are not allowed to use extra space, one simple way is to scan the elements one-by-one and for each element check whether that element appears in the remaining elements. If we find a match we return true.

```
int checkDuplicatesInArray(in A[], int n) {
    for (int i  =  0; i < n; i++)
        for (int j = i + 1; j < n; j++)
            if(A[i]==A[j])
                reutrn true;
    return false;
}
```

Each iteration of the inner, $j$-indexed loop uses O(1) space, and for a fixed value of $i$, the $j$ loop executes $n - i$ times. The outer loop executes $n - 1$ times, so the entire function uses time proportional to

$$\sum_{i=1}^{n-1} n - i = n(n-1) - \sum_{i=1}^{n-1} i = n(n-1) - \frac{n(n-1)}{2} = \frac{n(n-1)}{2} = O(n^2)$$

Time Complexity: $O(n^2)$. Space Complexity: O(1).

**Problem-2** Can we improve the time complexity of Problem-1?

**Solution**: **Yes**, using sorting technique.

```
int checkDuplicatesInArray(in A[], int n) {
    //for heap sort algorithm refer Priority Queues chapter
    Heapsort( A, n );
    for (int i  =  0; i < n-1; i++)
        if(A[i]==A[i+1])
            reutrn true;
    return false;
}
```

Heapsort function takes $O(nlogn)$ time, and requires O(1) space. The scan clearly takes $n - 1$ iterations, each iteration using O(1) time. The overall time is $O(nlogn + n) = O(nlogn)$.

Time Complexity: $O(nlogn)$. Space Complexity: O(1).

**Note:** For variations of this problem, refer to *Searching* chapter.

**Problem-3** Given an array $A[0 \ldots n-1]$, where each element of the array represents a vote in the election. Assume that each vote is given as an integer representing the ID of the chosen candidate. Give an algorithm for determining who wins the election.

**Solution:** This problem is nothing but finding the element which repeated the maximum number of times. The solution is similar to the Problem-1 solution: keep track of counter.

```
int CheckWhoWinsTheElection(in A[], int n) {
    int i, j, counter = 0, maxCounter = 0, candidate;
    candidate = A[0];
    for (i = 0; i < n; i++) {
        candidate = A[i];
        counter = 0;
        for (j = i + 1; j < n; j++) {
            if(A[i]==A[j]) counter++;
        }
        if(counter > maxCounter) {
            maxCounter = counter;
            candidate = A[i];
        }
    }
    return candidate;
}
```

Time Complexity: $O(n^2)$. Space Complexity: O(1).

**Note:** For variations of this problem, refer to *Searching* chapter.

**Problem-4** Can we improve the time complexity of Problem-3? Assume we don't have any extra space.

**Solution: Yes.** The approach is to sort the votes based on candidate ID, then scan the sorted array and count up which candidate so far has the most votes. We only have to remember the winner, so we don't need a clever data structure. We can use Heapsort as it is an in-place sorting algorithm.

```
int CheckWhoWinsTheElection(in A[], int n) {
    int i, j, currentCounter = 1, maxCounter = 1;
    int currentCandidate, maxCandidate;
    currentCandidate = maxCandidate= A[0];
    //for heap sort algorithm refer Priority Queues Chapter
    Heapsort( A, n );
    for (int i = 1; i <= n; i++) {
        if( A[i] == currentCandidate)
            currentCounter ++;
        else {
            currentCandidate = A[i];
            currentCounter = 1;
        }
        if(currentCounter > maxCounter)
            maxCandidate = currentCandidate;
            maxCounter = currentCounter;
        }
    }
    return candidate;
}
```

Since Heapsort time complexity is $O(nlogn)$ and in-place, so it only uses an additional O(1) of storage in addition to the input array. The scan of the sorted array does a constant-time conditional $n - 1$ times, thus using $O(n)$ time. The overall time bound is $O(nlogn)$.

**Problem-5** Can we further improve the time complexity of Problem-3?

**Solution:** In the given problem, number of candidates is less but the number of votes is significantly large. For this problem we can use counting sort.

Time Complexity: $O(n)$, $n$ is the number of votes (elements) in array.
Space Complexity: $O(k)$, $k$ is the number of candidates participated in election.

**Problem-6** Consider the voting problem from the previous exercise, but now suppose that we know the number k < n of candidates running. Describe an $O(nlogk)$-time algorithm for determining who wins the election.

**Solution:** In this case, the candidates can be stored in a balanced binary tree (for example, an AVL Tree). Each node should store a candidate ID and the number of votes they have received so far. As each vote in the sequence is processed, search the tree for the candidate ID of the chosen candidate (which takes $O(logk)$ time). If the ID is found, add one to its number of votes. Otherwise, create a new node with this ID and with one vote. At the end, go through all the nodes in the tree to find the one with the most votes. The process could be sped up even further in the average case (though not in the worst case) by replacing the AVL Tree with a Hash Table.

**Problem-7** Given an array $A$ of $n$ elements, each of which is an integer in the range $[1, n^2]$, how do we sort the array in $O(n)$ time?

**Solution**: If we subtract each number by 1 then we get the range $[0, n^2 - 1]$. If we consider all number as 2 –digit base $n$. Each digit ranges from 0 to $n^2$ - 1. Sort this using radix sort. This uses only two calls to counting sort. Finally, add 1 to all the numbers. Since there are 2 calls, the complexity is $O(2n) \approx O(n)$.

**Problem-8** For Problem-7, what if the range is $[1...n^3]$?

**Solution:** If we subtract each number by 1 then we get the range $[0, n^3 - 1]$. Considering all numbers as *3*-digit base $n$: each digit ranges from 0 to $n^3$ - 1. Sort this using radix sort. This uses only three calls to counting sort. Finally, add 1 to all the numbers. Since there are 3 calls, the complexity is $O(3n) \approx O(n)$.

**Problem-9** Given an array with $n$ integers, each of value less than $n^{100}$, can it be sorted in linear time?

**Solution: Yes.** The reasoning is the same as in of Problem-7 and Problem-8.

**Problem-10** Let $A$ and $B$ be two arrays of $n$ elements each. Given a number $K$, give an $O(nlogn)$ time algorithm for determining whether there exists a ∈ A and b ∈ B such that $a + b = K$.

**Solution:** Since we need $O(nlogn)$, it gives us a pointer that we need to sort. So, we will do that.

```
int find( int A[], int B[], int n, K ) {
	int i, c;
	Heapsort( A, n );                       // O(nlogn)
	for (i =0; i< n; i++) {                 // O(n)
		c = k-B[i];                         // O(1)
		if(BinarySearch(A, c))              // O(logn)
			return 1;
	}
	return 0;
}
```

**Note:** For variations of this problem, refer to *Searching* chapter.

**Problem-11** Let $A, B$ and $C$ be three arrays of $n$ elements each. Given a number $K$, give an $O(nlogn)$ time algorithm for determining whether there exists $a \in A$, $b \in B$ and $c \in C$ such that $a + b + c = K$.

**Solution:** Refer to *Searching* chapter.

**Problem-12** Given an array of $n$ elements, can we output in sorted order the $K$ elements following the median in sorted order in time $O(n + KlogK)$.

**Solution: Yes**. Find the median and partition the median. With this we can find all the elements greater than it. Now find the $K^{th}$ largest element in this set and partition it; and get all the elements less than it. Output the sorted list of the final set of elements. Clearly, this operation takes $O(n + KlogK)$ time.

**Problem-13** Consider the sorting algorithms: Bubble sort, Insertion sort, Selection sort, Merge sort, Heap sort, and Quick sort. Which of these are stable?

**Solution:** Let us assume that $A$ is the array to be sorted. Also, let us say $R$ and $S$ have the same key and $R$ appears earlier in the array than $S$. That means, $R$ is at $A[i]$ and $S$ is at $A[j]$, with $i < j$. To show any stable algorithm, in the sorted output $R$ must precede $S$.

**Bubble sort:** Yes. Elements change order only when a smaller record follows a larger. Since $S$ is not smaller than $R$ it cannot precede it.

**Selection sort:** No. It divides the array into sorted and unsorted portions and iteratively finds the minimum values in the unsorted portion. After finding a minimum $x$, if the algorithm moves $x$ into the sorted portion of the array by means of a swap, then the element swapped could be $R$ which then could be moved behind $S$. This would invert the positions of $R$ and $S$, so in general it is not stable. If swapping is avoided, it could be made stable but the cost in time would probably be very significant.

**Insertion sort:** Yes. As presented, when $S$ is to be inserted into sorted subarray $A[1..j - 1]$, only records larger than $S$ are shifted. Thus $R$ would not be shifted during $S$*'s* insertion and hence would always precede it.

**Merge sort:** Yes, In the case of records with equal keys, the record in the left subarray gets preference. Those are the records that came first in the unsorted array. As a result, they will precede later records with the same key.

**Heap sort:** No. Suppose $i = 1$ and $R$ and $S$ happen to be the two records with the largest keys in the input. Then $R$ will remain in location 1 after the array is heapified, and will be placed in location $n$ in the first iteration of Heapsort. Thus $S$ will precede $R$ in the output.

**Quick sort:** No. The partitioning step can swap the location of records many times, and thus two records with equal keys could swap position in the final output.

**Problem-14** Consider the same sorting algorithms as that of Problem-13. Which of them are in-place?

**Solution:**

**Bubble sort:** Yes, because only two integers are required.

**Insertion sort:** Yes, since we need to store two integers and a record.

**Selection sort:** Yes. This algorithm would likely need space for two integers and one record.

**Merge sort:** No. Arrays need to perform the merge. (If the data is in the form of a linked list, the sorting can be done in-place, but this is a nontrivial modification.)

**Heap sort:** Yes, since the heap and partially-sorted array occupy opposite ends of the input array.

**Quicksort:** No, since it is recursive and stores $O(logn)$ activation records on the stack. Modifying it to be non-recursive is feasible but nontrivial.

**Problem-15** Among Quick sort, Insertion sort, Selection sort, and Heap sort algorithms, which one needs the minimum number of swaps?

**Solution:** Selection sort – it needs $n$ swaps only (refer to theory section).

**Problem-16** What is the minimum number of comparisons required to determine if an integer appears more than $n/2$ times in a sorted array of $n$ integers?

**Solution:** Refer to *Searching* chapter.

**Problem-17** **Sort an array of 0's, 1's and 2's:** Given an array A[] consisting of 0*'s*, 1*'s* and 2*'s*, give an algorithm for sorting *A*[]. The algorithm should put all 0*'s* first, then all 1*'s* and all 2*'s* last.

**Example:** Input = {0,1,1,0,1,2,1,2,0,0,0,1}, Output = {0, 0, 0, 0, 0, 1, 1, 1, 1, 1, 2, 2}

**Solution:** Use Counting sort. Since there are only three elements and the maximum value is 2, we need a temporary array with 3 elements.

Time Complexity: $O(n)$. Space Complexity: O(1).

**Note:** For variations of this problem, refer to *Searching* chapter.

**Problem-18** Is there any other way of solving Problem-16?

**Solution:** Using Quick dort. Since we know that there are only 3 elements, 0, 1 and 2 in the array, we can select 1 as a pivot element for Quick sort. Quick sort finds the correct place for 1 by moving all 0's to the left of 1 and all 2's to the right of 1. For doing this it uses only one scan.

Time Complexity: $O(n)$. Space Complexity: O(1).

**Note:** For efficient algorithm, refer to *Searching* chapter.

**Problem-19** How do we find the number that appeared the maximum number of times in an array?

**Solution:** One simple approach is to sort the given array and scan the sorted array. While scanning, keep track of the elements that occur the maximum number of times.

**Algorithm**:
```
int mostFrequent(int A[], int n) {
    // Sort the Aay
    sort(A, A + n);
    // find the max frequency using linear traversal
    int maxCounter = 1, res = A[0], currentCounter = 1;
    for (int i = 1; i < n; i++) {
        if (A[i] == A[i - 1])
            currentCounter++;
        else {
            if (currentCounter > maxCounter) {
                maxCounter = currentCounter;
                res = A[i - 1];
            }
            currentCounter = 1;
        }
    }
    // If last element is most frequent
    if (currentCounter > maxCounter) {
        maxCounter = currentCounter;
        res = A[n - 1];
    }
```

```
        return res;
    }
```

Time Complexity = Time for Sorting + Time for Scan = $O(nlogn)$ +$O(n)$ = $O(nlogn)$. Space Complexity: O(1).

**Note:** For variations of this problem, refer to *Searching* chapter.

**Problem-20** Is there any other way of solving Problem-19?

**Solution: Using Binary Tree.** Create a binary tree with an extra field *count* which indicates the number of times an element appeared in the input. Let us say we have created a Binary Search Tree [BST]. Now, do the In-Order traversal of the tree. The In-Order traversal of BST produces the sorted list. While doing the In-Order traversal keep track of the maximum element.

Time Complexity: $O(n)$ +$O(n)$ ≈$O(n)$. The first parameter is for constructing the BST and the second parameter is for Inorder Traversal. Space Complexity: $O(2n)$ ≈$O(n)$, since every node in BST needs two extra pointers.

**Problem-21** Is there yet another way of solving Problem-19?

**Solution: Using Hash Table.** For each element of the given array we use a counter, and for each occurrence of the element we increment the corresponding counter. At the end we can just return the element which has the maximum counter.

Time Complexity: $O(n)$. Space Complexity: $O(n)$. For constructing the hash table we need $O(n)$.

**Note:** For the efficient algorithm, refer to the *Searching* chapter.

**Problem-22** Given a 2 GB file with one string per line, which sorting algorithm would we use to sort the file and why?

**Solution:** When we have a size limit of 2GB, it means that we cannot bring all the data into the main memory.

**Algorithm:** How much memory do we have available? Let's assume we have $X$ MB of memory available. Divide the file into $K$ chunks, where $X * K \sim 2\ GB$.

- Bring each chunk into memory and sort the lines as usual (any $O(nlogn)$ algorithm).
- Save the lines back to the file.
- Now bring the next chunk into memory and sort.
- Once we're done, merge them one by one; in the case of one set finishing, bring more data from the particular chunk.

The above algorithm is also known as *external sort*. Step 3 – 4 is known as K-way merge. The idea behind going for an external sort is the size of data. Since the data is huge and we can't bring it to the memory, we need to go for a disk-based sorting algorithm.

**Problem-23** **Nearly sorted:** Given an array of $n$ elements, each which is at most $K$ positions from its target position, devise an algorithm that sorts in $O(n\ logK)$ time.

**Solution:** Divide the elements into $n/K$ groups of size $K$, and sort each piece in $O(KlogK)$ time, let's say using Mergesort. This preserves the property that no element is more than $K$ elements out of position. Now, merge each block of $K$ elements with the block to its left.

**Problem-24** Is there any other way of solving Problem-23?

**Solution:** Insert the first $K$ elements into a binary heap. Insert the next element from the array into the heap, and delete the minimum element from the heap. Repeat.

**Problem-25** **Merging K sorted lists:** Given $K$ sorted lists with a total of $n$ elements, give an $O(nlogK)$ algorithm to produce a sorted list of all $n$ elements.

**Solution:** Simple Algorithm for merging $K$ sorted lists: Consider groups each having $\frac{n}{K}$ elements. Take the first list and merge it with the second list using a linear-time algorithm for merging two sorted lists, such as the merging algorithm used in merge sort. Then, merge the resulting list of $\frac{2n}{K}$ elements with the third list, and then merge the resulting list of $\frac{3n}{K}$ elements with the fourth list. Repeat this until we end up with a single sorted list of all $n$ elements.

Time Complexity: In each iteration we are merging $K$ elements.

$$T(n) = \frac{2n}{K} + \frac{3n}{K} + \frac{4n}{K} + \cdots \frac{Kn}{K}(n) = \frac{n}{K}\sum_{i=2}^{K} i$$

$$T(n) = \frac{n}{K}\left[\frac{K(K+1)}{2}\right] \approx O(nK)$$

**Problem-26** Can we improve the time complexity of Problem-25?

**Solution:** One method is to repeatedly pair up the lists and then merge each pair. This method can also be seen as a tail component of the execution merge sort, where the analysis is clear. This is called the Tournament Method. The maximum depth of the Tournament Method is $logK$ and in each iteration we are scanning all the $n$ elements.

Time Complexity: $O(n\log K)$.

**Problem-27** Is there any other way of solving Problem-25?

**Solution:** The other method is to use a *min* priority queue for the minimum elements of each of the *K* lists. At each step, we output the extracted minimum of the priority queue, determine from which of the *K* lists it came, and insert the next element from that list into the priority queue. Since we are using priority queue, that maximum depth of priority queue is *logK*.

Time Complexity: $O(n\log K)$.

**Problem-28** Which sorting method is better for Linked Lists?

**Solution:** Merge Sort is a better choice. At first appearance, merge sort may not be a good selection since the middle node is required to subdivide the given list into two sub-lists of equal length. We can easily solve this problem by moving the nodes alternatively to two lists (refer to *Linked Lists* chapter). Then, sorting these two lists recursively and merging the results into a single list will sort the given one.

```
typedef struct ListNode {
	int data;
	struct ListNode *next;
};
struct ListNode * LinkedListMergeSort(struct ListNode * first) {
	struct ListNode * list1HEAD = NULL;
	struct ListNode * list1TAIL = NULL;
	struct ListNode * list2HEAD = NULL;
	struct ListNode * list2TAIL = NULL;
	if(first==NULL || first→next==NULL)
			return first;
	while (first != NULL) {
			Append(first, list1HEAD, list1TAIL);
			if(first != NULL)
				Append(first, list2HEAD, list2TAIL);
	}
	list1HEAD = LinkedListMergeSort(list1HEAD);
	list2HEAD = LinkedListMergeSort(list2HEAD);
	return Merge(list1HEAD, list2HEAD);
}
```

**Note:** Append() appends the first argument to the tail of a singly linked list whose head and tail are defined by the second and third arguments.

All external sorting algorithms can be used for sorting linked lists since each involved file can be considered as a linked list that can only be accessed sequentially. We can sort a doubly linked list using its next fields as if it was a singly linked one and reconstruct the prev fields after sorting with an additional scan.

**Problem-29** Can we implement Linked Lists Sorting with Quick Sort?

**Solution:** The original Quick Sort cannot be used for sorting Singly Linked Lists. This is because we cannot move backward in Singly Linked Lists. But we can modify the original Quick Sort and make it work for Singly Linked Lists.

Let us consider the following modified Quick Sort implementation. The first node of the input list is considered a *pivot* and is moved to *equal*. The value of each node is compared with the *pivot* and moved *to less* (respectively, *equal* or *larger*) if the nodes value is smaller than (respectively, *equal* to or *larger* than) the *pivot*. Then, *less* and *larger* are sorted recursively. Finally, joining *less*, *equal* and *larger* into a single list yields a sorted one.

*Append*() appends the first argument to the tail of a singly linked list whose head and tail are defined by the second and third arguments. On return, the first argument will be modified so that it points to the next node of the list. *Join*() appends the list whose head and tail are defined by the third and fourth arguments to the list whose head and tail are defined by the first and second arguments. For simplicity, the first and fourth arguments become the head and tail of the resulting list.

```
typedef struct ListNode {
	int data;
	struct ListNode *next;
};
void Qsort(struct ListNode *first, struct ListNode * last) {
	struct ListNode *lesHEAD=NULL, lesTAIL=NULL;
	struct ListNode *equHEAD=NULL, equTAIL=NULL;
	struct ListNode *larHEAD=NULL, larTAIL=NULL;
```

```
        struct ListNode *current = *first;
        int pivot, info;
        if(current == NULL) return;
        pivot = current→data;
        Append(current, equHEAD, equTAIL);
        while (current != NULL) {
                info = current→data;
                if(info < pivot)
                        Append(current, lesHEAD, lesTAIL)
                else if(info > pivot)
                        Append(current, larHEAD, larTAIL)
                else    Append(current, equHEAD, equTAIL);
        }
        Quicksort(&lesHEAD, &lesTAIL);
        Quicksort(&larHEAD, &larTAIL);
        Join(lesHEAD, lesTAIL,equHEAD, equTAIL);
        Join(lesHEAD, equTAIL,larHEAD, larTAIL);
        *first = lesHEAD;
        *last = larTAIL;
}
```

**Problem-30** Given an array of $100,000$ pixel color values, each of which is an integer in the range $[0,255]$. Which sorting algorithm is preferable for sorting them?

**Solution:** Counting Sort. There are only 256 key values, so the auxiliary array would only be of size 256, and there would be only two passes through the data, which would be very efficient in both time and space.

**Problem-31** Similar to Problem-30, if we have a telephone directory with 10 million entries, which sorting algorithm is best?

**Solution:** Bucket Sort. In Bucket Sort the buckets are defined by the last 7 digits. This requires an auxiliary array of size 10 million and has the advantage of requiring only one pass through the data on disk. Each bucket contains all telephone numbers with the same last 7 digits but with different area codes. The buckets can then be sorted by area code with selection or insertion sort; there are only a handful of area codes.

**Problem-32** Give an algorithm for merging $K$-sorted lists.

**Solution:** Refer to *Priority Queues* chapter.

**Problem-33** Given a big file containing billions of numbers. Find maximum 10 numbers from this file.

**Solution:** Refer to *Priority Queues* chapter.

**Problem-34** There are two sorted arrays $A$ and $B$. The first one is of size $m + n$ containing only $m$ elements. Another one is of size $n$ and contains $n$ elements. Merge these two arrays into the first array of size $m + n$ such that the output is sorted.

**Solution:** The trick for this problem is to start filling the destination array from the back with the largest elements. We will end up with a merged and sorted destination array.

```
void Merge(int[] A[], int m, int B[], int n) {
        int count = m;
        int i = n – 1, j = count – 1, k = m - 1;
        for(;k>=0;k--) {
                if(B[i] > A[j] | | j < 0) {
                        A[k] =B[i];
                        i--;
                        if(i<0)
                                break;
                }
                else {
                        A[k] = A[j];
                        j--;
                }
        }
}
```

Time Complexity: $O(m + n)$. Space Complexity: $O(1)$.

**Problem-35** **Nuts and Bolts Problem:** Given a set of $n$ nuts of different sizes and $n$ bolts such that there is a one-to-one correspondence between the nuts and the bolts, find for each nut its corresponding bolt. Assume that we can only compare nuts to bolts: we cannot compare nuts to nuts and bolts to bolts.

**Alternative way of framing the question**: We are given a box which contains bolts and nuts. Assume there are $n$ nuts and $n$ bolts and that each nut matches exactly one bolt (and vice versa). By trying to match a bolt and a nut we can see which one is bigger, but we cannot compare two bolts or two nuts directly. Design an efficient algorithm for matching the nuts and bolts.

**Solution: Brute Force Approach:** Start with the first bolt and compare it with each nut until we find a match. In the worst case, we require $n$ comparisons. Repeat this for successive bolts on all remaining gives $O(n^2)$ complexity.

**Problem-36** For Problem-35, can we improve the complexity?

**Solution:** In Problem-35, we got $O(n^2)$ complexity in the worst case (if bolts are in ascending order and nuts are in descending order). Its analysis is the same as that of Quick Sort. The improvement is also along the same lines. To reduce the worst case complexity, instead of selecting the first bolt every time, we can select a random bolt and match it with nuts. This randomized selection reduces the probability of getting the worst case, but still the worst case is $O(n^2)$.

**Problem-37** For Problem-35, can we further improve the complexity?

**Solution:** We can use a divide-and-conquer technique for solving this problem and the solution is very similar to randomized Quick Sort. For simplicity let us assume that bolts and nuts are represented in two arrays $B$ and $N$.

The algorithm first performs a partition operation as follows: pick a random bolt $B[i]$. Using this bolt, rearrange the array of nuts into three groups of elements:

- First the nuts smaller than $B[i]$
- Then the nut that matches $B[i]$, and
- Finally, the nuts larger than $B[i]$.

Next, using the nut that matches $B[i]$, perform a similar partition on the array of bolts. This pair of partitioning operations can easily be implemented in $O(n)$ time, and it leaves the bolts and nuts nicely partitioned so that the "*pivot*" bolt and nut are aligned with each other and all other bolts and nuts are on the correct side of these pivots – smaller nuts and bolts precede the pivots, and larger nuts and bolts follow the pivots. Our algorithm then completes by recursively applying itself to the subarray to the left and right of the pivot position to match these remaining bolts and nuts. We can assume by induction on $n$ that these recursive calls will properly match the remaining bolts.

To analyze the running time of our algorithm, we can use the same analysis as that of randomized Quick Sort. Therefore, applying the analysis from Quick Sort, the time complexity of our algorithm is $O(nlogn)$.

**Alternative Analysis**: We can solve this problem by making a small change to Quick Sort. Let us assume that we pick the last element as the pivot, say it is a nut. Compare the nut with only bolts as we walk down the array. This will partition the array for the bolts. Every bolt less than the partition nut will be on the left. And every bolt greater than the partition nut will be on the right.

While traversing down the list, find the matching bolt for the partition nut. Now we do the partition again using the matching bolt. As a result, all the nuts less than the matching bolt will be on the left side and all the nuts greater than the matching bolt will be on the right side. Recursively call on the left and right arrays.

The time complexity is $O(2nlogn) \approx O(nlogn)$.

**Problem-38** Given a binary tree, can we print its elements in sorted order in $O(n)$ time by performing an In-order tree traversal?

**Solution: Yes,** if the tree is a Binary Search Tree [BST]. For more details refer to the *Trees* chapter.

**Problem-39** Given an array of elements, convert it into an array such that A < B > C < D > E < F and so on.

**Solution:** Sort the array, then swap every adjacent element to get the final result.

```
#include<algorithm>
convertArraytoSawToothWave(){
    int A[] = {0,-6,9,13,10,-1,8,12,54,14,-5};
    int n = sizeof(A)/sizeof(A[0]), i = 1, temp;
    sort(A, A+n);
    for(i=1; i < n; i+=2){
        if(i+1 < n){
            temp = A[i]; A[i] = A[i+1]; A[i+1] = temp;
        }
    }
    for(i=0; i < n; i++){
        printf("%d ", A[i]);
```

```
    }
  }
```

The time complexity is O(nlogn + n) ≈ O(nlogn), for sorting and a scan.

**Problem-40** Can we do Problem-39 with O(n) time?

**Solution**: Make sure all even positioned elements are greater than their adjacent odd elements, and we don't need to worry about odd positioned elements. Traverse all even positioned elements of input array, and do the following:

- If the current element is smaller than the previous odd element, swap previous and current.
- If the current element is smaller than the next odd element, swap next and current.

```
convertArraytoSawToothWave(){
    int A[] = {0,-6,9,13,10,-1,8,12,54,14,-5};
    int n = sizeof(A)/sizeof(A[0]), i = 1, temp;
    sort(A, A+n);
    for(i=1; i < n; i+=2){
        if (i>0 && A[i-1] > A[i] ){
            temp = A[i]; A[i] = A[i-1]; A[i-1] = temp;
        }
        if (i<n-1 && A[i] < A[i+1] ){
            temp = A[i]; A[i] = A[i+1]; A[i+1] = temp;
        }
    }
    for(i=0; i < n; i++){
        cout<<A[i]<< " ";
    }
}
```

The time complexity is $O(n)$.

**Problem-41** Merge sort uses

(a) Divide and conquer strategy (b) Backtracking approach (c) Heuristic search (d) Greedy approach

**Solution: (a)**. Refer theory section.

**Problem-42** Which of the following algorithm design techniques is used in the quicksort algorithm?

(a) Dynamic programming (b) Backtracking (c) Divide and conquer (d) Greedy method

**Solution: (c)**. Refer theory section.

**Problem-43** Sort the linked list elements in $O(n)$, where $n$ is the number of elements in the linked list.

**Solution**: As stated many times, the lower bound on comparison based sorting for general data is going to be $O(nlogn)$. So, for general data on a linked list, the best possible sort that will work on any data that can compare two objects is going to be $O(nlogn)$. However, if you have a more limited domain of things to work in, you can improve the time it takes (at least proportional to n). For instance, if you are working with integers no larger than some value, you could use Counting Sort or Radix Sort, as these use the specific objects you're sorting to reduce the complexity with proportion to $n$. Be careful, though, these add some other things to the complexity that you may not consider (for instance, Counting Sort and Radix sort both add in factors that are based on the size of the numbers you're sorting, $O(n + k)$ where $k$ is the size of largest number for Counting Sort, for instance).

Also, if you happen to have objects that have a perfect hash (or at least a hash that maps all values differently), you could try using a counting or radix sort on their hash functions. It is the application of counting sort.

Algorithm:

1) In the given linked list, find the maximum element ($k$). This would take $O(n)$ time.
2) Create a hash map of the size $k$. This would need $O(k)$ space.
3) Scan through the linked list elements, set 1 to the corresponding index in the array. Suppose element in the linked is 19, then H[4] = 1. This would take $O(n)$ time.
4) Now the array is sorted as similar to counting sort.
5) Read the elements from the array and add it back to the list with a time complexity of $O(k)$.

**Problem-44** For merging two sorted lists of sizes m and n into a sorted list of size m+n, we required comparisons of

(a) $O(m)$ (b) $O(n)$ (c) $O(m + n)$ (d) $O(logm + logn)$

**Solution: (c)**. We can use merge sort logic. Refer theory section.

**Problem-45** Quick-sort is run on two inputs shown below to sort in ascending order

(i) 1,2,3 ....n (ii) n, n – 1, n – 2, .... 2, 1

Let C1 and C2 be the number of comparisons made for the inputs (i) and (ii) respectively. Then,

(a) C1 < C2 (b) C1 > C2 (c) C1 = C2 (d) we cannot say anything for arbitrary $n$.

**Solution: (b)**. Since the given problems needs the output in ascending order, Quicksort on already sorted order gives the worst case ($O(n^2)$). So, (i) generates worst case and (ii) needs fewer comparisons.

**Problem-46** Give the correct matching for the following pairs:

(A) $O(logn)$ (P) Selection
(B) $O(n)$ (Q) Insertion sort
(C) $O(nlogn)$ (R) Binary search
(D) $O(n^2)$ (S) Merge sort

(a) A – R B – P C – Q D - S (b) A – R B – P C – S D - Q (c) A – P B – R C – S D - Q (d) A – P B – S C – R D - Q

**Solution: (b)**. Refer theory section.

**Problem-47** Let s be a sorted array of n integers. Let t(n) denote the time taken for the most efficient algorithm to determine if there are two elements with sum less than 1000 in s. which of the following statements is true?

a) $t(n)$ is O(1) b) $n < t(n) < nlog_2^n$ c) $nlog_2^n < t(n) < \binom{n}{2}$ d) $t(n) = \binom{n}{2}$

**Solution: (a)**. Since the given array is already sorted it is enough if we check the first two elements of the array.

**Problem-48** The usual $\Theta(n^2)$ implementation of Insertion Sort to sort an array uses linear search to identify the position where an element is to be inserted into the already sorted part of the array. If, instead, we use binary search to identify the position, the worst case running time will

(a) remain $\Theta(n^2)$ (b) become $\Theta(n(log\ n)^2)$ (c) become $\Theta(nlogn)$ (d) become $\Theta(n)$

**Solution: (a)**. If we use binary search then there will be $log_2^{n!}$comparisons in the worst case, which is $\Theta(nlogn)$. But the algorithm as a whole will still have a running time of $\Theta(n^2)$ on average because of the series of swaps required for each insertion.

**Problem-49** In quick sort, for sorting n elements, the $n/4^{th}$ smallest element is selected as pivot using an $O(n)$ time algorithm. What is the worst case time complexity of the quick sort?

(A) $\Theta(n)$ (B) $\Theta(nLogn)$ (C) $\Theta(n^2)$ (D) $\Theta(n^2logn)$

**Solution:** The recursion expression becomes: T(n) = T(n/4) + T(3n/4) + cn. Solving the recursion using *variant* of master theorem, we get $\Theta(nLogn)$.

**Problem-50** Consider the Quicksort algorithm. Suppose there is a procedure for finding a pivot element which splits the list into two sub-lists each of which contains at least one-fifth of the elements. Let T($n$) be the number of comparisons required to sort n elements. Then

A) T (n) ≤ 2T (n /5) + n B) T (n) ≤ T (n /5) + T (4n /5) + n C) T (n) ≤ 2T (4n /5) + n D) T (n) ≤ 2T (n /2) + n

**Solution: (C)**. For the case where n/5 elements are in one subset, T(n/5) comparisons are needed for the first subset with $n/5$ elements, T(4n/5) is for the rest 4n/5 elements, and $n$ is for finding the pivot. If there are more than $n/5$ elements in one set then other set will have less than 4n/5 elements and time complexity will be less than T(n/5) + T(4n/5) + n.

**Problem-51** Which of the following sorting algorithms has the lowest worst-case complexity?

(A) Merge sort (B) Bubble sort (C) Quick sort (D) Selection sort

**Solution: (A)**. Refer theory section.

**Problem-52** Which one of the following in place sorting algorithms needs the minimum number of swaps?

(A) Quick sort (B) Insertion sort (C) Selection sort (D) Heap sort

**Solution: (C)**. Refer theory section.

**Problem-53** You have an array of n elements. Suppose you implement quicksort by always choosing the central element of the array as the pivot. Then the tightest upper bound for the worst case performance is

(A) $O(n^2)$ (B) $O(nlogn)$ (C) $\Theta(nlogn)$ (D) $O(n^3)$

**Solution:** (A). When we choose the first element as the pivot, the worst case of quick sort comes if the input is sorted- either in ascending or descending order.

**Problem-54** Let P be a QuickSort Program to sort numbers in ascending order using the first element as pivot. Let t1 and t2 be the number of comparisons made by P for the inputs {1, 2, 3, 4, 5} and {4, 1, 5, 3, 2} respectively. Which one of the following holds?

(A) t1 = 5 (B) t1 < t2 (C) t1 > t2 (D) t1 = t2

**Solution:** (C). Quick Sort's worst case occurs when first (or last) element is chosen as pivot with sorted arrays.

**Problem-55** The minimum number of comparisons required to find the minimum and the maximum of 100 numbers is __

**Solution**: 147 (Formula for the minimum number of comparisons required is 3n/2 – 3 with n numbers).

**Problem-56** The number of elements that can be sorted in T($logn$) time using heap sort is

(A) Θ(1) (B) Θ(sqrt(logn)) (C) Θ(log n/(log log n)) (D) Θ(logn)

**Solution**: (D). Sorting an array with k elements takes time Θ(k log k) as k grows. We want to choose k such that Θ(k log k) = Θ(logn). Choosing k = Θ(logn) doesn't necessarily work, since Θ(k log k) = Θ(logn loglogn) ≠ Θ(logn). On the other hand, if you choose k = T(log n / log log n), then the runtime of the sort will be

$$= \Theta((\log n / \log\log n) \log (\log n / \log\log n))$$
$$= \Theta((\log n / \log\log n) (\log\log n - \log\log\log n))$$
$$= \Theta(\log n - \log n \log\log\log n / \log\log n)$$
$$= \Theta(\log n (1 - \log\log\log n / \log\log n))$$

Notice that 1 - logloglogn / loglogn tends toward 1 as n goes to infinity, so the above expression actually is Θ(log n), as required. Therefore, if you try to sort an array of size Θ(logn / loglogn) using heap sort, as a function of n, the runtime is Θ(logn).

**Problem-57** Which one of the following is the tightest upper bound that represents the number of swaps required to sort $n$ numbers using selection sort?
(A) $O(logn)$ (B) $O(n)$ (C) $O(nlogn)$ (D) $O(n^2)$

**Solution**: (B). Selection sort requires only $O(n)$ swaps.

**Problem-58** Which one of the following is the recurrence equation for the worst case time complexity of the Quicksort algorithm for sorting n(≥ 2) numbers? In the recurrence equations given in the options below, c is a constant.
(A)T(n) = 2T (n/2) + cn (B) T(n) = T(n – 1) + T(0) + cn (C) T(n) = 2T (n – 2) + cn (D) T(n) = T(n/2) + cn

**Solution**: (B). When the pivot is the smallest (or largest) element at partitioning on a block of size $n$ the result yields one empty sub-block, one element (pivot) in the correct place and sub block of size $n - 1$.

**Problem-59** True or False. In randomized quicksort, each key is involved in the same number of comparisons.

**Solution**: False.

**Problem-60** True or False: If Quicksort is written so that the partition algorithm always uses the median value of the segment as the pivot, then the worst-case performance is $O(nlogn)$.

**Soution:** True.

**Problem-61** **Squares of a sorted array**: Given an array of numbers A sorted in ascending order, return an array of the squares of each number, also in sorted ascending order. For array = [-6, -4, 1, 2, 3, 5], the output should be [1, 4, 9, 16, 25, 36].

**Solution**: **Intuitive approach**: One simplest approach to solve this problem is to create an array of the squares of each element, and sort them.

```
#include<bits/stdc++.h>
using namespace std;
void sortedSquaredArray(int A[], int n) {
   int result[n];
   for (int i = 0; i < n; ++i)
      result[i] = A[i] * A[i];
   sort(result, result+n);
   cout << "\nSorted squares array " << endl;
   for (int i = 0 ; i < n ; i++)
      cout << result[i] << " " ;
}
int main(){
   int A[] = { -4, -3, -1, 3, 4, 5 };
   int n = sizeof(A)/sizeof(A[0]);
   cout << "Given sorted array " << endl;
   for (int i = 0; i < n; i++)
      cout << A[i] << " " ;
   sortedSquaredArray(A, n);
   return 0;
}
```

Time complexity: $O(nlogn)$, for sorting the array. Space complexity: $O(n)$, for the result array.

**Elegant approach**: Since the given array A is sorted, it might have some negative elements. The squares of these negative numbers would be in decreasing order. Similarly, the squares of positive numbers would be in increasing order. For example, with [-4, -3, -1, 3, 4, 5], we have the negative part [-4, -3, -1] with squares [16, 9, 1], and the positive part [3, 4, 5] with squares [9, 16, 25]. Our strategy is to iterate over the negative part in reverse, and the positive part in the forward direction.

We can use two pointers to read the positive and negative parts of the array - one pointer i in the positive direction, and another j in the negative direction.

Now that we are reading two increasing arrays (the squares of the elements), we can merge these arrays together using a two-pointer technique.

```
#include<bits/stdc++.h>
using namespace std;
void sortedSquaredArray(int A[], int n) {
    int result[n];
    int j = 0;
    // Find the last index of the negative numbers
    while (j < n && A[j] < 0)
        j++;
    // i points to the last index of negative numbers
    int i = j-1;
    int t = 0;
    // j points to the first index of the positive numbers
    while (i >= 0 && j < n) {
        if (A[i] * A[i] < A[j] * A[j]) {
            result[t++] = A[i] * A[i];
            i--;
        } else {
            result[t++] = A[j] * A[j];
            j++;
        }
    }
    // add the remaining negative numbers squares to result
    while (i >= 0) {
        result[t++] = A[i] * A[i];
        i--;
    }
    // add the remaining positive numbers squares to result
    while (j < n) {
        result[t++] = A[j] * A[j];
        j++;
    }
    cout << "\nSorted squares array " << endl;
    for (int i = 0 ; i < n ; i++)
        cout << result[i] << " " ;
}
int main(){
    int A[] = { -4, -3, -1, 3, 4, 5 };
    int n = sizeof(A)/sizeof(A[0]);
    cout << "Given sorted array " << endl;
    for (int i = 0; i < n; i++)
        cout << A[i] << " " ;
    sortedSquaredArray(A, n);
    return 0;
}
```

Time complexity: O($n$). Space complexity: O($n$), for the result array.

**Problem-62** **Height Checker**: A school is trying to take an annual photo of all the students. The students are asked to stand in a single file line in non-decreasing order by height. Let this ordering be represented by the integer array expected where expected[i] is the expected height of the $i^{th}$ student in line. We are given an integer array *heights* representing the current order that the students are standing in. Each *heights*[i] is the height of the ith student in line (0-indexed). Return the number of indices where heights[i] != expected[i].

**Solution**: The goal of the problem is to count the number of students in a line who are not standing in non-decreasing order of height. We can create a sorted version of the line ("expected" order) using a sorting algorithm, and then compare it to the original line to count the number of differences. However, sorting the entire line can be inefficient for large inputs. Instead, we can use the counting sort algorithm to create a sorted array of heights.

- Find the maximum height in the heights array and store it in a variable max_height.

- Create a counting array count of length (max_height + 1) and initialize all its elements to zero.
- Loop through the heights array and use each value to increment the count of that value in the count array.
- Calculate the cumulative sum of the count array. This means that each element in the count array will contain the number of elements less than or equal to the index of that element.
- Initialize a variable result to zero.
- Loop through the heights array and compare each element with the expected height at the same index in the expected array. If they are not equal, increment the result variable.
- Return the result variable.

```
int heightChecker(int* heights, int heightsSize){
    int expected[101] = {0}; // initialize expected array with 0s
    int count = 0;
    // count the number of occurrences of each height in the heights array
    for (int i = 0; i < heightsSize; i++) {
        expected[heights[i]]++;
    }
    // compare the heights in the heights array with the expected heights
    // increment count for each height that is out of order
    int j = 0;
    for (int i = 1; i < 101; i++) {
        while (expected[i]-- > 0) {
            if (heights[j++] != i) {
                count++;
            }
        }
    }
}
```

The time complexity of the counting sort algorithm is O(n + k), where n is the length of the input array and k is the range of the input values. In this specific problem, the range is 100 since the heights are between 1 and 100. Therefore, the time complexity of the counting sort implementation for this problem is O(n + 100), which is equivalent to O(n). Additionally, there is a single pass over the input array to compare the sorted array with the original array, which takes O(n) time. Thus, the overall time complexity of the algorithm is O(n). The space complexity of the algorithm is O(k), which is equivalent to O(1) in this problem since the range is constant.

# SEARCHING

## 11.1 What is Searching?

In computer science, *searching* is the process of finding an item with specified properties from a collection of items. The items may be stored as records in a database, simple data elements in arrays, text in files, nodes in trees, vertices and edges in graphs, or they may be elements of other search spaces.

## 11.2 Why do we need Searching?

*Searching* is one of the core computer science algorithms. We know that today's computers store a lot of information. To retrieve this information proficiently we need very efficient searching algorithms. There are certain ways of organizing the data that improves the searching process. That means, if we keep the data in proper order, it is easy to search the required element. Sorting is one of the techniques for making the elements ordered. In this chapter we will see different searching algorithms.

## 11.3 Types of Searching

Following are the types of searches which we will be discussing in this book.

- Unordered Linear Search
- Sorted/Ordered Linear Search
- Binary Search
- Interpolation search
- Binary Search Trees (operates on trees and refer *Trees* chapter)
- Symbol Tables and Hashing
- String Searching Algorithms: Tries, Ternary Search and Suffix Trees

## 11.4 Unordered Linear Search

Let us assume we are given an array where the order of the elements is not known. That means the elements of the array are not sorted. In this case, to search for an element we have to scan the complete array and see if the element is there in the given list or not.

```
int unOrderedLinearSearch (int A[], int n, int data) {
    for (int i  = 0; i < n; i++) {
        if(A[i] == data)
            return i;
    }
    return -1;
}
```

Time complexity: O($n$), in the worst case we need to scan the complete array. Space complexity: O(1).

## 11.5 Sorted/Ordered Linear Search

If the elements of the array are already sorted, then in many cases we don't have to scan the complete array to see if the element is there in the given array or not. In the algorithm below, it can be seen that, at any point if the value at $A[i]$ is greater than the *data* to be searched, then we just return −1 without searching the remaining array.

```
int orderedLinearSearch(int A[], int n, int data) {
    for (int i  = 0; i < n; i++) {
        if(A[i] == data)
```

```
            return i;
        else if(A[i] > data)
            return -1;
    }
    return -1;
}
```

Time complexity of this algorithm is $O(n)$. This is because in the worst case we need to scan the complete array. But in the average case it reduces the complexity even though the growth rate is the same.

Space complexity: $O(1)$.

**Note:** For the above algorithm we can make further improvement by incrementing the index at a faster rate (say, 2). This will reduce the number of comparisons for searching in the sorted list.

## 11.6 Binary Search

Let us consider the problem of searching a word in a dictionary. Typically, we directly go to some approximate page [say, middle page] and start searching from that point. If the *name* that we are searching is the same then the search is complete. If the page is before the selected pages then apply the same process for the first half; otherwise apply the same process to the second half. Binary search also works in the same way. The algorithm applying such a strategy is referred to as *binary search* algorithm.

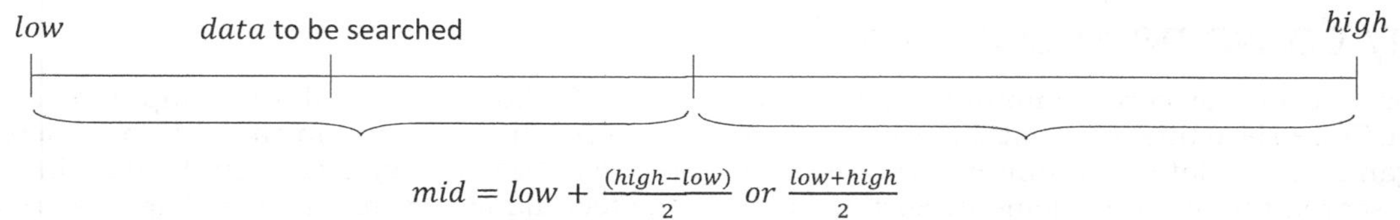


$$mid = low + \frac{(high-low)}{2} \; or \; \frac{low+high}{2}$$

```
//Iterative Binary Search Algorithm
int binarySearchIterative(int A[], int n, int data) {
    int low = 0;
    int high = n-1;
    while (low <= high) {
        mid = low + (high-low)/2; //To avoid overflow
        if(A[mid] == data)
            return mid;
        else if(A[mid] < data)
            low = mid + 1;
        else high = mid - 1;
    }
    return -1;
}
//Recursive Binary Search Algorithm
int binarySearchRecursive(int A[], int low, int high, int data) {
    int mid = low + (high-low)/2; //To avoid overflow
    if (low>high)
      return -1;
    if(A[mid] == data)
        return mid;
    else if(A[mid] < data)
        return BinarySearchRecursive (A, mid + 1, high, data);
    else   return BinarySearchRecursive (A, low, mid - 1 , data);
    return -1;
}
```

Recurrence for binary search is $T(n) = T(\frac{n}{2}) + \Theta(1)$. This is because we are always considering only half of the input list and throwing out the other half. Using *Divide and Conquer* master theorem, we get, $T(n) = O(logn)$.

Time Complexity: $O(logn)$. Space Complexity: $O(1)$ [for iterative algorithm].

## 11.7 Interpolation Search

Undoubtedly binary search is a great algorithm for searching with average running time complexity of $logn$. It always chooses the middle of the remaining search space, discarding one half or the other, again depending on the comparison between the key value found at the estimated (middle) position and the key value sought. The remaining search space is reduced to the part before or after the estimated position.

In the mathematics, interpolation is a process of constructing new data points within the range of a discrete set of known data points. In computer science, one often has a number of data points which represent the values of a function for a limited number of values of the independent variable. It is often required to interpolate (i.e. estimate) the value of that function for an intermediate value of the independent variable.

For example, suppose we have a table like this, which gives some values of an unknown function *f*. Interpolation provides a means of estimating the function at intermediate points, such as $x = 5.5$.

| $x$ | $f(x)$ |
|---|---|
| 1 | 10 |
| 2 | 20 |
| 3 | 30 |
| 4 | 40 |
| 5 | 50 |
| 6 | 60 |
| 7 | 70 |

There are many different interpolation methods, and one of the simplest methods is linear interpolation. Consider the above example of estimating $f(5.5)$. Since 5.5 is midway between 5 and 6, it is reasonable to take $f(5.5)$ midway between $f(5) = 50$ and $f(6) = 60$, which yields 55 ((50+60)/2).

Linear interpolation takes two data points, say $(x_1, y_1)$ and $(x_2, y_2)$, and the interpolant is given by:

$$y = y_1 + (y_2 - y_1)\frac{x - x_1}{x_2 - x_1} \text{ at point } (x, y)$$

With above inputs, what will happen if we don't use the constant ½, but another more accurate constant "K", that can lead us closer to the searched item.

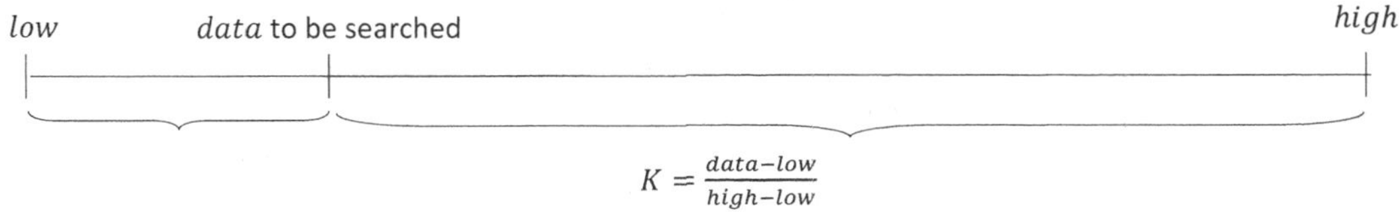


$$K = \frac{data - low}{high - low}$$

This algorithm tries to follow the way we search a name in a phone book, or a word in the dictionary. We, humans, know in advance that in case the name we're searching starts with a "m", like "monk" for instance, we should start searching near the middle of the phone book. Thus if we're searching the word "career" in the dictionary, you know that it should be placed somewhere at the beginning. This is because we know the order of the letters, we know the interval (a-z), and somehow we intuitively know that the words are dispersed equally. These facts are enough to realize that the binary search can be a bad choice. Indeed the binary search algorithm divides the list in two equal sub-lists, which is useless if we know in advance that the searched item is somewhere in the beginning or the end of the list. Yes, we can use also jump search if the item is at the beginning, but not if it is at the end, in that case this algorithm is not so effective.

The interpolation search algorithm tries to improve the binary search. The question is how to find this value? Well, we know bounds of the interval and looking closer to the image above we can define the following formula.

$$K = \frac{data - low}{high - low}$$

This constant $K$ is used to narrow down the search space. For binary search, this constant $K$ is $(low + high)/2$.

Now we can be sure that we're closer to the searched value. On average the interpolation search makes about $log(logn)$ comparisons (if the elements are uniformly distributed), where $n$ is the number of elements to be searched. In the worst case (for instance where the numerical values of the keys increase exponentially) it can make up to O($n$) comparisons. In interpolation-sequential search, interpolation is used to find an item near the one being searched for, then linear search is used to find the exact item. For this algorithm to give best results, the dataset should be ordered and uniformly distributed.

```
int interpolationSearch(int A[], int data){
    int low = 0, mid, high = sizeof(A) – 1;
    while (low <= high) {
        mid = low + (((data – A[low]) * (high – low))/(A[high] – A[low]));
        if (data == A[mid])
            return mid + 1;
        if (data < A[mid])
            high = mid - 1;
        else
```

```
            low = mid + 1;
        }
        return -1;
    }
```

## 11.8 Comparing Basic Searching Algorithms

| Implementation | Search-Worst Case | Search-Average Case |
|---|---|---|
| Unordered Array | $n$ | $n/2$ |
| Ordered Array (Binary Search) | $logn$ | $logn$ |
| Unordered List | $n$ | $n/2$ |
| Ordered List | $n$ | $n/2$ |
| Binary Search Trees (for skew trees) | $n$ | $logn$ |
| Interpolation search | $n$ | $log(logn)$ |

**Note:** For discussion on binary search trees refer to *Trees* chapter.

## 11.9 Symbol Tables and Hashing

Refer to *Symbol Tables* and *Hashing* chapters.

## 11.10 String Searching Algorithms

Refer to *String Algorithms* chapter.

## 11.11 Searching: Problems & Solutions

**Problem-1** Given an array of $n$ numbers, give an algorithm for checking whether there are any duplicate elements in the array or not?

**Solution:** This is one of the simplest problems. One obvious answer to this is exhaustively searching for duplicates in the array. That means, for each input element check whether there is any element with the same value. This we can solve just by using two simple *for* loops. The code for this solution can be given as:

```
void checkDuplicatesBruteForce(int A[], int n) {
    for(int i = 0; i < n; i++) {
        for(int j = i+1; j < n; j++) {
            if(A[i] == A[j])        {
                printf("Duplicates exist: %d", A[i]);
                return;
            }
        }
    }
    printf("No duplicates in given array.");
}
```

Time Complexity: $O(n^2)$, for two nested *for* loops. Space Complexity: O(1).

**Problem-2** Can we improve the complexity of Problem-1's solution?

**Solution: Yes.** Sort the given array. After sorting, all the elements with equal values will be adjacent. Now, do another scan on this sorted array and see if there are elements with the same value and adjacent.

```
void checkDuplicatesSorting(int A[], int n) {
    sort(A, n);                     //sort the array
    for(int i = 0; i < n-1; i++) {
        if(A[i] == A[i+1]) {
            printf("Duplicates exist: %d", A[i]);
            return;
        }
    }
    printf("No duplicates in given array.");
}
```

Time Complexity: $O(nlogn)$, for sorting (assuming $nlogn$ sorting algorithm). Space Complexity: O(1).

**Problem-3** Is there any alternative way of solving *Problem-1*?

**Solution: Yes**, using hash table. Hash tables are a simple and effective method used to implement dictionaries. *Average* time to search for an element is O(1), while worst-case time is O($n$). Refer to *Hashing* chapter for more details on hashing algorithms. As an example, consider the array, $A = \{3, 2, 1, 2, 2, 3\}$.

Scan the input array and insert the elements into the hash. For each inserted element, keep the *counter* as 1 (assume initially all entires are filled with zeros). This indicates that the corresponding element has occurred already. For the given array, the hash table will look like (after inserting the first three elements 3, 2 and 1):

| Key | | Counter |
|---|---|---|
| 1 | → | 1 |
| 2 | → | 1 |
| 3 | → | 1 |

Now if we try inserting 2, since the counter value of 2 is already 1, we can say the element has appeared twice.

Time Complexity: O($n$). Space Complexity: O($n$).

**Problem-4** Can we further improve the complexity of Problem-1 solution?

**Solution:** Let us assume that the array elements are positive numbers and also all the elements are in the range 0 to $n - 1$. For each element $A[i]$, go to the array element whose index is $A[i]$. That means select $A[A[i]]$ and mark - $A[A[i]]$ (negate the value at $A[A[i]]$). Continue this process until we encounter the element whose value is already negated. If one such element exists then we say duplicate elements exist in the given array. As an example, consider the array, $A = \{3, 2, 1, 2, 2, 3\}$.

Initially,

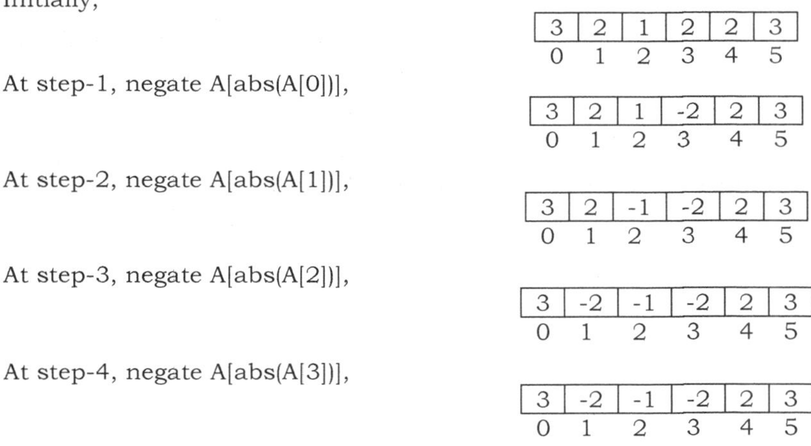

At step-1, negate A[abs(A[0])],

At step-2, negate A[abs(A[1])],

At step-3, negate A[abs(A[2])],

At step-4, negate A[abs(A[3])],

At step-4, observe that $A[abs(A[3])]$ is already negative. That means we have encountered the same value twice.

```
void checkDuplicates(int A[], int n) {
    for(int i = 0; i < n; i++) {
        if(A[abs(A[i])] < 0) {
            printf("Duplicates exist:%d", A[i]);
            return;
        }
        else A[A[i]] = - A[A[i]];
    }
    printf("No duplicates in given array.");
}
```

Time Complexity: O($n$). Since only one scan is required. Space Complexity: O(1).

**Notes:**

- This solution does not work if the given array is read only.
- This solution will work only if all the array elements are positive.
- If the elements range is not in 0 to $n - 1$ then it may give exceptions.

**Problem-5** Given an array of $n$ numbers. Give an algorithm for finding the element which appears the maximum number of times in the array?

**Brute Force Solution:** One simple solution to this is, for each input element check whether there is any element with the same value, and for each such occurrence, increment the counter. Each time, check the current counter with the *max* counter and update it if this value is greater than *max* counter. This we can solve just by using two simple *for* loops.

```
int maxRepetitions(int A[], int n) {
    int counter =0, max=0;
    for(int i = 0; i < n; i++) {
```

```
        counter=0;
        for(int j = 0; j < n; j++) {
            if(A[i] == A[j])
                counter++;
        }
        if(counter > max) max = counter;
    }
    return max;
}
```

Time Complexity: $O(n^2)$, for two nested *for* loops. Space Complexity: O(1).

**Problem-6** Can we improve the complexity of Problem-5 solution?

**Solution: Yes.** Sort the given array. After sorting, all the elements with equal values come adjacent. Now, just do another scan on this sorted array and see which element is appearing the maximum number of times.

Time Complexity: $O(nlogn)$. (for sorting). Space Complexity: O(1).

**Problem-7** Is there any other way of solving Problem-5?

**Solution: Yes,** using hash table. For each element of the input, keep track of how many times that element appeared in the input. That means the counter value represents the number of occurrences for that element.

Time Complexity: $O(n)$. Space Complexity: $O(n)$.

**Problem-8** For Problem-5, can we improve the time complexity? Assume that the elements' range is 1 to $n$. That means all the elements are within this range only.

**Solution: Yes.** We can solve this problem in two scans. We *cannot* use the negation technique of Problem-3 for this problem because of the number of repetitions. In the first scan, instead of negating, add the value $n$. That means for each occurrence of an element add the array size to that element. In the second scan, check the element value by dividing it by $n$ and return the element which gives the maximum value. The code based on this method is given below.

```
void maxRepetitions(int A[], int n) {
    int i = 0, max = 0, maxIndex;
    for(i = 0; i < n; i++)
        A[A[i]%n] +=n;
    for(i = 0; i < n; i++)
        if(A[i]/n > max) {
            max = A[i]/n;
            maxIndex =i;
        }
    return maxIndex;
}
```

**Notes:**

- This solution does not work if the given array is read only.
- This solution will work only if the array elements are positive.
- If the elements range is not in 1 to $n$ then it may give exceptions.

Time Complexity: $O(n)$. Since no nested *for* loops are required. Space Complexity: O(1).

**Problem-9** Given an array of $n$ numbers, give an algorithm for finding the first element in the array which is repeated. For example, in the array $A = \{3, 2, 1, 2, 2, 3\}$, the first repeated number is 3 (not 2). That means, we need to return the first element among the repeated elements.

**Solution:** We can use the brute force solution that we used for Problem-1. For each element, since it checks whether there is a duplicate for that element or not, whichever element duplicates first will be returned.

**Problem-10** For Problem-9, can we use the sorting technique?

**Solution:** No. For proving the failed case, let us consider the following array. For example, $A = \{3, 2, 1, 2, 2, 3\}$. After sorting we get $A = \{1, 2, 2, 2, 3, 3\}$. In this sorted array the first repeated element is 2 but the actual answer is 3.

**Problem-11** For Problem-9, can we use the hashing technique?

**Solution:** Yes. But the simple hashing technique which we used for Problem-3 will not work. For example, if we consider the input array as A = {3, 2, 1, 2, 3}, then the first repeated element is 3, but using our simple hashing technique we get the answer as 2. This is because 2 is coming twice before 3. Now let us change the hashing table behavior so that we get the first repeated element. Let us say, instead of storing 1 value, initially we store the position of the element in the array. As a result the hash table will look like (after inserting 3, 2 and 1):

| 1 | → 3 |
|---|---|

| | | |
|---|---|---|
| 2 | → | 2 |
| 3 | → | 1 |

Now, if we see 2 again, we just negate the current value of 2 in the hash table. That means, we make its counter value as −2. The negative value in the hash table indicates that we have seen the same element two times. Similarly, for 3 (the next element in the input) also, we negate the current value of the hash table and finally the hash table will look like:

| | | |
|---|---|---|
| 1 | → | 3 |
| 2 | → | -2 |
| 3 | → | -1 |

After processing the complete input array, scan the hash table and return the highest negative indexed value from it (i.e., −1 in our case). The highest negative value indicates that we have seen that element first (among repeated elements) and also repeating.

**What if the element is repeated more than twice?** In this case, just skip the element if the corresponding value $i$ is already negative.

**Problem-12** For Problem-9, can we use the technique that we used for Problem-3 (negation technique)?

**Solution: No.** As an example of contradiction, for the array $A = \{3, 2, 1, 2, 2, 3\}$ the first repeated element is 3. But with negation technique the result is 2.

**Problem-13** **Find the Missing Number:** We are given a list of $n - 1$ integers and these integers are in the range of 1 to $n$. There are no duplicates in the list. One of the integers is missing in the list. Given an algorithm to find the missing integer. **Example**: I/P: $[1, 2, 4, 6, 3, 7, 8]$ O/P: 5

**Alternative problem statement**: There is an array of numbers. A second array is formed by shuffling the elements of the first array and deleting a random element. Given these two arrays, find which element is missing in the second array.

**Brute Force Solution:** One naive way to solve this problem is for each number $i$ in the range 1 to $n$, check whether number $i$ is in the given array or not.

```
int findMissingNumber(int A[], int n) {
    int i, j, found=0;
    for (i = 1; i < =n; i ++) {
        found = 0;
        for (j = 0; j < n; j ++)
            if(A[j]==i)
                found = 1;
        if(!found) return i;
    }
    return -1;
}
```

Time Complexity: $O(n^2)$. Space Complexity: O(1).

**Problem-14** For **Error! Reference source not found.**, can we use the sorting technique?

**Solution: Yes.** More efficient solution is to sort the first array, so while checking whether an element in the range 1 to $n$ appears in the given array, we can do binary search.

Time Complexity: $O(nlogn)$, for sorting. Space Complexity: O(1).

**Problem-15** For **Error! Reference source not found.**, can we use the hashing technique?

**Solution: Yes.** Scan the input array and insert elements into the hash. For inserted elements, keep *counter* as 1 (assume initially all entires are filled with zeros). This indicates that the corresponding element has occurred already. Now, for each element in the range 1 to $n$ check the hash table and return the element which has counter value zero. That is, once hit an element with zero count that's the missing element.

Time Complexity: $O(n)$. Space Complexity: $O(n)$.

**Problem-16** For **Error! Reference source not found.**, can we improve the complexity?

**Solution: Yes**. We can use summation formula.

1) Get the sum of numbers, $sum = n \times (n + 1)/2$.
2) Subtract all the numbers from *sum* and you will get the missing number.

Time Complexity: $O(n)$, for scanning the complete array.

**Problem-17** In **Error! Reference source not found.**, if the sum of the numbers goes beyond the maximum allowed integer, then there can be integer overflow and we may not get the correct answer. Can we solve this problem?

**Solution:**

1) $XOR$ all the array elements, let the result of $XOR$ be $X$.
2) $XOR$ all numbers from 1 to $n$, let $XOR$ be Y.
3) $XOR$ of $X$ and $Y$ gives the missing number.

```
int findMissingNumber(int A[], int n) {
        int i, X, Y;
        for (i = 0; i < n; i ++)
            X ^= A[i];
      for (i = 1; i <= n; i ++)
            Y ^= i;
      //In fact, one variable is enough.
      return X ^ Y;
}
```

Let's analyze why this approach works. What happens when we XOR two numbers? We should think bitwise, instead of decimal. XORing a 4-bit number with 1101 would flip the first, second, and fourth bits of the number. XORing the result again with 1101 would flip those bits back to their original value. So, if we XOR a number two times with some number nothing will change. We can also XOR with multiple numbers and the order would not matter. For example, say we XOR the number number1 with number2, then XOR the result with number3, then XOR their result with number2, and then with number3. The final result would be the original number number1. Because every XOR operation flips some bits and when we XOR with the same number again, we flip those bits back. So the order of XOR operations is not important. If we XOR a number with some number an odd number of times, there will be no effect.

Above we XOR all the numbers in the given range 1 to $n$ and given array A. All numbers in given array A are from the range 1 to $n$, but there is an extra number in range 1 to $n$. So the effect of each XOR from array A is being reset by the corresponding same number in the range 1 to $n$ (remember that the order of XOR is not important). But we can't reset the XOR of the extra number in the range 1 to $n$, because it doesn't appear in array A. So the result is as if we XOR 0 with that extra number, which is the number itself. Since XOR of a number with 0 is the number. Therefore, in the end we get the missing number in array A. The space complexity of this solution is constant O(1) since we only use one extra variable. Time complexity is O($n$) because we perform a single pass from the array A and the range 1 to $n$.

Time Complexity: O($n$), for scanning the complete array. Space Complexity: O(1).

**Problem-18** **Find the Number Occurring an Odd Number of Times:** Given an array of positive integers, all numbers occur an even number of times except one number which occurs an odd number of times. Find the number in O($n$) time & constant space. **Example**: $I/P = [1, 2, 3, 2, 3, 1, 3]$ $O/P = 3$

**Solution:** Do a bitwise $XOR$ of all the elements. We get the number which has odd occurrences. This is because, $A\ XOR\ A = 0$.

Time Complexity: O($n$). Space Complexity: O(1).

**Problem-19** **Find the two repeating elements in a given array:** Given an array with $size$, all elements of the array are in range 1 to $n$ and also all elements occur only once except two numbers which occur twice. Find those two repeating numbers. For example: if the array is 4, 2, 4, 5, 2, 3, 1 with $size = 7$ and $n = 5$. This input has $n + 2 = 7$ elements with all elements occurring once except 2 and 4 which occur twice. So the output should be 4 2.

**Solution:** One simple way is to scan the complete array for each element of the input elements. That means use two loops. In the outer loop, select elements one by one and count the number of occurrences of the selected element in the inner loop. For the code below, assume that $PrintRepeatedElements$ is called with $n + 2$ to indicate the size.

```
void PrintRepeatedElements(int A[], int size) {
        for(int i = 0; i < size; i++)
                for(int j = i+1; j < size; j++)
                        if(A[i] == A[j])
                                printf("%d", A[i]);
}
```

Time Complexity: O($n^2$). Space Complexity: O(1).

**Problem-20** For Problem-19, can we improve the time complexity?

**Solution:** Sort the array using any comparison sorting algorithm and see if there are any elements which are contiguous with the same value.

Time Complexity: O($nlogn$). Space Complexity: O(1).

**Problem-21** For Problem-19, can we improve the time complexity?

**Solution:** Use Count Array. This solution is like using a hash table. For simplicity we can use array for storing the counts. Traverse the array once and keep track of the count of all elements in the array using a temp array *count*[] of size $n$. When we see an element whose count is already set, print it as duplicate. For the code below assume that *PrintRepeatedElements* is called with $n + 2$ to indicate the size.

```
void PrintRepeatedElements(int A[], int size) {
    int *count = (int *)calloc(sizeof(int), (size - 2));
    for(int i = 0; i < size; i++) {
            count[A[i]]++;
            if(count[A[i]] == 2)
                    printf("%d", A[i]);
    }
}
```

Time Complexity: O($n$). Space Complexity: O($n$).

**Problem-22** Consider Problem-19. Let us assume that the numbers are in the range 1 to $n$. Is there any other way of solving the problem?

**Solution: Yes, by using XOR Operation.** Let the repeating numbers be $X$ and $Y$, if we $XOR$ all the elements in the array and also all integers from 1 to $n$, then the result will be $X\ XOR\ Y$. The 1's in binary representation of $X\ XOR\ Y$ correspond to the different bits between $X$ and $Y$. If the $k^{th}$ bit of $X\ XOR\ Y$ is 1, we can $XOR$ all the elements in the array and also all integers from 1 to $n$ whose $k^{th}$ bits are 1. The result will be one of $X$ and $Y$.

```
void PrintRepeatedElements (int A[], int size) {
    int XOR = A[0];
    int i, right_most_set_bit_no, X= 0, Y = 0;
    for(i = 0; i < size; i++)                    // Compute XOR of all elements in A[]
            XOR ^= A[i];
    for(i = 1; i <= n; i++)                      // Compute XOR of all elements {1, 2 ..n}
            XOR ^= i;
    right_most_set_bit_no = XOR & ~( XOR -1);    // Get the rightmost set bit in right_most_set_bit_no
    // Now divide elements in two sets by comparing rightmost set
    for(i = 0; i < size; i++) {
            if(A[i] & right_most_set_bit_no)
                    X = X^ A[i];             // XOR of first set in A[]
            else    Y = Y ^ A[i];            // XOR of second set in A[]
    }
    for(i = 1; i <= n; i++) {
            if(i & right_most_set_bit_no)
                    X = X ^ i;                  // XOR of first set in A[] and {1, 2, ...n }
            else    Y = Y ^ i;                  // XOR of second set in A[] and {1, 2, ...n }
    }
    printf("%d and %d",X, Y);
}
```

Time Complexity: O($n$). Space Complexity: O(1).

**Problem-23** Consider Problem-19. Let us assume that the numbers are in the range 1 to $n$. Is there yet other way of solving the problem?

**Solution:** We can solve this by creating two simple mathematical equations. Let us assume that two numbers we are going to find are $X$ and $Y$. We know the sum of $n$ numbers is $n(n+1)/2$ and the product is $n!$. Make two equations using these sum and product formulae, and get values of two unknowns using the two equations. Let the summation of all numbers in array be $S$ and product be $P$ and the numbers which are being repeated are $X$ and $Y$.

$$X + Y = S - \frac{n(n+1)}{2}$$
$$XY = P/n!$$

Using the above two equations, we can find out $X$ and $Y$. There can be an addition and multiplication overflow problem with this approach.

Time Complexity: O($n$). Space Complexity: O(1).

**Problem-24** Can we solve this problem with negation technique?

**Solution**: This solution works only if array has positive integers and all the elements in the array are in range from 1 to $n$. The algorithm for this problem involces navigating the array and updating the array for every $i^{th}$index as $A[abs(A[i])] = A[abs(A[i])] * -1$. If $A[i]$ is already negative, then it means we are visiting it second time, means it is repeated.

```
void PrintRepeatedElementsWithNegationTechnique(int A[], int size) {
  int i;
  printf("n The repeating elements are");
  for(i = 0; i < size; i++) {
    if(A[abs(A[i])] > 0)
      A[abs(A[i])] = -A[abs(A[i])];
    else
      printf(" %d ", abs(A[i]));
  }
}
```

Time Complexity: O($n$). Space Complexity: O(1).

**Problem-25** Similar to Problem-19, let us assume that the numbers are in the range 1 to $n$. Also, $n - 1$ elements are repeated thrice and the remaining element repeated twice. Find the element which repeated twice.

**Solution:** If we $XOR$ all the elements in the array and all integers from 1 to $n$, then all the elements which are repeated thrice will become zero. This is because, since the element is repeating thrice and $XOR$ another time from range makes that element appear four times. As a result, the output of $a\, XOR\, a\, XOR\, a\, XOR\, a = 0$. It is the same case with all elements that are repeated three times.

With the same logic, for the element which repeated twice, if we $XOR$ the input elements and also the range, then the total number of appearances for that element is 3. As a result, the output of $a\, XOR\, a\, XOR\, a = a$. Finally, we get the element which repeated twice.

Time Complexity: O($n$). Space Complexity: O(1).

**Problem-26** Given an array of $n$ elements. Find two elements in the array such that their sum is equal to given element $K$.

**Brute Force Solution:** One simple solution to this is, for each input element, check whether there is any element whose sum is $K$. This we can solve just by using two simple for loops. The code for this solution can be given as:

```
void bruteForceSearch[int A[], int n, int K) {
    for (int i = 0; i < n; i++) {
            for(int j = i; j < n; j++) {
                    if(A[i]+A[j] == K) {
                            printf("Items Found:%d %d", i, j);
                            return;
                    }
            }
    }
    printf("Items not found: No such elements");
}
```

Time Complexity: O($n^2$). This is because of two nested $for$ loops. Space Complexity: O(1).

**Problem-27** For Problem-26, can we improve the time complexity?

**Solution: Yes.** Let us assume that we have sorted the given array. This operation takes O($n\, logn$). On the sorted array, maintain indices $loIndex = 0$ and hiIndex = $n - 1$ and compute $A[loIndex] + A[hiIndex]$. If the sum equals $K$, then we are done with the solution. If the sum is less than $K$, decrement $hiIndex$, if the sum is greater than $K$, increment $loIndex$.

```
void search[int A[], int n, int K) {
    int loIndex, hiIndex, sum;
    sort(A, n);
    for(loIndex = 0, hiIndex = n-1; loIndex < hiIndex) {
            sum = A[loIndex] + A[hiIndex];
            if(sum == K) {
                    printf("Elements Found: %d  %d", loIndex, hiIndex);
                    return;
            }
            else if(sum < K)
                    loIndex = loIndex + 1;
            else    hiIndex = hiIndex - 1;
```

```
        }
        return;
}
```

Time Complexity: $O(nlogn)$. If the given array is already sorted then the complexity is $O(n)$.
Space Complexity: $O(1)$.

**Problem-28** Does the solution of Problem-26 work even if the array is not sorted?

**Solution: Yes.** Since we are checking all possibilities, the algorithm ensures that we get the pair of numbers if they exist.

**Problem-29** Is there any other way of solving Problem-26?

**Solution: Yes,** using hash table. Since our objective is to find two indexes of the array whose sum is $K$. Let us say those indexes are $X$ and $Y$. That means, $A[X] + A[Y] = K$. What we need is, for each element of the input array $A[X]$, check whether $K - A[X]$ also exists in the input array. Now, let us simplify that searching with hash table.

**Algorithm:**

- For each element of the input array, insert it into the hash table. Let us say the current element is $A[X]$.
- Before proceeding to the next element we check whether $K$ - $A[X]$ also exists in the hash table or not.
- Ther existence of such number indicates that we are able to find the indexes.
- Otherwise proceed to the next input element.

Time Complexity: $O(n)$. Space Complexity: $O(n)$.

**Problem-30** Given an array A of $n$ elements. Find three indices, $i, j$ & $k$ such that $A[i]^2 + A[j]^2 = A[k]^2$?

**Solution:**

**Algorithm:**

- Sort the given array in-place.
- For each array index $i$ compute $A[i]^2$ and store in array.
- Search for 2 numbers in array from 0 to $i - 1$ which adds to $A[i]$ similar to Problem-26. This will give us the result in $O(n)$ time. If we find such a sum, return true, otherwise continue.

```
sort(A); // Sort the input array
for (int i=0; i < n; i++)
        A[i] = A[i]*A[i];
for (i=n; i > 0; i--) {
        res = false;
        if(res) {
                //Problem-11/12 Solution
        }
}
```

Time Complexity: Time for sorting + $n \times$ (Time for finding the sum) = $O(nlogn) + n \times O(n) = n^2$.
Space Complexity: $O(1)$.

**Problem-31** **Two elements whose sum is closest to zero.** Given an array with both positive and negative numbers, find the two elements such that their sum is closest to zero. For the below array, algorithm should give $-80$ and 85. Example: 1 60 $-10$ 70 $-80$ 85.

**Brute Force Solution:** For each element, find the *sum* with every other element in the array and compare sums. Finally, return the minimum sum.

```
void twoElementsWithMinSum(int A[], int n) {
        int i, j, min_sum, sum, min_i, min_j, inv_count = 0;
        if(n < 2) {
                printf("Invalid Input");
                return;
        }
        // Initialization
        min_i = 0;
        min_j = 1;
        min_sum = A[0] + A[1];
        for(i= 0; i < n - 1; i ++)      {
                for(j = i + 1; j < n; j++)      {
                        sum = A[i] + A[j];
                        if(abs(min_sum) > abs(sum)) {
                                min_sum = sum;
                                min_i = i;
```

```
                    min_j = j;
                }
            }
        }
        printf(" The two elements are %d and %d", A[min_i], A[min_j]);
}
```

Time complexity: O($n^2$). Space Complexity: O(1).

**Problem-32** Can we improve the time complexity of Problem-31?

**Solution:** Use Sorting.

**Algorithm:**

1. Sort all the elements of the given input array.
2. Maintain two indexes, one at the beginning ($i = 0$) and the other at the ending ($j = n - 1$). Also, maintain two variables to keep track of the smallest positive sum closest to zero and the smallest negative sum closest to zero.
3. While $i < j$:
   a. If the current pair sum is > zero and < postiveClosest then update the postiveClosest. Decrement $j$.
   b. If the current pair sum is < zero and > negativeClosest then update the negativeClosest. Increment $i$.
   c. Else, print the pair.

```
void twoElementsWithMinSum(int A[], int n) {
    int i = 0, j = n-1, temp, postiveClosest = INT_MAX, negativeClosest = INT_MIN;
    sort(A, n);
    while(i < j) {
        temp  = A[i] + A[j];
        if(temp  > 0) {
            if (temp < postiveClosest)
                postiveClosest = temp;
            j--;
        }
        else if (temp  < 0) {
            if (temp > negativeClosest)
                negativeClosest = temp;
            i++;
        }
        else printf("Closest Sum: %d ", A[i] + A[j]);
    }
    return (abs(negativeClosest)> postiveClosest: postiveClosest: negativeClosest);
}
```

Time Complexity: O($nlogn$), for sorting. Space Complexity: O(1).

**Problem-33** **Find elements whose sum is closest to given target.** Given an array with both positive and negative numbers, find the two elements such that their sum is closest to given target. Given A = [2, 7, 11, 15], target = 9. Because, A[0] + A[1] = 2 + 7 = 9, return [0, 1].

**Brute Force Solution:** The brute force approach is simple. Loop through each element $A[i]$ and find if there is another value that equals to $target - A[i]$.

```
int* twoSum(int* A, int numsSize, int target, int* returnSize){
    int i, j;
    int *result = (int*)malloc(2 * sizeof(int));
    *returnSize = 2;
    for(i=0; i < numsSize; i++){
        for(j=i+1; j < numsSize; j++){
            if(A[i] + A[j] == target){
                result[0] = i;
                result[1] = j;
            }
        }
    }
    return result;
}
```

Time complexity: O($n^2$). Space Complexity: O(1).

**Problem-34** Can we use sorting technique for solving the Problem-33?

**Solution**: We can use the sorting technique and solution is based on the binary search logic.

```
vector<int> twoSum(vector<int>& A, int target) {
    vector<int> ns = A;
    int l = 0, r = ns.size()-1;
    sort(ns.begin(), ns.end());
    while (l < r) {
        int s = ns[l]+ns[r];
        if (s > target)
            r--;
        else if (s < target)
            l++;
        else
            break;
    }
    vector<int> res;
    for (unsigned int i=0; i<A.size(); i++) {
        if (A[i] == ns[l])
            res.push_back(i+1);
        else if (A[i] == ns[r])
            res.push_back(i+1);
    }
    if (res[0] > res[1])
        swap(res[0], res[1]);
    return res;
}
```

**Problem-35** Can we use hash tables for solving the Problem-33?

**Solution**: To improve our run time complexity, we need a more efficient way to check if the complement exists in the array. If the complement exists, we need to look up its index. What is the best way to maintain a mapping of each element in the array to its index? A hash table.

We reduce the look up time from O($n$) to O(1) by trading space for speed. A hash table is built exactly for this purpose, it supports fast look up in near constant time. I say "near" because if a collision occurred, a look up could degenerate to O($n$) time. But, look up in hash table should be amortized O(1) time as long as the hash function was chosen carefully.

A simple implementation uses two iterations. In the first iteration, we add each element's value and its index to the table. Then, in the second iteration we check if each element's complement ($target - A[i]$) exists in the table. Beware that the complement must not be A[i] itself!

```
vector<int> twoSum(vector<int>& A, int target) {
    int len = A.size();
    vector<int> ans = {};
    unordered_map<int,int> mp;
    for(int i = 0; i < len ; i++) {
        ++mp[A[i]] = i;
    }
    for(int j = 0; j < len; j++) {
        if((mp.find(target - A[j]) != mp.end())&&(mp.find(target - A[j])->second != j)) {
            if(j < mp.find(target - A[j])->second) {
                ans.push_back(j + 1);
                ans.push_back(mp.find(target - A[j])->second + 1);
            } else {
                ans.push_back(mp.find(target - A[j])->second + 1);
                ans.push_back(j + 1);
            }
            return ans;
        }
    }
    return ans;
}
```

Time complexity: O($n$). We traverse the list containing nn elements exactly twice. Since the hash table reduces the look up time to O(1), the time complexity is O($n$).
Space complexity: O($n$). The extra space required depends on the number of items stored in the hash table, which stores exactly $n$ elements.

It turns out we can do it in one-pass. While we iterate and inserting elements into the table, we also look back to check if current element's complement already exists in the table. If it exists, we have found a solution and return immediately.

```
class Solution {
public:
    vector<int> twoSum(vector<int>& A, int target) {
        int i = 0, n = A.size();
        unordered_map<int, int> m;
        vector<int> ret;
        for (i = 0; i < n; ++i){
            if (m.find(target - A[i]) != m.end()){
                ret.push_back(m[target - A[i]]);
                ret.push_back(i);
                break;
            }
            m[A[i]] = i;
        }
        return ret;
    }
};
```

Time complexity: O($n$). We traverse the list containing $n$ elements only once. Each look up in the table costs only O(1) time.
Space complexity: O($n$). The extra space required depends on the number of items stored in the hash table, which stores at most $n$ elements.

**Problem-36** Given an array of $n$ elements. Find three elements in the array such that their sum is equal to given element $K$?

**Brute Force Solution:** The default solution to this is, for each pair of input elements check whether there is any element whose sum is $K$. This we can solve just by using three simple for loops. The code for this solution can be given as:

```
void bruteForceSearch[int A[], int n, int data) {
    for (int i = 0; i < n; i++) {
        for(int j = i+1; j < n; j++) {
            for(int k = j+1; k < n; k++)        {
                if(A[i] + A[j] + A[k]== data) {
                    printf("Items Found:%d %d %d", i, j, k);
                    return;
                }
            }
        }
    }
    printf("Items not found: No such elements");
}
```

Time Complexity: O($n^3$), for three nested $for$ loops. Space Complexity: O(1).

**Problem-37** Does the solution of Problem-36 work even if the array is not sorted?

**Solution: Yes.** Since we are checking all possibilities, the algorithm ensures that we can find three numbers whose sum is $K$ if they exist.

**Problem-38** Can we use the sorting technique for solving Problem-36?

**Solution: Yes.**

```
void search[int A[], int n, int data) {
    sort(A, n);
    for(int k = 0; k < n; k++) {
        for(int i =  k + 1, j = n-1; i < j;  ) {
            if(A[k] + A[i] + A[j]  == data) {
```

```
                    printf("Items Found:%d %d %d", i, j, k);
                    return;
               }
               else if(A[k] + A[i] + A[j]  < data)
                    i =  i + 1;
               else      j = j - 1;
          }
     }
     return;
}
```

Time Complexity: Time for sorting + Time for searching in sorted list = $O(nlogn) + O(n^2) \approx O(n^2)$. This is because of two nested *for* loops. Space Complexity: O(1).

**Problem-39** Can we use the hashing technique for solving Problem-36?

**Solution: Yes.** Since our objective is to find three indexes of the array whose sum is $K$. Let us say those indexes are $X, Y$ and $Z$. That means, $A[X] + A[Y] + A[Z] = K$.

Let us assume that we have kept all possible sums along with their pairs in hash table. That means the key to hash table is $K - A[X]$ and values for $K - A[X]$ are all possible pairs of input whose sum is $K - A[X]$.

**Algorithm:**

- Before starting the search, insert all possible sums with pairs of elements into the hash table.
- For each element of the input array, insert into the hash table. Let us say the current element is $A[X]$.
- Check whether there exists a hash entry in the table with key: $K - A[X]$.
- If such element exists then scan the element pairs of $K - A[X]$ and return all possible pairs by including $A[X]$ also.
- If no such element exists (with $K - A[X]$ as key) then go to next element.

Time Complexity: The time for storing all possible pairs in Hash table + searching = $O(n^2) + O(n^2) \approx O(n^2)$. Space Complexity: $O(n)$.

**Problem-40** Given an array of $n$ integers, the $3 - sum\ problem$ is to find three integers whose sum is closest to *zero*.

**Solution:** This is the same as that of Problem-36 with $K$ value is zero.

**Problem-41** Let A be an array of $n$ distinct integers. Suppose A has the following property: there exists an index $1 \le k \le n$ such that $A[1], \ldots, A[k]$ is an increasing sequence and $A[k+1], \ldots, A[n]$ is a decreasing sequence. Design and analyze an efficient algorithm for finding $k$.
**Similar question:** Let us assume that the given array is sorted but starts with negative numbers and ends with positive numbers [such functions are called monotonically increasing functions]. In this array find the starting index of the positive numbers. Assume that we know the length of the input array. Design a $O(logn)$ algorithm.

**Solution:** Let us use a variant of the binary search.

```
int search (int A[], int n, int first, int last) {
  int mid, first = 0, last = n-1;
  while(first <= last) {
     // if the current array has size 1
     if(first == last)
               return A[first];
     // if the current array has size 2
     else if(first == last-1)
               return max(A[first], A[last]);
     // if the current array has size 3 or more
     else {
               mid = first + (last-first)/2;
               if(A[mid-1] < A[mid] && A[mid] > A[mid+1])
                         return A[mid];
               else if(A[mid-1] < A[mid] && A[mid] < A[mid+1])
                         first = mid+1;
               else if(A[mid-1] > A[mid] && A[mid] > A[mid+1])
                         last = mid-1;
               else      return INT_MIN ;
      } // end of else
   } // end of while
```

```
}
```

The recursion equation is $T(n) = 2T(n/2) + c$. Using master theorem, we get $O(logn)$.

**Problem-42** If we don't know $n$, how do we solve the Problem-41?

**Solution:** Repeatedly compute $A[1], A[2], A[4], A[8], A[16]$ and so on, until we find a value of $n$ such that $A[n] > 0$.

Time Complexity: $O(logn)$, since we are moving at the rate of 2. Refer to *Introduction to Analysis of Algorithms* chapter for details on this.

**Problem-43** Given an input array of size unknown with all $1's$ in the beginning and $0's$ in the end. Find the index in the array from where $0's$ start. Consider there are millions of $1's$ and $0's$ in the array. E.g. array contents 1111111.......1100000.........0000000.

**Solution:** This problem is almost similar to Problem-42. Check the bits at the rate of $2^K$ where $k = 0, 1, 2 ....$ Since we are moving at the rate of 2, the complexity is $O(logn)$.

**Problem-44** Given a sorted array of $n$ integers that has been rotated an unknown number of times, give a $O(logn)$ algorithm that finds an element in the array.
**Example**: Find 5 in array (15 16 19 20 25 1 3 4 5 7 10 14) **Output**: 8 (the index of 5 in the array)

**Solution:** Let us assume that the given array is $A[]$and use the solution of Problem-41 with an extension. The function below *FindPivot* returns the $k$ value (let us assume that this function returns the index instead of the value). Find the pivot point, divide the array into two sub-arrays and call binary search.

The main idea for finding the pivot point is – for a sorted (in increasing order) and pivoted array, the pivot element is the only element for which the next element to it is smaller than it. Using the above criteria and the binary search methodology we can get pivot element in $O(logn)$ time.

**Algorithm:**
1) Find out the pivot point and divide the array into two sub-arrays.
2) Now call binary search for one of the two sub-arrays.
   a. if the element is greater than the first element then search in left subarray.
   b. else search in right subarray.
3) If element is found in selected sub-array, then return index *else* return −1.

```
int findPivot(int A[], int start, int finish) {
    if(finish - start == 0)
        return start;
    else if(start == finish - 1) {
        if(A[start] >= A[finish])
            return start;
        else    return finish;
    }
    else {
        mid = start + (finish-start)/2;
        if(A[start] >= A[mid])
            return findPivot(A, start, mid);
        else    return findPivot(A, mid, finish);
    }
}
int search(int A[], int n, int x) {
    int pivot = findPivot(A, 0, n-1);
    if(A[pivot] == x)
        return pivot;
    if(A[pivot] <= x)
        return BinarySearch(A, 0, pivot-1, x);
    else return BinarySearch(A, pivot+1, n-1, x);
}
int BinarySearch(int A[], int low, int high, int x) {
    if(high >= low)  {
        int mid = low + (high - low)/2;
        if(x == A[mid])
            return mid;
        if(x > A[mid])
            return binarySearch(A, (mid + 1), high, x);
        else    return binarySearch(A, low, (mid -1), x);
    }
```

```
    return -1;        //-1 if element is not found
}
```

Time complexity: $O(logn)$.

**Problem-45** For Problem-44, can we solve in one scan?

**Solution: Yes.**

```
int binarySearchRotated(int A[], int start, int finish, int data) {
    int mid = start + (finish - start) / 2;
    if(start > finish)
        return -1;
    if(data == A[mid])
        return mid;
    else if(A[start] <= A[mid]) {           // start half is in sorted order.
        if(data >= A[start] && data < A[mid])
            return binarySearchRotated(A, start, mid - 1, data);
        else    return binarySearchRotated(A, mid + 1, finish, data);
    }
    else {                                  // A[mid] <= A[finish], finish half is in sorted order.
        if(data > A[mid] && data <= A[finish])
            return binarySearchRotated(A, mid + 1, finish, data);
        else    return binarySearchRotated(A, start, mid - 1, data);
    }
}
```

Time complexity: $O(logn)$.

**Problem-46** **Bitonic search:** An array is *bitonic* if it is comprised of an increasing sequence of integers followed immediately by a decreasing sequence of integers. Given a bitonic array A of n distinct integers, describe how to determine whether a given integer is in the array in $O(logn)$ steps.

**Solution:** The solution is the same as that for Problem-41.

**Problem-47** Yet, another way of framing Problem-41.
Let $A[]$ be an array that starts out increasing, reaches a maximum, and then decreases. Design an $O(logn)$ algorithm to find the index of the maximum value.

**Problem-48** Give an $O(nlogn)$ algorithm for computing the median of a sequence of $n$ integers.

**Solution:** Sort and return element at $\frac{n}{2}$.

**Problem-49** Given two sorted lists of size $m$ and $n$, find the median of all elements in $O(log\,(m+n))$ time.

**Solution:** Refer to to *Divide and Conquer* chapter.

**Problem-50** Given a sorted array $A$ of $n$ elements, possibly with duplicates, find the index of the first occurrence of a number in $O(logn)$ time.

**Solution:** To find the first occurrence of a number we need to check for the following condition. Return the position if any one of the following is true:

```
mid == low && A[mid] == data  ||  A[mid] == data && A[mid-1] < data
```

```
int binarySearchFirstOccurrence(int A[], int low, int high, int data) {
    int mid;
    if(high >= low) {
        mid = low + (high-low) / 2;
        if((mid == low && A[mid] == data) || (A[mid] == data && A[mid - 1] < data))
            return mid;
        // Give preference to left half of the array
        else if(A[mid] >= data)
            return binarySearchFirstOccurrence (A, low, mid - 1, data);
        else    return binarySearchFirstOccurrence (A, mid + 1, high, data);
    }
    return -1;
}
```

Time Complexity: $O(logn)$.

**Problem-51** Given a sorted array $A$ of $n$ elements, possibly with duplicates. Find the index of the last occurrence of a number in $O(logn)$ time.

**Solution:** To find the last occurrence of a number we need to check for the following condition. Return the position if any one of the following is true:

mid == high && A[mid] == data || A[mid] == data && A[mid+1] > data

```
int binarySearchLastOccurrence(int A[], int low, int high, int data) {
    int mid;
    if(high >= low) {
        mid = low + (high-low) / 2;
        if((mid == high && A[mid] == data) || (A[mid] == data && A[mid + 1] > data))
            return mid;
        // Give preference to right half of the array
        else if(A[mid] <= data)
            return binarySearchLastOccurrence (A, mid + 1, high, data);
        else    return binarySearchLastOccurrence (A, low, mod - 1, data);
    }
    return -1;
}
```

Time Complexity: $O(logn)$.

**Problem-52** Given a sorted array of $n$ elements, possibly with duplicates. Find the number of occurrences of a number.

**Brute Force Solution:** Do a linear search of the array and increment count as and when we find the element data in the array.

```
int LinearSearchCount(int A[], int n, int data) {
    int count = 0;
    for (int i = 0; i < n; i++)
        if(A[i] == data)
            count++;
    return count;
}
```

Time Complexity: $O(n)$.

**Problem-53** Can we improve the time complexity of Problem-52?

**Solution: Yes.** We can solve this by using one binary search call followed by another small scan.

**Algorithm:**

- Do a binary search for the *data* in the array. Let us assume its position is $K$.
- Now traverse towards the left from K and count the number of occurrences of *data*. Let this count be $leftCount$.
- Similarly, traverse towards right and count the number of occurrences of *data*. Let this count be $rightCount$.
- Total number of occurrences = $leftCount + 1 + rightCount$

Time Complexity – $O(logn + S)$ where $S$ is the number of occurrences of *data*.

**Problem-54** Is there any alternative way of solving Problem-52?

**Solution:**

**Algorithm:**

- Find first occurrence of *data* and call its index as $firstOccurrence$ (for algorithm refer to Problem-50)
- Find last occurrence of *data* and call its index as $lastOccurrence$ (for algorithm refer to Problem-51)
- Return $lastOccurrence - firstOccurrence + 1$

Time Complexity = $O(logn + logn) = O(logn)$.

**Problem-55** What is the next number in the sequence 1, 11, 21, and why?

**Solution:** Read the given number loudly. This is just a fun problem.

One One
Two Ones
One two, one one→ 1211

So the answer is: the next number is the representation of the previous number by reading it loudly.

**Problem-56** Finding the second smallest number efficiently.

**Solution**: We can construct a heap of the given elements using up just less than $n$ comparisons (Refer to the *Priority Queues* chapter for the algorithm). Then we find the second smallest using $logn$ comparisons for the getMax() operation. Overall, we get $n + logn + constant$.

**Problem-57** Is there any other solution for Problem-56?

**Solution:** Alternatively, split the $n$ numbers into groups of 2, perform $n/2$ comparisons successively to find the largest, using a tournament-like method. The first round will yield the maximum in $n - 1$ comparisons. The second round will be performed on the winners of the first round and the ones that the maximum popped. This will yield $logn - 1$ comparison for a total of $n + logn - 2$. The above solution is called the *tournament problem*.

**Problem-58** An element is a majority if it appears more than $n/2$ times. Give an algorithm that takes an array of $n$ element as argument and identifies a majority (if it exists).

**Solution:** The basic solution is to have two loops and keep track of the maximum count for all different elements. If the maximum count becomes greater than $n/2$, then break the loops and return the element having maximum count. If maximum count doesn't become more than $n/2$, then the majority element doesn't exist.

Time Complexity: $O(n^2)$. Space Complexity: O(1).

**Problem-59** Can we improve Problem-58 time complexity to $O(nlogn)$?

**Solution:** Using binary search we can achieve this. Node of the Binary Search Tree (used in this approach) will be as follows.

```
struct TreeNode {
      int element;
      int count;
      struct TreeNode *left;
      struct TreeNode *right;
} BST;
```

Insert elements in BST one by one and if an element is already present then increment the count of the node. At any stage, if the count of a node becomes more than $n/2$, then return. This method works well for the cases where $n/2 + 1$ occurrences of the majority element are present at the start of the array, for example $\{1, 1, 1, 1, 1, 2, 3, \text{and } 4\}$.

Time Complexity: If a binary search tree is used then worst time complexity will be $O(n^2)$. If a balanced-binary-search tree is used then $O(nlogn)$. Space Complexity: $O(n)$.

**Problem-60** Is there any other of way of achieving $O(nlogn)$ complexity for Problem-58?

**Solution:** Sort the input array and scan the sorted array to find the majority element.

Time Complexity: $O(nlogn)$. Space Complexity: O(1).

**Problem-61** Can we improve the complexity for Problem-58?

**Solution:** If an element occurs more than $n/2$ times in $A$ then it must be the median of $A$. But, the reverse is not true, so once the median is found, we must check to see how many times it occurs in $A$. We can use linear selection which takes $O(n)$ time (for algorithm, refer to *Selection Algorithms* chapter).

```
int CheckMajority(int A[], in n) {
      1) Use linear selection to find the median m of A.
      2) Do one more pass through A and count the number of occurrences of m.
            a.   If m occurs more than n/2 times then return true;
            b.   Otherwise return false.
}
```

**Problem-62** Is there any other way of solving Problem-58?

**Solution:** We can find the majority element using linear time and constant space using Boyer–Moore majority vote algorithm. Since only one element is repeating, we can use a simple scan of the input array by keeping track of the count for the elements. If the count is 0, then we can assume that the element visited for the first time otherwise that the resultant element.

The algorithm can be expressed in pseudocode as the following steps. The algorithm processes each element of the sequence, one at a time. While processing an element:

- If the counter is 0, we set the current candidate to element and we set the counter to 1.
- If the counter is not 0, we increment or decrement the counter according to whether element is the current candidate.

At the end of this process, if the sequence has a majority, it will be the element stored by the algorithm. If there is no majority element, the algorithm will not detect that fact, and will still output one of the elements. We can modify the algorithm to verify that the element found is really is a majority element or not.

```
int MajorityNum(int[] A, int n) {
  int count = 0, element = -1;
  for(int i = 0; i < n; i++) {
    // If the counter is 0 then set the current candidate to majority num and set the counter to 1.
    if(count == 0) {
            element = A[i];
            count = 1;
    }
    else if(element == A[i]) {
            // Increment counter If the counter is not 0 and element is same as current candidate.
            count++;
    }
    else {
          // Decrement counter If the counter is not 0 and element is different from current candidate.
          count--;
    }
  }
  return element;
}
```

Time Complexity: O($n$). Space Complexity: O(1).

**Problem-63** Given an array of $2n$ elements of which $n$ elements are the same and the remaining $n$ elements are all different. Find the majority element.

**Solution:** The repeated elements will occupy half the array. No matter what arrangement it is, only one of the below will be true:

- All duplicate elements will be at a relative distance of 2 from each other. Ex: **n**, *1*, **n**, *100*, **n**, *54*, **n** ...
- At least two duplicate elements will be next to each other.
  Ex: $n, n, 1, 100, n, 54, n, \ldots$
  $n, 1, n, n, n, 54, 100 \ldots$
  $1, 100, 54, n, n, n, n \ldots$

In worst case, we will need two passes over the array:

- First Pass: compare $A[i]$ and $A[i + 1]$
- Second Pass: compare $A[i]$ and $A[i + 2]$

Something will match and that's your element. This will cost O($n$) in time and O(1) in space.

**Problem-64** Given an array with $2n + 1$ integer elements, $n$ elements appear twice in arbitrary places in the array and a single integer appears only once somewhere inside. Find the lonely integer with O($n$) operations and O(1) extra memory.

**Solution:** Except for one element, all elements are repeated. We know that $A\ XOR\ A = 0$. Based on this if we $XOR$ all the input elements then we get the remaining element.

```
int Solution(int* A) {
    int i, res;
    for (i = res = 0; i < 2n+1; i++)
        res = res ^ A[i];
    return res;
}
```

Time Complexity: O($n$). Space Complexity: O(1).

**Problem-65** **Throwing eggs from an n-story building:** Suppose we have an $n$ story building and a number of eggs. Also assume that an egg breaks if it is thrown from floor $F$ or higher, and will not break otherwise. Devise a strategy to determine floor $F$, while breaking O($logn$) eggs.

**Solution:** Refer to *Divide and Conquer* chapter.

**Problem-66** **Local minimum of an array:** Given an array $A$ of $n$ distinct integers, design an O($logn$) algorithm to find a *local minimum*: an index $i$ such that $A[i-1] < A[i] < A[i+1]$.

**Solution:** Check the middle value $A[n/2]$, and two neighbors $A[n/2 - 1]$ and $A[n/2 + 1]$. If $A[n/2]$ is local minimum, stop; otherwise search in half with smaller neighbor.

**Problem-67** Give an $n \times n$ array of elements such that each row is in ascending order and each column is in ascending order, devise an $O(n)$ algorithm to determine if a given element $x$ is in the array. You may assume all elements in the $n \times n$ array are distinct.

**Solution:** Let us assume that the given matrix is $A[n][n]$. Start with the last row, first column [or first row, last column]. If the element we are searching for is greater than the element at $A[1][n]$, then the first column can be eliminated. If the search element is less than the element at $A[1][n]$, then the last row can be completely eliminated. Once the first column or the last row is eliminated, start the process again with the left-bottom end of the remaining array. In this algorithm, there would be maximum $n$ elements that the search element would be compared with.

Time Complexity: $O(n)$. This is because we will traverse at most $2n$ points. Space Complexity: $O(1)$.

**Problem-68** Given an $n \times n$ array a of $n^2$ numbers, give an $O(n)$ algorithm to find a pair of indices $i$ and $j$ such that $A[i][j] < A[i+1][j], A[i][j] < A[i][j+1], A[i][j] < A[i-1][j]$, and $A[i][j] < A[i][j-1]$.

**Solution:** This problem is the same as Problem-67.

**Problem-69** Given $n \times n$ matrix, and in each row all 1's are followed by $0's$. Find the row with the maximum number of $0's$.

**Solution:** Start with first row, last column. If the element is 0 then move to the previous column in the same row and at the same time increase the counter to indicate the maximum number of $0's$. If the element is 1 then move to the next row in the same column. Repeat this process until your reach last row, first column.

Time Complexity: $O(2n) \approx O(n)$ (similar to Problem-67).

**Problem-70** Given an input array of size unknown, with all numbers in the beginning and special symbols in the end. Find the index in the array from where the special symbols start.

**Solution:** Refer to *Divide and Conquer* chapter.

**Problem-71** **Separate even and odd numbers:** Given an array $A[\,]$, write a function that segregates even and odd numbers. The functions should put all even numbers first, and then odd numbers. **Example**: Input = $\{12, 34, 45, 9, 8, 90, 3\}$ Output = $\{12, 34, 90, 8, 9, 45, 3\}$

**Note:** In the output, the order of numbers can be changed, i.e., in the above example 34 can come before 12, and 3 can come before 9.

**Solution:** The problem is very similar to *Separate* $0's$ *and* $1's$ (Problem-72) in an array, and both problems are variations of the famous *Dutch national flag problem*.

**Algorithm:** The logic is similar to Quick sort.

1) Initialize two index variables left and right: $left = 0$, $right = n - 1$
2) Keep incrementing the left index until you see an odd number.
3) Keep decrementing the right index until youe see an even number.
4) If $left < right$ then swap $A[left]$ and $A[right]$

```
void DutchNationalFlag(int A[], int n) {
    int left = 0, right = n-1;
    while(left < right) {
        // Increment left index while we see 0 at left
        while(A[left]%2 == 0 && left < right)
            left++;
        // Decrement right index while we see 1 at right
        while(A[right]%2 == 1 && left < right)
            right--;
        if(left < right) {
            // Swap A[left] and A[right]
            swap(&A[left], &A[right]);
            left++;
            right--;
        }
    }
}
```

Time Complexity: $O(n)$.

**Problem-72** The following is another way of structuring Problem-71, but with a slight difference.

**Separate 0's and 1's in an array:** We are given an array of 0's and 1's in random order. Separate 0's on the left side and 1's on the right side of the array. Traverse the array only once.

**Input array** = $[0, 1, 0, 1, 0, 0, 1, 1, 1, 0]$ **Output array** = $[0, 0, 0, 0, 0, 1, 1, 1, 1, 1]$

**Solution:** Counting 0's or 1's:

1. Count the number of $0's$. Let the count be $C$.
2. Once we have the count, put $C$ 0's at the beginning and $1's$ at the remaining $n - C$ positions in the array.

Time Complexity: O($n$). This solution scans the array two times.

**Problem-73** Can we solve Problem-72 in one scan?

**Solution: Yes.** Use two indexes to traverse: Maintain two indexes. Initialize the first index left as 0 and the second index right as $n-1$. Do the following while $left < right$:

1) Keep the incrementing index left while there are 0s in it
2) Keep the decrementing index right while there are 1s in it
3) If left < right then exchange $A[left]$ and $A[right]$

```
//Function to put all 0s on left and all 1s on right
void Separate0and1(int A[], int n) {
    /* Initialize left and right indexes */
    int left = 0, right = n-1;
    while(left < right) {
        // Increment left index while we see 0 at left
        while(A[left] == 0 && left < right)
            left++;
        // Decrement right index while we see 1 at right
        while(A[right] == 1 && left < right)
            right–;
        // If left is smaller than right then there is a 1 at left and a 0 at right.  Swap A[left] and A[right]
        if(left < right) {
            A[left] = 0;
            A[right] = 1;
            left++;
            right–;
        }
    }
}
```

Time Complexity: O($n$). Space Complexity: O(1).

**Problem-70** **Sort an array of 0's, 1's and 2's [or R's, G's and B's]:** Given an array A[] consisting of $0's$, $1's$ and $2's$, give an algorithm for sorting $A[]$.The algorithm should put all $0's$ first, then all $1's$ and finally all $2's$ at the end. **Example Input** = {0,1,1,0,1,2,1,2,0,0,0,1}, **Output** = {0, 0, 0, 0, 0, 1, 1, 1, 1, 1, 2, 2}

**Solution:** This problem is named the "Dutch national flag problem" because the flag of the Netherlands is comprised of the colors red, white, and blue in separate parts. Although we won't be using colors, the premise of the challenge is to develop a sorting algorithm that performs some form of separations of three kinds of elements.

A very basic approach to solve this problem can be keeping the count of number of zeroes, ones and twos in the given array and then manipulate the given array in accordance with the frequency of every number. This approach is a bit inspired by counting sort. No matter what the initial value of that particular index is, we first put all the zeroes we have in the array starting from index zero, then put all the ones and after that put all the twos.

**Algorithm**:

1.) Traverse the given array once and keep incrementing the count of the number encountered.
2.) Now Traverse the array again starting from index zero and keep changing the value of the element on current index first exhaust all the zeroes then ones and finally all the twos.

This way we have a sorted array where all the zeroes are in starting followed by all the ones and then in last section we have all the twos in a time complexity of O($n$). But the major drawback of this approach is, we have to traverse the given array twice once for counting the number of zeroes, ones and twos and second one for manipulating the array to make it sorted, which can be done only in a single pass.

As an alternative solution, called as Dutch national flag algorithm or Three way partitioning, in which elements of similar type are grouped together and their collective groups are also sorted in a the correct order. Now, we have three types of elements to be sorted, therefore, we divide the given array in four sections out of which 3 sections are designated to zeroes, Ones and twos respectively and one section is unknown or the section which is left to be explored. Now for traversing in these sections we need 3 pointers as well which will virtually divide the given array in four segments. Let us name these pointers as low, mid and high.

Now we can tell the starting and ending points of these segments.

1.) Segment-1 : zeroes
This will be a known section containing only zeroes with a range of [0, low-1].
2.) Segment-2: Ones
This will also be a know section containing only ones with a range of [low, mid-1].
3.) Segment-3 : Unexplored
This will be an unknown section as the elements in this sections are yet to be explored and hence it can contain all types of element that is, zeroes, ones and twos. Range of this segment will be [mid, high].
4.) Segment-4 : Twos
This will be the last and known area containing only twos having the range of [high+1, N] where N is the length of the given array or basically the last valid index of the given array.

Steps used in this Algorithm to sort the given array in a single pass:

- Initialize the low, *mid* and high pointers to, low = 0, *mid* = 0, high = n
- Now, run a loop and do the following until the *mid* pointer finally meets high pointer. As the *mid* pointer moves forward we keep putting the element at *mid* pointer to its right position by swapping that element with the element at pointers of respective sections.
- CASE – I: If the element at *mid*, that is, A[*mid*] == 0, this means the correct position of this element is in the range [0, *low*-1], therefore, we swap A[*mid*] with A[low] and increment *low* making sure that element with index lesser than *low* is a zero.
- CASE – II: If the element at *mid*, that is, A[*mid*] == 2, this means the correct position of this element is in the range [*high*+1, *n*], therefore, we swap A[*mid*] with A[*high*] and decrement *high* making sure that element with index greater than *high* is a two.
- CASE – III: If the element at *mid*, that is, A[*mid*] == 1, this means that the element is already in its correct segment because [*low*, *mid*-1] is the range where it needs to be. Therefore, we do nothing and simply increment the *mid* pointer.

So, there are total three cases, let us take a moment and emphasise on the fact that *mid* pointer gets only incremented only when the element A[*mid*] == 1. Let us discuss every case individually,

- For case – I: In this case, we increment *mid* as well along with increment low pointer, as we are sure that element at low pointer before swapping can surely only be one as had it been a two, it would have already got swapped with *high* pointer when mid pointer explored it as the only reason that *mid* pointer left it because it was a one.
- For case – II: Now, In this case we swap the element at *mid* and *high*, but unlike case – I, in this case we are not sure about the element which will come at *mid* index after swapping as the element at *high* index before swapping can be any of zero, one or two, therefore, we need to explore this swapped element and hence we do not increment *mid* pointer in this case.
- For case – III: There is no confusion regarding incrementing *mid* in this case as already discussed, as we know the element at *mid* is one therefore we definitely need to increment *mid* here.

Time complexity of this algorithm is also O(*n*) but it sorts the array in just a single pass and without any extra space unlike previous approach.

```
void sorting012sDutchFlagProblem(int A[],int n){
    int low=0,mid=0,high=n-1;
    while (mid <=high){
            switch(A[mid]){
                    case 0:
                            swap(A[low],A[mid]);
                            low++;mid++;
                            break;
                    case 1:
                            mid++;
                            break;
                    case 2:
                            swap(A[mid],A[high]);
                            high--;
                            break;
            }
    }
}
```

**Problem-71** **Maximum difference between two elements:** Given an array $A[]$ of integers, find out the difference between any two elements such that larger element appears after the smaller number in $A[]$.
**Examples**: If array is $[2, 3, 10, 6, 4, 8, 1]$ then returned value should be 8 (Difference between 10 and 2). If array is $[\,7, 9, 5, 6, 3, 2\,]$ then the returned value should be 2 (Difference between 7 and 9)

**Solution:** Refer to *Divide and Conquer* chapter.

**Problem-72** Given an array of 101 elements. Out of 101 elements, 25 elements are repeated twice, 12 elements are repeated 4 times, and one element is repeated 3 times. Find the element which repeated 3 times in O(1).

**Solution:** Before solving this problem, let us consider the following $XOR$ operation property: $a\ XOR\ a = 0$. That means, if we apply the $XOR$ on the same elements then the result is 0.

**Algorithm:**

- $XOR$ all the elements of the given array and assume the result is $A$.
- After this operation, 2 occurrences of the number which appeared 3 times becomes 0 and one occurrence remains the same.
- The 12 elements that are appearing 4 times become 0.
- The 25 elements that are appearing 2 times become 0.
- So just $XOR'ing$ all the elements gives the result.

Time Complexity: O($n$), because we are doing only one scan. Space Complexity: O(1).

**Problem-73** Given a number $n$, give an algorithm for finding the number of trailing zeros in $n!$.

**Solution:**

```
int numberOfTrailingZerosInNumber(int n) {
    int i, count = 0;
    if(n < 0) return -1;
    for (i = 5; n / i > 0; i *= 5)
        count += n / i;
    return count;
}
```

Time Complexity: O($logn$).

**Problem-74** Given an array of $2n$ integers in the following format $a1\ a2\ a3 \ldots an\ b1\ b2\ b3 \ldots bn$. Shuffle the array to $a1\ b1\ a2\ b2\ a3\ b3 \ldots an\ bn$ without any extra memory.

**Solution:** A brute force solution involves two nested loops to rotate the elements in the second half of the array to the left. The first loop runs $n$ times to cover all elements in the second half of the array. The second loop rotates the elements to the left. Note that the start index in the second loop depends on which element we are rotating and the end index depends on how many positions we need to move to the left.

```
void ShuffleArray() {
    int n = 4;
    int A[] = {1,3,5,7,2,4,6,8};
    for (int i = 0, q =1, k = n; i < n; i++, k++, q++) {
        for (int j = k; j > i + q; j--) {
            int tmp = A[j-1];
            A[j-1] = A[j];
            A[j] = tmp;
        }
    }
    for (int i = 0; i  < 2*n; i++)
        printf("%d", A[i]);
}
```

Time Complexity: O($n^2$).

**Problem-75** Can we improve the Problem-74 solution?

**Solution:** Refer to the *Divide and Conquer* chapter. A better solution of time complexity O($nlogn$) can be achieved using the *Divide and Concur* technique. Let us look at an example

1. Start with the array: $a1\ a2\ a3\ a4\ b1\ b2\ b3\ b4$
2. Split the array into two halves: $a1\ a2\ a3\ a4$ : $b1\ b2\ b3\ b4$
3. Exchange elements around the center: exchange $a3\ a4$ with $b1\ b2$ and you get: $a1\ a2\ b1\ b2\ a3\ a4\ b3\ b4$
4. Split $a1\ a2\ b1\ b2$ into $a1\ a2$ : $b1\ b2$. Then split $a3\ a4\ b3\ b4$ into $a3\ a4$ : $b3\ b4$
5. Exchange elements around the center for each subarray you get: $a1\ b1\ a2\ b2$ and $a3\ b3\ a4\ b4$

Note that this solution only handles the case when $n = 2^i$ where $i = 0, 1, 2, 3$, etc. In our example $n = 2^2 = 4$ which makes it easy to recursively split the array into two halves. The basic idea behind swapping elements around the center before calling the recursive function is to produce smaller size problems. A solution with linear time complexity may be achieved if the elements are of a specific nature. For example, if you can calculate the new position of the element using the value of the element itself. This is nothing but a hashing technique.

**Problem-76** Given an array A[], find the maximum j – i such that A[j] > A[i]. For example, Input: {34, 8, 10, 3, 2, 80, 30, 33, 1} and Output: 6 (j = 7, i = 1).

**Solution: Brute Force Approach:** Run two loops. In the outer loop, pick elements one by one from the left. In the inner loop, compare the picked element with the elements starting from the right side. Stop the inner loop when you see an element greater than the picked element and keep updating the maximum j-i so far.

```
int maxIndexDiff(int A[], int n){
    int maxDiff = -1;
    int i, j;
    for (i = 0; i < n; ++i){
        for (j = n-1; j > i; --j){
            if(A[j] > A[i] && maxDiff < (j - i))
                maxDiff = j - i;
        }
    }
    return maxDiff;
}
```

Time Complexity: O($n^2$). Space Complexity: O(1).

**Problem-77** Can we improve the complexity of Problem-76?

**Solution:** To solve this problem, we need to get two optimum indexes of A[]: left index $i$ and right index $j$. For an element A[i], we do not need to consider A[i] for the left index if there is an element smaller than A[i] on the left side of A[i]. Similarly, if there is a greater element on the right side of A[j] then we do not need to consider this j for the right index.

So we construct two auxiliary Arrays LeftMins[] and RightMaxs[] such that LeftMins[i] holds the smallest element on the left side of A[i] including A[i], and RightMaxs[j] holds the greatest element on the right side of A[j] including A[j]. After constructing these two auxiliary arrays, we traverse both these arrays from left to right.

While traversing LeftMins[] and RightMaxs[], if we see that LeftMins[i] is greater than RightMaxs[j], then we must move ahead in LeftMins[] (or do i++) because all elements on the left of LeftMins[i] are greater than or equal to LeftMins[i]. Otherwise we must move ahead in RightMaxs[j] to look for a greater $j$ - $i$ value.

```
int maxIndexDiff(int A[], int n){
    int maxDiff, i, j;
    int *LeftMins = (int *)malloc(sizeof(int)*n);
    int *RightMaxs = (int *)malloc(sizeof(int)*n);
    LeftMins[0] = A[0];
    for (i = 1; i < n; ++i)
        LeftMins[i] = min(A[i], LeftMins[i-1]);
    RightMaxs[n-1] = A[n-1];
    for (j = n-2; j >= 0; --j)
        RightMaxs[j] = max(A[j], RightMaxs[j+1]);
    i = 0, j = 0, maxDiff = -1;
    while (j < n && i < n){
        if (LeftMins[i] < RightMaxs[j]){
            maxDiff = max(maxDiff, j-i);
            j = j + 1;
        }
        else
            i = i+1;
    }
    return maxDiff;
}
```

Time Complexity: O($n$). Space Complexity: O($n$).

**Problem-78** Given an array of elements, how do you check whether the list is pairwise sorted or not? A list is considered pairwise sorted if each successive pair of numbers is in sorted (non-decreasing) order.

**Solution:**

```
int checkPairwiseSorted(int A[], int n) {
    if (n == 0 || n == 1)
        return 1;
    for (int i = 0; i < n - 1; i += 2){
        if (A[i] > A[i+1])
            return 0;
```

```
    }
    return 1;
}
```

Time Complexity: O($n$). Space Complexity: O(1).

**Problem-79** Given an array of $n$ elements, how do you print the frequencies of elements without using extra space. Assume all elements are positive, editable and less than $n$.

**Solution:** Use *negation* technique.

```
void frequencyCounter(int A[],int n){
    int pos = 0;
    while(pos < n){
        int expectedPos = A[pos] - 1;
        if(A[pos] > 0 && A[expectedPos] > 0){
            swap(A[pos], A[expectedPos]);
            A[expectedPos] = -1;
        }
        else if(A[pos] > 0){
            A[expectedPos] --;
            A[pos ++] = 0;
        }
        else{
            pos ++;
        }
    }
    for(int i = 0; i < n; ++i){
        printf("%d frequency is %d\n", i + 1 ,abs(A[i]));
    }
}
int main(int argc, char* argv[]){
    int A[] = {10, 10, 9, 4, 7, 6, 5, 2, 3, 2, 1};
    frequencyCounter(A, sizeof(A)/ sizeof(A[0]));
    return 0;
}
```

Array should have numbers in the range [1, $n$] (where $n$ is the size of the array). The if condition (A[$pos$] > 0 && A[$expectedPos$] > 0) means that both the numbers at indices $pos$ and $expectedPos$ are actual numbers in the array but not their frequencies. So we will swap them so that the number at the index $pos$ will go to the position where it should have been if the numbers 1, 2, 3, ...., $n$ are kept in 0, 1, 2, ..., $n-1$ indices. In the above example input array, initially $pos = 0$, so 10 at index 0 will go to index 9 after the swap. As this is the first occurrence of 10, make it to -1. Note that we are storing the frequencies as negative numbers to differentiate between actual numbers and frequencies.

The else if condition (A[$pos$] > 0) means A[$pos$] is a number and A[$expectedPos$] is its frequency without including the occurrence of A[$pos$]. So increment the frequency by 1 (that is decrement by 1 in terms of negative numbers). As we count its occurrence we need to move to next pos, so $pos++$, but before moving to that next position we should make the frequency of the number $pos + 1$ which corresponds to index $pos$ of zero, since such a number has not yet occurred.

The final else part means the current index pos already has the frequency of the number $pos + 1$, so move to the next $pos$, hence $pos++$.

Time Complexity: O($n$). Space Complexity: O(1).

**Problem-80** Which is faster and by how much, a linear search of only 1000 elements on a 5-GHz computer or a binary search of 1 million elements on a 1-GHz computer. Assume that the execution of each instruction on the 5-GHz computer is five times faster than on the 1-GHz computer and that each iteration of the linear search algorithm is twice as fast as each iteration of the binary search algorithm.

**Solution**: A binary search of 1 million elements would require $log_2^{1,000,000}$ or about 20 iterations at most (i.e., worst case). A linear search of 1000 elements would require 500 iterations on the average (i.e., going halfway through the array). Therefore, binary search would be $\frac{500}{20} = 25$ faster (in terms of iterations) than linear search. However, since linear search iterations are twice as fast, binary search would be $\frac{25}{2}$ or about 12 times faster than linear search overall, on the same machine. Since we run them on different machines, where an instruction on the 5-GhZ machine is 5 times faster than an instruction on a 1-GHz machine, binary search would be $\frac{12}{5}$ or about 2 times faster than linear search! The key idea is that software improvements can make an algorithm run much faster without having to use more powerful software.

**Problem-81** Given an array of integers, give an algorithm that returns the *pivot* index of this array. *Pivot* index is the index where the sum of the numbers to the left of the index is equal to the sum of the numbers to the right of the index. If no such index exists, we should return -1. If there are multiple pivot indexes, you should return the left-most pivot index.

Example 1: Input: A = [1, 8, 4, 7, 6, 7], Output: 3
Explanation: The sum of the numbers to the left of index 3 (A[3] = 7) is equal to the sum of numbers to the right of index 3. Also, 3 is the first index where this occurs.

Example 2: Input: A = [2, 3, 4], Output: -1
Explanation: There is no index that satisfies the conditions in the problem statement.

**Solution**: We need to quickly compute the sum of values to the left and the right of every index. Let's say we knew $totalSum$ as the sum of the numbers, and we are at index $i$. If we knew the sum of numbers leftsum that are to the left of index $i$, then the other sum to the right of the index would just be $totalSum - A[i] - leftsum$.

As such, we only need to know about $leftsum$ to check whether an index is a pivot index in constant time. Let's do that: as we iterate through candidate indexes i, we will maintain the correct value of leftsum.

```
class PivotIndex {
public:
    int pivotIndex(vector<int>& A) {
        int sum= accumulate(A.begin(),A.end(),0);
        int ls=0;
        for(int i=0;i<A.size();i++)
        {
            sum-=A[i];
            if(sum==ls) {return i; exit(0);}
            ls+=A[i];
        }
        return -1;
    }
};
```

Time Complexity: O($n$), where $n$ is the length of array A. Space Complexity: O(1), the space used by $leftsum$ and $totalSum$.

**Problem-82** Given two strings ***s*** and ***t*** which consist of only lowercase letters. String ***t*** is generated by random shuffling string ***s*** and then add one more letter at a random position. Find the letter that was added in ***t***.

Example Input: s = "abcd" t = "abcde" Output: e
Explanation: 'e' is the letter that was added.

**Solution**: Refer **Other Programming Questions** section in **Hacks on Bitwise Programming** chapter.

CHAPTER

# 12

# SELECTION ALGORITHMS [MEDIANS]

## 12.1 What are Selection Algorithms?

*Selection algorithm* is an algorithm for finding the $k^{th}$ smallest/largest number in a list (also called as $k^{th}$ order statistic). This includes finding the minimum, maximum, and median elements. For findingthe $k^{th}$ order statistic, there are multiple solutions which provide different complexities, and in this chapter we will enumerate those possibilities.

## 12.2 Selection by Sorting

A selection problem can be converted to a sorting problem. In this method, we first sort the input elements and then get the desired element. It is efficient if we want to perform many selections.

For example, let us say we want to get the minimum element. After sorting the input elements we can simply return the first element (assuming the array is sorted in ascending order). Now, if we want to find the second smallest element, we can simply return the second element from the sorted list.

That means, for the second smallest element we are not performing the sorting again. The same is also the case with subsequent queries. Even if we want to get $k^{th}$ smallest element, just one scan of the sorted list is enough to find the element (or we can return the $k^{th}$-indexed value if the elements are in the array).

From the above discussion what we can say is, with the initial sorting we can answer any query in one scan, $O(n)$. In general, this method requires $O(nlogn)$ time (for *sorting*), where $n$ is the length of the input list. Suppose we are performing $n$ queries, then the average cost per operation is just $\frac{n\, logn}{n} \approx O(logn)$. This kind of analysis is called *amortized* analysis.

## 12.3 Partition-based Selection Algorithm

For the algorithm check Problem-6. This algorithm is similar to Quick sort.

## 12.4 Linear Selection Algorithm - Median of Medians Algorithm

| Worst-case performance | $O(n)$ |
|---|---|
| Best-case performance | $O(n)$ |
| Worst-case space complexity | $O(1)$ auxiliary |

Refer to Problem-11.

## 12.5 Finding the K Smallest Elements in Sorted Order

For the algorithm check Problem-6. This algorithm is similar to Quick sort.

## 12.6 Selection Algorithms: Problems & Solutions

**Problem-1** Find the largest element in an array A of size $n$.

**Solution:** Scan the complete array and return the largest element.

```
void findLargestInArray(int n, const int A[]) {
    int i, large = A[0];
    for (int i = 1; i < n; i++)
```

```
        if(A[i] > large)
            large = A[i];
    printf("Largest:%d", large);
}
```

Time Complexity - O($n$). Space Complexity - O(1).

**Note:** Any deterministic algorithm that can find the largest of $n$ keys by comparison of keys takes at least $n - 1$ comparisons.

**Problem-2** Find the smallest and largest elements in an array $A$ of size $n$.

**Solution:**

```
void findSmallestAndLargestInArray (int A[], int n) {
    int small = A[0];
    int large =A[0];
    for (int i = 1; i <= n-1; i++)
        if(A[i] < small)
            small = A[i];
        else if(A[i] > large)
            large = A[i];
    printf("Smallest:%d, Largest:%d", small, large);
}
```

Time Complexity - O($n$). Space Complexity - O(1). The worst-case number of comparisons is $2(n - 1)$.

**Problem-3** Can we improve the previous algorithms?

**Solution: Yes.** We can do this by comparing in pairs.

```
// n is assumed to be even. Compare in pairs.
void findWithPairComparison (int A[], int n) {
    int large = small = -1;
    for (int i = 0; i <= n - 1; i = i + 2) {          // Increment i by 2.
        if(A[i] < A[i + 1]) {
            if(A[i] < small)
                small = A[i];
            if(A[i + 1] > large)
                large = A[i + 1];
        }
        else {
            if(A[i + 1] < small)
                small = A[i + 1];
            if(A[i] > large)
                large = A[i];
        }
    }
    printf("Smallest:%d, Largest:%d", small, large);
}
```

Time Complexity – O($n$). Space Complexity – O(1).

Number of comparisons: $\begin{cases} \frac{3n}{2} - 2, if\ n\ is\ even \\ \frac{3n}{2} - \frac{3}{2}\ if\ n\ is\ odd \end{cases}$

**Summary**

| Straightforward comparison – $2(n - 1)$ comparisons |
|---|
| Compare for min only if comparison for max fails |
| Best case: increasing order – $n - 1$ comparisons |
| Worst case: decreasing order – $2(n - 1)$ comparisons |
| Average case: $3n/2 - 1$ comparisons |

**Note:** For divide and conquer techniques refer to the *Divide and Conquer* chapter.

**Problem-4** Give an algorithm for finding the second largest element in the given input list of elements.

**Solution: Brute Force Method**

**Algorithm:**

- Find the largest element: needs $n - 1$ comparisons
- delete (discard) the largest element

- Again find the largest element: needs $n - 2$ comparisons

Total number of comparisons: $n-1+n-2 = 2n-3$

**Problem-5** Can we reduce the number of comparisons in Problem-4 solution?

**Solution: The Tournament method:** For simplicity, assume that the numbers are distinct and that $n$ is a power of 2. We pair the keys and compare the pairs in rounds until only one round remains. If the input has eight keys, there are four comparisons in the first round, two in the second, and one in the last. The winner of the last round is the largest key. The figure below shows the method.

The tournament method directly applies only when $n$ is a power of 2. When this is not the case, we can add enough items to the end of the array to make the array size a power of 2. If the tree is complete then the maximum height of the tree is $logn$. If we construct the complete binary tree, we need $n-1$ comparisons to find the largest. The second largest key has to be among the ones that were lost in a comparison with the largest one. That means, the second largest element should be one of the opponents of the largest element. The number of keys that are lost to the largest key is the height of the tree, i.e. $logn$ [if the tree is a complete binary tree]. Then using the selection algorithm to find the largest among them, take $logn - 1$ comparisons. Thus the total number of comparisons to find the largest and second largest keys is $n + logn - 2$.

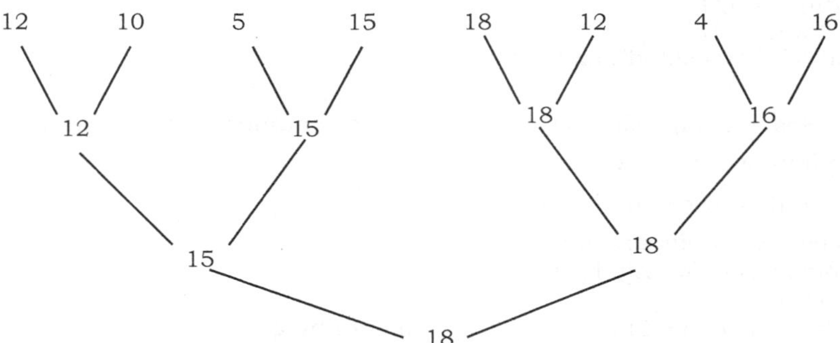


**Problem-6** Find the $k$-smallest elements in an array $S$ of $n$ elements using the partitioning method.

**Solution: Brute Force Approach**: Scan through the numbers $k$ times to have the desired element. This method is the one used in bubble sort (and selection sort), every time we find out the smallest element in the whole sequence by comparing every element. In this method, the sequence has to be traversed $k$ times. So the complexity is $O(n \times k)$.

**Problem-7** Can we use the sorting technique for solving Problem-6?

**Solution: Yes.** Sort and take the first $k$ elements.

1. Sort the numbers.
2. Pick the first $k$ elements.

The time complexity calculation is trivial. Sorting of $n$ numbers is of $O(nlogn)$ and picking $k$ elements is of $O(k)$. The total complexity is $O(nlogn + k) = O(nlogn)$.

**Problem-8** Can we use the *tree sorting* technique for solving Problem-6?

**Solution: Yes.**

1. Insert all the elements in a binary search tree.
2. Do an InOrder traversal and print $k$ elements which will be the smallest ones. So, we have the $k$ smallest elements.

The cost of creation of a binary search tree with $n$ elements is $O(nlogn)$ and the traversal up to $k$ elements is $O(k)$. Hence the complexity is $O(nlogn + k) = O(nlogn)$.

**Disadvantage**: If the numbers are sorted in descending order, we will be getting a tree which will be skewed towards the left. In that case, the construction of the tree will be $0 + 1 + 2 + \ldots + (n-1) = \frac{n(n-1)}{2}$ which is $O(n^2)$. To escape from this, we can keep the tree balanced, so that the cost of constructing the tree will be only $nlogn$.

**Problem-9** Can we improve the *tree sorting* technique for solving Problem-6?

**Solution: Yes.** Use a smaller tree to give the same result.

1. Take the first $k$ elements of the sequence to create a balanced tree of $k$ nodes (this will cost $klogk$).
2. Take the remaining numbers one by one, and
   a. If the number is larger than the largest element of the tree, return.
   b. If the number is smaller than the largest element of the tree, remove the largest element of the tree and add the new element. This step is to make sure that a smaller element replaces a larger

element from the tree. And of course the cost of this operation is $logk$ since the tree is a balanced tree of $k$ elements.

Once Step 2 is over, the balanced tree with $k$ elements will have the smallest $k$ elements. The only remaining task is to print out the largest element of the tree.

Time Complexity:

1. For the first $k$ elements, we make the tree. Hence the cost is $klogk$.
2. For the rest $n - k$ elements, the complexity is $O(logk)$.

Step 2 has a complexity of $(n - k)\ logk$. The total cost is $klogk + (n - k)\ logk = nlogk$ which is $O(nlogk)$. This bound is actually better than the ones provided earlier.

**Problem-10** Can we use the partitioning technique for solving Problem-6?

**Solution: Yes.**

**Algorithm**

1. Choose a pivot from the array.
2. Partition the array so that: $A[low...pivotpoint - 1] <= pivotpoint <= A[pivotpoint + 1..high]$.
3. if $k < pivotpoint$ then it must be on the left of the pivot, so do the same method recursively on the left part.
4. if $k = pivotpoint$ then it must be the pivot and print all the elements from $low$ to $pivotpoint$.
5. if $k > pivotpoint$ then it must be on the right of pivot, so do the same method recursively on the right part.

The top-level call would be kthSmallest = Selection(1, n, k).

```
int selection (int low, int high, int k) {
    int pivotpoint;
    if(low == high)
        return S[low];
    else {
        pivotpoint = partition(low, high);
        if(k == pivotpoint)
            return S[pivotpoint];  //we can print all the elements from low to pivotpoint.
        else if(k < pivotpoint)
            return selection (low, pivotpoint - 1, k);
        else return selection (pivotpoint + 1, high, k);
    }
}
void partition (int low, int high) {
    int i, j, pivotitem;
    pivotitem = S[low];
    j = low;
    for (i = low + 1; i <= high; i++)
        if(S[i] < pivotitem) {
            j++;
            Swap S[i] and S[j];
        }
    pivotpoint = j;
    Swap S[low] and S[pivotpoint];
    return pivotpoint;
}
```

Time Complexity: $O(n^2)$ in worst case as similar to Quicksort. Although the worst case is the same as that of Quicksort, this performs much better on the average [$O(nlogk)$ – Average case].

**Problem-11** Find the $k^{th}$-smallest element in an array $S$ of $n$ elements in the best possible way.

**Solution:** This problem is similar to Problem-6 and all the solutions discussed for Problem-6 are valid for this problem. The only difference is that instead of printing all the $k$ elements, we print only the $k^{th}$element. We can improve the solution by using the *median of medians* algorithm. Median is a special case of the selection algorithm. The algorithm Selection(A, $k$) to find the $k^{th}$ smallest element from set $A$ of $n$ elements is as follows:

**Algorithm:** *selection*(A, k)

1. Partition $A$ into $ceil\left(\frac{length(A)}{5}\right)$ groups, with each group having five items (the last group may have fewer items).
2. Sort each group separately (e.g., insertion sort).
3. Find the median of each of the $\frac{n}{5}$ groups and store them in some array (let us say $A'$).
4. Use *Selection* recursively to find the median of $A'$ (median of medians). Let us asay the median of medians is $m$.

$$m = Selection(A', \frac{\frac{length(A)}{5}}{2});$$

```
5. Let q = # elements of A smaller than m;
6. If(k == q + 1)
       return m;
   /* Partition with pivot */
7. Else partition A into X and Y
       • X = {items smaller than m}
       • Y = {items larger than m}

   /* Next,form a subproblem */
8. If(k < q + 1)
       return Selection(X, k);
9. Else
       return Selection(Y, k – (q+1));
```

Before developing recurrence, let us consider the representation of the input below. In the figure, each circle is an element and each column is grouped with 5 elements. The black circles indicate the median in each group of 5 elements. As discussed, sort each column using constant time insertion sort.

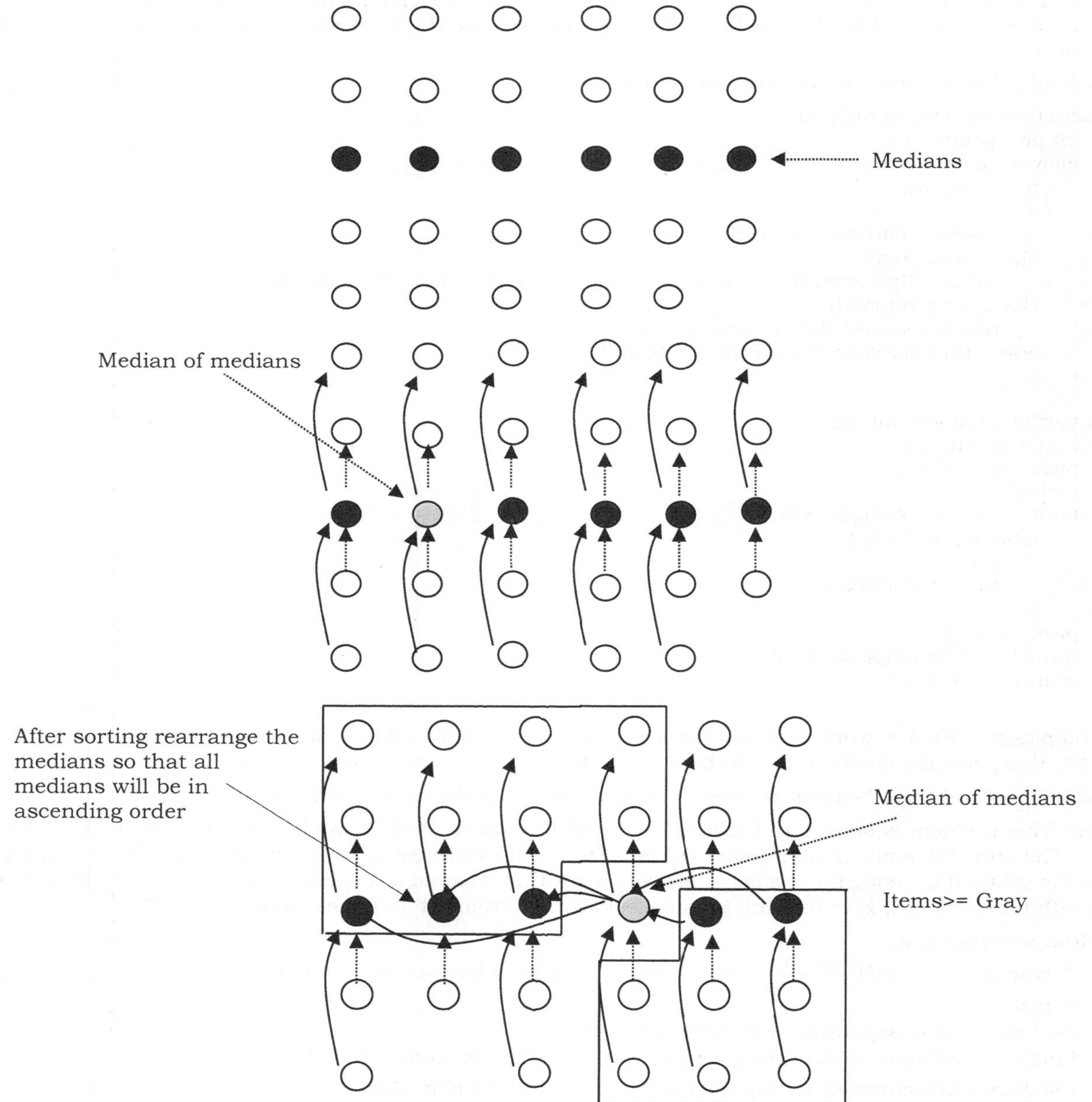

In the figure above the gray circled item is the median of medians (let us call this $m$). It can be seen that at least 1/2 of 5 element group medians $\leq m$. Also, these 1/2 of 5 element groups contribute 3 elements that are $\leq m$ except 2 groups [last group which may contain fewer than 5 elements, and other group which contains $m$]. Similarly, at least 1/2 of 5 element groups contribute 3 elements that are $\geq m$ as shown above. 1/2 of 5 element groups contribute 3 elements, except 2 groups gives: $3(\lceil\frac{1}{2}\lceil\frac{n}{5}\rceil\rceil-2) \approx \frac{3n}{10} - 6$. The remaining are $n - (\frac{3n}{10} - 6) \approx \frac{7n}{10} + 6$. Since $\frac{7n}{10} + 6$ is greater than $\frac{3n}{10} - 6$ we need to consider $\frac{7n}{10} + 6$ for worst.

**Components in recurrence:**

- In our selection algorithm, we choose $m$, which is the median of medians, to be a pivot, and partition A into two sets $X$ and $Y$. We need to select the set which gives maximum size (to get the worst case).
- The time in function *Selection* when called from procedure *partition*. The number of keys in the input to this call to *Selection* is $\frac{n}{5}$.
- The number of comparisons required to partition the array. This number is $length(S)$, let us say $n$.

We have established the following recurrence: $T(n) = T\left(\frac{n}{5}\right) + \Theta(n) + Max\{T(X), T(Y)\}$

From the above discussion we have seen that, if we select median of medians m as pivot, the partition sizes are: $\frac{3n}{10} - 6$ and $\frac{7n}{10} + 6$. If we select the maximum of these, then we get:

$$\begin{aligned} T(n) &= T\left(\frac{n}{5}\right) + \Theta(n) + T\left(\frac{7n}{10} + 6\right) \\ &\approx T\left(\frac{n}{5}\right) + \Theta(n) + T\left(\frac{7n}{10}\right) + O(1) \\ &\leq c\frac{7n}{10} + c\frac{n}{5} + \Theta(n) + O(1) \end{aligned}$$

Finally, $T(n) = \Theta(n)$.

**Problem-12** In Problem-11, we divided the input array into groups of 5 elements. The constant 5 play an important part in the analysis. Can we divide in groups of 3 which work in linear time?

**Solution:** In this case the modification causes the routine to take more than linear time. In the worst case, at least half of the $\lceil\frac{n}{3}\rceil$ medians found in the grouping step are greater than the median of medians $m$, but two of those groups contribute less than two elements larger than $m$. So as an upper bound, the number of elements larger than the pivotpoint is at least:

$$2(\lceil\frac{1}{2}\lceil\frac{n}{3}\rceil\rceil-2) \geq \frac{n}{3} - 4$$

Likewise this is a lower bound. Thus up to $n - (\frac{n}{3} - 4) = \frac{2n}{3} + 4$ elements are fed into the recursive call to *Select*. The recursive step that finds the median of medians runs on a problem of size $\lceil\frac{n}{3}\rceil$, and consequently the time recurrence is:

$$T(n) = T(\lceil\frac{n}{3}\rceil) + T(2n/3 + 4) + \Theta(n).$$

Assuming that $T(n)$ is monotonically increasing, we may conclude that $T(\frac{2n}{3} + 4) \geq T(\frac{2n}{3}) \geq 2T(\frac{n}{3})$, and we can say the upper bound for this as $T(n) \geq 3T(\frac{n}{3}) + \Theta(n)$, which is $O(nlogn)$. Therefore, we cannot select 3 as the group size.

**Problem-13** As in Problem-12, can we use groups of size 7?

**Solution:** Following a similar reasoning, we once more modify the routine, now using groups of 7 instead of 5. In the worst case, at least half the $\lceil\frac{n}{7}\rceil$ medians found in the grouping step are greater than the median of medians $m$, but two of those groups contribute less than four elements larger than $m$. So as an upper bound, the number of elements larger than the pivotpoint is at least:

$$4(\lceil 1/2\lceil n/7 \rceil\rceil-2) \geq \frac{2n}{7} - 8.$$

Likewise this is a lower bound. Thus up to $n - (\frac{2n}{7} - 8) = \frac{5n}{7} + 8$ elements are fed into the recursive call to Select. The recursive step that finds the median of medians runs on a problem of size $\lceil\frac{n}{7}\rceil$, and consequently the time recurrence is

$$\begin{aligned} T(n) &= T(\lceil\frac{n}{7}\rceil) + T(\frac{5n}{7} + 8) + O(n) \\ T(n) &\leq c\lceil\frac{n}{7}\rceil + c(\frac{5n}{7} + 8) + O(n) \\ &\leq c\frac{n}{7} + c\frac{5n}{7} + 8c + an, a \text{ is a constant} \\ &= cn - c\frac{n}{7} + an + 9c \end{aligned}$$

$$= (a + c)n - (c\frac{n}{7} - 9c).$$

This is bounded above by $(a + c)n$ provided that $c\frac{n}{7} - 9c \geq 0$. Therefore, we can select 7 as the group size.

**Problem-14** Given two arrays each containing $n$ sorted elements, give an $O(logn)$-time algorithm to find the median of all $2n$ elements.

**Solution:** The simple solution to this problem is to merge the two lists and then take the average of the middle two elements (note the union always contains an even number of values). But, the merge would be $\Theta(n)$, so that doesn't satisfy the problem statement. To get $logn$ complexity, let $medianA$ and $medianB$ be the medians of the respective lists (which can be easily found since both lists are sorted). If $medianA == medianB$, then that is the overall median of the union and we are done. Otherwise, the median of the union must be between $medianA$ and $medianB$. Suppose that $medianA < medianB$ (the opposite case is entirely similar). Then we need to find the median of the union of the following two sets:

$$\{x\ in\ A \mid x >= medianA\}\ \{x\ in\ B \mid x <= medianB\}$$

So, we can do this recursively by resetting the *boundaries* of the two arrays. The algorithm tracks both arrays (which are sorted) using two indices. These indices are used to access and compare the median of both arrays to find where the overall median lies.

```
void findMedian(int A[], int alo , int ahi, int B[], int blo int bhi) {
    amid = alo + (ahi-alo)/2;
    amed = a[amid];
    bmid = blo + (bhi-blo)/2;
    bmed = b[bmid];
    if( ahi - alo + bhi - blo < 4) {
        Handle the boundary cases and solve it smaller problem in O(1) time.
        return;
    }
    else if(amed < bmed)
        findMedian(A, amid, ahi, B, blo, bmid+1);
    else    findMedian(A, alo, amid+1,B, bmid+1, bhi);
}
```

Time Complexity: $O(logn)$, since we are reducing the problem size by half every time.

**Problem-15** Let $A$ and $B$ be two sorted arrays of $n$ elements each. We can easily find the $k^{th}$ smallest element in $A$ in $O(1)$ time by just outputting $A[k]$. Similarly, we can easily find the $k^{th}$ smallest element in $B$. Give an $O(logk)$ time algorithm to find the $k^{th}$ smallest element overall { *i.e.*, the $k^{th}$ smallest in the union of $A$ and $B$.

**Solution:** It's just another way of asking Problem-14.

**Problem-16** **Find the $k$ smallest elements in sorted order:** Given a set of $n$ elements from a totally-ordered domain, find the $k$ smallest elements, and list them in sorted order. Analyze the worst-case running time of the best implementation of the approach.

**Solution:** Sort the numbers, and list the $k$ smallest.

$T(n)$ = Time complexity of sort + listing $k$ smallest elements $= \Theta(nlogn) + \Theta(n) = \Theta(nlogn)$.

**Problem-17** For Problem-16, if we follow the approach below, then what is the complexity?

**Solution:** Using the priority queue data structure from heap sort, construct a min-heap over the set, and perform extract-min $k$ times. Refer to the *Priority Queues* (*Heaps*) chapter for more details.

**Problem-18** For Problem-16, if we follow the approach below then what is the complexity?
Find the $k^{th}$-smallest element of the set, partition around this pivot element, and sort the $k$ smallest elements.

**Solution:**

$$\begin{aligned} T(n) &= Time\ complexity\ of\ kth - smallest\ +\ Finding\ pivot\ +\ Sorting\ prefix \\ &= \Theta(n) + \Theta(n) + \Theta(klogk) = \Theta(n + klogk) \end{aligned}$$

Since, $k \leq n$, this approach is better than Problem-16 and Problem-17.

**Problem-19** Find $k$ nearest neighbors to the median of $n$ distinct numbers in $O(n)$ time.

**Solution:** Let us assume that the array elements are sorted. Now find the median of $n$ numbers and call its index as $X$ (since array is sorted, median will be at $\frac{n}{2}$ location). All we need to do is select $k$ elements with the smallest absolute differences from the median, moving from $X - 1$ to 0, and $X + 1$ to $n - 1$ when the median is at index $m$.

Time Complexity: Each step takes $\Theta(n)$. So the total time complexity of the algorithm is $\Theta(n)$.

**Problem-20** Is there any other way of solving Problem-19?

**Solution:** Assume for simplicity that n is odd and k is even. If set A is in sorted order, the median is in position $n/2$ and the $k$ numbers in A that are closest to the median are in positions $(n - k)/2$ through $(n + k)/2$.

We first use linear time selection to find the $(n - k)/2$, $n/2$, and $(n + k)/2$ elements and then pass through set A to find the numbers less than the $(n + k)/2$ element, greater than the $(n - k)/2$ element, and not equal to the $n/2$ element. The algorithm takes $O(n)$ time as we use linear time selection exactly three times and traverse the $n$ numbers in $A$ once.

**Problem-21** Given $(x, y)$ coordinates of $n$ houses, where should you build a road parallel to $x$-axis to minimize the construction cost of building driveways?

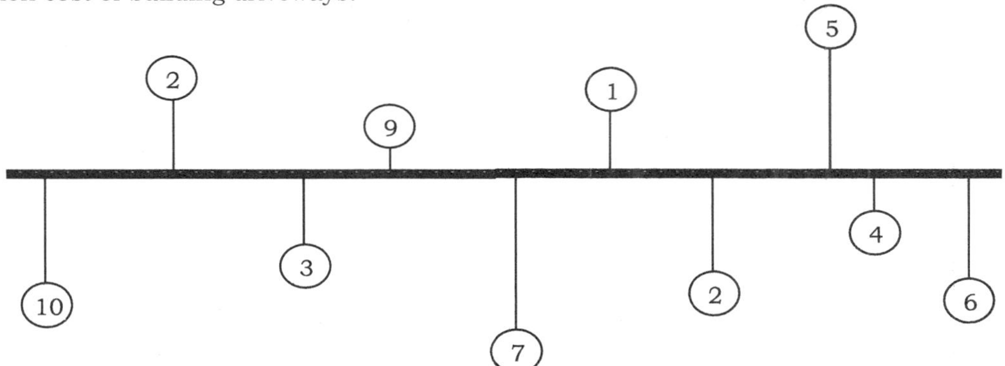


**Solution:** The road costs nothing to build. It is the driveways that cost money. The driveway cost is proportional to its distance from the road. Obviously, they will be perpendicular. The solution is to put the street at the median of the $y$ coordinates.

**Problem-22** Given a big file containing billions of numbers, find the maximum 10 numbers from that file.

**Solution:** Refer to the *Priority Queues* chapter.

**Problem-23** Suppose there is a milk company. The company collects milk every day from all its agents. The agents are located at different places. To collect the milk, what is the best place to start so that the least amount of total distance is travelled?

**Solution:** Starting at the median reduces the total distance travelled because it is the place which is at the center of all the places.

# CHAPTER 13

# SYMBOL TABLES

## 13.1 Introduction

Since childhood, we all have used a dictionary, and many of us have a word processor (say, Microsoft Word) which comes with a spell checker. The spell checker is also a dictionary but limited in scope. There are many real time examples for dictionaries and a few of them are:

- Spell checker
- The data dictionary found in database management applications
- Symbol tables generated by loaders, assemblers, and compilers
- Routing tables in networking components (DNS lookup)

In computer science, we generally use the term 'symbol table' rather than 'dictionary' when referring to the abstract data type (ADT).

## 13.2 What are Symbol Tables?

We can define the *symbol table* as a data structure that associates a *value* with a *key*. It supports the following operations:

- Search whether a particular name is in the table
- Get the attributes of that name
- Modify the attributes of that name
- Insert a new name and its attributes
- delete a name and its attributes

There are only three basic operations on symbol tables: searching, inserting, and deleting.

**Example:** DNS lookup. Let us assume that the key in this case is the URL and the value is an IP address.

- Insert URL with specified IP address
- Given URL, find corresponding IP address

| Key[Website] | Value [IP Address] |
|---|---|
| www.CareerMonks.com | 128.112.136.11 |
| www.AuthorsInn.com | 128.112.128.15 |
| www.AuthInn.com | 130.132.143.21 |
| www.klm.com | 128.103.060.55 |
| www.CareerMonk.com | 209.052.165.60 |

## 13.3 Symbol Table Implementations

Before implementing symbol tables, let us enumerate the possible implementations. Symbol tables can be implemented in many ways and some of them are listed below.

### Unordered Array Implementation

With this method, just maintaining an array is enough. It needs $O(n)$ time for searching, insertion and deletion in the worst case.

### Ordered [Sorted] Array Implementation

In this we maintain a sorted array of keys and values.

- Store in sorted order by key
- keys[i] = $i^{th}$ largest key
- values[i] = value associated with $i^{th}$ largest key

Since the elements are sorted and stored in arrays, we can use a simple binary search for finding an element. It takes O($logn$) time for searching and O($n$) time for insertion and deletion in the worst case.

### Unordered Linked List Implementation

Just maintaining a linked list with two data values is enough for this method. It needs O($n$) time for searching, insertion and deletion in the worst case.

### Ordered Linked List Implementation

In this method, while inserting the keys, maintain the order of keys in the linked list. Even if the list is sorted, in the worst case it needs O($n$) time for searching, insertion and deletion.

### Binary Search Trees Implementation

Refer to *Trees* chapter. The advantages of this method are: it does not need much code and it has a fast search [O($logn$) on average].

### Balanced Binary Search Trees Implementation

Refer to *Trees* chapter. It is an extension of binary search trees implementation and takes O($logn$) in worst case for search, insert and delete operations.

### Ternary Search Implementation

Refer to *String Algorithms* chapter. This is one of the important methods used for implementing dictionaries.

### Hashing Implementation

This method is important. For a complete discussion, refer to the *Hashing* chapter.

## 13.4 Comparison Table of Symbols for Implementations

Let us consider the following comparison table for all the implementations.

| Implementation | Search | Insert | Delete |
|---|---|---|---|
| Unordered Array | $n$ | $n$ | $n$ |
| Ordered Array (can be implemented with array binary search) | $logn$ | $n$ | $n$ |
| Unordered List | $n$ | $n$ | $n$ |
| Ordered List | $n$ | $n$ | $n$ |
| Binary Search Trees (O($logn$) on average) | $logn$ | $logn$ | $logn$ |
| Balanced Binary Search Trees (O($logn$) in worst case) | $logn$ | $logn$ | $logn$ |
| Ternary Search (only change is in logarithms base) | $logn$ | $logn$ | $logn$ |
| Hashing (O(1) on average) | 1 | 1 | 1 |

**Notes:**

- In the above table, $n$ is the input size.
- Table indicates the possible implementations discussed in this book. But, there could be other implementations.

CHAPTER

# HASHING 14

## 14.1 What is Hashing?

In this chapter we introduce so-called *associative arrays*, that is, data structures that are similar to arrays but are not indexed by integers, but other forms of data such as strings. One popular data structures for the implementation of associative arrays are hash tables. To analyze the asymptotic efficiency of hash tables we have to explore a new point of view, that of average case complexity. Hashing is a technique used for storing and retrieving information as quickly as possible. It is used to perform optimal searches and is useful in implementing symbol tables.

## 14.2 Why Hashing?

In the *Trees* chapter we saw that balanced binary search trees support operations such as *insert*, *delete* and *search* in O($logn$) time. In applications, if we need these operations in O(1), then hashing provides a way. Remember that worst case complexity of hashing is still O($n$), but it gives O(1) on the average.

## 14.3 Hash Table ADT

The hash table structure is an unordered collection of associations between a key and a data value. The keys in a hash table are all unique so that there is a one-to-one relationship between a key and a value. The operations are given below.

- HashTable: Creates a new hash table
- Get: Searches the hash table with key and return the value if it finds the element with the given key
- Put: Inserts a new key-value pair into hash table
- Delete: Deletes a key-value pair from hash table
- DeleteHashTable: Deletes the hash table

## 14.4 Understanding Hashing

In simple terms we can treat *array* as a hash table. For understanding the use of hash tables, let us consider the following example: Give an algorithm for printing the first repeated character if there are duplicated elements in it. Let us think about the possible solutions.

The simple and brute force way of solving is: given a string, for each character check whether that character is repeated or not. The time complexity of this approach is $O(n^2)$ with $O(1)$ space complexity.

Now, let us find a better solution for this problem. Since our objective is to find the first repeated character, what if we remember the previous characters in some array?

We know that the number of possible characters is 256 (for simplicity assume *ASCII* characters only). Create an array of size 256 and initialize it with all zeros. For each of the input characters go to the corresponding position and increment its count. Since we are using arrays, it takes constant time for reaching any location. While scanning the input, if we get a character whose counter is already 1 then we can say that the character is the one which is repeating for the first time.

```
char firstRepeatedChar ( char *str ) {
  int i, len=strlen(str);
  int count[256]; //additional array
  for(i=0; i<256; ++i)
    count[i] = 0;
  for(i=0; i<len; ++i) {
    if(count[str[i]]==1) {
      printf("%c", str[i]);
      break;
```

```
        }
        else    count[str[i]]++;
    }
    if(i==len)
        printf("No Repeated Characters");
    return 0;
}
```

## Why not Arrays?

Arrays can be seen as a mapping, associating with every integer in a given interval some data item. It is finitary, because its domain, and therefore also its range, is finite. There are many situations when we want to index elements differently than just by integers. Common examples are strings (for dictionaries, phone books, menus, data base records), or structs (for dates, or names together with other identifying information).

In many applications requiring associative arrays, we are storing complex data values and want to access them by a key which is derived from the data. A typical example of keys are strings, which are appropriate for many scenarios. For example, the key might be a student id and the data entry might be a collection of grades, perhaps another associative array where the key is the name of assignment or exam and the data is a score. We make the assumption that keys are unique in the sense that in an associative array there is at most one data item associated with a given key. In some applications we may need to complicate the structure of keys to achieve this uniqueness. This is consistent with ordinary arrays, which have a unique value for every valid index.

In the previous problem, we have used an array of size 256 because we know the number of different possible characters [256] in advance. Now, let us consider a slight variant of the same problem. Suppose the given array has numbers instead of characters, then how do we solve the problem?

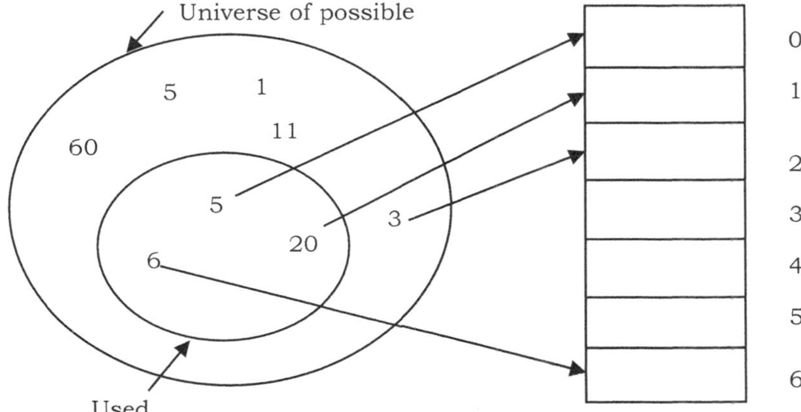


In this case the set of possible values is infinity (or at least very big). Creating a huge array and storing the counters is not possible. That means there are a set of universal keys and limited locations in the main memory. To solve this problem we need to somehow map all these possible keys to the possible memory locations.

From the above discussion and diagram it can be seen that we need a mapping of possible keys to one of the available locations. As a result, using simple arrays is not the correct choice for solving the problems where the possible keys are very big. The process of mapping the keys to available main memory locations is called *hashing*.

**Note:** For now, do not worry about how the keys are mapped to locations. That depends on the function used for conversions. One such simple function is *key % table size*.

## 14.5 Components of Hashing

Hashing has four key components:

1) Hash Table
2) Hash Functions
3) Collisions
4) Collision Resolution Techniques

## 14.6 Hash Table

Hash table is a generalization of array. With an array, we store the element whose key is $k$ at a position $k$ of the array. That means, given a key $k$, we find the element whose key is $k$ by just looking in the $k^{th}$ position of the array. This is called *direct addressing*.

Direct addressing is applicable when we can afford to allocate an array with one position for every possible key. But if we do not have enough space to allocate a location for each possible key, then we need a mechanism to handle this case. Another way of defining the scenario is: if we have less locations and more possible keys, then simple array implementation is not enough.

In these cases one option is to use hash tables. Hash table or hash map is a data structure that stores the keys and their associated values, and hash table uses a hash function to map keys to their associated values. The general convention is that we use a hash table when the number of keys actually stored is small relative to the number of possible keys.

A hash table is a collection of items which are stored in such a way as to make it easy to find them later. Each position of the hash table, often called a *slot* (or a *bucket*), can hold an item and is named by an integer value starting at 0.

For example, we will have a slot named 0, a slot named 1, a slot named 2, and so on. Initially, the hash table contains no items so every slot is empty. We can implement a hash table by using a list with each element initialized to the special NULL.

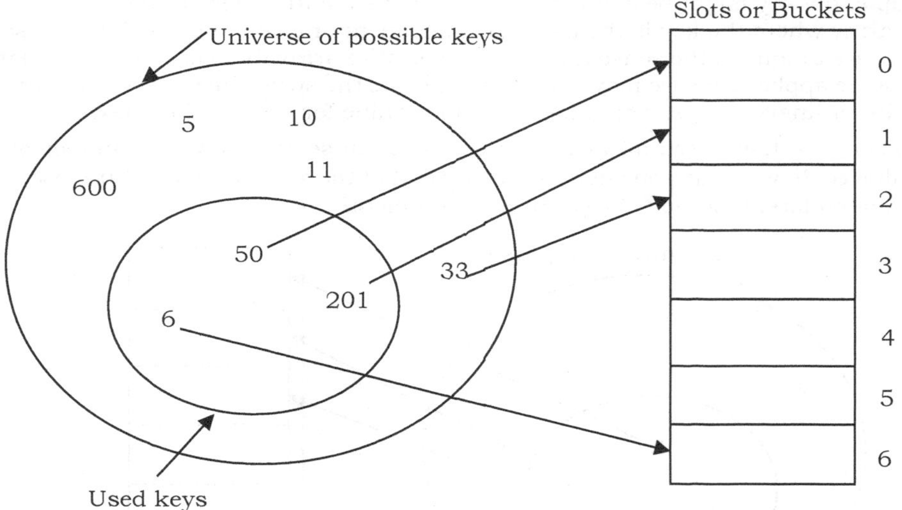


## 14.7 Hash Function

The first idea behind hash tables is to exploit the efficiency of arrays. So: to map a key to an entry, we first map a key to an integer and then use the integer to index an array A. The first map is called a *hash function*. The hash function is used to transform the key into the slot index (or bucket index). Ideally, the hash function should map each possible key to a unique slot index, but it is difficult to achieve in practice.

Given a collection of elements, a hash function that maps each item into a unique slot is referred to as a *perfect hash function*. If we know the elements and the collection will never change, then it is possible to construct a perfect hash function. Unfortunately, given an arbitrary collection of elements, there is no systematic way to construct a perfect hash function. Luckily, we do not need the hash function to be perfect to still gain performance efficiency.

One way to always have a perfect hash function is to increase the size of the hash table so that each possible value in the element range can be accommodated. This guarantees that each element will have a unique slot. Although this is practical for small numbers of elements, it is not feasible when the number of possible elements is large. For example, if the elements were nine-digit Social Security numbers, this method would require almost one billion slots. If we only want to store data for a class of 25 students, we will be wasting an enormous amount of memory.

Our goal is to create a hash function that minimizes the number of collisions, is easy to compute, and evenly distributes the elements in the hash table. There are a number of common ways to extend the simple remainder method. We will consider a few of them here.

The *folding method* for constructing hash functions begins by dividing the elements into equal-size pieces (the last piece may not be of equal size). These pieces are then added together to give the resulting hash value. For example, if our element was the phone number 436-555-4601, we would take the digits and divide them into groups of 2 (43,65,55,46,01). After the addition, 43+65+55+46+01, we get 210. If we assume our hash table has 11 slots, then we need to perform the extra step of dividing by 11 and keeping the remainder. In this case 210 % 11 is 1, so the phone number 436-555-4601 hashes to slot 1. Some folding methods go one step further and reverse every other piece before the addition. For the above example, we get 43+56+55+64+01=219 which gives 219 % 11=10.

### How to Choose Hash Function?

The basic problems associated with the creation of hash tables are:

- An efficient hash function should be designed so that it distributes the index values of inserted objects uniformly across the table.
- An efficient collision resolution algorithm should be designed so that it computes an alternative index for a key whose hash index corresponds to a location previously inserted in the hash table.
- We must choose a hash function which can be calculated quickly, returns values within the range of locations in our table, and minimizes collisions.

### Characteristics of Good Hash Functions

A good hash function should have the following characteristics:

- Minimize collisions
- Be easy and quick to compute
- Distribute key values evenly in the hash table
- Use all the information provided in the key
- Have a high load factor for a given set of keys

## 14.8 Load Factor

The load factor of a non-empty hash table is the number of items stored in the table divided by the size of the table. This is the decision parameter used when we want to rehash *or* expand the existing hash table entries. This also helps us in determining the efficiency of the hashing function. That means, it tells whether the hash function is distributing the keys uniformly or not.

$$Load\ factor = \frac{Number\ of\ elements\ in\ hash\ table}{Hash\ table\ size}$$

## 14.9 Collisions

Hash functions are used to map each key to a different address space, but practically it is not possible to create such a hash function and the problem is called *collision*. Collision is the condition where two keys are hashed to the same slot.

## 14.10 Collision Resolution Techniques

Fortunately, there are effective techniques for resolving the conflict created by collisions. The process of finding an alternate location for a key in the case of a collision is called *collision resolution*. Even though hash tables have collision problems, they are more efficient in many cases compared to all other data structures, like search trees. There are a number of collision resolution techniques, and the most popular are direct chaining and open addressing.

- **Direct Chaining (or Closed Addressing):** An array of linked list application
  - Separate chaining
- **Open Addressing:** Array-based implementation
  - Linear probing (linear search)
  - Quadratic probing (nonlinear search)
  - Double hashing (use multiple hash functions)

Of course, the ideal solution would be to avoid collisions altogether. We might try to achieve this goal by choosing a suitable hash function.

## 14.11 Separate Chaining

A first idea to explore is to implement the associative array as a linked list, called a chain or a linked list. Separate chaining is one of the most commonly used collision resolution techniques. It is usually implemented using linked lists. Collision resolution by chaining combines linked representation with hash table. When two or more elements hash to the same location, these elements are constituted into a singly-linked list called a *chain*. In chaining, we put all the elements that hash to the same slot in a linked list. If we have a key k and look for it in the linked list, we just traverse it, compute the intrisic key for each data entry, and compare it with k. If they are equal, we have found our entry, if not we continue the search. If we reach the end of the chain and do not find an entry with key k, then no entry with the given key exists.

In separate chaining, each slot of the hash table is a linked list. To store an element in the hash table you must insert it into a specific linked list. If there is any collision (i.e. two different elements have same hash value) then store both the elements in the same linked list.

As an example, consider the following simple hash function:

$$h(key) = key \ \% \ table \ size$$

In a hash table with size 7, keys 27 and 130 would get 6 and 4 as hash indices respectively.

| Slot | |
|---|---|
| 0 | |
| 1 | |
| 2 | |
| 3 | |
| 4 | → (130, "John") |
| 5 | |
| 6 | → (27, "Ram") |

If we insert a new element (18, "Saleem"), that would also go to the fourth index as 18%7 is 4.

| Slot | |
|---|---|
| 0 | |
| 1 | |
| 2 | |
| 3 | |
| 4 | → (130, "John") → (18, "Saleem") |
| 5 | |
| 6 | → (27, "Ram") |

The cost of a lookup is that of scanning the entries of the selected linked list for the required key. If the distribution of the keys is sufficiently uniform, then the average cost of a lookup depends only on the average number of keys per linked list. For this reason, chained hash tables remain effective even when the number of table entries ($n$) is much higher than the number of slots.

For separate chaining, the worst-case scenario is when all the entries are inserted into the same linked list. The lookup procedure may have to scan all its entries, so the worst-case cost is proportional to the number ($n$) of entries in the table.

The worst-case behavior of hashing with chaining is terrible: all $n$ keys hash to the same slot, creating a list of length $n$. The worst-case time for searching is thus )($n$) plus the time to compute the hash function--no better than if we used one linked list for all the elements. Clearly, hash tables are not used for their worst-case performance.

## 14.12 Open Addressing

In open addressing all keys are stored in the hash table itself. This approach is also known as *closed hashing*. This procedure is based on probing. A collision is resolved by probing.

### Linear Probing

The interval between probes is fixed at 1. In linear probing, we search the hash table sequentially. starting from the original hash location. If a location is occupied, we check the next location. We wrap around from the last table location to the first table location if necessary. The function for rehashing is the following:

$$rehash(key) = (n + 1)\% \ tablesize$$

One of the problems with linear probing is that table items tend to cluster together in the hash table. This means that the table contains groups of consecutively occupied locations that are called *clustering*.

Clusters can get close to one another, and merge into a larger cluster. Thus, the one part of the table might be quite dense, even though another part has relatively few items. Clustering causes long probe searches and therefore decreases the overall efficiency.

The next location to be probed is determined by the step-size, where other step-sizes (more than one) are possible. The step-size should be relatively prime to the table size, i.e. their greatest common divisor should be equal to 1. If we choose the table size to be a prime number, then any step-size is relatively prime to the table size. Clustering cannot be avoided by larger step-sizes.

### Quadratic Probing

The interval between probes increases proportionally to the hash value (the interval thus increasing linearly, and the indices are described by a quadratic function). The problem of clustering can be eliminated if we use the quadratic probing method. Quadratic probing is also referred to as $mid - square$ method.

In quadratic probing, we start from the original hash location $i$. If a location is occupied, we check the locations $i + 1^2$ , $i + 2^2$, $i + 3^2$, $i + 4^2$... We wrap around from the last table location to the first table location if necessary. The function for rehashing is the following:

$$rehash(key) = (n + k^2)\%\ tablesize$$

*Example*: Let us assume that the table size is 11 (0..10)

Hash Function: h(key) = key mod 11

*Insert keys*:

$31\ mod\ 11 = 9$
$19\ mod\ 11 = 8$
$2\ mod\ 11 = 2$
$13\ mod\ 11 = 2 \rightarrow 2 + 1^2 = 3$
$25\ mod\ 11 = 3 \rightarrow 3 + 1^2 = 4$
$24\ mod\ 11 = 2 \rightarrow 2 + 1^2, 2 + 2^2 = 6$
$21\ mod\ 11 = 10$
$9\ mod\ 11 = 9 \rightarrow 9 + 1^2,\ 9 + 2^2\ mod\ 11, 9 + 3^2\ mod\ 11 = 7$

| | |
|---|---|
| 0 | |
| 1 | |
| 2 | 2 |
| 3 | 13 |
| 4 | 25 |
| 5 | 5 |
| 6 | 24 |
| 7 | 9 |
| 8 | 19 |
| 9 | 31 |
| 10 | 21 |

Even though clustering is avoided by quadratic probing, still there are chances of clustering. Clustering is caused by multiple search keys mapped to the same hash key. Thus, the probing sequence for such search keys is prolonged by repeated conflicts along the probing sequence. Both linear and quadratic probing use a probing sequence that is independent of the search key.

### Double Hashing

The interval between probes is computed by another hash function. Double hashing reduces clustering in a better way. The increments for the probing sequence are computed by using a second hash function. The second hash function $h2$ should be:

$$h2(key) \neq 0 \text{ and } h2 \neq h1$$

We first probe the location $h1(key)$. If the location is occupied, we probe the location $h1(key) + h2(key)$, $h1(key) + 2 * h2(key)$, ...

*Example*:

Table size is 11 (0..10)
Hash Function: assume $h1(key) = key\ mod\ 11$ and
$h2(key) = 7 - (key\ mod\ 7)$

*Insert keys*:

$58\ mod\ 11 = 3$
$14\ mod\ 11 = 3 \rightarrow 3 + 7 = 10$
$91\ mod\ 11 = 3 \rightarrow 3 + 7, 3 + 2 * 7\ mod\ 11 = 6$
$25\ mod\ 11 = 3 \rightarrow 3 + 3, 3 + 2 * 3 = 9$

| | |
|---|---|
| 0 | |
| 1 | |
| 2 | |
| 3 | 58 |
| 4 | 25 |
| 5 | |
| 6 | 91 |
| 7 | |
| 8 | |
| 9 | 25 |
| 10 | 14 |

## 14.13 Comparison of Collision Resolution Techniques

### Comparisons: Linear Probing vs. Double Hashing

The choice between linear probing and double hashing depends on the cost of computing the hash function and on the load factor [number of elements per slot] of the table. Both use few probes but double hashing take more time because it hashes to compare two hash functions for long keys.

### Comparisons: Open Addressing vs. Separate Chaining

It is somewhat complicated because we have to account for the memory usage. Separate chaining uses extra memory for links. Open addressing needs extra memory implicitly within the table to terminate the probe sequence. Open-addressed hash tables cannot be used if the data does not have unique keys. An alternative is to use separate chained hash tables.

### Comparisons: Open Addressing methods

| Linear Probing | Quadratic Probing | Double hashing |
|---|---|---|

| | | |
|---|---|---|
| Fastest among three | Easiest to implement and deploy | Makes more efficient use of memory |
| Uses few probes | Uses extra memory for links and it does not probe all locations in the table | Uses few probes but takes more time |
| A problem occurs known as primary clustering | A problem occurs known as secondary clustering | More complicated to implement |
| Interval between probes is fixed - often at 1. | Interval between probes increases proportional to the hash value | Interval between probes is computed by another hash function |

## 14.14 How Hashing Gets O(1) Complexity

We stated earlier that in the best case hashing would provide a O(1), constant time search technique. However, due to collisions, the number of comparisons is typically not so simple. Even though a complete analysis of hashing is beyond the scope of this text, we can state some well-known results that approximate the number of comparisons necessary to search for an item. From the previous discussion, one doubts how hashing gets O(1) if multiple elements map to the same location.

The answer to this problem is simple. By using the load factor we make sure that each block (for example, linked list in separate chaining approach) on the average stores the maximum number of elements less than the *load factor*. Also, in practice this load factor is a constant (generally, 10 or 20). As a result, searching in 20 elements or 10 elements becomes constant.

If the average number of elements in a block is greater than the load factor, we rehash the elements with a bigger hash table size. One thing we should remember is that we consider average occupancy (total number of elements in the hash table divided by table size) when deciding the rehash.

The access time of the table depends on the load factor which in turn depends on the hash function. This is because hash function distributes the elements to the hash table. For this reason, we say hash table gives O(1) complexity on average. Also, we generally use hash tables in cases where searches are more than insertion and deletion operations.

## 14.15 Hashing Techniques

There are two types of hashing techniques: static hashing and dynamic hashing

### Static Hashing

If the data is fixed then static hashing is useful. In static hashing, the set of keys is kept fixed and given in advance, and the number of primary pages in the directory are kept fixed.

### Dynamic Hashing

If the data is not fixed, static hashing can give bad performance, in which case dynamic hashing is the alternative, in which case the set of keys can change dynamically.

## 14.16 Problems for which Hash Tables are not suitable

- Problems for which data ordering is required
- Problems having multidimensional data
- Prefix searching, especially if the keys are long and of variable-lengths
- Problems that have dynamic data
- Problems in which the data does not have unique keys.

## 14.17 Bloom Filters

A Bloom filter is a probabilistic data structure which was designed to check whether an element is present in a set with memory and time efficiency. It tells us that the element either definitely is *not* in the set or *may* be in the set. The base data structure of a Bloom filter is a *Bit Vector*. The algorithm was invented in 1970 by Burton Bloom and it relies on the use of a number of different hash functions.

### How it works?

A Bloom filter starts off with a bit array initialized to zero. To store a data value, we simply apply $k$ different hash functions and treat the resulting $k$ values as indices in the array, and we set each of the $k$ array elements to 1. We repeat this for every element that we encounter.

Now suppose an element turns up and we want to know if we have seen it before. What we do is apply the $k$ hash functions and look up the indicated array elements. If any of them are 0 we can be 100% sure that we have never encountered the element before - if we had, the bit would have been set to 1. However, even if all of them are one, we still can't conclude that we have seen the element before because all of the bits could have been set by the $k$ hash functions applied to multiple other elements. All we can conclude is that it is *likely* that we have encountered the element before.

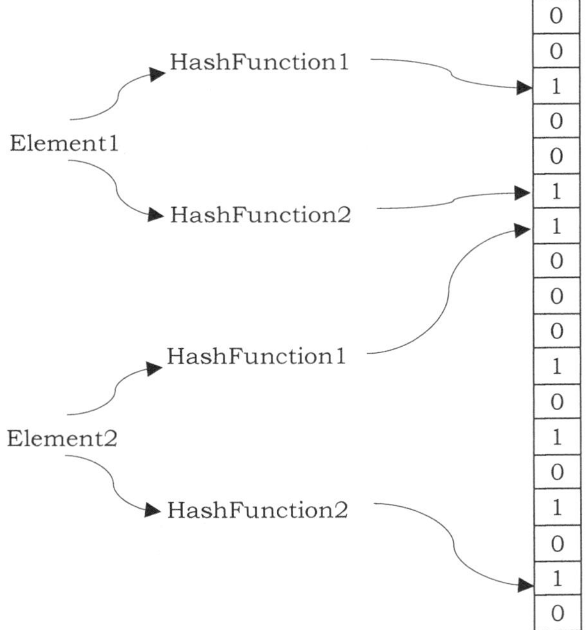


Now that the bits in the bit vector have been set for *Element*1 and *Element*2; we can query the bloom filter to tell us if something has been seen before.

The element is hashed but instead of setting the bits, this time a check is done and if the bits that would have been set are already set the bloom filter will return true that the element has been seen before.

Note that it is not possible to remove an element from a Bloom filter. The reason is simply that we can't unset a bit that appears to belong to an element because it might also be set by another element.

If the bit array is mostly empty, i.e., set to zero, and the $k$ hash functions are independent of one another, then the probability of a false positive (i.e., concluding that we have seen a data item when we actually haven't) is low. For example, if there are only $k$ bits set, we can conclude that the probability of a false positive is very close to zero as the only possibility of error is that we entered a data item that produced the same $k$ hash values - which is unlikely as long as the 'has' functions are independent.

As the bit array fills up, the probability of a false positive slowly increases. Of course when the bit array is full, every element queried is identified as having been seen before. So clearly we can trade space for accuracy as well as for time.

One-time removal of an element from a Bloom filter can be simulated by having a second Bloom filter that contains elements that have been removed. However, false positives in the second filter become false negatives in the composite filter, which may be undesirable. In this approach, re-adding a previously removed item is not possible, as one would have to remove it from the *removed* filter.

## Selecting hash functions

The requirement of designing $k$ different independent hash functions can be prohibitive for large $k$. For a good hash function with a wide output, there should be little if any correlation between different bit-fields of such a hash, so this type of hash can be used to generate multiple *different* hash functions by slicing its output into multiple bit fields. Alternatively, one can pass $k$ different initial values (such as 0, 1, ..., $k$ - 1) to a hash function that takes an initial value – or add (or append) these values to the key. For larger $m$ and/or $k$, independence among the hash functions can be relaxed with negligible increase in the false positive rate.

## Selecting size of bit vector

A Bloom filter with 1% error and an optimal value of k, in contrast, requires only about 9.6 bits per element — regardless of the size of the elements. This advantage comes partly from its compactness, inherited from arrays, and partly from its probabilistic nature. The 1% false-positive rate can be reduced by a factor of ten by adding only about 4.8 bits per element.

## Space advantages

While risking false positives, Bloom filters have a strong space advantage over other data structures for representing sets, such as self-balancing binary search trees, tries, hash tables, or simple arrays or linked lists of the entries. Most of these require storing at least the data items themselves, which can require anywhere from a small number of bits, for small integers, to an arbitrary number of bits, such as for strings (tries are an exception, since they can share storage between elements with equal prefixes). Linked structures incur an additional linear space overhead for pointers.

However, if the number of potential values is small and many of them can be in the set, the Bloom filter is easily surpassed by the deterministic bit array, which requires only one bit for each potential element.

### Time advantages

Bloom filters also have the unusual property that the time needed either to add items or to check whether an item is in the set is a fixed constant, $O(k)$, completely independent of the number of items already in the set. No other constant-space set data structure has this property, but the average access time of sparse hash tables can make them faster in practice than some Bloom filters. In a hardware implementation, however, the Bloom filter shines because its k lookups are independent and can be parallelized.

### Implementation

Refer to *Problems Section*.

## 14.18 Hashing: Problems & Solutions

**Problem-1** Implement a separate chaining collision resolution technique. Also, discuss time complexities of each function.

**Solution:** To create a hashtable of given size, say $n$, we allocate an array of $n/L$ (whose value is usually between 5 and 20) pointers to list, initialized to NULL. To perform *Search/Insert/Delete* operations, we first compute the index of the table from the given key by using *hashfunction* and then do the corresponding operation in the linear list maintained at that location. To get uniform distribution of keys over a hashtable, maintain table size as the prime number.

```
#include <stdio.h>
#include <stdlib.h>
#include <stdbool.h>
#include <string.h>
#include <assert.h>
/* elements */
struct element {
  int key;                    /* key */
  int value;                  /* data */
};
typedef struct element* element;
struct list {
  element data;
  struct list* next;
};
typedef struct list* list;
/* linked lists may be NULL (= end of list) and we do not check for circularity */
struct chain {
  list list;
};
/* Chains, implemented as linked lists */
typedef struct chain* chain;
struct table {
  int capacity;
  int size;
  chain* buckets;
};
/* Hash table interface */
typedef struct table* table;
table newHashTable (int capacity);
element put(table H, element e);
element get(table H, int key);
void deleteHashTable(table H);
chain newChain ();
element insertInChain(table H, chain C, element e);
```

```
element searchInChain(table H, chain C, int key);
void deleteChain(chain C);
void* xmalloc(size_t capacity) {
  void* p = malloc(capacity);
  if (p == NULL) {
    fprintf(stderr, "allocation failed\n");
    abort();
  }
  return p;
}
void* xcalloc(size_t nobj, size_t capacity) {
  void* p = calloc(nobj, capacity);
  if (p == NULL) {
    fprintf(stderr, "allocation failed\n");
    abort();
  }
  return p;
}
void deleteList(list p) {
  list q;
  while (p != NULL) {
    if (p->data != NULL)    /* free element, if such a function is supplied */
      free(p->data);
    q = p->next;
    free(p);
    p = q;
  }
}
chain newChain(){
  chain C = xmalloc(sizeof(struct chain));
  C->list = NULL;
  return C;
}
// findInChain(p, key) returns list element whosecdata field has key key, or NULL if none exists
list findInChain(table H, chain C, int key){
  list p = C->list;
  while (p != NULL) {
    if (key == p->data->key)
      return p;
    p = p->next;
  }
  return NULL;
}
element insertInChain(table H, chain C, element e){
  list p = findInChain(H, C, e->key);
  if (p == NULL) {
    /* insert new element at the beginning */
    list new_item = xmalloc(sizeof(struct list));
    new_item->data = e;
    new_item->next = C->list;
    C->list = new_item;
    return NULL;              /* did not overwrite entry */
  } else {
    /* overwrite existing entry with given key */
    element oldElement = p->data;
    p->data = e;
    return oldElement;                  /* return old entry */
  }
}
element searchInChain(table H, chain C, int key){
  list p = findInChain(H, C, key);
  if (p == NULL) return NULL;
```

```
    else return p->data;
}
void deleteChain(chain C){
  deleteList(C->list);
  free(C);
}
/* hash function */
int hash(int key, int capacity){
  return key % capacity;
}
table newHashTable(int capacity){
  chain* A = xcalloc(capacity, sizeof(chain));
  table H = xmalloc(sizeof(struct table));
  H->capacity = capacity;
  H->size = 0;
  H->buckets = A;                          /* all initialized to NULL; */
  return H;
}
element put(table H, element e){
  element oldElement;
  int key = e->key;
  int h = hash(key, H->capacity);
  if (H->buckets[h] == NULL)
    H->buckets[h] = newChain();
  oldElement = insertInChain(H, H->buckets[h], e);
  if (oldElement != NULL) return oldElement;
  H->size++;
  return NULL;
}
element get(table H, int key){
  int h = hash(key, H->capacity);
  if (H->buckets[h] == NULL) return NULL;
  element e = searchInChain(H, H->buckets[h], key);
  return e;
}
void deleteHashTable(table H){
  int i;
  for (i = 0; i < H->capacity; i++) {
    chain C = H->buckets[i];
    if (C != NULL) deleteChain(C);
  }
  free(H->buckets);
  free(H);
}
void deleteElement(element e) {
  free(e);
}
int main () {
  int n = 100, i, j;
  int capacity = num_tests = 5;
  printf("Testing buckets of capacity %d with %d values, %d times\n", capacity, n, num_tests);
  for (j = 0; j < num_tests; j++) {
    table H = newHashTable(capacity);
    for (i = 0; i < n; i++) {
      element e = xmalloc(sizeof(struct element));
      e->key = j*n+i;
      e->value = j*n+i;
      put(H, e);
    }
    for (i = 0; i < n; i++) {
      int key = j*n+i;
```

```
        assert(((element)get(H, key))->value == j*n+i);   /* "missed existing element" */
      }
      for (i = 0; i < n; i++) {
        int key = (j+1)*n+i;
        assert(get(H, key) == NULL);                   /* "found nonexistent element" */
      }
      deleteHashTable(H);
    }
    printf("All tests passed!\n");
    return 0;
  }
```

CreatHashTable – O($n$). HashSearch - O(1) average. HashInsert – O(1) average. HashDelete – O(1) average.

**Problem-2** Given an array of characters, give an algorithm for removing the duplicates.

**Solution:** Start with the first character and check whether it appears in the remaining part of the string using a simple linear search. If it repeats, bring the last character to that position and decrement the size of the string by one. Continue this process for each distinct character of the given string.

```
int elem(int *A, size_t n, int e){
   for (int i = 0; i < n; ++i)
     if (A[i] == e)
        return 1;
   return 0;
}
int RemoveDuplicates(int *A, int n){
   int m = 0;
   for (int i = 0; i < n; ++i)
     if (!elem(A, m, A[i]))
        A[m++] = A[i];
   return m;
}
```

Time Complexity: O($n^2$). Space Complexity: O(1).

**Problem-3** Can we find any other idea to solve this problem in better time than O($n^2$)? Observe that the order of characters in solutions do not matter.

**Solution:** Use sorting to bring the repeated characters together. Finally scan through the array to remove duplicates in consecutive positions.

```
int Compare(const void* a, const void *b) {
    return *(char*)a - *(char*)b;
}
void RemoveDuplicates(char s[]) {
    int last, current;
    QuickSort(s, strlen(s), sizeof(char), Compare);
    current = 0, last = 0;
    for(; s[current]; i++) {
        if(s[last] != s[current])
                s[++last] = s[current];
    }
    s[last] = '\0';
}
```

Time Complexity: $\Theta(nlogn)$. Space Complexity: O(1).

**Problem-4** Can we solve this problem in a single pass over given array?

**Solution:** We can use hash table to check whether a character is repeating in the given string or not. If the current character is not available in hash table, then insert it into hash table and keep that character in the given string also. If the current character exists in the hash table then skip that character.

```
void RemoveDuplicates(char s[]) {
    int src, dst;
    struct HastTable *h;
    h = CreatHashTable();
    current = last = 0;
    for(; s[current]; current++) {
        if( !HashSearch(h, s[current]))    {
```

```
                    s[last++] = s[current];
                    HashInsert(h, s[current]);
            }
    }
    s[last] = '\0';
}
```

Time Complexity: $\Theta(n)$ on average. Space Complexity: $O(n)$.

**Problem-5** Given two arrays of unordered numbers, check whether both arrays have the same set of numbers?

**Solution:** Let us assume that two given arrays are A and B. A simple solution to the given problem is: for each element of A, check whether that element is in B or not. A problem arises with this approach if there are duplicates. For example consider the following inputs:

$$A = \{2,5,6,8,10,2,2\}$$
$$B = \{2,5,5,8,10,5,6\}$$

The above algorithm gives the wrong result because for each element of A there is an element in B also. But if we look at the number of occurrences, they are not the same. This problem we can solve by moving the elements which are already compared to the end of the list. That means, if we find an element in B, then we move that element to the end of B, and in the next searching we will not find those elements. But the disadvantage of this is it needs extra swaps. Time Complexity of this approach is $O(n^2)$, since for each element of A we have to scan B.

**Problem-6** Can we improve the time complexity of Problem-5?

**Solution: Yes**. To improve the time complexity, let us assume that we have sorted both the lists. Since the sizes of both arrays are n, we need $O(n \log n)$ time for sorting them. After sorting, we just need to scan both the arrays with two pointers and see whether they point to the same element every time, and keep moving the pointers until we reach the end of the arrays.

Time Complexity of this approach is $O(n \log n)$. This is because we need $O(n \log n)$ for sorting the arrays. After sorting, we need $O(n)$ time for scanning but it is less compared to $O(n \log n)$.

**Problem-7** Can we further improve the time complexity of Problem-5?

**Solution: Yes**, by using a hash table. For this, consider the following algorithm.

**Algorithm:**

- Construct the hash table with array $A$ elements as keys.
- While inserting the elements, keep track of the number frequency for each number. That means, if there are duplicates, then increment the counter of that corresponding key.
- After constructing the hash table for $A's$ elements, now scan the array $B$.
- For each occurrence of $B's$ elements reduce the corresponding counter values.
- At the end, check whether all counters are zero or not.
- If all counters are zero, then both arrays are the same otherwise the arrays are different.

Time Complexity: $O(n)$ for scanning the arrays. Space Complexity: $O(n)$ for hash table.

**Problem-8** Given a list of number pairs; if $pair(i,j)$ exists, and $pair\ (j,i)$ exists, report all such pairs. For example, in $\{\{1,3\},\{2,6\},\{3,5\},\{7,4\},\{5,3\},\{8,7\}\}$, we see that {3,5} and {5,3} are present. Report this pair when you encounter {5,3}. We call such pairs 'symmetric pairs'. So, give an efficient algorithm for finding all such pairs.

**Solution:** By using hashing, we can solve this problem in just one scan. Consider the following algorithm.

**Algorithm:**

- Read the pairs of elements one by one and insert them into the hash table. For each pair, consider the first element as key and the second element as value.
- While inserting the elements, check if the hashing of the second element of the current pair is the same as the first number of the current pair.
- If they are the same, then that indicates a symmetric pair exits and output that pair.
- Otherwise, insert that element into that. That means, use the first number of the current pair as key and the second number as value and insert them into the hash table.
- By the time we complete the scanning of all pairs, we have output all the symmetric pairs.

Time Complexity: $O(n)$ for scanning the arrays. Note that we are doing a scan only of the input. Space Complexity: $O(n)$ for hash table.

**Problem-9** Given a singly linked list, check whether it has a loop in it or not.

**Solution: Using Hash Tables**

**Algorithm:**

- Traverse the linked list nodes one by one.
- Check if the node's address is there in the hash table or not.
- If it is already there in the hash table, that indicates we are visiting a node which was already visited. This is possible only if the given linked list has a loop in it.
- If the address of the node is not there in the hash table. then insert that node's address into the hash table.
- Continue this process until we reach the end of the linked list *or* we find the loop.

Time Complexity: $O(n)$ for scanning the linked list. Note that we are doing a scan only of the input. Space Complexity: $O(n)$ for hash table.

**Note:** for an efficient solution, refer to the *Linked Lists* chapter.

**Problem-10** Given an array of 101 elements. Out of them 50 elements are distinct, 24 elements are repeated 2 times, and one element is repeated 3 times. Find the element that is repeated 3 times in $O(1)$.

**Solution: Using Hash Tables**

**Algorithm:**

- Scan the input array one by one.
- Check if the element is already there in the hash table or not.
- If it is already there in the hash table, increment its counter value [this indicates the number of occurrences of the element].
- If the element is not there in the hash table, insert that node into the hash table with counter value 1.
- Continue this process until reaching the end of the array.

Time Complexity: $O(n)$, because we are doing two scans. Space Complexity: $O(n)$, for hash table.

**Note:** For an efficient solution refer to the *Searching* chapter.

**Problem-11** Given $m$ sets of integers that have $n$ elements in them, provide an algorithm to find an element which appeared in the maximum number of sets?

**Solution: Using Hash Tables**

**Algorithm:**

- Scan the input sets one by one.
- For each element keep track of the counter. The counter indicates the frequency of occurrences in all the sets.
- After completing the scan of all the sets, select the one which has the maximum counter value.

Time Complexity: $O(mn)$, because we need to scan all the sets. Space Complexity: $O(mn)$, for hash table. Because, in the worst case all the elements may be different.

**Problem-12** Given two sets $A$ and $B$, and a number $K$, Give an algorithm for finding whether there exists a pair of elements, one from $A$ and one from $B$, that add up to $K$.

**Solution:** For simplicity, let us assume that the size of $A$ is $m$ and the size of $B$ is $n$.

**Algorithm:**

- Select the set which has minimum elements.
- For the selected set create a hash table. We can use both key and value as the same.
- Now scan the second array and check whether *($K$-selected element)* exists in the hash table or not.
- If it exists then return the pair of elements.
- Otherwise continue until we reach the end of the set.

Time Complexity: $O(Max(m, n))$, because we are doing two scans.
Space Complexity: $O(Min(m, n))$, for hash table. We can select the small set for creating the hash table.

**Problem-13** Give an algorithm to remove the specified characters from a given string which are given in another string?

**Solution:** For simplicity, let us assume that the maximum number of different characters is 256. First we create an auxiliary array initialized to 0. Scan the characters to be removed, and for each of those characters we set the value to 1, which indicates that we need to remove that character.

After initialization, scan the input string, and for each of the characters, we check whether that character needs to be deleted or not. If the flag is set then we simply skip to the next character, otherwise we keep the character in the input string. Continue this process until we reach the end of the input string. All these operations we can do in-place as given below.

```
void removeChars(char str[], char removeTheseChars[]) {
    int srcInd, destInd;
    int auxi[256]; //additional array
    for(srcInd =0; srcInd<256; srcIndex++)
        auxi[srcInd]=0;
    //set true for all characters to be removed
    srcIndex=0;
    while(removeTheseChars[srcInd]) {
        auxi[removeTheseChars[srcInd]]=1;
        srcInd++;
    }
    //copy chars unless it must be removed
    srcInd=destInd=0;
    while(str[srcInd++]) {
        if(!auxi[str[srcInd]])
            str[destInd++]=str[srcInd];
    }
}
```

Time Complexity: Time for scanning the characters to be removed + Time for scanning the input array= $O(n)$ +$O(m)$ $\approx O(n)$. Where $m$ is the length of the characters to be removed and $n$ is the length of the input string.

Space Complexity: $O(m)$, length of the characters to be removed. But since we are assuming the maximum number of different characters is 256, we can treat this as a constant. But we should keep in mind that when we are dealing with multi-byte characters, the total number of different characters is much more than 256.

**Problem-14** Give an algorithm for finding the first non-repeated character in a string. For example, the first non-repeated character in the string "*abzddab*" is '*z*'.

**Solution:** The solution to this problem is trivial. For each character in the given string, we can scan the remaining string if that character appears in it. If it does not appears then we are done with the solution and we return that character. If the character appears in the remaining string, then go to the next character.

```
char firstNonRepeatedChar( char *str ) {
    int i, j, repeated = 0;
    int len = strlen(str);
    for(i = 0; i < len; i++ ){
        repeated = 0;
        for( j = 0; j < len; j++ ){
            if( i != j && str[i] == str[j] ){
                repeated = 1;
                break;
            }
        }
        if( repeated == 0 )    // Found the first non-repeated character
        return str[i];
    }
    return '';
}
```

Time Complexity: $O(n^2)$, for two for loops. Space Complexity: $O(1)$.

**Problem-15** Can we improve the time complexity of Problem-13?

**Solution: Yes**. By using hash tables we can reduce the time complexity. Create a hash table by reading all the characters in the input string and keeping count of the number of times each character appears. After creating the hash table, we can read the hash table entries to see which element has a count equal to 1. This approach takes $O(n)$ space but reduces the time complexity also to $O(n)$.

```
char firstNonRepeatedCharUsinghash( char * str ){
    int i, len=strlen(str);
    int count[256]; // additional array
    for(i=0;i<len;++i)
        count[i] = 0;
    for(i=0;i<len;++i)
        count[str[i]]++;
    for(i=0; i<len; ++i) {
        if(count[str[i]]==1) {
            printf("%c",str[i]);
```

```
                break;
            }
        }
        if(i==len)
            printf("No non-repeated characters");
        return 0;
    }
```

Time Complexity: We have $O(n)$ to create the hash table and another $O(n)$ to read the entries of hash table. So the total time is $O(n) + O(n) = O(2n) \approx O(n)$. Space Complexity: $O(n)$ for keeping the count values.

**Problem-16** Given a string, give an algorithm for finding the first repeating letter in a string?

**Solution:** The solution to this problem is somewhat similar to Problem-13 and Problem-15. The only difference is, instead of scanning the hash table twice we can give the answer in just one scan. This is because while inserting into the hash table we can see whether that element already exists or not. If it already exists then we just need to return that character.

```
    char firstRepeatedCharUsinghash( char * str ) {
        int i, len=strlen(str);
        int count[256]; // additional array
        for(i=0;i<len;++i)
            count[i] = 0;
        for(i=0; i<len; ++i) {
            if(count[str[i]]==1) {
                printf("%s",str[i]);
                break;
            }
            else count[str[i]]++;
        }
        if(i==len)
        printf("No Repeated Characters");
        return 0;
    }
```

Time Complexity: We have $O(n)$ for scanning and creating the hash table. Note that we need only one scan for this problem. So the total time is $O(n)$. Space Complexity: $O(n)$ for keeping the count values.

**Problem-17** Given an array of $n$ numbers, create an algorithm which displays all pairs whose sum is $S$.

**Solution:** This problem is similar to Problem-12. But instead of using two sets we use only one set.

**Algorithm:**

- Scan the elements of the input array one by one and create a hash table. Both key and value can be the same.
- After creating the hash table, again scan the input array and check whether ($S$ − *selected element)* exits in the hash table *or* not.
- If it exits then return the pair of elements.
- Otherwise continue and read all the elements of the array.

Time Complexity: We have $O(n)$ to create the hash table and another $O(n)$ to read the entries of the hash table. So the total time is $O(n) + O(n) = O(2n) \approx O(n)$. Space Complexity: $O(n)$ for keeping the count values.

**Problem-18** Is there any other way of solving Problem-17?

**Solution: Yes**. The alternative solution to this problem involves sorting. First sort the input array. After sorting, use two pointers, one at the starting and another at the ending. Each time add the values of both the indexes and see if their sum is equal to $S$. If they are equal then print that pair. Otherwise increase the left pointer if the sum is less than S and decrease the right pointer if the sum is greater than $S$.

Time Complexity: Time for sorting + Time for scanning = $O(nlogn) + O(n) \approx O(nlogn)$. Space Complexity: $O(1)$.

**Problem-19** We have a file with millions of lines of data. Only two lines are identical; the rest are unique. Each line is so long that it may not even fit in the memory. What is the most efficient solution for finding the identical lines?

**Solution:** Since a complete line may not fit into the main memory, read the line partially and compute the hash from that partial line. Then read the next part of the line and compute the hash. This time use the previous hash also while computing the new hash value. Continue this process until we find the hash for the complete line. Do this for each line and store all the hash values in a file [or maintain a hash table of these hashes]. If at any point you get same hash value, read the corresponding lines part by part and compare.

**Note:** Refer to *Searching* chapter for related problems.

**Problem-20** If $h$ is the hashing function and is used to hash $n$ keys into a table of size $s$, where $n <= s$, the expected number of collisions involving a particular key $X$ is :

(A) less than 1. (B) less than $n$. (C) less than $s$. (D) less than $\frac{n}{2}$.

**Solution:** A.

**Problem-21** Implement Bloom Filters.

**Solution:** A Bloom Filter is a data structure designed to tell, rapidly and memory-efficiently, whether an element is present in a set. It is based on a probabilistic mechanism where false positive retrieval results are possible, but false negatives are not. At the end we will see how to tune the parameters in order to minimize the number of false positive results.

Let's begin with a little bit of theory. The idea behind the Bloom filter is to allocate a bit vector of length $m$, initially all set to 0, and then choose $k$ independent hash functions, $h_1$, $h_2$, ..., $h_k$, each with range $[1..m]$. When an element a is added to the set then the bits at positions $h_1(a)$, $h_2$(a), ..., $h_k$(a) in the bit vector are set to 1. Given a query element $q$ we can test whether it is in the set using the bits at positions $h_1$(q), $h_2$(q), ..., $h_k$(q) in the vector. If any of these bits is 0 we report that $q$ is not in the set otherwise we report that $q$ is. The thing we have to care about is that in the first case there remains some probability that $q$ is not in the set which could lead us to a false positive response.

```
typedef unsigned int (*hashFunctionPointer)(const char *);
struct Bloom{
    int bloomArraySize;
    unsigned char *bloomArray;
    int nHashFunctions;
    hashFunctionPointer *funcsArray;
};
#define SETBLOOMBIT(a, n) (a[n/CHAR_BIT] |= (1<<(n%CHAR_BIT)))
#define GETBLOOMBIT(a, n) (a[n/CHAR_BIT] & (1<<(n%CHAR_BIT)))
struct Bloom *createBloom(int size, int nHashFunctions, ...){
    struct Bloom *blm;
    va_list l;
    int n;
    if(!(blm=malloc(sizeof(struct Bloom))))
        return NULL;
    if(!(blm→bloomArray=calloc((size+CHAR_BIT-1)/CHAR_BIT, sizeof(char)))) {
        free(blm);
        return NULL;
    }
    if(!(blm→funcsArray=(hashFunctionPointer*)malloc(nHashFunctions*sizeof(hashFunctionPointer)))) {
        free(blm→bloomArray);
        free(blm);
        return NULL;
    }
    va_start(l, nHashFunctions);
    for(n=0; n<nHashFunctions; ++n) {
        blm→funcsArray[n]=va_arg(l, hashFunctionPointer);
    }
    va_end(l);
    blm→nHashFunctions=nHashFunctions;
    blm→bloomArraySize=size;
    return blm;
}
int deleteBloom(struct Bloom *blm){
    free(blm→bloomArray);
    free(blm→funcsArray);
    free(blm);
    return 0;
}
int addElementBloom(struct Bloom *blm, const char *s){
    for(int n=0; n<blm→nHashFunctions; ++n) {
        SETBLOOMBIT(blm→bloomArray, blm→funcsArray[n](s)%blm→bloomArraySize);
    }
```

```
    return 0;
}
int checkElementBloom(struct Bloom *blm, const char *s){
    for(int n=0; n<blm→nHashFunctions; ++n) {
        if(!(GETBLOOMBIT(blm→bloomArray, blm→funcsArray[n](s)%blm→bloomArraySize))) return 0;
    }
    return 1;
}
unsigned int shiftAddXORHash(const char *key){
    unsigned int h=0;
    while(*key) h^=(h<<5)+(h>>2)+(unsigned char)*key++;
    return h;
}
unsigned int XORHash(const char *key){
    unsigned int h=0;
    hash_t h=0;
    while(*key) h^=*key++;
    return h;
}
int test(){
    FILE *fp;
    char line[1024];
    char *p;
    struct Bloom *blm;
    if(!(blm=createBloom(1500000, 2, shiftAddXORHash, XORHash))) {
        fprintf(stderr, "ERROR: Could not create Bloom filter\n");
        return -1;
    }
    if(!(fp=fopen("path", "r"))) {
        fprintf(stderr, "ERROR: Could not open file %s\n", argv[1]);
        return -1;
    }
    while(fgets(line, 1024, fp)) {
        if((p=strchr(line, '\r'))) *p='\0';
        if((p=strchr(line, '\n'))) *p='\0';
        addElementBloom(blm, line);
    }
    fclose(fp);
    while(fgets(line, 1024, stdin)) {
        if((p=strchr(line, '\r'))) *p='\0';
        if((p=strchr(line, '\n'))) *p='\0';
        p=strtok(line, " \t,.;:\r\n?!-/()");
        while(p) {
            if(!checkBloom(blm, p)) {
                printf("No match for ford \"%s\"\n", p);
            }
            p=strtok(NULL, " \t,.;:\r\n?!-/()");
        }
    }
    deleteBloom(blm);
    return 1;
}
```

**Problem-22** Given a hash table with size=11 entries and the following hash function $h_1$ and step function $h_2$:
$h_1(key)$ = $key$ % size
$h_2(key)$ = {key % (size-1)} + 1

Insert the keys {22, 1, 13, 11, 24, 33, 18, 42, 31} in the given order (from left to right) to the hash table using each of the following hash methods:

- Chaining with $h_1$ [$h(key)$ = $h_1(key)$]
- Linear-Probing with h1 --> $h(key$,i) = ($h_1(key)$+i) % size]
- Double-Hashing with $h_1$ as the hash function and $h_2$ as the step function [$h(key, i)$ = ($h_1(key)$ + i$h_2(key)$) % size].

**Solution:**

| | Chaining | Linear Probing | Double Hashing |
|---|---|---|---|
| 0 | 33 → 11→ 22 | 22 | 22 |
| 1 | 1 | 1 | 1 |
| 2 | 24 → 13 | 13 | 13 |
| 3 | | 11 | |
| 4 | | 24 | 11 |
| 5 | | 33 | 18 |
| 6 | | | 31 |
| 7 | 18 | 18 | 24 |
| 8 | | | 33 |
| 9 | 31→ 42 | 42 | 42 |
| 10 | | 31 | |

CHAPTER

# STRING ALGORITHMS

15

## 15.1 Introduction

To understand the importance of string algorithms let us consider the case of entering the URL (Uniform Resource Locator) in any browser (say, Internet Explorer, Firefox, or Google Chrome). You will observe that after typing the prefix of the URL, a list of all possible URLs is displayed. That means, the browsers are doing some internal processing and giving us the list of matching URLs. This technique is sometimes called *auto – completion*.

Similarly, consider the case of entering the directory name in the command line interface (in both *Windows* and *UNIX*). After typing the prefix of the directory name, if we press the *tab* button, we get a list of all matched directory names available. This is another example of auto completion.

In order to support these kinds of operations, we need a data structure which stores the string data efficiently. In this chapter, we will look at the data structures that are useful for implementing string algorithms.

We start our discussion with the basic problem of strings: given a string, how do we search a substring (pattern)? This is called a *string matching* problem. After discussing various string matching algorithms, we will look at different data structures for storing strings.

## 15.2 String Matching Algorithms

In this section, we concentrate on checking whether a pattern $P$ is a substring of another string $T$ ($T$ stands for text) or not. Since we are trying to check a fixed string $P$, sometimes these algorithms are called *exact string matching* algorithms. To simplify our discussion, let us assume that the length of given text $T$ is $n$ and the length of the pattern $P$ which we are trying to match has the length $m$. That means, $T$ has the characters from 0 to $n-1$ ($T[0 \ldots n-1]$) and $P$ has the characters from 0 to $m-1$ ($P[0 \ldots m-1]$). This algorithm is implemented in $C++$ as $strstr()$.

In the subsequent sections, we start with the brute force method and gradually move towards better algorithms.

- Brute Force Method
- Rabin-Karp String Matching Algorithm
- String Matching with Finite Automata
- KMP Algorithm
- Boyer-Moore Algorithm
- Suffix Trees

## 15.3 Brute Force Method

In this method, for each possible position in the text $T$ we check whether the pattern $P$ matches or not. Since the length of $T$ is $n$, we have $n - m + 1$ possible choices for comparisons. This is because we do not need to check the last $m - 1$ locations of $T$ as the pattern length is $m$. The following algorithm searches for the first occurrence of a pattern string $P$ in a text string $T$.

**Algorithm**

```
int bruteForceStringMatch (int T[], int n,  int P[], int m) {
    for (int i  = 0; i <=n - m; i++) {
        int j  = 0;
        while (j < m && P[j] == T[i + j])
            j  = j + 1;
        if(j == m )
            return i;
    }
```

```
        return -1;
    }
```

Time Complexity: $O((n-m+1) \times m) \approx O(n \times m)$. Space Complexity: $O(1)$.

## 15.4 Rabin-Karp String Matching Algorithm

In this method, we will use the hashing technique and instead of checking for each possible position in $T$, we check only if the hashing of $P$ and the hashing of $m$ characters of $T$ give the same result.

Initially, apply the hash function to the first $m$ characters of $T$ and check whether this result and $P$'s hashing result is the same or not. If they are not the same, then go to the next character of $T$ and again apply the hash function to $m$ characters (by starting at the second character). If they are the same then we compare those $m$ characters of $T$ with $P$.

### Selecting Hash Function

At each step, since we are finding the hash of $m$ characters of $T$, we need an efficient hash function. If the hash function takes $O(m)$ complexity in every step, then the total complexity is $O(n \times m)$. This is worse than the brute force method because first we are applying the hash function and also comparing.

Our objective is to select a hash function which takes $O(1)$ complexity for finding the hash of $m$ characters of $T$ every time. Only then can we reduce the total complexity of the algorithm. If the hash function is not good (worst case), the complexity of the Rabin-Karp algorithm is $O(n-m+1) \times m) \approx O(n \times m)$. If we select a good hash function, the complexity of the Rabin-Karp algorithm complexity is $O(m+n)$. Now let us see how to select a hash function which can compute the hash of $m$ characters of $T$ at each step in $O(1)$.

For simplicity, let's assume that the characters used in string $T$ are only integers. That means, all characters in $T \in \{0, 1, 2, \ldots, 9\}$. Since all of them are integers, we can view a string of $m$ consecutive characters as decimal numbers. For example, string '61815' corresponds to the number 61815. With the above assumption, the pattern $P$ is also a decimal value, and let us assume that the decimal value of $P$ is $p$. For the given text $T[0..n-1]$, let $t(i)$ denote the decimal value of length$-m$ substring $T[i..i+m-1]$ for $i = 0,1,\ldots,n-m-1$. So, $t(i) == p$ if and only if $T[i..i+m-1] == P[0..m-1]$.

We can compute $p$ in $O(m)$ time using Horner's Rule as:

$$p = P[m-1] + 10(P[m-2] + 10(P[m-3] + \ldots + 10\,(P[1] + 10\,P[0])\ldots))$$

The code for the above assumption is:

```
    value = 0;
    for (int i = 0; i < m-1; i++) {
        value = value * 10;
        value = value + P[i];
    }
```

We can compute all $t(i)$, for $i = 0,1,\ldots,n-m-1$ values in a total of $O(n)$ time. The value of $t(0)$ can be similarly computed from $T[0..m-1]$ in $O(m)$ time. To compute the remaining values $t(0), t(1), \ldots, t\,(n-m-1)$, understand that $t(i+1)$ can be computed from $t(i)$ in constant time.

$$t(i+1) = 10 * (t(i) - 10^{m-1} * T[i]) + T[i + m - 1]$$

For example, if $T =$ "123456" and $m = 3$

$$t(0) = 123$$
$$t(1) = 10 * (123 - 100 * 1) + 4 = 234$$

### Step by Step explanation

First : remove the first digit : $123 - 100 * 1 = 23$
Second: Multiply by 10 to shift it : $23 * 10 = 230$
Third: Add last digit : $230 + 4 = 234$

The algorithm runs by comparing, $t(i)$ with $p$. When $t(i) == p$, then we have found the substring $P$ in $T$, starting from position $i$.

## 15.5 String Matching with Finite Automata

In this method we use the finite automata which is the concept of the Theory of Computation (ToC). Before looking at the algorithm, first let us look at the definition of finite automata.

### Finite Automata

A finite automaton F is a 5-tuple $(Q, q_0, A, \Sigma, \delta)$, where

- $Q$ is a finite set of states
- $q_0 \in Q$ is the start state

- $A \subseteq Q$ is a set of accepting states
- $\sum$ is a finite input alphabet
- $\delta$ is the transition function that gives the next state for a given current state and input

## How does Finite Automata Work?

- The finite automaton $F$ begins in state $q_0$
- Reads characters from $\sum$ one at a time
- If $F$ is in state $q$ and reads input character $a$, $F$ moves to state $\delta(q, a)$
- At the end, if its state is in $A$, then we say, $F$ accepted the input string read so far
- If the input string is not accepted it is called the rejected string

**Example:** Let us assume that $Q = \{0,1\}, q_0 = 0, A = \{1\}, \Sigma = \{a, b\}$. $\delta(q, a)$ as shown in the transition table/diagram. This accepts strings that end in an odd number of $a$'s; e.g., *abbaaa* is accepted, *aa* is rejected.

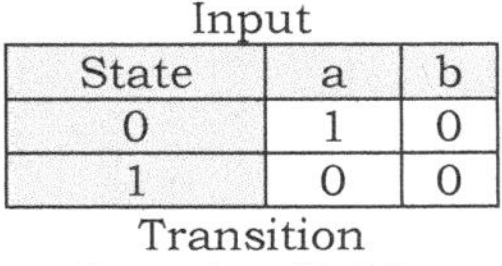

Input

| State | a | b |
|---|---|---|
| 0 | 1 | 0 |
| 1 | 0 | 0 |

Transition Function/Table

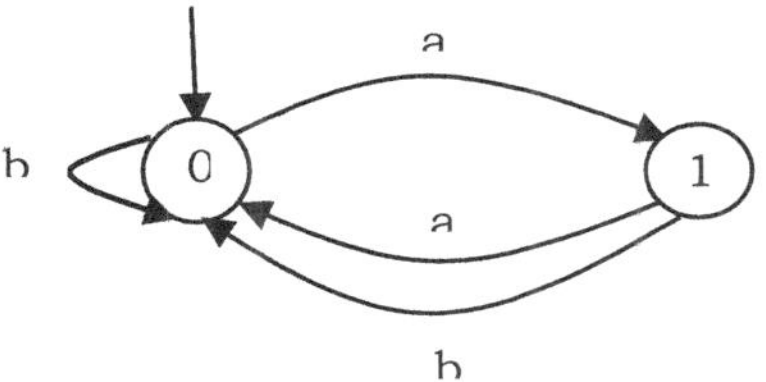


## Important Notes for Constructing the Finite Automata

For building the automata, first we start with the initial state. The FA will be in state $k$ if $k$ characters of the pattern have been matched. If the next text character is equal to the pattern character $c$, we have matched $k + 1$ characters and the FA enters state $k + 1$. If the next text character is not equal to the pattern character, then the FA go to a state $0, 1, 2, \ldots, or\ k$, depending on how many initial pattern characters match the text characters ending with $c$

## Matching Algorithm

Now, let us concentrate on the matching algorithm.

- For a given pattern $P[0..m-1]$, first we need to build a finite automaton $F$
  - The state set is $Q = \{0, 1, 2, \ldots, m\}$
  - The start state is 0
  - The only accepting state is $m$
  - Time to build $F$ can be large if $\sum$ is large
- Scan the text string $T[0..n-1]$ to find all occurrences of the pattern $P[0..m-1]$
- String matching is efficient: $\Theta(n)$
  - Each character is examined exactly once
  - Constant time for each character
  - But the time to compute $\delta$ (transition function) is O($m|\Sigma|$). This is because $\delta$ has O($m|\Sigma|$) entries. If we assume $|\Sigma|$ is constant then the complexity becomes O($m$).

**Algorithm:**

```
//Input: Pattern string P[0..m-1], δ and F
//Goal: All valid shifts displayed
FiniteAutomataStringMatcher(int P[], int m, F, δ) {
    q = 0;
    for (int i = 0; i < m; i++)
        q = δ(q,T[i]);
        if(q == m)
            printf("Pattern occurs with shift: %d", i-m);
}
```

Time Complexity: O($m$).

## 15.6 KMP Algorithm

As before, let us assume that $T$ is the string to be searched and $P$ is the pattern to be matched. This algorithm was presented by Knuth, Morris and Pratt. It takes O($n$) time complexity for searching a pattern. To get O($n$) time complexity, it avoids the comparisons with elements of $T$ that were previously involved in comparison with some element of the pattern $P$.

The algorithm uses a table and in general we call it *prefix function* or *prefix table* or *fail function* F. First we will see how to fill this table and later how to search for a pattern using this table. The prefix function F for a pattern stores the knowledge about how the pattern matches against shifts of itself. This information can be used to avoid useless shifts of the pattern $P$. It means that this table can be used for avoiding backtracking on the string $T$.

## Prefix Table

```
int F[];    //assume F is a global array
void Prefix-Table(int P[], int m) {
    int i=1,j=0, F[0]=0;
    while(i<m) {
        if(P[i]==P[j]) {
            F[i]=j+1;
            i++;
            j++;
        }
        else if(j>0)
            j=F[j-1];
        else {
            F[i]=0;
            i++;
        }
    }
}
```

As an example, assume that $P = a\ b\ a\ b\ a\ c\ a$. For this pattern, let us follow the step-by-step instructions for filling the prefix table F. Initially: $m = length[P] = 7, F[0] = 0$ and $F[1] = 0$.

**Step 1:** $i = 1, j = 0, \mathrm{F}[1] = 0$

| | 0 | 1 | 2 | 3 | 4 | 5 | 6 |
|---|---|---|---|---|---|---|---|
| P | a | b | a | b | a | c | a |
| F | 0 | 0 | | | | | |

**Step 2:** $i = 2, j = 0, \mathrm{F}[2] = 1$

| | 0 | 1 | 2 | 3 | 4 | 5 | 6 |
|---|---|---|---|---|---|---|---|
| P | a | b | a | b | a | c | a |
| F | 0 | 0 | 1 | | | | |

**Step 3:** $i = 3, j = 1, \mathrm{F}[3] = 2$

| | 0 | 1 | 2 | 3 | 4 | 5 | 6 |
|---|---|---|---|---|---|---|---|
| P | a | b | a | b | a | c | a |
| F | 0 | 0 | 1 | 2 | | | |

**Step 4:** $i = 4, j = 2, \mathrm{F}[4] = 3$

| | 0 | 1 | 2 | 3 | 4 | 5 | 6 |
|---|---|---|---|---|---|---|---|
| P | a | b | a | b | a | c | a |
| F | 0 | 0 | 1 | 2 | 3 | | |

**Step 5:** $i = 5, j = 3, \mathrm{F}[5] = 1$

| | 0 | 1 | 2 | 3 | 4 | 5 | 6 |
|---|---|---|---|---|---|---|---|
| P | a | b | a | b | a | c | a |
| F | 0 | 0 | 1 | 2 | 3 | 0 | |

**Step 6:** $i = 6, j = 1, \mathrm{F}[6] = 1$

| | 0 | 1 | 2 | 3 | 4 | 5 | 6 |
|---|---|---|---|---|---|---|---|
| P | a | b | a | b | a | c | a |
| F | 0 | 0 | 1 | 2 | 3 | 0 | 1 |

At this step the filling of the prefix table is complete.

## Matching Algorithm

The KMP algorithm takes pattern $P$, string $T$ and prefix function $F$ as input, and finds a match of $P$ in $T$.

```
int KMP(char T[], int n, int P[], int m) {
    int i=0,j=0;
    Prefix-Table(P,m);
    while(i<n) {
        if(T[i]==P[j]) {
            if(j==m-1)
                return i-j;
            else {
                i++;
                j++;
            }
        }
        else if(j>0)
            j=F[j-1];
        else i++;
    }
```

```
        return -1;
    }
```

Time Complexity: $O(m + n)$, where $m$ is the length of the pattern and $n$ is the length of the text to be searched. Space Complexity: $O(m)$.

Now, to understand the process let us go through an example. Assume that $T = b\,a\,c\,b\,a\,b\,a\,b\,a\,b\,a\,c\,a\,c\,a$ & $P = a\,b\,a\,b\,a\,c\,a$. Since we have already filled the prefix table, let us use it and go to the matching algorithm. Initially: $n = size\ of\ T = 15$; $m = size\ of\ P = 7$.

**Step 1:** $i = 0$, $j = 0$, comparing $P[0]$ with $T[0]$. $P[0]$ does not match with $T[0]$. $P$ will be shifted one position to the right.

| T | b | a | c | b | a | b | a | b | a | b | a | c | a | c | a |
|---|---|---|---|---|---|---|---|---|---|---|---|---|---|---|---|
| P | a | b | a | b | a | c | a | | | | | | | | |

**Step 2:** $i = 1$, $j = 0$, comparing $P[0]$ with $T[1]$. $P[0]$ matches with $T[1]$. Since there is a match, $P$ is not shifted.

| T | b | a | c | b | a | b | a | b | a | b | a | c | a | c | a |
|---|---|---|---|---|---|---|---|---|---|---|---|---|---|---|---|
| P | | a | b | a | b | a | c | a | | | | | | | |

**Step 3:** $i = 2$, $j = 1$, comparing $P[1]$ with $T[2]$. $P[1]$ does not match with $T[2]$. Backtracking on $P$, comparing $P[0]$ and $T[2]$.

| T | b | a | c | b | a | b | a | b | a | b | a | c | a | c | a |
|---|---|---|---|---|---|---|---|---|---|---|---|---|---|---|---|
| P | | a | b | a | b | a | c | a | | | | | | | |

**Step 4:** $i = 3$, $j = 0$, comparing $P[0]$ with $T[3]$. $P[0]$ does not match with $T[3]$.

| T | b | a | c | b | a | b | a | b | a | b | a | c | a | c | a |
|---|---|---|---|---|---|---|---|---|---|---|---|---|---|---|---|
| P | | | | a | b | a | b | a | c | a | | | | | |

**Step 5:** $i = 4$, $j = 0$, comparing $P[0]$ with $T[4]$. $P[0]$ matches with $T[4]$.

| T | b | a | c | b | a | b | a | b | a | b | a | c | a | c | a |
|---|---|---|---|---|---|---|---|---|---|---|---|---|---|---|---|
| P | | | | | a | b | a | b | a | c | a | | | | |

**Step 6:** $i = 5$, $j = 1$, comparing $P[1]$ with $T[5]$. $P[1]$ matches with T[5].

| T | b | a | c | b | a | b | a | b | a | b | a | c | a | c | a |
|---|---|---|---|---|---|---|---|---|---|---|---|---|---|---|---|
| P | | | | | a | b | a | b | a | c | a | | | | |

**Step 7:** $i = 6$, $j = 2$, comparing $P[2]$ with $T[6]$. $P[2]$ matches with $T[6]$.

| T | b | a | c | b | a | b | a | b | a | b | a | c | a | c | a |
|---|---|---|---|---|---|---|---|---|---|---|---|---|---|---|---|
| P | | | | | a | b | a | b | a | c | a | | | | |

**Step 8:** $i = 7$, $j = 3$, comparing $P[3]$ with $T[7]$. $P[3]$ matches with $T[7]$.

| T | b | a | c | b | a | b | a | b | a | b | a | c | a | c | a |
|---|---|---|---|---|---|---|---|---|---|---|---|---|---|---|---|
| P | | | | | a | b | a | b | a | c | a | | | | |

**Step 9:** $i = 8$, $j = 4$, comparing $P[4]$ with $T[8]$. $P[4]$ matches with $T[8]$.

| T | b | a | c | b | a | b | a | b | a | b | a | c | a | c | a |
|---|---|---|---|---|---|---|---|---|---|---|---|---|---|---|---|
| P | | | | | a | b | a | b | a | c | a | | | | |

**Step 10:** $i = 9$, $j = 5$, comparing $P[5]$ with $T[9]$. $P[5]$ does not match with $T[9]$. Backtracking on $P$, comparing $P[4]$ with $T[9]$ because after mismatch $j = F[4] = 3$.

| T | b | a | c | b | a | b | a | b | a | b | a | c | a | c | a |
|---|---|---|---|---|---|---|---|---|---|---|---|---|---|---|---|
| P | | | | | a | b | a | b | a | c | a | | | | |

Comparing $P[3]$ with $T[9]$.

| T | b | a | c | b | a | b | a | b | a | b | a | c | a | c | a |
|---|---|---|---|---|---|---|---|---|---|---|---|---|---|---|---|
| P | | | | | | | a | b | a | b | a | c | a | | |

**Step 11:** $i = 10$, $j = 4$, comparing $P[4]$ with $T[10]$. $P[4]$ matches with $T[10]$.

| T | b | a | c | b | a | b | a | b | a | b | a | c | a | c | a |
|---|---|---|---|---|---|---|---|---|---|---|---|---|---|---|---|
| P | | | | | | | a | b | a | b | a | c | a | | |

**Step 12:** $i = 11$, $j = 5$, comparing $P[5]$ with $T[11]$. $P[5]$ matches with $T[11]$.

| $T$ | b | a | c | b | a | b | a | b | a | b | a | c | a | c | a |
|---|---|---|---|---|---|---|---|---|---|---|---|---|---|---|---|
| $P$ | | | | | | | a | b | a | b | a | c | a | | |

**Step 13:** $i = 12$, $j = 6$, comparing $P[6]$ with $T[12]$. $P[6]$ matches with $T[12]$.

| $T$ | b | a | c | b | a | b | a | b | a | b | a | c | a | c | a |
|---|---|---|---|---|---|---|---|---|---|---|---|---|---|---|---|
| $P$ | | | | | | | a | b | a | b | a | c | a | | |

Pattern $P$ has been found to completely occur in string $T$. The total number of shifts that took place for the match to be found are: $i - m = 13 - 7 = 6$ shifts.

**Notes:**

- KMP performs the comparisons from left to right
- KMP algorithm needs a preprocessing (prefix function) which takes O($m$) space and time complexity
- Searching takes O($n + m$) time complexity (does not depend on alphabet size)

## 15.7 Boyer-Moore Algorithm

Like the KMP algorithm, this also does some pre-processing and we call it *last function*. The algorithm scans the characters of the pattern from right to left beginning with the rightmost character. During the testing of a possible placement of pattern $P$ in $T$, a mismatch is handled as follows: Let us assume that the current character being matched is $T[i] = c$ and the corresponding pattern character is $P[j]$. If $c$ is not contained anywhere in $P$, then shift the pattern $P$ completely past $T[i]$. Otherwise, shift P until an occurrence of character $c$ in $P$ gets aligned with $T[i]$. This technique avoids needless comparisons by shifting the pattern relative to the text.

The *last* function takes O($m + |\Sigma|$) time and the actual search takes O($nm$) time. Therefore the worst case running time of the Boyer-Moore algorithm is O($nm + |\Sigma|$). This indicates that the worst-case running time is quadratic, in the case of $n == m$, the same as the brute force algorithm.

- The Boyer-Moore algorithm is very fast on the large alphabet (relative to the length of the pattern).
- For the small alphabet, Boer-Moore is not preferable.
- For binary strings, the KMP algorithm is recommended.
- For the very shortest patterns, the brute force algorithm is better.

## 15.8 Data Structures for Storing Strings

If we have a set of strings (for example, all the words in the dictionary) and a word which we want to search in that set, in order to perform the search operation faster, we need an efficient way of storing the strings. To store sets of strings we can use any of the following data structures.

- Hashing Tables
- Binary Search Trees
- Tries
- Ternary Search Trees

## 15.9 Hash Tables for Strings

As seen in the *Hashing* chapter, we can use hash tables for storing the integers or strings. In this case, the keys are nothing but the strings. The problem with hash table implementation is that we lose the ordering information – after applying the hash function, we do not know where it will map to.

As a result, some queries take more time. For example, to find all the words starting with the letter "$K$", with hash table representation we need to scan the complete hash table. This is because the hash function takes the complete key, performs hash on it, and we do not know the location of each word.

## 15.10 Binary Search Trees for Strings

In this representation, every node is used for sorting the strings alphabetically. This is possible because the strings have a natural ordering: $A$ comes before $B$, which comes before $C$, and so on. This is because words can be ordered and we can use a Binary Search Tree (BST) to store and retrieve them. For example, let us assume that we want to store the following strings using BSTs:

*this is a career monk string*

For the given string there are many ways of representing them in BST. One such possibility is shown in the tree below.

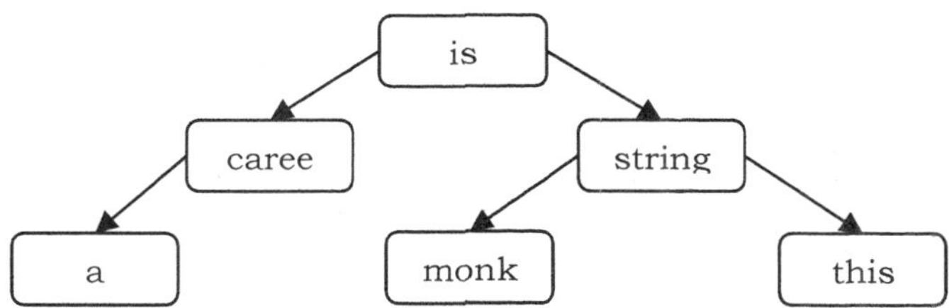


## Issues with Binary Search Tree Representation

This method is good in terms of storage efficiency. But the disadvantage of this representation is that, at every node, the search operation performs the complete match of the given key with the node data, and as a result the time complexity of the search operation increases. So, from this we can say that BST representation of strings is good in terms of storage but not in terms of time.

# 15.11 Tries

Now, let us see the alternative representation that reduces the time complexity of the search operation. The name *trie* is taken from the word re"trie".

## What is a Trie?

A *trie* is a tree and each node in it contains the number of pointers equal to the number of characters of the alphabet. For example, if we assume that all the strings are formed with English alphabet characters "*a*" to "*z*" then each node of the trie contains 26 pointers. A trie data structure can be declared as:

```
struct TrieNode {
    char data;                    // Contains the current node character.
    int is_End_Of_String;         // Indicates whether the string formed from root to current node is a string
or not
    struct TrieNode *child[26];   // Pointers to other tri nodes
};
```

Suppose we want to store the strings "*a*","*all*","*als*", and "*as*"": *trie* for these strings will look like:

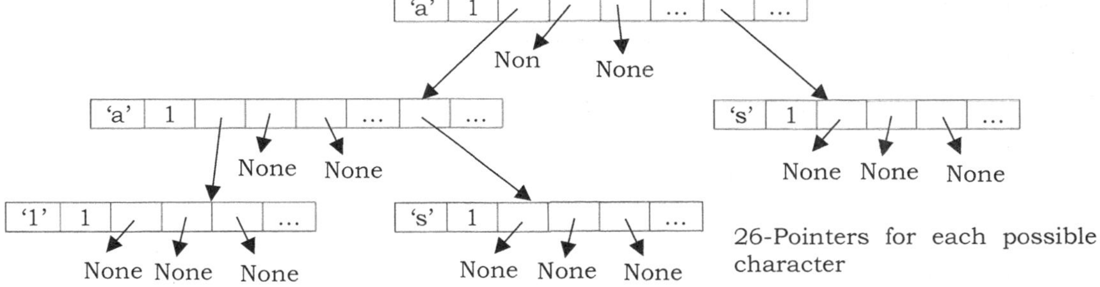


## Why Tries?

The tries can insert and find strings in O($L$) time (where $L$ represents the length of a single word). This is much faster than hash table and binary search tree representations.

## Trie Declaration

The structure of the TrieNode has data (char), is_End_Of_String (boolean), and has a collection of child nodes (Collection of TrieNodes). It also has one more method called subNode(char). This method takes a character as argument and will return the child node of that character type if that is present. The basic element - TrieNode of a TRIE data structure looks like this:

```
struct TrieNode {
    char data;
    int is_End_Of_String;
    struct TrieNode *child[];
};
struct TrieNode *TrieNode subNode(struct TrieNode *root, char c){
    if(root! = NULL){
        for(int i=0; i < 26; i++){
            if(root.child[i]→data == c)
                return root.child[i];
```

```
        }
    }
    return NULL;
}
```

Now that we have defined our TrieNode, let's go ahead and look at the other operations of TRIE. Fortunately, the TRIE data structure is simple to implement since it has two major methods: insert() and search(). Let's look at the elementary implementation of both these methods.

## Inserting a String in Trie

To insert a string, we just need to start at the root node and follow the corresponding path (path from root indicates the prefix of the given string). Once we reach the NULL pointer, we just need to create a skew of tail nodes for the remaining characters of the given string.

```
void insertInTrie(struct TrieNode *root, char *word) {
    if(!*word) return;
    if(!root) {
        struct TrieNode *newNode = (struct TrieNode *) malloc (sizeof(struct TrieNode *));
          newNode→data=*word;
          for(int i =0; i<26; i++)
                newNode→child[i]=NULL;
          if(!*(word+1))
                newNode→is_End_Of_String = 1;
          else
                newNode→child[*word] = insertInTrie(newNode→child[*word], word+1);
          return newNode;
    }
    root→child[*word] = insertInTrie(root→child[*word], word+1);
    return root;
}
```

Time Complexity: $O(L)$, where $L$ is the length of the string to be inserted.

**Note:** For real dictionary implementation, we may need a few more checks such as checking whether the given string is already there in the dictionary or not.

## Searching a String in Trie

The same is the case with the search operation: we just need to start at the root and follow the pointers. The time complexity of the search operation is equal to the length of the given string that want to search.

```
int searchInTrie(struct TrieNode *root, char *word) {
    if(!root) return -1;
    if(!*word) {
        if(root→ is_End_Of_String) return 1;
        else return -1;
    }
    if(root→data == *word)
        return  searchInTrie(root→child[*word], word+1);
    else  return -1;
}
```

Time Complexity: $O(L)$, where $L$ is the length of the string to be searched.

## Issues with Tries Representation

The main disadvantage of tries is that they need lot of memory for storing the strings. As we have seen above, for each node we have too many node pointers. In many cases, the occupancy of each node is less. The final conclusion regarding tries data structure is that they are faster but require huge memory for storing the strings.

**Note:** There are some improved tries representations called *trie compression techniques*. But, even with those techniques we can only reduce the memory at leaves but not at the internal nodes.

# 15.12 Ternary Search Trees

This representation was initially provided by Jon Bentley and Sedgewick. A ternary search tree takes the advantages of binary search trees and tries. That means it combines the memory efficiency of BSTs and the time efficiency of tries.

### Ternary Search Trees Declaration

```
struct TSTNode {
    char data;
```

```
        int is_End_Of_String;
        struct TSTNode *left;
        struct TSTNode *eq;
        struct TSTNode *right;
};
```

The Ternary Search Tree (TST) uses three pointers:

- The *left* pointer points to the TST containing all the strings which are alphabetically less than *data*.
- The *right* pointer points to the TST containing all the strings which are alphabetically greater than *data*.
- The *eq* pointer points to the TST containing all the strings which are alphabetically equal to *data*. That means, if we want to search for a string, and if the current character of the input string and the *data* of current node in TST are the same, then we need to proceed to the next character in the input string and search it in the subtree which is pointed by *eq*.

## Inserting strings in the Ternary Search Tree

For simplicity let us assume that we want to store the following words in TST (also assume the same order): *boats, boat, bat* and *bats*. Initially, let us start with the *boats* string.

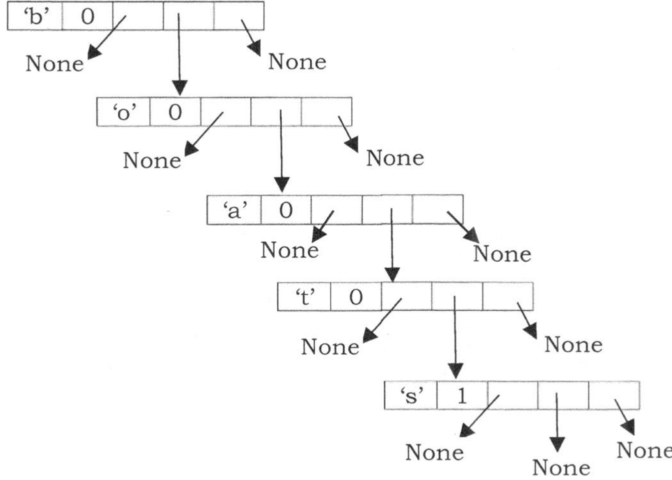


Now if we want to insert the string *boat*, then the TST becomes [the only change is setting the *isEndOfString* flag of "*t*" node to 1]:

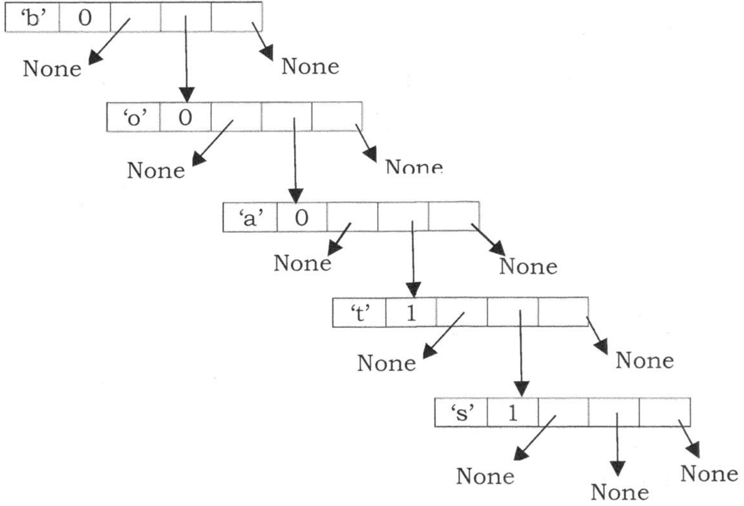


Now, let us insert the next string: *bat*

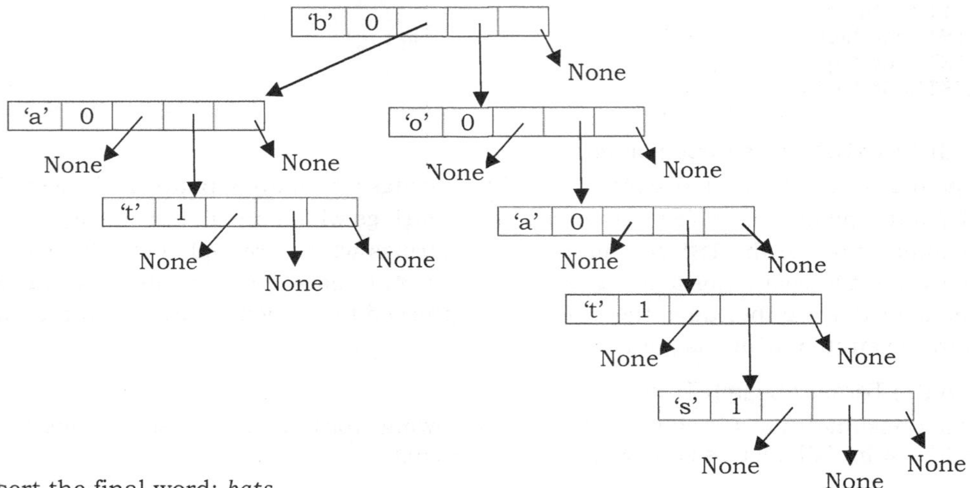


Now, let us insert the final word: *bats*.

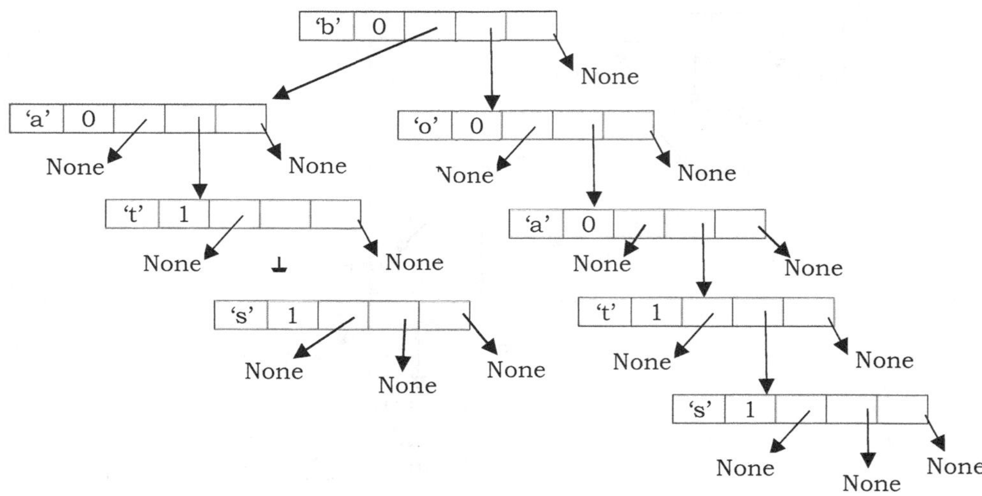


Based on these examples, we can write the insertion algorithm as below. We will combine the insertion operation of BST and tries.

```
struct TSTNode *insertInTST(struct TSTNode *root, char *word) {
    if(root == NULL) {
            root = (struct TSTNode *) malloc(sizeof(struct TSTNode));
            root→data = *word;
            root→is_End_Of_String = 1;
            root→left = root→eq = root→right = NULL;
    }
    if(*word < root→data)
            root→left = insertInTST (root→left, word);
    else if(*word == root→data) {
            if(*(word+1))
                root→eq = insertInTST (root→eq, word+1);
            else root→is_End_Of_String = 1;
    }
    else    root→right = insertInTST (root→right, word);
    return root;
}
```

Time Complexity: $O(L)$, where $L$ is the length of the string to be inserted.

## Searching in Ternary Search Tree

If after inserting the words we want to search for them, then we have to follow the same rules as that of binary search. The only difference is, in case of match we should check for the remaining characters (in *eq* subtree) instead of return. Also, like BSTs we will see both recursive and non-recursive versions of the search method.

```
int searchInTSTRecursive(struct TSTNode  *root, char *word) {
    if(!root)
        return -1;
    if(*word < root→data)
        return searchInTSTRecursive(root→left, word);
    else if(*word > root→data)
        return searchInTSTRecursive(root→right, word);
    else {
        if(root→is_End_Of_String && *(word+1)==0)
            return 1;
        return searchInTSTRecursive(root→eq, ++word);
    }
}
int searchInTSTNon-Recursive(struct TSTNode  *root, char *word) {
    while (root) {
        if(*word < root→data)
            root = root→left;
        else if(*word == root→data) {
            if(root→is_End_Of_String && *(word+1) == 0)
                return 1;
            word++;
            root = root→eq;
        }
        else root = root→right;
    }
    return -1;
}
```

Time Complexity: $O(L)$, where $L$ is the length of the string to be searched.

## Displaying All Words of Ternary Search Tree

If we want to print all the strings of TST we can use the following algorithm. If we want to print them in sorted order, we need to follow the inorder traversal of TST.

```
char word[1024];
void DisplayAllWords(struct TSTNode  *root) {
    if(!root)
        return;
    DisplayAllWords(root→left);
    word[i] = root→data;
    if(root→is_End_Of_String) {
        word[i] = '\0';
        printf("%c", word);
    }
    i++;
    DisplayAllWords(root→eq);
    i--;
    DisplayAllWords(root→right);
}
```

## Finding the Length of the Largest Word in TST

This is similar to finding the height of the BST and can be found as:

```
int maxLengthOfLargestWordInTST(struct TSTNode  *root) {
    if(!root) return 0;
    return max(maxLengthOfLargestWordInTST(root→left),
               maxLengthOfLargestWordInTST(root→eq)+1,
               maxLengthOfLargestWordInTST(root→right)));
}
```

# 15.13 Comparing BSTs, Tries and TSTs

- Hash table and BST implementation stores complete the string at each node. As a result they take more time for searching. But they are memory efficient.

- TSTs can grow and shrink dynamically but hash tables resize only based on load factor.
- TSTs allow partial search whereas BSTs and hash tables do not support it.
- TSTs can display the words in sorted order, but in hash tables we cannot get the sorted order.
- Tries perform search operations very fast but they take huge memory for storing the string.
- TSTs combine the advantages of BSTs and Tries. That means they combine the memory efficiency of BSTs and the time efficiency of tries.

## 15.14 Suffix Trees

Suffix trees are an important data structure for strings. With suffix trees we can answer the queries very fast. But this requires some preprocessing and construction of a suffix tree. Even though the construction of a suffix tree is complicated, it solves many other string-related problems in linear time.

**Note:** Suffix trees use a tree (suffix tree) for one string, whereas Hash tables, BSTs, Tries and TSTs store a set of strings. That means, a suffix tree answers the queries related to one string.

Let us see the terminology we use for this representation.

#### Prefix and Suffix

Given a string $T = T_1T_2 ... T_n$, the $prefix$ of $T$ is a string $T_1 ... T_i$ where $i$ can take values from 1 to $n$. For example, if $T = banana$, then the prefixes of $T$ are: $b, ba, ban$, $bana$, $banan, banana$. Similarly, given a string $T = T_1T_2 ... T_n$, the $suffix$ of T is a string $T_i ... T_n$ where $i$ can take values from $n$ to 1. For example, if $T = banana$, then the suffixes of $T$ are: $a, na, ana, nana$, $anana, banana$.

## Observation

From the above example, we can easily see that for a given text $T$ and pattern $P$, the exact string matching problem can also be defined as:

- Find a suffix of $T$ such that $P$ is a prefix of this suffix *or*
- Find a prefix of $T$ such that $P$ is a suffix of this prefix.

**Example:** Let the text to be searched be $T = accbkkbac$ and the pattern be $P = kkb$. For this example, $P$ is a prefix of the suffix $kkbac$ and also a suffix of the prefix $accbkkb$.

## What is a Suffix Tree?

In simple terms, the suffix tree for text $T$ is a Trie-like data structure that represents the suffixes of $T$. The definition of suffix trees can be given as: A suffix tree for a $n$ character string $T[1 ... n]$ is a rooted tree with the following properties.

- A suffix tree will contain $n$ leaves which are numbered from 1 to $n$
- Each internal node (except root) should have at least 2 children
- Each edge in a tree is labeled by a nonempty substring of $T$
- No two edges of a node (children edges) begin with the same character
- The paths from the root to the leaves represent all the suffixes of $T$

## The Construction of Suffix Trees

#### Algorithm

1. Let $S$ be the set of all suffixes of $T$. Append $ to each of the suffixes.
2. Sort the suffixes in S based on their first character.
3. For each group $S_c$ ($c \in \sum$):
   (i) If $S_c$ group has only one element, then create a leaf node.
   (ii) Otherwise, find the longest common prefix of the suffixes in $S_c$ group, create an internal node, and recursively continue with Step 2, S being the set of remaining suffixes from $S_c$ after splitting off the longest common prefix.

For better understanding, let us go through an example. Let the given text be $T = tatat$. For this string, give a number to each of the suffixes.

| Index | Suffix |
|---|---|
| 1 | $\$$ |
| 2 | $t\$$ |
| 3 | $at\$$ |
| 4 | $tat\$$ |
| 5 | $atat\$$ |
| 6 | $tatat\$$ |

Now, sort the suffixes based on their initial characters.

| Index | Suffix | |
|---|---|---|
| 1 | \$ | Group $S_1$ based on $a$ |
| 3 | $at\$$ | Group $S_2$ based on $a$ |
| 5 | $atat\$$ | |
| 2 | $t\$$ | Group $S_3$ based on $t$ |
| 4 | $tat\$$ | |
| 6 | $tatat\$$ | |

In the three groups, the first group has only one element. So, as per the algorithm, create a leaf node for it, as shown below.

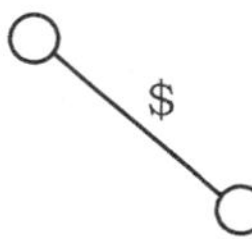


Now, for $S_2$ and $S_3$ (as they have more than one element), let us find the longest prefix in the group, and the result is shown below.

| Group | Indexes for this group | Longest Prefix of Group Suffixes |
|---|---|---|
| $S_2$ | 3, 5 | $at$ |
| $S_3$ | 2, 4, 6 | $t$ |

For $S_2$ and $S_3$, create internal nodes, and the edge contains the longest common prefix of those groups.

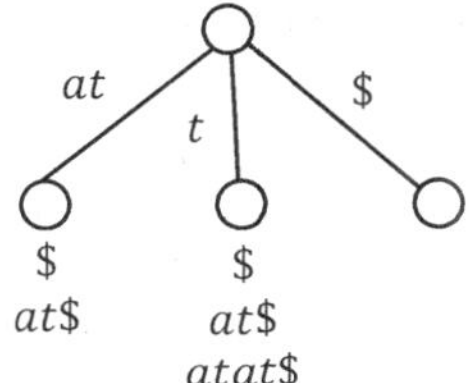


Now we have to remove the longest common prefix from the $S_2$ and $S_3$ group elements.

| Group | Indexes for this group | Longest Prefix of Group Suffixes | Resultant Suffixes |
|---|---|---|---|
| $S_2$ | 3, 5 | $at$ | \$, $at\$$ |
| $S_3$ | 2, 4, 6 | $t$ | \$, $at\$$, $atat\$$ |

Out next step is solving $S_2$ and $S_3$ recursively. First let us take $S_2$. In this group, if we sort them based on their first character, it is easy to see that the first group contains only one element \$, and the second group also contains only one element, $at\$$. Since both groups have only one element, we can directly create leaf nodes for them.

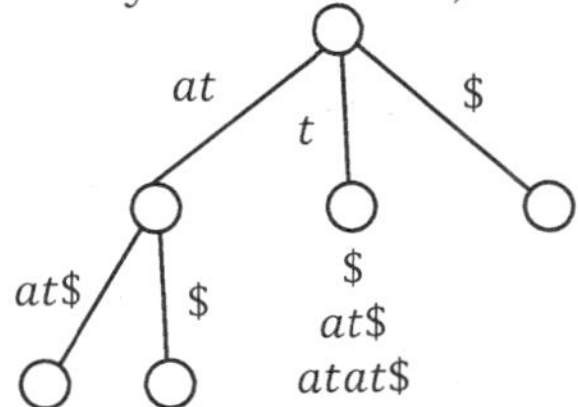


At this step, both $S_1$and $S_2$ elements are done and the only remaining group is $S_3$. As similar to earlier steps, in the $S_3$ group, if we sort them based on their first character, it is easy to see that there is only one element in the first group and it is \$. For $S_3$ remaining elements, remove the longest common prefix.

| Group | Indexes for this group | Longest Prefix of Group Suffixes | Resultant Suffixes |
|---|---|---|---|
| $S_3$ | 4, 6 | $at$ | \$, $at\$$ |

In the $S_3$ second group, there are two elements: \$ and $at\$$. We can directly add the leaf nodes for the first group element \$. Let us add $S_3$ subtree as shown below.

at
t
$
at$
$
at
$
$
at$
atat$
$
at$

Now, $S_3$ contains two elements. If we sort them based on their first character, it is easy to see that there are only two elements and among them one is \$ and other is *at\$*. We can directly add the leaf nodes for them. Let us add $S_3$ subtree as shown below.

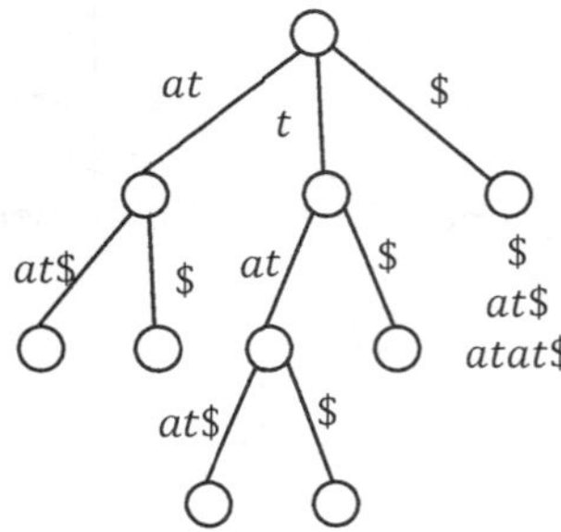


Since there are no more elements, this is the completion of the construction of the suffix tree for string $T = tatat$. The time-complexity of the construction of a suffix tree using the above algorithm is $O(n^2)$ where $n$ is the length of the input string because there are $n$ distinct suffixes. The longest has length $n$, the second longest has length $n - 1$, and so on.

**Note:**

- There are $O(n)$ algorithms for constructing suffix trees.
- To improve the complexity, we can use indices instead of string for branches.

## Applications of Suffix Trees

All the problems below (but not limited to these) on strings can be solved with suffix trees very efficiently (for algorithms refer to *Problems* section).

- **Exact String Matching:** Given a text $T$ and a pattern $P$, how do we check whether $P$ appears in $T$ or not?
- **Longest Repeated Substring:** Given a text $T$ how do we find the substring of $T$ that is the maximum repeated substring?
- **Longest Palindrome:** Given a text $T$ how do we find the substring of $T$ that is the longest palindrome of $T$?
- **Longest Common Substring:** Given two strings, how do we find the longest common substring?
- **Longest Common Prefix:** Given two strings $X[i \dots n]$ and $Y[j \dots m]$, how do we find the longest common prefix?
- How do we search for a regular expression in given text $T$?
- Given a text $T$ and a pattern $P$, how do we find the first occurrence of $P$ in $T$?

## 15.15 String Algorithms: Problems & Solutions

**Problem-1** Given a paragraph of words, give an algorithm for finding the word which appears the maximum number of times. If the paragraph is scrolled down (some words disappear from the first frame, some words still appear, and some are new words), give the maximum occurring word. Thus, it should be dynamic.

**Solution:** For this problem we can use a combination of priority queues and tries. We start by creating a trie in which we insert a word as it appears, and at every leaf of trie. Its node contains that word along with a pointer that points to the node in the heap [priority queue] which we also create. This heap contains nodes whose structure contains a *counter*. This is its frequency and also a pointer to that leaf of trie, which contains that word so that there is no need to store the word twice.

Whenever a new word comes up, we find it in trie. If it is already there, we increase the frequency of that node in the heap corresponding to that word, and we call it heapify. This is done so that at any point of time we can get the word of maximum frequency. While scrolling, when a word goes out of scope, we decrement the counter in heap. If the new frequency is still greater than zero, heapify the heap to incorporate the modification. If the new frequency is zero, delete the node from heap and delete it from trie.

**Problem-2** Given two strings, how can we find the longest common substring?

**Solution:** Let us assume that the given two strings are $T_1$ and $T_2$. The longest common substring of two strings, $T_1$ and $T_2$, can be found by building a generalized suffix tree for $T_1$ and $T_2$. That means we need to build a single suffix tree for both the strings. Each node is marked to indicate if it represents a suffix of $T_1$ or $T_2$ or both. This indicates that we need to use different marker symbols for both the strings (for example, we can use \$ for the first string and # for the second symbol). After constructing the common suffix tree, the deepest node marked for both $T_1$ and $T_2$ represents the longest common substring.

**Another way of doing this is:** We can build a suffix tree for the string $T_1\$T_2\#$. This is equivalent to building a common suffix tree for both the strings.

Time Complexity: $O(m + n)$, where $m$ and $n$ are the lengths of input strings $T_1$ and $T_2$.

**Problem-3** **Longest Palindrome:** Given a text $T$ how do we find the substring of $T$ which is the longest palindrome of $T$?

**Solution:** The longest palindrome of $T[1..n]$ can be found in $O(n)$ time. The algorithm is: first build a suffix tree for $T\$reverse(T)\#$ or build a generalized suffix tree for $T$ and $reverse(T)$. After building the suffix tree, find the deepest node marked with both \$ and #. Basically it means find the longest common substring.

**Problem-4** Given a string (word), give an algorithm for finding the next word in the dictionary.

**Solution:** Let us assume that we are using Trie for storing the dictionary words. To find the next word in Tries we can follow a simple approach as shown below. Starting from the rightmost character, increment the characters one by one. Once we reach $Z$, move to the next character on the left side.

Whenever we increment, check if the word with the incremented character exists in the dictionary or not. If it exists, then return the word, otherwise increment again. If we use $TST$, then we can find the inorder successor for the current word.

**Problem-5** Give an algorithm for reversing a string.

**Solution:**

```
//If the str is editable
char *ReversingString(char str[]) {
	char temp, start, end;
	if(str == NULL || *str == '\0')
		return str;
	for (end = 0; str[end]; end++);
	end--;
	for (start = 0; start < end; start++, end--) {
		temp = str[start]; str[start] = str[end]; str[end] = temp;
	}
	return str;
}
```

Time Complexity: $O(n)$, where $n$ is the length of the given string. Space Complexity: $O(n)$.

**Problem-6** If the string is not editable, how do we create a string that is the reverse of the given string?

**Solution:** If the string is not editable, then we need to create an array and return the pointer of that.

```
//If str is a const string (not editable)
char* ReversingString(char* str) {
	int start, end, len;
	char temp, *ptr=NULL;
	len=strlen(str);
	ptr=malloc(sizeof(char)*(len+1));
	ptr=strcpy(ptr,str);
	for (start=0, end=len-1; start<=end; start++, end--) {		//Swapping
		temp=ptr[start]; ptr[start]=ptr[end]; ptr[end]=temp;
	}
	return ptr;
}
```

Time Complexity: $O\left(\frac{n}{2}\right) \approx O(n)$, where $n$ is the length of the given string. Space Complexity: $O(n)$.

**Problem-7** Can we reverse the string without using any temporary variable?

**Solution: Yes**, we can use XOR logic for swapping the variables.

```
char* ReversingString(char *str) {
	int start = 0, end= strlen(str)-1;
	while( start<end ) {
		str[start] ^= str[end];  str[end] ^= str[start];  str[start] ^= str[end];
		++start;
		--end;
	}
	return str;
}
```

Time Complexity: $O\left(\frac{n}{2}\right) \approx O(n)$, where $n$ is the length of the given string. Space Complexity: $O(n)$.

**Problem-8** Given a text and a pattern, give an algorithm for matching the pattern in the text. Assume ? (single character matcher) and ∗ (multi character matcher) are the wild card characters.

**Solution: Brute Force Method.** For efficient method, refer to the theory section.

```
int PatternMatching(char *text, char *pattern) {
	if(*pattern == 0)
		return 1;
	if(*text == 0)
		return *p == 0;
	if('?' == *pattern)
		return PatternMatching(text+1,pattern+1) || PatternMatching(text,pattern+1);
	if('*' == *pattern)
		return PatternMatching(text+1,pattern) || PatternMatching(text,pattern+1);
	if(*text == *pattern)
		return PatternMatching(text+1,pattern+1);
	return -1;
}
```

Time Complexity: O($mn$), where $m$ is the length of the text and $n$ is the length of the pattern. Space Complexity: O(1).

**Problem-9** Give an algorithm for reversing words in a sentence.
**Example**: Input: "This is a Career Monk String" Output: "String Monk Career a is This"

**Solution:** Start from the beginning and keep on reversing the words. The below implementation assumes that ' ' (space) is the delimiter for words in given sentence.

```
void ReverseWordsInSentences(char *text) {
	int wordStart, wordEnd, length;
	length = strlen(text);
	ReversingString(text, 0, length-1);
	for(wordStart = wordEnd = 0; wordEnd < length; wordEnd ++) {
		if(text[wordEnd] ! = ' ') {
			wordStart = wordEnd;
			while (text[wordEnd] != ' ' && wordEnd < length)
				wordEnd ++;
			wordEnd--;
			ReversingString(text, wordStart, wordEnd); //Found current word, reverse it now.
		}
	}
}
void ReversingString(char text[], int start, int end) {
	for (char temp; start < end; start++, end--) {
		temp = str[end];
		str[end] = str[start];
		strstart] = temp;
	}
}
```

Time Complexity: O($2n$) ≈O($n$), where $n$ is the length of the string. Space Complexity: O(1).

**Problem-10** **Permutations of a string [anagrams]:** Give an algorithm for printing all possible permutations of the characters in a string. Unlike combinations, two permutations are considered distinct if they contain the same characters but in a different order. For simplicity assume that each occurrence of a repeated character is a distinct character. That is, if the input is "aaa", the output should be six repetitions of "aaa". The permutations may be output in any order.

**Solution:** The solution is reached by generating n! strings, each of length n, where n is the length of the input string.

```
void Permutations(int depth, char *permutation, int *used, char *original) {
	int length = strlen(original);
	if(depth == length)
		printf("%s",permutation);
	else {
		for (int i = 0; i < length; i++) {
			if(!used[i]) {
				used[i] = 1;
				permutation[depth] = original[i];
				Permutations(depth + 1, permutation, used, original);
				used[i] = 0;
			}
```

```
            }
        }
    }
```

**Problem-11** **Combinations of a String:** Unlike permutations, two combinations are considered to be the same if they contain the same characters, but may be in a different order. Give an algorithm that prints all possible combinations of the characters in a string. For example, "$ac$" and "$ab$" are different combinations from the input string "$abc$", but "$ab$" is the same as "$ba$".

**Solution:** The solution is achieved by generating $n!/r!\,(n-r)!$ strings, each of length between 1 and $n$ where $n$ is the length of the given input string.

**Algorithm:**

For each of the input characters

a. Put the current character in output string and print it.
b. If there are any remaining characters, generate combinations with those remaining characters.

```
void combinations(int depth, char *combination, int start, char *original) {
    int length = strlen(original);
    for (int i = start; i < length; i++) {
            combination[depth] = original[i];
        combination[depth +1] = '\0';
            printf("%s", combination);
            if(i < length -1)
          combinations(depth + 1, combination, start + 1, original);
    }
}
```

**Problem-12** Given a string "ABCCBCBA", give an algorithm for recursively removing the adjacent characters if they are the same. For example, ABCCBCBA --> ABBCBA-->ACBA

**Solution:** First we need to check if we have a character pair; if yes, then cancel it. Now check for next character and previous element. Keep canceling the characters until we either reach the start of the array, reach the end of the array, or don't find a pair.

```
void removeAdjacentPairs(char* str) {
    int len = strlen(str), i, j = 0;
    for (i=1; i <= len; i++) {
            while ((str[i] == str[j]) && (j >= 0)){        //Cancel pairs
                    i++;
                    j--;
            }
            str[++j] = str[i];
    }
    return;
}
```

**Problem-13** Given a set of characters $CHARS$ and a input string $INPUT$, find the minimum window in $str$ which will contain all the characters in $CHARS$ in complexity O($n$). For example, $INPUT$ = $ABBACBAA$ and $CHARS$ = $AAB$ has the minimum window $BAA$.

**Solution:** This algorithm is based on the sliding window approach. In this approach, we start from the beginning of the array and move to the right. As soon as we have a window which has all the required elements, try sliding the window as far right as possible with all the required elements. If the current window length is less than the minimum length found until now, update the minimum length. For example, if the input array is $ABBACBAA$ and the minimum window should cover characters $AAB$, then the sliding window will move like this:

| A | B | B | A | C | B | A | A |
|---|---|---|---|---|---|---|---|

| A | B | B | A | C | B | A | A |
|---|---|---|---|---|---|---|---|

| A | B | B | A | C | B | A | A |
|---|---|---|---|---|---|---|---|

**Algorithm:** The input is the given array and chars is the array of characters that need to be found.

1 Make an integer array shouldfind[] of len 256. The $i^{th}$ element of this array will have the count of how many times we need to find the element of ASCII value $i$.
2 Make another array hasfound of 256 elements, which will have the count of the required elements found until now.

3 Count <= 0
4 While input[i]
   a. If input[i] element is not to be found→ continue
   b. If input[i] element is required => increase count by 1.
   c. If count is length of chars[] array, slide the window as much right as possible.
   d. If current window length is less than min length found until now, update min length.

```
#define MAX 256
void minLengthWindow(char input[], char chars[]) {
	int shouldfind[MAX] = {0,}, hasfound[MAX] = {0,};
	int j=0, cnt = 0, start=0, finish, minwindow = INT_MAX;
	int charlen = strlen(chars), iplen = strlen(input);
	for (int i=0; i< charlen; i++)
		shouldfind[chars[i]] += 1;
	finish = iplen;
	for (int i=0; i< iplen; i++) {
		if(!shouldfind[input[i]])
			continue;
		hasfound[input[i]] += 1;
		if(shouldfind[input[i]] >= hasfound[input[i]])
			cnt++;
		if(cnt == charlen) {
			while (shouldfind[input[j]] == 0 || hasfound[input[j]] > shouldfind[input[j]])	{
				if(hasfound[input[j]] > shouldfind[input[j]])
					hasfound[input[j]]--;
				j++;
			}
			if(minwindow > (i - j +1)) {
				minwindow = i - j +1;
				finish = i;
				start = j;
			}
		}
	}
	printf("Start:%d and Finish: %d", start, finish);
}
```

Complexity: If we walk through the code, $i$ and $j$ can traverse at most $n$ steps (where $n$ is the input size) in the worst case, adding to a total of $2n$ times. Therefore, time complexity is $O(n)$.

**Problem-14** We are given a 2D array of characters and a character pattern. Give an algorithm to find if the pattern is present in the 2D array. The pattern can be in any order (all 8 neighbors to be considered) but we can't use the same character twice while matching. Return 1 if match is found, 0 if not. For example: Find "MICROSOFT" in the below matrix.

| A | C | P | **R** | C |
|---|---|---|---|---|
| X | **S** | **O** | P | **C** |
| V | **O** | V | N | **I** |
| W | G | **F** | **M** | N |
| Q | A | **T** | I | T |

**Solution:** Manually finding the solution of this problem is relatively intuitive; we just need to describe an algorithm for it. Ironically, describing the algorithm is not the easy part.

**How do we do it manually?** First we match the first element, and when it is matched we match the second element in the 8 neighbors of the first match. We do this process recursively, and when the last character of the input pattern matches, return true.

During the above process, take care not to use any cell in the 2D array twice. For this purpose, you mark every visited cell with some sign. If your pattern matching fails at some point, start matching from the beginning (of the pattern) in the remaining cells. When returning, you unmark the visited cells.

Let's convert the above intuitive method into an algorithm. Since we are doing similar checks for pattern matching every time, a recursive solution is what we need. In a recursive solution, we need to check if the substring passed is matched in the given matrix or not. The condition is not to use the already used cell, and to find the already used cell, we need to add another 2D array to the function (or we can use an unused bit in the input array itself.) Also, we need the current position of the input matrix from where we need to start. Since we need to pass a lot more information than is actually given, we should be having a wrapper function to initialize the extra information to be passed.

**Algorithm:**

If we are past the last character in the pattern
   Return true
If we get a used cell again
   Return false if we got past the 2D matrix

```
        Return false
    If searching for first element and cell doesn't match
        FindMatch with next cell in row-first order (or column-first order)
    Otherwise if character matches
        mark this cell as used
        res = FindMatch with next position of pattern in 8 neighbors
        mark this cell as unused
        Return res
    Otherwise
        Return false
```

```
#define MAX 100
boolean findMatch_wrapper(char mat[MAX][MAX], char *pat, int nrow, int ncol) {
        if(strlen(pat) > nrow*ncol) return false;
        int used[MAX][MAX] = {{0,},};
        return findMatch(mat, pat, used, 0, 0, nrow, ncol, 0);
}
//level: index till which pattern is matched & x, y: current position in 2D array
boolean findMatch(char mat[MAX][MAX], char *pat, int used[MAX][MAX],
                                    int x, int y, int nrow, int ncol, int level) {
    if(level == strlen(pat)) //pattern matched
        return true;
    if(nrow == x || ncol == y)  return false;
    if(used[x][y])        return false;
    if(mat[x][y] != pat[level] && level == 0) {
        if(x < (nrow - 1))
            return findMatch(mat, pat, used, x+1, y, nrow, ncol, level); //next element in same row
        else if(y < (ncol - 1))
            return findMatch(mat, pat, used, 0, y+1, nrow, ncol, level); //first element from same column
        else  return false;
    }
    else if(mat[x][y] == pat[level]) {
        boolean res;
        used[x][y] = 1;      //marking this cell as used
        //finding subpattern in 8 neighbors
        res = (x > 0  ? findMatch(mat, pat, used, x-1, y, nrow, ncol, level+1) :  false) ||
            (res = x < (nrow - 1)  ? findMatch(mat, pat, used, x+1, y, nrow, ncol, level+1) :  false) ||
            (res = y > 0 ? findMatch(mat, pat, used, x, y-1, nrow, ncol, level+1) :  false) ||
            (res = y < (ncol - 1)  ? findMatch(mat, pat, used, x, y+1, nrow, ncol, level+1) :  false) ||
            (res = x < (nrow - 1)&&(y < ncol -1)?findMatch(mat, pat, used, x+1, y+1, nrow, ncol, level+1) : false) ||
            (res = x < (nrow - 1) && y > 0  ?  findMatch(mat, pat, used, x+1, y-1, nrow, ncol, level+1) : false) ||
            (res = x > 0 && y < (ncol - 1) ?   findMatch(mat, pat, used, x-1, y+1, nrow, ncol, level+1) : false) ||
            (res = x > 0 && y > 0 ? findMatch(mat, pat, used, x-1, y-1, nrow, ncol, level+1) : false);
        used[x][y] = 0;                //marking this cell as unused
        return res;
    }
    else  return false;
}
```

**Problem-15** Given two strings $str1$ and $str2$, write a function that prints all interleavings of the given two strings. We may assume that all characters in both strings are different. Example: Input: $str1$ = "AB", $str2$ = "CD" and Output: ABCD ACBD ACDB CABD CADB CDAB. An interleaved string of given two strings preserves the order of characters in individual strings. For example, in all the interleavings of above first example, 'A' comes before 'B' and 'C' comes before 'D'.

**Solution:** Let the length of $str1$ be $m$ and the length of $str2$ be $n$. Let us assume that all characters in $str1$ and $str2$ are different. Let Count($m, n$) be the count of all interleaved strings in such strings. The value of Count($m, n$) can be written as following.

```
Count(m, n) = Count(m-1, n) + Count(m, n-1)
Count(1, 0) = 1 and Count(1, 0) = 1
```

To print all interleavings, we can first fix the first character of str1[0..m-1] in output string, and recursively call for str1[1..m-1] and str2[0..n-1]. And then we can fix the first character of str2[0..n-1] and recursively call for str1[0..m-1] and str2[1..n-1].

```
void PrintInterleavings(char *str1, char *str2, char *iStr, int m, int n, int i){
    // Base case: If all characters of str1 & str2 have been included in output string,
    // then print the output string
    if ( m==0 && n ==0 )
        printf("%s\n", iStr) ;
    // If some characters of str1 are left to be included, then include the
```

```
    // first character from the remaining characters and recur for rest
    if ( m != 0 )    {
        iStr[i] = str1[0];
        PrintInterleavings(str1 + 1, str2, iStr, m-1, n, i+1);
    }
    // If some characters of str2 are left to be included, then include the
    // first character from the remaining characters and recur for rest
    if ( n != 0 ) {
        iStr[i] = str2[0];
        PrintInterleavings(str1, str2+1, iStr, m, n-1, i+1);
    }
}
// Allocates memory for output string and uses PrintInterleavings() for printing all interleaving's
void Print(char *str1, char *str2, int m, int n){
    char *iStr= (char*)malloc((m+n+1)*sizeof(char));      // allocate memory for the output string
    iStr[m+n] = '\0';                                      // Set the terminator for the output string
    PrintInterleavings(str1, str2, iStr, m, n, 0);         // print all interleaving's using PrintInterleavings()
    free(iStr);
}
```

**Problem-16** Given a matrix with size $n \times n$ containing random integers. Give an algorithm which checks whether rows match with a column(s) or not. For example, if $i^{th}$ row matches with $j^{th}$ column, and $i^{th}$ row contains the elements - [2,6,5,8,9]. Then $j^{th}$ column would also contain the elements - [2,6,5,8,9].

**Solution:** We can build a trie for the data in the columns (rows would also work). Then we can compare the rows with the trie. This would allow us to exit as soon as the beginning of a row does not match any column (backtracking). Also this would let us check a row against all columns in one pass.

If we do not want to waste memory for empty pointers then we can further improve the solution by constructing a suffix tree.

**Problem-17** Write a method to replace all spaces in a string with '%20'. Assume string has sufficient space at end of string to hold additional characters.

**Solution**: Find the number of spaces. Then, starting from end (assuming string has enough space), replace the characters. Starting from end reduces the overwrites.

```
void encodeSpaceWithString(char* A){
    char *space = "%20";
    int stringLength = strlen(A);
    if(stringLength ==0){
        return;
    }
    int i, numberOfSpaces = 0;
    for(i = 0; i < stringLength; i++){
        if(A[i] == ' ' || A[i] == '\t'){
            numberOfSpaces ++;
        }
    }
    if(!numberOfSpaces)
        return;
    int newLength = len + numberOfSpaces * 2;
    A[newLength] = '\0';
    for(i = stringLength-1; i >= 0; i--){
        if(A[i] == ' ' || A[i] == '\t'){
            A[newLength--] = '0';
            A[newLength--] = '2';
            A[newLength--] = '%';
        }
        else{
            A[newLength--] = A[i];
        }
    }
}
```

Time Complexity: $O(n)$. Space Complexity: $O(1)$. Here, we do not have to worry about the space needed for extra characters.

**Problem-18** **Running length encoding**: Write an algorithm to compress the given string by using the count of repeated characters and if new com-pressed string length is not smaller than the original string then return the original string.

**Solution**:

*With extra space of* O(2):

```
string CompressString(string inputStr){
    char last = inputStr.at(0);
    int size = 0, count = 1;
    char temp[2];
    string str;
    for (int i = 1; i < inputStr.length(); i++){
        if(last == inputStr.at(i))
            count ++;
        else{
            itoa(count, temp, 10);
            str += last;
            str += temp;
            last = inputStr.at(i);
            count = 1;
        }
    }
    str = str + last + temp;
    // If the compresed string size is greater than input string, return input string
    if(str.length() >= inputStr.length())
        return inputStr;
    else return str;
}
```

Time Complexity: $O(n)$. Space Complexity: $O(1)$, but it uses a temporary array of size two.

*Without extra space (inplace)*:

```
char CompressString(char *inputStr, char currentChar, int lengthIndex, int& countChar, int& index){
    if(lengthIndex == -1)
        return currentChar;
    char lastChar = CompressString(inputStr, inputStr[lengthIndex], lengthIndex-1, countChar, index);
    if(lastChar == currentChar)
        countChar++;
    else {
        inputStr[index++] = lastChar;
        for(int i =0; i< NumToString(countChar).length(); i++)
            inputStr[index++] = NumToString(countChar).at(i);
        countChar = 1;
    }
    return currentChar;
}
```

Time Complexity: $O(n)$. Space Complexity: $O(1)$.

# ALGORITHMS DESIGN TECHNIQUES

CHAPTER 16

## 16.1 Introduction

In the previous chapters, we have seen many algorithms for solving different kinds of problems. Before solving a new problem, the general tendency is to look for the similarity of the current problem to other problems for which we have solutions. This helps us in getting the solution easily.

In this chapter, we will see different ways of classifying the algorithms and in subsequent chapters we will focus on a few of them (Greedy, Divide and Conquer, Dynamic Programming).

## 16.2 Classification

There are many ways of classifying algorithms and a few of them are shown below:

- Implementation Method
- Design Method
- Other Classifications

## 16.3 Classification by Implementation Method

### Recursion or Iteration

A *recursive* algorithm is one that calls itself repeatedly until a base condition is satisfied. It is a common method used in functional programming languages like $C, C++$, etc.

*Iterative* algorithms use constructs like loops and sometimes other data structures like stacks and queues to solve the problems.

Some problems are suited for recursive and others are suited for iterative. For example, the *Towers of Hanoi* problem can be easily understood in recursive implementation. Every recursive version has an iterative version, and vice versa.

### Procedural or Declarative (Non-Procedural)

In *declarative* programming languages, we say what we want without having to say how to do it. With *procedural* programming, we have to specify the exact steps to get the result. For example, SQL is more declarative than procedural, because the queries don't specify the steps to produce the result. Examples of procedural languages include: C, PHP, and PERL.

### Serial or Parallel or Distributed

In general, while discussing the algorithms we assume that computers execute one instruction at a time. These are called *serial* algorithms.

*Parallel* algorithms take advantage of computer architectures to process several instructions at a time. They divide the problem into subproblems and serve them to several processors or threads. Iterative algorithms are generally parallelizable.

If the parallel algorithms are distributed on to different machines then we call such algorithms *distributed* algorithms.

### Deterministic or Non-Deterministic

*Deterministic* algorithms solve the problem with a predefined process, whereas *non – deterministic* algorithms guess the best solution at each step through the use of heuristics.

#### Exact or Approximate

As we have seen, for many problems we are not able to find the optimal solutions. That means, the algorithms for which we are able to find the optimal solutions are called *exact* algorithms. In computer science, if we do not have the optimal solution, we give approximation algorithms.

Approximation algorithms are generally associated with NP-hard problems (refer to the *Complexity Classes* chapter for more details).

## 16.4 Classification by Design Method

Another way of classifying algorithms is by their design method.

#### Greedy Method

*Greedy* algorithms work in stages. In each stage, a decision is made that is good at that point, without bothering about the future consequences. Generally, this means that some *local best* is chosen. It assumes that the local best selection also makes for the *global* optimal solution.

#### Divide and Conquer

The D & C strategy solves a problem by:

1) Divide: Breaking the problem into sub problems that are themselves smaller instances of the same type of problem.
2) Recursion: Recursively solving these sub problems.
3) Conquer: Appropriately combining their answers.

Examples: merge sort and binary search algorithms.

### Dynamic Programming

Dynamic programming (DP) and memoization work together. The difference between DP and divide and conquer is that in the case of the latter there is no dependency among the sub problems, whereas in DP there will be an overlap of sub-problems. By using memoization [maintaining a table for already solved sub problems], DP reduces the exponential complexity to polynomial complexity (O($n^2$), O($n^3$), etc.) for many problems.

The difference between dynamic programming and recursion is in the memoization of recursive calls. When sub problems are independent and if there is no repetition, memoization does not help, hence dynamic programming is not a solution for all problems.

By using memoization [maintaining a table of sub problems already solved], dynamic programming reduces the complexity from exponential to polynomial.

### Linear Programming

Linear programming is not a programming language like C++, Java, or Visual Basic. Linear programming can be defined as:

> A method to allocate scarce resources to competing activities in an optimal manner when the problem can be expressed using a linear objective function and linear inequality constraints.

A linear program consists of a set of variables, a linear objective function indicating the contribution of each variable to the desired outcome, and a set of linear constraints describing the limits on the values of the variables. The *solution* to a linear program is a set of values for the problem variables that results in the best -- *largest or smallest* -- value of the objective function and yet is consistent with all the constraints. Formulation is the process of translating a real-world problem into a linear program.

Once a problem has been formulated as a linear program, a computer program can be used to solve the problem. In this regard, solving a linear program is relatively easy. The hardest part about applying linear programming is formulating the problem and interpreting the solution. In linear programming, there are inequalities in terms of inputs and *maximizing* (or *minimizing*) some linear function of the inputs. Many problems (example: maximum flow for directed graphs) can be discussed using linear programming.

### Reduction [Transform and Conquer]

In this method we solve a difficult problem by transforming it into a known problem for which we have asymptotically optimal algorithms. In this method, the goal is to find a reducing algorithm whose complexity is not dominated by the resulting reduced algorithms. For example, the selection algorithm for finding the median in a list involves first sorting the list and then finding out the middle element in the sorted list. These techniques are also called *transform and conquer*.

## 16.5 Other Classifications

## Classification by Research Area

In computer science each field has its own problems and needs efficient algorithms. Examples: search algorithms, sorting algorithms, merge algorithms, numerical algorithms, graph algorithms, string algorithms, geometric algorithms, combinatorial algorithms, machine learning, cryptography, parallel algorithms, data compression algorithms, parsing techniques, and more.

### Classification by Complexity

In this classification, algorithms are classified by the time they take to find a solution based on their input size. Some algorithms take linear time complexity ($O(n)$) and others take exponential time, and some never halt. Note that some problems may have multiple algorithms with different complexities.

#### Randomized Algorithms

A few algorithms make choices randomly. For some problems, the fastest solutions must involve randomness. Example: Quick Sort.

## Branch and Bound Enumeration and Backtracking

These were used in Artificial Intelligence and we do not need to explore these fully. For the Backtracking method refer to the *Recusion and Backtracking* chapter.

**Note:** In the next few chapters we discuss the Greedy, Divide and Conquer, and Dynamic Programming] design methods. These methods are emphasized because they are used more often than other methods to solve problems.

CHAPTER

# GREEDY ALGORITHMS

## 17.1 Introduction

Let us start our discussion with simple theory that will give us an understanding of the Greedy technique. In the game of *Chess*, every time we make a decision about a move, we have to also think about the future consequences. Whereas, in the game of *Tennis* (or *Volleyball*), our action is based on the immediate situation.

This means that in some cases making a decision that looks right at that moment gives the best solution (*Greedy*), but in other cases it doesn't. The Greedy technique is best suited for looking at the immediate situation.

## 17.2 Greedy Strategy

Greedy algorithms work in stages. In each stage, a decision is made that is good at that point, without bothering about the future. This means that some *local best* is chosen. It assumes that a local good selection makes for a global optimal solution.

## 17.3 Elements of Greedy Algorithms

The two basic properties of optimal Greedy algorithms are:

1) Greedy choice property
2) Optimal substructure

### Greedy choice property

This property says that the globally optimal solution can be obtained by making a locally optimal solution (Greedy). The choice made by a Greedy algorithm may depend on earlier choices but not on the future. It iteratively makes one Greedy choice after another and reduces the given problem to a smaller one.

### Optimal substructure

A problem exhibits optimal substructure if an optimal solution to the problem contains optimal solutions to the subproblems. That means we can solve subproblems and build up the solutions to solve larger problems.

## 17.4 Does Greedy Always Work?

Making locally optimal choices does not always work. Hence, Greedy algorithms will not always give the best solutions. We will see particular examples in the *Problems* section and in the *Dynamic Programming* chapter.

## 17.5 Advantages and Disadvantages of Greedy Method

The main advantage of the Greedy method is that it is straightforward, easy to understand and easy to code. In Greedy algorithms, once we make a decision, we do not have to spend time re-examining the already computed values. Its main disadvantage is that for many problems there is no greedy algorithm. That means, in many cases there is no guarantee that making locally optimal improvements in a locally optimal solution gives the optimal global solution.

## 17.6 Greedy Applications

- Sorting: Selection sort, Topological sort
- Priority Queues: Heap sort
- Huffman coding compression algorithm
- Prim's and Kruskal's algorithms
- Shortest path in Weighted Graph without Negative Edge Weights [Dijkstra's Algorithm]

- Coin change problem
- Fractional Knapsack problem
- Disjoint sets-UNION by size and UNION by height (or rank)
- Job scheduling algorithm
- Greedy techniques can be used as an approximation algorithm for complex problems

## 17.7 Understanding Greedy Technique

For better understanding let us go through an example.

## Huffman Coding Algorithm

### Definition

Given a set of $n$ characters from the alphabet A [each character c ∈ A] and their associated frequency $freq(c)$, find a binary code for each character c ∈ A, such that $\sum_{c \in A} freq(c)|binarycode(c)|$ is minimum, where /binarycode(c)/ represents the length of *binary code* of character c. That means the sum of the lengths of all character codes should be minimum [the sum of each character's frequency multiplied by the number of bits in the representation].

The basic idea behind the Huffman coding algorithm is to use fewer bits for more frequently occurring characters. The Huffman coding algorithm compresses the storage of data using variable length codes. We know that each character takes 8 bits for representation. But in general, we do not use all of them. Also, we use some characters more frequently than others. When reading a file, the system generally reads 8 bits at a time to read a single character. But this coding scheme is inefficient. The reason for this is that some characters are more frequently used than other characters. Let's say that the character $'e'$ is used 10 times more frequently than the character $'q'$. It would then be advantageous for us to instead use a 7 bit code for e and a 9 bit code for $q$ because that could reduce our overall message length.

On average, using Huffman coding on standard files can reduce them anywhere from 10% to 30% depending on the character frequencies. The idea behind the character coding is to give longer binary codes for less frequent characters and groups of characters. Also, the character coding is constructed in such a way that no two character codes are prefixes of each other.

### An Example

Let's assume that after scanning a file we find the following character frequencies:

| Character | Frequency |
|---|---|
| $a$ | 12 |
| $b$ | 2 |
| $c$ | 7 |
| $d$ | 13 |
| $e$ | 14 |
| $f$ | 85 |

Given this, create a binary tree for each character that also stores the frequency with which it occurs (as shown below).

b-2 c-7 a-12 d-13 e-14 f-85

The algorithm works as follows: In the list, find the two binary trees that store minimum frequencies at their nodes.

Connect these two nodes at a newly created common node that will store no character but will store the sum of the frequencies of all the nodes connected below it. So our picture looks like this:

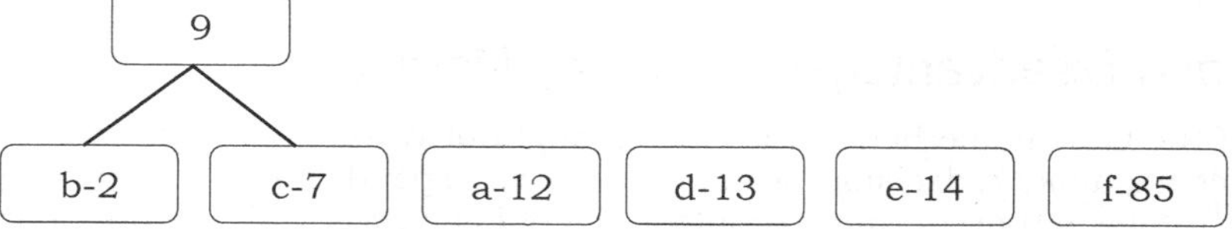


Repeat this process until only one tree is left:

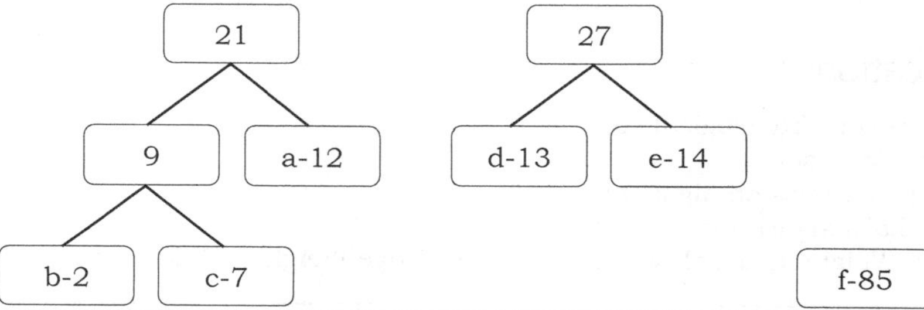

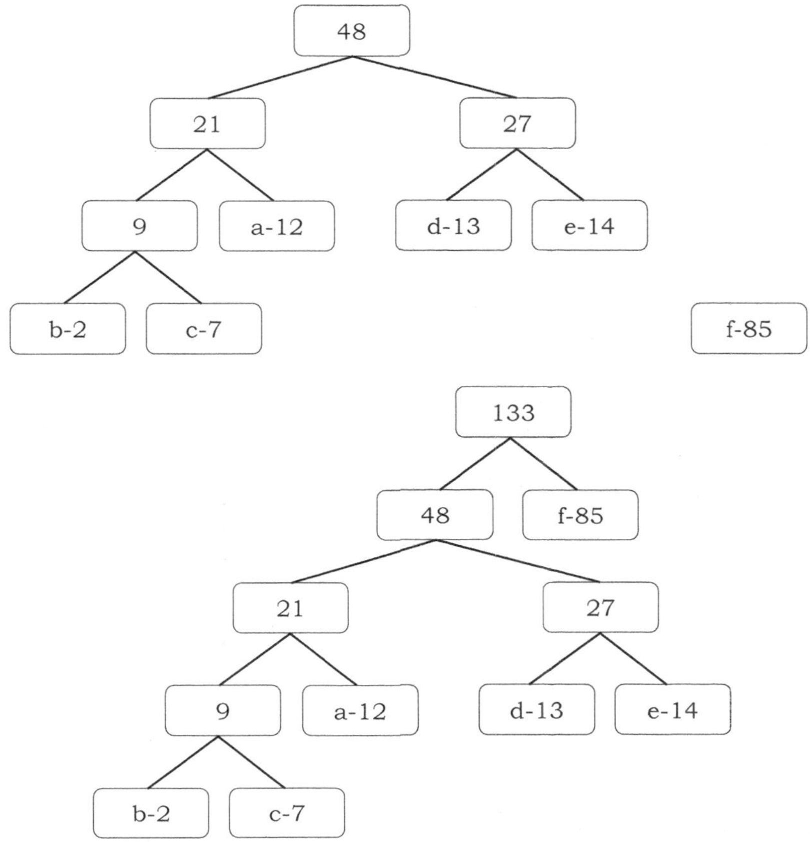


Once the tree is built, each leaf node corresponds to a letter with a code. To determine the code for a particular node, traverse from the root to the leaf node. For each move to the left, append a 0 to the code, and for each move to the right, append a 1. As a result, for the above generated tree, we get the following codes:

| Letter | Code |
|---|---|
| a | 001 |
| b | 0000 |
| c | 0001 |
| d | 010 |
| e | 011 |
| f | 1 |

## Calculating Bits Saved

Now, let us see how many bits that Huffman coding algorithm is saving. All we need to do for this calculation is see how many bits are originally used to store the data and subtract from that the number of bits that are used to store the data using the Huffman code. In the above example, since we have six characters, let's assume each character is stored with a three bit code. Since there are 133 such characters (multiply total frequencies by 3), the total number of bits used is $3 * 133 = 399$. Using the Huffman coding frequencies we can calculate the new total number of bits used:

| Letter | Code | Frequency | Total Bits |
|---|---|---|---|
| a | 001 | 12 | 36 |
| b | 0000 | 2 | 8 |
| c | 0001 | 7 | 28 |
| d | 010 | 13 | 39 |
| e | 011 | 14 | 42 |
| f | 1 | 85 | 85 |
| Total | | | 238 |

Thus, we saved $399 - 238 = 161$ bits, or nearly 40% of the storage space.

```
HuffmanCodingAlgorithm(int A[], int n) {
    Initialize a priority queue, PQ, to contain the n elements in A;
    struct BinaryTreeNode *temp;
    for (i =  1; i<n; i++) {
        temp   = (struct *)malloc(sizeof(BinaryTreeNode));
        temp→left =  delete-Min(PQ);
        temp→right =  delete-Min(PQ);
        temp→data = temp→left→data  +  temp→right→data;
        Insert temp to PQ;
    }
    return PQ;
}
```

Time Complexity: $O(nlogn)$, since there will be *one* build_heap, $2n - 2$ delete_mins, and $n - 2$ inserts, on a priority queue that never has more than $n$ elements. Refer to the *Priority Queues* chapter for details.

## 17.8 Greedy Algorithms: Problems & Solutions

**Problem-1** Given an array $F$ with size $n$. Assume the array content $F[i]$ indicates the length of the $i^{th}$ file and we want to merge all these files into one single file. Check whether the following algorithm gives the best solution for this problem or not?

**Algorithm:** Merge the files contiguously. That means select the first two files and merge them. Then select the output of the previous merge and merge with the third file, and keep going...

**Note:** Given two files $A$ and $B$ with sizes $m$ and $n$, the complexity of merging is $O(m + n)$.

**Solution:** This algorithm will not produce the optimal solution. For a counter example, let us consider the following file sizes array.

$$F = \{10,5,100,50,20,15\}$$

As per the above algorithm, we need to merge the first two files (10 and 5 size files), and as a result we get the following list of files. In the list below, 15 indicates the cost of merging two files with sizes 10 and 5.

$$\{15,100,50,20,15\}$$

Similarly, merging 15 with the next file 100 produces: $\{115,50,20,15\}$. For the subsequent steps the list becomes

$$\{165,20,15\},\{185,15\}$$

Finally, $\{200\}$

The total cost of merging = Cost of all merging operations $= 15 + 115 + 165 + 185 + 200 = 680$.

To see whether the above result is optimal or not, consider the order: $\{5, 10, 15, 20, 50,100\}$. For this example, following the same approach, the total cost of merging $= 15 + 30 + 50 + 100 + 200 = 395$. So, the given algorithm is not giving the best (optimal) solution.

**Problem-2** Similar to Problem-1, does the following algorithm give the optimal solution?

**Algorithm:** Merge the files in pairs. That means after the first step, the algorithm produces the $n/2$ intermediate files. For the next step, we need to consider these intermediate files and merge them in pairs and keep going.

**Note:** Sometimes this algorithm is called 2-way merging. Instead of two files at a time, if we merge $K$ files at a time then we call it $K$-way merging.

**Solution:** This algorithm will not produce the optimal solution and consider the previous example for a counter example. As per the above algorithm, we need to merge the first pair of files (10 and 5 size files), the second pair of files (100 and 50) and the third pair of files (20 and 15). As a result we get the following list of files.

$$\{15, 150, 35\}$$

Similarly, merge the output in pairs and this step produces [below, the third element does not have a pair element, so keep it the same]:

$$\{165,35\}$$

Finally, $\{200\}$

The total cost of merging = Cost of all merging operations $= 15 + 150 + 35 + 165 + 200 = 565$. This is much more than 395 (of the previous problem). So, the given algorithm is not giving the best (optimal) solution.

**Problem-3** In Problem-1, what is the best way to merge *all the files* into a single file?

**Solution:** Using the Greedy algorithm we can reduce the total time for merging the given files. Let us consider the following algorithm.

**Algorithm:**
1. Store file sizes in a priority queue. The key of elements are file lengths.
2. Repeat the following until there is only one file:
   a. Extract two smallest elements $X$ and $Y$.
   b. Merge $X$ and $Y$ and insert this new file in the priority queue.

**Variant of same algorithm:**
1. Sort the file sizes in ascending order.
2. Repeat the following until there is only one file:
   a. Take the first two elements (smallest) $X$ and $Y$.
   b. Merge $X$ and $Y$ and insert this new file in the sorted list.

To check the above algorithm, let us trace it with the previous example. The given array is:

$$F = \{10,5,100,50,20,15\}$$

As per the above algorithm, after sorting the list it becomes: $\{5, 10, 15, 20, 50,100\}$. We need to merge the two smallest files (5 and 10 size files) and as a result we get the following list of files. In the list below, 15 indicates the cost of merging two files with sizes 10 and 5.

$$\{15,15,20,50,100\}$$

Similarly, merging the two smallest elements (15 and 15) produces: $\{20,30,50,100\}$. For the subsequent steps the list becomes

{50,50,100} //merging 20 and 30
{100,100} //merging 20 and 30

Finally, {200}

The total cost of merging = Cost of all merging operations = 15 + 30 + 50 + 100 + 200 = 395. So, this algorithm is producing the optimal solution for this merging problem.

Time Complexity: $O(nlogn)$ time using heaps to find best merging pattern plus the optimal cost of merging the files.

**Problem-4** **Interval Scheduling Algorithm:** Given a set of $n$ intervals $S = \{(start_i, end_i)|1 \le i \le n\}$. Let us assume that we want to find a maximum subset $S'$ of $S$ such that no pair of intervals in $S'$ overlaps. Check whether the following algorithm works or not.

**Algorithm:** while ($S$ is not empty) {
Select the interval $I$ that overlaps the least number of other intervals.
Add $I$ to final solution set $S'$.
Remove all intervals from $S$ that overlap with $I$.
}

**Solution:** This algorithm does not solve the problem of finding a maximum subset of non-overlapping intervals. Consider the following intervals. The optimal solution is $\{M, O, N, K\}$. However, the interval that overlaps with the fewest others is $C$, and the given algorithm will select $C$ first.

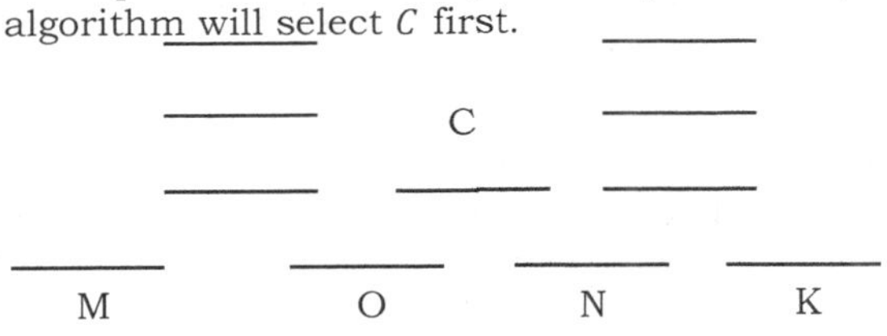

C

M O N K

**Problem-5** In Problem-4, if we select the interval that starts earliest (also not overlapping with already chosen intervals), does it give the optimal solution?

**Solution: No.** It will not give the optimal solution. Let us consider the example below. It can be seen that the optimal solution is 4 whereas the given algorithm gives 1.

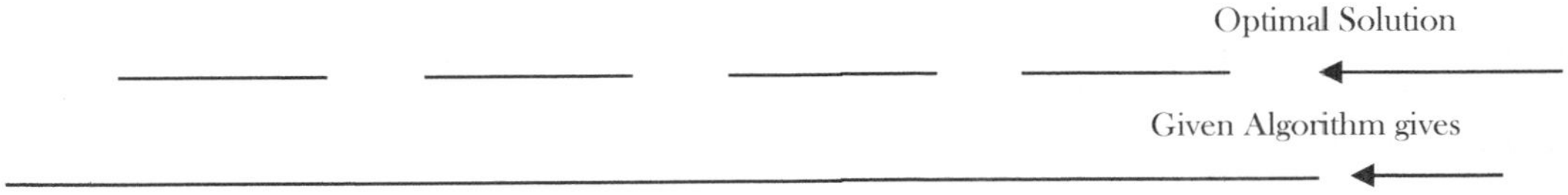

Optimal Solution

Given Algorithm gives

**Problem-6** In Problem-4, if we select the shortest interval (but it is not overlapping the already chosen intervals), does it give the optimal solution?

**Solution:** This also will not give the optimal solution. Let us consider the example below. It can be seen that the optimal solution is 2 whereas the algorithm gives 1.

Optimal Solution

Current Algorithm gives

**Problem-7** For Problem-4, what is the optimal solution?

**Solution:** Now, let us concentrate on the optimal greedy solution.

**Algorithm:**

Sort intervals according to the right-most ends [end times];
for every consecutive interval {
- If the left-most end is after the right-most end of the last selected interval then we select this interval
- Otherwise we skip it and go to the next interval

}

Time complexity = Time for sorting + Time for scanning = $O(nlogn + n) = O(nlogn)$.

**Problem-8** Consider the following problem.
Input: $S = \{(start_i, end_i) | 1 \leq i \leq n\}$ of intervals. The interval $(start_i, end_i)$ we can treat as a request for a room for a class with time $start_i$ to time $end_i$.
Output: Find an assignment of classes to rooms that uses the fewest number of rooms.
Consider the following iterative algorithm. Assign as many classes as possible to the first room, then assign as many classes as possible to the second room, then assign as many classes as possible to the third room, etc. Does this algorithm give the best solution?

**Note:** In fact, this problem is similar to the interval scheduling algorithm. The only difference is the application.

**Solution:** This algorithm does not solve the interval-coloring problem. Consider the following intervals:

A

B C D

E F G

Maximizing the number of classes in the first room results in having $\{B, C, F, G\}$ in one room, and classes $A, D,$ and $E$ each in their own rooms, for a total of 4. The optimal solution is to put $A$ in one room, $\{ B, C, D \}$ in another, and $\{E, F, G\}$ in another, for a total of 3 rooms.

**Problem-9** For Problem-8, consider the following algorithm. Process the classes in increasing order of start times. Assume that we are processing class $C$. If there is a room $R$ such that $R$ has been assigned to an earlier class, and $C$ can be assigned to $R$ without overlapping previously assigned classes, then assign $C$ to $R$. Otherwise, put $C$ in a new room. Does this algorithm solve the problem?

**Solution:** This algorithm solves the interval-coloring problem. Note that if the greedy algorithm creates a new room for the current class $c_i$, then because it examines classes in order of start times, $c_i$ start point must intersect with the last class in all of the current rooms. Thus when greedy creates the last room, $n$, it is because the start time of the current class intersects with $n - 1$ other classes. But we know that for any single point in any class it can only intersect with at most s other class, so it must then be that $n \leq S$. As $s$ is a lower bound on the total number needed, and greedy is feasible, it is thus also optimal.

**Note:** For optimal solution refer to Problem-7 and for code refer to Problem-10.

**Problem-10** Suppose we are given two arrays $Start[1..n]$ and $Finish[1..n]$ listing the start and finish times of each class. Our task is to choose the largest possible subset $X \in \{1, 2, \ldots, n\}$ so that for any pair $i, j \in X$, either $Start\ [i] > Finish[j]$ or $Start\ [j] > Finish\ [i]$

**Solution:** Our aim is to finish the first class as early as possible, because that leaves us with the most remaining classes. We scan through the classes in order of finish time, and whenever we encounter a class that doesn't conflict with the latest class so far, then we take that class.

```
int largestTasks(int Start[], int n, int Finish []) {
	sort Finish[];
	rearrange Start[] to match;
```

```
        count = 1;
        X[count] = 1;
        for (i = 2; i<n; i++) {
                if(Start[i] > Finish[X[count]]) {
                        count = count + 1;
                        X[count] = I;
                }
        }
        return X[1 .. count];
}
```

This algorithm clearly runs in $O(nlogn)$ time due to sorting.

**Problem-11** Consider the making change problem in the country of India. The input to this problem is an integer $M$. The output should be the minimum number of coins to make $M$ rupees of change. In India, assume the available coins are $1, 5, 10, 20, 25, 50$ rupees. Assume that we have an unlimited number of coins of each type.

**For this problem, does the following algorithm produce the optimal solution or not?** Take as many coins as possible from the highest denominations. So for example, to make change for 234 rupees the greedy algorithm would take four 50 rupee coins, one 25 rupee coin, one 5 rupee coin, and four 1 rupee coins.

**Solution:** The greedy algorithm is not optimal for the problem of making change with the minimum number of coins when the denominations are $1, 5, 10, 20, 25,$ and $50$. In order to make 40 rupees, the greedy algorithm would use three coins of $25, 10,$ and $5$ rupees. The optimal solution is to use two 20-shilling coins.

**Note:** For the optimal solution, refer to the *Dynamic Programming* chapter.

**Problem-12** Let us assume that we are going for a long drive between cities A and B. In preparation for our trip, we have downloaded a map that contains the distances in miles between all the petrol stations on our route. Assume that our car's tanks can hold petrol for $n$ miles. Assume that the value $n$ is given. Suppose we stop at every point. Does it give the best solution?

**Solution:** Here the algorithm does not produce optimal solution. Obvious Reason: filling at each petrol station does not produce optimal solution.

**Problem-13** For problem Problem-12, stop if and only if you don't have enough petrol to make it to the next gas station, and if you stop, fill the tank up all the way. Prove or disprove that this algorithm correctly solves the problem.

**Solution:** The greedy approach works: We start our trip from $A$ with a full tank. We check our map to determine the farthest petrol station on our route within $n$ miles. We stop at that petrol station, fill up our tank and check our map again to determine the farthest petrol station on our route within n miles from this stop. Repeat the process until we get to $B$.

**Note:** For code, refer to *Dynamic Programming* chapter.

**Problem-14** **Fractional Knapsack problem:** Given items $t_1, t_2, \ldots, t_n$ (items we might want to carry in our backpack) with associated weights $s_1, s_2, \ldots, s_n$ and benefit values $v_1, v_2, \ldots, v_n$, how can we maximize the total benefit considering that we are subject to an absolute weight limit $C$?

**Solution:**

**Algorithm:**

1) Compute value per size density for each item $d_i = \frac{v_i}{s_i}$.
2) Sort each item by its value density.
3) Take as much as possible of the density item not already in the bag

Time Complexity: $O(nlogn)$ for sorting and $O(n)$ for greedy selections.

**Note:** The items can be entered into a priority queue and retrieved one by one until either the bag is full or all items have been selected. This actually has a better runtime of $O(n + clogn)$ where $c$ is the number of items that actually get selected in the solution. There is a savings in runtime if $c = O(n)$, but otherwise there is no change in the complexity.

**Problem-15** **Number of railway-platforms:** At a railway station, we have a time-table with the trains' arrivals and departures. We need to find the minimum number of platforms so that all the trains can be accommodated as per their schedule.

**Example:** The timetable is as given below, the answer is 3. Otherwise, the railway station will not be able to accommodate all the trains.

| Rail | Arrival | Departure |
|---|---|---|
| Rail A | 0900 hrs | 0930 hrs |

| Rail B | 0915 hrs | 1300 hrs |
|---|---|---|
| Rail C | 1030 hrs | 1100 hrs |
| Rail D | 1045 hrs | 1145 hrs |

**Solution:** Let's take the same example as described above. Calculating the number of platforms is done by determining the maximum number of trains at the railway station at any time.

First, sort all the arrival($A$) and departure($D$) times in an array. Then, save the corresponding arrivals and departures in the array also. After sorting, our array will look like this:

| 0900 | 0915 | 0930 | 1030 | 1045 | 1100 | 1145 | 1300 |
|---|---|---|---|---|---|---|---|
| A | A | D | A | A | D | D | D |

Now modify the array by placing 1 for $A$ and -1 for $D$. The new array will look like this:

| 1 | 1 | -1 | 1 | 1 | -1 | -1 | -1 |
|---|---|---|---|---|---|---|---|

Finally make a cumulative array out of this:

| 1 | 2 | 1 | 2 | 3 | 2 | 1 | 0 |
|---|---|---|---|---|---|---|---|

Our solution will be the maximum value in this array. Here it is 3.

**Note:** If we have a train arriving and another departing at the same time, then put the departure time first in the sorted array.

**Problem-16** Consider a country with very long roads and houses along the road. Assume that the residents of all houses use cell phones. We want to place cell phone towers along the road, and each cell phone tower covers a range of 7 kilometers. Create an efficient algorithm that allow for the fewest cell phone towers.

**Solution:**

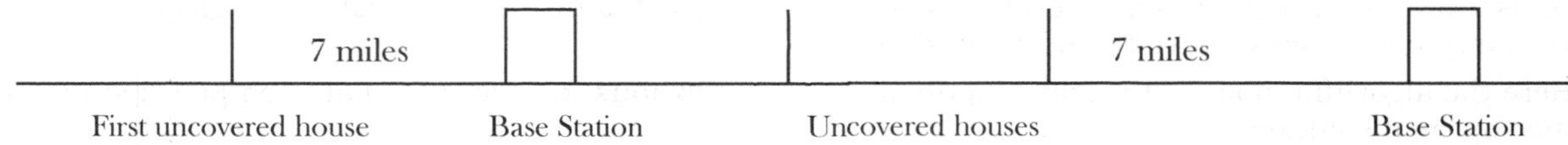


The algorithm to locate the least number of cell phone towers:

1) Start from the beginning of the road
2) Find the first uncovered house on the road
3) If there is no such house, terminate this algorithm. Otherwise, go to next step
4) Locate a cell phone tower 7 miles away after we find this house along the road
5) Go to step 2

**Problem-17** **Preparing Songs Cassette:** Suppose we have a set of $n$ songs and want to store these on a tape. In the future, users will want to read those songs from the tape. Reading a song from a tape is not like reading from a disk; first we have to fast-forward past all the other songs, and that takes a significant amount of time. Let $A[1..n]$ be an array listing the lengths of each song, specifically, song $i$ has length $A[i]$. If the songs are stored in order from 1 to $n$, then the cost of accessing the $k^{th}$ song is:

$$C(k) = \sum_{i=1}^{k} A[i]$$

The cost reflects the fact that before we read song $k$ we must first scan past all the earlier songs on the tape. If we change the order of the songs on the tape, we change the cost of accessing the songs, with the result that some songs become more expensive to read, but others become cheaper. Different song orders are likely to result in different expected costs. If we assume that each song is equally likely to be accessed, which order should we use if we want the expected cost to be as small as possible?

**Solution:** The answer is simple. We should store the songs in the order from shortest to longest. Storing the short songs at the beginning reduces the forwarding times for the remaining jobs.

**Problem-18** Let us consider a set of events at *HITEX* (*Hyderabad Convention Center*). Assume that there are $n$ events where each takes one unit of time. Event $i$ will provide a profit of $p_i$ ($p_i > 0$) if started at or before time $t_i$, where $t_i$ is an arbitrary number. If an event is not started by $t_i$ then there is no benefit in scheduling it at all. All events can start as early as time 0. Give the efficient algorithm to find a schedule that maximizes the profit.

**Solution:** This problem can be solved with greedy technique. The setting is that we have $n$ events, each of which takes unit time, and a convention center on which we would like to schedule them in as profitable a manner as possible. Each event has a profit associated with it, as well as a deadline; if the event is not scheduled by the deadline, then we don't get the profit.

Because each event takes the same amount of time, we will think of a *Schedule E* as consisting of a sequence of event "slots" 0, 2, 3, . . . where $E(t)$ is the event scheduled in slot t.

More formally, the input is a sequence $(t_0, p_0)$,$(t_1, p_1)$, $(t_2, p_2)$ $\cdots$ ,$(t_{n-1}, p_{n-1})$ where $p_i$ is a nonnegative real number representing the profit obtainable from event $i$, and $t_i$ is the deadline for event $i$. Notice that, even if some event deadlines were bigger than $n$, we can schedule them in a slot less than $n$ as each event takes only one unit of time.

**Algorithm:**

1. Sort the events according to their profits $p_i$ in the decreasing order.
2. Now, for each of the events:
   - Schedule event $i$ in the latest possible free slot meeting its deadline.
   - If there is no such slot, do not schedule event $i$.

The sort takes $O(nlogn)$ and the scheduling take $O(n)$ for $n$ events. So the overall running time of the algorithm is $O(nlogn)$ time.

**Problem-19** Let us consider a customer-care server (say, mobile customer-care) with $n$ customers to be served in the queue. For simplicity assume that the service time required by each customer is known in advance and it is $w_i$ minutes for customer $i$. So if, for example, the customers are served in order of increasing $i$, then the $i^{th}$ customer has to wait: $\sum_{j=1}^{n-1} w_j$ *minutes*. The total waiting time of all customers can be given as = $\sum_{i=1}^{n}\sum_{j=1}^{i-1} w_j$. What is the best way to serve the customers so that the total waiting time can be reduced?

**Solution:** This problem can be easily solved using greedy technique. Since our objective is to reduce the total waiting time, what we can do is, select the customer whose service time is less. That means, if we process the customers in the increasing order of service time then we can reduce the total waiting time.

Time Complexity: $O(nlogn)$.

CHAPTER

# 18

# DIVIDE AND CONQUER ALGORITHMS

## 18.1 Introduction

In the *Greedy* chapter, we have seen that for many problems the Greedy strategy failed to provide optimal solutions. Among those problems, there are some that can be easily solved by using the *Divide and Conquer* (D & *C*) technique. Divide and Conquer is an important algorithm design technique based on recursion.

The *D* & *C* algorithm works by recursively breaking down a problem into two or more sub problems of the same type, until they become simple enough to be solved directly. The solutions to the sub problems are then combined to give a solution to the original problem.

## 18.2 What is the Divide and Conquer Strategy?

The D & C strategy solves a problem by:

1) *Divide*: Breaking the problem into subproblems that are themselves smaller instances of the same type of problem.
2) *Conquer*: Conquer the subproblems by solving them recursively.
3) *Combine*: Combine the solutions to the subproblems into the solution for the original given problem.

## 18.3 Does Divide and Conquer Always Work?

It's not possible to solve all the problems with the Divide & Conquer technique. As per the definition of D & C, the recursion solves the subproblems which are of the same type. For all problems it is not possible to find the subproblems which are the same size and *D* & *C* is not a choice for all problems.

## 18.4 Divide and Conquer Visualization

For better understanding, consider the following visualization. Assume that $n$ is the size of the original problem. As described above, we can see that the problem is divided into sub problems with each of size $n/b$ (for some constant $b$). We solve the sub problems recursively and combine their solutions to get the solution for the original problem.

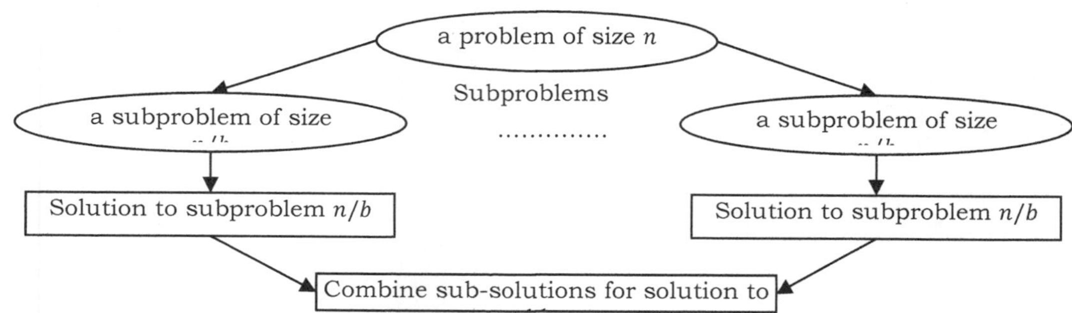


```
DivideAndConquer ( P ) {
    if( small ( P ) )
        // P is very small so that a solution is obvious
        return solution ( n );
        divide the problem P into k sub problems P1, P2, ..., Pk;
        return (
```

```
                Combine (
                DivideAndConquer ( P1 ),
                DivideAndConquer ( P2 ),
                ...
                DivideAndConquer ( Pk )
                )
        );
}
```

## 18.5 Understanding Divide and Conquer

For a clear understanding of $D \& C$, let us consider a story. There was an old man who was a rich farmer and had seven sons. He was afraid that when he died, his land and his possessions would be divided among his seven sons, and that they would quarrel with one another.

So he gathered them together and showed them seven sticks that he had tied together and told them that anyone who could break the bundle would inherit everything. They all tried, but no one could break the bundle. Then the old man untied the bundle and broke the sticks one by one. The brothers decided that they should stay together and work together and succeed together. The moral for problem solvers is different. If we can't solve the problem, divide it into parts, and solve one part at a time.

In earlier chapters we have already solved many problems based on $D \& C$ strategy: like Binary Search, Merge Sort, Quick Sort, etc.... Refer to those topics to get an idea of how $D \& C$ works. Below are a few other real-time problems which can easily be solved with $D \& C$ strategy. For all these problems we can find the subproblems which are similar to the original problem.

- Looking for a name in a phone book: We have a phone book with names in alphabetical order. Given a name, how do we find whether that name is there in the phone book or not?
- Breaking a stone into dust: We want to convert a stone into dust (very small stones).
- Finding the exit in a hotel: We are at the end of a very long hotel lobby with a long series of doors, with one door next to us. We are looking for the door that leads to the exit.
- Finding our car in a parking lot.

## 18.6 Advantages of Divide and Conquer

**Solving difficult problems:** $D \& C$ is a powerful method for solving difficult problems. As an example, consider the Tower of Hanoi problem. This requires breaking the problem into subproblems, solving the trivial cases and combining the subproblems to solve the original problem. Dividing the problem into subproblems so that subproblems can be combined again is a major difficulty in designing a new algorithm. For many such problems D & C provides a simple solution.

**Parallelism:** Since $D \& C$ allows us to solve the subproblems independently, this allows for execution in multi-processor machines, especially shared-memory systems where the communication of data between processors does not need to be planned in advance, because different subproblems can be executed on different processors.

**Memory access:** $D \& C$ algorithms naturally tend to make efficient use of memory caches. This is because once a subproblem is small, all its subproblems can be solved within the cache, without accessing the slower main memory.

## 18.7 Disadvantages of Divide and Conquer

One disadvantage of the $D \& C$ approach is that recursion is slow. This is because of the overhead of the repeated subproblem calls. Also, the $D \& C$ approach needs stack for storing the calls (the state at each point in the recursion). Actually this depends upon the implementation style. With large enough recursive base cases, the overhead of recursion can become negligible for many problems.

Another problem with $D \& C$ is that, for some problems, it may be more complicated than an iterative approach. For example, to add $n$ numbers, a simple loop to add them up in sequence is much easier than a $D \& C$ approach that breaks the set of numbers into two halves, adds them recursively, and then adds the sums.

## 18.8 Master Theorem

As stated above, in the $D \& C$ method, we solve the sub problems recursively. All problems are generally defined in terms of recursive definitions. These recursive problems can easily be solved using Master theorem. For details on Master theorem, refer to the *Introduction to Analysis of Algorithms* chapter. Just for continuity, let us reconsider the Master theorem.

If the recurrence is of the form $T(n) = aT(\frac{n}{b}) + \Theta(n^k log^p n)$, where $a \geq 1$, $b > 1, k \geq 0$ and $p$ is a real number, then the complexity can be directly given as:

1) If $a > b^k$, then $T(n) = \Theta(n^{log_b^a})$
2) If $a = b^k$
   a. If $p > -1$, then $T(n) = \Theta(n^{log_b^a} log^{p+1} n)$
   b. If $p = -1$, then $T(n) = \Theta(n^{log_b^a} loglogn)$
   c. If $p < -1$, then $T(n) = \Theta(n^{log_b^a})$
3) If $a < b^k$
   a. If $p \geq 0$, then $T(n) = \Theta(n^k log^p n)$
   b. If $p < 0$, then $T(n) = O(n^k)$

## 18.9 Divide and Conquer Applications

- Binary Search
- Merge Sort and Quick Sort
- Median Finding
- Min and Max Finding
- Matrix Multiplication
- Closest Pair problem

## 18.10 Divide and Conquer: Problems & Solutions

**Problem-1** Let us consider an algorithm $A$ which solves problems by dividing them into five subproblems of half the size, recursively solving each subproblem, and then combining the solutions in linear time. What is the complexity of this algorithm?

**Solution:** Let us assume that the input size is n and $T(n)$ defines the solution to the given problem. As per the description, the algorithm divides the problem into 5 sub problems with each of size $\frac{n}{2}$. So we need to solve $5T(\frac{n}{2})$ subproblems. After solving these sub problems, the given array (linear time) is scanned to combine these solutions. The total recurrence algorithm for this problem can be given as: $T(n) = 5T\left(\frac{n}{2}\right) + O(n)$. Using the Master theorem (of D & C), we get the complexity as $O(n^{log_2^5}) \approx O(n^{2+}) \approx O(n^3)$.

**Problem-2** Similar to Problem-1, an algorithm $B$ solves problems of size $n$ by recursively solving two subproblems of size $n - 1$ and then combining the solutions in constant time. What is the complexity of this algorithm?

**Solution:** Let us assume that the input size is n and $T(n)$ defines the solution to the given problem. As per the description of algorithm we divide the problem into 2 sub problems with each of size n – 1. So we have to solve $2T(n-1)$ sub problems. After solving these sub problems, the algorithm takes only a constant time to combine these solutions. The total recurrence algorithm for this problem can be given as:

$$T(n) = 2T(n-1) + O(1)$$

Using Master theorem (of *Subtract and Conquer*), we get the complexity as $O\left(n^0 2^{\frac{n}{1}}\right) = O(2^n)$. (Refer to *Introduction* chapter for more details).

**Problem-3** Again similar to Problem-1, another algorithm $C$ solves problems of size $n$ by dividing them into nine subproblems of size $\frac{n}{3}$, recursively solving each subproblem, and then combining the solutions in $O(n^2)$ time. What is the complexity of this algorithm?

**Solution:** Let us assume that input size is n and $T(n)$ defines the solution to the given problem. As per the description of algorithm we divide the problem into 9 sub problems with each of size $\frac{n}{3}$. So we need to solve $9T(\frac{n}{3})$ sub problems. After solving the sub problems, the algorithm takes quadratic time to combine these solutions. The total recurrence algorithm for this problem can be given as: $T(n) = 9T\left(\frac{n}{3}\right) + O(n^2)$. Using $D$ & $C$ Master theorem, we get the complexity as $O(n^2 logn)$.

**Problem-4** Write a recurrence and solve it.

```
void function(n) {
    if(n > 1) {
        printf(("*");
        function(n/2);
        function(n/2);
    }
}
```

**Solution:** Let us assume that input size is $n$ and $T(n)$ defines the solution to the given problem. As per the given code, after printing the character and dividing the problem into 2 subproblems with each of size $\frac{n}{2}$ and solving them. So we need to solve $2T(\frac{n}{2})$ subproblems. After solving these subproblems, the algorithm is not doing anything for combining the solutions. The total recurrence algorithm for this problem can be given as:

$$T(n) = 2T\left(\frac{n}{2}\right)+O(1)$$

Using Master theorem (of D & C), we get the complexity as $O\left(n^{log_2^2}\right) \approx O(n^1) = O(n)$.

**Problem-5** Given an array, give an algorithm for finding the maximum and minimum.

**Solution:** Refer to *Selection Algorithms* chapter.

**Problem-6** Discuss Binary Search and its complexity.

**Solution:** Refer to *Searching* chapter for discussion on Binary Search.

**Analysis:** Let us assume that input size is $n$ and $T(n)$ defines the solution to the given problem. The elements are in sorted order. In binary search we take the middle element and check whether the element to be searched is equal to that element or not. If it is equal then we return that element.

If the element to be searched is less than the middle element then we consider the left sub-array for finding the element and discard the right sub-array. Similarly, if the element to be searched is greater than the middle element then we consider the right sub-array for finding the element and discard the left sub-array.

What this means is, in both the cases we are discarding half of the sub-array and considering the remaining half only. Also, at every iteration we are dividing the elements into two equal halves.

As per the above discussion every time we divide the problem into 2 sub problems with each of size $\frac{n}{2}$ and solve one $T(\frac{n}{2})$ sub problem. The total recurrence algorithm for this problem can be given as:

$$T(n) = 2T\left(\frac{n}{2}\right) +O(1)$$

Using Master theorem (of D & C), we get the complexity as $O(logn)$.

**Problem-7** Consider the modified version of binary search. Let us assume that the array is divided into 3 equal parts (ternary search) instead of 2 equal parts. Write the recurrence for this ternary search and find its complexity.

**Solution:** From the discussion on Problem-5, binary search has the recurrence relation: $T(n) = T\left(\frac{n}{2}\right) +O(1)$. Similar to the Problem-5 discussion, instead of 2 in the recurrence relation we use "3". That indicates that we are dividing the array into 3 sub-arrays with equal size and considering only one of them. So, the recurrence for the ternary search can be given as:

$$T(n) = T\left(\frac{n}{3}\right) +O(1)$$

Using Master theorem (of $D$ & $C$), we get the complexity as $O(log_3^n) \approx O(logn)$ (we don't have to worry about the base of $log$ as they are constants).

**Problem-8** In Problem-5, what if we divide the array into two sets of sizes approximately one-third and two-thirds.

**Solution:** We now consider a slightly modified version of ternary search in which only one comparison is made, which creates two partitions, one of roughly $\frac{n}{3}$ elements and the other of $\frac{2n}{3}$. Here the worst case comes when the recursive call is on the larger $\frac{2n}{3}$ element part. So the recurrence corresponding to this worst case is:

$$T(n) = T\left(\frac{2n}{3}\right) + O(1)$$

Using Master theorem (of D & C), we get the complexity as $O(logn)$. It is interesting to note that we will get the same results for general $k$-ary search (as long as $k$ is a fixed constant which does not depend on $n$) as $n$ approaches infinity.

**Problem-9** Discuss Merge Sort and its complexity.

**Solution:** Refer to *Sorting* chapter for discussion on Merge Sort. In Merge Sort, if the number of elements are greater than 1, then divide them into two equal subsets, the algorithm is recursively invoked on the subsets, and the returned sorted subsets are merged to provide a sorted list of the original set. The recurrence equation of the Merge Sort algorithm is:

$$T(n) = \begin{cases} 2T\left(\frac{n}{2}\right) + O(n), if\ n > 1 \\ 0 \qquad\qquad\qquad , if n = 1 \end{cases}$$

If we solve this recurrence using D & C Master theorem it gives $O(nlogn)$ complexity.

**Problem-10** Discuss Quick Sort and its complexity.

**Solution:** Refer to *Sorting* chapter for discussion on Quick Sort. For Quick Sort we have different complexities for best case and worst case.

**Best Case:** In *Quick Sort,* if the number of elements is greater than 1 then they are divided into two equal subsets, and the algorithm is recursively invoked on the subsets. After solving the sub problems we don't need to combine them. This is because in *Quick Sort* they are already in sorted order. But, we need to scan the complete elements to partition the elements. The recurrence equation of *Quick Sort* best case is

$$T(n) = \begin{cases} 2T\left(\frac{n}{2}\right) + O(n), if\ n > 1 \\ 0 \qquad\qquad\qquad , if n = 1 \end{cases}$$

If we solve this recurrence using Master theorem of D & C gives $O(nlogn)$ complexity.

**Worst Case:** In the worst case, Quick Sort divides the input elements into two sets and one of them contains only one element. That means other set has $n-1$ elements to be sorted. Let us assume that the input size is $n$ and $T(n)$ defines the solution to the given problem. So we need to solve $T(n-1)$, $T(1)$ subproblems. But to divide the input into two sets Quick Sort needs one scan of the input elements (this takes $O(n)$).

After solving these sub problems the algorithm takes only a constant time to combine these solutions. The total recurrence algorithm for this problem can be given as:

$$T(n) = T(n-1) + O(1) + O(n).$$

This is clearly a summation recurrence equation. So, $T(n) = \frac{n(n+1)}{2} = O(n^2)$.

**Note:** For the average case analysis, refer to *Sorting* chapter.

**Problem-11** Given an infinite array in which the first $n$ cells contain integers in sorted order and the rest of the cells are filled with some special symbol (say, $). Assume we do not know the $n$ value. Give an algorithm that takes an integer $K$ as input and finds a position in the array containing $K$, if such a position exists, in $O(logn)$ time.

**Solution:** Since we need an $O(logn)$ algorithm, we should not search for all the elements of the given list (which gives $O(n)$ complexity). To get $O(logn)$ complexity one possibility is to use binary search. But in the given scenario we cannot use binary search as we do not know the end of the list. Our first problem is to find the end of the list. To do that, we can start at the first element and keep searching with doubled index. That means we first search at index 1 then, $2, 4, 8 \ldots$

```
int findInInfiniteSeries(int A[]) {
	int mid, l = r = 1;
	while( A[r] != '$') {
		l = r;
		r = r × 2;
	}
	while( (r – l > 1 ) {
		mid = (r – l)/2 + l;
		if( A[mid] == '$')
			r = mid;
		else	l = mid;
	}
}
```

It is clear that, once we have identified a possible interval $A[i,\ldots,2i]$ in which $K$ might be, its length is at most $n$ (since we have only $n$ numbers in the array $A$), so searching for $K$ using binary search takes $O(logn)$ time.

**Problem-12** Given a sorted array of non-repeated integers $A[1..n]$, check whether there is an index $i$ for which $A[i] = i$. Give a divide-and-conquer algorithm that runs in time $O(logn)$.

**Solution:** We can't use binary search on the array as it is. If we want to keep the $O(logn)$ property of the solution we have to implement our own binary search. If we modify the array (in place or in a copy) and subtract $i$ from A[i], we can then use binary search. The complexity for doing so is $O(n)$.

**Problem-13** We are given two sorted lists of size $n$. Give an algorithm for finding the median element in the union of the two lists.

**Solution:** We use the Merge Sort process. Use *merge* procedure of merge sort (refer to *Sorting* chapter). Keep track of the count while comparing elements of two arrays. If the count becomes $n$ (since there are $2n$ elements), we have reached the median. Take the average of the elements at indexes $n-1$ and $n$ in the merged array.

Time Complexity: $O(n)$.

**Problem-14** Can we give the algorithm if the size of the two lists are not the same?

**Solution:** The solution is similar to the previous problem. Let us assume that the lengths of two lists are $m$ and $n$. In this case we need to stop when the counter reaches $(m + n)/2$.

Time Complexity: $O((m + n)/2)$.

**Problem-15** Can we improve the time complexity of Problem-13 to $O(logn)$?

**Solution: Yes**, using the D & C approach. Let us assume that the given two lists are $L1$ and $L2$.

**Algorithm:**

1. Find the medians of the given sorted input arrays $L1[]$ and $L2[]$. Assume that those medians are $m1$ and $m2$.
2. If $m1$ and $m2$ are equal then return $m1$ (or $m2$).
3. If $m1$ is greater than $m2$, then the final median will be below two sub arrays.
4. From first element of $L1$ to $m1$.
5. From $m2$ to last element of $L2$.
6. If $m2$ is greater than $m1$, then median is present in one of the two sub arrays below.
7. From $m1$ to last element of $L1$.
8. From first element of $L2$ to $m2$.
9. Repeat the above process until the size of both the sub arrays becomes 2.
10. If size of the two arrays is 2, then use the formula below to get the median.
11. Median = $(max(L1[0], L2[0]) + min(L1[1], L2[1])/2$

Time Complexity: $O(logn)$ since we are considering only half of the input and throwing the remaining half.

**Problem-16** Given an input array $A$. Let us assume that there can be duplicates in the list. Now search for an element in the list in such a way that we get the highest index if there are duplicates.

**Solution:** Refer to *Searching* chapter.

**Problem-17** Discuss Strassen's Matrix Multiplication Algorithm using Divide and Conquer. That means, given two $n \times n$ matrices, $A$ and $B$, compute the $n \times n$ matrix $C = A \times B$, where the elements of $C$ are given by

$$C_{i,j} = \sum_{k=0}^{n-1} A_{i,k} B_{k,j}$$

**Solution:** Before Strassen's algorithm, first let us see the basic divide and conquer algorithm. The general approach we follow for solving this problem is given below. To determine, $C[i, j]$ we need to multiply the $i^{th}$ row of $A$ with $j^{th}$ column of $B$.

```
// Initialize C.
for i = 1 to n
  for j = 1 to n
    for k = 1 to n
        C[i, j] += A[i, k] * B[k, j];
```

The matrix multiplication problem can be solved with the D & C technique. To implement a D & C algorithm we need to break the given problem into several subproblems that are similar to the original one. In this instance we view each of the $n \times n$ matrices as a $2 \times 2$ matrix, the elements of which are $\frac{n}{2} \times \frac{n}{2}$ submatrices. So, the original matrix multiplication, $C = A \times B$ can be written as:

$$\begin{bmatrix} C_{1,1} & C_{1,2} \\ C_{2,1} & C_{2,2} \end{bmatrix} = \begin{bmatrix} A_{1,1} & A_{1,2} \\ A_{2,1} & A_{2,2} \end{bmatrix} \times \begin{bmatrix} B_{1,1} & B_{1,2} \\ B_{2,1} & B_{2,2} \end{bmatrix}$$

where each $A_{i,j}$, $B_{i,j}$, and $C_{i,j}$ is a $\frac{n}{2} \times \frac{n}{2}$ matrix.

From the given definition o f $C_{i,j}$, we get that the result sub matrices can be computed as follows:

$$C_{1,1} = A_{1,1} \times B_{1,1} + A_{1,2} \times B_{2,1}$$
$$C_{1,2} = A_{1,1} \times B_{1,2} + A_{1,2} \times B_{2,2}$$
$$C_{2,1} = A_{2,1} \times B_{1,1} + A_{2,2} \times B_{2,1}$$
$$C_{2,2} = A_{2,1} \times B_{1,2} + A_{2,2} \times B_{2,2}$$

Here the symbols + and $\times$ are taken to mean addition and multiplication (respectively) of $\frac{n}{2} \times \frac{n}{2}$ matrices.

In order to compute the original $n \times n$ matrix multiplication we must compute eight $\frac{n}{2} \times \frac{n}{2}$ matrix products (*divide*) followed by four $\frac{n}{2} \times \frac{n}{2}$ matrix sums (*conquer*). Since matrix addition is an $O(n^2)$ operation, the total running time for the multiplication operation is given by the recurrence:

$$T(n) = \begin{cases} O(1) & , for\ n = 1 \\ 8T\left(\frac{n}{2}\right) + O(n^2) & , for\ n > 1 \end{cases}$$

Using master theorem, we get $T(n) = O(n^3)$.

Fortunately, it turns out that one of the eight matrix multiplications is redundant (found by Strassen). Consider the following series of seven $\frac{n}{2} \times \frac{n}{2}$ matrices:

$$M_0 = (A_{1,1} + A_{2,2}) \times (B_{1,1} + B_{2,2})$$
$$M_1 = (A_{1,2} - A_{2,2}) \times (B_{2,1} + B_{2,2})$$
$$M_2 = (A_{1,1} - A_{2,1}) \times (B_{1,1} + B_{1,2})$$
$$M_3 = (A_{1,1} + A_{1,2}) \times B_{2,2}$$
$$M_4 = A_{1,1} \times (B_{1,2} - B_{2,2})$$
$$M_5 = A_{2,2} \times (B_{2,1} - B_{1,1})$$
$$M_6 = (A_{21} + A_{2,2}) \times B_{1,1}$$

Each equation above has only one multiplication. Ten additions and seven multiplications are required to compute $M_0$ through $M_6$. Given $M_0$ through $M_6$, we can compute the elements of the product matrix $C$ as follows:

$$C_{1,1} = M_0 + M_1 - M_3 + M_5$$
$$C_{1,2} = M_3 + M_4$$
$$C_{2,1} = M_5 + M_6$$
$$C_{2,2} = M_0 - M_2 + M_4 - M_6$$

This approach requires seven $\frac{n}{2} \times \frac{n}{2}$ matrix multiplications and 18 $\frac{n}{2} \times \frac{n}{2}$ additions. Therefore, the worst-case running time is given by the following recurrence:

$$T(n) = \begin{cases} O(1) & , for\ n = 1 \\ 7T\left(\frac{n}{2}\right) + O(n^2) & , for\ n = 1 \end{cases}$$

Using master theorem, we get, $T(n) = O(n^{log_2^7}) = O(n^{2.81})$.

**Problem-18** **Stock Pricing Problem:** Consider the stock price of *CareerMonk.com* in $n$ consecutive days. That means the input consists of an array with stock prices of the company. We know that the stock price will not be the same on all the days. In the input stock prices there may be dates where the stock is high when we can sell the current holdings, and there may be days when we can buy the stock. Now our problem is to find the day on which we can buy the stock and the day on which we can sell the stock so that we can make maximum profit.

**Solution:** As given in the problem, let us assume that the input is an array with stock prices [integers]. Let us say the given array is $A[1], \ldots, A[n]$. From this array we have to find two days [one for buy and one for sell] in such a way that we can make maximum profit. Also, another point to make is that the buy date should be before sell date. One simple approach is to look at all possible buy and sell dates.

```
void stockStrategy(int A[], int n, int *buyDateIndex, int *sellDateIndex) {
    int j, profit=0;
    *buyDateIndex =0; *sellDateIndex =0;
    for (int i  = 1; i < n; i++) //indicates buy date
        //indicates sell date
        for( j  =  i; j < n;  j++)
            if(A[j] - A[i] > profit)      {
                profit = A[j] - A[i];
                *buyDateIndex = i;
                *sellDateIndex = j;
            }
}
```

The two nested loops take $n(n + 1)/2$ computations, so this takes time $\Theta(n^2)$.

**Problem-19** For Problem-18, can we improve the time complexity?

**Solution: Yes,** by opting for the Divide-and-Conquer $\Theta(nlogn)$ solution. Divide the input list into two parts and recursively find the solution in both the parts. Here, we get three cases:

- *buyDateIndex* and *sellDateIndex* both are in the earlier time period.
- *buyDateIndex* and *sellDateIndex* both are in the later time period.
- *buyDateIndex* is in the earlier part and *sellDateIndex* is in the later part of the time period.

The first two cases can be solved with recursion. The third case needs care. This is because *buyDateIndex* is one side and *sellDateIndex* is on other side. In this case we need to find the minimum and maximum prices in the two sub-parts and this we can solve in linear-time.

```
void stockStrategy(int A[], int left, int right) {
    //Declare the necessary variables;
    if(left + 1 == right)
            return (0, left, left);
```

```
        mid  = left + (right - left) / 2;
        (profitLeft, buyDateIndexLeft, sellDateIndexLeft) = stockStrategy(A, left, mid);
        (profitRight, buyDateIndexRight, sellDateIndexRight) = stockStrategy(A, mid, right);
        minLeft  = min(A, left, mid);
        maxRight  = max(A, mid, right);
        profit  = A[maxRight] - A[minLeft];
        if(profitLeft > max{profitRight, profit})
                return (profitLeft, buyDateIndexLeft, sellDateIndexLeft);
        else if(profitRight > max{profitLeft, profit})
                return (profitRight, buyDateIndexRight, sellDateIndexRight);
        else    return (profit, minLeft, maxRight);
}
```

Algorithm *StockStrategy* is used recursively on two problems of half the size of the input, and in addition $\Theta(n)$ time is spent searching for the maximum and minimum prices. So the time complexity is characterized by the recurrence $T(n) = 2T(n/2) + \Theta(n)$ and by the Master theorem we get O(nlogn).

**Problem-20** We are testing "unbreakable" laptops and our goal is to find out how unbreakable they really are. In particular, we work in an $n$-story building and want to find out the lowest floor from which we can drop the laptop without breaking it (call this "the ceiling"). Suppose we are given two laptops and want to find the highest ceiling possible. Give an algorithm that minimizes the number of tries we need to make $f(n)$ (hopefully, $f(n)$ is sub-linear, as a linear $f(n)$ yields a trivial solution).

**Solution:** For the given problem, we cannot use binary search as we cannot divide the problem and solve it recursively. Let us take an example for understanding the scenario. Let us say 14 is the answer. That means we need 14 drops to find the answer. First we drop from height 14, and if it breaks we try all floors from 1 to 13. If it doesn't break then we are left 13 drops, so we will drop it from $14 + 13 + 1 = 28^{th}$ floor. The reason being if it breaks at the $28^{th}$ floor we can try all the floors from 15 to 27 in 12 drops (total of 14 drops). If it did not break, then we are left with 11 drops and we can try to figure out the floor in 14 drops.

From the above example, it can be seen that we first tried with a gap of 14 floors, and then followed by 13 floors, then 12 and so on. So if the answer is $k$ then we are trying the intervals at $k, k-1, k-2 \ldots .1$. Given that the number of floors is $n$, we have to relate these two. Since the maximum floor from which we can try is $n$, the total skips should be less than $n$. This gives:

$$k + (k-1) + (k-2) + \cdots + 1 \leq n$$
$$\frac{k(k+1)}{2} \leq n$$
$$k \leq \sqrt{n}$$

Complexity of this process is $O(\sqrt{n})$.

**Problem-21** Given $n$ numbers, check if any two are equal.

**Solution:** Refer to *Searching* chapter.

**Problem-22** Give an algorithm to find out if an integer is a square? E.g. 16 is, 15 isn't.

**Solution:** Initially let us say $i = 2$. Compute the value $i \times i$ and see if it is equal to the given number. If it is equal then we are done; otherwise increment the **i** vlaue. Continue this process until we reach $i \times i$ greater than or equal to the given number.

Time Complexity: $O(\sqrt{n})$. Space Complexity: O(1).

**Problem-23** Given an array of $2n$ integers in the following format $a1\ a2\ a3 \ldots an\ b1\ b2\ b3 \ldots bn$. Shuffle the array to $a1\ b1\ a2\ b2\ a3\ b3 \ldots an\ bn$ without any extra memory [MA].

**Solution:** Let us take an example (for brute force solution refer to *Searching* chapter)

1. Start with the array: $a1\ a2\ a3\ a4\ b1\ b2\ b3\ b4$
2. Split the array into two halves: $a1\ a2\ a3\ a4 : b1\ b2\ b3\ b4$
3. Exchange elements around the center: exchange $a3\ a4$ with $b1\ b2$ you get: $a1\ a2\ b1\ b2\ a3\ a4\ b3\ b4$
4. Split $a1\ a2\ b1\ b2$ into $a1\ a2 : b1\ b2$ then split $a3\ a4\ b3\ b4$ into $a3\ a4 : b3\ b4$
5. Exchange elements around the center for each subarray you get: $a1\ b1\ a2\ b2$ and $a3\ b3\ a4\ b4$

Please note that this solution only handles the case when $n = 2^i$ where $i = 0, 1, 2, 3$, etc. In our example $n = 2^2 = 4$ which makes it easy to recursively split the array into two halves. The basic idea behind swapping elements around the center before calling the recursive function is to produce smaller size problems. A solution with linear time complexity may be achieved if the elements are of a specific nature. For example you can calculate the new position of the element using the value of the element itself. This is a hashing technique.

```
void shuffleArray(int A[], int l, int r) {
    //array center
    int c = l + (r-l)/2, q = 1 + l + (c-l)/2;
    if(l == r) //base case when the array has only one element
        return;
    for (int k = 1, i = q; i <= c; i++, k++) {
        //swap elements around the center
        int tmp = A[i];         A[i] = A[c + k];    A[c + k] = tmp;
    }
    shuffleArray(A, l, c);          //Recursively call the function on the left and right
    shuffleArray(A, c + 1, r); );   //Recursively call the function on the right
}
```

Time Complexity: $O(nlogn)$.

Problem-24 **Nuts and Bolts Problem:** Given a set of $n$ nuts of different sizes and $n$ bolts such that there is a one-to-one correspondence between the nuts and the bolts, find for each nut its corresponding bolt. Assume that we can only compare nuts to bolts (cannot compare nuts to nuts and bolts to bolts).

**Solution:** Refer to *Sorting* chapter.

Problem-25 **Maximum Value Contiguous Subsequence:** Given a sequence of $n$ numbers $A(1) \ldots A(n)$, give an algorithm for finding a contiguous subsequence $A(i) \ldots A(j)$ for which the sum of elements in the subsequence is maximum. **Example**: {-2, **11, -4, 13**, -5, 2} → 20 and {1, -3, **4, -2, -1, 6**} → 7.

**Solution:** Divide this input into two halves. The maximum contiguous subsequence sum can occur in one of 3 ways:

- Case 1: It can be completely in the first half
- Case 2: It can be completely in the second half
- Case 3: It begins in the first half and ends in the second half

We begin by looking at case 3. To avoid the nested loop that results from considering all $n/2$ starting points and $n/2$ ending points independently, replace two nested loops with two consecutive loops. The consecutive loops, each of size $n/2$, combine to require only linear work. Any contiguous subsequence that begins in the first half and ends in the second half must include both the last element of the first half and the first element of the second half. What we can do in cases 1 and 2 is apply the same strategy of dividing into more halves. In summary, we do the following:

1. Recursively compute the maximum contiguous subsequence that resides entirely in the first half.
2. Recursively compute the maximum contiguous subsequence that resides entirely in the second half.
3. Compute, via two consecutive loops, the maximum contiguous subsequence sum that begins in the first half but ends in the second half.
4. Choose the largest of the three sums.

```
int maxSumRec(int A[], int left, int right) {
    int MaxLeftBorderSum = 0, MaxRightBorderSum = 0, LeftBorderSum = 0, RightBorderSum = 0;
    int mid = left + (right - left) / 2;
    if(left == right) // Base Case
        return A[left] > 0 ? A[left] : 0;
    int MaxLeftSum = maxSumRec(A, left, mid);
    int MaxRightSum = maxSumRec(A, mid + 1, right);
    for (int i = mid; i >= left; i--) {
        LeftBorderSum += A[i];
        if(LeftBorderSum > MaxLeftBorderSum)
            MaxLeftBorderSum = LeftBorderSum;
    }
    for (int j = mid + 1; j <= right; j++) {
        RightBorderSum += A[j];
        if(RightBorderSum > MaxRightBorderSum)
            MaxRightBorderSum = RightBorderSum;
    }
    return max(MaxLeftSum, MaxRightSum,MaxLeftBorderSum + MaxRightBorderSum);
}
int maxSubsequenceSum(int A, int n) {
    return n > 0 ? maxSumRec(A, 0, n – 1) : 0;
}
```

The base case cost is 1. The program performs two recursive calls plus the linear work involved in computing the maximum sum for case 3. The recurrence relation is:

$$T(1) = 1$$
$$T(n) = 2T(n/2) + n$$

Using $D \& C$ Master theorem, we get the time complexity as $T(n) = O(nlogn)$.

**Note:** For an efficient solution refer to the *Dynamic Programming* chapter.

Problem-26 **Closest-Pair of Points:** Given a set of $n$ points, $S = \{p_1, p_2, p_3, \ldots, p_n\}$, where $p_i = (x_i, y_i)$. Find the pair of points having the smallest distance among all pairs (assume that all points are in one dimension).

**Solution:** Let us assume that we have sorted the points. Since the points are in one dimension, all the points are in a line after we sort them (either on $X$-axis or $Y$-axis). The complexity of sorting is $O(nlogn)$. After sorting we can go through them to find the consecutive points with the least difference. So the problem in one dimension is solved in $O(nlogn)$ time which is mainly dominated by sorting time.

Time Complexity: $O(nlogn)$.

Problem-27 For Problem-26, how do we solve it if the points are in two-dimensional space?

**Solution:** Before going to the algorithm, let us consider the following mathematical equation:

$$distance(p_1, p_2) = \sqrt{(x_1 - x_2)^2 - (y_1 - y_2)^2}$$

The above equation calculates the distance between two points $p_1 = (x_1, y_1)$ and $p_2 = (x_2, y_2)$.

**Brute Force Solution**:

- Calculate the distances between all the pairs of points. From $n$ points there are $n_{c_2}$ ways of selecting 2 points. ($n_{c_2} = O(n^2)$).
- After finding distances for all $n^2$ possibilities, we select the one which is giving the minimum distance and this takes $O(n^2)$.

The overall time complexity is $O(n^2)$.

Problem-28 Give $O(nlogn)$ solution for the *closest pair* problem (Problem-27)?

**Solution:** To find $O(nlogn)$ solution, we can use the D & C technique. Before starting the divide-and-conquer process let us assume that the points are sorted by increasing $x$-coordinate. Divide the points into two equal halves based on median of $x$-coordinates. That means the problem is divided into that of finding the closest pair in each of the two halves. For simplicity let us consider the following algorithm to understand the process.

**Algorithm:**

1) Sort the given points in $S$ (given set of points) based on their $x$ –coordinates. Partition $S$ into two subsets, $S_1$ and $S_2$, about the line $l$ through median of $S$. This step is the *Divide* part of the $D \& C$ technique.
2) Find the closest-pairs in $S_1$ and $S_2$ and call them $L$ and $R$ recursively.
3) Now, steps 4 to 8 form the Combining component of the $D \& C$ technique.
4) Let us assume that $\delta = min\ (L, R)$.
5) Eliminate points that are farther than $\delta$ apart from $l$.
6) Consider the remaining points and sort based on their $y$-coordinates.
7) Scan the remaining points in the $y$ order and compute the distances of each point to all its neighbors that are distanced no more than $2 \times \delta$ (that's the reason for sorting according to $y$).
8) If any of these distances is less than $\delta$ then update $\delta$.

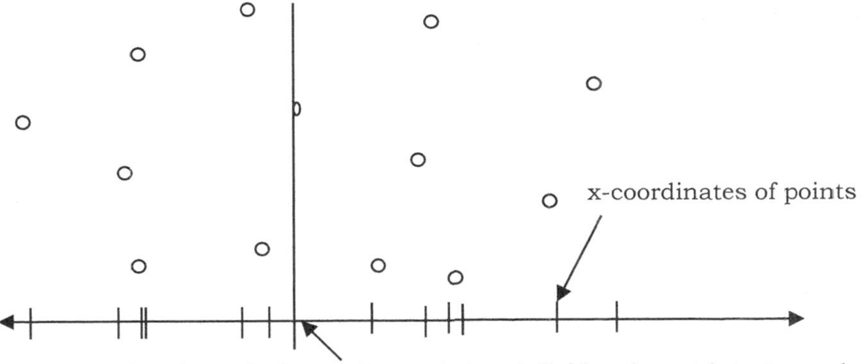

Line $l$ passing through the median point and divides the set into 2 equal parts

**Combining the results in linear time**

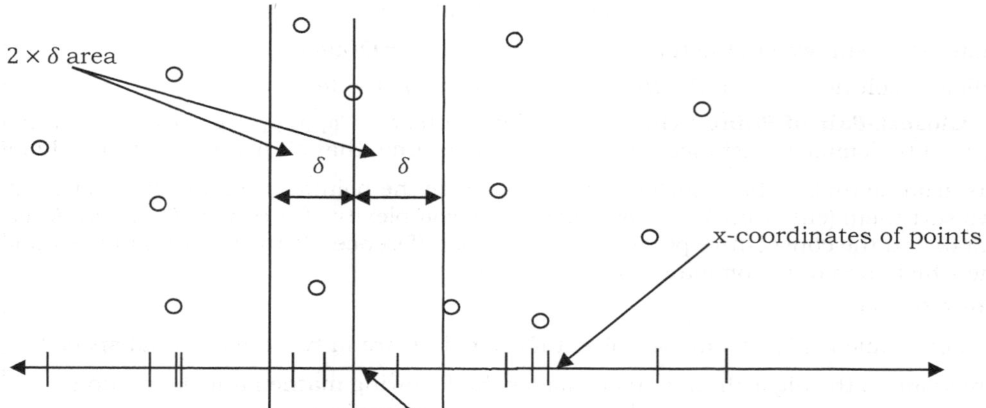


Line $l$ passing through the median point and divides the set into 2 equal parts

Let $\delta = min(L, R)$, where L is the solution to first sub problem and R is the solution to second sub problem. The possible candidates for closest-pair, which are across the dividing line, are those which are less than δ distance from the line. So we need only the points which are inside the $2 \times \delta$ area across the dividing line as shown in the figure. Now, to check all points within distance δ from the line, consider the following figure.

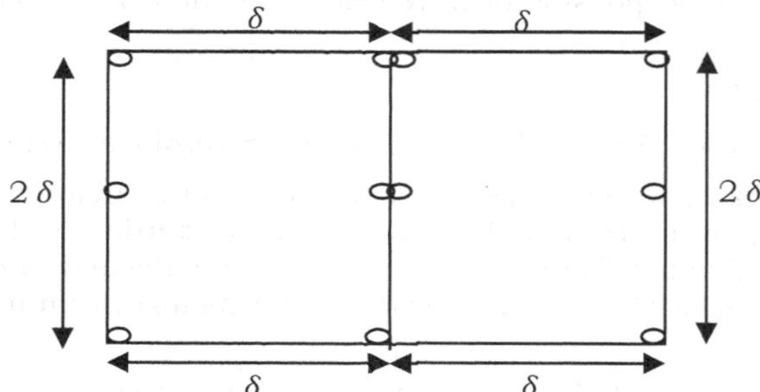


From the above diagram we can see that a maximum of 12 points can be placed inside the square with a distance not less than $\delta$. That means, we need to check only the distances which are within 11 positions in the sorted list. This is similar to the one above, but with the difference that in the above combining of subproblems, there are no vertical bounds. So we can apply the 12-point box tactic over all the possible boxes in the $2 \times \delta$ area with the dividing line as the middle line. As there can be a maximum of $n$ such boxes in the area, the total time for finding the closest pair in the corridor is $O(n)$.

**Analysis:**

1) Step-1 and Step-2 take $O(nlogn)$ for sorting and recursively finding the minimum.
2) Step-4 takes O(1).
3) Step-5 takes $O(n)$ for scanning and eliminating.
4) Step-6 takes $O(nlogn)$ for sorting.
5) Step-7 takes $O(n)$ for scanning.

The total complexity: $T(n) = O(nlogn) + O(1) + O(n) + O(n) + O(n) \approx O(nlogn)$.

**Problem-29** To calculate $k^n$, give the algorithm and discuss its complexity.

**Solution:** The naive algorithm to compute $k^n$ is: start with 1 and multiply by $k$ until reaching $k^n$. For this approach; there are $n - 1$ multiplications and each takes constant time giving a $\Theta(n)$ algorithm. But there is a faster way to compute $k^n$. For example,

$$9^{24} = (9^{12})^2 = ((9^6)^2)^2 = (((9^3)^2)^2)^2 = (((9^2.9)^2)^2)^2$$

Note that taking the square of a number needs only one multiplication; this way, to compute $9^{24}$ we need only 5 multiplications instead of 23.

```
int exponential(int k, int n) {
    if (k == 0) return 1;
    else{
        if (n%2 == 1){
            a = exponential(k, n-1);
            return a*k;
        }
```

```
        else{
            a= exponential(k, n/2);
            return a*a;
        }
    }
}
```

Let T($n$) be the number of multiplications required to compute $k^n$. For simplicity, assume $k = 2^i$ for some $i \geq 1$.

$$T(n) = T(\frac{n}{2}) + 1$$

Using master theorem we get T($n$) = O ($logn$).

Problem-30 **The Skyline Problem**: Given the exact locations and shapes of $n$ rectangular buildings in a 2-dimensional city. There is no particular order for these rectangular buildings. Assume that the bottom of all buildings lie on a fixed horizontal line (bottom edges are collinear). The input is a list of triples; one per building. A building $B_i$ is represented by the triple ($l_i$, $h_i$, $r_i$) where $l_i$ denote the $x$-position of the left edge and $r_i$ denote the $x$-position of the right edge, and $h_i$ denotes the building's height. Give an algorithm that computes the skyline (in 2 dimensions) of these buildings, eliminating hidden lines. In the diagram below there are 8 buildings, represented from left to right by the triplets (1, 14, 7), (3, 9, 10), (5, 17, 12), (14, 11, 18), (15, 6, 27), (20, 19, 22), (23, 15, 30) and (26, 14, 29).

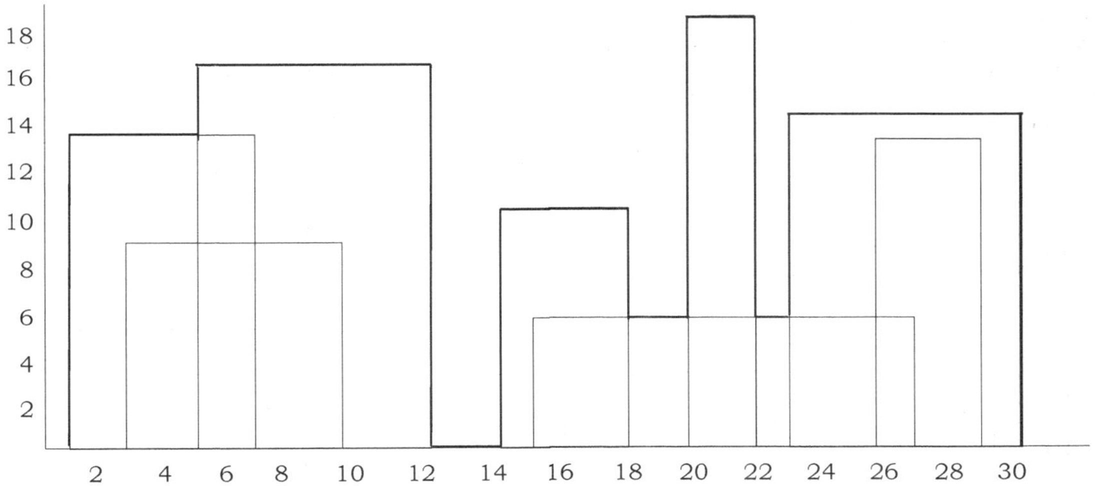


The output is a collection of points which describe the path of the skyline. In some versions of the problem this collection of points is represented by a sequence of numbers $p_1$, $p_2$, ..., $p_n$, such that the point $p_i$ represents a horizontal line drawn at height $p_i$ if $i$ is even, and it represents a vertical line drawn at position $p_i$ if $i$ is odd. In our case the collection of points will be a sequence of $p_1$, $p_2$, ..., $p_n$ pairs of ($x_i$, $h_i$) where $p_i$($x_i$, $h_i$) represents the $h_i$ height of the skyline at position $x_i$. In the diagram above the skyline is drawn with a thick line around the buildings and it is represented by the sequence of position-height pairs (1, 14), (5, 17), (12, 0), (14, 11), (18, 6), (20, 19), (22, 6), (23, 15) and (30, 0). Also, assume that $R_i$ of the right most building can be maximum of 1000. That means, the $L_i$ co-ordinate of left building can be minimum of 1 and $R_i$ of the right most building can be maximum of 1000.

**Solution**: The most important piece of information is that we know that the left and right coordinates of each and every building are non-negative integers less than 1000. Now why is this important? Because we can assign a height-value to every distinct $x_i$ coordinate where $i$ is between 0 and 9,999.

**Algorithm**:

- Allocate an array for 1000 elements and initialize all of the elements to 0. Let's call this array *auxHeights*.
- Iterate over all of the buildings and for every $B_i$ building iterate on the range of [$l_i$.. $r_i$) where $l_i$ is the left, $r_i$ is the right coordinate of the building $B_i$.
- For every $x_j$ element of this range check if $h_i$>*auxHeights*[xj], that is if building $B_i$ is taller than the current height-value at position $x_j$. If so, replace *auxHeights*[$x_j$] with $h_i$.

Once we checked all the buildings, the *auxHeights* array stores the heights of the tallest buildings at every position. There is one more thing to do: convert the *auxHeights* array to the expected output format, that is to a sequence of position-height pairs. It's also easy: just map each and every $i$ index to an (i, *auxHeights*[i]) pair.

```
#include<stdio.h>
#define MaxRightMostBuildingRi 1000
int auxHeights[MaxRightMostBuildingRi];
int skyLineBruteForce(){
    int left,h,right,i,prev;
```

```
        int rightMostBuildingRi = 0;
        while(scanf("%d %d %d", &left, &h, &right)==3){
            for(i=left;i<right;i++)
                if(auxHeights[i]<h)
                    auxHeights[i]=h;
                if(rightMostBuildingRi<right)
                    rightMostBuildingRi=right;
        }
        prev = 0;
        for(i=1;i<rightMostBuildingRi;i++){
            if(prev!=auxHeights[i]){
                printf("%d %d ", i, auxHeights[i]);
                prev=auxHeights[i];
            }
        }
        printf("%d %d\n", rightMostBuildingRi, auxHeights[rightMostBuildingRi]);
        return 0;
    }
```

Let's have a look at the time complexity of this algorithm. Assume that, $n$ indicates the number of buildings in the input sequence and $m$ indicates the maximum coordinate (right most building $r_i$). From the above code, it is clear that for every new input building, we are traversing from $left$ ($l_i$) to $right$ ($r_i$) to update the heights. In the worst case, with $n$ equal-size buildings, each having $l = 0$ left and $r = m - 1$ right coordinates, that is every building spans over the whole $[0..m)$ interval. Thus the running time of setting the height of every position is $O(n \times m)$. The overall time-complexity is $O(n \times m)$, which is a lot larger than $O(n^2)$ if $m > n$.

**Problem-31** Can we improve the solution of the Problem-30?

**Solution**:

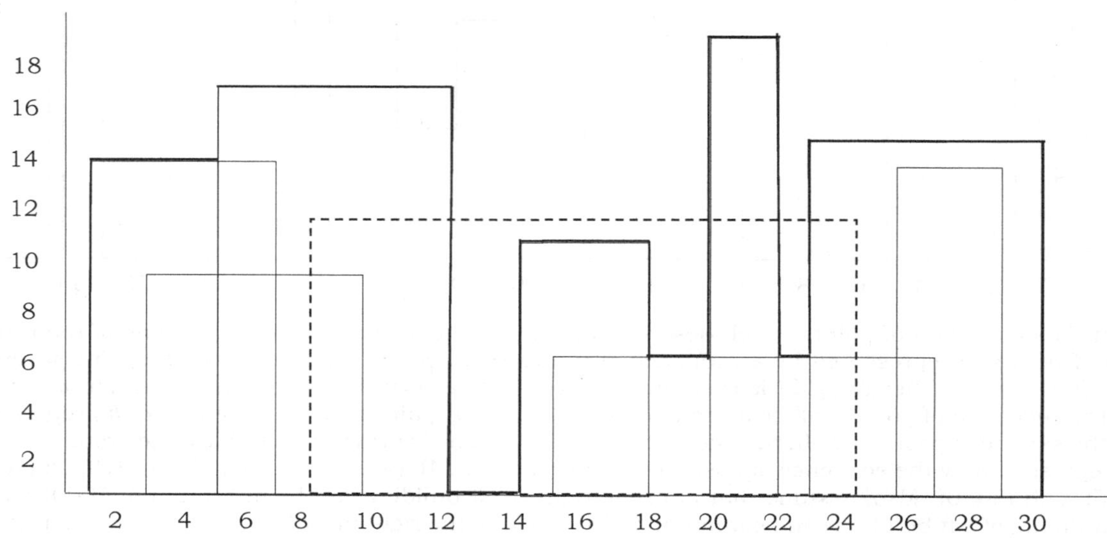


It would be a huge speed-up if somehow we could determine the skyline by calculating the height for those coordinates only where it matters, wouldn't it? Intuition tells us that if we can insert a building into an *existing skyline* then instead of all the coordinates the building spans over we only need to check the height at the left and right coordinates of the building plus those coordinates of the skyline the building overlaps with and may modify.

Is merging two skylines substantially different from merging a building with a skyline? The answer is, of course, No. This suggests that we use divide-and-conquer. Divide the input of $n$ buildings into two equal sets. Compute (recursively) the skyline for each set then merge the two skylines. Inserting the buildings one after the other is not the fastest way to solve this problem as we've seen it above. If, however, we first merge pairs of buildings into skylines, then we merge pairs of these skylines into bigger skylines (and not two sets of buildings), and then merge pairs of these bigger skylines into even bigger ones, then - since the problem size is halved in every step - after $logn$ steps we can compute the final skyline.

```
class SkyLineDivideandConquer {
 public:
 vector<pair<int, int>> getSkyline(int start, int end, vector<vector<int>>& buildings) {
    if (start == end) {
        vector<pair<int, int>> result;
        result.push_back(pair<int, int>(buildings[start][0], buildings[start][1]));
        result.push_back(pair<int, int>(buildings[start][2], 0));
```

```
            return result;
        }
        int mid = (end + start) / 2;
        vector<pair<int, int>> leftSkyline = getSkyline(start, mid, buildings);
        vector<pair<int, int>> rightSkyline = getSkyline(mid + 1, end, buildings);
        vector<pair<int, int>> result = mergeSkylines(leftSkyline, rightSkyline);
        return result;
    }
    vector<pair<int, int>> mergeSkylines(vector<pair<int, int>>& leftSkyline, vector<pair<int, int>>& rightSkyline) {
        vector<pair<int, int>> result;
        int i = 0, j = 0, currentHeight1 = 0, currentHeight2 = 0;
        int maxH = max(currentHeight1, currentHeight2);
        while (i != leftSkyline.size() && j != rightSkyline.size()) {
            if (leftSkyline[i].first < rightSkyline[j].first) {
                currentHeight1 = leftSkyline[i].second;
                if (maxH != max(currentHeight1, currentHeight2))
                    result.push_back(pair<int, int>(leftSkyline[i].first, max(currentHeight1, currentHeight2)));
                maxH = max(currentHeight1, currentHeight2);
                i++;
            }
            else if (leftSkyline[i].first > rightSkyline[j].first) {
                currentHeight2 = rightSkyline[j].second;
                if (maxH != max(currentHeight1, currentHeight2))
                    result.push_back(pair<int, int>(rightSkyline[j].first, max(currentHeight1, currentHeight2)));
                maxH = max(currentHeight1, currentHeight2);
                j++;
            } else {
                if(leftSkyline[i].second >= rightSkyline[j].second) {
                    currentHeight1 = leftSkyline[i].second;
                    currentHeight2 = rightSkyline[j].second;
                    if(maxH != max(currentHeight1, currentHeight2))
                        result.push_back(pair<int, int>(leftSkyline[i].first, leftSkyline[i].second));
                    maxH = max(currentHeight1, currentHeight2);
                    i++;
                    j++;
                } else {
                    currentHeight1 = leftSkyline[i].second;
                    currentHeight2 = rightSkyline[j].second;
                    if(maxH != max(currentHeight1, currentHeight2))
                        result.push_back(pair<int, int>(rightSkyline[j].first, rightSkyline[j].second));
                    maxH = max(currentHeight1, currentHeight2);
                    i++;
                    j++;
                }
            }
        }
        while (j < rightSkyline.size()) {
            result.push_back(rightSkyline[j]);
            j++;
        }
        while (i != leftSkyline.size()) {
            result.push_back(leftSkyline[i]);
            i++;
        }
        return result;
    }
};
```

For example, given two skylines A=($a_1$, h$a_1$, $a_2$, h$a_2$, ..., $a_n$, 0) and B=($b_1$, h$b_1$, $b_2$, h$b_2$, ..., $b_m$, 0), we merge these lists as the new list: ($c_1$, h$c_1$, $c_2$, h$c_2$, ..., $c_{n+m}$, 0). Clearly, we merge the list of $a$'s and $b$'s just like in the standard Merge algorithm. But, in addition to that, we have to decide on the correct height in between these boundary values. We use two variables $currentHeight1$ and $currentHeight2$ (note that these are the heights prior to encountering the heads of the lists) to store the current height of the first and the second skyline, respectively. When comparing the head entries ($currentHeight1$, $currentHeight2$) of the two skylines, we introduce a new strip (and append to the output skyline) whose x-coordinate is the minimum of the entries' x-coordinates and whose height is the maximum of $currentHeight1$ and $currentHeight2$. This algorithm has a structure similar to Mergesort. So the overall running time of the divide and conquer approach will be O($nlogn$).

CHAPTER

# DYNAMIC PROGRAMMING

19

## 19.1 Introduction

In this chapter, we will try to solve few of the problems for which we failed to get the optimal solutions using other techniques (say, *Greedy* and *Divide & Conquer* approaches). Dynamic Programming is a simple technique but it can be difficult to master. Being able to tackle problems of this type would greatly increase your skill.

Dynamic programming (usually referred to as DP) is a very powerful technique to solve a particular class of problems. It demands very elegant formulation of the approach and simple thinking and the coding part is very easy. The idea is very simple, if you have solved a problem with the given input, then save the result for future reference, so as to avoid solving the same problem again. Simply, we need to remember the past.

One easy way to identify and master DP problems is by solving as many problems as possible. The term DP is not related to coding, but it is from literature, and means filling tables.

## 19.2 What is Dynamic Programming Strategy?

Dynamic programming is typically applied to *optimization problems*. In such problems there can be many possible solutions. Each solution has a value, and we wish to find a solution with the optimal (minimum or maximum) value. We call such a solution an optimal solution to the problem, as opposed to the optimal solution, since there may be several solutions that achieve the optimal value.

The development of a dynamic-programming algorithm can be broken into a sequence of four steps.

1. Characterize the structure of an optimal solution.
2. Recursively define the value of an optimal solution.
3. Compute the value of an optimal solution in a bottom-up fashion.
4. Construct an optimal solution from computed information.

Steps 1-3 form the basis of a dynamic-programming solution to a problem. Step 4 can be omitted if only the value of an optimal solution is required. When we do perform step 4, we sometimes maintain additional information during the computation in step 3 to ease the construction of an optimal solution.

If the given problem can be broken up into smaller sub-problems and these smaller subproblems are in turn divided into still-smaller ones, and in this process, if you observe some over-lapping subproblems, then it's a big hint for DP. Also, the optimal solutions to the subproblems contribute to the optimal solution of the given problem.

## 19.3 Properties of Dynamic Programming Strategy

The two dynamic programming properties which can tell whether it can solve the given problem or not are:

- *Optimal substructure*: An optimal solution to a problem contains optimal solutions to sub problems.
- *Overlapping sub problems*: A recursive solution contains a small number of distinct sub problems repeated many times.

## 19.4 Greedy vs Divide and Conquer vs DP

All algorithmic techniques construct an optimal solution of a subproblem based on optimal solutions of smaller subproblems.

Greedy algorithms are one which finds optimal solution at each and every stage with the hope of finding global optimum at the end. The main difference between DP and greedy is that, the choice made by a greedy algorithm may depend on choices made so far but not on future choices or all the solutions to the sub problem. It iteratively makes one greedy choice after another, reducing each given problem into a smaller one.

In other words, a greedy algorithm never reconsiders its choices. This is the main difference from dynamic programming, which is exhaustive and is guaranteed to find the solution. After every stage, dynamic programming makes decisions based on all the decisions made in the previous stage, and may reconsider the previous stage's algorithmic path to solution.

The main difference between dynamic programming and divide and conquer is that in the case of the latter, sub problems are independent, whereas in DP there can be an overlap of sub problems.

## 19.5 Can DP solve all problems?

Like greedy and divide and conquer techniques, DP cannot solve every problem. There are problems which cannot be solved by any algorithmic technique [greedy, divide and conquer and DP].

The difference between DP and straightforward recursion is in memoization of recursive calls. If the sub problems are independent and there is no repetition then DP does not help. So, dynamic programming is not a solution for all problems.

## 19.6 Dynamic Programming Approaches

Dynamic programming is all about ordering computations in a way that we avoid recalculating duplicate work. In dynamic programming, we have a main problem, and subproblems (subtrees). The subproblems typically repeat and overlap. The major components of DP are:

- Overlapping subproblems: Solves sub problems recursively.
- Storage: Store the computed values to avoid recalculating already solved subproblems.

By using extra storage, DP reduces the exponential complexity to polynomial complexity ($O(n^2)$, $O(n^3)$, etc.) for many problems.

Basically, there are two approaches for solving DP problems:

- Top-down approach [Memoization]
- Bottom-up approach [Tabulation]

These approaches were classified based on the way we fill the storage and reuse them.

$$Dynamic\ Programming = Overlapping\ subproblems + \text{Memoization or } Tabulation$$

## 19.7 Understanding DP Approaches

### Top-down Approach [Memoization]

In this method, the problem is broken into sub problems; each of these subproblems is solved; and the solutions remembered, in case they need to be solved. Also, we save each computed value as the final action of the recursive function, and as the first action we check if pre-computed value exists.

### Bottom-up Approach [Tabulation]

In this method, we evaluate the function starting with the smallest possible input argument value and then we step through possible values, slowly increasing the input argument value. While computing the values we store all computed values in a table (memory). As larger arguments are evaluated, pre-computed values for smaller arguments can be used.

### Example: Fibonacci Series

Let us understand how DP works through an example; Fibonacci series.

In Fibonacci series, the current number is the sum of previous two numbers. The Fibonacci series is defined as follows:

$$\begin{aligned} Fib(\text{n}) &= 0, & for\ n = 0 \\ &= 1, & for\ n = 1 \\ &= Fib(\text{n}-1) + Fib(\text{n}-2), & for\ n > 1 \end{aligned}$$

Calling $fib(5)$ produces a call tree that calls the function on the same value many times:

$fib(5)$
$fib(4) + fib(3)$
$(fib(3) + fib(2)) + (fib(2) + fib(1))$
$((fib(2) + fib(1)) + (fib(1) + fib(0))) + ((fib(1) + fib(0)) + fib(1))$
$(((fib(1) + fib(0)) + fib(1)) + (fib(1) + fib(0))) + ((fib(1) + fib(0)) + fib(1))$

In the above example, $fib(2)$ was calculated three times (overlapping of subproblems). If $n$ is big, then many more values of $fib$ (subproblems) are recalculated, which leads to an exponential time algorithm. Instead of solving the same subproblems again and again we can store the previous calculated values and reduce the complexity.

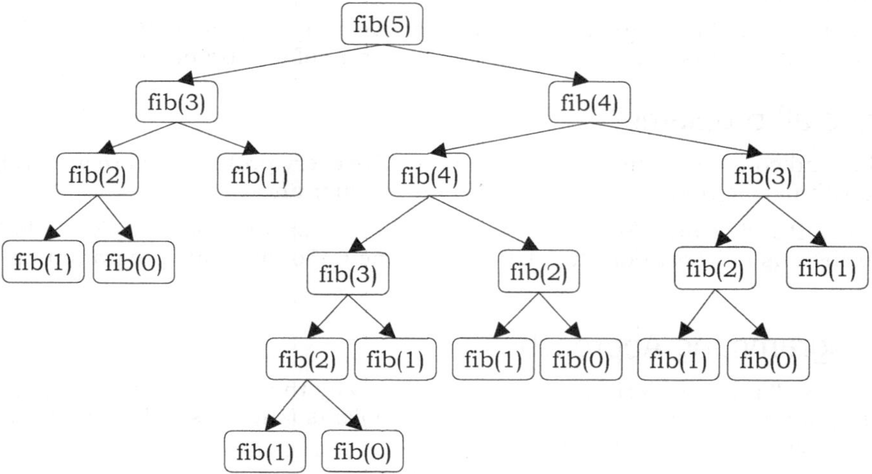


The recursive implementation can be given as:

```
int recursiveFibonacci(int n) {
    if(n == 0) return 0;
    if(n == 1) return 1;
    return recursiveFibonacci(n -1) + recursiveFibonacci(n -2);
}
```

Solving the above recurrence gives:

$$T(n) = T(n-1) + T(n-2) + 1 \approx \left(\frac{1+\sqrt{5}}{2}\right)^n \approx 2^n = O(2^n)$$

## Memoization Solution [Top-down]

*Memoization* works like this: Start with a recursive function and add a table that maps the function's parameter values to the results computed by the function. Then if this function is called twice with the same parameters, we simply look up the answer in the table.

In this method, we preserve the recursive calls and use the values if they are already computed. The implementation for this is given as:

```
int fib[n];
int fibonacci( int n ) {
    if(n == 1)
        return 1;
    if(n == 2)
        return 1;
    if( fib[n] != 0) return fib[n] ;
    return fib[n] = fibonacci(n-1) + fibonacci(n -2) ;
}
```

## Tabulation Solution [Bottom-up]

The other approach is bottom-up. Now, we see how DP reduces this problem complexity from exponential to polynomial. This method start with lower values of input and keep building the solutions for higher values.

```
int fib[n];
int fib(int n) {
    // Check for base cases
    if(n == 0 || n == 1) return 1;
    fib[0] = 1;
    fib[1] = 1;
    for (int i = 2; i < n; i++)
        fib[i] = fib[i - 1] + fib[i - 2];
    return fib[n - 1];
}
```

**Note:** For all problems, it may not be possible to find both top-down and bottom-up programming solutions.

Both versions of the Fibonacci series implementations clearly reduce the problem complexity to $O(n)$. This is because if a value is already computed then we are not calling the subproblems again. Instead, we are directly taking its value from the table.

Time Complexity: $O(n)$. Space Complexity: $O(n)$, for table.

## Further Improving

One more observation from the Fibonacci series is: The current value is the sum of the previous two calculations only. This indicates that we don't have to store all the previous values. Instead, if we store just the last two values, we can calculate the current value. The implementation for this is given below:

```
int fibonacci(int n) {
    int a = 0, b = 1, sum, i;
    for (i=0;i < n;i++) {
        sum = a + b;
        a = b;
        b = sum;
    }
    return sum;
}
```

Time Complexity: $O(n)$. Space Complexity: $O(1)$.

**Note:** This method may not be applicable (available) for all problems.

## Observations

While solving the problems using DP, try to figure out the following:

- See how the problems are defined in terms of subproblems recursively.
- See if we can use some table [memoization] to avoid the repeated calculations.

## Example: Factorial of a Number

As another example, consider the factorial problem: $n!$ is the product of all integers between $n$ and 1. The definition of recursive factorial can be given as:

$$n! = n * (n-1)!$$
$$1! = 1$$
$$0! = 1$$

This definition can easily be converted to implementation. Here the problem is finding the value of $n!$, and the sub-problem is finding the value of $(n - l)!$. In the recursive case, when $n$ is greater than 1, the function calls itself to find the value of $(n - l)!$ and multiplies that with $n$. In the base case, when $n$ is 0 or 1, the function simply returns 1.

```
int fact(int n) {
    if(n == 1)
      return 1;
    else if(n == 0)
      return 1;
    else    // recursive case: multiply n by (n -1) factorial
        return n *fact(n -1);
}
```

The recurrence for the above implementation can be given as:

$$T(n) = n \times T(n-1) \approx O(n)$$

Time Complexity: $O(n)$. Space Complexity: $O(n)$, recursive calls need a stack of size $n$.

In the above recurrence relation and implementation, for any $n$ value, there are no repetitive calculations (no overlapping of sub problems) and the factorial function is not getting any benefits with dynamic programming. Now, let us say we want to compute a series of $m!$ for some arbitrary value $m$. Using the above algorithm, for each such call we can compute it in $O(m)$. For example, to find both $n!$ and $m!$ we can use the above approach, wherein the total complexity for finding $n!$ and $m!$ is $O(m + n)$.

Time Complexity: $O(n + m)$. Space Complexity: $O(\max(m, n))$, recursive calls need a stack of size equal to the maximum of $m$ and $n$.

## Improving with Dynamic Programming

Now let us see how DP reduces the complexity. From the above recursive definition it can be seen that $fact(n)$ is calculated from $fact(n-1)$ and $n$ and nothing else. Instead of calling $fact(n)$ every time, we can store the previous calculated values in a table and use these values to calculate a new value. This implementation can be given as:

```
int facto[n];
int fact(int n) {
    if(n == 1) return 1;
    else if(n == 0)
        return 1;
    //Already calculated case
    else if(facto[n]!=0)
            return facto[n];
    else    // recursive case: multiply n by (n -1) factorial
    return facto[n]= n *fact(n -1);
}
```

For simplicity, let us assume that we have already calculated $n!$ and want to find $m!$. For finding $m!$, we just need to see the table and use the existing entries if they are already computed. If $m < n$ then we do not have to recalculate $m!$. If $m > n$ then we can use $n!$ and call the factorial on the remaining numbers only.

The above implementation clearly reduces the complexity to $O(max(m, n))$. This is because if the $fact$(n) is already there, then we are not recalculating the value again. If we fill these newly computed values, then the subsequent calls further reduce the complexity.

Time Complexity: $O(max(m, n))$. Space Complexity: $O(max(m, n))$ for table.

## Bottom-up versus Top-down Programming

With *tabulation* (bottom-up), we start from smallest instance size of the problem, and *iteratively* solve bigger problems using solutions of the smaller problems (i.e., by reading from the table), until we reach our starting instance.

With *memoization* (top-down) we start right away at original problem instance and solve it by breaking it down into smaller instances of the same problem (*recursion*). When we must solve smaller instances, we first check in a look-up table to see if we already solved it. If we did, we just read it up and return value without solving it again and branching into recursion. Otherwise, we solve it recursively, and save the result into table for further use.

In bottom-up approach, the programmer has to select values to calculate and decide the order of calculation. In this case, all subproblems that might be needed are solved in advance and then used to build up solutions to larger problems.

In top-down approach, the recursive structure of the original code is preserved, but unnecessary recalculation is avoided. The problem is broken into subproblems, these subproblems are solved and the solutions are remembered, in case they need to be solved again.

Recursion with memoization is better whenever the state is sparse space (number of different subproblems are less). In other words, if we don't need to solve all smaller subproblems but only some of them. In such cases recursive implementation can be much faster. Recursion with memoization is also better whenever the state space is irregular, i.e., whenever it is hard to specify an order of evaluation iteratively. Recursion with memoization is faster because only subproblems that are necessary in each problem instance are solved.

Tabulation methods are better whenever the state space is dense and regular. If we need to compute the solutions to all the subproblems anyway, we may as well do it without all the function calling overhead. An additional advantage of the iterative approach is that we are often able to save memory by forgetting the solutions to subproblems we won't need in the future. For example, if we only need row $k$ of the table to compute row $k + 1$, there is no need to remember row $k - 1$ anymore. On the flip side, in the tabulation method, we solve all subproblems although some subproblems may not be needed for a given problem instance.

## 19.8 Examples of DP Algorithms

- Many string algorithms including longest common subsequence, longest increasing subsequence, longest common substring, edit distance.
- Algorithms on graphs can be solved efficiently: Bellman-Ford algorithm for finding the shortest distance in a graph, Floyd's All-Pairs shortest path algorithm, etc.
- Chain matrix multiplication
- Subset Sum
- 0/1 Knapsack

- Travelling salesman problem, and many more

## 19.9 Longest Common Subsequence

Given two strings: string $X$ of length $m$ $[X(1..m)]$, and string $Y$ of length $n$ $[Y(1..n)]$, find the longest common subsequence: the longest sequence of characters that appear left-to-right (but not necessarily in a contiguous block) in both strings. For example, if $X$ = "ABCBDAB" and $Y$ = "BDCABA", the $LCS$(X, Y) = {"BCBA", "BDAB", "BCAB"}. We can see there are several optimal solutions.

**Brute Force Approach:** One simple idea is to check every subsequence of $X[1..m]$ ($m$ is the length of sequence $X$) to see if it is also a subsequence of $Y[1..n]$ ($n$ is the length of sequence $Y$). Checking takes O($n$) time, and there are $2^m$ subsequences of $X$. The running time thus is exponential O($n.2^m$) and is not good for large sequences.

**Recursive Solution:** Before going to DP solution, let us form the recursive solution for this and later we can add memoization to reduce the complexity. Let's start with some simple observations about the LCS problem. If we have two strings, say "ABCBDAB" and "BDCABA", and if we draw lines from the letters in the first string to the corresponding letters in the second, no two lines cross:

A B C B D A B

B D C A B A

From the above observation, we can see that the current characters of $X$ and $Y$ may or may not match. That means, suppose that the two first characters differ. Then it is not possible for both of them to be part of a common subsequence - one or the other (or maybe both) will have to be removed. Finally, observe that once we have decided what to do with the first characters of the strings, the remaining sub problem is again a $LCS$ problem, on two shorter strings. Therefore, we can solve it recursively.

The solution to $LCS$ should find two sequences in $X$ and $Y$ and let us say the starting index of sequence in $X$ is $i$ and the starting index of sequence in $Y$ is $j$. Also, assume that $X[i \dots m]$ is a substring of $X$ starting at character $i$ and going until the end of $X$, and that $Y[j \dots n]$ is a substring of $Y$ starting at character $j$ and going until the end of $Y$.

Based on the above discussion, here we get the possibilities described below:

1) If $X[i] == Y[j]$ : $1 + LCS(i+1, j+1)$
2) If $X[i] \neq Y[j]$: $LCS(i, j+1)$ // skipping $j^{th}$ character of $Y$
3) If $X[i] \neq Y[j]$: $LCS(i+1, j)$ // skipping $i^{th}$ character of $X$

In the first case, if $X[i]$ is equal to $Y[j]$, we get a matching pair and can count it towards the total length of the $LCS$. Otherwise, we need to skip either $i^{th}$ character of $X$ or $j^{th}$ character of $Y$ and find the longest common subsequence. Now, $LCS(i, j)$ can be defined as:

$$LCS(i,j) = \begin{cases} 0, & if\ i = m\ or\ j = n \\ Max\{LCS(i, j+1), LCS(i+1, j)\}, & if\ \text{X[i]} \neq \text{Y[j]} \\ 1 + LCS[i+1, j+1], & if\ \text{X[i]} == \text{Y[j]} \end{cases}$$

LCS has many applications. In web searching, if we find the smallest number of changes that are needed to change one word into another. A *change* here is an insertion, deletion, or replacement of a single character.

```
//Initial Call: LCSLength(X, 0, m-1, Y, 0, n-1);
int LCSLength( int X[], int i, int m, int Y[], int j, int n) {
    if (i == m || j == n)
        return 0;
    else if (X[i] == Y[j]) return 1 + LCSLength(X, i+1, m, Y, j+1, n);
    else return max( LCSLength(X, i+1, m, Y, j, n),  LCSLength(X, i, m, Y, j+1, n));
}
```

This is a correct solution, but it is very time consuming. For example, if the two strings have no matching characters, the last line always gets executed which gives (if $m == n$) close to $O(2^n)$.

**DP Solution: Adding Memoization:** The problem with the recursive solution is that the same subproblems get called many different times. A subproblem consists of a call to LCSLength, with the arguments being two suffixes of $X$ and $Y$, so there are exactly $(i+1)(j+1)$ possible subproblems (a relatively small number). If there are nearly $2^n$ recursive calls, some of these subproblems must be solved over and over.

The DP solution is to check, whenever we want to solve a sub problem, whether we've already done it before. So, we look up the solution instead of solving it again. Implemented in the most direct way, we just add some code to our recursive solution. To do this, look up the code. This can be given as:

```
int LCS[1024][1024];
int LCSLength( int X[], int m, int Y[], int n) {
```

```
        for( int i = 0; i <= m; i++ )
            LCS[i][n] = 0;
        for( int j = 0; j <= n; j++ )
            LCS[m][j] = 0;
        for( int i = m - 1; i >= 0; i--) {
            for( int j = n - 1; j >= 0; j--) {
                LCS[i][j] = LCS[i + 1][j + 1]; // matching X[i] to Y[j]
                if( X[i] == Y[j] )
                    LCS[i][j]++; // we get a matching pair
                // the other two cases - inserting a gap
                if(LCS[i][j + 1] > LCS[i][j] )
                    LCS[i][j] = LCS[i][j + 1];
                if(LCS[i + 1][j] > LCS[i][j] )
                    LCS[i][j] = LCS[i + 1][j];
            }
        }
        return LCS[0][0];
    }
```

First, take care of the base cases. We have created an $LCS$ table with one row and one column larger than the lengths of the two strings. Then run the iterative DP loops to fill each cell in the table. This is like doing recursion backwards, or bottom up.

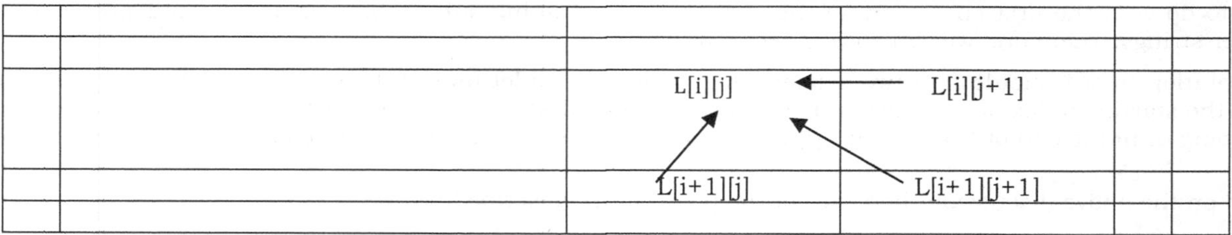


The value of $LCS[i][j]$ depends on 3 other values ($LCS[i+1][j+1]$, $LCS[i][j+1]$ and $LCS[i+1][j]$), all of which have larger values of $i$ or $j$. They go through the table in the order of decreasing $i$ and $j$ values. This will guarantee that when we need to fill in the value of $LCS[i][j]$, we already know the values of all the cells on which it depends.

Time Complexity: $O(mn)$, since $i$ takes values from 1 to $m$ and and $j$ takes values from 1 to $n$. Space Complexity: $O(mn)$.

**Note:** In the above discussion, we have assumed $LCS(i,j)$ is the length of the $LCS$ with $X[i \dots m]$ and $Y[j \dots n]$. We can solve the problem by changing the definition as $LCS(i,j)$ is the length of the $LCS$ with $X[1 \dots i]$ and $Y[1 \dots j]$.

**Printing the subsequence:** The above algorithm can find the length of the longest common subsequence but cannot give the actual longest subsequence. To get the sequence, we trace it through the table. Start at cell $(0,0)$. We know that the value of $LCS[0][0]$ was the maximum of 3 values of the neighboring cells. So we simply recompute $LCS[0][0]$ and note which cell gave the maximum value. Then we move to that cell (it will be one of $(1,1)$, $(0,1)$ or $(1,0)$) and repeat this until we hit the boundary of the table. Every time we pass through a cell $(i,j)$ where $X[i] == Y[j]$, we have a matching pair and print $X[i]$. At the end, we will have printed the longest common subsequence in $O(mn)$ time.

An alternative way of getting path is to keep a separate table for each cell. This will tell us which direction we came from when computing the value of that cell. At the end, we again start at cell $(0,0)$ and follow these directions until the opposite corner of the table.

From the above examples, I hope you understood the idea behind DP. Now let us see more problems which can be easily solved using the DP technique.

**Note:** As we have seen above, in DP the main component is recursion. If we know the recurrence then converting that to code is a minimal task. For the problems below, we concentrate on getting the recurrence.

## 19.10 Dynamic Programming: Problems & Solutions

**Problem-1** Convert the following recurrence to code.

$$T(0) = T(1) = 2$$

$$T(n) = \sum_{i=1}^{n-1} 2 \times \mathrm{T(i)} \times \mathrm{T(i-1)}, \text{for n} > 1$$

**Solution:** The code for the given recursive formula can be given as:

```
int f(int n) {
    int sum = 0;
    if(n==0 || n==1) //Base Case
        return 2;
    //recursive case
    for(int i=1; i < n;i++)
        sum += 2 * f(i) * f(i-1);
    return sum;
}
```

**Problem-2** Can we improve the solution to Problem-1 using memoization of DP?

**Solution: Yes.** Before finding a solution, let us see how the values are calculated.

$$T(0) = T(1) = 2$$
$$T(2) = 2 * T(1) * T(0)$$
$$T(3) = 2 * T(1) * T(0) + 2 * T(2) * T(1)$$
$$T(4) = 2 * T(1) * T(0) + 2 * T(2) * T(1) + 2 * T(3) * T(2)$$

From the above calculations it is clear that there are lots of repeated calculations with the same input values. Let us use a table for avoiding these repeated calculations, and the implementation can be given as:

```
int f(int n) {
    T[0] = T[1] = 2;
    for(int i=2; i <= n; i++) {
        T[i] = 0;
        for (int j=1; j < i; j++)
            T[i] +=2 * T[j] * T[j-1];
    }
    return T[n];
}
```

Time Complexity: O($n^2$), two *for* loops. Space Complexity: O($n$), for table.

**Problem-3** Can we further improve the complexity of Problem-2?

**Solution: Yes**, since all sub-problem calculations are dependent only on previous calculations, the code can be modified as:

```
int f(int n) {
    T[0] = T[1] = 2;
    T[2] = 2 * T[0] * T[1];
    for(int i=3; i <= n; i++)
        T[i]=T[i-1] + 2 * T[i-1] * T[i-2];
    return T[n];
}
```

Time Complexity: O($n$), since only one *for* loop. Space Complexity: O($n$).

**Problem-4** **Maximum Value Contiguous Subsequence:** Given an array of $n$ numbers, give an algorithm for finding a contiguous subsequence $A(i)...A(j)$ for which the sum of elements is maximum.
**Example**: {-2, **11, -4, 13**, -5, 2} → 20 and {1, -3, **4, -2, -1, 6**} → 7

**Solution: Goal**: If there are no negative numbers, then the solution is just the sum of all elements in the given array. If negative numbers are there, then our aim is to maximize the sum [there can be a negative number in the contiguous sum].

One simple and brute force approach is to see all possible sums and select the one which has maximum value.

```
int maxContiguousSum(int A[], in n) {
    int maxSum = 0;
    for(int i = 0; i < n; i++)                // for each possible start point
            for(int j = i; j < n; j++) {      // for each possible end point
                int currentSum = 0;
                for(int k = i; k <= j; k++)
                        currentSum += A[k];
                if(currentSum > maxSum)
                        maxSum = currentSum;
            }
    }
    return maxSum;
```

```
}
```

Time Complexity: $O(n^3)$. Space Complexity: O(1).

**Problem-5** Can we improve the complexity of Problem-4?

**Solution: Yes.** One important observation is that, if we have already calculated the sum for the subsequence $i, ..., j-1$, then we need only one more addition to get the sum for the subsequence $i, ..., j$. But, the Problem-4 algorithm ignores this information. If we use this fact, we can get an improved algorithm with the running time $O(n^2)$.

```
int maxContiguousSum(int A[], int n) {
    int maxSum = 0;
    for( int i = 0; i < n;   i++) {
        int currentSum = 0;
        for( int j = i; j < n; j++)   {
            currentSum += a[j];
            if(currentSum > maxSum)
                maxSum = currentSum;
        }
    }
    return maxSum;
}
```

Time Complexity: $O(n^2)$. Space Complexity: O(1).

**Problem-6** Can we solve Problem-4 using Dynamic Programming?

**Solution: Yes.** For simplicity, let us say, $M(i)$ indicates maximum sum over all windows ending at $i$.

Given Array, $A$: recursive formula considers the case of selecting $i^{th}$ element

To find maximum sum we have to do one of the following and select maximum among them.

- Either extend the old sum by adding $A[i]$
- or start new window starting with one element $A[i]$

$$M(i) = Max\begin{cases} M(i-1) + A[i] \\ 0 \end{cases}$$

Where, $M(i-1) + A[i]$ indicates the case of extending the previous sum by adding $A[i]$ and 0 indicates the new window starting at $A[i]$.

```
int maxContiguousSum(int A[], int n) {
    int M[n] = 0, maxSum = 0;
    if(A[0] > 0)
        M[0] = A[0];
    else M[0] = 0;
    for( int i = 1; i < n; i++) {
        if( M[i-1] + A[i] > 0)
            M[i] = M[i-1] + A[i];
        else    M[i] = 0;
    }
    for( int i = 0; i < n; i++)
        if(M[i] > maxSum)
            maxSum = M[i];
    return maxSum;
}
```

Time Complexity: $O(n)$. Space Complexity: $O(n)$, for table.

**Problem-7** Is there any other way of solving Problem-4?

**Solution: Yes.** We can solve this problem without DP too (without memory). The algorithm is a little tricky. One simple way is to look for all positive contiguous segments of the array (*sumEndingHere*) and keep track of the maximum sum contiguous segment among all positive segments (*sumSoFar*). Each time we get a positive sum compare it (*sumEndingHere*) with *sumSoFar* and update *sumSoFar* if it is greater than *sumSoFar*. Let us consider the following code for the above observation.

```
int maxContiguousSum(int A[], int n) {
```

```
    int sumSoFar = 0, sumEndingHere = 0;
    for(int i = 0; i < n; i++)  {
        sumEndingHere = sumEndingHere + A[i];
            if(sumEndingHere < 0) {
                sumEndingHere = 0;
                continue;
            }
        if(sumSoFar < sumEndingHere)
            sumSoFar = sumEndingHere;
    }
    return sumSoFar;
}
```

**Note:** The algorithm doesn't work if the input contains all negative numbers. It returns 0 if all numbers are negative. To overcome this, we can add an extra check before the actual implementation. The phase will look if all numbers are negative, and if they are it will return maximum of them (or smallest in terms of absolute value).

Time Complexity: O($n$), because we are doing only one scan. Space Complexity: O(1), for table.

Problem-8 In the Problem-7 solution, we have assumed that $M(i)$ indicates maximum sum over all windows ending at $i$. Can we assume $M(i)$ indicates maximum sum over all windows starting at $i$ and ending at $n$?

**Solution**: Yes. For simplicity, let us say, $M(i)$ indicates maximum sum over all windows starting at $i$.

Given Array, A: recursive formula considers the case of selecting $i^{th}$ element

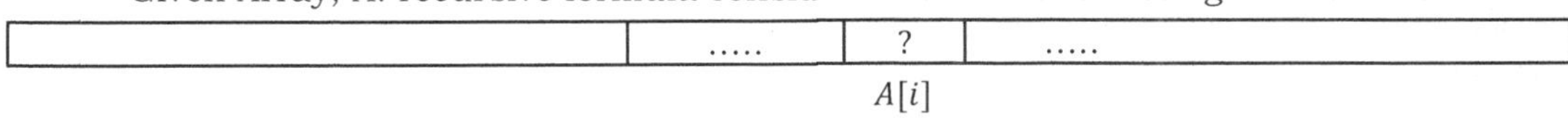

To find maximum window we have to do one of the following and select maximum among them.

- Either extend the old sum by adding $A[i]$
- Or start new window starting with one element A[i]

$$M(i) = Max\begin{cases} M(i+1) + A[i], & if\ M(i+1) + A[i] > 0 \\ 0 \quad , & if\ M(i+1) + A[i] <= 0 \end{cases}$$

Where, $M(i+1) + A[i]$ indicates the case of extending the previous sum by adding $A[i]$, and 0 indicates the new window starting at $A[i]$.

Time Complexity: *O(n)*. Space Complexity: O($n$), for table.

**Note:** For O($nlogn$) solution, refer to the *Divide and Conquer* chapter.

Problem-9 Given a sequence of $n$ numbers $A(1) \ldots A(n)$, give an algorithm for finding a contiguous subsequence $A(i) \ldots A(j)$ for which the sum of elements in the subsequence is maximum. Here the condition is we should not select *two* contiguous numbers.

**Solution:** Let us see how DP solves this problem. Assume that $M(i)$ represents the maximum sum from 1 to $i$ numbers without selecting two contiguous numbers. While computing $M(i)$, the decision we have to make is, whether to select the $i^{th}$ element or not. This gives us two possibilities and based on this we can write the recursive formula as:

$$M(i) = \begin{cases} Max\{A[i] + M(i-2), M(i-1)\}, if\ i > 2 \\ A[1], \quad if\ i = 1 \\ Max\{A[1], A[2]\}, \quad if\ i = 2 \end{cases}$$

- The first case indicates whether we are selecting the $i^{th}$ element or not. If we don't select the $i^{th}$ element then we have to maximize the sum using the elements 1 to $i-1$. If $i^{th}$ element is selected then we should not select $i-1^{th}$ element and need to maximize the sum using 1 to $i-2$ elements.
- In the above representation, the last two cases indicate the base cases.

Given Array, A: recursive formula considers the case of selecting $i^{th}$ element

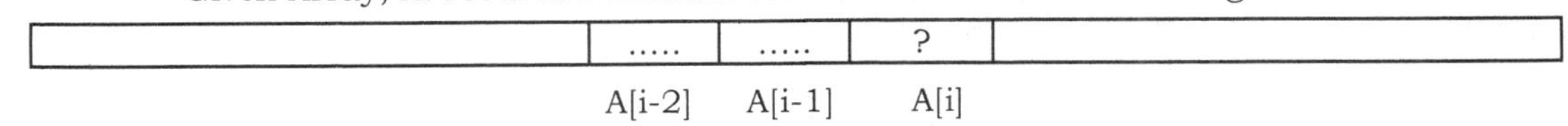

```
int maxSumWithNoTwoContinuousNumbers(int A[], int n) {
    int M[n+1];
    M[0]=A[0];
    M[1]=(A[0]>A[1]?A[0]:A[1]);
    for(i=2, i<n; i++)
        M[i]= (M[i-1]>M[i-2]+A[i]? M[i-1]: M[i-2]+A[i]);
```

```
    return M[n-1];
}
```

Time Complexity: O($n$). Space Complexity: O($n$).

**Problem-10** In Problem-9, we assumed that $M(i)$ represents the maximum sum from 1 to $i$ numbers without selecting two contiguous numbers. Can we solve the same problem by changing the definition as: $M(i)$ represents the maximum sum from $i$ to $n$ numbers without selecting two contiguous numbers?

**Solution: Yes.** Let us assume that $M(i)$ represents the maximum sum from $i$ to $n$ numbers without selecting two contiguous numbers.

Given Array, A: recursive formula considers the case of selecting $i^{th}$ element

| | ? | ..... | ..... | |
|---|---|---|---|---|
| | A[i] | A[i+1] | A[i+2] | |

As similar to Problem-9 solution, we can write the recursive formula as:

$$M(i) = \begin{cases} Max\{A[i] + M(i+2), M(i+1)\}, if\ i > 2 \\ A[1], & if\ i = 1 \\ Max\{A[1], A[2]\}, & if\ i = 2 \end{cases}$$

- The first case indicates whether we are selecting the $i^{th}$ element or not. If we don't select the $i^{th}$ element then we have to maximize the sum using the elements $i+1$ to $n$. If $i^{th}$ element is selected then we should not select $i+1^{th}$ element need to maximize the sum using $i+2$ to $n$ elements.
- In the above representation, the last two cases indicate the base cases.

Time Complexity: O($n$). Space Complexity: O($n$).

**Problem-11** Given a sequence of $n$ numbers $A(1) \ldots A(n)$, give an algorithm for finding a contiguous subsequence $A(i) \ldots A(j)$ for which the sum of elements in the subsequence is maximum. Here the condition is we should not select *three* continuous numbers.

**Solution:** Input: Array $A(1) \ldots A(n)$ of $n$ numbers.

Given Array, A: recursive formula considers the case of selecting $i^{th}$ element

| | ..... | ..... | ..... | ? | |
|---|---|---|---|---|---|
| | A[i-3] | A[i-2] | A[i-1] | A[i] | |

Assume that $M(i)$ represents the maximum sum from 1 to $i$ numbers without selecting three contiguous numbers. While computing $M(i)$, the decision we have to make is, whether to select $i^{th}$ element or not. This gives us the following possibilities:

$$M(i) = Max\begin{cases} A[i] + A[i-1] + M(i-3) \\ A[i] + M(i-2) \\ M(i-1) \end{cases}$$

- In the given problem the restriction is not to select three continuous numbers, but we can select two elements continuously and skip the third one. That is what the first case says in the above recursive formula. That means we are skipping $A[i-2]$.
- The other possibility is, selecting $i^{th}$ element and skipping second $i-1^{th}$ element. This is the second case (skipping $A[i-1]$).
- The third term defines the case of not selecting $i^{th}$ element and as a result we should solve the problem with $i-1$ elements.

Time Complexity: O($n$). Space Complexity: O($n$).

**Problem-12** In Problem-11, we assumed that $M(i)$ represents the maximum sum from 1 to $i$ numbers without selecting three contiguous numbers. Can we solve the same problem by changing the definition as: $M(i)$ represents the maximum sum from $i$ to $n$ numbers without selecting three contiguous numbers?

**Solution: Yes.** The reasoning is very much similar. Let us see how DP solves this problem. Assume that $M(i)$ represents the maximum sum from $i$ to $n$ numbers without selecting three contiguous numbers.

Given Array, A: recursive formula considers the case of selecting $i^{th}$ element

| | ? | ..... | ..... | ..... | |
|---|---|---|---|---|---|
| | A[i] | A[i+1] | A[i+2] | A[i+3] | |

While computing $M(i)$, the decision we have to make is, whether to select $i^{th}$ element or not. This gives us the following possibilities:

$$M(i) = Max \begin{cases} A[i] + A[i+1] + M(i+3) \\ A[i] + M(i+2) \\ M(i+1) \end{cases}$$

- In the given problem the restriction is to not select three continuous numbers, but we can select two elements continuously and skip the third one. That is what the first case says in the above recursive formula. That means we are skipping $A[i+2]$.
- The other possibility is, selecting $i^{th}$ element and skipping second $i-1^{th}$ element. This is the second case (skipping $A[i+1]$).
- And the third case is not selecting $i^{th}$ element and as a result we should solve the problem with $i+1$ elements.

Time Complexity: O($n$). Space Complexity: O($n$).

Problem-13 **Catalan Numbers:** How many binary search trees are there with $n$ vertices?

**Solution:** Binary Search Tree (BST) is a tree where the left subtree elements are less than the root element, and the right subtree elements are greater than the root element. This property should be satisfied at every node in the tree. The number of BSTs with $n$ nodes is called *Catalan Number* and is denoted by $C_n$. For example, there are 2 BSTs with 2 nodes (2 choices for the root) and 5 BSTs with 3 nodes.

| Number of nodes, $n$ | Number of Trees |
|---|---|
| 1 | 1 |
| 2 | 2 1 / 1 2 |
| 3 | 3 2 1 / 1 2 3 / 3 1 2 / 1 2 3 / 2 1 3 |

Let us assume that the nodes of the tree are numbered from 1 to $n$. Among the nodes, we have to select some node as root, and then divide the nodes which are less than root node into left sub tree, and elements greater than root node into right sub tree. Since we have already numbered the vertices, let us assume that the root element we selected is $i^{th}$ element.

If we select $i^{th}$ element as root then we get $i-1$ elements on left sub-tree and $n-i$ elements on right sub tree. Since $C_n$ is the Catalan number for $n$ elements, $C_{i-1}$ represents the Catalan number for left sub tree elements ($i-1$ elements) and $C_{n-i}$ represents the Catalan number for right sub tree elements. The two sub trees are independent of each other, so we simply multiply the two numbers. That means, the Catalan number for a fixed $i$ value is $C_{i-1} \times C_{n-i}$.

Since there are $n$ nodes, for $i$ we will get $n$ choices. The total Catalan number with $n$ nodes can be given as:

$$C_n = \sum_{i=1}^{n} C_{i-1} \times C_{n-i}$$

```
int CatalanNumber( int n ) {
    if( n == 0 ) return 1;
    int count = 0;
    for( int i = 1; i <= n; i++ )
            count += CatalanNumber (i -1) * CatalanNumber (n -i);
    return count;
}
```

Time Complexity: O($4^n$). For proof, refer to *Introduction* chapter.

Problem-14 Can we improve the time complexity of Problem-13 using DP?

**Solution:** The recursive call $C_n$ depends only on the numbers $C_0$ to $C_{n-1}$ and for any value of $i$, there are a lot of recalculations. We will keep a table of previously computed values of $C_i$. If the function $CatalanNumber()$ is called with parameter i, and if it has already been computed before, then we can simply avoid recalculating the same subproblem.

```
int Table[1024];
int CatalanNumber( int n ) {
    if( Table[n] ) != 1 )
        return Table[n];
    Table[n] = 0;
    for( int i = 1; i <= n; i++ )
            Table[n] += CatalanNumber( i -1) * CatalanNumber(n -i);
    return Table[n];
}
```

The time complexity of this implementation $O(n^2)$, because to compute $CatalanNumber(n)$, we need to compute all of the $CatalanNumber(i)$ values between 0 and $n-1$, and each one will be computed exactly once, in linear time.

In mathematics, Catalan Number can be represented by direct equation as: $\frac{(2n)!}{n!(n+1)!}$.

Problem-15 **Matrix Product Parenthesizations:** Given a series of matrices: $A_1 \times A_2 \times A_3 \times \ldots \times A_n$ with their dimensions, what is the best way to parenthesize them so that it produces the minimum number of total multiplications. Assume that we are using standard matrix and not Strassen's matrix multiplication algorithm.

**Solution:** Input: Sequence of matrices $A_1 \times A_2 \times A_3 \times \ldots \times A_n$, where $A_i$ is a $P_{i-1} \times P_i$. The dimensions are given in an array P.

**Goal**: Parenthesize the given matrices in such a way that it produces the optimal number of multiplications needed to compute $A_1 \times A_2 \times A_3 \times \ldots \times A_n$.

We could write a function which tries all possible parenthesizations. Unfortunately, the number of ways of parenthesizing an expression is very large. If you have just one or two matrices, then there is only one way to parenthesize. If you have $n$ items, then there are $n - 1$ places where you could break the list with the outermost pair of parentheses, namely just after the first item, just after the second item, etc., and just after the $(n - 1)^{st}$ item.

When we split just after the $i^{th}$ item, we create two sublists to be parenthesized, one with $i$ items, and the other with $n - i$ items. Then we could consider all the ways of parenthesizing these. Since these are independent choices, if there are $L$ ways to parenthesize the left sublist and $R$ ways to parenthesize the right sublist, then the total is $L \times R$. This suggests the following recurrence for $P(n)$, the number of different ways of parenthesizing $n$ items:

$$P(n) = \sum_{i=1}^{n} P(i) \times P(n-i)$$

The base case would be $P(1)$, and obviously, the number of ways to parenthesize the two matrices is 1.

$$P(1) = 1$$

This is related to the Catalan numbers (which in turn is related to the number of different binary trees on $n$ nodes). As said above, applying Stirling's formula, we find that $C(n)$ is $O\left(\frac{4^n}{n^{\frac{3}{2}}\sqrt{\pi}}\right)$. Since $4^n$ is exponential and $n^{3/2}$ is just polynomial, the exponential will dominate, implying that function grows very fast. Thus, this will not be practical except for very small $n$. In summary, brute force is not an option.

Now let us use DP to improve this time complexity. Assume that, $M[i,j]$ represents the least number of multiplications needed to multiply $A_i \cdots A_j$.

$$M[i,j] = \begin{cases} 0 & ,if\ i = j \\ Min\{M[i,k] + M[k+1,j] + P_{i-1}P_kP_j\}, & if\ i < j \end{cases}$$

The above recursive formula says that we have to find point $k$ such that it produces the minimum number of multiplications. After computing all possible values for $k$, we have to select the $k$ value which gives minimum value. We can use one more table (say, $S[i,j]$) to reconstruct the optimal parenthesizations. Compute the $M[i,j]$ and $S[i,j]$ in a bottom-up fashion.

```
/* P is the sizes of the matrices, Matrix i has the dimension P[i-1] x P[i].
M[i,j] is the best cost of multiplying matrices i through j
S[i,j] saves the multiplication point and we use this for back tracing */
void MatrixChainOrder(int P[], int length) {
    int n = length – 1, M[n][n], S[n][n];
```

```
        for (int i = 1; i <= n; i++)
                M[i][i] = 0;
        // Fills in matrix by diagonals
        for (int l=2; l<= n; l++)   {           // l is chain length
                for (int i=1; i<= n -l+1; i++) {
                        int j = i+l-1;
                        M[i][j] = MAX_VALUE;
                        // Try all possible division points i..k and k..j
                        for (int k=i; k<=j-1; k++) {
                                int thisCost = M[i][k] + M[k+1][j] + P[i-1]*P[k]*P[j];
                                if(thisCost < M[i][j]) {
                                        M[i][j] = thisCost;
                                        S[i][j] = k;
                                }
                        }
                }
        }
}
```

**How many sub problems are there?** In the above formula, $i$ can range from $1$ $to$ $n$ and $j$ can range from $1$ $to$ $n$. So there are a total of $n^2$ subproblems, and also we are doing $n-1$ such operations [since the total number of operations we need for $A_1 \times A_2 \times A_3 \times . . . \times A_n$ ise $n-1$]. So the time complexity is $O(n^3)$.
Space Complexity: $O(n^2)$.

Problem-16 For Problem-15, can we use greedy method?

**Solution:** *Greedy* method is not an optimal way of solving this problem. Let us go through some counter example for this. As we have seen already, *greedy* method makes the decision that is good locally and it does not consider the future optimal solutions. In this case, if we use *Greedy*, then we always do the cheapest multiplication first. Sometimes it returns a parenthesization that is not optimal.

**Example:** Consider $A_1 \times A_2 \times A_3$ with dimensions $3 \times 100$, $100 \times 2$ and $2 \times 2$. Based on *greedy* we parenthesize them as: $A_1 \times (A_2 \times A_3)$ with $100 \cdot 2 \cdot 2 + 3 \cdot 100 \cdot 2 = 1000$ multiplications. But the optimal solution to this problem is: $(A_1 \times A_2) \times A_3$ with $3 \cdot 100 \cdot 2 + 3 \cdot 2 \cdot 2 = 612$ multiplications. $\therefore$ we cannot use *greedy* for solving this problem.

Problem-17 **Integer Knapsack Problem [Duplicate Items Permitted]:** Given $n$ types of items, where the $i^{th}$ item type has an integer size $s_i$ and a value $v_i$. We need to fill a knapsack of total capacity $C$ with items of maximum value. We can add multiple items of the same type to the knapsack.
**Note:** For Fractional Knapsack problem refer to *Greedy Algorithms* chapter.

**Solution:** Input: $n$ types of items where $i^{th}$ type item has the size $s_i$ and value $v_i$. Also, assume infinite number of items for each item type.

**Goal**: Fill the knapsack with capacity $C$ by using $n$ types of items and with maximum value.

One important note is that it's not compulsory to fill the knapsack completely. That means, filling the knapsack completely [of size $C$] if we get a value V and without filling the knapsack completely [let us say C – 1] with value U and if V < U then we consider the second one. In this case, we are basically filling the knapsack of size C – 1. If we get the same situation for $C-1$ also, then we try to fill the knapsack with $C-2$ size and get the maximum value.

Let us say M(j) denotes the maximum value we can pack into a $j$ size knapsack. We can express M(j) recursively in terms of solutions to sub problems as follows:

$$M(j) = \begin{cases} max\{M(j-1), max_{i=1\ to\ n}(M(j-s_i)) + v_i\}, & if\ j \geq 1 \\ 0, & if\ j \leq 0 \end{cases}$$

For this problem the decision depends on whether we select a particular $i^{th}$ item or not for a knapsack of size $j$.

- If we select $i^{th}$ item, then we add its value $v_i$ to the optimal solution and decrease the size of the knapsack to be solved to $j - s_i$.
- If we do not select the item then check whether we can get a better solution for the knapsack of size $j-1$.

The value of $M(C)$ will contain the value of the optimal solution. We can find the list of items in the optimal solution by maintaining and following "back pointers".

Time Complexity: Finding each $M(j)$ value will require $\Theta(n)$ time, and we need to sequentially compute $C$ such values. Therefore, total running time is $\Theta(nC)$.
Space Complexity: $\Theta(C)$.

Problem-18 **0-1 Knapsack Problem:** For Problem-17, how do we solve it if the items are not duplicated (not having an infinite number of items for each type, and each item is allowed to be used for 0 or 1 time)?

**Real-time example:** Suppose we are going by flight, and we know that there is a limitation on the luggage weight. Also, the items which we are carrying can be of different types (like laptops, etc.). In this case, our objective is to select the items with maximum value. That means, we need to tell the customs officer to select the items which have more weight and less value (profit).

**Solution:** Input is a set of $n$ items with sizes $s_i$ and values $v_i$ and a Knapsack of size $C$ which we need to fill with a subset of items from the given set. Let us try to find the recursive formula for this problem using DP. Let $M(i,j)$ represent the optimal value we can get for filling up a knapsack of size $j$ with items $1 \dots i$. The recursive formula can be given as:

$$M(i,j) = Max\,\{\underbrace{M(i-1,j)}_{i^{th} \text{ item is not used}}, \underbrace{M(i-1,j-s_i)+v_i}_{i^{th} \text{ item is used}}\}$$

Time Complexity: O($nC$), since there are $nC$ subproblems to be solved and each of them takes O(1) to compute. Space Complexity: O($nC$), where as Integer Knapsack takes only O($C$).

Now let us consider the following diagram which helps us in reconstructing the optimal solution and also gives further understanding. Size of below matrix is $M$.

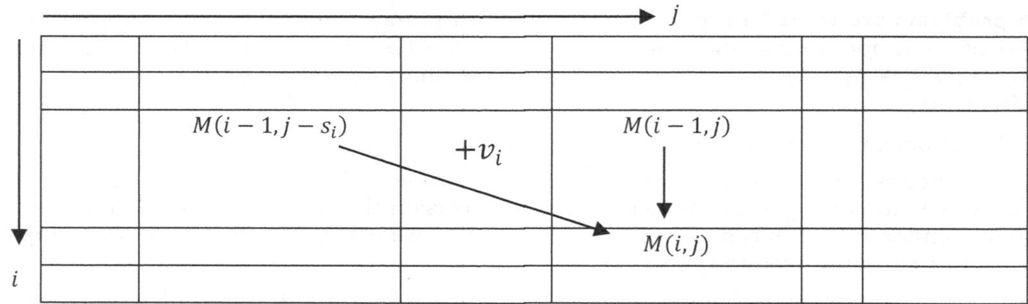


Since $i$ takes values from $1 \dots n$ and $j$ takes values from $1 \dots C$, there are a total of $nC$ subproblems. Now let us see what the above formula says:

- $M(i-1,j)$: Indicates the case of not selecting the $i^{th}$ item. In this case, since we are not adding any size to the knapsack we have to use the same knapsack size for subproblems but excluding the $i^{th}$ item. The remaining items are $i-1$.
- $M(i-1,j-s_i)+v_i$ indicates the case where we have selected the $i^{th}$ item. If we add the $i^{th}$ item then we have to reduce the subproblem knapsack size to $j-s_i$ and at the same time we need to add the value $v_i$ to the optimal solution. The remaining items are $i-1$.

Now, after finding all $M(i,j)$ values, the optimal objective value can be obtained as: $Max_j\{M(n,j)\}$
This is because we do not know what amount of capacity gives the best solution.

In order to compute some value $M(i,j)$, we take the maximum of $M(i-1,j)$ and $M(i-1,j-s_i)+v_i$. These two values ($M(i,j)$ and $M(i-1,j-s_i)$) appear in the previous row and also in some previous columns. So, $M(i,j)$ can be computed just by looking at two values in the previous row in the table.

Problem-19 **Making Change:** Given $n$ types of coin denominations of values $v_1 < v_2 < \dots < v_n$ (integers). Assume $v_1 = 1$, so that we can always make change for any amount of money $C$. Give an algorithm which makes change for an amount of money $C$ with as few coins as possible.

**Solution:**

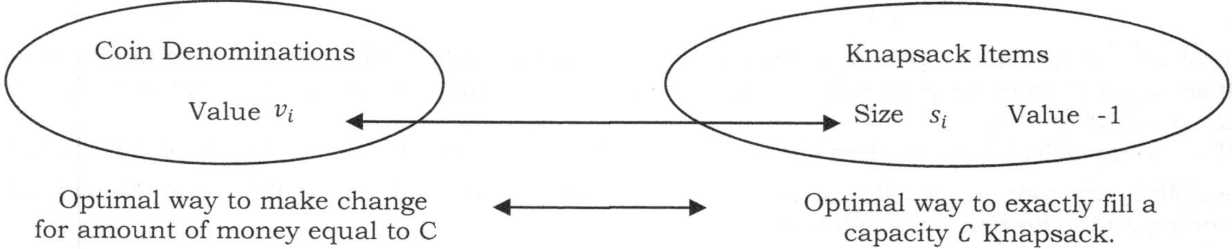


This problem is identical to the Integer Knapsack problem. In our problem, we have coin denominations, each of value $v_i$. We can construct an instance of a Knapsack problem for each item that has a size $s_i$, which is equal to the value of $v_i$ coin denomination. In the Knapsack we can give the value of every item as $-1$.

Now it is easy to understand an optimal way to make money $C$ with the fewest coins is completely equivalent to the optimal way to fill the Knapsack of size $C$. This is because since every value has a value of $-1$, and the Knapsack algorithm uses as few items as possible which correspond to as few coins as possible.

Let us try formulating the recurrence. Let $M(j)$ indicate the minimum number of coins required to make change for the amount of money equal to $j$.

$$M(j) = Min_i\{M(j - v_i)\} + 1$$

What this says is, if coin denomination $i$ was the last denomination coin added to the solution, then the optimal way to finish the solution with that one is to optimally make change for the amount of money $j - v_i$ and then add one extra coin of value $v_i$.

```
int Table[128] ; //Initialization
int makingChange(int n) {
    if(n < 0) return -1;
    if(n == 0)
            return 0;
    if(Table[n] != -1)
            return Table[n];
    int ans = -1;
    for ( int i = 0 ; i < num_denomination ; ++i )
            ans = min( ans , makingChange(n - denominations [ i ] ) ) ;

    return Table[ n ] = ans + 1 ;
}
```

Time Complexity: $O(nC)$. Since we are solving $C$ sub-problems and each of them requires minimization of $n$ terms. Space Complexity: $O(nC)$.

Problem-20 **Longest Increasing Subsequence (LIS):** Given a sequence of $n$ numbers $A_1 \ldots A_n$, determine a subsequence (not necessarily contiguous) of maximum length in which the values in the subsequence form a strictly increasing sequence.

**Solution: Goal**: To find a subsequence that is just a subset of elements and does not happen to be contiguous. But the elements in the subsequence should form a strictly increasing sequence and at the same time the subsequence should contain as many elements as possible.

For example, if the sequence is (5,6,2,3,4,1,9,9,8,9,5), then (5,6), (3,5), (1,8,9) are all increasing sub-sequences. The longest one of them is (2, 3, 4, 8, 9), and we want an algorithm for finding it.

First, let us concentrate on the algorithm for finding the longest subsequence. Later, we can try printing the sequence itself by tracing the table. Our first step is finding the recursive formula. First, let us create the base conditions. If there is only one element in the input sequence then we don't have to solve the problem and we just need to return that element. For any sequence we can start with the first element ($A[1]$). Since we know the first number in the LIS, let's find the second number ($A[2]$). If $A[2]$ is larger than $A[1]$ then include $A[2]$ also. Otherwise, we are done – the LIS is the one element sequence ($A[1]$).

Now, let us generalize the discussion and decide about $i^{th}$ element. Let $L(i)$ represent the optimal subsequence which is starting at position $A[1]$ and ending at $A[i]$. The optimal way to obtain a strictly increasing subsequence ending at position $i$ is to extend some subsequence starting at some earlier position $j$. For this the recursive formula can be written as:

$$L(i) = Max_{j<i \text{ and } A[j]<A[i]}\{L(j)\} + 1$$

The above recurrence says that we have to select some earlier position $j$ which gives the maximum sequence. The 1 in the recursive formula indicates the addition of $i^{th}$ element.

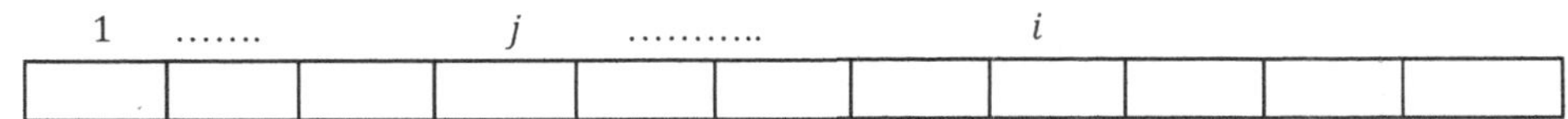


Now after finding the maximum sequence for all positions we have to select the one among all positions which gives the maximum sequence and it is defined as:

$$Max_i\{L(i)\}$$

```
int LISTable [1024];
int LongestIncreasingSequence( int A[], int n ) {
    int i, j, max = 0;
    for ( i = 0; i < n; i++ )
            LISTable[i] = 1;
```

```
    for ( i = 0; i< n; i++ ) {
        for ( j = 0; j < i; j++ ) {
            if( A[i] > A[j] && LISTable[i] < LISTable[j] + 1 )
                LISTable[i] = LISTable[j] + 1;
        }
    }
    for ( i = 0; i < n; i++) {
        if( max < LISTable[i] )
            max = LISTable[i];
    }
    return max;
}
```

Time Complexity: $O(n^2)$, since two *for* loops. Space Complexity: $O(n)$, for table.

Problem-21 **Longest Increasing Subsequence:** In Problem-20, we assumed that $L(i)$ represents the optimal subsequence which is starting at position $A[1]$ and ending at $A[i]$. Now, let us change the definition of $L(i)$ as: $L(i)$ represents the optimal subsequence which is starting at position $A[i]$ and ending at $A[n]$. With this approach can we solve the problem?

**Solution: Yes.**

Let $L(i)$ represent the optimal subsequence which is starting at position $A[i]$ and ending at $A[n]$. The optimal way to obtain a strictly increasing subsequence starting at position $i$ is going to be to extend some subsequence starting at some later position $j$. For this the recursive formula can be written as:

$$L(i) = Max_{i<j \text{ and } A[i]<A[j]}\{L(j)\} + 1$$

We have to select some later position $j$ which gives the maximum sequence. The 1 in the recursive formula is the addition of $i^{th}$ element. After finding the maximum sequence for all positions select the one among all positions which gives the maximum sequence and it is defined as:

$$Max_i\{L(i)\}$$

```
int LISTable [1024];
int LongestIncreasingSequence( int A[], int n ) {
    int i, j, max = 0;
    for ( i = 0; i < n; i++ )
        LISTable[i] = 1;
    for(i = n – 1; i >= 0; i++) {
        // try picking a larger second element
        for( j = i + 1; j < n; j++ ) {
            if( A[i] < A[j] && LISTable [i] < LISTable [j] + 1)
                LISTable[i] = LISTable[j] + 1;
        }
    }
    for ( i = 0; i < n; i++ ) {
        if( max < LISTable[i] )
            max = LISTable[i];
    }
    return max;
}
```

Time Complexity: $O(n^2)$, since two nested *for* loops. Space Complexity: $O(n)$, for table.

Problem-22 Is there an alternative way of solving *Problem-21?*

**Solution: Yes**. The other method is to sort the given sequence and save it into another array and then take out the "Longest Common Subsequence" (LCS) of the two arrays. This method has a complexity of $O(n^2)$. For the LCS problem refer to the *theory section* of this chapter.

Problem-23 **Box Stacking:** Assume that we are given a set of $n$ rectangular $3-D$ boxes. The dimensions of $i^{th}$ box are height $h_i$, width $w_i$ and depth $d_i$. Now we want to create a stack of boxes which is as tall as possible, but we can only stack a box on top of another box if the dimensions of the $2-D$ base of the lower box are each strictly larger than those of the $2-D$ base of the higher box. We can rotate a box so that any side functions as its base. It is possible to use multiple instances of the same type of box.

**Solution:** Box stacking problem can be reduced to LIS *[Problem-21]*.

**Input**: $n$ boxes where $i^{th}$ with height $h_i$, width $w_i$ and depth $d_i$. For all $n$ boxes we have to consider all the orientations with respect to rotation. That is, if we have, in the original set, a box with dimensions $1 \times 2 \times 3$, then we consider 3 boxes,

$$1 \times 2 \times 3 \Longrightarrow \begin{cases} 1 \times (2 \times 3), with\ height\ 1, base\ 2\ and\ width\ 3 \\ 2 \times (1 \times 3), with\ height\ 2, base\ 1\ and\ width\ 3 \\ 3 \times (1 \times 2), with\ height\ 3, base\ 1\ and\ width\ 2 \end{cases}$$

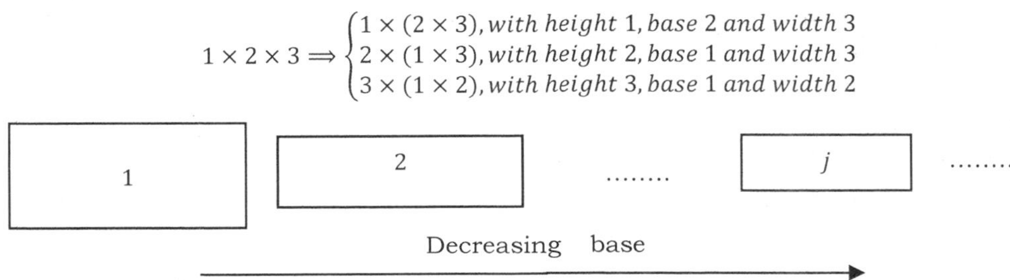


This simplification allows us to forget about the rotations of the boxes and we just focus on the stacking of n boxes with each height as $h_i$ and a base area of $(w_i \times d_i)$. Also assume that $w_i \le d_i$. Now what we do is, make a stack of boxes that is as tall as possible and has maximum height. We allow a box $i$ on top of box $j$ only if box $i$ is smaller than box $j$ in both the dimensions. That means, if $w_i < w_j$ && $d_i < d_j$. Now let us solve this using DP. First select the boxes in the order of decreasing base area.

Now, let us say $H(j)$ represents the tallest stack of boxes with box $j$ on top. This is very similar to the LIS problem because the stack of $n$ boxes with ending box $j$ is equal to finding a subsequence with the first $j$ boxes due to the sorting by decreasing base area. The order of the boxes on the stack is going to be equal to the order of the sequence.

Now we can write $H(j)$ recursively. In order to form a stack which ends on box $j$, we need to extend a previous stack ending at $i$. That means, we need to put $j$ box at the top of the stack [$i$ box is the current top of the stack]. To put $j$ box at the top of the stack we should satisfy the condition $w_i > w_j and\ d_i > d_j$ [this ensures that the low level box has more base than the boxes above it]. Based on this logic, we can write the recursive formula as:

$$H(j) = Max_{i<j\ and\ w_i>w_j and\ d_i>d_j} \{H(i)\} + h_i$$

Similar to the LIS problem, at the end we have to select the best $j$ over all potential values. This is because we are not sure which box might end up on top.

$$Max_j\{H(j)\}$$

Time Complexity: $O(n^2)$.

Problem-24 **Building Bridges in India:** Consider a very long, straight river which moves from north to south. Assume there are $n$ cities on both sides of the river: $n$ cities on the left of the river and $n$ cities on the right side of the river. Also, assume that these cities are numbered from 1 to $n$ but the order is not known. Now we want to connect as many left-right pairs of cities as possible with bridges such that no two bridges cross. When connecting cities, we can only connect city $i$ on the left side to city $i$ on the right side.

**Solution:**

**Input**: Two pairs of sets with each numbered from 1 to $n$.

**Goal**: Construct as many bridges as possible without any crosses between the cities on the left side of the river and the cities on the right side.

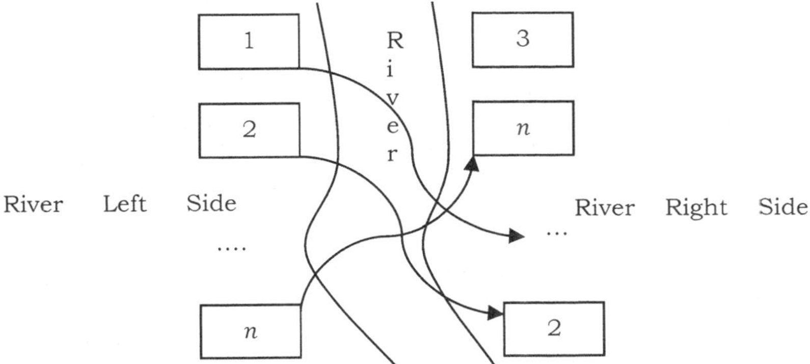


To understand better let us consider the diagram below. In the diagram it can be seen that there are $n$ cities on the left side of river and $n$ cities on the right side of river. Also, note that we are connecting the cities which have the same number [a requirement in the problem]. Our goal is to connect the maximum cities on the left side of river to cities on the right side of the river, without any cross edges. Just to make it simple, let us sort the cities on one side of the river.

If we observe carefully, since the cities on the left side are already sorted, the problem can be simplified to finding the maximum increasing sequence. That means we have to use the LIS solution for finding the maximum increasing sequence on the right side cities of the river.

Time Complexity: $O(n^2)$, *(same as LIS)*.

Problem-25 **Subset Sum:** Given a sequence of $n$ positive numbers $A_1 \ldots A_n$, give an algorithm which checks whether there exists a subset of $A$ whose sum of all numbers is $T$?

**Solution:** This is a variation of the Knapsack problem. As an example, consider the following array:

$$A = [3, 2, 4, 19, 3, 7, 13, 10, 6, 11]$$

Suppose we want to check whether there is any subset whose sum is 17. The answer is yes, because the sum of $4 + 13 = 17$ and therefore $\{4, 13\}$ is such a subset.

Let us try solving this problem using DP. We will define $n \times T$ matrix, where $n$ is the number of elements in our input array and $T$ is the sum we want to check.

Let, $M[i,j] = 1$ if it is possible to find a subset of the numbers 1 through $i$ that produce sum $j$ and $M[i,j] = 0$ otherwise.

$$M[i,j] = Max(M[i - 1,j], M[i - 1,j - A_i])$$

According to the above recursive formula similar to the Knapsack problem, we check if we can get the sum $j$ by not including the element $i$ in our subset, and we check if we can get the sum $j$ by including $i$ and checking if the sum $j - A_i$ exists without the $i^{th}$ element. This is identical to Knapsack, except that we are storing 0/1's instead of values. In the below implementation we can use binary OR operation to get the maximum among $M[i - 1,j]$ and $M[i - 1,j - A_i]$.

```
int SubsetSum( int A[], int n, int T ) {
    int i, j, M[n+1][T +1];
    M[0][0]=0;
    for (i=1; i<= T; i++)
        M[0][i]= 0;
    for (i=1; i<=n; i++) {
        for (j = 0; j<= T; j++) {
            M[i][j] = M[i-1][j] || M[i-1][j - A[i]];
        }
    }
    return M[n][T];
}
```

**How many subproblems are there?** In the above formula, $i$ can range from $1$ *to* $n$ and $j$ can range from $1$ *to* $T$. There are a total of $nT$ subproblems and each one takes O(1). So the time complexity is $O(nT)$ and this is not polynomial as the running time depends on two variables [$n$ and $T$], and we can see that they are an exponential function of the other.

Space Complexity: $O(nT)$.

Problem-26 Given a set of $n$ integers and the sum of all numbers is at most $K$. Find the subset of these $n$ elements whose sum is exactly half of the total sum of $n$ numbers.

**Solution:** Assume that the numbers are $A_1 \ldots A_n$. Let us use DP to solve this problem. We will create a boolean array $T$ with size equal to $K + 1$. Assume that $T[x]$ is 1 if there exists a subset of given $n$ elements whose sum is $x$. That means, after the algorithm finishes, $T[K]$ will be 1, if and only if there is a subset of the numbers that has sum $K$. Once we have that value then we just need to return $T[K/2]$. If it is 1, then there is a subset that adds up to half the total sum.

Initially we set all values of $T$ to 0. Then we set $T[0]$ to 1. This is because we can always build 0 by taking an empty set. If we have no numbers in $A$, then we are done! Otherwise, we pick the first number, $A[0]$. We can either throw it away or take it into our subset. This means that the new $T[]$ should have $T[0]$ and $T[A[0]]$ set to 1. This creates the base case. We continue by taking the next element of $A$.

Suppose that we have already taken care of the first i – 1 elements of A. Now we take A[i] and look at our table T[]. After processing i – 1 elements, the array T has a 1 in every location that corresponds to a sum that we can make from the numbers we have already processed. Now we add the new number, A[i]. What should the table look like? First of all, we can simply ignore A[i]. That means, no one should disappear from T[] – we can still make all those sums. Now consider some location of T[j] that has a 1 in it. It corresponds to some subset of the previous numbers that add up to j. If we add A[i] to that subset, we will get a new subset with total sum j + A[i]. So we should set T[j + A[i]] to 1 as well. That's all. Based on the above discussion, we can write the algorithm as:

```
bool T[10240];
bool SubsetHalfSum( int  A[], int n ) {
    int K = 0;
    for( int i = 0; i < n; i++ )
            K += A[i];
    T[0] = 1;          // initialize the table
    for( int i = 1; i <= K; i++ )
            T[i] = 0;
    // process the numbers one by one
    for( int i = 0; i < n; i++ ) {
            for( int j = K - A[i]; j >= 0; j--)      {
                    if( T[j] )
                            T[j + A[i]] = 1;
            }
    }
    return T[K / 2];
}
```

In the above code, $j$ loop moves from right to left. This reduces the double counting problem. That means, if we move from left to right, then we may do the repeated calculations.

Time Complexity: $O(nK)$, for the two *for* loops. Space Complexity: $O(K)$, for the boolean table $T$.

Problem-27 Can we improve the performance of Problem-26?

**Solution: Yes**. In the above code what we are doing is, the inner $j$ loop is starting from $K$ and moving left. That means, it is unnecessarily scanning the whole table every time.
What we actually want is to find all the 1 entries. At the beginning, only the $0^{th}$ entry is 1. If we keep the location of the rightmost 1 entry in a variable, we can always start at that spot and go left instead of starting at the right end of the table.

To take full advantage of this, we can sort $A[]$ first. That way, the rightmost 1 entry will move to the right as slowly as possible. Finally, we don't really care about what happens in the right half of the table (after $T[K/2]$) because if $T[x]$ is 1, then $T[Kx]$ must also be 1 eventually – it corresponds to the complement of the subset that gave us $x$. The code based on above discussion is given below.

```
int T[10240];
int SubsetHalfSumEfficient( int  A[], int n ) {
    int K = 0;
    for( int i = 0; i < n; i++ )
            K += A[i];
    sort(A,n));
    T[0] = 1;          // initialize the table
    for( int i = 1; i <= sum; i++ )
        T[i] = 0;
    int R = 0; // rightmost 1 entry
    for( int i = 0; i < n; i++)  {          // process the numbers one by one
        for( int j = R; j >= 0; j--) {
            if( T[j] )
                T[j + A[i]] = 1;
                R = min(K / 2, R + C[i] );
        }
    }
    return T[K / 2];
}
```

After the improvements, the time complexity is still $O(nK)$, but we have removed some useless steps.

Problem-28 The partition problem is to determine whether a given set can be partitioned into two subsets such that the sum of elements in both subsets is the same [the same as the previous problem but a different way of asking]. For example, if A[] = {1, 5, 11, 5}, the array can be partitioned as {1, 5, 5} and {11}. Similarly, if A[] = {1, 5, 3}, the array cannot be partitioned into equal sum sets.

**Solution:** Let us try solving this problem another way. Following are the two main steps to solve this problem:

1. Calculate the sum of the array. If the sum is odd, there cannot be two subsets with an equal sum, so return false.
2. If the sum of the array elements is even, calculate $sum/2$ and find a subset of the array with a sum equal to $sum/2$.

The first step is simple. The second step is crucial, and it can be solved either using recursion or Dynamic Programming.

**Recursive Solution**: Following is the recursive property of the second step mentioned above. Let subsetSum(A, n, sum/2) be the function that returns true if there is a subset of A[0..n-1] with sum equal to $sum/2$. The isSubsetSum problem can be divided into two sub problems:

a) isSubsetSum() without considering last element (reducing $n$ to $n - 1$)
b) isSubsetSum considering the last element (reducing sum/2 by A[n-1] and $n$ to $n - 1$)

If any of the above sub problems return true, then return true.

$$subsetSum\ (A, n, sum/2)\ =\ isSubsetSum\ (A, n-1, sum/2)\ ||\ subsetSum\ (A, n-1, sum/2\ -\ A[n-1])$$

```
// A utility function that returns true if there is a subset of A[] with sum equal to given sum
bool subsetSum(int A[], int n, int sum){
    if (sum == 0)
      return true;
    if (n == 0 && sum != 0)
      return false;
    // If last element is greater than sum, then ignore it
    if (A[n-1] > sum)
      return subsetSum (A, n-1, sum);
    return subsetSum (A, n-1, sum) || subsetSum (A, n-1, sum-A[n-1]);
}
// Returns true if A[] can be partitioned in two subsets of equal sum, otherwise false
bool findPartition(int A[], int n){
     // Calculate sum of all elements
     int sum = 0;
     for (int i = 0; i < n; i++)
        sum += A[i];
     // If sum is odd, there cannot be two subsets with equal sum
     if (sum%2 != 0)
        return false;
     // Find if there is subset with sum equal to half of total sum
     return subsetSum(A, n, sum/2);
}
```

Time Complexity: $O(2^n)$ In worst case, this solution tries two possibilities (whether to include or exclude) for every element.

**Dynamic Programming Solution**: The problem can be solved using dynamic programming when the sum of the elements is not too big. We can create a 2D array $part[][]$ of size $(sum/2)*(n + 1)$. And we can construct the solution in a bottom-up manner such that every filled entry has a following property

$$part[i][j]\ =\ true\ if\ a\ subset\ of\ \{A[0], A[1], .. A[j-1]\}\ has\ sum\ equal\ to\ sum/2, otherwise\ false$$

```
// Returns true if A[] can be partitioned in two subsets of equal sum, otherwise false
bool findPartition (int A[], int n){
    int sum = 0;
    int i, j;
    // calculate sum of all elements
    for (i = 0; i < n; i++)
      sum += A[i];
    if (sum%2 != 0)
      return false;
    bool part[sum/2+1][n+1];
    // initialize top row as true
    for (i = 0; i <= n; i++)
      part[0][i] = true;
    // initialize leftmost column, except part[0][0], as 0
    for (i = 1; i <= sum/2; i++)
```

```
        part[i][0] = false;
    // Fill the partition table in bottom up manner
    for (i = 1; i <= sum/2; i++) {
        for (j = 1; j <= n; j++) {
            part[i][j] = part[i][j-1];
            if (i >= A[j-1])
                part[i][j] = part[i][j] || part[i - A[j-1]][j-1];
        }
    }
    return part[sum/2][n];
}
```

Time Complexity: $O(sum \times n)$. Space Complexity: $O(sum \times n)$. Please note that this solution will not be feasible for arrays with a big sum.

Problem-29 **Counting Boolean Parenthesizations:** Let us assume that we are given a boolean expression consisting of symbols $'true', 'false', 'and', 'or', and\ 'xor'$. Find the number of ways to parenthesize the expression such that it will evaluate to $true$. For example, there is only 1 way to parenthesize $'true\ and\ false\ xor\ true'$ such that it evaluates to $true$.

**Solution:** Let the number of symbols be n and between symbols there are boolean operators like and, or, xor, etc. For example, if $n = 4$, $T\ or\ F\ and\ T\ xor\ F$. Our goal is to count the numbers of ways to parenthesize the expression with boolean operators so that it evaluates to $true$. In the above case, if we use $T\ or\ ((F\ and\ T)\ xor\ F)$ then it evaluates to true.

$$T\ or(\ (F\ and\ T) xor\ F) = True$$

Now let us see how DP solves this problem. Let $T(i,j)$ represent the number of ways to parenthesize the sub expression with symbols $i \dots j$ [symbols means only $T$ and $F$ and not the operators] with boolean operators so that it evaluates to $true$. Also, $i$ and $j$ take the values from 1 to $n$. For example, in the above case, $T(2,4) = 0$ because there is no way to parenthesize the expression $F\ and\ T\ xor\ F$ to make it $true$.

Just for simplicity and similarity, let $F(i,j)$ represent the number of ways to parenthesize the sub expression with symbols $i \dots j$ with boolean operators so that it evaluates to $false$. The base cases are $T(i,i)$ and $F(i,i)$.

Now we are going to compute $T(i, i+1)$ and $F(i, i+1)$ for all values of $i$. Similarly, $T(i, i+2)$ and $F(i, i+2)$ for all values of $i$ and so on. Now let's generalize the solution.

$$T(i,j) = \sum_{k=i}^{j-1} \begin{cases} T(i,k)T(k+1,j), & for\ "and" \\ Total(i,k)Total(k+1,j) - F(i,k)F(k+1,j), & for\ "or" \\ T(i,k)F(k+1,j) + F(i,k)T(k+1,j), & for\ "xor" \end{cases}$$

Where, $Total(i,k) = T(i,k) + F(i,k)$.

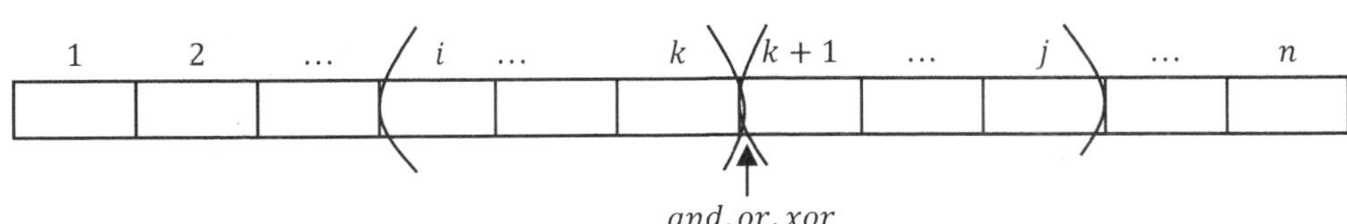


What this above recursive formula says is, $T(i,j)$ indicates the number of ways to parenthesize the expression. Let us assume that we have some sub problems which are ending at $k$. Then the total number of ways to parenthesize from $i\ to\ j$ is the sum of counts of parenthesizing from $i\ to\ k$ and from $k+1\ to\ j$. To parenthesize between $k$ and $k+1$ there are three ways: "$and$", "$or$" and "$xor$".

- If we use "$and$" between $k$ and $k+1$, then the final expression becomes $true$ only when both are $true$. If both are $true$ then we can include them to get the final count.
- If we use "$or$", then if at least one of them is $true$, the result becomes $true$. Instead of including all three possibilities for "$or$", we are giving one alternative where we are subtracting the "false" cases from total possibilities.
- The same is the case with "$xor$". The conversation is as in the above two cases.

After finding all the values we have to select the value of $k$, which produces the maximum count, and for $k$ there are $i\ to\ j-1$ possibilities.

**How many subproblems are there?** In the above formula, $i$ can range from 1 $to$ $n$, and $j$ can range from 1 $to$ $n$. So there are a total of $n^2$ subproblems, and also we are doing summation for all such values. So the time complexity is $O(n^3)$.

Problem-30 **Optimal Binary Search Trees:** Given a set of $n$ (sorted) keys $A[1..n]$, build the best binary search tree for the elements of $A$. Also assume that each element is associated with $frequency$ which indicates the number of times that a particular item is searched in the binary search trees. That means we need to construct a binary search tree so that the total search time will be reduced.

**Solution:** Before solving the problem let us understand the problem with an example. Let us assume that the given array is A = [3, 12, 21, 32, 35]. There are many ways to represent these elements, two of which are listed below.

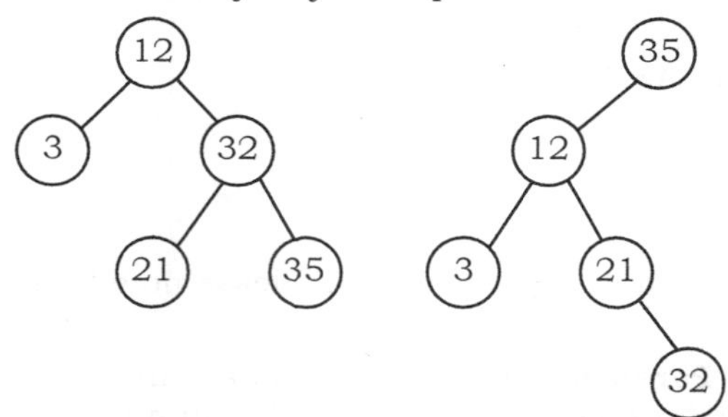


**Of the two, which representation is better?** The search time for an element depends on the depth of the node. The average number of comparisons for the first tree is: $\frac{1+2+2+3+3}{5} = \frac{11}{5}$ and for the second tree, the average number of comparisons is: $\frac{1+2+3+3+4}{5} = \frac{13}{5}$. Of the two, the first tree gives better results.

If frequencies are not given and if we want to search all elements, then the above simple calculation is enough for deciding the best tree. If the frequencies are given, then the selection depends on the frequencies of the elements and also the depth of the elements. An obvious way to find an optimal binary search tree is to generate each possible binary search tree for the keys, calculate the search time, and keep that tree with the smallest total search time. This search through all possible solutions is not feasible, since the number of such trees grows exponentially with $n$.

An alternative would be a recursive algorithm. Consider the characteristics of any optimal tree. Of course it has a root and two subtrees. Both subtrees must themselves be optimal binary search trees with respect to their keys and frequencies. First, any subtree of any binary search tree must be a binary search tree. Second, the subtrees must also be optimal.

For simplicity let us assume that, the given array is $A$ and the corresponding frequencies are in array $F$. $F[i]$ indicates the frequency of $i^{th}$ element $A[i]$. With this, the total search time S(root) of the tree with *root* can be defined as:

$$S(root) = S(r) = \sum_{i=1}^{n} (depth(root, i) + 1) \times F[i])$$

In the above expression, $depth(root, i) + 1$ indicates the number of comparisons for searching the $i^{th}$ element. Since we are trying to create a binary search tree, the left subtree elements are less than root element and the right subtree elements are greater than root element. If we separate the left subtree time and right subtree time, then the above expression can be written as:

$$S(root) = \sum_{i=1}^{r-1} (depth(root, i) + 1) \times F[i] + \sum_{i=1}^{n} F[i] + \sum_{i=r+1}^{n} (depth(root, i) + 1) \times F[i]$$

Where $r$ indicates the position of the root element in the array.

If we replace the left subtree and right subtree times with their corresponding recursive calls, then the expression becomes:

$$S(root) = S(r) = S(root \rightarrow left) + S(root \rightarrow right) + \sum_{i=1}^{n} F[i]$$

Since, $r$ can vary from 1 to $n$, we need to minimize the total search time for the given keys 1 to $n$ considering all possible values for $r$. Let $OBST(1, n)$ is the optimal binary search tree with keys 1 to $n$

$$OBST(1, n) = min_{1 \le r \le n}\{S(r)\}$$
$$OBST(i, i) = F[i]$$

On the similar lines, the optimal binary search tree with keys from $i$ to $j$ can be given as:

$$OBST(i, j) = min_{i \le r \le j}\{S(r)\}$$

**Binary Search Tree node declaration**

Refer to *Trees* chapter.

**Implementation:**

```
    struct BinarySearchTreeNode *OptimalBST(int A[], int F[], int low, int high) {
        int r, minTime = 0;
        struct BinarySearchTreeNode *newNode=(struct BinarySearchTreeNode *) malloc(sizeof(struct
BinarySearchTreeNode));
        if(!newNode) {
            printf("Memory Error");
            return;
        }
        for (r =0, r <= n-1; r++)            {
            root→left = OptimalBST(A, F, low, r-1);
            root→left = OptimalBST(A, F, r+1, high)
            root→data = A[r];
            if(minTime > S(root))
                minTime = S(root);
        }
        return minTime;
    }
```

Problem-31 **Edit Distance:** Given two strings $A$ of length $m$ and $B$ of length $n$, transform $A$ into $B$ with a minimum number of operations of the following types: delete a character from $A$, insert a character into $A$, or change some character in $A$ into a new character. The minimal number of such operations required to transform $A$ into $B$ is called the *edit distance* between $A$ and $B$.

**Solution: Input**: Two text strings $A$ of length $m$ and $B$ of length $n$. **Goal**: Convert string $A$ into $B$ with minimal conversions.

Before going to a solution, let us consider the possible operations for converting string $A$ into $B$.

- If $m > n$, we need to remove some characters of $A$
- If $m == n$, we may need to convert some characters of $A$
- If $m < n$, we need to remove some characters from $A$

So the operations we need are the insertion of a character, the replacement of a character and the deletion of a character, and their corresponding cost codes are defined below.

**Costs of operations:**

| Insertion of a character | $c_i$ |
|---|---|
| Replacement of a character | $c_r$ |
| Deletion of a character | $c_d$ |

Now let us concentrate on the recursive formulation of the problem. Let, $T(i,j)$ represents the minimum cost required to transform first $i$ characters of $A$ to first $j$ characters of $B$. That means, $A[1 ... i]$ to $B[1 ... j]$.

$$T(i,j) = min \begin{cases} c_d + T(i-1,j) \\ T(i,j-1) + c_i \\ \begin{cases} T(i-1,j-1), & if\ A[i] == B[j] \\ T(i-1,j-1) + c_r & if\ A[i] \neq B[j] \end{cases} \end{cases}$$

Based on the above discussion we have the following cases.

- If we delete $i^{th}$ character from $A$, then we have to convert remaining $i-1$ characters of $A$ to $j$ characters of $B$
- If we insert $i^{th}$ character in $A$, then convert these $i$ characters of $A$ to $j-1$ characters of $B$
- If $A[i] == B[j]$, then we have to convert the remaining $i-1$ characters of $A$ to $j-1$ characters of $B$
- If $A[i] \neq B[j]$, then we have to replace $i^{th}$ character of $A$ to $j^{th}$ character of B and convert remaining $i-1$ characters of $A$ to $j-1$ characters of $B$

After calculating all the possibilities we have to select the one which gives the lowest cost.

**How many subproblems are there?** In the above formula, $i$ can range from $1\ to\ m$ and $j$ can range from $1\ to\ n$. This gives $mn$ subproblems and each one takes O(1) and the time complexity is O($mn$). Space Complexity: O($mn$) where $m$ is number of rows and $n$ is number of columns in the given matrix.

Problem-32 **All Pairs Shortest Path Problem: Floyd's Algorithm:** Given a weighted directed graph $G = (V, E)$, where $V = \{1, 2, ..., n\}$. Find the shortest path between any pair of nodes in the graph. Assume the weights are represented in the matrix $C[V][V]$, where $C[i][j]$ indicates the weight (or cost) between the nodes $i$ and $j$. Also, $C[i][j] = \infty$ or -1 if there is no path from node $i$ to node $j$.

**Solution:** Let us try to find the DP solution (Floyd's algorithm) for this problem. The Floyd's algorithm for all pairs shortest path problem uses matrix $A[1..n][1..n]$ to compute the lengths of the shortest paths. Initially,

$$A[i,j] = C[i,j]\ if\ i \neq j$$

$$= 0 \quad if\ i = j$$

From the definition, $C[i,j] = \infty$ if there is no path from $i$ to $j$. The algorithm makes $n$ passes over A. Let $A_0, A_1, ..., A_n$ be the values of $A$ on the $n$ passes, with $A_0$ being the initial value.

Just after the $k-1^{th}$ iteration, $A_{k-1}[i,j]$ = smallest length of any path from vertex $i$ to vertex $j$ that does not pass through the vertices $\{k+1, k+2, .... n\}$. That means, it passes through the vertices possibly through $\{1, 2, 3, ..., k-1\}$.

In each iteration, the value $A[i][j]$ is updated with minimum of $A_{k-1}[i,j]$ and $A_{k-1}[i,k] + A_{k-1}[k,j]$.

$$A[i,j] = \min \begin{cases} A_{k-1}[i,j] \\ A_{k-1}[i,k] + A_{k-1}[k,j] \end{cases}$$

The $k^{th}$ pass explores whether the vertex $k$ lies on an optimal path from $i$ to $j$, for all $i, j$. The same is shown in the diagram below.

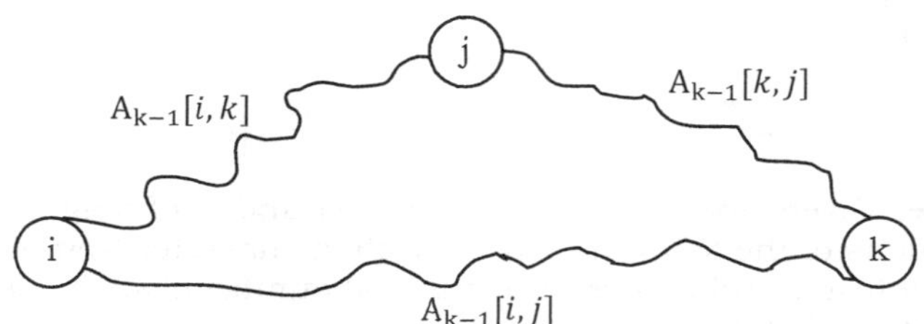


```
void Floyd(int C[][], int A[][], int n) {
    int i, j, k;
    for(i = 0, i <= n - 1;i + +)
        for(j = 0; j <= n - 1, j + +)
            A[i][j] = C[i][j];
    for(i = 0;i <= n - 1;i + +)
        A[i][i] = 0;
    for(k = 0;k <= n - 1;k + +) {
        for(i = 0;i <= n - 1;i + +) {
            for(j = 0;j <= n - 1, j + +)
                if(A[i][k] + A[k][j] < A[i][j])
                    A[i][j] = A[i][k] + A[k][j];
        }
    }
}
```

Time Complexity: $O(n^3)$.

Problem-33 **Optimal Strategy for a Game:** Consider a row of $n$ coins of values $v_1 \ldots v_n$, where $n$ is even [since it's a two player game]. We play this game with the opponent. In each turn, a player selects either the first or last coin from the row, removes it from the row permanently, and receives the value of the coin. Determine the maximum possible amount of money we can definitely win if we move first.

**Alternative way of framing the question:** Given n pots, each with some number of gold coins, are arranged in a line. You are playing a game against another player. You take turns picking a pot of gold. You may pick a pot from either end of the line, remove the pot, and keep the gold pieces. The player with the most gold at the end wins. Develop a strategy for playing this game.

**Solution:** Let us solve the problem using our DP technique. For each turn either we *or* our opponent selects the coin only from the ends of the row. Let us define the subproblems as:

$V(i,j)$: denotes the maximum possible value we can definitely win if it is our turn and the only coins remaining are $v_i \ldots v_j$.

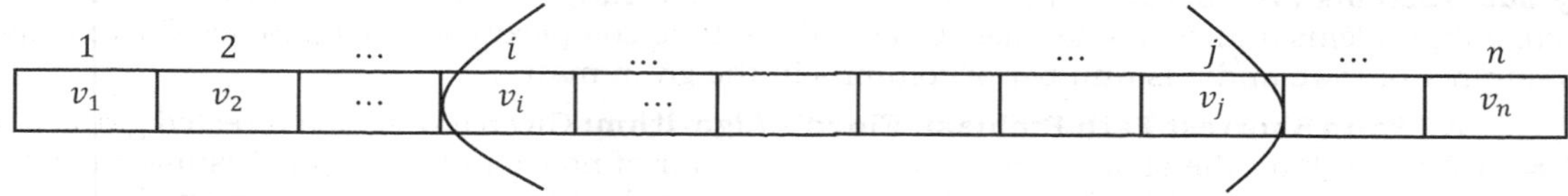


Base Cases: $V(i,i), V(i,i+1)$ for all values of $i$.

From these values, we can compute $V(i,i+2), V(i,i+3)$ and so on. Now let us define $V(i,j)$ for each sub problem as:

$$V(i,j) = Max\left\{Min\begin{Bmatrix} V(i+1,j-1) \\ V(i+2,j) \end{Bmatrix} + v_i, Min\begin{Bmatrix} V(i,j-2) \\ V(i+1,j-1) \end{Bmatrix} + v_j\right\}$$

In the recursive call we have to focus on $i^{th}$ coin to $j^{th}$ coin ($v_i \dots v_j$). Since it is our turn to pick the coin, we have two possibilities: either we can pick $v_i$ or $v_j$. The first term indicates the case if we select $i^{th}$ coin ($v_i$) and the second term indicates the case if we select $j^{th}$ coin ($v_j$). The outer $Max$ indicates that we have to select the coin which gives maximum value. Now let us focus on the terms:

- Selecting $i^{th}$ coin: If we select the $i^{th}$ coin then the remaining range is from $i+1$ $to$ $j$. Since we selected the $i^{th}$ coin we get the value $v_i$ for that. From the remaining range $i+1$ $to$ $j$, the opponents can select either $i+1^{th}$ coin or $j^{th}$ coin. But the opponents selection should be minimized as much as possible [the $Min$ term]. The same is described in the below figure.

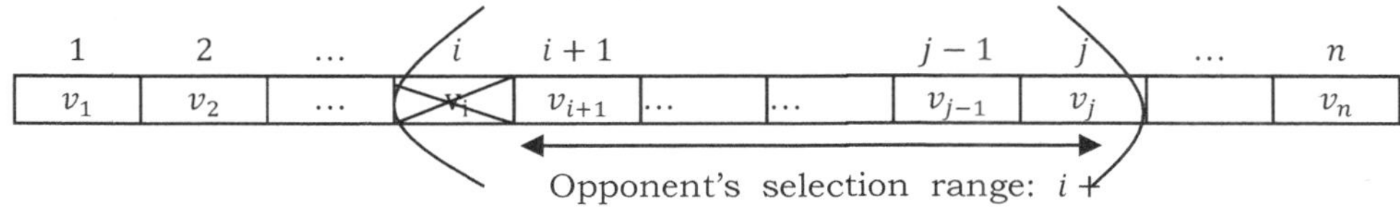


- Selecting the $j^{th}$ coin: Here also the argument is the same as above. If we select the $j^{th}$ coin, then the remaining range is from i to j − 1. Since we selected the $j^{th}$ coin we get the value $v_j$ for that. From the remaining range i to j − 1, the opponent can select either the $i^{th}$ coin or the $j-1^{th}$ coin. But the opponent's selection should be minimized as much as possible [the $Min$ term].

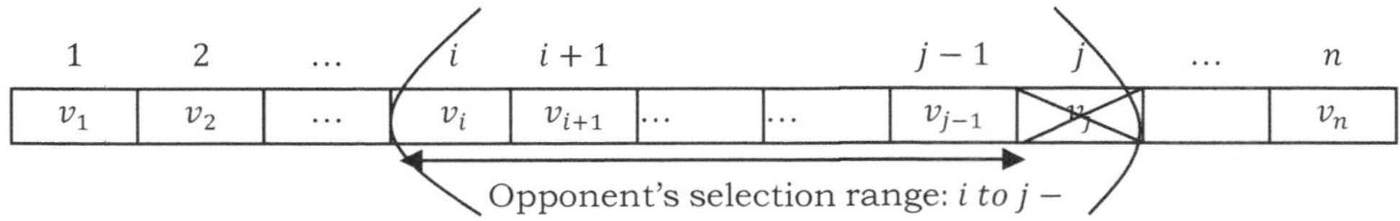


**How many subproblems are there?** In the above formula, $i$ can range from $1$ $to$ $n$ and $j$ can range from $1$ $to$ $n$. There are a total of $n^2$ subproblems and each takes O(1) and the total time complexity is O($n^2$).

Problem-34 **Tiling:** Assume that we use dominoes measuring $2 \times 1$ to tile an infinite strip of height 2. How many ways can one tile a $2 \times n$ strip of square cells with $1 \times 2$ dominoes?

**Solution:** Notice that we can place tiles either vertically or horizontally. For placing vertical tiles, we need a gap of at least $2 \times 2$. For placing horizontal tiles, we need a gap of $2 \times 1$. In this manner, the problem is reduced to finding the number of ways to partition $n$ using the numbers 1 and 2 with order considered relevant [1]. For example: $11 = 1 + 2 + 2 + 1 + 2 + 2 + 1$.

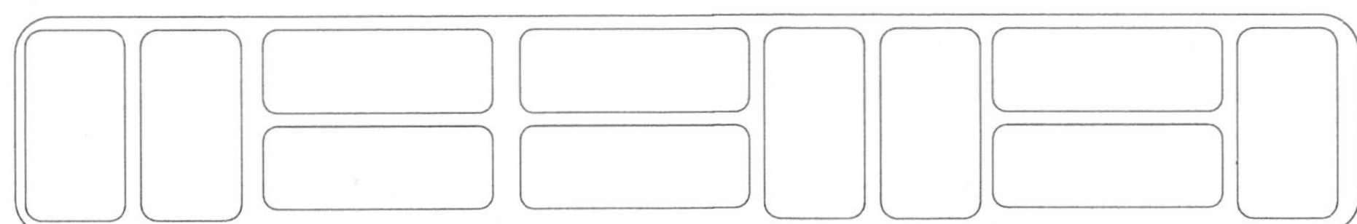

If we have to find such arrangements for 12, we can either place a 1 at the end or we can add 2 in the arrangements possible with 10. Similarly, let us say we have $F_n$ possible arrangements for n. Then for $(n+1)$, we can either place just 1 at the end $or$ we can find possible arrangements for $(n-1)$ and put a 2 at the end. Going by the above theory:

$$F_{n+1} = F_n + F_{n-1}$$

Let's verify the above theory for our original problem:

- In how many ways can we fill a $2 \times 1$ strip: $1 \rightarrow$ Only one vertical tile.
- In how many ways can we fill a $2 \times 2$ strip: $2 \rightarrow$ Either 2 horizontal or 2 vertical tiles.
- In how many ways can we fill a $2 \times 3$ strip: $3 \rightarrow$ Either put a vertical tile in the 2 solutions possible for a $2 \times 2$ strip, or put 2 horizontal tiles in the only solution possible for a $2 \times 1$ strip. $(2 + 1 = 3)$.
- Similarly, in how many ways can we fill a $2 \times n$ strip: Either put a vertical tile in the solutions possible for $2\ X\ (n-1)$ strip or put 2 horizontal tiles in the solution possible for a $2 \times (n-2)$ strip. $(F_{n-1} + F_{n-2})$.
- That's how we verified that our final solution is: $F_n = F_{n-1} + F_{n-2}$ with $F_1 = 1$ and $F_2 = 2$.

Problem-35 **Longest Palindrome Subsequence:** A sequence is a palindrome if it reads the same whether we read it left to right or right to left. For example $A, C, G, G, G, G, C, A$. Given a sequence of length $n$, devise an algorithm to output the length of the longest palindrome subsequence. For example, the string

$A,G,C,T,C,B,M,A,A,C,T,G,G,A,M$ has many palindromes as subsequences, for instance: $A,G,T,C,M,C,T,G,A$ has length 9.

**Solution:** Let us use DP to solve this problem. If we look at the sub-string A[i,..,j] of the string $A$, then we can find a palindrome sequence of length at least 2 if A[i] == A[j]. If they are not the same, then we have to find the maximum length palindrome in subsequences A[i + 1,...,j] and A[i,...,j – 1]. Also, every character $A[i]$ is a palindrome of length 1. Therefore the base cases are given by $A[i,i]$ = 1. Let us define the maximum length palindrome for the substring A[i,...,j] as L(i,j).

$$L(i,j) = \begin{cases} L(i+1,j-1)+2, & if\ A[i] == A[j] \\ Max\{L(i+1,j), L(i,j-1)\}, & otherwise \end{cases}$$

$$L(i,i) = 1 \text{ for all } i = 1\ to\ n$$

```
int longestPalindromeSubsequence(int A[], int n) {
    int max = 1;
    int i,k, L[n][ n];
    for (i = 1; i<= n -1; i++) {
        L[i][i] =1;
        if(A[i]==A[i+1]) {
            L[i][i + 1] = 1;
            max = 2;
        }
        else
            L[i][i + 1] = 0;
    }
    for (k=3;k<= n;k++) {
        for (i = 1;i <= n-k +1; i++) {
            j = i + k - 1;
            if(A[i] == A[j])    {
                L[i, j] = 2 + L[i + 1][j - 1];
                max = k;
            }
            else
                L[i, j] = max(L[i + 1][j - 1], L[i][j - 1]);
        }
    }
    return max;
}
```

Time Complexity: First *for* loop takes O($n$) time while the second 'for' loop takes O($n - k$) which is also O($n$). Therefore, the total running time of the algorithm is given by O($n^2$).

Problem-36 **Longest Palindrome Substring:** Given a string $A$, we need to find the longest sub-string of $A$ such that the reverse of it is exactly the same.

**Solution:** The basic difference between the longest palindrome substring and the longest palindrome subsequence is that, in the case of the longest palindrome substring, the output string should be the contiguous characters, which gives the maximum palindrome; and in the case of the longest palindrome subsequence, the output is the sequence of characters where the characters might not be contiguous but they should be in an increasing sequence with respect to their positions in the given string.

Brute-force solution exhaustively checks all $n\,(n+1)/2$ possible substrings of the given n-length string, tests each one if it's a palindrome, and keeps track of the longest one seen so far. This has worst-case complexity O($n^3$), but we can easily do better by realizing that a palindrome is centered on either a letter (for odd-length palindromes) or a space between letters (for even-length palindromes). Therefore we can examine all $n + 1$ possible centers and find the longest palindrome for that center, keeping track of the overall longest palindrome. This has worst-case complexity O($n^2$).

Let us use DP to solve this problem. It is worth noting that there are no more than O($n^2$) substrings in a string of length $n$ (while there are exactly $2^n$ subsequences). Therefore, we could scan each substring, check for a palindrome, and update the length of the longest palindrome substring discovered so far. Since the palindrome test takes time linear in the length of the substring, this idea takes $O(n^3)$ algorithm. We can use DP to improve this. For $1 \le i \le j \le n$, define

$$L(i,j) = \begin{cases} 1, & if\ A[i] \ldots . A[j] \text{ is a palindrome substring,} \\ 0, & \text{otherwise} \end{cases}$$

$$L[i,i] = 1,$$

$$L[i,j] = L[i,i+1], if\ A[i] == A[i+1], for\ 1 \le i \le j \le n-1$$

Also, for string of length at least 3,

$$L[i,j] = (L[i + 1, j - 1] \; and \; A[i] = A[j])$$

Note that in order to obtain a well-defined recurrence, we need to explicitly initialize two distinct diagonals of the boolean array $L[i,j]$, since the recurrence for entry $[i,j]$ uses the value $[i - 1, j - 1]$, which is two diagonals away from $[i,j]$ (that means, for a substring of length $k$, we need to know the status of a substring of length $k - 2$).

```
int longestPalindromeSubstring(int A[], int n) {
    int max = 1;
    int i,k, L[n][n];
    for (i = 1; i<=n-1; i++) {
        L[i][i] =1;
        if(A[i]==A[i+1]) {
            L[i][i + 1] = 1;
            max = 2;
        }
        else
            L[i][i + 1] = 0;
    }
    for (k=3;k<=n;k++) {
        for (i = 1;i <= n-k +1; i++) {
            j = i + k - 1;
            if(A[i] == A[j] && L[i + 1][j - 1]) {
                L[i][j] = 1;
                max = k;
            }
            else
                L[i][j] = 0;
        }
    }
    return max;
}
```

Time Complexity: First for loop takes $O(n)$ time while the second for loop takes $O(n - k)$ which is also $O(n)$. Therefore the total running time of the algorithm is given by $O(n^2)$.

Problem-37 Given two strings $S$ and $T$, give an algorithm to find the number of times $S$ appears in $T$. It's not compulsory that all characters of S should appear contiguous to $T$. For example, if $S = ab$ and $T = abadcb$ then the solution is 4, because $ab$ is appearing 4 times in $abadcb$.

**Solution:** **Input**: Given two strings $S[1..m]$ and $T[1 ... m]$. **Goal**: Count the number of times that $S$ appears in $T$.

Assume $L(i,j)$ represents the count of how many times $i$ characters of $S$ are appearing in $j$ characters of $T$.

$$L(i,j) = Max \begin{cases} 0, & if \; j = 0 \\ 1, & if \; i = 0 \\ L(i-1, j-1) + L(i, j-1), & if \; S[i] == T[j] \\ L(i-1, j), & if \; S[i] \neq T[j] \end{cases}$$

If we concentrate on the components of the above recursive formula,

- If $j = 0$, then since $T$ is empty the count becomes 0.
- If $i = 0$, then we can treat empty string $S$ also appearing in $T$ and we can give the count as 1.
- If S[i] == T[j], it means $i^{th}$ character of $S$ and $j^{th}$ character of $T$ are the same. In this case we have to check the subproblems with $i - 1$ characters of S and $j - 1$ characters of $T$ and also we have to count the result of $i$ characters of $S$ with $j - 1$ characters of $T$. This is because even all $i$ characters of $S$ might be appearing in $j - 1$ characters of $T$.
- If S[i] ≠ T[j], then we have to get the result of subproblem with $i - 1$ characters of $S$ and $j$ characters of $T$.

After computing all the values, we have to select the one which gives the maximum count.

**How many subproblems are there?** In the above formula, $i$ can range from $1 \; to \; m$ and $j$ can range from $1 \; to \; n$. There are a total of $mn$ subproblems and each one takes $O(1)$. Time Complexity is $O(mn)$.
Space Complexity: $O(mn)$ where $m$ is number of rows and $n$ is number of columns in the given matrix.

Problem-38 Given a matrix with $n$ rows and $m$ columns ($n \times m$). In each cell there are a number of apples. We start from the upper-left corner of the matrix. We can go down or right one cell. Finally, we need to arrive at the bottom-right corner. Find the maximum number of apples that we can collect. When we pass through a cell, we collect all the apples left there.

**Solution:** Let us assume that the given matrix is $A[n][m]$. The first thing that must be observed is that there are at most 2 ways we can come to a cell - from the left (if it's not situated on the first column) and from the top (if it's not situated on the most upper row).

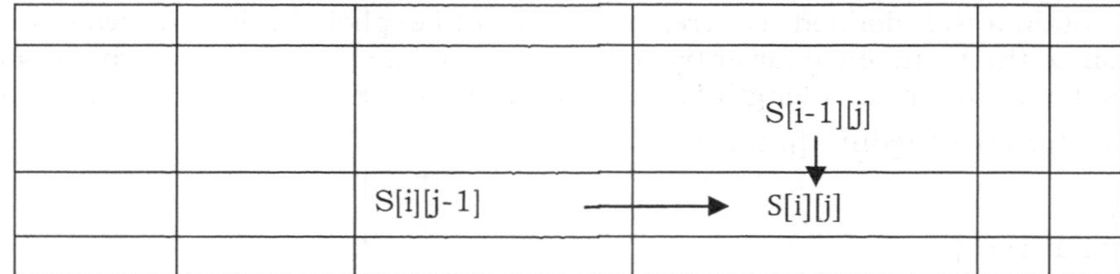


To find the best solution for that cell, we have to have already found the best solutions for all of the cells from which we can arrive to the current cell. From above, a recurrent relation can be easily obtained as:

$$S(i,j) = \left\{A[i][j] + Max\begin{cases} S(i,j-1), & if\ j > 0 \\ S(i-1,j), & if\ i > 0 \end{cases}\right\}$$

$S(i,j)$ must be calculated by going first from left to right in each row and process the rows from top to bottom, or by going first from top to bottom in each column and process the columns from left to right.

```
int findApplesCount(int A[][], int n, int m) {
    int S[n][m];
    for( int i = 1;i<=n;i++) {
            for(int j = 1;i<=m;j++) {
                S[i][j] = A[i][j];
                if(j>0 && S[i][j] < S[i][j] + S[i][j-1])
                    S[i][j] += S[i][j-1];
                if(i>0 && S[i][j] < S[i][j] + S[i-1][j])
                    S[i][j] +=S[i-1][j];
            }
    }
    return S[n][m];
}
```

**How many such subproblems are there?** In the above formula, $i$ can range from $1$ *to* $n$ and $j$ can range from $1$ *to* $m$. There are a total of $nm$ subproblems and each one takes O(1).

Time Complexity is O($nm$). Space Complexity: O($nm$), where $m$ is number of rows and $n$ is number of columns in the given matrix.

Problem-39 Similar to Problem-38, assume that we can go down, right one cell, or even in a diagonal direction. We need to arrive at the bottom-right corner. Give DP solution to find the maximum number of apples we can collect.

**Solution: Yes.** The discussion is very similar to Problem-38. Let us assume that the given matrix is A[n][m]. The first thing that must be observed is that there are at most 3 ways we can come to a cell - from the left, from the top (if it's not situated on the uppermost row) or from the top diagonal. To find the best solution for that cell, we have to have already found the best solutions for all of the cells from which we can arrive to the current cell. From above, a recurrent relation can be easily obtained:

$$S(i,j) = \left\{A[i][j] + Max\begin{cases} S(i,j-1), & if\ j > 0 \\ S(i-1,j), & if\ i > 0 \\ S(i-1,j-1), if\ i > 0\ and\ j > 0 \end{cases}\right\}$$

$S(i,j)$ must be calculated by going first from left to right in each row and process the rows from top to bottom, or by going first from top to bottom in each column and process the columns from left to right.

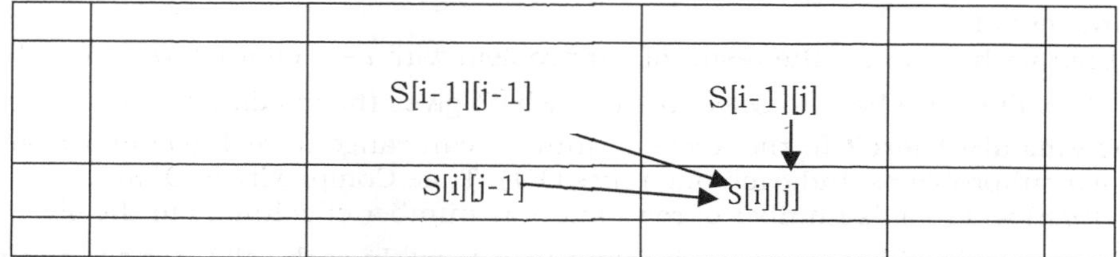


**How many such subproblems are there?** In the above formula, $i$ can range from 1 to $n$ and $j$ can range from 1 *to* $m$. There are a total of $nm$ subproblems and and each one takes O(1). Time Complexity is O($nm$).
Space Complexity: O($nm$) where $m$ is number of rows and $n$ is number of columns in the given matrix.

Problem-40 **Maximum size square sub-matrix with all 1's:** Given a matrix with 0's and 1's, give an algorithm for finding the maximum size square sub-matrix with all 1s. For example, consider the binary matrix below.

```
0 1 1 0 1
1 1 0 1 0
0 1 1 1 0
1 1 1 1 0
1 1 1 1 1
0 0 0 0 0
```

The maximum square sub-matrix with all set bits is

```
1 1 1
1 1 1
1 1 1
```

**Solution:** Let us try solving this problem using DP. Let the given binary matrix be $B[m][m]$. The idea of the algorithm is to construct a temporary matrix $L[\,][\,]$ in which each entry $L[i][j]$ represents size of the square sub-matrix with all $1's$ including $B[i][j]$ and $B[i][j]$ is the rightmost and bottom-most entry in the sub-matrix.

**Algorithm**

1) Construct a sum matrix $L[m][n]$ for the given matrix $B[m][n]$.
   a. Copy first row and first columns as is from $B[\,][\,]$ to $L[\,][\,]$.
   b. For other entries, use the following expressions to construct L[ ][ ]
      if($B[i][j]$ )
         $L[i][j] = min(L[i][j-1], L[i-1][j], L[i-1][j-1]) + 1;$
      else $L[i][j] = 0;$
2) Find the maximum entry in $L[m][n]$.
3) Using the value and coordinates of maximum entry in $L[i]$, print sub-matrix of $B[\,][\,]$.

```
void MatrixSubSquareWithAllOnes(int B[][], int m, int n) {
    int i, j, L[m][n], max_of_s, max_i, max_j;
    // Setting first column of L[][]
    for(i = 0; i < m; i++)
            L[i][0] = B[i][0];
    // Setting first row of L[][]
    for(j = 0; j < n; j++)
            L[0][j] = B[0][j];
    // Construct other entries of L[][]
    for(i = 1; i < m; i++) {
            for(j = 1; j < n; j++) {
                    if(B[i][j] == 1)
                            L[i][j] = min(L[i][j-1], L[i-1][j], L[i-1][j-1]) + 1;
                    else    L[i][j] = 0;
            }
    }
    max_of_s = L[0][0]; max_i = 0; max_j = 0;
    for(i = 0; i < m i++) {
            for(j = 0; j < n; j++) {
                    if(L[i][j] > max_of_s){
                        max_of_s = L[i][j];
                        max_i = i;
                        max_j = j;
                    }
            }
    }
    printf("Maximum sub-matrix");
    for(i = max_i; i > max_i - max_of_s; i--) {
            for(j = max_j; j > max_j - max_of_s; j--)
                    printf("%d",B[i][j]);
    }
}
```

**How many subproblems are there?** In the above formula, $i$ can range from 1 to $n$ and $j$ can range from 1 to $m$. There are a total of $nm$ subproblems and each one takes O(1). Time Complexity is O($nm$). Space Complexity is O($nm$), where $n$ is number of rows and $m$ is number of columns in the given matrix.

**Problem-41** **Maximum size sub-matrix with all 1's:** Given a matrix with 0's and 1's, give an algorithm for finding the maximum size sub-matrix with all 1s. For example, consider the binary matrix below.

```
1 1 0 0 1 0
0 1 1 1 1 1
1 1 1 1 1 0
0 0 1 1 0 0
```

The maximum sub-matrix with all set bits is

```
1 1 1 1
1 1 1 1
```

**Solution:** If we draw a histogram of all $1's$ cells in the above rows for a particular row, then maximum all $1's$ sub-matrix ending in that row will be equal to maximum area rectangle in that histogram. Below is an example for $3^{rd}$row in the above discussed matrix [1]:

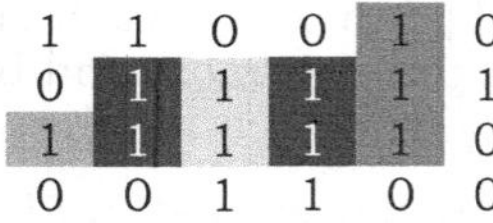


If we calculate this area for all the rows, maximum area will be our answer. We can extend our solution very easily to find start and end co-ordinates. For this, we need to generate an auxiliary matrix $S[][]$ where each element represents the number of 1s above and including it, up until the first 0. $S[][]$ for the above matrix will be as shown below:

```
1 1 0 0 1 0
0 2 1 1 2 1
1 3 2 2 3 0
0 0 3 3 0 0
```

Now we can simply call our maximum rectangle in histogram on every row in $S[][]$ and update the maximum area every time. Also we don't need any extra space for saving $S$. We can update original matrix ($A$) to $S$ and after calculation, we can convert $S$ back to $A$.

```
#define ROW 10
#define COL 10
int find_max_matrix(int A[ROW][COL]) {
	int max, cur_max = 0;
	//Calculate Auxilary matrix
	for (int i=1; i<ROW; i++)
		for(int j=0; j<COL; j++) {
			if(A[i][j] == 1)
				A[i][j] = A[i-1][j] + 1;
		}
	//Calculate maximum area in S for each row
	for (int i=0; i<ROW; i++) {
		max = maxRectangleArea(A[i], COL);		//Refer Stacks Chapter
		if(max > cur_max)
			cur_max = max;
	}
	//Regenerate Original matrix
	for (int i=ROW-1; i>0; i--)
		for(int j=0; j<COL; j++) {
			if(A[i][j])
				A[i][j] = A[i][j] - A[i-1][j];
		}
	return cur_max;
}
```

**Problem-42** **Maximum sum sub-matrix:** Given an $n \times n$ matrix $M$ of positive and negative integers, give an algorithm to find the sub-matrix with the largest possible sum.

**Solution**: Let $Aux[r, c]$ represent the sum of rectangular subarray of $M$ with one corner at entry $[1, 1]$ and the other at $[r, c]$. Since there are $n^2$ such possibilities, we can compute them in $O(n^2)$ time. After computing all possible sums, the sum of any rectangular subarray of $M$ can be computed in constant time. This gives an $O(n^4)$ algorithm: we simply guess the lower-left and the upper-right corner of the rectangular subarray and use the $Aux$ table to compute its sum.

**Problem-43** Can we improve the complexity of Problem-42?

**Solution:** We can use the Problem-4 solution with little variation, as we have seen that the maximum sum array of a 1 – D array algorithm scans the array one entry at a time and keeps a running total of the entries. At any point, if this total becomes negative, then set it to 0. This algorithm is called *Kadane's* algorithm. We use this as an auxiliary function to solve a two-dimensional problem in the following way.

```
public void findMaximumSubMatrix(int[][] A, int n){
    //computing the vertical prefix sum for columns
    int[][] M = new int[n][n];
    for (int i = 0; i < n; i++) {
        for (int j = 0; j < n; j++) {
            if (j == 0)
                M[j][i] = A[j][i];
            else
                M[j][i] = A[j][i] + M[j - 1][i];
        }
    }
    int maxSoFar = 0, min, subMatrix;
    //iterate over the possible combinations applying Kadane's Alg.
    for (int i = 0; i < n; i++) {
        for (int j = i; j < n; j++) {
            min = 0;
            subMatrix = 0;
            for (int k = 0; k < n; k++) {
                if (i == 0)
                    subMatrix += M[j][k];
                else    subMatrix += M[j][k] - M[i - 1 ][k];
                if(subMatrix < min)
                    min = subMatrix;
                if((subMatrix - min) > maxSoFar)
                    maxSoFar = subMatrix - min;
            }
        }
    }
}
```

Time Complexity: $O(n^3)$.

Problem-44 Given a number $n$, find the minimum number of squares required to sum a given number $n$.
*Examples*: min[1] = 1 = $1^2$, min[2] = 2 = $1^2 + 1^2$, min[4] = 1 = $2^2$, min[13] = 2 = $3^2 + 2^2$.

**Solution:** This problem can be reduced to a coin change problem. The denominations are 1 to $\sqrt{n}$. Now, we just need to make change for $n$ with a minimum number of denominations.

Problem-45 **Finding Optimal Number of Jumps To Reach Last Element:** Given an array, start from the first element and reach the last by jumping. The jump length can be at most the value at the current position in the array. The optimum result is when you reach the goal in the minimum number of jumps. **Example**: Given array A = {2,3,1,1,4}. Possible ways to reach the end (index list) are:

- 0,2,3,4 (jump 2 to index 2, and then jump 1 to index 3, and then jump 1 to index 4)
- 0,1,4 (jump 1 to index 1, and then jump 3 to index 4)

Since second solution has only 2 jumps it is the optimum result.

**Solution:** This problem is a classic example of Dynamic Programming. Though we can solve this by brute-force, it would be complex. We can use the LIS problem approach for solving this. As soon as we traverse the array, we should find the minimum number of jumps for reaching that position (index) and update our result array. Once we reach the end, we have the optimum solution at last index in result array.

**How can we find the optimum number of jumps for every position (index)?** For first index, the optimum number of jumps will be zero. Please note that if value at first index is zero, we can't jump to any element and return infinite. For $n + 1^{th}$ element, initialize result[$n + 1$] as infinite. Then we should go through a loop from 0 ... $n$, and at every index $i$, we should see if we are able to jump to $n + 1$ from i or not. If possible, then see if total number of jumps (result[i] + 1) is less than result[$n + 1$], then update result[$n + 1$], else just continue to next index.

```
//Define MAX 1 less so that adding 1 doesn't make it 0
#define MAX 0xFFFFFFFE;
unsigned int jump(int *array, int n) {
    unsigned answer, int *result = new unsigned int[n];
    int i, j;
    //Boundary conditions
```

```
    if(n==0 || array[0] == 0)
        return MAX;
    result[0] = 0;                                          //no need to jump at first element
    for (i = 1; i < n; i++) {
            result[i] = MAX; //Initialization of result[i]
            for (j = 0; j < i; j++) {
                    //check if jump is possible from j to is
                    if(array[j] >= (i-j)) {
                            //check if better solution available
                            if((result[j] + 1) < result[i])
                                    result[i] = result[j] + 1;          //updating result[i]
                    }
            }
    }
    answer = result[n-1];                                   //return result[n-1]
    delete[] result;
    return answer;
}
```

The above code will return optimum number of jumps. To find the jump indexes as well, we can very easily modify the code as per requirement.

Time Complexity: Since we are running 2 loops here and iterating from 0 to $i$ in every loop, then total time takes will be $1 + 2 + 3 + 4 + ... + n - 1$. So time efficiency $O(n) = O(n * (n-1)/2) = O(n^2)$.
Space Complexity: $O(n)$ space for result array.

Problem-46 Explain what would happen if a dynamic programming algorithm is designed to solve a problem that does not have overlapping sub-problems.

**Solution**: It will be just a waste of memory, because the answers of sub-problems will never be used again. And the running time will be the same as using the Divide & Conquer algorithm.

**Problem-47** Christmas is approaching. You're helping Santa Claus to distribute gifts to children. For ease of delivery, you are asked to divide $n$ gifts into two groups such that the weight difference of these two groups is minimized. The weight of each gift is a positive integer. Please design an algorithm to find an optimal division minimizing the value difference. The algorithm should find the minimal weight difference as well as the groupings in $O(nS)$ time, where $S$ is the total weight of these $n$ gifts. Briefly justify the correctness of your algorithm.

**Solution**: This problem can be converted into making one set as close to $\frac{S}{2}$ as possible. We consider an equivalent problem of making one set as close to W=$\left\lfloor\frac{S}{2}\right\rfloor$ as possible. Define FD($i, w$) to be the minimal gap between the weight of the bag and W when using the first $i$ gifts only. WLOG, we can assume the weight of the bag is always less than or equal to W. Then fill the DP table for $0 \le i \le n$ and $0 \le w \le W$ in which F(0, $w$) = W for all $w$, and

$$FD(i,w) = min\{FD(i-1, w-w_i) - w_i, FD(i-1,w)\} \; if \; \{FD(i-1, w-w_i) \ge w_i$$
$$= FD(i-1,w) \text{ otherwise}$$

This takes $O(nS)$ time. $FD(n, W)$ is the minimum gap. Finally, to reconstruct the answer, we backtrack from $(n, W)$. During backtracking, if $FD(i,j) = FD(i-1,j)$ then $i$ is not selected in the bag and we move to F($i-1, j$). Otherwise, $i$ is selected and we move to F($i-1, j-w_i$).

**Problem-48** A circus is designing a tower routine consisting of people standing atop one another's shoulders. For practical and aesthetic reasons, each person must be both shorter and lighter than the person below him or her. Given the heights and weights of each person in the circus, write a method to compute the largest possible number of people in such a tower.

**Solution**: It is same as Box stacking and Longest increasing subsequence (LIS) problem.

# COMPLEXITY CLASSES

## 20.1 Introduction

In the previous chapters we have solved problems of different complexities. Some algorithms have lower rates of growth while others have higher rates of growth. The problems with lower rates of growth are called *easy* problems (or *easy solved problems*) and the problems with higher rates of growth are called *hard* problems (or *hard solved problems*). This classification is done based on the running time (or memory) that an algorithm takes for solving the problem.

| Time Complexity | Name | Example | Problems |
|---|---|---|---|
| $O(1)$ | Constant | Adding an element to the front of a linked list | Easy solved problems |
| $O(logn)$ | Logarithmic | Finding an element in a binary search tree | |
| $O(n)$ | Linear | Finding an element in an unsorted array | |
| $O(nlogn)$ | Linear Logarithmic | Merge sort | |
| $O(n^2)$ | Quadratic | Shortest path between two nodes in a graph | |
| $O(n^3)$ | Cubic | Matrix Multiplication | |
| $O(2^n)$ | Exponential | The Towers of Hanoi problem | Hard solved problems |
| $O(n!)$ | Factorial | Permutations of a string | |

There are lots of problems for which we do not know the solutions. All the problems we have seen so far are the ones which can be solved by computer in deterministic time. Before starting our discussion let us look at the basic terminology we use in this chapter.

## 20.2 Polynomial/Exponential Time

Exponential time means, in essence, trying every possibility (for example, backtracking algorithms) and they are very slow in nature. Polynomial time means having some clever algorithm to solve a problem, and we don't try every possibility. Mathematically, we can represent these as:

- Polynomial time is $O(n^k)$, for some $k$.
- Exponential time is $O(k^n)$, for some $k$.

## 20.3 What is a Decision Problem?

A decision problem is a question with a *yes/no* answer and the answer depends on the values of input. For example, the problem "Given an array of $n$ numbers, check whether there are any duplicates or not?" is a decision problem. The answer for this problem can be either *yes* or *no* depending on the values of the input array.

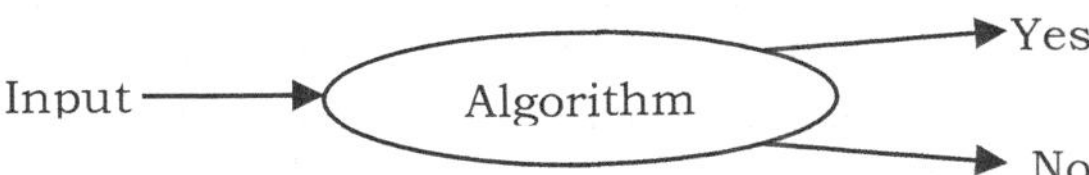


## 20.4 Decision Procedure

For a given decision problem let us assume we have given some algorithm for solving it. The process of solving a given decision problem in the form of an algorithm is called a *decision procedure* for that problem.

## 20.5 What is a Complexity Class?

In computer science, in order to understand the problems for which solutions are not there, the problems are divided into classes and we call them as complexity classes. In complexity theory, a *complexity class* is a set of problems with related complexity. It is the branch of theory of computation that studies the resources required during computation to solve a given problem.

The most common resources are time (how much time the algorithm takes to solve a problem) and space (how much memory it takes).

## 20.6 Types of Complexity Classes

### P Class

The complexity class $P$ is the set of decision problems that can be solved by a deterministic machine in polynomial time ($P$ stands for polynomial time). $P$ problems are a set of problems whose solutions are easy to find.

### NP Class

The complexity class $NP$ ($NP$ stands for non-deterministic polynomial time) is the set of decision problems that can be solved by a non-deterministic machine in polynomial time. $NP$ class problems refer to a set of problems whose solutions are hard to find, but easy to verify.

For better understanding let us consider a college which has 500 students on its roll. Also, assume that there are 100 rooms available for students. A selection of 100 students must be paired together in rooms, but the dean of students has a list of pairings of certain students who cannot room together for some reason.

The total possible number of pairings is too large. But the solutions (the list of pairings) provided to the dean, are easy to check for errors. If one of the prohibited pairs is on the list, that's an error. In this problem, we can see that checking every possibility is very difficult, but the result is easy to validate.

That means, if someone gives us a solution to the problem, we can tell them whether it is right or not in polynomial time. Based on the above discussion, for $NP$ class problems if the answer is *yes*, then there is a proof of this fact, which can be verified in polynomial time.

### Co-NP Class

$Co - NP$ is the opposite of $NP$ (complement of $NP$). If the answer to a problem in $Co - NP$ is *no*, then there is a proof of this fact that can be checked in polynomial time.

| | |
|---|---|
| $P$ | Solvable in polynomial time |
| $NP$ | *Yes* answers can be checked in polynomial time |
| $Co - NP$ | *No* answers can be checked in polynomial time |

### Relationship between P, NP and Co-NP

Every decision problem in $P$ is also in $NP$. If a problem is in $P$, we can verify YES answers in polynomial time. Similarly, any problem in P is also in $Co - NP$.

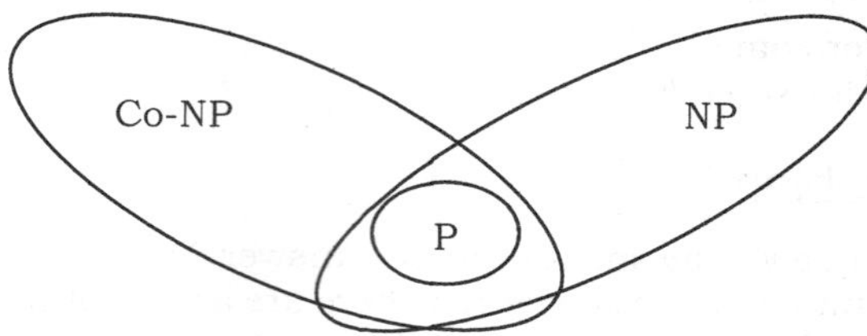


One of the important open questions in theoretical computer science is whether or not $P = NP$. Nobody knows. Intuitively, it should be obvious that $P \neq NP$, but nobody knows how to prove it.

Another open question is whether $NP$ and $Co - NP$ are different. Even if we can verify every YES answer quickly, there's no reason to think that we can also verify NO answers quickly.

It is generally believed that $NP \neq Co - NP$, but again nobody knows how to prove it.

#### NP-hard Class

It is a class of problems such that every problem in $NP$ reduces to it. All $NP$-hard problems are not in $NP$, so it takes a long time to even check them. That means, if someone gives us a solution for $NP$-hard problem, it takes a long time for us to check whether it is right or not.

A problem $K$ is $NP$-hard indicates that if a polynomial-time algorithm (solution) exists for $K$ then a polynomial-time algorithm for every problem is $NP$. Thus:

$K$ is $NP$-hard implies that if $K$ can be solved in polynomial time, then $P = NP$

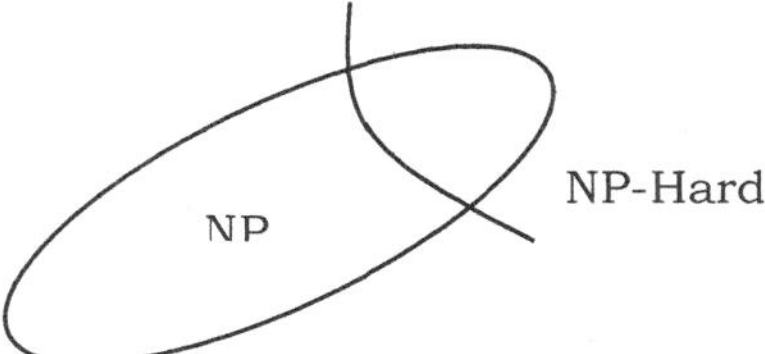


## NP-complete Class

Finally, a problem is $NP$-complete if it is part of both $NP$-hard and $NP$. $NP$-complete problems are the hardest problems in $NP$. If anyone finds a polynomial-time algorithm for one $NP$-complete problem, then we can find polynomial-time algorithm for every $NP$-complete problem. This means that we can check an answer fast and every problem in $NP$ reduces to it.

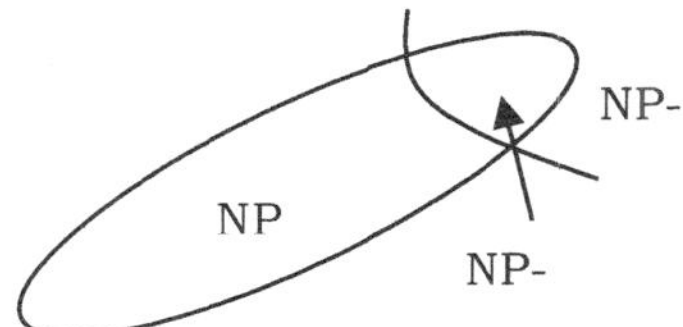


## Relationship between P, NP Co-NP, NP-Hard and NP-Complete

From the above discussion, we can write the relationships between different components as shown below (remember, this is just an assumption).

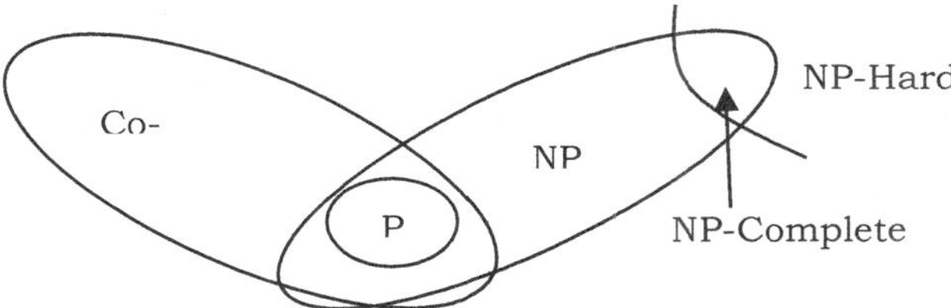


The set of problems that are $NP$-hard is a strict superset of the problems that are $NP$-complete. Some problems (like the halting problem) are $NP$-hard, but not in $NP$. $NP$-hard problems might be impossible to solve in general. We can tell the difference in difficulty between $NP$-hard and $NP$-complete problems because the class $NP$ includes everything easier than its "toughest" problems – if a problem is not in $NP$, it is harder than all the problems in $NP$.

## Does P==NP?

If $P = NP$, it means that every problem that can be checked quickly can be solved quickly (remember the difference between checking if an answer is right and actually solving a problem).

This is a big question (and nobody knows the answer), because right now there are lots of $NP$-complete problems that can't be solved quickly. If $P = NP$, that means there is a way to solve them fast. Remember that "quickly" means not trial-and-error. It could take a billion years, but as long as we didn't use trial and error, it was quick. In future, a computer will be able to change that billion years into a few minutes.

## 20.7 Reductions

Before discussing reductions, let us consider the following scenario. Assume that we want to solve problem $X$ but feel it's very complicated. In this case what do we do?

The first thing that comes to mind is, if we have a similar problem to that of $X$ (let us say $Y$), then we try to map $X$ to $Y$ and use $Y's$ solution to solve $X$ also. This process is called reduction.

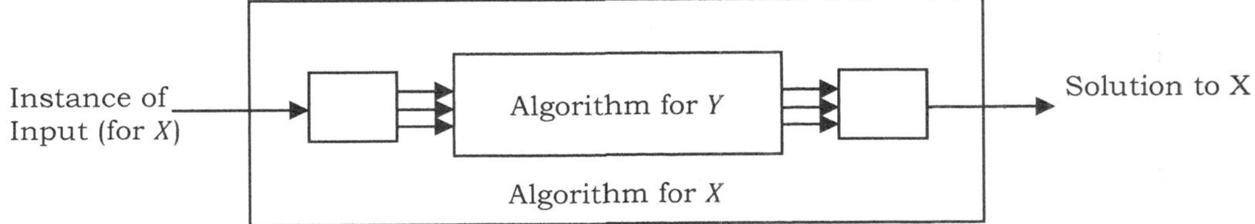


In order to map problem $X$ to problem $Y$, we need some algorithm and that may take linear time or more. Based on this discussion the cost of solving problem $X$ can be given as:

$$Cost\ of\ solving\ X = Cost\ of\ solving\ Y + Reduction\ time$$

Now, let us consider the other scenario. For solving problem $X$, sometimes we may need to use $Y's$ algorithm (solution) multiple times. In that case,

$$Cost\ of\ solving\ X = Number\ of\ Times\ *\ Cost\ of\ solving\ X\ +\ Reduction\ time$$

The main thing in $NP$-Complete is reducibility. That means, we reduce (or transform) given $NP$-Complete problems to other known $NP$-Complete problem. Since the $NP$-Complete problems are hard to solve and in order to prove that given $NP$-Complete problem is hard, we take one existing hard problem (which we can prove is hard) and try to map given problem to that and finally we prove that the given problem is hard.

**Note:** It's not compulsory to reduce the given problem to known hard problem to prove its hardness. Sometimes, we reduce the known hard problem to given problem.

## Important NP-Complete Problems (Reductions)

**Satisfiability Problem:** A boolean formula is in *conjunctive normal form* (CNF) if it is a conjunction (AND) of several clauses, each of which is the disjunction (OR) of several literals, each of which is either a variable or its negation. For example: $(a \vee b \vee c \vee d \vee e) \wedge (b \vee \sim c \vee \sim d) \wedge (\sim a \vee c \vee d) \wedge (a \vee \sim b)$

A 3-CNF formula is a CNF formula with exactly three literals per clause. The previous example is not a 3-CNF formula, since its first clause has five literals and its last clause has only two.

2-SAT Problem: 3-SAT is just SAT restricted to 3-CNF formulas: Given a 3-CNF formula, is there an assignment to the variables so that the formula evaluates to TRUE?

2-SAT Problem: 2-SAT is just SAT restricted to 2-CNF formulas: Given a 2-CNF formula, is there an assignment to the variables so that the formula evaluates to TRUE?

**Circuit-Satisfiability Problem:** Given a boolean combinational circuit composed of AND, OR and NOT gates, is it satisfiable?. That means, given a boolean circuit consisting of AND, OR and NOT gates properly connected by wires, the Circuit-SAT problem is to decide whether there exists an input assignment for which the output is TRUE.

**Hamiltonian Path Problem (Ham-Path):** Given an undirected graph, is there a path that visits every vertex exactly once?

**Hamiltonian Cycle Problem (Ham-Cycle):** Given an undirected graph, is there a cycle (where start and end vertices are same) that visits every vertex exactly once?

**Directed Hamiltonian Cycle Problem (Dir-Ham-Cycle):** Given a directed graph, is there a cycle (where start and end vertices are same) that visits every vertex exactly once?

**Travelling Salesman Problem (TSP):** Given a list of cities and their pair-wise distances, the problem is to find the shortest possible tour that visits each city exactly once.

**Shortest Path Problem (Shortest-Path)**: Given a directed graph and two vertices s and t, check whether there is a shortest simple path from $s$ to $t$.

**Graph Coloring:** A $k$-coloring of a graph is to map one of $k$ 'colors' to each vertex, so that every edge has two different colors at its endpoints. The graph coloring problem is to find the smallest possible number of colors in a legal coloring.

3-Color problem: Given a graph, is it possible to color the graph with 3 colors in such a way that every edge has two different colors?

**Clique (also called complete graph):** Given a graph, the $CLIQUE$ problem is to compute the number of nodes in its largest complete subgraph. That means, we need to find the maximum subgraph which is also a complete graph.

**Independent Set Problem (Ind_Set):** Let $G$ be an arbitrary graph. An independent set in $G$ is a subset of the vertices of $G$ with no edges between them. The maximum independent set problem is the size of the largest independent set in a given graph.

**Vertex Cover Problem (Vertex-Cover):** A vertex cover of a graph is a set of vertices that touches every edge in the graph. The vertex cover problem is to find the smallest vertex cover in a given graph.

**Subset Sum Problem (Subset-Sum):** Given a set $S$ of integers and an integer $T$, determine whether $S$ has a subset whose elements sum to $T$.

**Integer Programming:** Given integers $b_i$, $a_{ij}$ find 0/1 variables $x_i$ that satisfy a linear system of equations.

$$\sum_{j=1}^{N} a_{ij}x_j = b_i \quad 1 \le i \le M$$
$$x_j \in \{0,1\} \; 1 \le j \le N$$

In the figure, arrows indicate the reductions. For example, Ham-Cycle (Hamiltonian Cycle Problem) can be reduced to CNF-SAT. Same is the case with any pair of problems. For our discussion, we can ignore the reduction process for each of the problems. There is a theorem called *Cook's Theorem* which proves that Circuit satisfiability problem is NP-hard. That means, Circuit satisfiability is a known $NP$-hard problem.

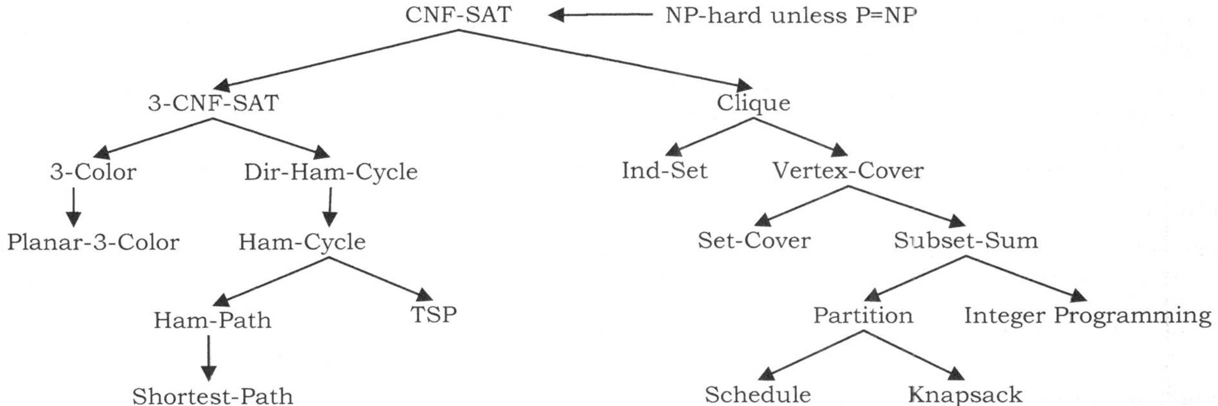


**Note:** Since the problems below are $NP$-Complete, they are $NP$ and $NP$-hard too. For simplicity we can ignore the proofs for these reductions.

## 20.8 Complexity Classes: Problems & Solutions

**Problem-1** What is a quick algorithm?

**Solution:** A quick algorithm (solution) means not trial-and-error solution. It could take a billion years, but as long as we do not use trial and error, it is efficient. Future computers will change those billion years to a few minutes.

**Problem-2** What is an efficient algorithm?

**Solution:** An algorithm is said to be efficient if it satisfies the following properties:

- Scale with input size.
- Don't care about constants.
- Asymptotic running time: polynomial time.

**Problem-3** Can we solve all problems in polynomial time?

**Solution**: **No**. The answer is trivial because we have seen lots of problems which take more than polynomial time.

**Problem-4** Are there any problems which are $NP$-hard?

**Solution:** By definition, $NP$-hard implies that it is very hard. That means it is very hard to prove and to verify that it is hard. Cook's Theorem proves that Circuit satisfiability problem is $NP$-hard.

**Problem-5** For 2-SAT problem, which of the following are applicable?
(a) $P$ (b) $NP$ (c) $CoNP$ (d) $NP$-Hard
(e) $CoNP$-Hard (f) $NP$-Complete (g) $CoNP$-Complete

**Solution**: 2-SAT is solvable in poly-time. So it is $P$, $NP$, and $CoNP$.

**Problem-6** For 3-SAT problem, which of the following are applicable?
(a) $P$ (b) $NP$ (c) $CoNP$ (d) $NP$-Hard
(e) $CoNP$-Hard (f) $NP$-Complete (g) $CoNP$-Complete

**Solution**: 3-SAT is NP-complete. So it is NP, NP-Hard, and NP-complete.

**Problem-7** For 2-Clique problem, which of the following are applicable?
(a) $P$ (b) $NP$ (c) $CoNP$ (d) $NP$-Hard
(e) $CoNP$-Hard (f) $NP$-Complete (g) $CoNP$-Complete

**Solution**: 2-Clique is solvable in poly-time (check for an edge between all vertex-pairs in $O(n^2)$ time). So it is $P, NP$, and $CoNP$.

**Problem-8** For 3-Clique problem, which of the following are applicable?
(a) $P$ (b) $NP$ (c) $CoNP$ (d) $NP$-Hard
(e) $CoNP$-Hard (f) $NP$-Complete (g) $CoNP$-Complete

**Solution**: 3-Clique is solvable in poly-time (check for a triangle between all vertex-triplets in $O(n^3)$ time). So it is $P$, $NP$, and $CoNP$.

**Problem-9** Consider the problem of determining. For a given boolean formula, check whether every assignment to the variables satisfies it. Which of the following is applicable?

(a) $P$ (b) $NP$ (c) $CoNP$ (d) $NP$-Hard
(e) CoNP-Hard (f) $NP$-Complete (g) $CoNP$-Complete

**Solution**: Tautology is the complimentary problem to Satisfiability, which is NP-complete, so Tautology is $CoNP$-complete. So it is $CoNP$, $CoNP$-hard, and $CoNP$-complete.

**Problem-10** Let $S$ be an $NP$-complete problem and $Q$ and $R$ be two other problems not known to be in $NP$. $Q$ is polynomial time reducible to $S$ and $S$ is polynomial-time reducible to $R$. Which one of the following statements is true?
(a) $R$ is $NP$-complete (b) $R$ is $NP$-hard (c) $Q$ is $NP$-complete (d) $Q$ is $NP$-hard.

**Solution:** $R$ is $NP$-hard (b).

**Problem-11** Let $A$ be the problem of finding a Hamiltonian cycle in a graph $G = (V, E)$, with $|V|$ divisible by 3 and $B$ the problem of determining if Hamiltonian cycle exists in such graphs. Which one of the following is true?
(a) Both $A$ and $B$ are $NP$-hard (b) $A$ is $NP$-hard, but $B$ is not
(c) $A$ is $NP$-hard, but $B$ is not (d) Neither $A$ nor $B$ is $NP$-hard

**Solution:** Both $A$ and $B$ are $NP$-hard (a).

**Problem-12** Let $A$ be a problem that belongs to the class $NP$. State which of the following is true?
(a) There is no polynomial time algorithm for $A$.
(b) If $A$ can be solved deterministically in polynomial time, then $P = NP$.
(c) If $A$ is $NP$-hard, then it is $NP$-complete.
(d) $A$ may be undecidable.

**Solution:** If $A$ is $NP$-hard, then it is $NP$-complete (c).

**Problem-13** Suppose we assume $Vertex - Cover$ is known to be $NP$-complete. Based on our reduction, can we say $Independent - Set$ is $NP$-complete?

**Solution: Yes**. This follows from the two conditions necessary to be $NP$-complete:

- Independent Set is in $NP$, as stated in the problem.
- A reduction from a known $NP$-complete problem.

**Problem-14** Suppose *Independent Set* is known to be $NP$-complete. Based on our reduction, is *Vertex Cover* $NP$-complete?

**Solution: No**. By reduction from Vertex-Cover to Independent-Set, we do not know the difficulty of solving Independent-Set. This is because Independent-Set could still be a much harder problem than Vertex-Cover. We have not proved that.

**Problem-15** The class of NP is the class of languages that cannot be accepted in polynomial time. Is it true? Explain.

**Solution**:

- The class of NP is the class of languages that can be *verified* in *polynomial time*.
- The class of P is the class of languages that can be *decided* in *polynomial time*.
- The class of P is the class of languages that can be *accepted* in *polynomial time*.

$P \subseteq NP$ and "languages in P can be accepted in polynomial time", the description "languages in NP cannot be accepted in polynomial time" is wrong.

The term NP comes from nondeterministic polynomial time and is derived from an alternative characterization by using nondeterministic polynomial time Turing machines. It has nothing to do with "cannot be accepted in polynomial time".

**Problem-16** Different encodings would cause different time complexity for the same algorithm. Is it true?

**Solution**: True. The time complexity of the same algorithm is different between unary encoding and binary encoding. But if the two encodings are polynomially related (e.g. base 2 & base 3 encodings), then changing between them will not cause the time complexity to change.

**Problem-17** If P = NP, then NPC (NP Complete) ⊆ P. Is it true?

**Solution**: True. If P = NP, then for any language L ∈ NP C (1) L ∈ NPC (2) L is NP-hard. By the first condition, L ∈ NPC ⊆ NP = P ⇒ NPC ⊆ P.

**Problem-18** If NPC ⊆ P, then P = NP. Is it true?

**Solution**: True. All the NP problem can be reduced to arbitrary NPC problem in polynomial time, and NPC problems can be solved in polynomial time because NPC ⊆ P. ⇒ NP problem solvable in polynomial time ⇒ NP ⊆ P and trivially P ⊆ NP implies NP = P..

# MISCELLANEOUS CONCEPTS

## 21.1 Introduction

In this chapter we will cover the topics which are useful for interviews and exams.

## 21.2 Hacks on Bit-wise Programming

In $C$ and $C++$ we can work with bits effectively. First let us see the definitions of each bit operation and then move onto different techniques for solving the problems. Basically, there are six operators that $C$ and $C++$ support for bit manipulation:

| Symbol | Operation |
|---|---|
| & | Bitwise AND |
| \| | Bitwise OR |
| ^ | Bitwise Exclusive-OR |
| ≪ | Bitwise left shift |
| ≫ | Bitwise right shift |
| ~ | Bitwise complement |

### 21.2.1 Bitwise AND

The bitwise AND tests two binary numbers and returns bit values of 1 for positions where both numbers had a one, and bit values of 0 where both numbers did not have one:

```
   01001011
&  00010101
   ----------
   00000001
```

### 21.2.2 Bitwise OR

The bitwise OR tests two binary numbers and returns bit values of 1 for positions where either bit or both bits are one, the result of 0 only happens when both bits are 0:

```
   01001011
|  00010101
   ----------
   01011111
```

### 21.2.3 Bitwise Exclusive-OR

The bitwise Exclusive-OR tests two binary numbers and returns bit values of 1 for positions where both bits are different; if they are the same then the result is 0:

```
   01001011
^  00010101
   ----------
   01011110
```

### 21.2.4 Bitwise Left Shift

The bitwise left shift moves all bits in the number to the left and fills vacated bit positions with 0.

```
        01001011
<< 2
        --------
        00101100
```

### 21.2.5 Bitwise Right Shift

The bitwise right shift moves all bits in the number to the right.

```
         01001011
  >> 2
         --------
           ??010010
```

Note the use of ? for the fill bits. Where the left shift filled the vacated positions with 0, a right shift will do the same only when the value is unsigned. If the value is signed then a right shift will fill the vacated bit positions with the sign bit or 0, whichever one is implementation-defined. So the best option is to never right shift signed values.

### 21.2.6 Bitwise Complement

The bitwise complement inverts the bits in a single binary number.

```
       01001011
  ~
       ---------
       10110100
```

### 21.2.7 Checking Whether K-th Bit is Set or Not

Let us assume that the given number is $n$. Then for checking the $K^{th}$ bit we can use the expression: $n \,\&\, (1 \ll K - 1)$. If the expression is true then we can say the $K^{th}$ bit is set (that means, set to 1).

| *Example*: | $n$ | 01001011 | $K = 4$ |
|---|---|---|---|
| | $1 \ll K - 1$ | 00001000 | |
| | $n \,\&\, (1 \ll K - 1)$ | 00001000 | |

### 21.2.8 Setting K-th Bit

For a given number $n$, to set the $K^{th}$ bit we can use the expression: $n \mid 1 \ll (K - 1)$

| *Example*: | $n$ | 01001011 | $K = 3$ |
|---|---|---|---|
| | $1 \ll K - 1$ | 00000100 | |
| | $n \mid (1 \ll K - 1)$ | 01001111 | |

### 21.2.9 Clearing K-th Bit

To clear $K^{th}$ bit of a given number $n$, we can use the expression: $n \,\&\, {\sim}(1 \ll K - 1)$

| *Example*: | $n$ | 01001011 | $K = 4$ |
|---|---|---|---|
| | $1 \ll K - 1$ | 00001000 | |
| | ${\sim}(1 \ll K - 1)$ | 11110111 | |
| | $n \,\&\, {\sim}(1 \ll K - 1)$ | 01000011 | |

### 21.2.10 Toggling K-th Bit

For a given number $n$, for toggling the $K^{th}$ bit we can use the expression: $n$ ^$(1 \ll K - 1)$

| *Example*: | $n$ | 01001011 | $K = 3$ |
|---|---|---|---|
| | $1 \ll K - 1$ | 00000100 | |
| | $n$ ^ $(1 \ll K - 1)$ | 01001111 | |

### 21.2.11 Toggling Rightmost One Bit

For a given number $n$, for toggling rightmost one bit we can use the expression: $n \,\&\, n - 1$

| *Example*: | $n$ | 01001011 |
|---|---|---|
| | $n - 1$ | 01001010 |
| | $n \,\&\, n - 1$ | 01001010 |

### 21.2.12 Isolating Rightmost One Bit

For a given number $n$, for isolating rightmost one bit we can use the expression: $n \,\&\, -n$

| *Example*: | $n$ | 01001011 |
|---|---|---|
| | $-n$ | 10110101 |
| | $n \,\&\, -n$ | 00000001 |

**Note:** For computing $-n$, use two's complement representation. That means, toggle all bits and add 1.

### 21.2.13 Isolating Rightmost Zero Bit

For a given number $n$, for isolating rightmost zero bit we can use the expression: $\sim n \,\&\, n+1$

| *Example:* | | |
|---|---|---|
| | $n$ | 01001011 |
| | $\sim n$ | 10110100 |
| | $n+1$ | 01001100 |
| | $\sim n \,\&\, n+1$ | 00000100 |

### 21.2.14 Checking Whether Number is Power of 2 or Not

Given number $n$, to check whether the number is in $2^n$ form for not, we can use the expression: $if(n \,\&\, n-1 == 0)$

| *Example:* | | |
|---|---|---|
| | $n$ | 01001011 |
| | $n-1$ | 01001010 |
| | $n \,\&\, n-1$ | 01001010 |
| | $if(n \,\&\, n-1 == 0)$ | 0 |

### 21.2.15 Multiplying Number by Power of 2

For a given number $n$, to multiply the number with $2^K$ we can use the expression: $n \ll K$

| *Example:* | | | |
|---|---|---|---|
| | $n$ | 00001011 | $K = 2$ |
| | $n \ll K$ | 00101100 | |

### 21.2.16 Dividing Number by Power of 2

For a given number $n$, to divide the number with $2^K$ we can use the expression: $n \gg K$

| *Example:* | | | |
|---|---|---|---|
| | $n$ | 00001011 | $K = 2$ |
| | $n \gg K$ | 00000010 | |

### 21.2.17 Finding Modulo of a Given Number

For a given number $n$, to find the %8 we can use the expression: $n \,\&\, 0x7$. Similarly, to find %32, use the expression: $n \,\&\, 0x1F$

**Note:** Similarly, we can find modulo value of any number.

### 21.2.18 Reversing the Binary Number

For a given number $n$, to reverse the bits (reverse (mirror) of binary number) we can use the following code snippet:

```
unsigned int n, nReverse = n;
int s = sizeof(n);
for (; n; n >>= 1) {
    nReverse <<= 1;
    nReverse |= n & 1;
    s--;
}
nReverse <<= s;
```

Time Complexity: This requires one iteration per bit and the number of iterations depends on the size of the number.

### 21.2.19 Counting Number of One's in Number

For a given number $n$, to count the number of $1's$ in its binary representation we can use any of the following methods.

**Method1:** Process bit by bit with bitwise and operator

```
unsigned int n;
unsigned int count=0;
while(n) {
    count += n & 1;
    n >>= 1;
}
```

Time Complexity: This approach requires one iteration per bit and the number of iterations depends on system.

**Method2:** Using modulo approach

```
unsigned int n;
unsigned int count=0;
```

```
while(n) {
    if(n%2 ==1)
        count++;
    n = n/2;
}
```

Time Complexity: This requires one iteration per bit and the number of iterations depends on system.

**Method3:** Using toggling approach: $n \& n - 1$

```
unsigned int n;
unsigned int count=0;
while(n) {
    count++;
    n &= n - 1;
}
```

Time Complexity: The number of iterations depends on the number of 1 bits in the number.

**Method4:** Using preprocessing idea. In this method, we process the bits in groups. For example if we process them in groups of 4 bits at a time, we create a table which indicates the number of one's for each of those possibilities (as shown below).

| | | | |
|---|---|---|---|
| 0000→0 | 0100→1 | 1000→1 | 1100→2 |
| 0001→1 | 0101→2 | 1001→2 | 1101→3 |
| 0010→1 | 0110→2 | 1010→2 | 1110→3 |
| 0011→2 | 0111→3 | 1011→3 | 1111→4 |

The following code to count the number of 1s in the number with this approach:

```
int Table = {0,1,1,2,1,2,2,3,1,2,2,3,2,3,3,4};
int count = 0;
for(; n; n >>= 4)
    count = count + Table[n & 0xF];
return count;
```

Time Complexity: This approach requires one iteration per 4 bits and the number of iterations depends on system.

## 21.2.20 Creating Mask for Trailing Zero's

For a given number $n$, to create a mask for trailing zeros, we can use the expression: $(n \& -n) - 1$

| | |
|---|---|
| *Example*: $n$ | 01001011 |
| $-n$ | 10110101 |
| $n \& -n$ | 00000001 |
| $(n \& -n) - 1$ | 00000000 |

**Note:** In the above case we are getting the mask as all zeros because there are no trailing zeros.

## 27.2.21 Swap All Odd and Even Bits

| | |
|---|---|
| *Example*: $n$ | 01001011 |
| Find even bits of given number (evenN) = $n$ & 0xAA | 00001010 |
| Find odd bits of given number (oddN) = $n$ & 0x55 | 01000001 |
| evenN >>= 1 | 00000101 |
| oddN <<= 1 | 10000010 |
| Final Expression: evenN \| oddN | 10000111 |

## 21.2.22 Performing Average without Division

Is there a bit-twiddling algorithm to replace $mid = (low + high) / 2$ (used in Binary Search and Merge Sort) with something much faster?

We can use $mid = (low + high) >> 1$. Note that using $(low + high) / 2$ for midpoint calculations won't work correctly when integer overflow becomes an issue. We can use bit shifting and also overcome a possible overflow issue: $low + ((high - low)/ 2)$ and the bit shifting operation for this is $low + ((high - low) >> 1)$.

# 21.3 Other Programming Questions

**Problem-1** Give an algorithm for printing the matrix elements in spiral order.

**Solution**: Non-recursive solution involves directions right, left, up, down, and dealing their corresponding indices. Once the first row is printed, direction changes (from right) to down, the row is discarded by incrementing the upper limit. Once the last column is printed, direction changes to left, the column is discarded by decrementing the right hand limit.

```
void spiral(int **A, int n) {
    int rowStart=0, columnStart=0;
    int rowEnd=n-1, columnEnd=n-1;
    while(rowStart<=rowEnd && columnStart<=columnEnd) {
        int i=rowStart, j=columnStart;
        for(j=columnStart; j<=columnEnd; j++)
            printf("%d ",A[i][j]);
        for(i=rowStart+1, j--; i<=rowEnd; i++)
            printf("%d ",A[i][j]);
        for(j=columnEnd-1, i--; j>=columnStart; j--)
            printf("%d ",A[i][j]);
        for(i=rowEnd-1, j++; i>=rowStart+1; i--)
            printf("%d ",A[i][j]);
        rowStart++; columnStart++; rowEnd--; columnEnd--;
    }
}
```

Time Complexity: $O(n^2)$. Space Complexity: O(1).

**Problem-2** Give an algorithm for shuffling the deck of cards.

**Solution:** Assume that we want to shuffle an array of 52 cards, from 0 to 51 with no repeats, such as we might want for a deck of cards. First fill the array with the values in order, then go through the array and exchange each element with a randomly chosen element in the range from itself to the end. It's possible that an element will swap with itself, but there is no problem with that.

```
void shuffle(int cards[], int n){
    srand(time(0));                         // initialize seed randomly
    for (int i=0; i<n; i++)
        cards[i] = i;                       // filling the array with card number
    for (int i=0; i<n; i++) {
        int r = i + (rand() % (52-i));      // Random remaining position.
        int temp = cards[i];
        cards[i] = cards[r];
        cards[r] = temp;
    }
    printf("Shuffled Cards:" );
    for (int i=0; i<n; i++)
        printf("%d ", cards[i]);
}
```

Time Complexity: $O(n)$. Space Complexity: O(1).

**Problem-3** Reversal algorithm for array rotation: Write a function rotate(A[], d, n) that rotates A[] of size $n$ by $d$ elements. For example, the array $1, 2, 3, 4, 5, 6, 7$ becomes $3, 4, 5, 6, 7, 1, 2$ after 2 rotations.

**Solution**: Consider the following algorithm.

**Algorithm**:

```
rotate(Array[], d, n)
reverse(Array[], 1, d) ;
reverse(Array[], d + 1, n);
reverse(Array[], l, n);
```

Let AB be the two parts of the input Arrays where A = Array[0..d-1] and B = Array[d..n-1]. The idea of the algorithm is:

Reverse A to get ArB. /* Ar is reverse of A */
Reverse B to get ArBr. /* Br is reverse of B */
Reverse all to get (ArBr) r = BA.
For example, if Array[] = [1, 2, 3, 4, 5, 6, 7], d =2 and n = 7 then, A = [1, 2] and B = [3, 4, 5, 6, 7]
Reverse A, we get ArB = [2, 1, 3, 4, 5, 6, 7], Reverse B, we get ArBr = [2, 1, 7, 6, 5, 4, 3]
Reverse all, we get (ArBr)r = [3, 4, 5, 6, 7, 1, 2]

**Implementation**:

```
//function to left rotate Array[] of size n by d
void leftRotate(int Array[], int d, int n) {
    rvereseArrayay(Array, 0, d-1);
    rvereseArrayay(Array, d, n-1);
```

```
        rvereseArrayay(Array, 0, n-1);
    }
    //UTILITY FUNCTIONS: function to print an Arrays
    void printArrayay(int Array[], int size){
        for(int i = 0; i < size; i++)
            printf("%d ", Array[i]);
        printf("%\n ");
    }
    //function to reverse Array[] from index start to end
    void rvereseArrayay(int Array[], int start, int end) {
      int i;
      int temp;
      while(start < end){
          temp = Array[start];
          Array[start] = Array[end];
          Array[end] = temp;
          start++;
          end--;
      }
    }
```

**Problem-4** Suppose you are given an array s[1...n] and a procedure reverse (s,i,j) which reverses the order of elements in between positions i and j (both inclusive). What does the following sequence do, where 1 < k <= n:

```
reverse (s, 1, k);
reverse (s, k + 1, n);
reverse (s, 1, n);
```

a) Rotates s left by k positions b) Leaves s unchanged c) Reverses all elements of s d) None of the above

**Solution**: (b). Effect of the above 3 reversals for any $k$ is equivalent to left rotation of the array of size $n$ by $k$ [refer to Problem-3].

**Problem-5** Finding Anagrams in Dictionary: you are given these 2 files: dictionary.txt and jumbles.txt

The jumbles.txt file contains a bunch of scrambled words. Your job is to print out those jumbles words, 1 word to a line. After each jumbled word, print a list of real dictionary words that could be formed by unscrambling the jumbled word. The dictionary words that you have to choose from are in the dictionary.txt file. Sample content of jumbles.txt:

```
nwae: wean anew wane
eslyep: sleepy
rpeoims: semipro imposer promise
ettniner: renitent
ahicryrhe: hierarchy
dica: acid cadi caid
dobol: blood
......
%
```

**Solution**: Step-By-Step

*Step* 1: Initialization

- Open the dictionary.txt file and read the words into an array (before going further verify by echoing out the words back from the array out to the screen).
- Declare a hash table variable.

*Step* 2: Process the Dictionary for each dictionary word in the array. Do the following:
We now have a hash table where each key is the sorted form of a dictionary word and the value associated to it is a string or array of dictionary words that sort to that same key.

- Remove the newline off the end of each word via chomp($word);
- Make a sorted copy of the word - i.e. rearrange the individual chars in the string to be sorted alphabetically
- Think of the sorted word as the key value and think of the set of all dictionary words that sort to the exact same key word as being the value of the key
- Query the hashtable to see if the sortedWord is already one of the keys
- If it is not already present then insert the sorted word as key and the unsorted original of the word as the value
- Else concat the unsorted word onto the value string already out there (put a space in between)

*Step* 3: Process the jumbled word file

- Read through the jumbled word file one word at a time. As you read each jumbled word chomp it and make a sorted copy (the sorted copy is your key)
- Print the unsorted jumble word
- Query the hashtable for the sorted copy. If found, print the associated value on same line as key and then a new line.

*Step* 4: Celebrate, we are all done

Sample code in Perl:

```
#step 1
open("MYFILE",<dictionary.txt>);
while(<MYFILE>){
    $row = $_;
    chomp($row);
    push(@words,$row);
}
my %hashdic = ();
#step 2
foreach $words(@words){
    @not_sorted=split (//, $words);
     @sorted = sort (@not_sorted);
    $name=join("",@sorted);
     if (exists $hashdic{$name})     {
        $hashdic{$name}.=" $words";
    }
    else {
        $hashdic{$name}=$words;
    }
}
$size=keys %hashdic;
#step 3
open("jumbled",<jumbles.txt>);
while(<jumbled>){
    $jum = $_;
    chomp($jum);
    @not_sorted1=split (//, $jum);
    @sorted1 = sort(@not_sorted1);
    $name1=join("",@sorted1);
    if(length($hashdic{$name1})<1) {
        print "\n$jum : NO MATCHES";
    }
    else {
        @value=split(/ /,$hashdic{$name1});
        print "\n$jum : @values";
    }
}
```

Problem-6 **Pathways:** Given a matrix as shown below, calculate the number of ways for reaching destination *B* from *A*.

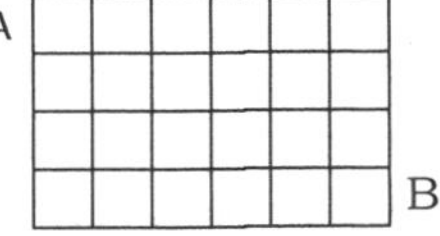


**Solution:** Before finding the solution, we try to understand the problem with a simpler version. The smallest problem that we can consider is the number of possible routes in a 1×1 grid.

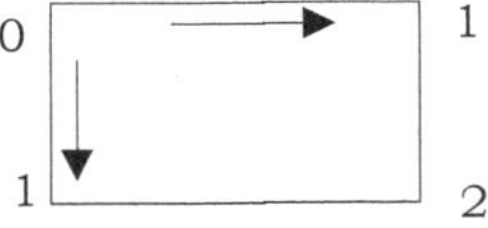


From the above figure, it can be seen that:

- From both the bottom-left and the top-right corners there's only one possible route to the destination.
- From the top-left corner there are trivially two possible routes.

Similarly, for 2x2 and 3x3 grids, we can fill the matrix as:

| **0** | 1 |
|---|---|
| 1 | **2** |

| **0** | 1 | 1 |
|---|---|---|
| 1 | 2 | 3 |
| 1 | 3 | **6** |

From the above discussion, it is clear that to reach the bottom right corner from left top corner, the paths are overlapping. As unique paths could overlap at certain points (grid cells), we could try to alter the previous algorithm, as a way to avoid following the same path again. If we start filling 4x4 and 5x5, we can easily figure out the solution based on our childhood mathematics concepts.

| **0** | 1 | 1 | 1 |
|---|---|---|---|
| 1 | 2 | 3 | 4 |
| 1 | 3 | 6 | 10 |
| 1 | 4 | 10 | **20** |

| **0** | 1 | 1 | 1 | 1 |
|---|---|---|---|---|
| 1 | 2 | 3 | 4 | 5 |
| 1 | 3 | 6 | 10 | 15 |
| 1 | 4 | 10 | 20 | 35 |
| 1 | 5 | 15 | 35 | **70** |

Are you able to figure out the pattern? It is the same as *Pascals* triangle. So, to find the number of ways, we can simply scan through the table and keep counting them while we move from left to right and top to bottom (starting with left-top). We can even solve this problem with mathematical equation of *Pascals* triangle.

Problem-7 Given a string that has a set of words and spaces, write a program to move the spaces to *front* of string. You need to traverse the array only once and you need to adjust the string in place.
*Input* = "move these spaces to beginning" *Output* ="    movethesepacestobeginning"

**Solution**: Maintain two indices *i* and *j*; traverse from end to beginning. If the current index contains char, swap chars in index *i* with index *j*. This will move all the spaces to beginning of the array.

```
void mySwap(char A[],int i,int j){
    char temp=A[i];
    A[i]=A[j];
    A[j]=temp;
}
void moveSpacesToBegin(char A[]){
    int i=strlen(A)-1;
    int j=i;
    for(; j>=0; j--){
        if(!isspace(A[j]))
            mySwap(A,i--,j);
    }
}
```

```
void testCode(int argc, char * argv[]){
    char sparr[]="move these spaces to beginning";
    printf("Value of A is: %s\n", sparr);
    moveSpacesToBegin(sparr);
    printf("Value of A is: %s", sparr);
}
```

Time Complexity: O($n$) where $n$ is the number of characters in input array. Space Complexity: O(1).

Problem-8 For Problem-7, can we improve the complexity?

**Solution**: We can avoid a swap operation with a simple counter. But, it does not reduce the overall complexity.

```
void moveSpacesToBegin(char A[]){
    int n=strlen(A)-1,count=n;
    int i=n;
    for(;i>=0;i--){
        if(A[i]!=' ')
            A[count--]=A[i];
    }
    while(count>=0)
        A[count--]=' ';
}
```

```
int testCode(){
    char sparr[]="move these spaces to beginning";
    printf("Value of A is: %s\n", sparr);
    moveSpacesToBegin(sparr);
    printf("Value of A is: %s", sparr);
}
```

Time Complexity: O($n$) where $n$ is the number of characters in input array. Space Complexity: O(1).

Problem-9 Given a string that has a set of words and spaces, write a program to move the spaces to *end* of string. You need to traverse the array only once and you need to adjust the string in place.
*Input* = "move these spaces to end" *Output* = "movethesepacestoend    "

**Solution**: Traverse the array from left to right. While traversing, maintain a counter for non-space elements in array. For every non-space character A[*i*], put the element at A[*count*] and increment *count*. After complete traversal, all non-space elements have already been shifted to front end and *count* is set as index of first 0. Now, all we need to do is run a loop which fills all elements with spaces from *count* till end of the array.

```
void moveSpacesToEnd(char A[]){
    // Count of non-space elements
```

```
void testCode(int argc, char * argv[]){
    char sparr[]="move these spaces to end";
```

```
        int count = 0;
        int n =strlen(A)-1;
        int i =0;
        for (; i <= n; i++)
            if (!isspace(A[i]))
                A[count++] = A[i];
        while (count <= n)
            A[++count] = ' ';
    }
```

```
        printf("Value of A is: %s\n", sparr);
        moveSpacesToEnd(sparr);
        printf("Value of A is: %s", sparr);
    }
```

Time Complexity: O($n$) where $n$ is number of characters in input array. Space Complexity: O(1).

Problem-10 Moving Zeros to end: Given an array of $n$ integers, move all the zeros of a given array to the end of the array. For example, if the given array is {1, 9, 8, 4, 0, 0, 2, 7, 0, 6, 0}, it should be changed to {1, 9, 8, 4, 2, 7, 6, 0, 0, 0, 0}. The order of all other elements should be the same.

**Solution**: Maintain two variables $i$ and $j$; and initialize with 0. For each of the array element $A[i]$, if $A[i]$ non-zero element, then replace the element $A[j]$ with element $A[i]$. Variable $i$ will always be incremented till $n$ - 1 but we will increment $j$ only when the element pointed by $i$ is non-zero.

```
void moveZerosToEnd(int A[], int size){
    int i=0,j=0;
    while (i <= size - 1){
        if (A[i] != 0){
            A[j++] = A[i];
        }
        i++;
    }
    while (j <= size - 1)
        A[j++] = 0;
}
```

```
int testCode(){
    int A[ ] = {1,9,8,4,0,0,2,7,0,6,0};
    int i;
    int size = sizeof(A) / sizeof(A[0]);
    moveZerosToEnd(A, size);
    for (i = 0; i <= size - 1; i++)
        printf("%d ", A[i]);
    return 0;
}
```

Time Complexity: O($n$). Space Complexity: O(1).

Problem-11 For Problem-10, can we improve the complexity?

**Solution**: Using simple swap technique we can avoid the unnecessary second *while* loop from the above code.

```
void mySwap(int A[],int i,int j){
    int temp=A[i]; A[i]=A[j]; A[j]=temp;
}
void moveZerosToEnd(int A[], int len){
    int i, j;
    for(i=0,j=0; i<len; i++)    {
        if (A[i] !=0)
            mySwap(A,j++,i);
    }
}
```

Time Complexity: O($n$). Space Complexity: O(1).

Problem-12 Variant of Problem-10 and Problem-11: Given an array containing negative and positive numbers; give an algorithm for separating positive and negative numbers in it. Also, maintain the relative order of positive and negative numbers.
Input: -5, 3, 2, -1, 4, -8 Output: -5 -1 -8 3 4 2

**Solution**: In the *moveZerosToEnd* function, just replace the condition $A[i]$ !=0 with $A[i] < 0$.

Problem-13 Given a number, swap odd and even bits.

**Solution**: To swap the odd and even bits of a given number, we can follow the following steps:

- Create two bit masks: one to select all even bits, and one to select all odd bits. The even bit mask would be a binary number with all even bits set to 1 and odd bits set to 0 (in binary notation, this would be 1010...10). The odd bit mask would be a binary number with all odd bits set to 1 and even bits set to 0 (in binary notation, this would be 0101...01).
- Perform a bitwise AND operation with the given number and the even bit mask to extract all the even bits.
- Perform a bitwise AND operation with the given number and the odd bit mask to extract all the odd bits.
- Shift the even bits to the right by one position and shift the odd bits to the left by one position.
- Combine the shifted even and odd bits using a bitwise OR operation to get the result.

```
unsigned int swap_bits(unsigned int num) {
    // Create bit masks
```

```
        unsigned int even_mask = 0xAAAAAAAA;            // Binary 101010...10
        unsigned int odd_mask = 0x55555555;             // Binary 010101...01
        // Extract even and odd bits
        unsigned int even_bits = num & even_mask;
        unsigned int odd_bits = num & odd_mask;
        // Shift even and odd bits
        even_bits >>= 1;
        odd_bits <<= 1;
        // Combine shifted even and odd bits
        unsigned int result = even_bits | odd_bits;
        return result;
}
```

The time complexity of the swap_bits function (in all the implementations provided in previous answers) is O(1), because it performs a fixed number of operations that do not depend on the size of the input. Specifically, it performs 3 bitwise operations, 2 bit mask operations, and 2 bit shifting operations, which can be considered constant time operations.

Therefore, the time complexity of the overall program is also O(1), since the function is the only significant operation performed. Note that space complexity is also O(1), since the function only uses a fixed number of variables to store the bit masks, bit shifts, and intermediate results.

Problem-14 Count the number of set bits in all numbers from 1 to n.

**Solution**: We can use the technique of section 21.2.19 and iterate through all the numbers from 1 to n.

```
int countingNumberofOnesIn1toN(unsigned int n){
    int count =0, i = 0, j;
    for (i = 1; i <= n; i++){
        j = i;
        while(j){
            j = j & (j-1);
            count++;
        }
    }
    return count;
}
```

Problem-15 **Flower bed**: Suppose you have a long flowerbed in which some of the plots are planted and some are not. However, flowers cannot be planted in adjacent plots - they would compete for water and both would die. Given a flowerbed (represented as an array containing 0 and 1, where 0 means empty and 1 means not empty), and a number *n*, return if n new flowers can be planted in it without violating the no-adjacent-flowers rule.

Example 1: Input: flowerbed = [1,0,0,0,1], n = 1 Output: True
Example 2: Input: flowerbed = [1,0,0,0,1], n = 2 Output: False

**Solution**: Planting additional flowers in a given flowerbed arrangement can be easily accomplished by determining the maximum number of extra flowers that can be planted. To do so, we simply need to examine each element in the flowerbed and identify the 0s, which represent empty positions. For each empty position, we can check if both of its adjacent positions are also empty. If this condition is met, we can plant a flower in the current position without violating the no-adjacent-flowers-rule. We do not need to check the adjacent positions for the first and last elements.

If the count of empty positions where flowers can be planted is greater than or equal to the number of flowers required (n), then we can plant n flowers in the empty spaces. Otherwise, we cannot plant n flowers.

```
bool canPlaceFlowers(vector<int>& flowerbed, int n) {
    for (int i = 0; i < flowerbed.size(); i++) {
        if (!flowerbed[i] && (i == 0 || !flowerbed[i - 1]) && (i == flowerbed.size() - 1 || !flowerbed[i + 1])) {
            flowerbed[i] = 1;
            n--;
        }
    }
    return n <= 0;
}
```

Time complexity: O(*n*). A single scan of the flowerbed array of size *n* is done. Space complexity: O(1).

**Problem-16** Given two strings ***s*** and ***t*** which consist of only lowercase letters. String ***t*** is generated by random shuffling string ***s*** and then add one more letter at a random position. Find the letter that was added in ***t***.

Example Input: s = "abcd" t = "abcde" Output: e
Explanation: 'e' is the letter that was added.

**Solution**: Since there is only character difference between the two given strings, we can simply perform the XOR of all the characters from both the strings to get the difference.

```
char findTheDifference(string s, string t) {
    char r=0;
    for(char c:s) r ^=c;
    for(char c:t) r ^=c;
    return r;
}
```

Time Complexity: O($n$), where $n$ is the length of arrays. Space Complexity: O(1).

**Problem-17** Given an integer array, sort the integers in the array in ascending order by the number of 1's in their binary representation and in case of two or more integers having the same number of 1's you must sort them in ascending order.

**Solution**: Refer the solution section of *Priority Queues* chapter.

# REFERENCES


[1] Akash. Programming Interviews. tech-queries.blogspot.com.
[2] Alfred V.Aho,J. E. (1983). Data Structures and Algorithms. Addison-Wesley.
[3] Algorithms.Retrieved from cs.princeton.edu/algs4/home
[4] Anderson., S. E. Bit Twiddling Hacks. Retrieved 2010, from Bit Twiddling Hacks: graphics.stanford.edu
[5] Bentley, J. AT&T Bell Laboratories. Retrieved from AT&T Bell Laboratories.
[6] Bondalapati, K. Interview Question Bank. Retrieved 2010, from Interview Question Bank: halcyon.usc.edu/~kiran/msqs.html
[7] Chen. Algorithms hawaii.edu/~chenx.
[8] Database, P.Problem Database. Retrieved 2010, from Problem Database: datastructures.net
[9] Drozdek, A. (1996). Data Structures and Algorithms in C++.
[10] Ellis Horowitz, S. S. Fundamentals of Data Structures.
[11] Gilles Brassard, P. B. (1996). Fundamentals of Algorithmics.
[12] Hunter., J. Introduction to Data Structures and Algorithms. Retrieved 2010, from Introduction to Data Structures and Algorithms.
[13] James F. Korsh, L. J. Data Structures, Algorithms and Program Style Using C.
[14] John Mongan, N. S. (2002). Programming Interviews Exposed. Wiley-India. .
[15] Judges. Comments on Problems and Solutions. http://www.informatik.uni-ulm.de/acm/Locals/2003/html/judge.html.
[16] Kalid. P, NP, and NP-Complete. Retrieved from P, NP, and NP-Complete.: cs.princeton.edu/~kazad
[17] Knuth., D. E. (1973). Fundamental Algorithms, volume 1 of The Art of Computer Programming. Addison-Wesley.
[18] Leon, J. S. Computer Algorithms. Retrieved 2010, from Computer Algorithms : math.uic.edu/~leon
[19] Leon., J. S. Computer Algorithms. math.uic.edu/~leon/cs-mcs401-s08.
[20] OCF. Algorithms. Retrieved 2010, from Algorithms: ocf.berkeley.edu
[21] Parlante., N. Binary Trees. Retrieved 2010, from cslibrary.stanford.edu: cslibrary.stanford.edu
[22] Patil., V. Fundamentals of data structures. Nirali Prakashan.
[23] Poundstone., W. HOW WOULD YOU MOVE MOUNT FUJI? New York Boston.: Little, Brown and Company.
[24] Pryor, M. Tech Interview. Retrieved 2010, from Tech Interview: techinterview.org
[25] Questions, A. C. A Collection of Technical Interview Questions. Retrieved 2010, from A Collection of Technical Interview Questions
[26] S. Dasgupta, C. P. Algorithms cs.berkeley.edu/~vazirani.
[27] Sedgewick., R. (1988). Algorithms. Addison-Wesley.
[28] Sells, C. (2010). Interviewing at Microsoft. Retrieved 2010, from Interviewing at Microsoft
[29] Shene, C.-K. Linked Lists Merge Sort Implementation.
[30] Sinha, P. Linux Journal. Retrieved 2010, from: linuxjournal.com/article/6828.
[31] Structures., d. D. www.math-cs.gordon.edu. Retrieved 2010, from www.math-cs.gordon.edu
[32] T. H. Cormen, C. E. (1997). Introduction to Algorithms. Cambridge: The MIT press.
[33] Tsiombikas, J. Pointers Explained. nuclear.sdf-eu.org.
[34] Warren., H. S. (2003). Hackers Delight. Addison-Wesley.
[35] Weiss., M. A. (1992). Data Structures and Algorithm Analysis in C.
[36] SANDRASI http://sandrasi-sw.blogspot.in/